JOURNAL FOR THE STUDY OF THE OLD TESTAMENT
SUPPLEMENT SERIES
285

Sheffield Academic Press

The History of the
Second Temple Period

Paolo Sacchi

Journal for the Study of the Old Testament
Supplement Series 285

Copyright © 2000 Sheffield Academic Press

Published by Sheffield Academic Press Ltd
Mansion House
19 Kingfield Road
Sheffield S11 9AS
England
http://www.shef-ac-press.co.uk

Typeset by Sheffield Academic Press
and
Printed on acid-free paper in Great Britain
by Biddles Ltd
Guildford, Surrey

British Library Cataloguing in Publication Data

A catalogue record for this book is available
from the British Library

ISBN 1-85075-938-3

CONTENTS

Preface to the English Edition   9
Translator's Note   23
Abbreviations   24

Introduction   27

PART I
THE AGE OF EXILE

Chapter 1
THE EVENTS   46

Chapter 2
THE JEWISH CULTURE OF THE SIXTH CENTURY BCE   69

PART II
THE ZADOKITE PERIOD

Chapter 3
EARLY ZADOKITISM (C. 520–400 BCE)   114

Chapter 4
NEHEMIAH   130

Chapter 5
THE SAMARITANS   152

Chapter 6
LATE ZADOKITISM (C. 400–200 BCE)   160

PART III
PALESTINE FROM THE ADVENT OF SELEUCID DOMINATION
TO THE DESTRUCTION OF THE SECOND TEMPLE

Chapter 7
PALESTINE UNDER THE SELEUCIDS: THE MACCABEES   214

Chapter 8
THE HASMONAEANS   250

Chapter 9
JUDAEA AT THE TIME OF JESUS OF NAZARETH   284

PART IV
THE THEMES OF MIDDLE JUDAISM

Chapter 10
INTRODUCTION TO THE PROBLEMS   304

Chapter 11
THE PROBLEM OF KNOWLEDGE   316

Chapter 12
PREDETERMINISM AND THE PROBLEM OF EVIL   328

Chapter 13
SALVATION   355

Chapter 14
MESSIANISM   380

Chapter 15
THE RIGHTEOUS   409

Chapter 16
LIFE BEYOND DEATH: THE IMMORTAL SOUL AND THE
RESURRECTION OF THE BODY   426

Chapter 17
THE SACRED AND THE PROFANE, THE IMPURE AND THE PURE   439

Chapter 18
THE TWO CALENDARS   477

Chapter 19
JESUS IN HIS TIME   485

Bibliography   496
Index of References   517
Index of Authors   529

Five years have gone by since my book on the history of the Second Temple period first came out in Italian, and six or seven years have passed since I finished the bibliography. Some updating of the bibliography would therefore seem in order (see the added bibliography), with a few considerations both on studies which I saw only after my own work was too far along to be modified, and also studies that have come out since the publication of my book. Of course, these observations only take some fundamental questions into consideration, or, at any rate, questions that are particularly interesting from my point of view. In what follows, I will point out the elements that I agree with, as well as those that I do not, and in some cases I accept solutions that are different from those I propose in this book. However, in order to fully understand this preface it is necessary to read the book first, making this something of an afterword rather than a preface.

1. *The Importance of the Exile and the Persian Period*

First of all I think it is worth emphasizing the fact that, unlike in the past, scholarly interest has come more and more to be focused on the history of the Second Temple period instead of the history of Israel in general. In fact, the classic histories of Israel are centred on pre-exile Israel, as Grabbe has rightly pointed out.[1] My *Storia del mondo giudaico* (Turin 1976), which deals with the same period in Israel's history as this history, has shown itself to represent a valid intuition regarding the needs of the modern historiography of Israel. I believe that part of the reason for this new interest is that indicated by Grabbe: the need for a more comprehensive understanding of the Second Temple period. I also believe, though, that there is a growing awareness that the texts of the Bible were given their present form only during the Persian and

---

1. L.L. Grabbe, *Judaism from Cyrus to Hadrian* (2 vols.; Minneapolis: Fortress Press, 1992, 1994), I, p. xxv.

Hellenistic periods. The Persian period is no longer a 'desert sea' as Ricciotti called it,[2] but has come to be seen as a very creative period in Jewish history. While the sources are often ancient, the criteria that led to the definitive structure date from after the exile. Judaism was born during the Persian period, though I feel that the importance of the Hellenistic period in the development of Judaism remains to be fully appreciated. The trend, however, to lower the dates of all the biblical books seems to me to depend more on the current intellectual climate than on scientific proofs.[3]

There is a whole series of books and articles that present as certain that not only the texts of the Bible were formed during the Persian period, but also the ideology, or rather ideologies, that gave them the structure that they have. This no longer needs to be demonstrated, it has become a 'given' for scholars. Along this line of thought see, for example, the book by Davies[4] and Rouillard-Bonraisin's article.[5] Diana V. Edelman has even written that the way of referring to Yhwh as Elohim cannot date from before the Persian period.[6] What was once called 'monolatry' is now called 'inclusive monotheism' with a slight semantic difference, while the classic 'monotheism' has become 'exclusive monotheism', whose origin has been moved forward to the Hellenistic period. It would seem that Deutero-Isaiah's anti-idolatric thought carries no weight. Although I am convinced that the Persian period was culturally an extremely active period and that the roots of Judaism are to be found there, I still have the impression that there has

2. G. Ricciotti, *Storia d'Israele* (2 vols.; Torino: Società Editrice Internazionale, 1932, 1934), p. 150. This book has recently been reprinted by the same publisher in a single volume (Turin, 1997).

3. See the same opinon in E. Noort, *Das Buch Josua; Forschungsgeschichte und Problemfelder* (Darmstadt: Wissenschaftliche Buchgesellschaft, 1998): 'Wir müssen wohl dankbar sein, dass es eine feststellbare Reception der Josuatexte in Qumran und im Neuen Testament gibt. Ansonsten wäre in Kürze der Vorschlag zu erwarten, das Josuabuch sei ein Blaudruck für den Bar-Kochba-Aufstand' (p. 245).

4. P.R. Davies, *In Search of 'Ancient Israel'* (Sheffield: Sheffield Academic Press, 1992), especially pp. 94-112.

5. H. Bouillard-Bonraisin, 'Les livres bibliques d'époque perse', in E.M. Laperrousaz (ed.), *La Palestine à l'époque perse* (Paris: Cerf, 1994), pp. 157-88. Some space is also given to the formation of the Pentateuch.

6. D.V. Edelman, in the Introduction to *The Triumph of Elohim: From Yahavisms to Judaisms* (Grand Rapids: Eerdmans, 1995), pp. 15-26, in particular pp. 22-23.

been some exaggeration in attributing to it works and ideas which must be considered much older. I feel that the exile was very important in the production of material; later epochs would have the task of structuring and organizing that material.

I know of only one book on this period of the history of Israel that has the defect of presenting a history of pre-exile Israel in the traditional manner, the book by C. and F. Jullien.[7] Even the studies by Gosse, now synthesized in a book, place all the formation of the most ancient parts of the Bible in the Hellenistic period.[8]

2. *The Edict of Cyrus*

The authenticity of the Edict of Cyrus is a basic question for understanding the period of the Exile. While C. and F. Jullien, Nodet[9] and also Grabbe[10] favour the Edict's authenticity, I continue to have many doubts. The main argument against its authenticity is the fact that no people living west of the Euphrates are mentioned in the Cyrus Cylinder among the peoples allowed to return home. It is clear that the authorization to return home addressed only the peoples of Mesopotamia, those who had been persecuted by Nabonidus, the Babylonian king deposed by Cyrus.

3. *The Jews Remaining in the Homeland*

It is a fact, more than a common opinion, that all traces of the Jews remaining in the Homeland had been lost. Direct heirs of the most ancient Palestinian tradition, all memory of them had been cancelled by the Babylonian Judaism which gained the upper hand with Nehemiah, so much so that the book of Chronicles even says that all of Israel was sent into exile. Anyhow, it is only reasonable to believe that the Jews who remained in Palestine must have had a culture and some weight in the history of Judaism. Noth[11] wrote that the Jews who remained in

---

7. C. and F. Jullien, *La Bible en exil* (Neuchâtel: Recherches et Publications, 1996). See also my review article in *Mesopotamia* 31 (1996), pp. 305-307.

8. B. Gosse, *Structuration des grands ensembles bibliques et intertextualité à l'époque perse* (Berlin: de Gruyter, 1997).

9. E. Nodet, *A Search for the Origins of Judaism: From Joshua to the Mishnah* (Sheffield: Sheffield Academic Press, 1997 [French edn 1992]), p. 7.

10. Grabbe, *Judaism*, pp. 35-36, 123 and 127.

11. M. Noth, *The History of Israel* (London: A. & C. Black, 1958), p. 359.

their homeland were certainly important in the history of Israel and in the formation of Judaism, even though we have lost trace of them. In 1982 I put forth the hypothesis that these traces could possibly be found in the Apocalyptic tradition,[12] following the terminology that I used then; today I would speak of Enochism. But once the Enochic tradition too has been brought into the realm of Babylonian culture,[13] it is worth taking Nodet's extremely complex hypothesis into consideration. For Nodet some elements of pre-exilic theology survived without being filtered by the Babylonian tradition, and are to be found in Samaritanism. This is an attractive hypothesis, but a long control period will be necessary due to the large number of indications drawn from new interpretations of the texts, each of which needs to be studied again. Along different lines, R. Albertz[14] singles out Palestinian ideas in the redaction of Jeremiah made around 550 BCE.

4. *The Deuteronomist and R1*

No one seems to have taken into consideration my hypothesis that Noth's Deuteronomist only makes sense if the historical work is taken separately from Deuteronomy. Research continues to make progress, examining individual questions, but the general structure suggested by Noth, that is the existence of a global work beginning from Deuteronomy and ending with the last verse of the books of Kings, is taken for granted as having a solid basis. Römer and De Pury state that the historical work of the Deuteronomist as proposed by Noth is a sure result of modern exegetical research.[15] Only E.A. Knauf's contribution[16]

12. P. Sacchi, 'Per una storia dell'apocalittica', in *Atti del tertio Convegno dell'Associazione Italiana per lo studio del giudaismo* (Rome: Carucci, 1987), pp. 59-78, republished in *L'apocalittica giudaica e la sua storia* (Brescia: Paideia, 1990), pp. 99-130, in particular pp. 128-29 (English translation: *Jewish Apocalyptic and its History* [Sheffield: Sheffield Academic Press, 1997], pp. 88-108, in particular pp. 107-108).

13. See J.C. VanderKam, *Enoch and the Growth of an Apocalyptic Tradition* (Washington: Catholic Biblical Association of America, 1984).

14. 'Le milieu des Detéronomistes', in A. de Pury (ed.), *Israël construit son histoire* (Geneva: Labor et Fides, 1996), pp. 377-418, esp. p. 400.

15. 'L'historiographie deutéronomiste (HD): Histoire de la recherche et enjeux du débat', in de Pury (ed.), *Israël construit son histoire*, pp. 9-120 (9).

16. 'L' "historiographie deutéronomiste" existe-t-elle?', in de Pury (ed.), *Israël construit son histoire*, pp. 409-18 (415).

contains the clear statement that Deuteronomy cannot be part of the Deuteronomist's historical work. He also refers to an article by H. Donner.[17] However, the fundamental literary argument, in my opinion, lies in the abundant traces of what Cortese[18] has called the 'buttoning' of Deuteronomy with the works that precede it and those that follow[19]. The ideological argument can be seen in the non-Davidic construction of Deuteronomy in comparison with the rest of the so-called work of the Deuteronomist. It is precisely for this reason that I decided to call the 'Deuteronomist' 'R1', because it is senseless to call a work Deuteronomistic if Deuteronomy is not a part of it. As concerns the place where R1's work was composed, it seems that Babylon has won a new consensus,[20] as has the characterization of R1's thought as well.[21]

I feel that much if not most of today's scholarly contributions regarding the history of the Old Testament tradition are distorted by a certain pre-understanding (*Vorverständnis*) that there was a tradition running from Moses to the Ezra of the tradition, in other words to the end of the exile.[22] But it is not to be assumed that R1's existed in substantially its present form prior to the exile. Before the exile separate written documents and oral traditions certainly existed, but normally we are completely unable to distinguish what derives from the earlier and what from the later period. It is also impossible to single out earlier editions, and even less so to assign a precise date to them.[23]

17. ' "Wie geschrieben steht": Herkunft und Sinn einer Formel', in *idem, Aufsätze zum Alten Testament aus vier Jahrzehnten* (Berlin: W. de Gruyter, 1994), pp. 224-38.

18. See E. Cortese, 'Gios. 21 e Giud. 1 (TM o LXX?) e l'abbottonatura del "Tetrateuco" con l'opera deuteronomistica', *RivB* 33 (1985), pp. 375-94 in the general bibliography. See also E. Cortese, *Da Mosè ad Ezra: I libri storici di Israele* (Bologna: EDB, 1985).

19. Cf. P. Sacchi, 'Giosuè 1, 1-9: Dalla critica storica a quella letteraria', in D. Garrone and F. Israel (eds.), *Storia e tradizioni di Israele* (Scritti in onore di J. Alberto Soggin; Brescia: Paideia 1991), pp. 237-54 (251).

20. See Albertz, 'Le milieu des Detéronomistes', p. 405

21. See Albertz, 'Le milieu des Detéronomistes', p. 401.

22. See P. Sacchi, 'The Pentateuch, the Deuteronomist, and Spinoza', *Henoch* 20 (1998), pp. 259-71.

23. Cf. R. Rendtorff, 'L'histoire biblique des origines (Gen 1–11) dans le contexte de la rédaction "sacerdotale" du Pentateuque', in A. de Pury (ed.), *Le Pentateuque en question: Les origines et la composition des cinq premiers livres de la*

5. *The Beginnings of the Republic*

One fundamental point for understanding the history of early Judaism is establishing just what the structure of the Jewish state of Jerusalem was. Was it, following Flavius Josephus's commonly accepted description, a theocratic republic, or rather a diarchy, that continued the structures of the times of Zerubbabel and Joshua? I tended to lean toward the latter opinion, convinced not only by the information given by Nehemiah about the governors who had preceded him (Neh. 5.15), but also by the *bullae* published by Avigad. Some doubts remained, though, since the question of the *bullae*'s authenticity had been raised. I now see, however, that an expert of Lemaire's calibre has no difficulty in accepting their authenticity.[24] In this case I feel that it is fair, following Lemaire, to reconstruct the governorship in Judaea with a decent margin of error as follows: after Zerubbabel most probably came the governorship of his brother Hananah, and then Elnathan, the husband of Hananah's sister, Shelomit.[25] Accepting the value of the *bullae* as documents, then, it becomes clear that the end of the Davidic dynasty was rather gradual, certainly more so than we used to believe. It thus becomes clearer why memory of that dynasty lasted so long after 515 BCE.

6. *Ezra*

The figure of Ezra continues to pose some difficult problems; see the Eskenazi and Richards collection.[26] Davies makes an acute critique of the problem of the books of Ezra and Nehemiah,[27] concluding: 'it is

Bible à la lumière des recherches récentes (Geneva: Labor et Fides, 1989), pp. 83-94 (84).

24. See A. Lemaire, 'Histoire et administration de la Palestine à l'époque perse', in Laperrousaz (ed.), *La Palestine à l'époque perse*, pp. 11-54.

25. See Lemaire, 'Histoire et administration'.

26. See T. Eskenazi and K.H. Richards (eds.), *Second Temple Studies*. II. *Temple Community in the Persian Period* (Sheffield: Sheffield Academic Press, 1994). The contributions that deal with Ezra are: S. Japhet, 'Composition and Chronology in the Book of Ezra-Nehemiah', pp. 189-216; D. Smith Christopher, 'The Mixed Marriage Crisis in Ezra 9–10 and Nehemiah 13', pp. 243-65; Grabbe, 'What Was Ezra's Mission?', pp. 276-89. See also P.R. Davies, 'Scenes from Early History of Judaism', in Edelman (ed.), *The Triumph*, pp. 145-84.

27. Davies, 'Scenes from Early History of Judaism'.

surely more productive for the historian of Judaism to accept the clear evidence that these books are far removed from the time they describe and to ask about the function of stories and of characters such as these in a later period'.[28] In my book I have attempted to solve this question. Even though, as Grabbe maintains,[29] the problems of Ezra are desperate, I feel that we must continue to accept the historical existence of this person and that his life must be situated during the time of Artaxerxes II.[30] On the one hand it seems beyond doubt that the unity of Ezra–Nehemiah is late and served the purpose of explaining the origins of Judaism, or of accrediting a certain form of Judaism at the expense of another, Ezra's Judaism over Nehemiah's. On the other hand, I cannot see why the fact that Ezra–Nehemiah is late should mean that the book in its present form is not the fusion of two pre-existing works[31] which addressed different aims. The simple fact, then, that the author has a particular point of view and a particular aim in mind does not mean that the events narrated contain no 'historical truth'.

7. Judaism and Judaisms

The idea is now so widely accepted that it is hardly worth discussing the fact that Judaism was not monolithic, but was rather a complex reality, with a wealth of different, rival ideologies (or theologies) and reciprocal adjustments, as takes place within every culture of the world. This fact has had very strong repercussions on the understanding of the origins of Christianity. Had Judaism been monolithic then Christianity could only have inherited from Judaism or broken away from it. But, if Judaism contained various different and at times even opposite tendencies within itself, then our comprehension of the Christian phenomenon changes. Christianity becomes one group among many with complex affinities and oppositions.

In my book I indicate the various tensions and parties that animated the Jewish world with the term 'currents', in keeping with the most

28. See Davies, 'Scenes from Early History of Judaism', p. 160.

29. Grabbe, *Judaism*, I, p. 138.

30. Japhet shares this view, see 'Composition and Chronology in the Book of Ezra–Nehemiah', in Eskenazi and Richards (eds.), *Second Temple Studies*, II, pp. 189-216.

31. See also my article 'La questione di Ezra', in G. Busi (ed.), *We-zo't le-Angelo* (Bologna: Fattoadarte, 1993), pp. 461-70.

common usage. Neusner, followed with great enthusiasm and coherence by Boccaccini, coined the term 'Judaisms' in order to indicate the
currents within Judaism. Each of these is a Judaism. In a recent article
P.R. Davies[32] has approached the problem from a theoretical point of
view, pointing out that 'the replacement of the concept of "Judaism" by
the concept of "Judaisms" solves one problem only to create another'.[33]
Analysing the concept of 'Judaisms' as it appears in the works of Boccaccini and Schiffman, he sees the risk of considering the most ancient
form of Judaism as a sort of 'biblical religion': 'Behind his [Bocca-
ccini's] interpretation of Ben Sira might be suspected the common
assumption that the earliest form of Judaism was some kind of "biblical
Judaism" '.[34]

In reality, not even the definition of Judaism is an easy one, as it is
not easy to define any culture. Judaism is linked to the life of the Jewish
people. Historically, however, there are also varieties of Judaism that
have developed among non-Jews. If we claim that there is a Latin culture whose origins are only Latin, then it is only because we are unaware of all the elements that produced that culture. And Latin
civilization also developed away from Rome, and outside of Italy; fragments of Latinity can be found in non-Latin countries like Germany, or
the Anglo-Saxon world. But those things that get called Latin in the
Anglo-Saxon world could have originally been imported into Latin
civilization. 'Person' is a word derived from the Latin *persona*, but the
Latin word was borrowed from Etruscan. Even still, in modern languages we can say that we are dealing with a Latin word, since it is
from Latin that we have taken it. A culture is in continual diachronic
variation, whose development is based on both internal and external
elements. It is said that the resurrection is an element that came from
Iran, but today we say that it was a typical element of the Jewish religion beginning from a certain point in time, and this is true even if a
rabbi can interpret in such a metaphorical way as to in fact deny it.[35]

Judaism, therefore, is a historical reality with characteristics that vary
over time, or within a particular time; between the inhabitants of Qumran and the followers of the Hasmonaeans there were enormous

32. Davies, 'Scenes from Early History of Judaism'.
33. See Davies, 'Scenes from Early History of Judaism', p. 147.
34. See Davies, 'Scenes from Early History of Judaism', p. 149.
35. See B.Z. Bokser, *Judaism: Profile of a Faith* (New York: Knopf, 1963),
ch. 9.

differences in both thought and behaviour. We can also say that wherever Christianity exists Judaism exists as well. It is because of this unity across difficult to define borders (though they are easily *discerned*) that I feel it is more useful to speak of 'currents' within Judaism rather than of different Judaisms, but I am sure that beyond the labels and the philosophical pre-understandings that each person carries, many similar thoughts are shared.

8. *The Problem of the Jewish 'Currents' of the Second Temple: Their Identification and Name*

While the existence of different forms of thought within Jewish society of the Second Temple is clear, both inside and outside Palestine, it is more difficult to come up with adequate names for them and, especially in recent times, new names have been suggested in keeping with the way each author sees most fit for the individual realities. Essentially the problem is constituted by the fact that our information comes from two different types of sources, direct and indirect (in the terminology currently in use in Italian philology). Direct sources are those texts where the author expresses his thought directly, as in the non-historical books of the Bible, or the pseudepigrapha, or most of the Qumran texts. Narrations are indirect sources, or at least the information provided by authors speaking of other authors' ideas. We can find the names of Jewish groups or currents in the indirect sources, such as the Jewish-Hellenistic historians or Philo. It is impossible to find these names in the texts where the authors speak directly of their ideas; the attribution of a text to one group or another is always the fruit of an inductive process and is destined, therefore, to remain a hypothesis. Thus, at one time we said that we only knew of the Essenes but did not possess any of their works. With the discovery of the Dead Sea Scrolls the typical material of Qumran has been identified with the Essenism of the indirect sources. Today the idea has been formulated[36] that the typical texts of Qumran are not Essenic, but rather belong to an extremist Essene group, to be distinguished from mainstream Essenism by their strong belief in predeterminism. Many texts which until not too long ago were called 'apocalyptic' now seem rather to be Essenic, in keeping with the value assigned that term by Philo and Flavius Josephus.

---

36. G. Boccaccini, *Beyond the Essene Hypothesis: The Parting of the Ways between Qumran and Enochic Judaism* (Grand Rapids: Eerdmans, 1998).

With apocalyptic we are faced with a case that is the opposite of that of the Essenes. With the Essenes we had a name, but we were unable to attribute any known Jewish works to them until the discovery of the Dead Sea Scrolls. The name 'apocalyptic' was born at the beginning of the nineteenth century; it is, therefore, a modern creation used to indicate works that are stylistically comparable to the Apocalypse of John, and which were thought to have some common elements in their ideology. In reality there is no common ideology, and part of the works that were once called 'apocalyptic' are now listed under the labels of Enochism or Essenism, as recently suggested (and I agree) by Boccaccini.

The advantage of Boccaccini's labelling lies in the fact that finally there are some works known to the tradition that correspond to the Essenes of the Jewish-Hellenistic writers. Use of the term 'apocalyptic current' entails the difficulty of having a body of works that, however numerous and important, were unknown as such to the ancients.

It is a historical datum that the writers of the Qumran scrolls were in effect ignored by the ancients; their production was not only ignored by the rabbis, but by Christians as well, though those preserved the Enochian literature. If the people of Qumran were forgotten by the ancients, it is necessary to give them a conventional name; it is necessary to understand one another when we speak! When the Qumran sect broke away from the Enochians for complex reasons, the Enochians forcefully reconfirmed their faith in the individual's freedom of choice, in contrast to Qumranic determinism. Thus two currents were born from one, and the principal one of these was none other than the Essenism spoken of by the ancient historians.

9. *The Library and the Occupation of Qumran*

A discussion of fundamental importance revolves around the structure of the Qumran library. First of all, it seems that the 'Groningen hypothesis' is being confirmed.[37] The collection of essays by Laperrousaz[38]

37. See F. García Martínez, 'Qumran Origins and Early History: A Groningen Hypothesis', *Folia Orientalia* 25 (1988), pp. 113-36, an article taken up again and lengthened in *RevQ* 14 (1990), pp. 522-41, under the title 'A Groningen Hypothesis of Qumran Origins and Early History'.

38. See E.M. Laperrousaz (ed.), *Qoumrân et les manuscrits de la Mer Morte* (Paris: Cerf, 1997).

and Boccaccini's recent book[39] confirm it completely. On the one hand Golb's hypothesis[40] of the library's composite and eclectic nature has been put aside, while on the other the need to make some distinctions within the library has been confirmed: typically sectarian texts to be attributed to the inhabitants of Qumran, texts whose origin cannot be attributed to members of the sect, and, among these, texts which may be labelled as Zadokite and texts which may rather be labelled as Enochic. The collection of studies edited by Laperrousaz and in particular his own articles in that collection lower the date of Qumran's occupation, though not those of the sect's origin, on an archaeological and historical basis to around the year 100 BCE. In my opinion, this later date is certain.

10. *Enochians and Hasmonaeans*

Another development that seems very important is the new evaluation made of the relations between Enochians, Qumranians and Hasmonaeans. It now seems that in the beginning that was not as negative as it has been presented in the past, and as I myself have presented it.[41] There is strong evidence that Enochism came close to becoming the religion of Israel. The book of Jubilees bears witness to an attempt to fuse the Zadokite tradition with the Enochic one in a single whole where the basic values and structure were Enochic. The Law of Moses which had become the Law with the Maccabbaean revolt remained the Law, but it was placed below that of the heavenly tablets of the Enochians.[42]

11. *Is the Pentateuch a Late Work?*

The question of when the Pentateuch received the form it now has and of when it became part of the Bible can be seen behind Boccaccini's

39. See Boccaccini, *Beyond the Essene Hypothesis.*

40. See N. Golb, 'L'origine des Manuscrits de la Mer Morte', *Annales* 40 (1985), pp. 1133-79. The theme is taken up again several times: see 'Who Hid the Dead Sea Scrolls?', *BA* 48 (1985), pp. 68-82; 'Hypothesis of Jerusalem Origin of the Dead Sea Scrolls—Synopsis', in Z.J. Kapera (ed.), *Mogilany 1989 Papers on the Dead Sea Scrolls* (Cracow: Enigma Press, 1993), pp. 53-58.

41. See A.I. Baumgarten, *The Flourishing of Jewish Sects in the Maccabean Era: An Interpretation* (Leiden: E.J. Brill, 1997), pp. 31-32.

42. See Boccaccini, *Beyond the Essene Hypothesis*, pp. 86-98.

historical reconstruction, and this refers back to Nodet's hypothesis and the recurring theme in Garbini's work.[43] I believe that R1's work began well before the book of Joshua, but this does not necessarily mean that it began with the myth of Eden. At any rate I would like to draw attention to the fact (see Chapter 12 §4) that in the *Book of Dreams* (approx. 160 BCE) the myth of Adam and Eve is known, but not the story of Eden. Had it been suppressed, or was it not yet considered a founding myth, part of the sacred tradition? I feel that this important question is still open. I would like to remind the reader, however, that in any case the story of Eden is mentioned in the Book of Watchers, even though in its later stage (*1 En.* 32.6).

12. *Dating the Eleazar Episode*

In the *Antiquities of the Jews* (12.288-98) Flavius Josephus tells of a certain Eleazar who accused John Hyrcanus of occupying the throne illegitimately. The same episode is recounted in a rabbinic source in relation to Alexander Jannaeus, shifting the date by several years. Depending on the date that one chooses, the perspective on the origin of Pharisaism changes.[44] I remain faithful to my choice in favour of Flavius Josephus's dating, in company, it seems, with Grabbe as well.[45]

13. *The Origins of Christianity*

The date assigned to the Enochic *Book of Parables* is of particular importance in the study of the origins of Christianity. The central figure of that book was created before time with the dual function of protecting the righteous of this world and holding the Great Judgment at the end of time. This character is indicated by three names during the course of the work: 'the Righteous One', 'the Chosen One' and the 'Son of Man'. The last name is how Jesus referred to himself. Hence the importance of the book's dating, because it is very different if the *Book of Parables* depends (in this case literarily) on the New Testament, or if the New Testament bears witness to an expression used by

43. See in English Garbini's work, in many ways a summary, *History and Ideology in Ancient Israel* (trans. J. Bowden; London: SCM Press, 1988).

44. Cf. G. Stemberger, *Pharisäer, Sadduzäer, Essener* (Stuttgart: Katholisches Bibelwerk, 1991).

45. Grabbe, *Judaism*, II, p. 470.

Jesus' contemporaries for indicating a mysterious figure, placed above the very angels, for whom the *Book of Parables* provides an interpretation. In any case the importance of the fact remains, that Jesus did not indicate himself in direct reference to Daniel, but by way of this Enochic interpretation of a passage in Daniel. This interpretation of the question of the 'Son of Man' in the New Testament is linked, obviously, to the date assigned to the *Book of Parables*. It seems to me that this dating is coming to be definitively accepted. I defended it recently at the Congress held at Princeton in November 1997; the same position is to be found in the book by Chialà[46] and in an article by Charlesworth.[47] Now it is certain that the words 'Son of Man' on the lips of Jesus were an expression indicating someone that the people of the day knew. Clearly, the semantic area of the expression in the language of Palestine of the day remains to be determined; did it really indicate a character, or only a function, or was it even more vague?

I believe that the best way of furthering study on the New Testament, seen as an integral part of first century CE Jewish society, is to concentrate attention on the major themes.[48] The work of Chilton and Evans follows this line.[49] This methodological line can also be seen in Ben F. Meyer's article summarizing the teachings of John the Baptist as preaching penitence and purification to all Israel.[50]

46. S. Chialà, *Libro delle Parabole di Enoch* (Brescia: Paideia, 1997).

47. J.H. Charlesworth, 'The Date of the Parables of Enoch', *Henoch* 20 (1998), pp. 93-98.

48. See P. Sacchi, Introduction to the *Apocrifi dell'Antico Testamento* (Turin: UTET, 1989), II, pp. 14-15.

49. B. Chilton and C.A. Evans, *Jesus in Context: Temple, Purity and Restoration* (Leiden: E.J. Brill, 1997). 'It is the conviction of the authors that despite good intentions all around Jesus research continues to be defective at crucial points because of a general lack of awareness of the importance of purity in the teaching and conduct of Jesus and his contemporaries' (p. 2). Peter, Paul and John are studied in the light of their interpretation of purity. The sacrifice of the cross is of central importance; see in B. Chilton and C.A. Evans (eds.), *Studying the Historical Jesus: Evaluation of the State of Current Research* (Leiden: E.J. Brill, 1994), the article by Ben F. Meyer, 'Jesus' Ministry and Self-Understanding', pp. 337-52. 'The problem was the sunkenness in sin of Israel and the nations; the revealed solution, the death of the appointed messianic savior as ransom, expiatory and covenant sacrifice' (p. 352). Against this interpretation of Jesus' mission, which I hold to be at least historically correct, see now the important work of S. Dianich, *Il messia sconfitto* (Casale: Piemme, 1997).

50. 'Jesus' Ministry and Self-Understanding'.

I am also pleased to point out an important series of studies on Alexandrian Judaism, that have strong implications for the history of the origins of Christianity. These are the studies of Lucio Troiani, a synthesis of which is available in the introduction to the fifth volume of the *Apocrifi dell'Antico Testamento*.[51]

Troiani begins with an examination of some of the Jewish-Hellenistic works (the *Letter of Aristeas* and the *Antiquities of the Jews*). He attempts a description of the circles where they originated, and has discovered the multilingual, cosmopolitan and international character of these texts. He thus describes the general situation of Judaism, especially of the Greek language, which was very articulate and more rooted in individual, local realities than is usually recognized. The sense of Jewish self-identification reveals itself to be a complex phenomenon, in which different geographical locations created a sense of nationality which was linked to a sense of belonging to Judaism. The world reached by the first Christian mission was the variegated world of Judaism that had fought for the 'rights of citizenship'; it was the Judaism of Alexandria and Ephesus, of Cyrene and Antioch, of Rome and Corinth. In the light of these studies an analysis of the contents of the Acts of the Apostles and the letters of Paul allows for a new and fascinating interpretation not only of the recipients of the first *kerygma* but also of its meaning. The fact that the studies are very complex and not yet entirely finished, and above all that they change ideas that have perhaps always been accepted, imposes a certain degree of caution and the need for careful review. In any case, Troiani is a scholar whose work deserves to be known outside Italy.

I would like to thank Sheffield Academic Press for the interest they have shown in my work, and Thomas Kirk who translated it. Particular thanks are due to Corrado Martone, who took on the task of chasing down the English versions of works referred to in Italian in the original edition of this book.

51. See L. Troiani, 'Introduction', in P. Sacchi (ed.), *Apocrifi dell'Antico Testamento* (Brescia: Paideia, 1997), V, pp. 17-72.

TRANSLATOR'S NOTE

In the original Italian edition of this book the author provides new translations of the many quotations, made directly from the original languages. I unfortunately do not possess the same linguistic ability to do the same for this English edition. Biblical quotations, therefore, have been taken from the Revised Standard Version and the New Revised Standard Version of the Bible, adapting them where necessary in order to make them correspond to the author's interpretation of the original language texts. J.H. Charlesworth's *The Old Testament Pseudepigrapha* (2 vols.; Garden City: New York, 1983–85) has been used for quotations from the pseudepigraphical works, again modifying them in some cases due to differing interpretations of the original. In the case of the Qumran manuscripts, in most cases the author and I have provided new translations, though G. Vermes, *The Dead Sea Scrolls in English* (Harmondsworth: Penguin Books, 1968), and J.H. Charlesworth (ed.), *The Dead Sea Scrolls: Hebrew, Aramaic and Greek Texts with English Translation* (Tübingen: J.C.B. Mohr, 1994–), were used as constant points of reference.

ABBREVIATIONS

AfO	*Archiv für Orientforschung*
AION	*Annali dell'istituto orientale di Napoli*
AISG	Associazione italiana per lo studio del Giudaismo
ANET	James B. Pritchard (ed.), *Ancient Near Eastern Texts Relating to the Old Testament* (Princeton: Princeton University Press, 1950)
AR(R)AST	*Atti della (Reale) Accademia delle Scienze di Torino*
ASNSP	*Annali della Scuola Normale Superiore di Pisa*
ASE	*Annali di Storia dell'Esegesi*
BA	*Biblical Archaeologist*
BA	Book of Astronomy
BASOR	*Bulletin of the American Schools of Oriental Research*
BD	*Book of Dreams*
BeO	*Bibbia e oriente*
BHK	R. Kittel (ed.), *Biblia hebraica* (Stuttgart: Württembergische Bibelanstalt, 1937)
BHS	*Biblia hebraica stuttgartensia*
BJRL	*Bulletin of the John Rylands University Library of Manchester*
BN	*Biblische Notizen*
BO	*Bibliotheca orientalis*
BP	*Book of Parables*
BW	*Book of Watchers*
CAH	Cambridge Ancient History
CBQ	*Catholic Biblical Quarterly*
CEI	Conferenza episcopale italiana
CHJ	Cambridge History of Judaism
DBSup	*Dictionnaire de la Bible, Supplément*
DJD	Discoveries in the Judaean Desert
EC	*Enciclopedia Cattolica*
ER	*Enciclopedia delle Religioni*
EVO	*Egitto e Vicino Oriente*
ExpTim	*Expository Times*
HR	*History of Religions*
HTR	*Harvard Theological Review*
HUCA	*Hebrew Union College Annual*
ICC	International Critical Commentary

IEJ	*Israel Exploration Journal*
JBL	*Journal of Biblical Literature*
JfBT	*Jahrbuch für biblische Theologie*
JJS	*Journal of Jewish Studies*
JQR	*Jewish Quarterly Review*
JNES	*Journal of Near Eastern Studies*
JSJ	*Journal for the Study of Judaism in the Persian, Hellenistic and Roman Period*
JSOT	*Journal for the Study of the Old Testament*
LA	*Libera Annuus*
NovT	*Novum Testamentum*
OrAnt	*Oriens antiquus*
PdP	*La Parola del Passato*
RB	*Revue biblique*
REJ	*Revue des études juives*
RevQ	*Revue de Qumran*
RGG	*Religion in Geschichte und Gegenwart*
RivB	*Rivista biblica*
RSO	*Rivista degli studi orientali*
RSB	*Ricerche storico-bibliche*
RSLR	*Rivista di storia e litteratura religiosa*
RStI	*Rivista storica italiana*
SBLSP	SBL Seminar Papers
SBT	Studies in Biblical Theology
Sem	*Semitica*
StAns	*Studia Anselmiana*
StIr	*Studia Irannica*
ThRund	*Theologische Rundschau*
TSK	*Theologische Studien und Kritiken*
ThWAT	G.J. Botterweck and H.-J. Fabry, *Theologisches Wörterbuch zum Alten Testament* (Stuttgart: Kohlhammer)
TWNT	Gerhard Kittel and Gerhard Friedrich (eds.), *Theologisches Wörterbuch zum Neuen Testament* (11 vols.; Stuttgart, Kohlhammer, 1932–79)
VO	*Vicino oriente*
VT	*Vetus Testamentum*
VTSup	*Vetus Testamentum*, Supplements
WdO	*Welt des Orients*
WMANT	Wissenschaftliche Monographien zum Alten und Neuen Testament
ZA	*Zeitschrift für Assyriologie*
ZAW	*Zeitschrift für die alttestamentliche Wissenschaft*
ZDMG	*Zeitschrift der deutschen morgenländischen Gesellschaft*

INTRODUCTION

1. *Origin, Audience and Aims of the Present Volume*

This book is the product of teaching experience gained in a number of courses at the University of Turin. I have tried in those courses to present the main themes that belaboured Hebrew and Jewish thought before the rise of Christianity to students of classical Hebrew, many of whom also studied the history of Christianity. I feel that in order to understand the origins of Christianity it is necessary to know the fundamental themes of Jewish thought which, of course, did not arise in any systematic fashion. They have undergone a long and difficult evolution, an evolution of spiritual experiences, which, like all things human, has been conditioned by historical events. While a great deal of space in this book is dedicated to the history of thought, it does not overlook the fundamental events of the history of Palestine. It is not, however, a history of Palestine, nor is it simply a history of Judaism. Its aim is rather to illustrate, to place certain aspects of pre-Christian Jewish thought in their proper context in order to better understand the earliest positions of Christianity. By this I do not mean to say that there is any reasonable hope of grasping the deepest nature of any event through its antecedents, but a certain spirituality can be understood within the limits of historical study, both through the choices that spirituality determines in the realm of its own traditions, and through the innovations it brings about in those same traditions. The historian must try to understand the unity of the forces that have a modelling effect on tradition, including all ideas and currents of thought encountering that tradition, together with the freedom of innovation. These two terms are to be understood through comparison; any autonomy between the two is purely rational inasmuch as it is their complete and intimate fusion that constitutes the very essence of history.

It is useful therefore, for the goals of this book, to go back in time and shed light on a number of elements of ideology and political facts that gave birth to the tensions and the divisions of Jesus of Nazareth's time. In spite of the book's broadly chronological presentation, our discussion is organized by themes.

In Jesus' time, the Jewish religion was deeply rooted in the spiritual and political life of Judaea. The religion was permeated with deep tensions whose historical manifestations are to be seen both in the formation of various sects and parties, and in political choices very closely linked to theological motivations. We are reminded of the Pharisees and the Sadducees, both mentioned in the Gospels, but also of the Essenes who are not. A number of problems arose in the midst of these groups and were to influence Christianity, either in terms of the adoption of their ideas or through conscious opposition to them.

This then is the context for the book's subject; the choice of themes to be dealt with, which is greater than might at first appear after an initial glance at the table of contents, has been determined primarily by the importance they have had on the formation of early Christian thought.

'Parties' and 'sects': both terms can be found in the work of the various scholars. The choice of one term or the other is determined by the author's point of view. Those scholars who tend to see the political weight that the groups of Jesus' time had on their day rather than taking into consideration the religious matrix of their formation, which, in effect, is not always easy to see in their political choices, prefer the term 'parties'. I shall use, however, the term 'sect' because the religious component always seems to be extremely strong in the formation of such groups' ideologies.

While the Essenes are not mentioned in the Gospels, it is unthinkable that neither Jesus nor the authors of the Gospels knew of them. See the articles by Daniel on the possibility that the Essenes actually are present in the Gospel.[1] The term ἐσσηνός or ἐσσαῖος is Greek and does not have a sure equivalent term in either Hebrew or in Aramaic. The most probable hypothesis is that it is derived form the Aramaic word *ḥsy'*. At any rate the problem of Essenism is purely one of the historical comparison of ideologies; beginning with Essenism as described by

---

1.   C. Daniel, 'Une mention paulienne des esséniens de Qumran', *RevQ* 5 (1966), pp. 553-68; *idem*, 'Esséniens, zélots et sicaires et leur mention par paronymie dans le NT', *Numen* 13 (1966), pp. 88-115; *idem*, 'Les hérodiens du NT, sont-ils des esséniens?', *RevQ* 6 (1967), pp. 31-54; *idem*, 'Les esséniens et l'arrière-fond historique de la parabole du bon Samaritain', *NovT* 11 (1969), pp. 71-104; *idem*, 'Nouveaux arguments en faveur de l'identification des hérodiens et des esséniens', *RevQ* 7 (1970), pp. 397-402.

Hellenistic Jewish writers such as Philo and Flavius Josephus, we look for an ideological matrix similar to the one provided by these authors in pre-Christian Jewish works, no matter which language was used in their composition.[2]

2. *Terminology*

First of all we should give a precise definition of a few words used in this book.

It can be useful to distinguish between Hebrew and Hebraism (in a restricted sense) on the one hand, and Jewish/Judaism on the other. We use the noun Hebraism and the adjective Hebrew in reference to the Hebrew religion and civilization prior to the exile. We use Judaism and Jewish when we speak of the religion and civilization after the exile. Following the great crisis of the first century CE we should use the term Rabbinical Judaism, or quite simply Rabbinism.[3]

It should be pointed out, however, that the term 'Jewish' can be used to mean all of the religion and civilization of the Jews from their origins right down to the present. The distinction between Hebrew and Jewish can be justified by the fact that during the exile new problems were posed which opened up new horizons for the Hebrew religion.

I am rather perplexed regarding the use of the word 'Messiah' as it has taken on a whole set of values in Christian theology which are

2.   On the question of etymology, see G. Vermes, 'The Etymology of "Essenes"', *RevQ* 2 (1960), pp. 427-43; see also J.T. Milik, *Ten Years of Discovery in the Wilderness of Judaea* (London: SCM Press, 1959), p. 80 n. 1, and F.M. Cross, *The Ancient Library of Qumran and Modern Biblical Studies* (Garden City, NY: Doubleday, 2nd edn, 1960), p. 51 n. 1. See also the justified position taken in favour of the traditional *ḥsy'* by T. Muraoka, ' "Essene" in the Septuagint', *RevQ* 8 (1973), pp. 267-68. Now see also E. Puech, *La croyance des Esséniens en la vie future: Immortalité, résurrection, vie éternelle? Histoire d'une croyance dans le judaïsme ancien* (Paris: Gabalda, 1993), I, pp. 22-24; Puech demonstrates that *ḥsy'* is the Aramaic form of the Hebrew *ḥsyd*.

3.   On the distinction between Hebrew and Jewish, see M. Simon and A. Benoit, *Le judaïsme et le christianisme antique d'Antiochus Epiphane à Constantin* (Paris: Presses Universitaires de France, 1968), p. 4. Now see also G. Boccaccini, 'History of Judaism: Its Periods in Antiquity', in J. Neusner (ed.), *Judaism in Late Antiquity* (Leiden: E.J. Brill, 1995), pp. 285-308. Boccaccini proposes a distinction between 'Jewish', which should be used in reference to history and culture, and 'Judaic' for use in reference only to religion.

extraneous to the Old Testament. I have chosen the solution of using the word 'anointed' where the Old-Testament Hebrew uses *mašiaḥ* and the word 'Messiah' for the figure without a precise name who dominates some passages of the Old Testament and the pseudepigraphical literature, that figure who is supposed to come in the future and bring salvation to the people of Israel, or even to all people. I reserve the term 'Messiah', which by the way should not be seen as a simple phonetic adaptation of *mašiaḥ*, for that future figure sometimes called 'prophet' (Deut. 18.9-22), at other times with a variety of names: 'star' (Num. 24.17), 'shoot' (Isa. 11.1), etc.

Regarding the passage from Deuteronomy, in the intentions of the author the word 'prophet' does not refer to a future figure, but the permanent institution of Israel. This becomes clear from the context: first it speaks of the monarchy, secondly of the priesthood, and thirdly of prophetism. The messianic interpretation of the passage originated with the Samaritans who, having excluded the Prophets from the canon, interpreted the passage as though there were only two prophets: Moses and a later one equal to Moses who would come as a restorer.[4] The great antiquity of the Samaritan conception of the messianic figure as 'prophet' is extremely probable.[5]

On the problem of the lack of a precise term indicating the messianic figure in the Old Testament and the related problem of indicating all the characteristics and functions the Old Testament attributes to him, see the introductory pages of J. Coppens's study on messianism.[6]

3. *Basic Orientations in Hebrew Thought*

Through a general broadening of the horizons of a series of individual disciplines and a widespread feeling that a deeper understanding of humanity must necessarily lie at the basis of any historical knowledge, during the last few decades the problem of 'Hebrew thought' has been posed.

The aim of such studies is not so much to understand Hebrew thought as objectivised in a system, a task which seems to be left mainly to the-

4. See J. MacDonald, *The Theology of the Samaritans* (London: SCM Press, 1964).

5. MacDonald, *Theology of the Samaritans*, pp. 360-62.

6. J. Coppens, *Le messianisme royal: Ses origines, son développement, son accomplissement* (Paris: Cerf, 1968).

ologians and historians of theology, as it is to understand the underlying ways of thinking, the ways in which thought flows and confronts the real world.

These studies, while often quite stimulating, are generally unacceptable in the way they pose the problem. They should be discussed, however, since their basic principles are very common. The school of thought which best represents this trend is the so-called 'Biblical Theology' school. It attempts to grasp the structure of Hebrew thought in the very structure of the language. It is built on the supposition that there is a complete correspondence between the rhythm of thought and the rhythm of language. While perhaps this is not impossible, as demonstrated by the new discipline of psycholinguistics, we are still a long way from having the means necessary for reconstructing the mentality of a people through the structure of its language. It is much easier to intuit a relationship between language and ways of thinking than it is to pinpoint just exactly what constitutes that relationship.

Let us look at a few of the most widespread ideas, those most capable of influencing culture in a broad sense. Even a superficial knowledge of Greek and Hebrew literature is enough to notice that the two cultures are very different, and that the differences go well beyond what scholars of literature call themes and interests. The two literatures, and the two cultures, present completely different ways of reasoning and of seeing the world. In order to identify and understand the phenomenon some maintain, for example, that the defining characteristic of Hebrew thought compared to Greek thought is that the former is dynamic while the latter is static.

That would be easy enough to see in the structure of the Hebrew language where, unlike in Greek, everything is in continual movement. The demonstration of this idea is seen to lie in the nature of the Hebrew verb whose fundamental meaning always expresses the idea of movement, even in the case of verbs denoting immobility such as 'to stay', 'to sit' and 'to lie'. The argument is that these verbs can be used in the sense of 'putting oneself in the indicated position'.

Of course, the existence of such a possibility is taken to be of primary importance. This, however, is an argument which confuses linguistic and philosophical elements and in the end is useless. It is easily disproved by the simple phenomenon of verbs that can be used for both entering into a particular state and for continuity in that state. As far as I know this phenomenon is common to all languages and meaning is determined by the use of verb tenses and also by context. Let's take, for example, the expression 'I cannot sit' which, depending on its context, can mean that it is impossible to sit down, that is, perhaps there are no chairs or not enough space. The expression could also mean that I am already seated but cannot remain in a seated position, or the impossibility of ever sitting down, because for some reason it is forbidden that I ever sit. Furthermore, expressive necessity or simple stylistic taste can lead to the use of different verb forms which in normal use have opposite values. 'Napoleon was to die that year' can easily be used in place of 'Napoleon died that year'. The relation between logic and syntax is none too clear.[7]

Another idea which is to be rejected at all costs is that the root of the word in Hebrew has some particular function, something like that of the idea in Platonic thought. 'If it is true that the Hebrew roots express the concept or the idea, it means that that which Plato arrived at only after long and difficult thought, was offered freely to the Semites in their language'.[8] This has all led to a way of studying Hebrew thought usually based on a sort of metaphysical digression on the study of the roots of words rather than on the meanings of the words in their written context. A typical example of this way of proceeding is Snaith's reading of Ps. 1.1, which begins with 'Blessed...' But the Hebrew word translated, *'ašrê*, is an abstract derivative of a root which in other Semitic languages lies at the base of words meaning 'step', 'to go ahead, to advance'.

> This all goes to show how suitable the first word is. The psalm in fact speaks of the true way as opposed to the false one. Happy is the man who walks straight ahead, because, as the last verse says, 'for the Lord knows the way of the righteous, but the way of the wicked will perish'.[9]

It is clear that we are talking about notions which must have been entirely unknown to the poet who wrote these verses, but also to his

---

7.   The original Italian text contraposes the imperfect tense of the verb 'morire' (to die) with the remote past tense, a stylistic mutation common in Italian prose. 'In quell'anno moriva Napoleon', and 'In quell'anno morì Napoleone' [Translator's note].

8.   T. Boman, *Das Hebräische Denken im Vergleich mit dem Griechischen* (Göttingen: Vandenhoeck & Ruprecht, 1965), p. 57 (ET: *Hebrew Thought Compared with Greek* [London: SCM Press, 1960]).

9.   N.H. Snaith, 'The Language of the Old Testament', in *The Interpreter's Bible* (Nashville, New York: Abingdon Press, 1952), I, p. 224.

readers, whether his contemporaries or all of those who have lived in the centuries before the birth of modern linguistics.

This methodological problem is very important for a certain line of studies which, however, seems to have lost momentum recently.[10]

Even though these attempts at characterizing Hebrew thought are not acceptable, that does not change the fact that there are some fundamental attitudes underlying Hebrew and Jewish thought through the generations. We are not talking about a deep structure of thought, but rather of demonstrating an orientation, of individuating the idea which guides the Jew's thought and which at the same time is the object of a constant effort for clarifying that idea.

We can state that both Hebrew and Jewish thought are oriented toward the search for salvation. The fundamental problem is 'how to be saved'. Truth is rooted in this 'how to be saved' and in its dimensions which can go well beyond the individual and even the very people of Israel. Greek thought always seeks a universal element in the truth. Single events and single individuals (all of that which scholastic philosophy defines as existing *per accidens*), therefore, remain external to the discourse of Greek thought which is able to take the individual in consideration only inasmuch as he or she participates in the universal. The Jew's attention, alternatively, regards the single event in exactly the same way and perhaps with even greater force than the unchanging laws of the cosmos. It is this which is usually defined as the practical attitude of Hebrew thought, or sometimes as its particular attention to historical facts.

While Hebrew thought was always more or less consciously centred on the idea of 'salvation', it should be pointed out right away that the very concept of 'salvation' changed over time. During the Hebrew period it was essentially the 'salvation of the people'. Later, beginning with Ezekiel, beyond 'salvation of the people' it became 'salvation of the individual'. In 'canonic' Judaism, however, until the second century

---

10. See J. Barr, *Semantics of Biblical Language* (Oxford: Oxford University Press, 2nd edn, 1962) (which I translated into Italian under the title *La semantica del linguaggio biblico* [Bologna: Il Mulino, 1968]; see also my introduction to the Italian translation which puts some radical criticisms of the most recent and most important tradition of studies in a more correct perspective); Boman, *Hebrew Thought*; J. Pedersen, *Israel, its Life and Culture* (4 vols.; London: G. Cumberlege; Copenhagen: B.Og Korch, 1926–40); C. Tresmontant, *Essai sur la pensée hébraïque* (Paris: Cerf, 1953).

BCE it was never 'otherworldly salvation'. And then, the passage from one concept of salvation to another accompanied a deep transformation in the concept of the individual human being; it is very different to view a person's existence as limited between birth and death or to see the same person against an eternal backdrop. The passage from one concept to the other is marked by belief in life after death, which did not exist in the Hebrew period or in canonic Judaism prior to the second century BCE. We shall see the terms of the problem later on.

Salvation is the idea/matrix of Hebrew thought independently of any form which it could take throughout history and independently of all the reflections which were developed around the theme. The Hebrews dwelt on the means of reaching salvation, means which can be grouped together in two fundamental categories under the very modern names of 'Theology of the Covenant' and 'Theology of the Promise'. These categories represent two different, if not opposite, ways of conceiving religion, and both can be perceived even in the most ancient extant texts of Jewish literature.

For the Theology of the Promise there is a special relationship between God and the people of Israel whose existence and survival are guaranteed by God's promise. In this vision of things human guilt can arouse the wrath of the offended divinity, but cannot lead to the definitive catastrophe. Moreover, the authors working within this sphere tend to emphasize God's plan of salvation which is destined to come about entirely independently of human guilt.

Human beings are seen as being dominated by a force which drives them toward evil, which can in some cases be identified with impurity. At any rate, it is human nature itself which is inclined toward evil (Gen. 8.21). For this reason the punishment of the flood was useless. It would have been necessary not only to eliminate human beings from the face of the Earth but also to renew them as well. Salvation, therefore, can come only when God desires to bestow it upon humankind, whether through direct intervention or by means of a particularly charismatic personality. Every messianic movement is rooted in an anthropological concept of this type. The more one has a sense of the infinite power of God and of the individual's utter insufficiency, the more salvation tends to be considered a gratuitous gift of God which could never obtain through human forces alone.

Even righteousness, which remains the fundamental aspiration of the Hebrew soul, can be realized on Earth only through one who is anointed

by God. 'There shall come forth a shoot from the stump of Jesse...
They shall neither hurt nor do wrong' (Isa. 11.1, 9 [passages from different time periods]).

Those who experience religion in this way are led to emphasize the
unpredictability of God's action: 'I will be gracious to whom I will be
gracious, and I will show mercy on whom I will show mercy' (Exod.
33.19 [from a Yahwist source, in the common academic terminology]).
This concept often contains universalistic aspects; for example God's
call to Abraham,

> Go from your country and your kindred and your father's house to the
> land that I will show you. And I will make of you a great nation, and I
> will bless you, and make your name great, so that you will be a blessing.
> I will bless those who bless you, and him who curses you I will curse;
> and by you all the families of the earth shall be blessed (Gen. 12.1-3).

The God of the Promise is a God much closer to humans than the
God of the Covenant. Yhwh has elected his people because he loves
them and, if he has given them the Law, it is in order to sanction this
union between him and his people. He could even suspend the terrible
force of the sacred by letting himself be seen by the elders of Israel:

> Then Moses and Aaron, Nadab, and Abihu, and seventy of the elders of
> Israel went up, and they saw the God of Israel; and there was under his
> feet as it were a pavement of sapphire stone, like the very heaven for
> clearness. And he did not lay his hand on the chief men of the people of
> Israel; they beheld God, and ate and drank (Exod. 24.9-11).

David sinned, but God did not for this deny him the promise of an
eternal reign.

The Theology of the Covenant, on the other hand, is centred around
human freedom and responsibility. God chose the people of Israel and
offered them his Law. The people of Israel accepted it and the Law thus
became the sum of all the clauses regulating the Covenant binding God
to the Jews. A passage traditionally attributed to the Elohist reads:

> Moses came and told the people all the words of the Lord and all the
> ordinances; and all the people answered with one voice, and said, 'All
> the words which the Lord has spoken we will do'. And Moses wrote all
> the words of the Lord. And he rose early in the morning, and built an
> altar at the foot of the mountain [Sinai], and twelve pillars, according to
> the twelve tribes of Israel. And he sent young men of the people of
> Israel, who offered burnt offerings and sacrificed peace offerings of oxen
> to the Lord. And Moses took half of the blood and put it in basins, and

half of the blood he sprinkled on the altar. Then he took the book of the
covenant, and read it aloud to the people; and they said, 'All that the
Lord has spoken we will do, and we will be obedient'. And Moses took
the blood and sprinkled it upon the people, and said, 'Behold the blood
of the Covenant which Yhwh has made with you in accordance with all
these words' (Exod. 24.3-8).

Moses thus contaminated God, invisible on the altar, and the people
with the *blood of the Covenant*. The meaning of Moses' act is that each
time that Israel breaks the Covenant (the Covenant was made 'in accordance with all these words') contamination by blood will be unleashed
against Israel. Salvation of the people chosen by God, the elect, after
Abraham is no longer a gratuitous gift, but rather is based on the
people's observation of the commandments.

Human freedom is of great importance in this theological vision,
freedom in the sense of freedom of choice between good and evil. In
Hebrew terms, the choice lay between 'doing' God's commandments
and refusing them. Human beings manage history together with God, so
to speak; or rather, arrival at salvation seems to be placed essentially in
the hands of the humans. While it is true that God has given the commandments necessary for attaining salvation, they are only effective if
observed. Responsibility for salvation or ruin weighs heavily on the
fragile shoulders of the human beings.

The words of Deuteronomy follow in the path of the Theology of the
Covenant: 'See, I have set before you this day life and good, death and
evil' (30.15). Salvation and ruin depend on the choices to be made by
Israel, whether or not they choose to follow the commandments of
Yhwh their God.

During the Persian period the Theology of the Covenant grew more
and more important within what was to become canonical Judaism.
Outside of this line of thought, though, the presuppositions of the Theology of the Promise continued to develop. During the Hellenistic and
Roman periods the presence of two distinct basic modes of thought
becomes ever more clear within Jewish society. That this division
should correspond, however, to the ancient division between 'Promise'
texts and 'Covenant' texts is debatable and improbable. The problem is
an ancient one, though, and the meaning of the Promise of an eternal
reign compared to God's request for fidelity to him and his commandments is a problem which resurfaces often, each time with new and different nuances.

I feel compelled to insist that the terms 'Theology of the Covenant' and 'Theology of the Promise' do not indicate two separate theological systems, but simply two underlying attitudes of the Hebrew soul. Positions typical of the Theology of the Covenant can be found in texts which do not deal with the Covenant, and the Theology of the Promise in texts which do not even mention promises. Not only that, but within the Theology of the Covenant it is necessary to distinguish the point where the accent is placed more heavily on the concept of 'Covenant' from those where it tends to fall more on the idea of the 'Law'.

I am perfectly aware that in presenting these matrices in Jewish thought as those which characterize it and distinguish it from Greek culture, it is important to avoid all schematizations, because it is possible to find similar positions in the Greek world, and, even though only sporadically, it is not impossible to find positions in the Hebrew world which by definition should be Greek. For example, in Aeschylus's conception of ὕβρις [*hybris*] which leads the Persians to the disaster of Salamis we find an interpretation of history able to locate in a single event a logic governing all of history in a religious light.[11] Qohelet, on the other hand, basing his thought on meditations on the laws of the cosmos, accepts some ideas from the other side. I feel that the terms of the contraposition between an oriental mentality (Hebrew-Semitic) and the western one (Greek) were formulated quite well by Cumont:[12] the East was religious, the West was (or became) rationalist. The characteristic of rationalism being that of claiming to 'judge all sacred traditions in order to either condemn or approve them'. Its centre therefore is to be found in an 'I' which presents itself as absolute. It seems to me that rationalistic human struggle is that of trying to create a world through rationality which ends up colliding with very human, but non-rationalizable, needs. The risk, then, of the human who acts in accordance only with reason is that of becoming a non-human, as represented in the final steps of Platonic thought, from the rationalism of the *Republic* to the greater historicism of the *Laws*.[13]

11. On the richness and complexity of Aeschylus's thought see E. Severino, *Interpretazione e traduzione dell'Orestea di Eschilo* (Milan: Rizzoli, 1985).

12. F. Cumont, *Les religions orientales dans le paganisme romain: Conférences faites au Collège de France en 1905* (Paris: Librairie Orientaliste Paul Geuthner, 2nd edn, 1929 [1906]), pp. 26-27.

13. See E.R. Dodds, *The Greeks and the Irrational* (Berkeley: University of California Press, 1951). See in particular ch. 7.

Unlike Greek thought, Hebrew thought never distanced itself from the presupposition of the existence of a theodicy. In my opinion, it is for this reason, and no other, that Hebrew thought has always been centred around the question of salvation. Such a quest makes sense only if the divinity in some way lives with humans and cares about human things. Only in this way do events avoid falling into the void; in principle they are absurd, but inasmuch as they are traces of divine will they are the only means for understanding God, history and the life of the individual.

God is not experienced as a metaphysical reality, the author of some beginning which has subsequently undergone an independent development, but as the will lying at the basis of all reality, both in its cosmic structure (the sacred) and in its daily contingencies (history). Furthermore, there is another principle at work in history which is derived from God, but with considerable autonomy: the profane. Profanity is the essential and authentic characteristic of human beings and it reveals itself in their freedom of action and judgment. Humans can argue with God and can either accept or refuse God's proposals; if God has chosen Israel, then the individual Jew must in turn choose to accept or reject God.

In the Bible the pair 'sacred/profane' is placed in relationship to another pair, 'impure/pure' (see Lev. 10.10, and Ezek. 44.23 which is derived from it). All things that attach themselves to humans in some way and violate them, or better that weaken them, are called impure. A blow is not impure, but a disease is, especially leprosy. It was also a conviction among the ancients that sight of the divinity killed. While an encounter with the sacred in its most immediate and direct manifestation, contact with the divinity, could kill, then an encounter with reduced forms, that is with objects which are sacred inasmuch as belonging to God, transmitted a sort of fluid capable of undermining one's strength or of doing harm. Contact with such a 'weakened sacredness', present in the things called impure, contaminates, weakens humanity.

The question of the impurity of blood and male semen must be seen in this light. In the same manner all animals that crawl with their bellies on the ground are in contact with the earth which is of God (see pp. 439-42 below) and therefore they are impure. Such animals include all snakes and animals with a similar form: eels, lizards, etc. The classification of animals as either pure or impure can be confused in its details, but the inspiring principle is not (see Lev. 11).

In the set 'sacred–profane/impure–pure' the original analogous relationship was that between sacred and impure. The prohibition against planting different kinds of seeds in the same field echoes the rule in Deuteronomy against sowing other plants among the vines, and, as an explanation of the prohibition adds, 'so that the whole yield does not become sacred, the crop which you have sown and the yield of the vineyard' (Deut. 22.9).

Since all things that belong to God are sacred, Israel itself is sacred among all the other peoples. The conception of sacrality, its value, is profoundly different in this case in that being sacred to God is a value. Thus there is a certain ambivalence in the idea of the sacred which was, and remains, the *tremendum*, but also becomes more and more the *fascinans*.[14] There is the ontological sacred which kills, but also the anthropological sacred which is the privileged condition before God. In this new value, the Hebrew word *qodeš* (sacrality) could also be translated as 'holiness',[15] but I prefer to remain faithful to a single translation of the term, not only because it renders the original meaning of the Hebrew better, but also because the word 'holiness' has become more and more charged with the idea of 'good to the highest degree', a value which was unknown for the biblical *qodeš*. In short, 'holiness' would become a code word for use by experts exactly like 'sacrality'; at that point it is better to leave the term which better expresses the word's original value: 'sacrality'.

With the passage of time, towards the end of the Persian period, the two concepts of 'sacred' and 'pure' became more and more similar. Israel is sacred to God and belongs to him in a peculiar way; therefore the people of Israel must avoid everything which could contaminate them and undermine the force necessary to stay next to God, to belong to him. In this sense all the Jews are priests (Exod. 19.6), but only the

14. See R. Otto, *Das Heilige: Über das Irrationale in der Idee des Göttlichen und sein Verhältnis zum Rationalen* (Stuttgart/Gotha: Verlag Friederich Andreas Perthes A.-G., 1923), pp. 13-21, 38-49 (ET: *The Idea of the Holy* [Oxford: Oxford University Press, 1923]).

15. The problem of translating the Hebrew *qodeš* is perhaps best rendered by the English pair 'sacrality'/'saintliness', since the English 'saintly' tends to hold the same problem of banalization as the Italian 'santità'. I have chosen to use 'holy/holiness', however, because 'saintly/saintliness' are usually used in reference to persons and not objects, while both uses are possible for the original 'santo/santità' [Translator's note].

priest can perform religious rites and in order to perform them he must maintain a higher state of purity than the people.

The original idea of impure things, which weaken because they are sacred, in other words which belong to God in a peculiar way, gives way to an idea of the impure which weakens inasmuch as, being bad in its origin, it hinders closeness to God. Impure no longer means 'bad for man', but 'bad in itself'. It is a complex story to which we shall dedicate ample space later in the book. For now, let us just say that the idea of impurity as an evil force is as old as the story of the snake's punishment for having tempted Eve in the Garden of Eden. In fact it was condemned to slither; apparently it had had four legs which God took away as a form of punishment. Forcing it to slither God made it impure. This idea of impurity is at the basis of the early Enochic literature and is developed more fully later in Essenism. If impurity is evil it is to be avoided; the path toward God is made of purity, which now coincides with sacrality.

The problem of impurity is one of the fundamental problems of the great pre-Christian crisis years and is faced when the sequence 'sacred–profane/impure–pure', following the word-order of Leviticus, has come to be thought of as 'sacred–profane/pure–impure'. Many modern versions of the Bible translate the series of words in this latter order without realizing the deep modernization they are performing on the text, a modernization which in turn corresponds to a precise scheme of values.

The analytical category for approaching reality through the double yet analogous system 'sacred–profane/impure–pure' is a good key for understanding many problems of Jewish thought. We shall return to this topic in Chapter 17 for an analysis of some of this category's historical manifestations.[16]

Writing a history of Jewish thought is always more or less a question of writing a history of the conception the Jews had of salvation. Writing a history of Jewish thought means describing the various ways of conceiving salvation and the tools that seemed most adapt for reaching it. The problems of judgment, of retribution, of the Law, of the Messiah

---

16. On the problem of the 'sacred' and the 'pure' in the history of religions, see Cazeneuve, Durkheim, Eliade, Lévi-Strauss. On the power of the truth being revealed to humans as a threat of annihilation, see C.G. Jung, *L'io e l'inconscio* (Torino: Boringhieri, 1948), pp. 31-40. (ET: *Two Essays on Analytical Pscyhology* [London: Balliere Tundall and Cox, 1928].)

and of the value of purity were all closely linked to the idea of salvation, and any modification made to the solution of any of these problems was inevitably felt by all the others.

Furthermore, the very image of salvation varied over time and from one place to another. There was the salvation of the individual on earth and of the individual beyond the earth, the salvation of Israel and that of all peoples.

The formulations of the problem are rich and complex and vary according to the point of view of the one posing the questions. It is certain that salvation is given by God in his omnipotence; but are the motives behind God's judgment regarding salvation hidden from humankind, or can human beings in some way grasp them?

Supposing that God has a criterion for his judgment, what can it be? Is it based on the Law? Or perhaps on other criteria? Or does salvation consist in avoiding judgment?

As a consequence, just who is it that is saved? The righteous or the chosen? And what does it mean to be righteous if no one is without sin?

Again, must humanity present itself before God's judgment in order to answer for its transgressions, or can it present its righteous deeds in its own defence?

Or again, salvation is given by God, but is it given directly or through a mediator, anointed or prophet? And in the latter case, can a human suffice for such mediation?

To be near God purity is essential, but just what exactly is pure and what is not? Is contamination a transgression of the Law, or is transgression of the Law to be seen as merely one of the many impurities that can weaken and annihilate human beings? And just how far from humans lies the boundary between the sacred and the profane? What, then, is the sphere of human freedom of initiative?

In the great spiritual and historical crisis which shook first-century Judaism leading up to the catastrophe of 70 CE, the two currents of Judaism that survived the catastrophe, Pharisaism and Christianity, both take up a position on each of these questions. Both maintain elements of the great Jewish tradition, both in a selective fashion.

4. *The New Elements of this Edition*

The present volume could be considered as a rewriting of a book I wrote several years ago, *Storia del mondo giudaico* (History of the Jewish World), which was never translated into English. While the wider goals of the book and, I believe, the method I have used have not changed, there are still some novelties to this work which derive from the broadening of my knowledge and interests over the years.

While I was writing *Storia del mondo giudaico* and in the years since then, the idea that Christianity was originally only one of the many sects in the Jewish world of the day has become increasingly prevalent. This approach has been developed in the works of Neusner, Charlesworth, Vermes, Carmignac and, recently, Boccaccini and continues to gain ground. While it is obvious that Jesus was a Jew, the whole range of consequences leading from this fact had never been fully studied. Jesus' Jewishness seemed to lack historical value in that Jesus' teachings brought about a revolution great enough for him to be considered the founder of an entirely new religion. Partly for apologetical reasons and partly for the meagre knowledge of the ideas circulating in Palestine during his day, Jesus was considered a complete innovator and as such Jewish only by blood.

Many scholars had already decried the need for a historical study of the origins of Christianity, but it seemed to be a task taken on only by atheists who were looking for a historical justification of the religion's origin.[17] Today, even believers are aware of the need to place the figure of Jesus in the context of the facts and ideas of his time. Penna observes that 'Christianity was not born in a test tube as the artificial fruit of a laboratory experiment, nor did it fall from the sky like a meteorite'.[18] Whether one believes in Jesus of Nazareth's divinity or not, he spoke the language of his time to the men of his time, directly addressing the problems of his time. The Dead Sea manuscripts and renewed study of pseudepigraphical literature have made possible a knowledge of that world which would have been unthinkable just 50 years ago. Of course, I am not a New Testament scholar and when I arrived at the point in *Storia del mondo giudaico* where I had to talk about Jesus I wrote very little, because I realized that I have a great deal more to learn. I did, however, want to at least illustrate the degree to which I saw him clearly immersed in his world, from the vantage point of one who has studied the Qumran texts and the pseudepigraphical literature at length.

I have also changed my opinion radically regarding the date to be

17. P. Sacchi, 'L'eredità giudaica nel cristianesimo', *Augustinianum* 28 (1988), pp. 23-50.

18. R. Penna, *L'ambiente storico culturale delle origini cristiane* (Bologna: Dehoniane, 2nd edn, 1986), p. 7.

assigned to the pre-exilic texts. I believe that far fewer things can be confidently attributed to North Israel than I thought 20 years ago. As a result certain expressions like 'Theology of the North' as opposed to a 'Theology of the South' have disappeared in favour of terms such as 'Theology of the Covenant' and 'Theology of the Promise'.

Rereading texts that I was already familiar with has also been of the utmost importance. In particular, the fact that Babylonian sources of an administrative nature, and therefore immune to suspicion of an ideological bias, indicate that the king of Judah, Jehoiachin, maintained his royal title in exile was very important. This has allowed me to reread the Hebrew sources in a new light.

The early dating of the *Book of Watchers* imposed by the Aramaic Qumran texts has also been of extreme importance. If the *Book of Watchers* and all its baggage of ideas already existed before 200 BCE, and probably long before, then the whole evolution of Jewish thought in the Persian period had to be re-evaluated. That evolution comes to take on a previously unsuspected colour and vivacity.

At any rate, the problem of dating remains an open question for many biblical and apocryphal books, even when all the text books have come to agree on the same, yet still hypothetical date. Moving any one of these dates could provoke future shifts in the interpretation of Judaism.

Among these, the book of Ezra is of particular importance. The book in the form that it has been handed down to us, closely linked to the book of Nehemiah, is decidedly late, but I am convinced that Ezra the person really existed, though it is a difficult undertaking to recuperate his works from later books with a heavy ideological charge.

The reader should also be reminded that most of the dates assigned to the pseudepigraphical works are uncertain as well. Many doubts have also been raised regarding the dating of many parts of the Qumran texts, the *Community Rule* for example. And what should we say about a book like Wisdom which could even have been written during the Christian era? For this reason the organization by themes in the discussion of the Hellenistic period has been left intact in this edition. Where greater certainty was not possible, it seemed more opportune to adopt an elastic approach in relation to the time periods. If we have only limited knowledge then it doesn't make sense to ask the historian for a greater degree of precision than that which philology can guarantee, or at least present with a respectable margin of probability.

I was already writing this book when Boccaccini proposed calling the period running from the third century BCE to the second century CE 'Middle Judaism'. The criterion which led Boccaccini to use this label corresponds more to the needs of a history of thought rather than a history of the facts, and is useful for this book as well. It helps in illustrating an interpretation of the history of Israel which I too hold. I have appropriated this definition, especially when referring to the history of ideas. In fact this label will be used most of all for the period after 175 BCE, the year I take to mark the end of the Zadokite period.

Perhaps my *Storia del mondo giudaico* already presented a new solution to a two hundred-year-old problem, that of the rupture between Judaism and Christianity. The awareness of such a division has always been present in both Christian and Jewish culture since the earliest times. However, it became a historical question only with Reimarus in the eighteenth century. Reimarus placed the break between Judaism and Christianity not between Jesus and his world, as a long tradition would have it, but between Jesus and his disciples. Others moved the breaking point to a period prior to the life of Jesus, collocating him in an Essenism which was already to be considered a deviated form of Judaism. Perhaps the roots of Christian theology should be sought out only in that face of the Bible that we have called the Theology of the Promise, and which is just as old as the Theology of the Covenant: two sides of Israel's soul. It is clear that the Theology of the Promise underwent considerable development in some pre-Christian Jewish sects. This is very important. Boccaccini's work has been particularly useful in making me aware of this possible interpretation of my work.

Part I
THE AGE OF EXILE

Chapter 1

THE EVENTS

1. *The Events Leading up to the Catastrophe*

In 609 BCE Josiah died from wounds received in the disastrous battle of Megiddo fought against the Pharaoh Necho. Josiah had rushed to block Necho's northward march because he knew that the pharaoh was going to help the Assyrians, Israel's great enemies and the enemies of mono-latric Yahwism who had supported Manasseh's 'syncretistic' policy. Josiah did not understand that the situation had changed, that the Assyrians were no longer a threat and that the real threat would come from the power that was to succeed the Assyrians. According to 1 Esdras (1.26), Jeremiah had been opposed to the decision, but was unable to convince Josiah. Catastrophe followed.

Josiah was succeeded by his son Joahaz who reigned for only a few months. The pharaoh had him imprisoned and deported to Egypt, placing another of Josiah's sons, Eliakim, on the throne, and in sign of vassalage his name was changed to Jehoiakim. Jehoiakim's reign, which lasted until 598, was marked by shifts in fortune and strong internal contrast. He maintained Judah within Egypt's sphere of influence until 605 when the Egyptian defeat at Carchemish at the hands of Nebuchadnezzar, king of Babylon, forced the Egyptians to withdraw from the Syro-Palestinian area. Jehoiakim then became vassal to Nebuchadnezzar until 600 when Necho II invaded Palestine from the South. Jehoiakim's hopes of freedom led him to support Necho, who was defeated. The king of Judah died shortly before Nebuchadnezzar's army arrived before Jerusalem's walls.

When the Babylonian king arrived in 598 he found Jehoiakim's son, Jehoiachin, on the throne and had him immediately arrested and sent prisoner to Babylon, apparently, however, without mistreating him; it was his father who had been guilty of rebellion.[1]

1. A passage from Chronicles (2 Chron. 36.5-8) speaks of an anti-Babylonian

The city of Jerusalem and its temple were sacked.

> [The king of Babylon] carried off all the treasures of the temple, and the
> treasures of the king's house... He carried away all Jerusalem, and all
> the princes (*śarim*), and all the mighty men of valour (*gibborim*), ten
> thousand captives, and all the craftsmen and the smiths; none remained,
> except the poorest people of the land (2 Kgs 24.13-14).

The number of deportees is uncertain; in v. 16 the soldiers (here called
'anše haḥayl) have become seven thousand and the craftsmen one thousand: round figures. In Jer. 52.28 we find a precise number, 3023, for
all the male adults. Whether we accept one figure or the other, though,
the general picture hardly changes. Many of the important officials of
the state and the temple left Jerusalem and were immediately replaced
by immigrants from the surrounding areas. Life in Jerusalem carried on.

Jehoiachin was 18 years old when he ascended to and stepped down
from the throne, too young to have sons who were old enough to reign.
Thus Nebuchadnezzar placed one of Jehoiachin's uncles on the throne,
one of Jehoiakim's brothers, Mattaniah, whose name was changed to
Zedekiah. His juridical position before the Great King of Babylon is not
clear. According to the Bible, he maintained the title of king (*melek*),
though he was probably only a *naśi'*, a 'vassal king', as his trip to
Babylon in 593 seems to demonstrate (see Jer. 51.59). As we shall see
more clearly below, it was Jehoiachin who was considered the legitimate heir to the throne by the Babylonians. The deportees counted the
years based on Jehoiachin's reign and not on that of Zedekiah (see
Ezek. 1.1, 2). Prophecies of Jehoiachin's return circulated in Judah,
demonstrating that he was still considered the king even for the Jews
remaining in their homeland and that his return was awaited (see Jer.
28.4). Apparently Nebuchadnezzar was waiting to see how the situation
would develop before deciding in favour of one or the other. Therefore,
the hopes of restoration and freedom did have some concrete basis in
the historical situation itself.

In 588 Pharaoh Hophra ascended to the throne and abandoned the
prudent policy of non-intervention in Syria-Palestine followed by his
predecessors Necho II and Psammetichus II in the wake of the defeat of

insurrection on the part of Jehoiakim without providing any dates (but see also Dan.
1.1-2). Following the insurrection Jehoiakim was deported to Babylon and the
Temple was sacked for the first time. However, since we know that Jehoiakim died
in Jerusalem, if we accept this as true, we must also admit that he was sent back to
Judah shortly thereafter. Perhaps this would not be impossible.

600. All of Syria rose up against the Babylonians and Zedekiah followed the enthusiasm of the revolt. A year later Hophra was defeated and Syria reconquered. Jerusalem was again occupied and sacked. The temple was again profaned and again sacked; it was even burned.

> And the pillars of bronze that were in the temple, and the stands and the bronze sea that were in the temple, the Chaldeans broke in pieces, and carried the bronze to Babylon…and all the vessels of bronze used in the temple service… They took away everything that was made of gold or silver (2 Kgs 25.13-15).

A second deportation followed; again the book of Jeremiah (52.29) gives a precise figure for the number of men sent away: 832 adult males. Five years later a third deportation followed, a sign that at least from the Babylonian point of view Jerusalem was not yet peaceful. This last deportation involved even fewer people than the previous one: 745 men (Jer. 52.30).

Zedekiah did not receive the same treatment as Jehoiachin; he had been a traitor.

> Then they captured [Zedekiah], and brought him up to the king of Babylon at Riblah, who passed sentence upon him. They slew the sons of Zedekiah before his eyes, and put out the eyes of Zedekiah, and bound him in fetters, and took him to Babylon (2 Kgs 25.6-7).

Even though Jehoiachin held the title of 'son of the vassal king' and later that of 'vassal king' (see §3, pp. 56-58 below), he did not resume his royal functions, not even within the sphere of Babylonian sovereignty. At any rate, no sooner had Zedekiah been deported than a new governor of Judaea was appointed. His name was Gedaliah,[2] a Jew, not a Babylonian, descendent of a philo-Babylonian family as witnessed by the fact that his father had defended Jeremiah from persecution at the hands of the philo-Egyptian ruling class (Jer. 26.24 and 2 Kgs 25.22). Given the fact that Nebuchadnezzar named a Jew as governor, even a

2.   In reality we do not know the title under which Gedaliah governed Judaea. The text in the Bible says only that Nebuchadnezzar 'put him at their head' (2 Kgs 25.22). There was probably uncertainty in the Babylonian court concerning Judaea's political and administrative organization and the idea of sending Jehoiachin, who was considered the legitimate heir to the throne, must have been taken into consideration. Gedaliah's assassination and the permanent tension must have discouraged sending Jehoiachin back to Judaea even though his royal prerogatives were not taken away.

philo-Babylonian Jew, leads us to believe that the Babylonians did not intend to rule Judaea with their own functionaries. Judaea maintained its national identity since it still had a territory, even though limited, a Jew as governor, even though philo-Babylonian, and a ruling house, even though in exile.

2. *Judaea under Babylonian Domination*

As we have seen, the deportees were not so very numerous. Furthermore, unlike the Assyrians before them, the Babylonians did not introduce foreign elements into Jerusalem. That means that the property belonging to the deportees was occupied only by other Jews left behind. The Babylonians themselves saw to distributing the deportees' property to those remaining in Jerusalem. See Jer. 39.10; 2 Kgs 25.12; Ezek. 33.21-27. This means that those remaining at home, that is the majority of the population, were not mistreated by the Babylonians. The deportees were for the most part inhabitants of Jerusalem (2 Kgs 25.11), in other words the rich, the ruling class both in political and economic terms. Their goods must have been abundant and the advantages to those remaining behind, therefore, must have been great. The property must have been divided up (Jer. 39.10 and 2 Kgs 25.12). In other words, a new social situation was created in Judah which may not have displeased the people who lived there, once memory of the violence undergone had faded. The country was in a state of ruin after having so disastrously lost the war, but the basis for continuation and for reconstruction existed. It is certain that Jerusalem continued to be inhabited, as can be seen in Lam. 1.4, where it speaks of mourning on the roads to Zion.

The situation must not have been too different for the temple either. It is certain that the priests who controlled it in 587 were all deported to Babylon, but worship of some kind must have remained and, therefore, new priests must have taken the place of those who had been carried away. The book of Jeremiah (41.5) mentions that not long after the destruction a pilgrimage was made to the temple by a group of Jews. Thus, even after having been sacked and burned, the temple and its rites in some way still existed. The verse of Lamentations quoted above also mentions 'groaning priests', so some priests were still there. It is unthinkable that there would not be a place of worship in a city which was still inhabited.

If we read the history of the period in the light of later sources such as the book of Nehemiah, the documents opening the book of Ezra and, most of all, 2 Chronicles, we get the idea that all the Jews were carried off to Babylon and that when they then returned home they once again filled the empty spaces that they had been forced to leave behind. These empty spaces, which the documents closer to the facts (in chronological terms) never mention, did not exist. Their existence is limited to the realm of postexilic ideology and it is the merit of the most recent historiography to have emphasized the important role that Jerusalem continued to play for all Jews, even during the exile.

Even though Noth wrote, along with all of modern historiography at least since Wellhausen, that everything came to an end with the death of Zedekiah,[3] he adds that the later vision of history, that of the

---

3.   Let us look at other contemporary historians' expressions. Ricciotti wrote in 1934 that with the death of Zedekiah 'the last monarch of the dynasty of David died' (Ricciotti, *Storia d'Israele*, I, p. 493). B. Oded: 'The kingdom of Judah had ceased to exist' ('Judah and the Exile', in J.H. Hayes and J.M. Miller (eds.), *Israelite and Judaean History* [London: SCM Press, 1977], pp. 435-88 [477]). 'The year 587/8 BCE marks a turning point in the history of Israel. The burning of the temple, the destruction of the city of Jerusalem, and the end of the Davidic dynasty's rule surely brought about fundamental changes in the people's thinking, which was nourished on the belief in the eternity of the house of David and in the invulnerability of the temple in Jerusalem' (Oded, 'Judah and the Exile', p. 479). Soggin in his *Storia di Israele*, is less decisive, but he doesn't seem to say anything different. The same can be said of H. Donner in his *Geschichte des Volkes Israël*. Wellhausen's dramatic and effective expression also comes to mind (*Israelitische und jüdische Geschichte* [Berlin: W. de Gruyter, 9th edn, 1958], p. 142) 'jetzt zerfiel Jahve mit Israel'. The great scholar's way of conducting the discussion demonstrates that he considered the exile a continuation of Josiah's reforms: 'Die Reformation ist schliesslich gerade durch das Exil zum Ziel gekommen' (p. 144). In a broad sense the exile represents continuity in the history of Israel, and not a moment of decisive rupture between the monarchy and the priesthood. 'Der Staat war zerstört', Wellhausen continues. Outside of their homeland and outside of their own state, the people could only rely on the ancient blood ties (p. 145). 'Waren die Propheten früher den Illusionen der Zeit entgegen getreten, so traten sie nun ihrer Hoffnungslosigkeit entgegen und richteten den Glauben an die Zukunft auf' (p. 147). Return then came about in a void, even in the narrow region around Jerusalem (p. 160). Those returning home joined those who had remained. 'Sie waren nicht spröde gegen sie, sondern nahmen sie mit offenen Armen auf und zogen sie an sich heran' (p. 162). See also E. Janssen, *Juda in der Exilszeit* (Göttingen: Vandenhoeck & Ruprecht, 1956), p. 61. In reality, this interpretation dates from postexilic Judaism itself, from the fourth or third century BCE. In 2 Chron. 36.20 we read, 'He

Chronicler and the books of Ezra and Nehemiah, was only partial. 'The history of Israel was and continued to be centred around Palestine'. Noth's conclusion rests essentially on the fact that Jerusalem remained the ideal centre of Hebraism.[4] In reality it was much more.

3. *The King of Judah in Exile*

At this point it is natural to pose a question: if all things lead us to believe that the Jews, both in their homeland and in exile, kept the consciousness of their identity alive, is this phenomenon to be ascribed to their tradition and their culture, or also because their king remained a concrete reference point? According to Nathan's prophecy, which no matter the precise date when it was formulated already existed at the time of the exile, the king was son of David and depository of the promise of an eternal reign. It can be reasonably claimed that the Jews of the time considered their period a particularly difficult one, but one which had all the appearances of being transitory. They could reasonably hope for the return of their king since he had not disappeared from their horizon; Israel still had a king, even though he was being held away from the homeland. It was a transient situation which could change and had to change.

Many elements lend credibility to this reconstruction of the situation. Ezekiel, who did not have a great sympathy for the reigning house and who blamed it, rightly or wrongly, for a great deal of the disaster, does not explicitly call Jehoiachin king. The vision given in the first chapter, though, is dated to the fifth year since Jehoiachin's exile, not of Zedekiah's reign. Apparently Ezekiel considered the real king of Israel to be Jehoiachin. This is confirmed by other biblical and Babylonian documents.

Even the last words of 2 Kings confirm that Jehoiachin had remained 'king of Judah' even in exile. Unlike Ezekiel's words, here a certain sympathy is evident, a solid hope for Israel was founded on the sorts of its king: 'And in the thirty-seventh year of the exile of Jehoiachin king (*melek*) of Judah' (2 Kgs 25.27). Therefore, for the author writing these things in Babylon towards the middle of the sixth century or not much

[Nebuchadnezzar] took into exile in Babylon those who had escaped from the sword, and they became servants to him and to his sons until the establishment of the kingdom of Persia'.

4.   M. Noth, *The History of Israel* (London: A. & C. Black, 1958), p. 291.

later, Jehoiachin could still be called the king of Judah. Years could be
counted by his exile, the exile of the king of Israel. Thus, Jehoiachin's
thirty-seventh year was 561; it is clear that in 561, roughly 25 years
after the conquest of Jerusalem, Jehoiachin still held the title of 'king of
Judah'.

The title of king attributed to Jehoiachin in the Bible could seem the
product of chauvinism carried to the point of distorting the facts, but the
truth of the matter is that Jehoiachin *was* the king of Judah because
even the Babylonians considered him king. If there is a trace of an
excess of hope on the author's part, it is only in the use of the term
melek instead of *naśi'*. We have irrefutable proof from Mesopotamian
administrative documents conserving lists of the rations destined to
vassal kings deported to Babylon. Jehoiachin is listed among these
kings. The rations were destined to Jehoiachin and his sons, and he is
always referred to, in some way, as '(vassal) king of Judah'.

These lists are on four administrative tablets, published by Weidner
in 1939, registering the passage of rations of foodstuffs to Jehoiachin
and his court. The four tablets are indicated with the first four letters of
the alphabet, and of these only tablet C is dated. It was written in 592
BCE and therefore dates from the period when Zedekiah sat on the
throne in Jerusalem. On this tablet Jehoiachin is not given the title
sharru, 'vassal king' (the king of Babylon had the title *sharru rabu*,
literally 'Great King'), but 'son of a vassal king', that is 'heir prince'.
This confirms the biblical information that Zedekiah was actually king
and not governor, but it also tells us more. It also tells us that the Babylonians intended to re-establish the normal line of descent in Judah as
soon as the situation seemed to be more stable.

In the other three tablets, which bear no date, Jehoiachin is given the
title 'vassal king'. Given the use of this title, these tablets must date to
after Zedekiah's death. All of this indicates a precise evolution of
events in favour of Jehoiachin who, however, was not allowed to leave
his forced place of residence until 561. Other governors must have
remained in Judah, but we do not know whether they were Jews or
Babylonians. At any rate, in Babylon the situation in Judaea under
Zedekiah's rule must have continued to appear unstable since another
deportation was made in 592. But that the expression 'king of Judah'
should be simply the fruit of imprecise bureaucratic language, as proposed by Weidner, is to be excluded since the names of Jehoiachin's
sons are listed next to his own, and on one of the tablets eight 'men of

Judah', who must have had some duties toward Jehoiachin, are also indicated. In other words, Jehoiachin had a small court in exile with eight functionaries.

If the rations of foodstuffs allotted to the king of Judah were much greater than those given to other vassal kings who were in Babylon under more or less the same conditions as Jehoiachin,[5] this means that he must have been attributed considerable importance by the Babylonian Great King.

If the Babylonians never denied Jehoiachin the title of king, then it is clear that he remained such for the people of Judah as well. In him they had a natural reference point for national unity and hope for the restoration. This created a very close relationship between the inhabitants of Judah and their king, a relationship which did not last between the king and the other exiles. For as much as the juridical status of the exiles is difficult to decipher today—and it was probably not very well defined at the time either—a network of interests created by the very structure of the empire brought the ruling house to deal with Judah, but not with the other exiles. The subjects of the dynasty of David, recognized as such by the Babylonians, were the Jews in their homeland. The deportees were wicked and in some way had to be punished.

In this situation the monarchy must have appeared as a traitor to Israel in the eyes of the deportees, and the contacts, which must have existed, could only have been stormy. Jehoiachin governed over a Judaea which had been reorganized administratively and socially by the Babylonians and he accepted this situation. The exiles, in contrast, could not accept it; it would have meant renouncing their rights as priests of the temple and, among both priests and laymen, renouncing their claims to the property they had lost in Judaea which was now held by others.

In Judaea it was still held that Yhwh had remained in the temple and continued to protect Israel with his presence. As far as the exiles were concerned, it was believed that Yhwh had caused them to be sent away, that they were no longer under his protection. In Palestine it was said: 'They have gone far from the Lord; to us this land is given for a possession' (Ezek. 11.15). History was the *locus* of divine judgment and the deportees were those who had been punished by God. Even

---

5. For the size of the rations allotted to Jehoiachin as being greater than those of the other kings in Babylon, see I. Eph'al, 'On the Political and Social Organization of the Jews in Babylonian Exile', *ZDMG* suppl. 5 (1983), pp. 106-12.

some prophets, called 'foxes' by Ezekiel (13.4), were busy pronouncing oracles in favour of the stability of the situation. Ezekiel, in exile, proclaimed the opposite to the exiles (11.17; chs. 15, 20 and 38); the Glory of God had left the temple (chs. 1 and 10). The interests behind both Ezekiel's prophecy and behind the 'foxes' of Jerusalem can be seen clearly. And it is equally clear that they were making the rift even deeper. However, the ruling house had no choices; choosing the interests of those remaining in Israel meant choosing not only the favour of the subjects but also the favour of the Great King. This was the only policy allowing the Davidic dynasty's survival. Or at least that is how the situation appeared to the Davidians at the time.

Ezekiel's reaction against those remaining in the homeland and against the monarchy was characterized by harsh tones (22.6 and 45.9)[6] and radical theology. He demolishes the idea that Israel's salvation is bound to the house of David, as prophesied by Isaiah (11.1 for example) and Jeremiah (23.5). David was no longer considered the Messiah's ancestor, but only his figure. The real David was yet to come, but not necessarily from the house of David. Thus the memory of the great king of the past was safe, but the current monarchy no longer had the function of preserving the line believed in Nathan's prophecy (2 Sam. 7) to be Israel's salvation. This belief must have been a fairly widespread idea, together with an analogous belief which saw in the temple a guarantee of salvation (see Ps. 46.5-6).

The historical David thus became a pure figure of the ideal king that will one day come to save Israel; that future king will be the real David. In Ezek. 34.23-24 we read,

> And I will set up over them one shepherd, my servant David, and he
> shall feed them: he shall feed them and be their shepherd. And I, Yhwh,

---

6.   Ezek. 22.6: 'Behold, the kings of Israel in you, every one according to his power, have been bent on shedding blood'. The usual translation 'princes of Israel' can be misleading. The term *neśi'im* does not refer to a very high dignity, but to the kings themselves. Technically, the term was used during the times of the exile to indicate a vassal king of the Great King, but the term is also used as a synonym of *melek*. Here, the presence of the perfect form of the verb seems to indicate only the past, and not the present, but the general meaning of the passage very definitely includes the present as well. In 45.9, certainly later than the former verse, Ezekiel is even more explicit in condemning both the past and the present: 'Enough, O kings of Israel! Put away violence and oppression'. In this passage the current king was certainly Jehoiachin, or, if the text is from the school of Ezekiel, even one of Jehoiachin's successors.

will be their God, and my servant David shall be prince among them; I, Yhwh, have spoken.

David, the real one, is yet to come to be Israel's shepherd. At first David had been the messiah-king's ancestor. Now he has become only a figure; while the fundamental theological underpinnings remain the same, the political ideology based on them has been overturned.

Again in Ezek. 37.24-26:

> My servant David shall be king over them; and they shall all have one shepherd. They shall follow my ordinances and be careful to observe my statutes…and David my servant shall be their king for ever. I will make a covenant of peace with them; it shall be an everlasting covenant with them.

No word is made of the Davidic dynasty; Ezekiel awaits a new David who will fulfill the hopes once placed in the historical descendants of David's house.

The exiles had only to resist and to wait and hope for some kind of change in the empire's general political situation. If they did not lose their identity, it was because the Babylonians, unlike the Assyrians before them, did not introduce foreign elements into Judaea from other parts of the empire, nor did they do anything to undermine the exiles' sense of identity. The exiles were left united in villages in order to bring certain regions under cultivation. The fact, though, that the priests were able to maintain not only their national identity but were also able to keep up their traditions without the temple is to be attributed to the tenacity of certain men like Ezekiel and his group. This tendency must also have been aided by the fact that the Jews were particularly active and some must have already reached good economic positions during the course of the sixth century BCE as attested to, for that century, by the archive of the Egibi, as yet unpublished; but some information is available. The development of the priestly tradition (*Priestercodex*) would be unthinkable without adequate economic support, which certainly did not come from the empire's public finances.

Jehoiachin's position in regard to the Babylonian empire and Judaea can seem unusual to us today, but it can also be explained by the structure of the Babylonian empire. The central organ of government in the empire was the council known as the 'Grandees of the land of Akkad'.[7]

---

7. *Rabutu* (GAL.MEŠ) *ša ma-at Ak-ka-di-in*, poorly translated as 'officials' in *ANET*. Given the spelling of *mat*, the translation 'Grandees of Akkad' must be

Both a consultative and an executive body, the council was formed by governors of provinces, but it also included vassal kings who were considered both governors and kings, kings for their subjects, governors for the Great King.

The custom of keeping defeated kings on the throne as governors had already been present in the Assyrian empire, as documented by a bilingual inscription (Akkadian-Aramaic) recently discovered at El-Fekheriye and dating from the ninth century BCE.[8] This inscription has perplexed many critics because the figure referred to in the Akkadian text as governor, in the Aramaic text, to be read by the subjects, is called king. This should come as no surprise, though, since it was the normal condition of vassal kings. Jehoiachin's relations with the Babylonian court on the one hand and his subjects on the other must have been regulated by a structure of this kind.

The favours that Jehoiachin obtained from Awil Marduk, Nebuchadnezzar's successor, as narrated in the Bible must be interpreted in the light of the structure of the Mesopotamian empires. Jehoiachin was released from prison (2 Kgs 25.27, Hebrew *bet kele'*) and allowed to dine at the king's table, or rather, according to the Greek text, he was released from the house where he had been kept (ἐξήγαγεν αὐτὸν ἐξ οἴκου φυλακῆς αὐτοῦ) and allowed to dine at the king's table. The general meaning of the passage is that Jehoiachin's title as king was confirmed, but he was also given something more; apart from the privilege of dining with the Great King, he was granted freedom of

considered imprecise. On the Grandees of Akkad, see R. Labat, 'L'Assiria e i suoi vicini dal 1000 a.C. al 617. Il regno babilonese fino al 539 a.C'., in *Storia Universale Feltrinelli* (Milano: Feltrinelli, 1969), IV, pp. 7-114 (109). Alongside the Grandees of Akkad proper, stood the priests of certain temples, the prefects of the cities and the vassal kings. See also M. Liverani, *Antico Oriente: Storia, società, economia* (Bari: Laterza, 1988), p. 887. Liverani, in his description of the administrative organization of the Babylonian kingdom, seems to indicate a hierarchical order among functionaries dealing with the cities of Babylon and functionaries working alongside local kings in peripheral territories. Still, even though the vassal kings are at the bottom of the list of Babylonian functionaries, the fact remains that they are considered royal functionaries.

8.   On the El-Fekheriye inscription see A.R. Millard and P. Bordeuil, 'A Statue from Syria with Assyrian and Aramaic Inscriptions', *BA* 45 (1982), pp. 135-43; J.C. Greenfield and A. Shaffer, 'Notes on the Akkadian-Aramaic Bilingual Statue from Tell Fekherye', *Iraq* 45 (1983), pp. 109-16; T. Muraoka, 'The Tell Fekherye Bilingual Inscription and Early Aramaic', *Abr-Nahrain* 22 (1983–84), pp. 79-117.

movement. He came out of the house where he had been kept. How he used this freedom is not clear. We do not even know how long after 561 he lived, but we do know how his successors used such freedom. They travelled between the seat of the central government and Judaea.

If Jehoiachin maintained his title as king and was able to become a 'Grandee of the Land of Akkad', then we can exclude Alt's classic theory that Judaea became a district of the province of Samaria. Judaea had remained in some way an autonomous province, and in any case a well-defined unit within the Babylonian empire.[9] Turning now to the Hebrew language, we see that the word used for 'king' is not the same as in the past. In this period the title *melek* is reserved almost exclusively for the Great King, while the vassal kings are called *neśi'im*. The term could also be used in a non-technical sense, though, in which case *melek* and *naśi'* are synonyms. Thinking of David, Ezekiel could use *melek* (37.25) and *naśi* (34.24) indifferently. As for the people of Judah, the *naśi'* was what they had once called the *melek*: he was their king.

---

9. On the existence of an autonomous province of Judaea see G. Widengren, 'The Persian Period', in Hayes and Miller (eds.), *Israelite and Judaean History*, pp. 489-538 (esp. 489, 510-11). Widengren takes the opposite view of A. Alt who would have Judaea as an appendix to the province of Samaria ('Die Rolle Samarias bei der Entstehung des Judentums', in *Kleine Schriften* [3 vols.; Munich, 1953–59 (1934)], II, pp. 316-37. See also A. Alt, 'Zur Geschichte der Grenze zwischen Judäa und Samaria', *ibidem*, pp. 346-62 [1st edn 1935]). Widengren bases himself exclusively on the titles given to the governors of Judaea; the fact that Jehoiachin was able to maintain his royal title lends certainty to this hypothesis. Stern ('The Persian Period', in *The Cambridge Ancient History* [12 vols.; Cambridge: Cambridge University Press, 1965–71; repr. 20 vols.; Cambridge, 1969–73], I, p. 72) accepts the administrative autonomy of Judaea from Samaria only for the period of Zerubbabel and again beginning with Nehemiah, in other words for the periods referred to by the extant information, but we have no evidence of any changes. This seems to be a compromise with the old and accepted theory of Alt and there is no reason for accepting it. Its only support could be the fact of documented Samarian interference in Judaea in periods other than those of Zerubbabel, but interference can be explained in many ways without believing in Jerusalem's direct dependence on Samaria—the least likely explanation of such interference.

Peoples from the surrounding areas, most of all the Edomites, did penetrate the southern territories of Judah giving rise to the district of Idumaea of later periods (see B. Oded, 'Judah and the Exile', in Hayes and Miller [eds.], *Israelite and Judaean History*, pp. 435-88 [477], but the region of Judah may have undergone disorganized raids, not systematic invasions.

Thus, in keeping with the biblical and Mesopotamian documentation, the common opinion that the kingdom of Judah came to an end with the death of Zedekiah in 587 is no longer sustainable.

4. *Jehoiachin's Successors under the Persian Empire*

In 539 BCE Cyrus occupied Babylon and the Persian empire took the place of the Babylonian one. This event was bound, in the future, to have a deep effect on the situation of the Jews, but for the moment nothing changed, at least not on a political level. It is true that in questions regarding religious freedom Cyrus had much more liberal ideas than the Babylonians, but this did not lead him to renounce founding an empire. It is probable that he had a monotheistic idea of the divinity and, as a consequence, a universalistic vision of the structure his empire was to take. His monotheism did not imply the compulsory worship of the same divinity honoured by Cyrus since, no matter what name was attributed to the divinity, it was held to be the one God. While it is possible that this way of seeing things dates to a slightly later period, to Darius, in any case Cyrus' liberal policy towards the peoples, formerly subjected to the Babylonians, and their religions is well documented. For Cyrus this approach also had a precise political value, that of exploiting the dissatisfaction of the peoples who had lived under Babylonian rule.[10]

In following this ideology, and in order to confirm the role of sovereign/liberator from the Babylonian yoke which the Persian propaganda had spread, Cyrus gave back the sacred images taken away from many peoples and carried off to Babylon. He also allowed the return to their homeland of those who had been forcibly expatriated. But Nabonidus remains the reference point, and the peoples mentioned are all Mesopotamian; no mention is made of the Jews, or of any other Western

---

10. Discontent in Babylon had both economic and religious causes. Even under Nebuchadnezzar state control over the land had already been reinforced through the institution of a kind of farm system directly dependent on the Palace, placed alongside the farms administered by the temple which paid only 10 per cent of their produce as taxation. Nebuchadnezzar's first edict on the matter dates to the twenty-third year of his reign (583 BCE). Nabonidus insisted on furthering this policy, which brought him into conflict with the Babylonian priesthood. Furthermore, Nabonidus favoured worship of the god Sin of Haran which was extraneous to the Babylonian tradition.

people. A list of 'liberated' peoples has survived in the so-called 'Cylinder of Cyrus'.[11] This has led to some doubt concerning the historicity of the Edict of Cyrus in favour of the Jews. In effect, it is probable that such an edict was never issued: the Jewish tradition itself seems to indicate that the first return of the exiles came about only with the rise of Darius I to the throne (521 BCE). Cyrus wanted to remedy the situation created by Nabonidus, and not the pre-existent one. Furthermore, since the vassal kings had been integrated into the state apparatus of the Babylonian empire, liberating them would not have made political sense. They were integrated into the state, their liberation had come about at the moment when Babylon itself had been liberated.

At any rate, Cyrus saw to it that the sacred ornaments of the temple were returned to Jerusalem, and the way in which this return took place is of interest. Let us follow the account given in the Bible which, even

---

11. The Cylinder of Cyrus (see R.P. Berger, 'Der Kyros-Zylinder mit dem Zusatzfragment BIN II, nr. 32 und die akkadischen Personennamen im Danielbuch', *ZA* 64 [1975], pp. 192-234, and *ANET*, II, p. 316) in a long paragraph (lines 28-34) narrates that Cyrus received 'all the kings of the world from the Upper Sea to the Lower one' in Babylon, both those that governed sedentary peoples and those who governed nomads, who had come to kiss his feet and bear to him their heavy tributes. The expression 'all the kings of the world' is global, but the text only mentions peoples of Mesopotamia and the region to the east of the Tigris. Cyrus called all the inhabitants together and sent them home with their gods, but the text only refers clearly to the area indicated in the examples. Furthermore, mention is made of the fact that Cyrus gave back the images of the gods, but the Jews seem to be excluded, along with the other peoples of the West who maintained their vassal kings.

The biblical information regarding the Edict of Cyrus is usually held to be reliable, even though it contains the difficulty arising from the fact that an interval of 18 years passed between the Edict of Cyrus and the return of the first exiles to the homeland, an interval which is hard to explain. Doubts have therefore been raised concerning the authenticity of such information, even in the past. The problem has been studied thoroughly, though, and resolved in favour of its authenticity; see E.J. Bickerman, 'The Edict of Cyrus in Ezra I', *JBL* 65 (1946), pp. 249-75. Some scholars continue to have reservations on the matter; see O. Kaiser, *Einleitung in das Alte Testament* (Gütersloh: Gütersloher Verlagshaus, 4th edn, 1978), p. 164 (ET: *Introduction to the Old Testament* [Oxford: Basil Blackwell, 1975]), and G. Garbini, *History and Ideology in Ancient Israel* (London: SCM Press, 1998), p. 134 n. On the history of the problem, see K. Galling, *Studien zur Geschichte Israels im persischen Zeitalter* (Tübingen: Mohr [Paul Siebeck], 1964), pp. 61-68.

though debated, appears to be beyond doubt. Its reliability stems from the fact that it contrasts the Zadokite ideology which dominated the Jewish-biblical tradition in the following century and gave rise to some variations on the information contained in Ezra 1, which we will here follow.

In Ezra 1.7-8 we read:

> Cyrus the king brought out the vessels of the house of Yhwh which Nebuchadnezzar had carried away from Jerusalem and placed in the house of his god. Cyrus king of Persia brought these out in charge of Mithredath the treasurer, who counted them out to Sheshbazzar the vassal king of Judah.[12]

From this information we learn not only of an event, but also of an institutional structure: the highest overseer of the temple of Jerusalem was not a priest, but the king, vassal or not. This is still the same social structure of pre-exile Israel. In this context we are not speaking about the (re)construction of the temple. There are no random elements: Sheshbazzar did not have to (re)construct a temple because he already had one with a priesthood faithful to him. He limited himself to returning the ornaments carried off during the sack.

Sheshbazzar, son of Jehoiachin, was on the throne of Judah as vassal king when Cyrus occupied Babylon. In Ezra 1.8 he is mentioned as *naśi'* of Judah; this expression must be understood in its technical sense: 'vassal king of Judah'. The same Sheshbazzar is referred to in the same book of Ezra with the title of *peḥah*, 'governor' (5.14), and in the 1 Esdras 2.8 he is called προστάτης τῆς Ἰουδαίας. These are not errors of transmission, nor are they signs of confusion on the part of the authors, as has often been said. They are the two faces, the two functions, of the same person.

---

12. On the identification of Sheshbazzar, called Sanabasaros both in Josephus's *Antiquities of the Jews* and in 1 Esdras (which is Josephus's source), with the Shen'azzar of 1 Chronicles (3.18), transcribed by the LXX as Sanesar, see E. Stern, 'The Persian Empire and the Political and Social History of Palestine in the Persian Period', CHJ, pp. 70-87 (70). 1 Chron. 3.17 mentions that this Shen'azzar was the son of Jeconiah *the captive*. Therefore, we must be dealing with Jehoiachin of the book of Kings; this latter version of the name's spelling is confirmed by the Akkadian sources. It is difficult not to make the connection with Sheshbazzar of the book of Ezra. The Greek form of the name adopted by the LXX should also be pointed out: Sasabasar, Sabanasar.

Sheshbazzar was succeeded by a nephew, Zerubbabel, the son of a brother. The Bible mentions him only as *peḥah* (see the Hebrew text[13] of Hag. 1.1 and 2.2, 21), and not as *naśi'*, though he certainly held the title of *naśi'* as well. As will be seen below, Zerubbabel was at the centre of a difficult struggle, which he lost. The tradition, written by the winners of that struggle, maintains the memory of the fact that he led a column of exiles, the first (520 BCE), but has censured his royal title. In some passages even the title has been maintained, but where the text is not to be interpreted in a political key, but in a messianic one. See Hag. 2.23 and Zech. 4.14 (the anointed) and 6.12 (the Branch); both of these are royal titles.

Unlike his predecessors, Zerubbabel did not only have two titles, he had three, and the third was the cause of his downfall and his dynasty's ruin. Alongside the title of 'governor of Judaea' he also held that of 'governor of the Jews' which, at first glance, can seem to be no more than a literary variation of the first. In reality it is quite different, as Josephus noticed. This title is documented in Ezra 6.7 in its Aramaic form *peḥat Yehudaye'*, 'governor of the Jews', in reference to a governor of Judaea normally identified, given the context, as Zerubbabel.

Josephus, when speaking of Zerubbabel, paraphrases the title as τῶν αἰχμαλώτων Ἰουδαίων ἡγεμών (*Ant.* 11.32), which can be translated as 'governor of the Jewish captives', that is 'governor of the Jews in exile'. This function did not, of course, replace the others; he remained king and governor of Judea, but he also had a new duty.

---

13. In the same passages the LXX have always used ἐκ φυλῆς Ἰουδα, 'of the tribe of Judah', in place of 'the governor of Judah'. The difference between the Hebrew and Greek texts consists in only three (or two) consonants at the beginning of the expression as it is written in Hebrew: *pḥt Yhwdh*, 'governor of Judah', and *(m)mšpḥt Yhwdh*, 'of the tribe of Judah'. Since this variant is repeated in every passage, its existence cannot be accidental, but the fruit of reflection. Recently attempts have been made to explain the Greek variant in terms of an affirmation of Zerubbabel's royalty (F. Bianchi, 'Zorobabele, re di Giuda', *Henoch* 13 [1991], pp. 133-50), but the discourse's structure and the Greek expression 'of the tribe of Judah' create some problems. (1) Zerubbabel is parallel to Joshua; the latter is the son of Jehozedek, the former the son of Shealtiel, the latter is high priest, the former is *pḥh*. (2) 'Of the house of Judah' is not an office and it remains to be demonstrated that it could be a messianic title at such an early date. It would be the only example before the *Testament of the Twelve Patriarchs* (in part dating from the second century BCE, in part from the first).

The importance of the new title and corresponding functions is enormous. It sheds light on the motivations that brought the Davidic dynasty to ruin. It shows that Zerubbabel's authority was extended from Judaea to the Jews of the Babylonian diaspora. In other words, they went back to being unconditional Jews, free to return or to stay, restored to their legitimate authority. This is the formal substance of the new title, a formal substance which probably lies at the basis of the territorial claims documented in some biblical texts written during this period and according to which the land of Israel spread from the Euphrates to the western sea (Josh. 1.4).[14] The political substance, however, was different.

As we have seen, the interests of the kings of Judah in exile were directed exclusively towards their subjects in the homeland for very solid political reasons. They pursued ancient customs and traditions in their relationship with their subjects. What it was that pushed Zerubbabel to take interest in the Jews in exile we do not know, but some considerations seem to stand out. Since the dynasty had no real reason, at least when seen in hindsight, to assume responsibility for the new subjects, and given the fact that Zerubbabel's authority over the exiles came from a title which could only have been given him by the Persians, it would seem that dynasty–exile relations were imposed by Persia. Furthermore, since it is not very probable that the Persians would have concerned themselves with the Jewish exiles if the exiles themselves had not made some request, we must think that the Jews took advantage of the favourable situation which had been created between them and the Persians in order to obtain permission to become full Jewish citizens once again.[15]

In reality they even obtained something more, another proof that dynasty–exile relations were imposed from above. A true compromise on the basis of demands for power was reached between Zerubbabel and the priests who had been given back their rights. At one time the priests' demands would have been inconceivable. The priests and the exiles in general knew that real freedom to return to the homeland and to be Jews there would remain in the realm of theory if they did not have the power to recuperate the belongings and the roles that they had

14. See Gen. 15.18; Deut. 1.7, 11.24; Josh. 1.4.
15. See J. Maier, *Zwischen den Testamenten: Geschichte und Religion in der Zeit des zweiten Tempels* (Würzburg: Echter Verlag, 1990), p. 49, where he speaks of this as an initiative of the priests.

lost with exile. In order to do this, though, they had to have some kind of authority.

During the exile the priesthood had taken on a rigidly hierarchical structure following Ezekiel's inspiration. Only one family or group of priests descendent from Zadok had full priestly functions (Ezek. 44.15), the others became second-order priests with subordinate functions. Among the Zadokite priests, one was the high priest and his position remained hereditary until Onias III, forced from power around 175 BCE. The first of these high priests was Joshua. The agreement foresaw a sort of diarchy; both Zerubbabel and Joshua held the title of 'anointed one' (Zech. 4.11-14), once an exclusively royal attribute. Perhaps Zerubbabel felt satisfied in that at least in the weight of tradition he was the first of the two anointed.

The exiled priests returned to Jerusalem with the charge, authorized by the Persians, to rebuild the temple even bigger than it had been before. This detail is clearly evident in 1 Esdras 6.24 (see also Ezra 6.3) and it makes perfect sense, because only with Persian authorization to build a temple different from the previous one could the exiled priests dominate the new temple. Nor is it strange that the temple's dimensions have been omitted by the later tradition, since for that tradition this temple was supposed to be a continuation of the ancient one destroyed in 587 BCE. The exiles probably did not like the new measurements much either, because they were not a part of their tradition. Though the text of 1 Esdras is mutilated, the temple must have been square in shape, extraneous to Judaic culture, but deeply rooted in the Mesopotamian tradition. It seems that the temple was to be square like the Ziggurat. A document like this one was not invented by a later epoch.

Work on the temple's (re)construction was begun under Zerubbabel (Hag. 1.15) in 520 BCE. This confirms that the old order was still in place in Jerusalem at that date. The principal affairs of the temple still regarded the sovereign and this confirms the pre-eminent position that Zerubbabel must have assured for himself in the agreement with the priests in exile. But the exiled priests were kept apart from the priests of Judah not only by divisions which Zerubbabel must have been able to overcome, since the atmosphere of these years is essentially one of national harmony, but also by theological and liturgical differences which had probably escaped the king's attention. The Priestly tradition had developed during the exile, a theology which included measures for purity and rules of worship that the priests in the homeland knew nothing about. Theological debate was inevitable. Traces of one of these debates on purity can still be found in Hag. 2.10-14; the prophet presents the priests with a problem of purity and from their answers deduces that the entire people is impure and that the very offerings in the sanctuary are contaminated. 'Then Haggai said, "So it is with this people [that they are impure], and with this nation before me, says Yhwh; and so with every work of their hands; and what they offer there [in the temple] is impure".' This is the first sign of the rupture between the returned exiles and those who had remained in the homeland.

The community was organized, at first, according to Ezekiel's ideal scheme (Ezek. 45), under the leadership of two heads, the two anointed ones: the vassal king from the line of David and the high priest from the line of Zadok. In fact, during the exile it had become an established principle (Ezek. 44.15) that the position of high priest be the appanage of a single priestly family, that of Zadok. The result was the hierarchization of the priesthood and the birth of the figure of the high priest in accordance with Ezekiel's plan.

Initially the two anointed ones enjoyed an air of great enthusiasm. The people knew that they were being guided by a descendant of David and the prophet Zechariah saw all the obstacles before Zerubbabel dissolve (4.6-7) by God's miraculous intervention. The kingdom of David was undergoing a second birth. A miracle was felt in the air; God's presence was felt 'watching over them to build and to plant' as foretold by the prophet Jeremiah (31.28). The desert crossing was the antitype of that of the Red Sea; the dedication of the new and larger temple must have seemed a tangible sign from God that the New Order spoken of in certain prophecies was about to begin, if it hadn't begun already.

> Consider what will come to pass from this day onward.
> Before a stone was placed upon a stone in the temple of Yhwh, how did you fare?
> When one came to a heap of twenty measures, there were but ten;
> when one came to the winevat to draw fifty measures, there were but twenty.
> I smote you and all the products of your toil with blight and mildew and hail
> …Consider from this day onward…There is seed in the barn,
> the vine, the fig tree, the pomegranate, and the olive tree yield their fruits.
> From this day on I will bless you (Hag. 2.15-19).

The words of Zechariah echo those of Haggai:

Thus says Yhwh Sabaoth:
'Let your hands be strong...
For before these days there was no wage for man...
neither was there any safety from the foe
for him who went out or came in [that is for anyone who carried on any
    activity];
for I set every man against his fellow.
But now I will not deal with the remnant of this people
as in the former days,
Oracle of Yhwh Sabaoth.

For there shall be a sowing of peace;
the vine shall yield its fruit,
and the ground shall give its increase,
and the heavens shall give their dew;
and I will cause the remnant of this people to possess all these things.
And as you have been a byword of cursing among the nations,
O house of Judah and house of Israel,
so, since I shall save you,
you shall be a blessing.
Fear not, but let your hands be strong' (Zech. 8.9-13).

The kingdom of David was born again. The people of Judah and Israel would again be united, the times of plenty would return in a grandiose and undefined time of waiting for the revelation of the God of Israel to all peoples through Israel. Zerubbabel's triumph was not going to come about through armed force and it had no importance that Jerusalem could not be fortified. God himself would be the true and impregnable defence against all enemies (Zech. 2.8-9). The return of the exiles must have been presented as offering benefits to those who had remained, and it is even possible that the community as a whole did initially receive some benefit.

In reality, though, things went quite differently than the way Haggai and Zechariah had originally hoped, and this because there were also the premises for civil war: contrasting interests had been radicalized in divergent ideologies. Some traces of this war, which the later tradition has tried to hide, have remained in the book of Zechariah, especially in chs. 12 and 3. Chapter 12 belongs to the so-called Deutero-Zechariah, a distinct prophet from the First, but probably his contemporary,[16] and is

16. On the early date of Deutero-Zechariah, see M. Smith, *Palestinian Parties and Politics that Shaped the Old Testament* (London: SCM Press, 1971), pp. 115-16. Smith bases his evaluation on P. Lamarche, *Zacharie IX–XIV: Structure*

a particularly corrupted text. And the corruptions are certainly not accidental. This sentence, for example, has remained in v. 2: 'Lo, I am about to make Jerusalem a cup of reeling to all the peoples round about; furthermore, Judah will be in the siege against Jerusalem'. And shortly thereafter: 'Then the generals of Judah shall say to themselves, "The inhabitants of Jerusalem have strength through Yhwh of the hosts, *their* God"' (v. 5); 'On that day I will make the generals of Judah like a blazing pot in the midst of wood, like a flaming torch among sheaves; and they shall devour to the right and to the left all the peoples round about, while Jerusalem shall remain in its place, in Jerusalem' (v. 6). Yhwh is the God of Jerusalem, not of Judah, naturally from the point of view of the winners.

The existence of a civil war between Jerusalem and Judah is certain, as it is certain that initially Judah was more successful. What is not clear from the texts though is which side the king was on. He probably took the side of Judah, although he surely tried to mediate between the two sides. Zechariah 3 narrates the self-accusal of the high priest Joshua and God's pardon. This passage, in a somewhat figurative manner, but really not too figurative, recounts that there was a moment when Joshua was able to maintain the high priesthood only at the price of making a self-accusal: 'I have taken your iniquity away from you... Put a clean turban on his head' (Zech. 3.4-5). It was a compromise, but it represented only a temporary pause in the war, because in the end Joshua was the complete victor. When Josephus mentions the end of the temple's reconstruction, he places it exclusively in relation to the priests (*Ant.* 11.79).

The passage beginning with Zech. 12.9 is very interesting as well. It speaks of someone who has fallen victim to a murder and who will be mourned like an only child or like a first-born child. Everyone will mourn him. It would seem that peace came to Judah only after this murder. If we identify this anonymous murder victim with Zerubbabel then there can be no doubts about the meaning of the passage. Zerubbabel's death marked the end of the civil war and the beginning of reconciliation. The reconciliation was only superficial though: in reality it only served to put off, for roughly half a century, the final destiny of those who had remained in the homeland. Power then passed entirely into the hands of the former exiles who set about reconstructing the

littéraire et messianisme (Paris: Lecoffre, 1961). He does not accept the unity of Deutero-Zechariah, but he does accept the antiquity of the passages.

former dominant class, that of the *ḥorim* and the elders, but this time without the king. The monarchy had become too compromised with the *dallim*, with those whom today we would call the petite bourgeoisie and the proletariat who had benefited the most from the redistribution of the exiles' property in the wake of the Babylonian conquest (see §2 of this chapter, pp. 49-51).

Of course the disappearance of the line of David must have caused a number of problems since the idea that the reigning house constituted a guarantee of salvation for the whole people was quite widespread. In forms which are more or less conscious, every society has a certain image of itself based on certain principles. The contrast which had taken place in Babylon between the sphere of the court and that of the priests had brought about a deepening of the values of each of the two groups and the radicalization of their ideologies. The agreement reached between the two groups marking the end of the civil war had to elaborate a new ideology of Israel appropriate for the new situation. We will come back to this in the next chapter which is dedicated to the culture and thought of the period of the exile.

Memory of Zerubbabel in the atmosphere of national unity which followed his death was cumbersome. His figure was a reminder to all of the Davidic dynasty, its powers and its divine favour. The desire to eliminate the memory of David's last descendant, the 'anointed' king, emerges through the history of the most ancient tradition of the passage in Zech. 6.9-15. The text has been retouched with the precise intent of making the anointed one of the house of David disappear. This passage was corrupted by a very ancient and deliberate alteration aimed at diminishing the importance of the anointed one of the line of David in favour of the priestly one. Through the prophet God says,

> 'Take from them silver and gold, and make *crowns*, and set them upon the head of Joshua...the High Priest...' You will say to him: 'Behold, the man whose name is the Branch...he shall build the temple...and shall sit and rule upon his throne, and the priest shall be upon his throne, and the counsel of peace shall be between them both. And the *crown* shall be...'

It is clear that in the original text it was written that the prophet was to make two crowns, one of silver and one of gold, one for Joshua and one for Zerubbabel. The words which follow seem now to be addressed to Joshua, but must have originally been addressed to Zerubbabel; the name 'the Branch' comes from the ideology of royal messianism (see

Zech. 3.8 and 4.10). It was he who should have governed, while Joshua was to be 'the priest upon his [own] throne'. Some other words have remained in the Greek text which better betray the meaning of the original text, composed when work on the temple's reconstruction was about to begin; in addition to the Hebrew text's 'upon his throne' the Greek text says 'to his right'.

The corrections are fairly naïve, but they are clearly corrections. They bear witness to a chapter in the story of the Zadokite priesthood's affirmation.

At this point a very serious question is raised; was the power that had belonged to the vassal king assumed by the priests and the high priest in particular, or did the Persians entrust what had been the royal responsibility of government to their own governors? If we follow the biblical texts which, with only one exception (Neh. 5.15), do not ever mention the existence of such governors, it would seem that all the power that could be exercised in a society under foreign domination lay in the hands of the Zadokite priesthood. This was also Josephus's classic interpretation.[17] The opposite interpretation, however, seems to be the most plausible, since the existence of such governors is recorded in the Bible, even if in only one passage, and because sources outside the Bible demonstrate the governors' existence (see pp. 116-17). Naturally, we have no idea what the division of powers between the two was, but we do not even know what it had been in the Joshua–Zerubbabel diarchate. Since Montesquieu had not yet been born, the distinction between the spheres of power were probably very ill-defined and vague. It should also be borne in mind that immediately after the fall of the monarchy there was a period, probably a very brief one, when Jewish society gave itself a constitution based on the Law. Even the highest authorities had to observe the Law. This is the regime foreseen in the final version of Deuteronomy, which I believe dates to the years immediately after 515 and which mirrors a process analogous to the one which had already taken place in Greece with the first written legislation.

17. πολιτείᾳ χρώμενοι ἀριστοκρατικῇ μετ᾽ ὀλιγαρχίας (*Ant.* 11.111).

Chapter 2

THE JEWISH CULTURE OF THE SIXTH CENTURY BCE

1. *Jeremiah*

The figure of Jeremiah, whose prophecy can be dated to between 627 (Jer. 1.1-3) and the sack of Jerusalem in 587, was very important in the history of Jewish thought. Important for the development of thought during the period of the exile, some of his intuitions were also to be taken up again and developed more fully in later times. He had lived the exciting years of the decline of Assyrian power and the new vigour of Judah under the rule of Josiah. He had nurtured great hopes in the return of the Jews of the North, of Israel in the narrowest sense, those who had been deported to Assyria at the end of the kingdom of the North. In Jer. 30.1-10 we can read:[1]

> The word that came to Jeremiah from Yhwh: 'Thus says Yhwh, the God of Israel: Write in a book all the words that I have spoken to you. For behold, days are coming, oracle of Yhwh, when I will restore the fortunes of my people, Israel [and Judah],[2] says Yhwh, and I will bring them back to the land which I gave to their fathers, and they shall take possession of it... Alas! that day shall be great, there shall be none like it; it will be a time of distress for Jacob; yet he shall be saved out of it.

1.   The text of Jeremiah is usually presented in the form it has in the Masoretic text. The LXX differs considerably from the Masoretic version in both the order of the parts and in dimensions (the LXX text is shorter). The quoted passage is 37.1-10 in the LXX.

2.   The interpolation 'and of Judah' is present in the LXX as well, and must be considered very ancient. It betrays a reinterpretation of Jeremiah's oracle which was originally destined only for North Israel. The text's readaptation to the state of exile must be contemporaneous to the events and it seems probable to me that the author of the interpolation was Jeremiah himself. See P. Sacchi, *Storia del mondo giudaico* (Turin: Società Editrice Internazionale, 1976), p. 279, which substantially follows the thesis put forth by Angelo Penna in his edition of Jeremiah (Turin: Marietti, 1964).

And it shall come to pass in that day, says Yhwh Sabaoth, that I will break his[3] [Israel's] yoke from off your neck, and I will burst your bonds, and they shall no more be servants of him nor strangers. But they shall serve Yhwh their God and David their king, whom I will raise up for them. Then fear not, O Jacob my servant, oracle of Yhwh, nor be dismayed, O Israel; for lo, I will save you[4] from afar, and your offspring from the land of their captivity. Jacob shall return and have quiet and ease, and none shall make him afraid'.

The mention of Judah in this text is a clear but very ancient interpolation. It is a clear example of how oracles could over time be reinterpreted and in some cases rewritten. This oracle, originally concerning Israel in the narrowest sense came to gain new meaning when referred to 'all of Israel', that is to both Israel and Judah together. That it is an interpolation can, in fact, be seen in the very grammatical structure; in general it speaks only of Jacob ('your neck').

Jeremiah's sureness was perhaps strengthened by the knowledge that Judah was being ruled at that time by a righteous king, Josiah (Jer. 22.15).[5] He had accepted the palace doctrine that the dynasty of David was destined to reign over Israel forever and be its guarantee of salvation. The Jews of the North would return to their homeland, but they would no longer find the kingdom of the North. They would find a single Israel under the leadership of a descendant of David. Jerusalem would be the capital for all. Then the righteous king was defeated and fell at the battle of Megiddo in 609. Why? Perhaps he was being punished for the sins of his fathers. Josiah was the son of Amon, son of Manasseh, the vassal of Assyria who had allowed worship of other gods to enter the temple of Yhwh. But the fact that God punished the sins of the fathers on the sons gave rise to injustice, an absurdity that God's mercy and justice could not allow to continue forever.

If in Jeremiah's day there was already a theology which we could define a Theology of the Covenant, even in embryonic form, that is the promise of salvation in return for observance of the divine commandments, there was also another theology, another way of living one's

3.   The LXX omits 'his'. 'His' must have referred to an enemy, whose name has been lost. For the two influences of 'your' the LXX gives 'their', which is the normalized form of the text.

4.   'You' is singular in the original Hebrew text, as is the possessive adjective 'your' refering to offspring.

5.   The LXX provides a different interpretation.

own religion, which we can call the Theology of the Promise. God loves Israel, he gave it land and a dynasty to rule over it forever. The Covenant was such that by its very nature salvation could be brought about only on condition that men observed the divine commandments, first among them not to worship other gods. In other words, the Covenant was a sure means of salvation only within the limits of human behaviour, a possibility which seemed highly improbable to Jeremiah. 'Can the Ethiopian change his skin or the leopard his spots? Then also can you do good who are accustomed to do evil?' (Jer. 13.23). The Covenant led to an inevitable failure, which God's mercy could only delay.

The Covenant promised salvation to those who observed God's commandments, but the sins of the fathers were laid out before the Jews as an insuperable barrier. The Covenant would never lead the Jews to salvation, because humans would always break the commandments. Thus the idea of imperfection unfolds before Jeremiah, and with it the provisory nature of all present things. He looks towards a future which will necessarily be characterized by the disappearance of all the contradictions of his age. Today the fathers eat sour grapes and yet it is the children's teeth that are set on edge (Jer. 31.29), but this fact contains an imperfection, something that God will eliminate. There will be a time when this aphorism will no longer be valid, because God will reward each person according to his or her deeds (Jer. 31.30). But there is an imperfection in this solution too, because humans will continue to disobey and, therefore, God's punishment will continue as well.

Already in the past, around 700 BCE, in the wake of the fall of Samaria, the problem had already been posed concerning the meaning of the loss of such a large part of Israel. An answer was given through what we call today the 'doctrine of the remnant'. Traces of this doctrine can be found in Amos (5.15), in Micah (4.7) and in Isaiah. In Isa. 4.3 we read, 'And he who is left in Zion and remains in Jerusalem will be called sacred, every one who (has been or) will be recorded for life in Jerusalem'. And in Isa. 6.13, 'And though a tenth remain in it, it will be burned again, like a terebinth or an oak, whose stump remains standing when it is felled. The sacred seed is its stump' (along the same lines, see Isa. 10.20). This doctrine is able to explain what for the Jews are even terrible defeats, catastrophe and destruction, without the Jews being scandalized with God, who is searching for the sacred remnant. This doctrine excludes the idea that the destruction of Israel can be brought about through human unfaithfulness, because God has promised Israel salvation.

The two certainties must have clashed in the heart and mind of Jeremiah, who may have already known the story of the flood according to the so-called Yahwist tradition. In the end God realized the useless-ness of his punishment, because 'the nature (*yeṣer*) of man's heart is evil from his youth' (Gen. 8.21).[6] Were these words of hope or of despair for Israel and for all of humanity?

Whether he knew this passage or not, Jeremiah was well aware of the problem it contained. On the one hand, he was led to foretell the destruction and end of Jerusalem, which for him had an enormous, ideal value going well beyond the historical event, while on the other hand he was led to formulate a great hope in renewal. And again, the terms of renewal went beyond political restoration. Men of Jeremiah's magni-tude, though their thought begins with reflections on the events that they are called to live through, broaden that thought to reach universal dimensions.

Destruction is necessary because of Judah's wickedness which is human wickedness, but it will only be the first act of a new human history, and perhaps it will come about soon. A completely different world, characterized by a new Covenant must be born and the new Covenant will be structured in such a way that humans cannot disobey it. In this way the Promise and the Covenant will come to coincide without being mutually exclusive. In the meantime, however, between the present and future eras, between the time of imperfection and the one of perfection, there is an abyss, a clean break that only God can cross and make man cross. 'I will forgive their iniquity' (Jer. 31.34), but when will this come about?

It is precisely in this question, between the boldest of hopes and the most bewildering of uncertainties, that Jeremiah's thought reaches its acme. He leaves the future generations with a word of boundless hope. The present era is bearable as the era of imperfection. This explains the failures and the losses, everything that seemed to represent the end. In fact, the end of this order of things appeared inevitable, precisely

---

6. The LXX provides a much more nuanced text, with the desire of maintaining humanity's freedom of choice at a moment when the early apocalyptic literature was clearly raising doubts on the matter. See below. The Greek text reads: ὅτι ἔγκειται ἡ διάνοια τοῦ ἀνθρώπου ἐπιμελῶς ἐπὶ τὰ πονερὰ ἐκ νεότητος, 'because man's thought attaches itself to evil from his youth'.

because the end of this era was necessary. Every end is painful ('it is a time of distress for Jacob; yet he shall be saved out of it', Jer. 30.7b), but the end of imperfection is an inevitable step in the passage towards real salvation. The end, or better *an* end, of the history of Judah and its order of things had to come, because everything was marked by the seal of imperfection and that seal had to be removed, no matter how painful that process would be.

In ch. 27, which has certainly undergone many modifications and contains many later additions, Jeremiah insists that God has put all the land in the hands of Nebuchadnezzar, king of Babylon. He was God's 'servant',[7] in other words his instrument. Nebuchadnezzar's role could be precisely that of preparing the way for the end.

> In the fourth year of Zedekiah's reign[8] [i.e. four years after the first fall of Jerusalem] the son of Josiah, king of Judah, this word came to Jeremiah from Yhwh. Thus Yhwh said to me: 'Make yourself thongs and yoke-bars, and put them on your neck [signs of submission and defeat]. Send them to the king of Edom, the king of Moab, the king of Tyre, and the king of Sidon by the hand of the envoys who have come to Jerusalem to Zedekiah King of Judah. Give them this charge for their masters: 'Thus says Yhwh Sabaoth, God of Israel: This is what you shall say to your masters: "It is I who by my great power and my outstretched arm have made the earth, with the men and animals that are on the earth, and I give it to whomever it seems right to me. Now I have given all these lands into the hand of Nebuchadnezzar, the king of Babylon, my servant..." '[9] (Jer. 27.1-6).

On a human level, two profound problems emerge in Jewish culture with Jeremiah: that of God's justice and that of knowledge. The first of these problems runs through all of Jeremiah's work. It lays as a background to all of his thought, in every passage regarding the imperfection of the present, which is also injustice. It is even present in his difficult relationship with his own prophetic inspiration, experienced completely as something external to him. Why had God forced him to be a prophet and hated by all, having to proclaim destruction (Jer. 20.8,

---

7.   'My servant': the LXX avoids attributing this title to Nebuchadnezzar and, with only a slight variation on the Hebrew text, reads 'to serve him'.

8.   'In the fourth year of Zedekiah's reign' is a conjecture (see *BHK* [Rudolph] and *BHS* [Rüger]). The Hebrew text reads: 'In the beginning of the reign of Jehoiakim'. The LXX omits the verse. The conjecture is very probable since the text continues to speak of Zedekiah (see v. 3).

9.   See n. 7.

10)? He felt that he was the instrument of a project that he did not understand. This for him meant a pain that he could not understand, and which was therefore unjust. God's injustice did not appear to Jeremiah only when he saw himself immersed in a suffering that could not be explained in human terms. The entire structure of human society and history seemed unjust to him, even though it lay under the rule of God. 'You are too righteous, Yhwh, that I should plead with You, yet I would like to talk with You of [Your] judgments [that is the way You govern history and society]. Why does the way of the wicked prosper?... You planted them, and they have taken root...' (Jer. 12.1-2). Everything that comes about in the world is the work of God, just as Amos had already claimed (Amos 3.6; 5.8-9), so what sense can there be to the injustice that dominates the world? What relationship is there between God and injustice, or why does God use even injustice to realize his plans? What meaning is there to pain if it cannot always be interpreted as punishment?

Jeremiah knew that in some way his words were dictated by the divinity. He would willingly have done without being a prophet (Jer. 20.7-11), so if he continued to preach it was only because he was unable to do otherwise; it came from a force that was greater than him. It came from God. But this experience came into conflict daily with another experience that left him speechless. Why were there so many others who, like him, claimed to speak in the name of God yet they claimed that Judah would never be subjected to Babylon (for example Jer. 23.25 and 27.14)? Was there some way of determining, first of all to himself, who was right? Otherwise, how would he be able to firmly declare that the others were false prophets and that they had not been sent by God? In some way the problem of criteria of truth had been posed, a problem that had been solved in a very simple manner in Deuteronomy. 'When a prophet speaks in the name of Yhwh, if the word does not come to pass or come true, that is a word which Yhwh has not spoken' (Deut. 18.22).

In Jeremiah the situation is more hard-felt and therefore more complicated, but the solution is similar. God gives Jeremiah a sign that he is the one speaking the truth. It is a sign regarding the future, but that does not seem to bother Jeremiah. It follows the same logic found in Exod. 3.12, 'He said, "Certainly I will be with you [Moses]; and this shall be the sign for you, that I have sent you: when you have brought forth the people out of Egypt, you *shall serve* [future!] God upon this mountain" '. The prophet realizes that there is a gap between his own way of thinking and the Word of God. He can even try to oppose the Word that he feels as present in his mind; he understood perfectly well the difficulties for the people represented by the fact that there were others who made prophecies different from his own. In some way he poses the question of the criterion of truth and in order to resolve it he uses the idea of the sign, as a guarantee that God will cause his prophecies to come true.

Therefore, when someone asked Jeremiah what importance (*maśśa'*, 'burden') God's word had, he could answer, 'You are the burden of Yhwh...and I will cast you off [you who say such things]' (Jer. 23.33-34). The word *maśśa'* on the lips of his interlocutor becomes the sign that one day the things that Jeremiah has said will come true. His is the true word, not that of the other prophets, and it is true for the sole reason that it comes from God. This principle of truth later expands to the point of invading all realms of knowledge.

2. *Jewish Cultural Movements during the Exile*

After the grave separation between the kingdom of the North and the kingdom of the South, the Jews experienced another serious fracture at the time of the exile, as we have already seen above in the pages concerning the events. Opposing interests and physical distance led quickly to two separate ideologies, each one of them explaining 'rationally' that 'the others' had been abandoned by God and that they therefore no longer belonged to the same people. 'The others' had lost their rights. Like all rationalizations this one too deepened the divide by shifting emphasis away from human interests, toward questions of ideology. In the words of Ezekiel we have already seen not only the defence of the exiles' interests, but also threats for those who had remained in the homeland.

This threat is even more clear in a passage from Jeremiah composed sometime between the first and the second sack of Jerusalem. It was therefore destined, when written, only for those who had remained in the homeland after the first conquest at the hand of Nebuchadnezzar. Later the passage easily lent itself to the interpretation that it referred to those who had remained even after the second conquest.

> Yhwh showed me two baskets of figs placed before the temple of Yhwh, after Nebuchadnezzar king of Babylon had taken into exile from Jerusalem Yeconia [= Jehoiachin], son of Jehoiakim, king of Judah... One basket had very good figs...but the other basket had very bad figs...

> Thus says Yhwh, God of Israel, 'Like these good figs, so I will regard as
> good the exiles from Judah, whom I have sent away from this place to
> the land of the Chaldeans. I will set my eyes upon them for good, and I
> will bring them back to this land... Like the bad figs which are so bad
> they cannot be eaten, so will I treat Zedekiah the king of Judah... I will
> send sword, famine, and pestilence upon them, until they shall be utterly
> destroyed from the land which I gave to them and their fathers' (Jer.
> 24.1-10).

The threat is one of total ruin. This passage demonstrates that the
prophet did not approve of the policies of his compatriots who had
remained in Judaea.

The Jewish tradition has not conserved anything representing the
elaboration of an ideology of those who remained, which leads us to
believe that it was either completely eliminated or absorbed by the
theology of the returned exiles. We will therefore have to content ourselves with examining what the exiles did and what they thought. Concerning the thought of those who remained in the homeland, we can
only make conjectures, which will always remain such.

3. *The Priests, the Elders and Ezekiel*

It is possible to individuate two or three centres of culture and of power
in Babylon. The first area that can be singled out is that of the priests,
with Ezekiel at their head. He was the first to become active, motivated
by the need to defend interests that no one else was interested in
defending. The second area was that of the court. It is more difficult to
establish whether or not we can speak of a third, cultural area centred
around the elders of Israel. The laymen in exile must have looked first
to the king as the centre of their hopes, but the policies of Jehoiachin,
after the death of Zedekiah, must have seemed suspicious to the elders
for the same reasons that Ezekiel, with great lucidity, was opposed to
the same policies. A convergence between the priests and the elders
was born from this, but it was a convergence that required some clarification.

The elders' rather nearsighted aim was simply that of returning to the
homeland, and they imagined that they would be able to return to a
Judaea in exactly the same state as they had left it. Ezekiel undeceived
them in extremely clear terms, as can be seen in ch. 20 of the book of
Ezekiel. A group of elders went to the place where Ezekiel lived in
order to consult with Yhwh. The text does not say exactly what they

asked, though it can be deduced from the response; they wanted to know about the possibilities of a return home. At least in appearance, Ezekiel receives them exceedingly rudely. In one passage, where the prophet's thoughts concerning Israel and its destiny are synthesized, Ezekiel answers that Yhwh will not allow them to consult him, apparently because they are unworthy. And they were unworthy, because they looked upon Israel and its destiny with the same eyes as when they had lived in the homeland. They were simply asking if God would allow them to return.

Instead of answering the elders' question directly, Ezekiel made a brief summary of the history of Israel from its origins, emphasizing that Israel was unworthy of election. The election lay at the base of Ezekiel's thought, and he insisted on the idea that Israel had been unworthy of election. Israel was the daughter of 'an Amorite and a Hittite' (Ezek. 16.3). God's election should have brought about the abandonment of the Egyptian idols (v. 7). The Jews had rebelled many times against God. He would have liked to pour out his wrath on Israel, but he had not done so out of respect for his own name, so that the Gentiles would not have believed him to be an impotent God. 'So I led them out of the land of Egypt and brought them into the wilderness. I gave them my statutes and showed them my ordinances, by whose observance man shall live' (Ezek. 20.10-11).

In spite of this, Israel's rebellions had continued right up to the prophet's own day. Ezekiel's goal is clear; he wants to explain two things to the elders. First he wanted to explain that the religious and moral structure of Israel as it had been under the monarchy was not that which God had desired. Given the stubbornness of his elected people, God in the end had given Israel bad laws in order to hasten the end of that shameful order of things; 'Moreover I gave them statutes that were not good and ordinances by which they could not have life; and I defiled them through their very gifts in making them offer by fire all their first-born...' (Ezek. 20.25-26). Secondly, the Jews in exile, as a consequence, should not think that return to the homeland meant simply recuperating lost goods and picking up where they had left off. Israel would return to its land, but once there it would have to create a new society unlike the preceding one:

> And you shall know that I am Yhwh, when I bring you (again) into the land of Israel, the country which I swore to give to your fathers. And there you shall remember your ways and all the doings with which you

have polluted yourselves; and you shall loathe yourselves for all the evils
that you have committed (Ezek. 20.42-43).

For Ezekiel there were laws which needed to be abolished, others to
be added and reformed. He envisioned a truly different society.

The situation seemed all but fixed to Ezekiel, and history proved him
right. For the moment it was enough to have clarified to the elders that a
return would only have been possible with a complete renewal of the
structures of society. The priesthood in exile, by now completely separated from the priests in Judaea, was to have a primary role in this
renewal. In a later period Ezekiel (or a faithful writer continuing Ezekiel's text) was to draw the guidelines for the future state. As time went
by, in spite of the better position enjoyed by the Davidic dynasty with
the Babylonians and then the Persians, Ezekiel had become more and
more certain that the return was certain. It was blocked only by a political situation that he rightly considered to be contingent and destined to
be overcome at the first favourable moment.

Ezekiel thought therefore of a new constitution for Israel which did
not exclude the ruling house's continuation (as, in fact, came about),
but that did place it in a specific condition with marked limits to its
authority. The text of the book of Ezekiel was certainly written before
520–515 BCE, since its author does not know of the situation then coming about in Palestine. Ezekiel (or perhaps a faithful writer continuing
the text) felt that the king (*naśi'*!) should have some kind of privileged
role in the temple (44.3). The temple, however, was to be governed by a
select group of priests referred to as the 'sons of Zadok'. Anyone who
was not a Zadokite would be a priest of only secondary status. He
insists that the Jews had committed several abominations, and among
them particular importance is given to having admitted uncircumcised
foreigners into the temple; the exiles' concern with saving the identity
of the people, and not just the culture and religion, seems clear.
Furthermore, Ezekiel draws up a liturgy based on a complex theory of
the sacred (44.17 and following verses), which had complex consequences for the structure of Jewish society in favour of the priesthood, whose sacredness was greater than that of the layperson. In fact
the authority of establishing just what is sacred and what profane, what
pure and what impure belongs to the priesthood alone (Ezek. 44.23).
The priests are to be the only judges in Israel. They cannot be married
following the laws of the other Jews. Their sacrality had to put them in
a pre-eminent position, marked by a certain isolation.

The king would be given a wide strip of land with the temple at its centre and its eastern and western boundaries coinciding with the state's borders. 'It is to be his property in Israel. And my kings shall no more oppress my people; but they shall let the house of Israel have the land according to their tribes' (Ezek. 45.8). The kings of Israel had in the past oppressed God's people with their authority, which must have been more or less absolute. Now, Ezekiel advocates a constitution that greatly limits royal powers. The king will possess vast stretches of land, but only in order to dispose of the means necessary for defending the temple and the people, without having to impose taxes or military conscription. The tribes of Israel will have to be free. The constitution envisaged by Ezekiel was vaguely oligarchical, with power in the hands of the heads of the tribes, and with the temple as a central point of reference. The temple, unlike the kings, will have the right to receive the offerings (more or less compulsory) of the faithful. All of this, of course, implied the complete centralization of worship.

The king, who once considered the temple his own property, was now only its protector. He does carry out particularly important roles there, but always within the organization desired and controlled by the Zadokite priesthood. The temple will have a special door reserved for the prince (44.3),[10] and the prince will carry out particular sacrifices, especially that of Passover, which for Ezekiel seems to be a case of state worship and not family worship (45.16, 18 and following verses). If the temple was to lie at the centre of Israel, then the priesthood lay at the centre of the temple. The priesthood gathered in its hand the powers of justice, of handing down and modifying laws, of interpreting them and of collecting taxes.

While Ezekiel's constitution was directed most of all at protecting certain interests coinciding with those of the exiles, it also contained strong theoretical elements. The collection of commandments that was later to become the Torah is at the very centre of Ezekiel's thought, because it is the instrument destined to bring salvation to the people as well as (and in Ezekiel the idea is very clear) to the individual. Observation of the Law is fundamental in function of life. Chapter 18 is

---

10. Even though there is a door reserved for the king who has the special right to enter and exit by the same door, unlike the others who must enter and exit through separate doors, the king is not free to go to the temple when he likes, but only when the people go there. This is my interpretation of Ezek. 46.8-10.

developed entirely around this theme. Jeremiah had already foreseen
the new world which would be born from the new Covenant, a world
free from the human and divine injustices characterizing the time in
which he had been called to live. He had foreseen that in those blessed
future days no one would repeat the bitter saying, ' "The fathers have
eaten sour grapes, and the children's teeth are set on edge". But every
one shall die for his own sin; each man who eats sour grapes, his teeth
shall be set on edge' (Jer. 31.29-30).

For Jeremiah, the new form of the retributive principle would only be
brought about in the future, once God had established the new order.
For the time he lived in, the application of this principle was unthinkable. When Jeremiah turns to God in prayer he exclaims, 'You who are
merciful to thousands of generations and requite the wickedness of
fathers in their children... You are great, and incomprehensible in your
designs' (Jer. 32.18-19). The way in which God metes out retributory
justice is a mystery, but in the time of the new order it will no longer be
so. The human condition Jeremiah lived in was acceptable only if he
bore in mind that the world carried a seal of imperfection which was
destined to disappear.

Ezekiel, however, was categorical; God had already put the new
retributory principle into effect, each person paid according to his own
guilt. The new order has not yet begun, but this first element of the
future order is already in place.

> What do you mean by repeating this proverb concerning the land of
> Israel, 'The fathers have eaten sour grapes, and the children's teeth are
> set on edge'? As I live, oracle of Adonai Yhwh, this proverb shall no
> more be used by you in Israel. Behold, all souls are mine; the soul of the
> father as well as the soul of the son is mine: the soul that sins shall die
> (Ezek. 18.2-4).

The early death, which must punish the sinner, will strike the sinner
only, not his descendants. And if someone sins and then repents and
returns to doing right, he will be safe as well, 'for the righteousness
which he has done he shall live' (Ezek. 18.22). Therefore justice, that is
observance of the commandments, saves and salvation is not too far off.
It does not regard future generations, but is nearby, just behind observance of the Law.

Perhaps with these claims Ezekiel aimed at removing a motive of
disturbance and fear from his friends, a fear which could impede their
actions. Perhaps it was aimed at annulling the fear that the sins of their

fathers that they heard the prophet speak of so often could fall on them, rendering vain their works, their attempts at personal redemption and at recuperating the homeland. Ezekiel, however, proclaimed a principle whose importance went well beyond the contingent moment and that was to give new reason for reflection to later generations. For Jeremiah the divine principle of retribution based on the righteousness of the individual was a sign of the beginning of a future time which would lack the contradictions afflicting history up until his own day. For Ezekiel it was something that had already come about, at least in part. But was it possible to find evidence of this fact in the life of his times? His claims were verifiable in daily reality. And it was precisely in this area that doubts and problems were bound to arise.

Another extremely interesting point in Ezekiel's preachings is the following: for him observance of the Law saves, if we can say that, in itself. The Law is not seen as the sum total of the clauses in the Covenant. Inasmuch as Ezekiel's thought can be placed in the vein of spirituality that we have called 'Theology of the Covenant', he lacks an important element of the Theology of the Covenant. This lack perhaps becomes more understandable if we look at the way in which another ideology of Israel was being created at court.

Ezekiel of course knew the idea of the 'Covenant', but he did not identify it with the Law. *B^{e}rît* is the term indicating the peculiar and extremely close relationship between God and Israel, a bond sworn to by God (Ezek. 16.8) in the moment when he chose Israel, because Israel (which is feminine in the Hebrew language) became such only when God 'spread his skirt over her', according to a nuptial image already used by Hosea. For this particular relationship idol worship is an extremely grave sin and it is the sin that Ezekiel insists upon the most, at least in ch. 16. But pride and neglecting the poor are sins as well (Ezek. 16.49). In the prophet's teachings the ethical and social motive is tied to the betrayal inherent in idolatry forming a solid context for behaviour; by doing evil Israel broke the Covenant (16.59), in the sense that it broke this special relationship with God.[11] The radical identification of the Law with the Covenant, in the sense that the com-

---

11. See the text of Ezek. 20.37, which, however, does not have a unitary tradition: 'I will make you pass under the rod and I will bring you into the bond of the Covenant'. The Hebrew text surely presents the original version. The LXX has lost the word *b^{e}rît*, 'Covenant', and in the place of *bm(')srt*, 'bond', it reads *bmspr*, 'by number'.

mandments of the Law constitute the clauses of the Covenant, is apparently a later phenomenon.

4. *Ezekiel and the New Culture*

Ezekiel provided a very strong stimulus to the Jewish culture of the exiles. More than one current of later Jewish thought referred back to him. Some currents, however, developed certain aspects of his thought while other currents developed others.

Ezekiel moves within the Jewish tradition, but he also conceives of a number of innovative elements, fruit of contact with the great Akkadic civilization. Like the prophets that came before him, he too expresses his most original ideas in connection with visions or with hearing the Word. There is also symbolic action. But the vision assumes a cognitive importance that it did not have before (chs. 4–5). With Ezekiel the relationship between the heavens and the earth assumes new dimensions. Up until this point visions had always taken place on earth. Even the vision in Isaiah 6, which says so much about the divine, takes place in the temple, that is on earth. God spoke into the prophet's ear and showed something to his eye, but in a terrestrial dimension. Even that which went beyond the realm of the human was expressed in earthly terms.

As early as the first verse of the first chapter the book of Ezekiel speaks of *mar'ôt 'ᵉlōhîm*, 'divine visions'. I do not believe that Ezekiel wanted to place himself in opposition to tradition and claim that previous visions had not come from God. He merely wanted to say that his visions had a more vast dimension: 'the heavens were opened'. His gaze reaches beyond this world. The roof of the firmament no longer has, or no longer only has, the role of separating the upper waters from the lower, but that of separating the world of God from the world of men. This corresponds to a greater awareness of divine transcendence, but it also corresponds to a widening of human cognitive interests. For the pre-exile Jew God lived on the clouds and therefore under the heavens; he moved about in space riding the cherubim (see, for example, Judg. 5.4; Isa. 19.1; 37.16). Beginning with Ezekiel God is situated beyond that; the idea of God, the vision of the world and the circle of human interests have grown broader and more complex.

Ezekiel was still interested in the events that took place around him, but his interest took on characteristics which were different from those of his predecessors. First of all, he is aware of living *after* a period of Israel's history has come to a close. The Covenant has been violated and, says Ezekiel, it is as though Israel were dead (ch. 37), but it will rise again for a future that will be different from the past. There is a clean break in history. In this vision of things the past does not hold its value in being that which precedes and conditions the future, but in being what today we call the type of the future. In other words, its value transcends history; the past and the future are no longer two independent realities, but rather two realities bound together by a middle term which, even though it is dependent on God's will, assumes an autonomous value. An example of this is the drastic condemnation of the monarchic period, destined to never return again, at least not in its past forms (45.9). Unlike the tradition that saw the dynasty's continuity in the passage from father to son as a rhythm that would last until the coming of the Messiah (Prophecy of Nathan, 2 Sam. 7, a text which probably dates to the seventh century BCE), David is no longer seen as the Messiah's forebear. For Ezekiel David is the type of the messiah (34.23 and 37.24-25), not his forebear. This indicates a profound novelty in the conceptual structures, a greater capacity of abstraction; though not verbalized, we have the concept of 'type' with all that that brings with it.

This means seeing reality through new eyes. This new kind of knowledge is fully realized in the vision of the chariot.

The vision of the chariot (Ezek. 1) is structured differently from the visions of previous prophets and is distinguished from them by the breadth and richness of meanings of the details. The elements of this vision provide a complex theology, even though its particulars escape us.

In Isaiah (ch. 6) the vision provides a backdrop for the words and furnishes *some* elements on the relationship between humans and God. In Jeremiah (ch. 1) the vision is enclosed in the spoken message which it illustrates. In Ezekiel (ch. 1), to a large degree the vision has an autonomous value and meaning which normally goes beyond history, in harmony with the new conception of the divine, now placed above and not below the heavens. The chariot's four wheels could have been suggested by an ordinary, earthly chariot, but the fact that they are able to move in all directions shows us that the wheels of this celestial chariot are different from those of an earthly one. In the vision the number '4' appears too many times for it to be, even in the case of the wheels, the pure transposition of an earthly chariot's four wheels: the beings have four faces and four wings each. '4' is above all a cosmic symbol.

In 1.14 we are told that the beings of the vision move like lightening,[12] that is with instant speed. Even this detail is meant to emphasize the fact that the chariot of the vision belongs to a world where the laws of this one do not apply. The divine world is different from ours, ruled by different laws than this world, all of them desired by God, of course. At any rate the upper world exists and acts upon ours.

In other words, in Ezekiel we see an interest for the upper world, for the world of God, where God does not live alone, but where other beings live as well. Even the existence of a celestial court is not new though, but the complexity of its conception here is new and most of all its relationship with God and with the world is new. For example, we see *kî rûah hahayyâ bᵉ'opannîm* in 1.21. This means more or less that the same spirit as in the angelic beings is also in the wheels of the chariot. This detail points out a search for unity in the upper world, even though I would not be able to explain it in more rational terms.[13] Ezekiel is a new man in Israel, but he says new things through the old schemas, which are still the image, the symbol and the myth.

Even the fact that the day in which Ezekiel's visions and hearings take place is mentioned is important for the newness of the spiritual dimension within which Ezekiel acts. His visions usually take place on Sunday, the first day of the week, when time leaves the sacredness of the Sabbath and returns to humans. Or they take place on Friday when time is about to enter the realm of the sacred. The week is not only a period of seven days, it is also the earthly projection of a cosmic structure, that of the creation.[14]

12. The authenticity of this verse has been put in doubt by the *BHK* based on its omission in the Vatican Codex of the LXX. It is put in doubt on more solid grounds in the *BHS* inasmuch as it is attributed to the original Greek. See Rahlfs and Ziegler. It is certain that the verse should be eliminated from the original Greek, but it is less sure whether or not it belongs to the original Hebrew. This is a difficult passage with rare words and perhaps some errors which even created problems when it was inserted, based on the Hebrew, in the Greek tradition. It is one of those typical passages that bother a translator and, in fact, Origen left it out.

13. In this case the translation of *rûah* with 'wind' is impossible. 'The wind of the living creatures was in the wheels' does not make sense and calls for some intervention on the part of the translator.

14. According to the Hebrew text visions 1.1; 3.16; 29.1; 31.1; 32.1 and 33.21 take place on Sunday. Visions 8.1; 24.1 and 40.1 take place on Friday, that is just

In this epoch the Sabbath is no longer a reminder of delivery from Egypt, as in Deuteronomy (Deut. 5.15),[15] but the actualization and repetition of the seventh day of the creation as in Exodus (Exod. 20.11). The liturgy is no longer a simple act of homage to God: it links the upper world to this one. The exact day becomes a fundamental element of the liturgy, because the positions of the stars lay behind each day: while for us the firmament is a physical concept, for the ancients it was much less so. The term 'heaven(s)' did not exist only in relation to God, but 'heaven' was an entire cosmos of powers whose influence could be felt even down here. It should not surprise us that Ezekiel dedicates so much attention to the question of what is sacred in the liturgy; sacredness is a cosmic force.

Within this framework, even the problem of the validity of knowledge, which Jeremiah had already posed, is resolved in a different manner. Like all of his predecessors, Ezekiel knows the voice, but at the beginning of his book he describes, in a symbolic manner, a new way of understanding knowledge that does not depend on the senses. Ezekiel is presented with a scroll with writing on it and he is invited to

before entering the Sabbath. The texts of the LXX are normally in concordance with the Hebrew texts. The LXX, though, would have 33.21 take place on Friday as well, but this could be an error due to the repetition of a number, and therefore the Hebrew text is to be preferred. The case of 29.1 is interesting; the LXX has Wednesday. Here the possibility of errors (the repetition of the same number twice) goes against the Hebrew text, although the fact that an anomalous result is obtained leaves some perplexity. It should be pointed out that liturgically Wednesday is the most important day of the week according to the solar calendar since it is the day of the creation of the stars and therefore of the beginning of time. In the solar calendar all years begin with Wednesday. All in all though, I feel that the Hebrew text is to be preferred; if Wednesday had had the same importance for Ezekiel that it was later given, his visions would probably not have taken place in relation to the sabbath.

15. In pre-exile times the word *šabbāt* did not indicate the seventh day of the week, but rather the day of the full moon. According to Deuteronomy the sabbath marked the memory of escape from Egypt, but this did not take place on Saturday. Following a tradition documented in the Priestly source (Exod. 12), it took place on a day of the full moon according to the pre-exile lunar/solar calendar (the 15th of the first month). Only in the post-exile period was the word placed in relation to the root *šbt*, 'rest'. The double consonant indicates the root *šbb*, which has been put in relation with a semitic root meaning 'to get up'. On this problem see A. Lemaire, 'Le sabbat à l'époque royale israélite', *RB* 80 (1973), pp. 161-85; G. Bettenzoli, 'Lessemi ebraici di radice -shabat-', *Henoch* 4 (1982), pp. 129-62; Bettenzoli, 'La tradizione del shabbat', *Henoch* 4 (1982), pp. 265-93.

eat it (2.8). He absorbs the scroll's contents and he 'knows' that he has assimilated the Word, which in turn becomes both his and God's. Faced with the Word of the older prophets one could believe that something had been left out or altered, but with Ezekiel that is impossible. He has the Word in him, it is part of him. For Jeremiah the words of the prophet could be confirmed by an objective and divine sign, for Ezekiel certainty is inside him, and he alone experiences it.

5. *The King and his Court in Exile*

Jehoiachin's court seems to have been passive with regard to the events, at least at first, substantially contented not to have completely lost all their own rights. We have no proof that any culture was produced there under the reign of Nebuchadnezzar. Beginning with the reign of Awil Marduk and then under Cyrus, though, there was some movement in the Davidic court. Attempts were made to interpret the position and role of the monarchy for the Jewish people. The history of the dynasty and of Israel were put down in writing with the purpose of binding the two solidly together. The consequence of this operation was the creation of a precise interpretation of Israel. Among the people at work at court, or at least in the same sphere of interests, was the historian who compiled the history of the kings of Judah and Israel and perhaps even of the patriarchs, the man whom Noth calls the Deuteronomist. I prefer to call him R1, because I do not believe that he ever dealt with Deuteronomy, which reflects a different ideology than that of R1 and also presupposes an equally different historical situation.

Deuteronomy, at least in its current structure, is a later work. It is of a different hand than R1 not only because it has a peculiar literary structure, unique in biblical literature, with the theme divided into speeches, but also because it is derived from a different ideology. Deuteronomy's author not only admits that any Jew could sit on the throne of Israel, and therefore could not have been an exponent of the Davidic court, but he also admits it as a pure possibility (Deut. 17.14-15). He lets a republican spirit show, which is easier to explain in a later historical context than that of R1 or his follower R2.[16] For Deut. 17.14 there will be a

---

16. With 'R2' I indicate the interpolator of the universalistic passages in accordance with the thesis of J. Hoftijzer, *Die Verheissungen an die drei Erzväter* (Leiden: E.J. Brill, 1956). R2 would seem, however, to be very close to R1. The milieu is still the same, that of the court in exile, but we are now in the last years of the monarchy before 515.

king in Israel only if Israel itself wants one; Moses was chosen by God, but the monarchy was not. In the case, then, that Israel should want a king, then it is enough that he should be a Jew and not a foreigner. This sort of text does not come from the Davidic court, nor does it come from the times of Josiah, nor from the time of the exile. Nor is it an artifact of the monarchical tradition of the North. This text's background is a republican one that concedes the possibility of becoming a monarchy, but not necessarily a Davidic one. That is the situation in Israel during the years around 515 BCE.

Furthermore, Deuteronomy differs both from Ezekiel and his school and from R1 in that it has the Covenant coincide with the very moment in which the Law was given to Israel. And this is stated polemically. The Covenant was *not* made with the fathers, 'but with us, who are all of us here alive this day' (Deut. 5.3). This passage is clearly to be attributed to a nomistic writer who sees Israel as governed solely by the Law of God. All institutions, including the priesthood, are to be regulated by the Law. Even the power of passing judgment is not in the hands of the priests, but of the elders (Deut. 1.15-17). If there is to be a king, he must live by the law regarding kings (Deut. 17.19) and therefore could not pass laws. In any case he can be elected only if the people so desire (Deut. 17.14). The Covenant and the Law coincide completely only from this point on, at least for one current of Judaism.

Deutero-Isaiah, who belonged to the same court milieu, created a true royal ideology. The acme of his activity may be situated, I believe, near the great crisis years of 520–515 BCE.

The circles nearest the court elaborated an image of Israel too, but theirs was very different from the one elaborated by the priests. If the reconstruction of the court that we have proposed is exact, then the court functionaries must have felt much more attached to the homeland than the priesthood or the elders. They *knew*, just as the king knew, that their exile was only temporary. They were merely waiting to re-obtain freedom of movement, which was conceded, as we have seen, by Awil-Marduk. Their drama was lesser than that of the others. We have even tried to understand why they were not on good terms with the priests and the other laymen in exile. If the king was still to be considered king of Judah, then he had to be careful to maintain the situation created by the Babylonians. This precluded dialogue with the common deportees and the priesthood. The court was in exile, which was a sad reality, but the exile was contingent and temporary. And just as the means for dedicating themselves to culture were not lacking for the priesthood, they were not lacking for the circle of the court either. The 'rations of foodstuffs' destined for the court could have corresponded to some amount of tribute that Judaea surely paid to Babylon.

In imitation of the Assyrian annals and the Babylonian Chronicles, but mostly the latter, a Jewish historiography was born with the goal of collecting the nation's memory. An Israel without a history would not have had a mirror for recognizing itself, especially from the point of view of the cultural elite in exile. It is not necessary here to repeat my ideas about the breadth of the work of Israel's first historian. I believe that his work covered the period from the origin of the world up until his own day. The last event known to the author regards the year 561 BCE. He must have been writing after that date, but not long after, probably in the period around the fall of the Babylonian Empire and the rise of the Persian one. Some parts of the work in fact contain a universalism that would seem to be a consequence of contact with Persian culture. Since these parts appear to have been inserted into the completed work,[17] we could be dealing with a second author, R2, who retouched the work of the great master for the first time. The figure of R1 coincides more or less, in the current terminology, with Noth's Deuteronomist, with the differences noted above.

The central theme of R1's thought is the idea that God promised an eternal reign to David and his descendants, as stated in the story of Nathan's prophecy (2 Sam. 7). The history of the Davidic monarchy has three central figures: David, Hezekiah and Josiah. Josiah made a solemn covenant with Yhwh based on a book found in the temple and that the author calls the 'Book of the Covenant' (2 Kgs 23.2). Josiah commits himself and, in his name, the people to observing the commandments, that is the laws that are written in that book. By this it is understood that God would protect the people if the people observed the laws. The laws thus became the clauses in the Covenant with God, but in a very different way than the totalizing vision of the post-exilic Deuteronomy.

The Law is presented to the people as being given by God, but first of all it has been accepted by the king and issued by him. Inserting the Law in the Covenant with Yhwh, in that particular bond tying God to his people, was a gesture made with the intention of favouring the

17. See Hoftijzer, *Die Verheissungen*.

acceptance of the new laws. Their innovative value (regarding the family, for example: women, Jewish slaves—Deut. 24.1 and 15.12-18) must not have been welcomed by everyone. In other words, the Covenant of Josiah seems to be an attempt to insert the laws that he issued, or at least that he had wanted, into the very structure of the state, substituting previous legislation. It was the people's duty to observe them, and the king's duty to enforce them for collective salvation. Whether as a result of a political move a religious principle was born and then developed independently of original intentions is another question.

The Davidic dynasty, then, was necessary for Israel's salvation because David had been chosen king by God himself. The choice was not dependent on whether the king was good or not, just as with the election of Israel. David may have sinned; in fact, it was the same prophet, Nathan, who both reproached David for having killed Uriah, and pronounced the prophecy of eternal reign for David. God's grace and his promise are above the kings' guilt, a fact that R1 does not ever try to hide. He does not even try to hide the sins of Jehoiachin (2 Kgs 24.9) at whose court he must have spent much of his life. In the same way that David sinned and was also promised eternal reign for his dynasty, so too Jehoiachin was not a good king during the brief time he ruled in Judah, but that does not mean that God, through his grace, did not show him salvation through the favour obtained under Awil Marduk. The favour is emphasized, in the same way as the sin.

When a city of Judah was saved in what could seem a miraculous manner R1 uses a typical formula of his thought: 'I will defend this city to save it [says God], for my own sake and for the sake of my servant David' (2 Kgs 19.34; see also 1 Kgs 11.13, 32 and 2 Kgs 20.6).

This is the application to history of the ideology of Davidic messianism which arose in the court circles of Judah.

> There shall come forth a shoot from the stump of Jesse,
> and a branch shall grow out of his roots.
> And the spirit of Yhwh shall rest upon him... (Isa. 11.1-2).[18]

18. The dating of the text of Isa. 11 is debated. At one time common opinion held it to be authentic, but today many believe it to date from the post-exilic period in that it speaks of a stump, that is the image of something that has been cut, thus corresponding to a period in which the monarchy no longer exists in Israel. But the rare word *geza'* does not seem to mean 'trunk of a tree that has been cut down' (see Isa. 40.24). I do not feel that there is sufficient reason to accept this later dating. In any case, the idea that a descendent will come forth from the stump of Jesse just as

Of the increase of his government and of peace there will be no end, upon
the throne of David, and over his kingdom, to establish it, and to uphold it
with justice and with righteousness from this time forth and for ever-
more… (Isa. 9.7).

Bring no more vain offerings…When you spread forth your hands, I will
hide my eyes from you; even though you make many prayers…your hands
are full of blood (Isa. 1.13-15).

According to Isaiah human injustice makes God insensitive to prayer
and makes every sacrifice useless. Therefore the wrath of God falls on
his people and punishes them, searching for the remains that can be
holy and righteous. In Isaiah's vision, though, this cannot come about
through human justice, but only when God will cause to be born from
among David's descendants a king to whom God will give the power to
establish justice in Israel and free the people from their enemies. In like
manner, for R1 Israel's salvation is tied to the Davidic dynasty, in that
the promise of justice that one day God will give to his people has been
deposited with that dynasty. R1 mixes the moral teachings of the
prophets with expectations of grace, in turn tied to God's love for his
servant David.

6. *The Court Historian's Method*

We do not know the names of all the Jewish authors, and perhaps of
only a very few. One of the greatest anonymous works is the one that
narrates the history of the world and of Israel from its origins up to 561
BCE, the year that Jehoiachin's conditions bettered from those of a
beaten king held by the victor.

If we work our way backwards in time from the last verse of 2 Kings
to the first verse of Genesis it is quite easy to notice a single narrative
thread broken only by Deuteronomy, which clearly breaks the line of
the story.[19] Furthermore, there is some reasonable doubt that some or

David did, and therefore equal to David in dignity, was a deeply rooted idea at court
in Jerusalem, as witnessed by the prophecy of Nathan (probably no older than the
seventh century BCE). The same idea is found in all of Isaiah's prophetic ideology,
which awaits Israel's salvation through an exceptional king, capable of imposing
justice on the people, in a discoursive procedure opposite to that of Amos.

19. The idea that the real problem of the Pentateuch is Deuteronomy, that is a
book inserted into a greater work running from Genesis to the last book of Kings,
was already formulated by Spinoza. See ch. 8 of the *Tractatus politico-religiosus*:

even many of the law collections could have been inserted in the body of the work at a later moment or moments, along with some smaller additions. I have given the name R1 to the author of this work, based on the idea of a compiler (*redattore*), a term which clearly falls short of indicating the complexity of his work.

The general outline of the work is clear. It begins with the origin of the world and of humanity, it continues with the genealogy of the antediluvian patriarchs with few details but a great many numbers. Then comes Noah and the flood and a new humankind, the election of Abraham and the promise of descendants and the Land. Then comes Joseph in Egypt and escape from Egypt under Moses' guidance. This is followed by the desert crossing and the Law given to Moses by God, which guaranteed the obedience of the people to the king. Then comes Joshua and various texts recounting the conquest, and then remembrance of a time when Israel had no king and 'every man did what was right in his own eyes' (Judg. 21.25); the monarchy was clearly a guarantee of order. Finally we have the story of the monarchy up to Jehoiachin. It should be borne in mind that the author dedicates a great deal of attention to the monarchy of the North. In his ideology, which repeats that of Josiah and Jeremiah, there was only one Israel, not the divided Kingdoms of Israel in the North and Judah in the South. Of course it is perfectly possible that the work was written by more than one person.

Van Seters's thesis is similar to mine; he maintains that the tetrateuch was added later, but not long after the work of the author of history of the books of Samuel and of the Kings, in order to complete and fill out the first work. If I continue to uphold my own hypothesis over van Seters's, it is only because mine presents a more unitary structure and

'Ex his igitur tribus consideratis—nempe simplicitate argumenti horum omnium librorum, connexione, et quod sint apographa multis post saeculis a rebus gestis scripta, concludimus...eos omnes *ab uno solo historico* scriptos fuisse'. This historian must have lived after the last event narrated. In keeping with a widely held view of his day, Spinoza mentions the name of Ezra, but not without some uncertainty. Of course, we must bear in mind that Spinoza held Ezra to be much more ancient than we believe today. He had placed him around the end of the period of exile, following the genealogy provided in Ezra 7.1, where he is called the son of Seraiah, who must be the father of Jozedek, father of Joshua (see Ezra 3.2).

Regarding the meaning of the word 'apographa', see A. Droetto and E. Giancotti Boscherini's *Commento al Tractatus theologico-Politicus di Spinoza* (Turin: Einaudi, 1972), p. 254: ' "*Apographi*" for Spinoza means that the books examined belong neither to the authors nor to the époques to which they have been attributed'.

somehow includes and confirms Van Seters's intuition: without the tetrateuch somethng would have been lacking. In other words, the work makes sense only as it is and this is the strongest indicator of a unity of conception and therefore of a single author. The chronological continuity, which beyond the year 1000 more or less is absolutely abstract, derives from speculation and not from a bundle of stories piled up or added one after the other over the course of pre-exilic history. Additions existed, but they were added in a framework that had already been laid out. This does not mean that the author had no sources, and it is interesting to see how he used them. It is informative for understanding the man, his aims and his ideology.

Above all, the work presents a solid chronological frame. If it has been possible to establish a date for the creation, it is only because the biblical account allows it. Even though the calculations made in antiquity and in more recent times differ, it cannot be denied that the differences are small.[20] That means that our author considered the beginning of the world a historical event, described according to a memory of the facts in some way handed down to the author. Our author never claims to have had any revelations concerning the content of his story.[21] He knew the origins of the world only through the myths that he could read and that were told in his milieu. Whether he heard them told orally or whether he read them written on papyrus or clay tablets is of little importance. What matters is that, wherever the myths of the origin came from, and in whatever language,[22] he interpreted them in a his-

20. According to the calculations made recently by T.L. Thompson, *The Historicity of the Patriarchal Narratives* (Berlin: W. de Gruyter, 1974), the creation took place in the year 4164 BCE, which diverges from both the *Jubilees* and the Rabbinical calendar. For the *Jubilees* the exodus took place in 1300 CM (*Creatio Mundi*) while for Thompson it happened in 2666 CM. During the eighteenth century Musanti had established the date for the exodus in 2564 CM (*Fax chronologica* [Pistoia, 1706], p. 32).

21. On R1's philosophy, see P. Sacchi, 'Knowledge among the Jews from Amos to the Essenes', in *Jewish Apocalyptic and its History* (Sheffield: Sheffield Academic Press, 1997), pp. 168-99 and 'Storicizzazione e rivelazione alle origini del giudaismo', *RSLR* 24 (1988), pp. 68-77, now in *Jewish Apocalyptic*, with the elimination of a number of typographical errors that impaired comprehension, pp. 200-10.

22. On the relationship between Babylonian and Jewish literature, see the famous book *Babel und Bibel* by F. Delitzsch (Stuttgart: Hinrichs, 1905), a work which remains a milestone in research, even though its approach is dated. In some

torical manner. The abstract chronology begins with the unified kingdom and continues through the period of the judges, which in common
opinion belongs to the work of the Deuteronomist. The chronology
continues back in time, though, penetrating the Pentateuch by way of
the years indicated for both the ante- and post-diluvian patriarchs. The
historiographical method does not change; this is a sign that there is a
single author.

Our author is, therefore, witness to a period of profound social evolution which most probably did not regard only the Jews. The myth was
no longer understood as such and required reading with different categories. During the same time the problem of the *archè* appeared in
Greece, which was explained through the idea that water lay at the
origin of all things. That is, they read the oriental texts that spoke of primordial chaos as being made of water as though they were what we
today would call scientific or philosophical documents. Was it any
more *logical* that water should lay at the origin of things and not air, or,
in an even a more abstract thought, the infinite (see the ἄπειρον of
Anaximander)?

In Jewish culture the fall of the myth produced historiography; myths
were read as the narration of events that had really taken place. All that
was left to be done was to find some indication or approximation, even
very rough, of the dates. Where the Greeks sought the logical scheme
of things, shifting attention and discourse from the myths' contents to
logic, the Jews sought to individuate the times of the mythical contents
and saw God's hand at work in time and space. Our author deduced the
facts, which make up the stuff of his history writing, from texts that
today we cannot identify, but that he surely had available to him in one
form or another, even oral. At any rate, the means of assimilation and
reception is of little importance to us and in most cases it is also difficult to distinguish what he received in one form and what in another,
what he received from the Jewish tradition and what from direct contact
with Babylonian culture.

The totality of the conceptual elaboration and the interpretation of the
data is all the work of our Jewish author though. It is possible that his
interpretation was already to be found in one of his sources, but it is
equally possible that it was not. At times it is quite easy to see his hand
transcribe and modify the original text, but in most cases it would be a

passages the story of the flood in the Hebrew text seems to be a translation of a
Babylonian text.

desperate undertaking to even attempt an analysis. The globality of his ideology, however, remains a given.

From a reconstruction of his work beginning with the books of Kings and of Samuel, commonly considered to be his work,[23] his historical method can be recuperated. The information regarding the most recent events recounted, Jehoiachin's imprisonment for example, may seem few in number, but they are exact. As we have seen in the previous chapter, in fact, traces of Jehoiachin's imprisonment can be found even in the documents of the Babylonian administration. He was always attributed the title of king and even had some ministers. Following this analysis of the fundamental events, we find that the information given by our author can be considered exact as far back as the destruction of Samaria. Going backward in time, between the destruction of Samaria and the foundation of the divided kingdom there is some imprecision. While we are unable to rectify his imprecision, it is there nonetheless; the dates, though, are not more than 20 years off.

The author's method is that of providing information concerning the kings of Judah and the kings of Israel in a parallel fashion. He must have come up against insurmountable problems, however, when he came to the last phase of the kingdom of Israel's history. The name of one sovereign appears doubled (Peqah and Peqahyah), while the name of another was unknown to the author even though his existence is certain, since he has left his name on a seal.[24] The author knew the date of Samaria's destruction with certainty, 721 BCE, and tried to fill the gaps in his information with conjectures.

If we should want to pass judgment on his work, we could say that he

23. Today there is a tendency to see the end of the Deuteronomist's work at 2 Kgs 23.23, though I feel that Noth's unitary thesis placing the Deuteronomist in the Babylon of the sixth century and not at the time of Josiah is to be upheld in that it still allows for a better explanation of the text. I have defended this position in *Henoch* 12 (1990), pp. 380-85 (a review article for the book by M.A. O'Brien, *The Deuteronomistic History Hypothesis: A Reassessment* (Freiburg/Göttingen: Vandenhoeck & Ruprecht, 1989).

24. See G. Garbini, 'I sigilli del regno di Israele', *OrAnt* 21 (1982), pp. 163-76 (173). Names of kings of Israel appear in three seals. One contains the name of Jeroboam who is present in the book of Kings. The other two seals contain the names of two different ministers of a king Uzziyaw (seals V 65 and V 67), who is not mentioned in the book of Kings. It is interesting to note that the book of Kings, in 15.13, 34 gives this name, in some manuscripts, to Azariah of Judah, as that king is commonly referred to in the Chronicles. See also Isa. 6.1.

made a very careful reconstruction of the dates, but it is a reconstruction. His calculations are always based on more and more subjective
rational elements the further he got from his own time. In other words,
the further back in time he went the more gaps there must have been in
the documents he had available.

His way of constructing the historical narrative changes abruptly, in
fact, with the passage moving back from the two kingdoms to the united monarchy. On the one hand there is much more information, and in
greater detail, regarding the kings of the united kingdom as opposed to
their successors. On the other hand it is clear that R1 no longer has
access to dated or datable documents. Both David and Solomon are
attributed forty-year reigns (1 Kgs 2.11 and 11.42). The manuscript
tradition has lost the information concerning the length of Saul's reign
(see 1 Sam. 13.1, the text is corrupt in the Hebrew and missing in most
of the Greek tradition), but around the beginning of the Christian era
word had it that Saul too had reigned 40 years (see Josephus, *Ant.* 6.378
and Acts 13.21). According to another passage of the *Antiquities*
(10.143) Saul only reigned for 20 years. It is clear, though, that we are
dealing with round figures based roughly on the length of a generation.
Our author knows that history is made with dates and, therefore, when
he does not have any available he makes conjectures following an
abstract criterion. There is a criterion though, based on the number 40.
He creates small periods of 40 years which are inserted into a scheme
of longer periods dominated by multiples of the number 40. Between
escape from Egypt and the construction of the temple 480 years go by
(1 Kgs 6.1) while the stay in Egypt lasted 400 years (Gen. 15.13).[25]

Working backward in time, it becomes more and more difficult to
understand the criteria adopted by R1 in creating a scheme in which to
insert the events recounted, but it must have been rooted in the idea that
the world had to have a certain duration. This is the only way to explain
why for the first five prediluvian patriarchs the LXX give figures greater
than those of the Hebrew text, but only regarding the digit representing
hundreds (which is increased by one), and not the tens or the ones. But
this was cosmic speculation.[26] They could seem to be merely symbolic

---

25. As for the 430 years attributed to the stay in Egypt in Exod. 12.40, it should
be noted that the tradition here is uncertain (see LXX and the Samaritan text).

26. See J. Hughes, *Secrets of the Times: Myth and History in Biblical Chronology* (Sheffield: Sheffield Academic Press, 1990), and D. Cerutti, 'Vecchi e nuovi
approcci per lo studio del rapporto tra Pentateuco e libri storici: Il contributo

numbers for the author, but this is not the case. He was convinced that he had found a method for reconstructing his people's history. Yefte's ambassadors tell the king of Moab that the Jews have been in that area for 300 years (Judg. 11.26). The figure is roughly correct, if we consider our author's chronology as real. And so on back to the world's creation.

The greatest problem for our historian was that of taking old accounts of the origins of his people that I do not know how he possessed, but he certainly did possess them, and placing them in time. He situated all of these episodes in an indeterminate time of nomadic and desert life. He had the value of these stories as providing a foundation; they were what today we would call 'sagas'. And since the saga is a myth of the foundation, its contents must be placed *before* the history reconstructed on the bases of dated texts.

In one case we are able to check up on his way of proceeding. Our author tells of an episode concerning Balaam bar Beor, an uncommon name. We now possess an inscription regarding this character which on the one hand confirms his existence, but on the other excludes the chronology built up by the author. Balaam lived around the middle of the eighth century BCE,[27] several centuries later than the date supposed by our author. The error is fairly easy to explain if we think of the logic

---

dell'analisi della cronologia' (unpublished dissertation: Turin, 1991).

27. This is the inscription of Deir 'Alla. It has been suggested that the date of the inscription is no more than a *terminus ante quem* for the text, and that, therefore, even though the Balaam inscription is from the eighth century BCE, it still does not tell us when this pagan prophet lived. While this suggestion is possible, chances are against it, because (a) the case of copied inscriptions is not as frequent as with literary texts and (b) the language of the text with the presence of Aramaisms cannot be back-dated much further than the century of the inscription.

On the Deir 'Alla inscription see J. Hoftijzer and B. van der Kooj, *Aramaic Texts from Deir Alla* (Leiden: E.J. Brill, 1976); J. Hoftijzer, 'The Prophet Balaam in a 6th Century Aramaic Inscription', *BA* 39 (1976), pp. 11-17; G. Garbini, 'L'iscrizione di Balaam Bar Beor', *Henoch* 1 (1979), pp. 166-88; J.A. Hackett, 'Some Observations on the Balaam Tradition at Deir 'Alla', *BA* 49 (1986), pp. 216-23; S.A. Kaufman, 'The Aramaic Texts from Deir 'Alla', *BASOR* 239 (1980), pp. 71-74; P.K. McCarter, 'The Balaam Texts from Deir 'Alla', *BASOR* 239 (1980), pp. 49-60; E. Puech, 'Le texte "ammonite" de Deir 'Alla: Les admonitions de Balaam (première partie)', in P. Grelot (ed.), *La vie de la Parole: De l'Ancien au Nouveau Testament* (Paris: Desclée de Brouwer, 1987), pp. 13-30; A. Zeron, 'Pseudophilonic Parallels to the Inscriptions of Deir 'Alla', *VT* 41 (1991), pp. 186-91.

behind our author's procedure; since he had found no link between the Balaam episode and the chronology of his annals, and since the character of this episode was that of a founding myth, one of those episodes that miraculously founded Israel, he therefore projected the episode to the ideal time of the origins, to the times of the desert.

This process makes sense and in all probability our author applied it systematically. The result is that the modern reader has the impression that in an early period Israel was nomadic, or semi-nomadic, and only with the passage of time did it become sedentary. It is more probable that the two phases, nomadic or semi-nomadic and sedentary, were contemporaneous. While it is true that a nomadic life lies as the background to the stories of Abraham, it is also true, according to our author, that he departed from *Ur Kasdim*, 'Ur of the Chaldeans'. The Chaldeans, though, did not arrive in Mesopotamia before the first millennium. While the name of Abraham could date from the second millennium, his bond with Mesopotamia must date from our author's day, when it became opportune to unite one's own origins with the land of the great Babylonian civilization.

One single element seems to link R1's thought to that of Ezekiel and his school: their common interest for Israel. If it was important for Ezekiel to trace out a history of the origins of Israel (ch. 20 and the narratives of the P source concerning the most ancient times of Israel), it was even more important for R1 to delineate all of history. The reality of Israel is never put in discussion by either one, and for both of them it is the very foundation for any and all hopes for the future. Only Israel's existence in history, and the presupposition of its continued future existence, could justify the claims made by the king, but also those made by the priesthood. But while Ezekiel is interested mostly in the stories of the desert, when the traditional figure of Moses handed down all the laws regulating the temple and the power of the priesthood, R1 was mostly interested in the history of Israel under the kings. For R1 the reign of David and his dynasty at least, if not all the kings, had been willed by God himself. David had been anointed king by the great Samuel, and another prophet, Nathan, had assured him, in God's name, an eternal reign. This story had its antecedents in the tradition of the patriarchs who had handed down the patrimony of Israel from father to son just as the kings and, just as in the case of the ruling house of the Davidic dynasty, not always to the eldest son. Israel's destiny lay under the same norms established by God at the time of its origins, which dated back to Abraham. Our author's evaluation of Moses is difficult to find in the work as it stands now, because the Moses that has come down to us is essentially the Moses of the priestly tradition.

R1's eye, however, did not look to Israel alone. He was interested in the history of all of humanity, at least in the period prior to the election of Abraham, because that election had taken place in the context of the broader history of humankind. It is possible that certain universalistic tones are fruit of later additions given the fact, mentioned above, that they are spread here and there throughout the work. At any rate they are additions made only shortly after the original version of the text. The general plan of the opus, though, which can only be the work of its author, was made by someone gazing through Israel at all of humanity. God made a covenant regarding all of humankind and Noah received commandments that were valid for all men (Gen. 9). Abraham was destined to be a benediction for all men (Gen. 12.3, probably by R2). The kings of Israel had, in the eyes of our author, an elevated role which was to be made even clearer by Deutero-Isaiah who would declare that the Servant of Yhwh, in other words the king, was a light for all the pagans (Isa. 42.6 and 49.6). This was a great hope and an incredible faith in a little people like Israel, it is, however, clearly documented in the texts.

7. *Deutero-Isaiah and the Highest Development of the Royal Ideology*

R1 had tried to bind the Davidic dynasty to its people through historical reflection. An anonymous prophet, one of Israel's greatest, Deutero-Isaiah, more commonly called Deutero-Isaiah, attempted a different approach. Deutero-Isaiah's method took the development of the thought of his day into account and tried to avoid certain pitfalls that seemed serious to him, that is the possibility that the conviction should take root that the essence of the Covenant binding Yhwh to his people was independent of the king.

Given the difficulty of dating many texts, we do not have a precise date for the first time this idea was put forth in Israel. We do know, however, that King Josiah had made a covenant with Yhwh based on the contents of a book called the 'Book of the Covenant'. This book certainly contained some laws (2 Kgs 23.3), because the king solemnly committed himself before the people 'to walk after Yhwh and to keep his commandments…with all his heart and all his soul, to perform the words of this covenant that were written in this book; and all the people joined in [this] covenant'.

Though, while it had been easy for the king to proclaim himself the protector of God's will and of his Law prior to the exile, during the exile the situation had changed. The priests had developed their reflection on the Law, considering it the only instrument of salvation for the whole people and for the individual.

Faced with this situation which completely sidestepped the king with regard to the problem of salvation, Deutero-Isaiah strongly asserts that the very essence of the Covenant was constituted by the king himself. Thus, the founding ideas of Israel were saved, but their contents were adapted to defending the interests of the monarchy. I interpret Isa. 42.6 in this way:

> I, Yhwh, have called you [sing.] *b*'ṣedeq [?]; I have taken you by the hand; I have made you Covenant of the people, a light to the Gentiles; to open the eyes that are blind, to bring out the prisoners from the prison, and from their place of confinement those who live in darkness.

Taken in its context, the passage reveals a decidedly universalistic attitude coupled with very convinced monotheistic formulations, in any case stronger than those of R1. He addresses himself to a person referred to as 'Servant of Yhwh' and the 'chosen of Yhwh', and that person can be no other than Zerubbabel, the king. He alone could be defined 'Covenant' between God and the people. He alone could have been seen as capable of taking Yahwism to other peoples in a peaceful form, given the historical situation of the moment that excluded the use of force. Universalistic ideas were circulating in the Persian empire and traces of a strong link between the Jewish king and the Persian court can be found in the episode of the 'Three Page-boys' narrated in 1 Esdras 3–4. As the backdrop for the passage mentioned above of Deutero-Isaiah, I see Zerubbabel's position as he and Joshua are about to take the exiles back to their homeland. He is the unifying element of a divided people, the tangible reality binding God to his people. All those who hope and who refuse the use of violence must look to him (42.2-3). He will bring social peace to Judah (42.3-4) and his doctrine, its practical application, will be such that even the Gentiles will appreciate it ('toward his doctrine [*tōrātô*] the islands shall look with hope').

These words of Deutero-Isaiah are directed to all the Jews, both the exiles and those who had remained. This was a project for general pacification based on a new law, a new social order which would have to take everyone into account, at least in its best intentions. In other words it was a compromise that should have saved the monarchy first of all, along with all of its privileges deriving from the promise of eternal reign, and secondly Judah itself, composed of the returnees and the remainees. The existence of a compromise regarding the exiles, those who had remained behind, and the monarchy itself, is comfirmed by the fact that Deutero-Isaiah accepted an idea dear to the exiles. The acceptance of this idea also demonstrates the force with which the exiles negotiated the agreement. That idea was that God had truly left Jerusalem and now he had to return. Deutero-Isaiah's expression nuances as much as possible the anthropomorphism underlying this idea, but he does not refuse it: 'A voice cries: "In the wilderness prepare the way of Yhwh, make straight in the desert a highway for our God... Behold the Lord Yhwh comes with might... His reward is with Him, and His recompense before Him" ' (Isa. 40.3, 10). The meaning of the passage is clear; the prophet invokes that there should be no obstacles to Yhwh's return because 'His reward is with Him'.

It would therefore seem very likely that one of the fruits of the negotiations between the ruling house and the priesthood in exile was that the ruling house accepted the priesthood's legislation, that is the fundamental parts of P, more or less P^G of our academic tradition.

As we have seen in the previous chapter, the prophet's hopes were dashed. There was a war and, after various episodes, the victory of the exiles over those who had remained, Jerusalem over Judah, the priesthood over the monarchy. If not an actor in the events, Deutero-Isaiah was at the least a sad spectator watching on as the safety of Israel and its tradition, in which the people's self-consciousness were rooted, were threatened. At any rate, Deutero-Isaiah knew how to save the situation: 'the privileges of David' remained valid as in the past, only now they were transmitted directly to the people as a whole (Isa. 5.3). This was a solution that both guaranteed and explained Israel's continuity, even with the fall of the 'eternal dynasty', and that probably had contingent political aspects as well. The new formulation, while everything leads us to believe that it was accepted by all concerned parties, denied the primacy that the priesthood aspired to. It confirmed that the instrument of salvation was not the Law, understood as the foundation and essence of the Covenant, but the divine Promise once made to David, and now extended (again by divine goodness) to the entire people—to the whole people, not to the temple. Behind certain statements, besides the genius of the thought there is always a political aspect. On this basis of reconciliation Israel began its new life.

8. *The Problems Left Open*

The Covenant

The concept of the Covenant had been extremely important for the monarchy. It had given the ruling house a unique position in the relationship between God and his people. Seen in this light, the Covenant was important for both the ruling house and for the people; the Covenant was a guarantee of the 'salvation' of both.

This theology of the Covenant had been carried to a radical extreme by Deutero-Isaiah when he declared that the king was the Covenant itself, using a formula which later lent itself to the interpretation that the Covenant was the people, identifying the Servant of Yhwh with the entire people. This 'democratic' element is quite visible in the final version of Deuteronomy, where it claims that the Covenant had not been made with the fathers, one by one as in the formulation dear to the monarchy, but with the entire people (5.3). In this way, the contrast between the monarchy and the priesthood after 515 BCE became a contrast between the people and the temple. Neither of the two solutions was entirely to the liking of the priesthood, which aspired to inheriting the privileges of David.

The priests must have tried to make themselves the direct heirs of the monarchy, but they did not succeed. Traces of this have been left in Mal. 2.8 where it speaks of priests who have broken 'the covenant of Levi'. There is no later mention of this covenant, which seems to represent only an abortive attempt to make Levi, as archetype and symbol of the priesthood, the denominator of the Covenant.

In the theology of Deuteronomy Covenant and Law seem to have become synonyms and, in fact, anyone reading the Bible today as it has been handed down to us has the impression that the whole of its discourse presupposes the coinciding of the Covenant of Sinai (or of Horeb) and the Law. We have already seen, though, that Ezekiel did not know of such an identification which apparently came about later.

I believe that the passage of Exod. 24.3-8 can be dated to the beginning of the republican period. It is clearly later than the 'Jahwist' (for me R1) passage that it has been inserted into, since it breaks it up

(Exod. 24.1-2, 9-11). The characteristic element of this Covenant with God is the absolute clarity with which it is identified with the Law, that only the priesthood had the right to interpret (see Hag. 2.10-13). With this formula the priesthood assumed, or tried to assume, the role of heir to the monarchy.

The passage narrates how Moses told the people all the things that he had heard from the voice of God and how he put them down in writing after the people had promised to observe Yhwh's commandments. Moses then had some oxen killed and he separated the blood into two basins. One was poured on the altar and the other was sprinkled on the people. The blood of the Covenant thus formed an indivisible bond between the two parties, God and the people, but the clauses which were to allow the continuance of the Covenant were represented by the legislation taken as a whole, which was in the hands of the priesthood. This can be deduced from Ezekiel, but also from the first legal problems arising in the homeland in 520 BCE (see passage of Haggai mentioned above). In this way the priesthood did not directly proclaim itself heir to the monarchy as the representatives of the Covenant in the same way that the monarchy had been before, but the priesthood did possess the instruments binding the people to God.

After 515 BCE the monarchical interpretation of the Covenant fell from the foreground, though it did in some way remain alive, having entered into Israel's tradition; it could be born again. But it did not follow that there was a new unified conception of the Covenant. On the one hand the Deuteronomic idea that the Covenant and the Law coincided seems to be confirmed, that is, that the Law was considered to be the sum of the clauses making up the Covenant. At the same time, on the other hand, the idea that the Law had its own value independent of the Covenant remained alive as well. In other words, in some circles the idea that the Law was the only instrument of salvation remained alive, while the concept of the Covenant seems to have been assimilated into that of election. The two concepts are not mutually exclusive, but the latter attributes an eternal value and sureness to the Covenant that the former could not.

Characteristic of this situation during the early years of the republic is the idea of the Covenant as presented in Genesis 17. Here too the Covenant is not attached to the monarchy, but rather it is a rite, that of circumcision, that binds the people to God. The imposition of circumcision as an obligation distinguishing the Jews only makes sense during the exile, in Babylon, where the Jews found themselves living among the uncircumcised people of Mesopotamia. In Palestine the practice was widespread and the commandment did not make sense; much less was it a sign of distinction and separation.[28]

The terminology of Genesis 17 follows the palace style more than the priestly style, but the meaning of the passage is clear; the Covenant was made with the entire people, but each Jew must demonstrate having accepted it. Circumcision is the first commandment that every Jew must observe, in order to demonstrate that he is a Jew, in order to be one.

> Behold, my Covenant is with you [Abraham], and you shall be the father of a multitude of nations [v. 4]... I will make you exceedingly fruitful...and kings shall come forth from you [v. 6]. And I will establish my Covenant between me and you and your descendants after you throughout their generations... [v. 7]. And I will give to you, and to your descendants after you, the land of your sojournings...for an everlasting possession...[v. 8]...you shall keep my Covenant, you and your descendants after you throughout their generations [v. 9]. This is my Covenant... Every male among you shall be circumcised... [v. 10]. Any uncircumcised male...shall be cut off from his people [v. 14].

Retribution

The problem of the relationship between human actions and recompense by the gods was very deeply felt in Middle Eastern thought, particularly that of Mesopotamia.

It is the problem of theodicy, the very human attempt on man's part to understand God, not in his essence, but as a subject acting among men and on men, at times in their favour and at times, at least in appearances, acting against them.[29] Let us refer to the following maxims taken from the book of Proverbs.

---

28. On circumcision in the Syro-Palestinian region see P. Arata Mantovani, 'Circoncisi e incirconcisi', *Henoch* 10 (1988), pp. 51-68.

29. A good presentation of these problems in the history of Egyptian and Mesopotamian thought can be found in O. Loretz, *Qohélet und der alte Orient* (Freiburg: Herder, 1964), and H.H. Schmid, *Wesen und Geschichte der Weisheit* (Berlin: Töpelmann, 1966). Jewish wisdom had also touched on the problem long before. See, for example, the passages taken from the oldest part of the book of Proverbs, from the pre-exile period, running from 10.1 to 22.16 (see J.A. Soggin, *Introduzione all'Antico Testamento* [Brescia: Paideia, 4th edn, 1987], p. 470) (ET: *Introduction to the Old Testament* [London: SCM Press, 1987]).

What the wicked dreads will come upon him,
but the desire of the righteous will be granted (Prov. 10.24).

The fear of Yhwh prolongs life,
but the years of the wicked will be short (Prov. 10.27).

The righteous will never be removed (Prov. 10.30).

And again:

The righteous is delivered from trouble,
and the wicked gets into it instead (Prov. 11.8).

He who is steadfast in righteousness will live,
but he who pursues evil will die (Prov. 11.19).

For as much as the wise men were more interested in the problems of the single individual rather than those of whole peoples, it seems clear that for them the law of retributory justice held true both for the individual and for entire peoples:

Righteousness exalts a people,
but sin is the poverty[30] of nations (Prov. 14.34).

The idea, then, of a divine Law by which the righteous and the wicked, individuals and peoples are given their recompense each according to his just deserts was well established in Israel. Before the exile this Law of retributory justice was inserted in a whole conception of history that allowed them to overcome, or to not even notice or consider certain contradictions as obvious. The conception of the history of Israel as dominated by Yhwh both in his wrath and his mercy is an ancient idea. In fact, while his wrath can reach as far as the fourth generation, his mercy can arrive as far as the thousandth.

The text of the Ten Commandments states this:

For I Yhwh, your God am a jealous God, visiting the iniquity of the fathers upon the children to the third and the fourth generation of those who hate me, but showing steadfast love to thousands of generations of those who love me and keep my commandments (Exod. 20.5-6; Deut. 5.9-10).

Divine retributory intervention is not tied to the righteous or the iniquitous person, but more flexibly to the family and the offspring of the righteous or the iniquitous person. Thus the single figure of the right-

---

30. 'Poverty' as in the LXX. The Hebrew text reads *ḥsd*, 'mercy', which does not make sense. The Greek translator correctly read *ḥsr*.

eous or the wicked person is dissolved, carrying with it the very elements making up the basis of the problem. This ancient vision of life was summed up in a popular saying that must have been repeated often in order to try to understand God's logic and to reconcile themselves with the unexplainable: 'The fathers have eaten sour grapes, and the children's teeth are set on edge' (Jer. 31.29; Ezek. 18.2).

In this sense Hebraism can be considered a closed system inasmuch as it is capable of providing an answer to humanity's most elementary and urgent problems; every event in life, good or bad, happened because it was right for it to happen. At the beginning of the Zadokite period, however, the injustice of this behaviour attributed to God began to be felt. The development of the Theology of the Covenant demanded that God's behaviour always be 'just', even when linked to his great mercy. In Deut. 7.9-11 it states that God maintains his Covenant and mercy for as many as one thousand generations with those who love him, but punishes immediately those who hate him, thus correcting the older text of the Ten Commandments. It seems that God extends his mercy infinitely and eternally over the descendance of those who love him, but that he immediately punishes those who hate him. In this case the sins of the fathers would no longer be punished on the sons, yet the relationship between God's lasting mercy and the statement that at any rate God's punishment of sins falls immediately on the guilty person remains to be clarified. Anyhow, this is an idea that was not fruitful in Israel, because the tendency was to be that of recognizing all retribution (remuneration and punishment) as being bound immediately to the individual.

Jeremiah (20.7-14) describes his own sufferings and lucidly feels that the question of his pains must be seen as such, and not as punishment. Pain is a new element coming into play in the mechanisms used to interpret history, it becomes an element of the value system. It is an absurd element, because it cannot be rationalized.

Logic would have it, it seemed, that pain was a consequence of guilt, but one text put forth the hypothesis that it could even fall upon a person other than the sinner, that there could be an expiating intermediary. Moses had interceded on behalf of the people's sin of idolatry (Exod. 32.11-14), but he too was subjected to divine punishment for a sin he had not committed.

Moses invokes Yhwh, that he should let him enter into the Promised land:

> Let me go over, I pray, and see the good land beyond the Jordan, that goodly hill country, and Lebanon'. But Yhwh was angry with me on your account, and did not hearken to me; and Yhwh said to me, 'Let it suffice you; speak no more to me of this matter' (Deut. 3.23-27).

Moses, according to the text, had only once and in the past drawn the wrath of God onto himself, turning it away from the people; he had suffered for the others. The possibility of attributing a value to suffering presented itself, but it was not taken up by Jewish thought, with the exception of Deutero-Isaiah. With Deutero-Isaiah the figure of the 'Servant of Yhwh', righteous and suffering outside of all retributory logic, opened up a new possibility for the Jewish religion, a possibility which was to remain fruitless for many centuries. The figure of the righteous man who suffered appeared to the prophet as a matter of fact that could even be compared to an analogous historical figure; Jerusalem had paid for its guilt twice (Isa. 40.2). This intuition opens the book of Deutero-Isaiah and constitutes the centre of his reflection: 'The ways of Yhwh are not your ways' (Isa. 55.8). This is an intuition which cannot be integrated into the Jewish ideological constellation. It remains an element of rupture and renewal for a time in which it could have been taken up as idea-matrix, the basis for new values.

In the last years of Hebraism a greater sensitivity for moral values tied to the individual can be noted. This leads to hope in a future world in which retribution regards the life of each individual and does not fall on later generations. Jeremiah speaks of the end of the great punishment (Jer. 31.25-28). God will abundantly provide for those who are weary with hunger and the land of Judah will be peopled with men and animals and in those blessed days no one will repeat the proverb 'The fathers have eaten sour grapes, and the children's teeth have been set on edge. But every one shall die for his own sin; each man who eats sour grapes, his teeth shall be set on edge' (Jer. 31.29-30).

The idea that pain is a sign of guilt, committed either by the one who suffers or by his parents was still alive in Palestine during Jesus' day; before the man who was blind from birth the desciples ask Jesus whether the man had sinned or his parents (Jn 9.2; see also Lk. 13.1-5).

In the world to come, in the world of the New Covenant, everyone will have to pay for his own sins. The prophet's absurd suffering will therefore vanish. To Jeremiah, the concept of 'suffering because of others' seems to be an imperfect element of the imperfect age in which he lives. The epoch of the First Covenant must be overcome by a new order of things. For Jeremiah, the new form of the retributory principle was destined to be realized only in the future, when God had established the new order, the wonderful and definitive order of the world to be called that of the 'eschaton' and, by the rabbis, '*ha'olam habbah*'.

At this point, the application of this principle was not even imaginable, and in fact it was not realized. When Jeremiah turns to God in prayer, he exclaims, 'You who show mercy to thousands of generations, and punish the wickedness of the fathers on the sons... You are great, incomprehensible in your plans' (Jer. 32.18). Jeremiah's solution appears to lie halfway between the Ten Commandments (God punishes the sins of the fathers on the sons up to the third or fourth generation) and the solution of Deut. 7.9-10 (God punishes only the sins of the guilty). How God brings about retributory justice, then, is a mystery, but in the epoch of the new order it will no longer be thus, because the former form was imperfect, if not unjust. It was understandable only in that the age of the First Covenant was an age of imperfection, as could easily be seen in common experience.

The great leap comes about with Ezekiel. God has already applied the new retributory principle, that of the new order.

> What do you mean by repeating this proverb... 'The fathers have eaten sour grapes, and the children's teeth are set on edge?' As I live, says Adonay Yhwh, this proverb shall no more be used by you in Israel. Behold, all souls are mine; the soul of the father as well as the soul of the son is mine: the soul that sins shall die (Ezek. 18.2-4).

The premature death that punishes sin will only strike the sinner, and not his descendants. And if someone sins, and then repents and goes back to doing what is right, then he too will be saved; 'for the righteousness he has done he shall live' (Ezek. 18.22). Therefore, righteousness, that is observance of the Law, saves and salvation is not far off. It does not regard future generations, but is nearby, placed just behind observance of the Law.

The ethical demands, which were already clear in Jeremiah, create a schematization of the ancient idea of retribution. The former conception left considerable room to God's initiative; sin was always to be punished, but not necessarily right away, and mercy was used even to the thousandth generation (Ezek. 34.16-17). The space left for God's initiative now becomes very narrow. More than ever before in Hebraism, suffering is understood only as punishment. This is the atmosphere that Job and his friends/enemies live in.

The idea of the divine retributory principle as sustained by Ezekiel inevitably leads to new problems. Whether God repaid individuals according to their actions was, for the pre-exile Jew, essentially a question of faith. There was no way of empirically verifying whether this principle was valid or not. For the postexilic Jew the situation was different. The space between action and retribution had become very narrow and humans therefore had the possibility of verifying the retributory principle. This principle, therefore, was no longer founded on faith, but on the series of events lived and witnessed by all. From this point on the validity of the system could be checked. If there is suffering, a sin must have been committed and, if there is happiness, there must be righteousness.

In order to better understand this new spirituality let us turn to Lamentations. God has caused the downfall of Jerusalem only because he is just: 'Yhwh is in the right, for I have rebelled against His word' (Lam. 1.8).

'Let us test and examine our ways, and return to Yhwh' (Lam. 3.40). But once Israel has expiated its sins, salvation will follow: 'The punishment of your iniquity, O daughter of Zion, is accomplished. He will keep you in exile no longer' (Lam. 4.22). The sole hope for Israel is righteousness, because God punishes sin immediately; only observance of the Law can allow life to continue.

The main problem of some books of later wisdom literature was that of understanding how to verify this principle. This led to the complete negation of the retributory principle, shifting the entire axis of Jewish thought toward new ideological equilibria.

This conception of the retributory principle necessarily sinks its roots in a complete sense of human freedom and its complete ability to choose between Good and Evil. Let us reread the words of Deuteronomy (30.15), 'I have set before you this day life and good, death and evil...', or the words of the book of Joshua (24.15), 'Choose this day whom you will serve...'

This does not mean that the problem of whether or not humans are free, and if so to what degree, had already been formulated or resolved. This only means that should the problem of human freedom be called into question, as it later was, then the basis of the retributory principle would necessarily be called into question as well.

It is clear that, following the Theology of the Covenant's line of thought, God's intervention to save humanity must be seen in a different light than when following the discourse of the Theology of the Promise. According to the former (Isa. 40.2) Jerusalem received double the punishment that was her due. In the end, then, Jerusalem's punishment lies outside a rigid idea of retribution and this in turn leads to a new conception of suffering which was eventually to blend with the messianic idea of the righteous sufferer (see the destiny of the Servant). There was a manifest contradiction in the order of things that would later be brought to light by Qohelet. Consciousness of this contradiction was to push Judaism toward new and different solutions in a search for that New Covenant that Jeremiah had talked about (Jer. 31.31) and that alone could bring an end to the intrinsic contradictions of the human condition.

Ezekiel's discourse is based on a rigid conception of the law of retribution (Ezek. 18) and thus renders the break between the old and the new a bit more blurred and a bit less dramatic. In the new and righteous order of things the retributory law that always lay at the basis of Israel's soul will be realized finally and completely. In this new order the Law must be realized by men who have been reborn after death through God's exceptional and saving intervention (Ezek. 37). It does not seem, however, that these men are destined to have any particular help in this undertaking, which is their only means of salvation. After the miraculous rebirth of Israel the Law will remain written in the book and it will be the Law of before and forever. Jeremiah had foreseen a new order based on a Law that was to be the same as always in its contents, but which was to be written in the individuals' hearts; a new humanity was to be reborn ontologically as well.

With the development of the Theology of the Covenant, the most characteristic elements of the Theology of the Promise were eventually forgotten or neglected. Let us reread, for example, Nehemiah's prayer beginning in Neh. 1.5. Upon hearing news of Jerusalem's tragic situation, Nehemiah saw this as the consequence of some new sin and therefore of the necessity to re-establish the Law, the sole means of salvation.

> Yhwh, God of heaven... Who keep the Covenant [an allusion to the Sinai covenant, not Jeremiah's new one] and mercy with those who love You and keep Your commandments [that is who observe the commandments inasmuch as they love You]... We have sinned against You... Remember the word which You commanded Your servant Moses, saying 'If you are unfaithful, I will scatter you among the peoples; but if you return to Me and keep My commandments and do them... I will gather them thence and bring them to the place which I have chosen' [This is

the conception of history typical of Deuteronomy, showing the influence
of that tradition on Nehemiah].[31]

Many years would have to go by before the idea was accepted that
misfortune did not depend directly on sin according to the retributory
principle, at least as it had been understood up to that point (Qohelet
and Ps. 44). And even more years would have to pass before all the
consequences were to be drawn and problems posed regarding the
value of the Law in relation to salvation. Either the value of the Law
had to change, or that of salvation, or even both terms together, including the middle term, judgment.

It goes without saying that when we speak of the Law for such an
ancient time, we are talking about a value rather than a series of contents. What those contents were is impossible to determine. It was
material in evolution and it is highly probable that different groups had
different laws. The Dead Sea Scrolls have left a trace of a discussion
concerning the norms which was destined never to come to a complete
close in rabbinical Judaism, nor in Christianity.[32]

I have emphasized these contrasting aspects of Hebrew theology of
the time of the exile to some extent to show their intimate and deep
contradictoriness: Theology of the Promise and Theology of the
Covenant.

In reality the two theologies are more two aspects of the same discourse on God rather than two contrasting theologies. The Promise is
essentially 'Promise of a Covenant, or of the Covenant' and the Covenant only makes sense in light of a promise guaranteeing in some way

31. See H. Cazelles, 'La mission d'Esdras', *VT* 4 (1954), pp. 113-40.

32. On the recently discovered Halakhic Letter, see the interesting presentations
of E. Qimron, and J. Strugnell, 'An Unpublished Halakhic Letter from Qumran', in
J. Amitai (ed.), *Biblical Archaeology Today: Proceedings of the International Congress on Biblical Archaeology, Jerusalem, April 1984* (Jerusalem: Israel Exploration Society, 1985), pp. 400-407; L.H. Schiffman, 'The New Halachic Letter
(4QMMT) and the Origins of the Dead Sea Sect', *The Qumran Chronicle* 1 (1990),
pp. 47-48, and *idem*, 'The New Halakhic Letter (4QMMT) and the Origins of the
Dead Sea Sect', *BA* 53 (1990), pp. 64-73. See also J.M. Baumgarten, 'Recent
Qumran Discoveries and Halakhah in the Hellenistic-Roman Period', in S. Talmon
(ed.), *Jewish Civilization in the Hellenistic-Roman Period* (Sheffield: Sheffield
Academic Press, 1991), pp. 147-58. The letter itself has been published recently by
E. Qimron and J. Strugnell, in consultation with Y. Sussman and with contributions
by Y. Sussman and A. Yardeni, *Qumran Cave 4. V. Miqṣat ma'aśe ha-torah* (DJD,
10; Oxford: Oxford University Press, 1994).

that if the clauses are respected the benefits foreseen will be realized.

That which our critical and modern spirit feels the need to put in order organically was described by the prophets, but not analysed. And just how difficult it is to organize these two aspects of theological discourse in an organic system is demonstrated by the history of speculation on God right up to our own times. Essenes and Pharisees, Pelagius and Luther represent the continued and troubled re-emergence in human consciousness through the centuries of a dilemma whose premisses are felt in the human being's very deepest roots.

Part II
THE ZADOKITE PERIOD

Chapter 3

EARLY ZADOKITISM (C. 520–400 BCE)

1. *The Beginnings*

The period running from the events that brought about the fall of the Davidic monarchy until the consolidation of Nehemiah's work is very poorly known.

We can, however, formulate some idea of what must have happened during this period by comparing the situation at the beginning of the period with the one at its end. For the intervening time essentially we have only the scarce information that can be drawn from the text of Malachi. The beginning point can be illustrated by the situation as it appears in the book of Deuteronomy, considered in its form as it has been handed down to us, which has been dated[1] to the end of the sixth century BCE, in other words just after the end of the monarchy.

The fundamental element for dating Deuteronomy to the years immediately after 515 BCE is the fact that it presupposes a situation in which the monarchy does not exist: it is a republican text. It is significant that the Covenant uniting God and the people is polemically considered as being made at Sinai (Horeb) between God and the entire people and not with one of the patriarchs (Deut. 5.3). Equally significant is the position assumed regarding the monarchy. The possibility of a monarchy is not excluded (in a certain sense Israel always remained a monarchy),[2] but

---

1. The late dating of Deuteronomy has been upheld by G. Hölscher, 'Komposition und Ursprung des Deuteronomiums', *ZAW* 40 (1922), pp. 161-225; T. Oestreicher, *Das Deuteronomische Grundgesetz* (Gütersloh: C. Bertelsmann, 1923); A.C. Welch, *The Code of Deuteronomy* (London: J. Clarke, 1924); *idem*, 'When Was the Worship of Israel Centralized in the Temple?', *ZAW* 43 (1925), pp. 250-55; *idem*, *Deuteronomy, the Framework to the Code* (London: Oxford University Press, H. Milford, 1932).

2. See A. Tosato, 'Israele nell'ideologia politica del Cronista', *RSB* 1 (1989), pp. 257-68.

the declaration that there *may* be a king and that the only limitation is that he be a Jew (Deut. 17.15) would be unimaginable in the historical context of the Davidic dynasty, and merely betrays the fear that foreigners could gain power in Judah. And the shadow of Persia fully justifies that fear.

But, while the republican topic aids in dating the text, a reading of the text as composed in this period sheds some light on the situation created in Judaea after the end of the monarchy. In Deuteronomy we can discern a society desirous of subjecting itself to the written law, understood roughly as a constitution. The judge still seems to judge by justice and therefore without a written law.

The atmosphere of compromise as the basis for pacification is expressed in Deuteronomy with two measures which appear to counterbalance one another; on the one hand we have the disappearance of the monarchy, which must have defended the interests of those who had remained in the homeland, and on the other hand the priests are forbidden from owning property in Judaea (Deut. 18.1). Thus the priests returning from exile cannot repossess the lands which had belonged to their fathers. No mention is made of laymen, but they must have been able to settle in their home villages[3] and hold property. Even regarding the authority to pass judgment, we see in Deut. 16.18 that it is clearly delegated to local judges who will pass judgment according to justice, that is without written law, and that they will be laymen, as is made clear from the compromise solution. In case of difficulty, appeal could be made to the temple where alongside an unidentified judge sat Levite judges as well (Deut. 17.8-9). Furthermore, no mention is made of worship as being centralized in Jerusalem. The principle of unified worship is accepted, at least in theory, but it is not established just exactly where it should take place. The priesthood did have an arm for defending its prerogatives, though, because the principle of unified worship was accepted by all, even by those who had remained during the exile, since it had been desired by Josiah. Jerusalem was refused, though, as the site and the question was left for divine judgment, which would come about when God so desired. In fact, though, the temple remained in Jerusalem.

For reasons of stability of the state, an effort was also made to limit prophetic activity. Each generation would have one prophet with the same authority as that of Moses (Deuteronomy's author gives a guaran-

---

3. For the settlements of returned exiles in Judaean villages see Ezra 2.70, Neh. 7.72; 1 Esdras 9.37.

tee for himself). Obedience should be given to that prophet, but if anyone should speak in God's name, his words should be verified, and he
can do so only at great risk (Deut. 18.20-22). Deutero-Zechariah[4] is
even more explicit:

> On that day... I will remove from the land the prophets and the spirit of
> impurity. And if anyone again appears as a prophet, his father and
> mother who bore him will say to him, 'You shall not live, for you speak
> lies in the name of Yhwh' (Zech. 13.1-6).

Even though the text seems to refer to eschatological time ('On that
day'), the context demonstrates that it is rooted in the situation of the
author's day.

Of course, prophetism was too deeply rooted an institution in Israel
to disappear, as would have been convenient for some, and in fact it did
not go away. Even Nehemiah found himself hindered in his work by a
number of prophets (Neh. 6.14).

It is not clear what the high priest's authority originally was. The
question of the relationship of authority between the priesthood and the
governor, which in certain periods certainly did exist, remains an open
question, and one which is currently unresolvable. While until recently
it could be sustained that all exercisable authority in a province of the
Persian empire, Judaea, was held by the priesthood, following Josephus's classic interpretation, today, after the publication of Avigad's
bullae[5] it is possible to believe that alongside the high priest there also
stood a governor nominated by Persia, as confirmed by a passage of
Malachi (1.8) and one of Nehemiah (Neh. 5.15; see also Pap. Cowley
no. 30 and *Ant.* 11.297-301).

Apart from the problem of the authenticity of the *bullae*, the question
of the Persian governor's duties remains to be clarified. From the *bullae*
he appears normally to have been a Jew. Was his role limited to that of
representing Persian interests, primarily through surveillance and
through coordinating ties between Jerusalem and the centre and

4.   On the early dating of Deutero-Zechariah, see p. 65 n. 16.
5.   See N. Avigad, *Bullae and Seals from a Post-exilic Judean Archive* (Jerusalem: Institute of Archaeology—The Hebrew University of Jerusalem, 1976). See
also F. Bianchi, 'Monete giudaiche di età ellenistica', *RSO* 63 (1989), pp. 213-29.
Bianchi considers the *bullae* to be later. At any rate, mention made by Nehemiah of
previous governors, the name of a governor drawn from the letters of Elephantine
and the history of successive periods all favour the hypothesis of the existence of a
governor alongside the high priest.

between Jerusalem and the other provinces of the empire, or did he also represent particular interests within Jewish society? And again, what was the ratio of power between the high priest and the governor?

It would seem that the diarchy installed in 521 BCE following the plans made by Ezekiel and certainly with Persian approval during the initial phase did not disappear with the Davidic dynasty. It is probable that the king's duties passed to the governor. At any rate, in respect to the empire, first the Babylonian one and then the Persian one, even the kings held the title of governor. The diarchy, however, certainly hides a degree of conflict which cannot be seen in terms of an opposition, though. That being the case, the priesthood still must have aimed at domination from the very beginning of the period, a tendency which was accentuated toward the end of the fourth century BCE when the high priest assumed the office of governor, at least according to coins bearing the inscription 'Yehezqiyah the governor'. Yehezqiyah is the name of a high priest.[6]

The first phase, which can be called that of Early Zadokitism, draws to a close around 400 BCE, when the work of Nehemiah must have been finished. The second Zadokite phase was to last to the end of the Zadokite high priesthood, that is until the deposition of Onias III, which took place around 175 BCE. The difference between the two phases consists in the fact that during the first phase the problems of Jerusalem and Judaea were internal problems within Judaean society, while during the second phase the problems were general to all of Judaism. In other words, the Jews of the Diaspora made their voice heard in Jerusalem in such a way that from being the capital of the inhabitants of Judaea the city became the capital of the Jews throughout the world.

2. The Environment and Movements of the Early Zadokite Period

The situation of the priesthood in Jerusalem was unique. The desire for power clashed with two aspects of reality: the fact that Judaea, as a dependent province of the Persian empire, was disarmed and, at least in theory and initially in practice, the priests could not own property, at least not landed property. The only instrument of power that they possessed was the temple and interpretation of the Law, an authority recognized them at least in part in Deuteronomy (17.9). The fact that they

---

6. See A. Kindler, 'Silver Coins Bearing the Name of Judea from the Early Hellenistic Period', *IEJ* 24 (1974), pp. 73-76.

were unable to control the wealth of the land and the lack of armed forces necessarily led them to seek contact and ties with the neighbouring peoples, because without money and military might it is impossible to seize or to exercise power. A trace of the poverty of the priesthood can be found in Malachi's complaint to the priests that in sacrifice to God they offered lame or sick animals that the governor would refuse (1.8). This situation led to the practice of mixed marriages, that is to political and economic alliances binding the priesthood of Jerusalem to the powerful families of Samaria and Ammon. This was a financial activity that control of the temple permitted, since in antiquity the temples also functioned as banks.

The archaeology of Palestine for this period confirms this general situation. On the one hand there was consistent building activity, while on the other new fortifications were rare. The Palestinian region was kept in peace by the Persian empire in an economic situation which at least at first must have been rather precarious.

A reading of Malachi provides a fairly clear picture of the situation in Jerusalem during the first half of the fifth century BCE. Malachi recognizes the leading role of the priesthood and their monopoly on interpretation of the Law. 'For the lips of a priest should guard knowledge [that is the Law, and its interpretation]' (Mal. 2.7); the people must turn to the priest for instruction, since the priest 'is the messenger of Yhwh Sabaoth [therefore his direct voice] on earth'. Even the title given to the covenant has changed; it has become the 'Covenant of Levi' (Mal. 2.4), in the sense that it had been given through Moses as a Levite and because he was a Levite, in other words a priest.

Behind this new formulation of the Covenant it is easy to make out the priesthood's attempt to entirely substitute the Davidic dynasty. As long as there had been a king the Covenant had always been a sign of the bond between the ruling family and God. Turned upside down, the Covenant was a sign of legitimation of power.

As time went by the class of the priesthood gained more and more power in Jerusalem and in Judaea. As long as there had been a king, he had also held authority over the temple, but now the temple became more and more the one chosen by God, and his priesthood interpreted his will on earth. Yhwh, then, from God of the Jews became more and more god of the region. Malachi writes that the name of Yhwh is great in the entire region and that everyone, from all peoples, make 'pure', that is legitimate, offerings to the divinity (1.11).

In the area around Jerusalem the practice of offering incense to Yhwh, the God of Jerusalem, must have been spreading even among people who were not Jews. This was not only allowed, but perhaps even favoured by the Zadokites, who aimed at extending their authority more over the territory than over the Jews. This was in conformity with a new conception of state that was then in formation in Greece as well (the constitution of Clistenes was based on territory and not on blood relations; the passage was made from the *phratria* to the *demos* without abolishing the former). Malachi is neither scandalized by these sacrifices nor does he hold anything against the priests' authority, since by this time a sort of universalism must have entered the theology of the Jerusalem priesthood, excluding the impurity of the Gentile. In the recent past, however, to varying degrees such an impurity was recognized by the Law, especially in the Deuteronomic tradition (for the example of an extreme case, see Deut. 23.4).

Those governing Jerusalem could not content themselves with governing only a part of the inhabitants in their territory. It was inevitable that they seek to extend their authority to all peoples, but this presupposed the creation of a certain communion with the alien peoples.

Ezekiel, who had foreseen and encouraged the return from exile, and had seen it in an aura of triumph, was also worried about the settlement of aliens in the middle of Israel (47.22). Had the Jews returning from exile had effective control over the land they lived on, then the solution proposed by Ezekiel would have been possible. The foreigners who owned possessions in the territory of Jerusalem had to be made in all ways equivalent to the Jews. This probably would have meant a forced conversion to Judaism, but they would have been made equivalent. Anyhow, in order to realize this policy, power had to lie entirely in Jewish hands. If that were not the case, then any solution would have always held the taste of synchretism.

Given the impossibility of carrying out Ezekiel's plan, the teachings of Trito-Isaiah become clear. I believe that Trito-Isaiah lived at the end of the sixth century BCE, after Haggai and Zechariah, when the problems of rebuilding Jerusalem as an administrative unit, and not only as a religious unit, became more and more pressing. Trito-Isaiah (Isa. 56.1-8) claims that all people can follow Yhwh. It is interesting that this passage, unlike the essentially eschatalogical ones that speak of a final reunion of all peoples under Yhwh, approaches the problem as belonging to the present, and therefore as a question of purity. Even the impure man, such as the eunuch, can become pure by will of God. From a contingent fact an innovative principle with vast possible repercussions has been born. The essence of the Hebrew doctrine of purity as being indispensable for encounter with Yhwh is thus threatened at its very base. Equality between Jews and non-Jews must be absolute; it was even held that in the future the priesthood would be open to these foreigners (Isa. 66.20-21). It is clear that the priesthood that Trito-Isaiah has in mind has a different ontology than the traditional one requiring descendance from Aaron through the Zadokite line. Trito-Isaiah's idea represents a bold and radical development of a similar idea in First Isaiah, who had said that all peoples would have come to the temple of the God of Jacob (Isa. 2.3), but in Trito-Isaiah's thought the new universal reality even involved the priesthood.

Zechariah invites all the Jews to be faithful to God in order to avoid his wrath in the future, and gives brief advice insisting on mutual goodwill among the Jews:

> These are the things that you shall do:
> Speak the truth to one another,
> render in your gates [of the city, where there was sufficient space for hold-
> ing assemblies] judgments that are true and make for peace,
> do not devise evil in your hearts against one another,
> and love no false oath,
> for all these things I hate (Zech. 8.16-17).

No mention is made of the norms of purity, but on the contrary there is a manifest opening to all peoples, who can enter into the temple:

> Peoples shall yet come,
> even the inhabitants of many cities;
> the inhabitants of one city shall go
> to another saying,
> 'Let us go at once
> to entreat the favour of Yhwh,
> and to seek Yhwh Sabaoth;
> I am going too'...
> In those days ten men from the nations of every tongue shall take hold of
> the robe of a Jew, saying, 'Let us go with you, for we have heard that God
> is with you' (Zech. 8.20-23).

In the portrayal Malachi makes of Zadokite Jerusalem, the prophet never speaks of infringement of the sabbath, observation of which had been of extreme importance for Trito-Isaiah (Isa. 56.2, 4, 6) and was to be fundamental for Nehemiah (Neh. 13.15 and following). Was an effort being made to make some concessions to the aliens?

Thus a union of all the peoples living in the territory of Jerusalem was formed around the city. This too was seen as a sign of new times, the realization of past aspirations (Gen. 12.1-3) and ancient prophecies (Isa. 2.2). The union that was emerging was a new community where the Jewish element was only one of many elements. This was a position of openness and, from a certain point of view, in effect it presented some risks.

Mixed marriages were favoured, especially in the ruling class, that is among the Zadokites. On the other hand, such marriages, which must have been frequent during the fifth century BCE (see Neh. 13.23 and Mal. 2.11-12), were certainly not made in order to carry out the teachings of Trito-Isaiah who had touched upon this specific topic. It was the weight of the situation that brought the leading class to bind itself to the most powerful families of the area, from Ammon to Samaria. They were political marriages that helped the priests to maintain their power in the middle of an extremely fluid situation (see Neh. 6.17-19).

It is likely that a counterposition was being created for economic reasons which saw the priests of Jerusalem pitted against the *horim*, landowners. The latter group saw their only opportunity to defend their privileges in the exclusion of the aliens from what we would call their civil rights. Appeal was made to a rigid interpretation of the law of Deuteronomy that imposed, or could be interpreted to impose, a strict separation between Jews and aliens.[7] The internal politics of Judea unfold around this problem and the two opposing parties can be defined 'segregationists' and 'anti-segregationists' or 'universalists'.

The two books of Ruth and Jonah are to be placed in this atmosphere of Early Zadokitism. I am not sure, though, whether they are to be placed in the initial phase of the period or during its decline. The former in particular seems to place in evidence a debate against those contrary to mixed marriages and against the segregationists in general. In this sense it could be placed near the end of Early Zadokitism, when the work of Nehemiah was being more and more broadly accepted (the end of the fifth century BCE).

7. See, for example, Deut. 7. Moses imposes the destruction of all the peoples living in Palestine. In the final version, the blessing reserved for those who observe the Law is promised on the condition that the aliens be destroyed. See the link between vv. 15 and 16.

The book of Ruth narrates that Boaz married a Moabite woman. Not only was she foreign, but she belonged to one of the peoples that Deuteronomy had excluded forever from any possible communion with Israel (Deut. 23.3-4). And still, David was one of her descendants. Was the greatest figure of all of Israel perhaps a Moabite? What, then, was an alien?

The debate presented by the book of Jonah is more broad. The author touches upon a theme approached by Malachi as well, that by which Gentiles can please God just as the Jews. Here though the theme is treated with a certain sense of humour that does not, however, conceal the debate which is developed differently by Malachi, who appeals to the same principle, but for a different reason: the moral decadence of the priesthood. Jonah wants to flee God in order to avoid following his will, which seems absurd, if not immoral. His sadness, then, before the effects of Nineveh's conversion is the sadness of a Jew who does not accept the political and spiritual openness of Jerusalem, presented as a consequence of Yhwh's care for all men equally.

Anyhow, in the reality of daily life, the nobles of Samaria and the sheiks of the steppe had to be dealt with. Wanting to govern and being disarmed was the great tragedy of the early Zadokites. The only alternatives available were agreement and compromise; the teachings of Trito-Isaiah and the faith of Zechariah (Zech. 4.6), and perhaps the books of Ruth and Jonah, if they had already been written, constituted the acceptance of this doctrine which was universalistic only within the limits of Jerusalem's boundaries. The first person to protest against mixed marriages, if not against this policy in general was Malachi (Mal. 2.11).[8] Such marriages went against established and perhaps ancient tradition, at any rate a tradition that had been consolidated during the exile. But mixed marriages were, or seemed to be (which from a political viewpoint is the same thing) a necessity for founding a social group which is more than merely a mixture of isolated members condemned to losing their power. This was the case among the upper classes; in the lower ones it was merely a consequence of the fact that they lived on the same land.

It should be noted that with the exception of Deut. 7.3-4, which I think is the product of a current of thought of this very period, there are

---

8.   This passage is considered to be a later interpolation (see *BHS* at this verse), but it could well represent a moment of debate within the Judaism of the fifth century BCE.

no explicit injunctions against marrying foreign women in the Torah. In fact, in the case of women taken prisoner during wars marriages were governed by ancient rules, recorded even in Deuteronomy (21.10-14), which guaranteed respect of the woman's grief. At any rate, marriage with a foreign woman had been presented with some scorn even in passages clearly antedating the exile. Marrying a foreigner must have been considered something like contaminating oneself with idols. In order to condemn mixed marriages, Malachi (2.11)[9] uses the expression, 'Judah has profaned the sanctuary loved by Yhwh, and has married the daughter of a foreign god'.

The same type of observation can be seen in Judg. 3.4-6:

> These peoples were for the testing of Israel, to know whether Israel would obey the commandments of Yhwh, which He commanded their fathers by Moses. So the people of Israel dwelt among the Canaanites, the Hittites, the Amorites... and they took their daughters to themselves for wives, and their own daughters they gave to their sons; and they served their gods.

It is the mentality of the historian of the exile that gives importance to the continuation of the group and that has lifted up the breaking of God's commandments as the cause of Israel's misadventures. The situation of monolatry combined with worship of other gods and idolatrous practices is interpreted by R1 as the fruit of a synchretism to be blamed on the kings and the people, rather than as an earlier, more ancient phase of the religious history of Israel.

Serving foreign gods and marrying foreign women were felt as being closely related and it seems that tradition would attribute this prohibition to Moses himself. This in spite of the fact that the book of Numbers tells us that Moses married a Cushite woman and that God himself defended Moses against those who condemned that union (Num. 12.1, 6-8).

The prohibition against marrying alien women was not so much an explicit commandment as it was a direct consequence of Israel's sacrality before its God on a theological level, and a consequence of the particular situation that Israel lived in on a practical level.

From the historical outline drawn up in this way, we get the impression that in Zadokite Jerusalem the legal norms that we are used to considering as characteristic of Hebraism from its very beginnings had

9.　See the preceding note.

not yet been codified. The very fact that the Torah was later to be formed by the first four books of R1's history with the addition of Deuteronomy demonstrates that there was no real legal code. The Pentateuch contains many laws, but they often contradict one another. It was a historical collection of traditions, but not a law code. Even Deuteronomy itself, which must have been held as a sort of constitutional law at the time it was promulgated later became *one* law code among others. The teaching and interpretation of the Law, however, had been handed back over entirely to the priests after only a brief period (Mal. 2.7). A certain degree of tension can be seen between a Deuteronomic current and a priestly current within Israel, but this is a situation that should not be overly schematized since, as we shall see shortly, there were also other ideas in Israel that cannot be reduced to the common denominator of 'priestly' or 'lay-Deuteronomic'.

3. *The Economic and Social Situation*

For as much as there is a lack of precise data concerning the economic situation of Jerusalem during the Early Zadokite period, it was certainly not good. A number of indicators point this out: the slowness with which the exiles moved back from Babylon, the neglect of worship which, besides depending on ethical factors, certainly depended on the lack of earnings for the priests in their functions. In his reform, Nehemiah considered on the one hand binding the priests to the temple, and on the other guaranteeing them the regular income from taxation (Neh. 10.39). The lack of an army worsened the situation of disorder. Being disarmed, which had seemed a manifest sign of God's protection to Zechariah (Zech. 4.6), must have worried the Zadokite priesthood who attempted to remedy the situation by trying to restore the walls around the city.

Josephus places the attempt to reconstruct the walls during the time of Cambyses (*Ant.* 11.26-31). The chronology presented by 1 Esdras (2.23-26) and by Ezra (4.8-23) is much more likely. According to this source the attempt is to be situated during the reign of Artaxerxes I, and therefore during the early years of his reign. This hypothesis is favoured by the fact that during Zechariah's day, and therefore after Cambyses, the walls did not yet exist, and by the fact that Nehemiah must have found himself before a work of restoration and not of reconstruction proper. Nehemiah arrived in Jerusalem during the twentieth year of Artaxerxes' reign, and therefore the reconstruction of the walls must have already taken place.

This situation forced the Zadokite priesthood to insist more and more in their good-neighbour policy toward a fusion of the area's various peoples, the only guarantee for their domination over the district of Jerusalem. But this policy, which the landowners did not like, was disliked by the Jews of the Diaspora as well; this latter group sought to maintain as much as possible a separate society in Jerusalem. This is the message drawn from Neh. 10.28, that defines the only real citizens of Judah with this expression: 'All who have separated themselves from the peoples of the lands to the Law of God'. The Law of God and ethnic fusion are two irreconcilable terms for the Jews of the Diaspora, because Jerusalem can be their spiritual and economic point of reference only inasmuch as it remains a fully Jewish city. In reality, as we shall see, the returned exiles ended up coming more and more into conflict with those who had remained, to the point of excluding the latter from the community and considering them foreigners.

4. *New Ideas: The 'In-between World'*

After having come into contact with the Persian world, and especially after the reign of Darius I, Jewish thought became more complex. This enrichment of Jewish thought was not only influenced by Iranian ideas which perhaps arrived by way of Deutero-Isaiah, but also by more ancient ideas such as those of Ezekiel. These ideas now took on a new dimension since they were reconsidered and remeditated in a new atmosphere. The new ideas fermented in the reflective thought of the day and led to the formation of different currents within Judaism.

The problem of the influence of Babylonian and Persian thought on Jewish thought is a difficult one to resolve in its details due to the difficulty in dating the Iranian works. This difficulty even leaves some doubt as to the very direction of influence.[10]

The following are some of the elements that later Judaism held in

10. See R.N. Frye, 'Iran und Israel', in *Festschrift für Wilhelm Eilers: Ein Dokument der internationalen Forschung zum 27. September 1966* (Wiesbaden: Harrassowitz, 1967), pp. 74-84. See also M.V. Cerutti, 'Tematiche encratite nello zoroastrismo pahlavico', in U. Bianchi (ed.), *La tradizione dell'enkrateia: Motivazioni ontologiche e protologiche: Atti del colloquio internazionale: Milano, 20–23 aprile 1982* (Rome: Edizioni dell'Ateneo, 1985), pp. 637-70.

some way in common with the Persian religion and which it could have borrowed from the Persians: 1) the tendency toward dualism; 2) the tendency to complicate angelology and demonology, giving them theological importance; 3) the idea that there is a divine or at least, in Jewish thought, a superhuman mediator between God and humanity; 4) the idea of the resurrection of the body, or at least that human life does not end with its corporal death. These elements, if they are of Persian origin, were absorbed very slowly by Judaism, because they became clear only during the Hellenistic period, that is after the disappearance of Persian domination. On the other hand, the subject of history (and the object of the historian's studies) is humanity, as it presents itself concretely in time and space. In order to understand Judaism in all its peculiarity, it is not as important to know the origin of every single theme, every single idea, as it is to grasp the way in which the single ideas were structured into forming the Judaic ideology. The value of every idea changes according to the system that it is inserted in. Not only that, but that value depends in turn on the particular position that the idea assumes within the system, becoming a measure for other ideas. These are the ideas that I call 'mother ideas', and that other scholars call by other names. Depending on whether the Promise or the Covenant is taken as 'mother idea', Judaic ideas can be structured differently, while at the same time individual ideas remain substantially the same. To take a classic example, let us think of the problem of the 'Plautinisches in Plautus' and the enormous originality of the Roman author, even though he was clearly influenced by Greek models. The historical value of an idea does not depend on the idea itself, but on the ideological constellation that it is a part of and of which it is a function.

In the atmosphere characterizing the first years after the return from exile, the divinity was felt to be particularly near to human events, an ancient motif in Israel, but one that was now filtered and considered in the light of two new facts. The first of these was the civil war, and the other was the intuition that God lived in a sky further away than the clouds where he once flew, riding on his cherubim (1 Sam. 4.4; 2 Kgs 19.15; Isa. 37.15; Ps. 18.11; etc.). The images seen by Ezekiel in his visions were from beyond the roof of the heavens (Ezek. 1.1). The sense of the greatness and transcendance of God grew and this brought about deep reflections concerning his interventions on earth.

God dominated history in a way that had been well known to the ancient prophets (Amos 5.8-9), but in this period alongside the growing dimensions of God, the idea that he was beyond human comprehension began to be emphasized as well (Isa. 55.8-11). In the past, God's action in history seemed to be by way of direct intervention, determined by his will at the moment in question. God could change his mind; there was a dialogue between God and humans. More than once the prophets had told the Jews to return to God if they wanted to avoid being punished. Nothing was preordained; divine foresight did not cause problems. Now, though, the idea of the existence of a divine plan going beyond the single event began to take root, and such a plan was clearly beyond humanity's grasp.

We have seen that during the exile history of the past had been placed in a particular relationship with the future, called a relationship between type and antitype. But, in order for this relationship to be truly valid, divine will must be placed between the type and the antitype guaranteeing the latter by way of the former. Historical events become symbols of a higher will which, in the end, is the only true reality. In the process of emptying this world's reality in favour of another reality to be placed beyond this world a step forward is made with Zechariah. At times, future events are not preannounced through a type or through the formula, 'God has said', but are seen as already having taken place in an order of things superior to terrestial reality. This order is not in God, nor is it in our world, therefore we shall call it 'the in-between world'. The fact that they have already taken place is the best guarantee that they will come about on the earth as well, since on earth they are clearly only repetitions of the reality of the in-between world. Let us read Zechariah's own words:

> Then the angel who talked with me came forward and said to me, 'Lift your eyes, and see what this is that goes forth'. And I said, 'What is it?' He said, 'This is the ephah that goes forth'. And he said, 'This is their iniquity[11] in all the land'. And behold, the leaden cover was lifted, and there was a woman sitting in the ephah! And he said, 'This is Wickedness'. And he thrust her back into the ephah, and thrust down the leaden weight upon its mouth. Then I lifted my eyes and saw, and behold, two women coming forward! The wind was in their wings; they had wings like the wings of a stork, and they lifted up the ephah between earth and heaven. Then I said to the angel who talked with me, 'Where are they taking the ephah?' He said to me, 'To the land of Shinar, to build a house for it...' (Zech. 5.5-11).

11. *iniquity*: *'wn*, according to part of the Greek and Syriac tradition. The Masoretic Text reads *'yn*: 'eye'.

Wickedness, then, will leave Israel, or rather, it has already left. In this vision, the event as seen in the in-between world is still somewhat veiled, somewhere between reality and symbol, but in another vision we find the same characters who act in our world speaking with angels and with God. In Zech. 3.1-8 we read:

> Then (the angel who talked with me) showed me Joshua the high priest standing before the angel of Yhwh, and Satan standing at his right hand to accuse him. [The angel of] Yhwh said to Satan, 'Yhwh rebuke you, O Satan!... Is Joshua not a brand plucked from the fire?'

The trial, therefore, is about to begin and Joshua would be in for trouble if Satan were to be allowed to carry out the prosecution. Joshua's salvation consists in the fact that God does not judge him, he does not even listen to the accusation, thanks to the intercession of the defending angels.

> Joshua was standing before the angel [of Yhwh], clothed in filthy garments. And the angel said to those who were standing before him, 'Remove the filthy garments from him and clothe him[12] with rich apparel. Put a clean turban on his head'. So they put a clean turban on his head and clothed him with candid garments...and the angel of Yhwh said to him, 'Behold, I have taken your iniquity away from you...behold, I will bring my servant the Branch'.

The underlying events are not what interests us here, but rather the new cognitive process. In this passage the step from the in-between world to our world is made with extreme ease. The certainty that by now the time of divine wrath against Joshua has come to an end is contained in the scene which unfolds in the in-between world. Joshua is recognized as being righteous and is confirmed in his role as high priest. Here on the earth that which has already begun can only continue. Historical events can be interpreted as projections of another reality and as manifestations of divine will.

Later, apocalyptic literature places itself along this same line of thought, carrying its premises to their extreme consequences; understanding history means understanding God's plan concerning humans.

---

12. *clothe him*: as in the Greek text. The Masoretic text reads as follows: 'I will clothe you'. In this scene there are two angelic figures as well as Satan. The two angels are referred to as 'the angel who talked with me' (Zech. 1.9), and the other as 'the angel of Yhwh'. The translation attempts to clarify the account based on this observation. The order of the verses differs too from the Masoretic text.

It is also interesting that Joshua is recognized as worthy of the position of high priest through a divine judgment that has all the trappings of a human trial. Satan carries out a role similar to that of a public prosecutor and, inasmuch as he participates in Joshua's trial, must be considered a member in full of the celestial court. In short, he occupies the same position before God as he will have later in the book of Job. He has not yet become Satan, the Devil.

5. *The End of Early Zadokitism*

While the policy of the Zadokites was disliked by Malachi for essentially moral reasons and by the landowners for practical interests, the Jews of the Diaspora disliked it because they wanted Jerusalem to remain their spiritual centre, and therefore entirely Jewish. Their opposition, however, could not be felt until a greater failure in Jerusalem than previous ones, and a particularly favourable situation for a Jew at the emperor Artaxerxes' court allowed the Jews of the Diaspora to intervene in the internal affairs of Jerusalem. That Jew was Nehemiah.

Nehemiah himself narrates the story of the failure that led him to action in the first chapter of the book that bears his name. It is impossible to establish precisely what happened, but it is clear that the gates of Jerusalem, which had in some way been put to use again, had been burned. The walls were dilapidated even after the attempt to rebuild them, which apparently was never finished. During the rule of the Zadokites who governed without force, some sheik, on the pretext of some offence, must have committed some abuse against the defenceless lands of Jerusalem. The damage was probably none too great, at least not on this single occasion, since Nehemiah was able to repair the walls within less than two months (Neh. 6.15). Powerful minister of the emperor, Nehemiah, however, was able to exploit the episode in order to get *carte blanche* and reorganize the situation in Jerusalem. After bringing his work to a close Nehemiah had given Judaism a new face. With Nehemiah the Theology of the Covenant was imposed in Jerusalem in its Deuteronomic form.

Chapter 4

NEHEMIAH

1. *The Books of Ezra and Nehemiah*

Traditionally the books of Ezra and Nehemiah form a single whole. If ever there was a case of complete agreement among scholars, though, it is that these two books were originally distinct and that they were fused by a redactor.

In order to trace the history of these texts back in time, then, we must begin with the last phase, that of the works as a single whole. The fusion of the two books may have taken place even during a very late period, perhaps even in our own era, but we do not know anything for certain. Josephus did not use the fused version, but from the fact that he did not use the book Ezra–Nehemiah we can neither deduce that he did not know the book, nor, much the less, that it did not yet exist. In the section of the *Antiquities of the Jews* dedicated to Jeremiah, we can see that Josephus followed the long text (the Hebrew text today) and not the shorter version (documented in the Septuagint and in some Qumran fragments),[1] which, however, is probably the older of the two. There is a sufficient margin of likelihood that Josephus did not follow the single text of Ezra–Nehemiah, because it had not yet been affirmed, that is he probably made his choice following the fashion of the day rather than personal opinion. This is possible, but it still does not tell us anything about the real date of the two books' fusion, even though it could not have come about much earlier. This is because neither the author of the Chronicles, nor Ben Sira, nor 2 Maccabees knows Ezra, while Ben Sira and 2 Maccabees both know Nehemiah (see the genealogy of the sons of Levi in 1 Chron. 5.27-41; 2 Macc. 1.18-36 and 2.9-12; Sir. 44–50). The fact that the name of Ezra is missing in each of these authors

1. See P. Piovanelli, 'Le texte de Jérémie utilisé par Flavius Josèphe dans le X livre des Antiquités juives', *Henoch* 14 (1992), pp. 11-36.

cannot be assigned to chance. If the united work already existed when these authors were writing it would have been very difficult indeed to ignore half of it. The *terminus post quem* for the fusion of the two works should therefore be placed tentatively around 100 BCE. We shall try to give a more precise and better documented dating below (see Chapter 6 §3; pp. 169-73).

Turning now to the two books separately. Their contents, in the sense of the basis of the fusion, have been reconstructed with an ample margin of surety. In fact, part of the original work of Ezra is contained within the book of Nehemiah. It should also be borne in mind that there is a double, so to speak, to the book of Ezra known as 1 Ezra in the Latin tradition and as 1 Esdras in the Greek one. Here we shall call it simple 1E. This is the text that Josephus used in writing the story of Ezra in the *Antiquities of the Jews*. The problem to be solved is the relationship between the two books; is 1E an enlargement with some modifications of Ezra, or is it the other way around?

If Ezra, and not 1E, was taken as the basis for the fusion, then we must conclude that the ideology behind the fusion (that was to become canonical) was an ideology that fitted well into the period after 100 BCE. We shall examine the details later, but for now let it suffice to say that 1E shows such an interest in Zerubbabel, the last descendant of the Davidic dynasty, that it is scarcely probable that it could have been used during the first century BCE. It was impossible that the Hasmonaeans could have used it, but not even the Pharisees could have had much interest in David's dynasty either. Only rebels such as the author of the Psalms of Solomon, which was not followed up in the history of ideas, could have had some interest in it. We must conclude, therefore, that the original form of the book of Ezra was the apocryphal one.[2] It is even possible that the author of the fusion was the same person who retouched Ezra based on 1E. In fact, the text of 1E does exist as an autonomous text in the tradition, while Ezra as an autonomous text does not.

2.   See Bianchi, 'Zorobabele, re di Giuda', who takes up Garbini's arguments. I believe that the original work is 1E and that Ezra is the copyist's adaptation (whether this coincides or not with its fusion with the book of Nehemiah) for various reasons: 1E is a work with a precise beginning and end (from the Passover of Josiah to Ezra's reform), and therefore one author, while Ezra is fragmentary and the fruit of an operation aimed at eliminating the parts in common with the Chronicles as useless repetitions and those regarding Zerubbabel as dangerous for an eventual rebirth of the monarchy.

I feel that the better part of the introduction I made to my Italian translation of 1E[3] still holds today. The analysis of the book's literary structure is still valid. One thing that I believe, however, that we can no longer accept is that 1E is posterior to the canonic book of Ezra–Nehemiah. The fundamental, and only, reason behind that conclusion was that a verse from the book of Nehemiah can be found in the pseudepigraphical Ezra, Neh. 7.72 and 1E 9.37. I deduced that the author of 1E must have known the canonical Ezra–Nehemiah.[4]

I have now gone back to fully accepting the analysis of the sources made by de Vaux[5] which continue to be a reference point in research on the matter; the sources for the stories of Ezra and Nehemiah represent two autonomous groups. The attempt to make the two characters appear linked stems from the redactor's intentions to present the two in parallel fashion.

No weight should be given, therefore, to Neh. 8.9, from which it could be deduced that Ezra and Nehemiah were together in Jerusalem at least on one occasion. But, since the story of the two books unfolds without implying any contact between Ezra and Nehemiah, it follows that this verse should even be considered the work of the redactor who made the single book of Ezra–Nehemiah. The fusion of the two books was made with the idea of placing the figures of the two protagonists more and more on the same plane, after having purged the work of 1E of a few elements that the redactor did not agree with. The problem of Ezra's and Nehemiah's chronologies should therefore be approached separately, taking account of the information given in each book independently of the other. It is clear that the author of the fusion considered Ezra to be the earlier work and that both books were closely linked to the end of the exile.

In an effort to give an even more precise date to the work of 1E, it should be observed that the book was certainly written after the Chronicles, since the author uses broad passages of them. His work should be placed prior to the Maccabaean period, though, since the references to Zerubbabel would no longer have made sense at that time. All in all we can maintain that the book was composed not long after the Chronicles, because for the Chronicles Israel was still, at least by law, a monarchy and David still represented an ideal. At any rate, the author had

---

3.   Sacchi, *Apocrifi*, I, pp. 99-121.
4.   Sacchi, *Apocrifi*, I, p. 112.
5.   See *DBSup*, IV, p. 766.

completely lost the idea of the chronology of the events whose narration he puts together.

It is obvious that, the discourse being constructed in this way, we are forced to keep the problem of dating the work separate from that of the sources and their value. Furthermore, I consider the idea that the book of Ezra–Nehemiah could have been the work of the Chronicler, separated from the Chronicles only later, to be a completely superseded problem.

The question of 1E's sources can be taken seriously into consideration, since the facts narrated could not have been invented by the author since they contradict the chronology that he conjectured. He placed the story of Ezra after Cyrus, Artaxerxes and Darius, but since he wanted to take Ezra back to the beginning of the postexilic period he invented a genealogy that made him live in that period. He could have been helped in this 'error' by the fact that there was an Artaxerxes between Cyrus and Darius in the chronology that he possessed. However, it is clear that he knew that Ezra lived after Darius. He clearly says 'after' (1E 8.1 = Ezra 7.1).

The discrepancy between the information given in the story and the genealogies does not show that the facts were written as a function of the genealogies, but rather that the genealogies were written as a function of the facts in a time when the Jews no longer had any chronological information for the period after 500 BCE. They had no work containing a continuous account of events. What appears evident is the author of 1E's desire to place Ezra back at the beginning of the postexilic period.

Inasmuch as the author of 1E knows the book of Chronicles and copies parts of it, he diverges from it in the genealogy of the descendants of Levi, because rather than giving Yosedeq, father of Joshua the founder of the Zadokite dynasty, as the son of Seraiah (1 Chron. 5.40 and Ezra 7.1 = 1E 8.1), he gives Ezra.[6] With this the author of 1E polemicizes with the book of Chronicles which represents, as we shall see, a further development of the Deuteronomic doctrine identifying the Law with the Covenant, which in turn implied an identification of the Law of God with that of the state.

1E was completely unaware of Nehemiah. The Nehemiah mentioned in 5.8 cannot be the Nehemiah of the book of the same name due to

6. See Tosato, 'Israele nell'ideologia politica del Cronista'.

problems of dates. And if today a 'with' appears before Nehemiah, this is to be attributed to the manuscript tradition which certainly took him for the historical Nehemiah. The Hebrew text (Ezra 2.2) does not present the 'with' and places this Nehemiah on a lower level than Zerubbabel and Joshua. The original lesson must be the one left in Ezra, which only places Zerubbabel in a position of relief, with all the other names following on the same plane, though Joshua is the first name to follow.

The other mention of Nehemiah in 1E (5.40) should be deleted since the verb is in the singular. The subject was Attharias; here the problem is one of an error in the late manuscript tradition which already knew the single work of Ezra–Nehemiah. In other words, 1E did not know Nehemiah at all, he was not aware of him.

It could be said, and indeed it has been said, that the figure of Ezra is merely an invention of the author of the book of the same name, but this is not possible. No one gives the name of an unknown person to a pseudepigraphical book. Ezra was unknown to the official tradition, the tradition that was affirmed with Nehemiah, because in some way his ideas must not have coincided with those of the priesthood in Jerusalem, who had already accepted Nehemiah's reforms. Proof of this hypothesis must be sought through an analysis of the principal ideas of the books of Nehemiah and 1E. The revision of the book of Ezra in connection with the book of Nehemiah, then, must correspond to the ideological necessities of a decidedly later period. During the first century CE Ezra, in the form of the above-mentioned cliché, was famous and a number of pseudepigraphical texts were even given his name. The most famous of these is *4 Ezra*. These are pseudepigraphical texts, but the first one cannot be considered such, because Ezra's glory began at the time of the unification of the books of Ezra and Nehemiah in a single work.

The later author who combined the two in a single work certainly believed in the existence of both of the reformers, but it is clear that he wanted to give precedence to and therefore pre-eminence to Ezra. We shall see what reasons pushed him to do this. Without refusing either form of Judaism, he gives primacy to the form set forth in Ezra.

It seems that for him Ezra and Nehemiah were the progenitors, the emblems of two different forms of Judaism. One of these forms, that associated with Nehemiah, descended from Saraiah by way of Joshua and Jozedek. This was the form of Judaism that immediately prevailed.

The other form, that of Ezra, seemed to have lost out, but apparently still counted some followers around the beginning of the Hellenistic period, and became central during the times of the book of Ezra's author. Ezra follows the priestly line of thought while Nehemiah follows that of Deuteronomy, two lines of thought that share many points in common, but also hold many differences. An analogous phenomenon is that of messianism, which after a long parenthesis re-emerged in the first century BCE.

I also believe that Neh. 12.26, where we see both Ezra and Nehemiah together, this time as contemporaries of the priest Joiakim, son of Joshua, is the work of the author who united the two books. Once again we are presented with a chronology in contrast with the general outline of the stories. The priest that Nehemiah was in contact with was Eliashib. This element then should be attributed to the later desire to place the two figures on the same plane. It was a compromise between two currents of thought.

The same can be said for Neh. 8.9, which is part of Ezra; this verse contains the name of Nehemiah, while 1E only mentions the governor who speaks to Ezra. The name of Nehemiah was clearly included by the author of the united work.

2. *The Chronology of Nehemiah and Ezra*

From the information given in the texts, Nehemiah left Persia for Jerusalem during the twentieth year of Artaxerxes' reign, and Ezra during the seventh. Neither of the books tells us, however, which Artaxerxes it is talking about. There were three sovereigns with that name who reigned respectively from 465 to 424, 405 to 358 and 358 to 337 BCE.

If, then, we assume that the two books originated independently of one another, the fundamental element for resolving the problem of Nehemiah's date is the following. The papyrus Cowley no. 30 from Elephantine, dated to 408 BCE, is addressed to the governor of Judaea, Bagohi, and mentions the high priest Yehohanan. In Neh. 12.10-11, 22 the following line of high priests of Jerusalem is given: Eliashib, Joiada, Johanan, Jaddua (see *Ant.* 11.297 where the order is given: Eliashib, Jaddua, Johanan [Ioannes]). Eliashib's priesthood, therefore, was a thing of the past in 408 BCE, and an Eliashib was high priest at the time of Nehemiah's mission. As a consequence, the sons of Sanballat mentioned in the papyrus are the sons of Sanballat 'governor of

Samaria', Nehemiah's adversary. It is therefore certain that Nehemiah's first mission is to be placed in the year 445 BCE, the twentieth year of Artaxerxes I's reign.

As for Ezra, 1E 9.1 (see Ezra 10.6) tells us that he was active under the high priesthood of Johanan, son of Eliashib, also mentioned in Neh. 12.23 (see *Ant.* 11.147). This could be the Johanan of the Elephantine letter, supposing that 'son' should read 'grandson', or, following Cross's hypothesis, that two names, erroneously considered repetitions, have been dropped from the genealogy in our possession,[7] since for both Neh. 12.11 and Josephus, Johanan's father was Jaddua, son of Eliashib. Furthermore, Josephus tells us that the governor of Jerusalem at the time of this Johanan was Bagoses (or Bagoas), confirming the first-hand information drawn from the Elephantine letter which Josephus certainly did not know. Josephus also adds that this Bagoses held power up until the time of Artaxerxes II. The most probable date for Ezra's mission, then, would be 398 BCE, the seventh year of Artaxerxes II's reign. That the information contained in the book of Ezra refers to a later period than that of Nehemiah (excluding of course the first chapters) is revealed clearly from the series of internal traces listed by Soggin.[8]

Some scholars have suggested that the seventh year of the reign of Artaxerxes, when Ezra arrived in Jerusalem, contains an error in transmission and that it should read 'the thirty-seventh year'. This has been done in order to avoid the situation where the two missions, that of Nehemiah and that of Ezra, become too distant from one another in time. In this way Ezra's mission could be placed in the thirty-seventh year of Artaxerxes I's reign, in 428 BCE. This suggestion is to be attributed to the desire to safeguard the idea that Nehemiah and Ezra were in Jerusalem at the same time, at least a few times. We have already

---

7.   According to F.M. Cross, 'A Reconstruction of the Judaean Restoration', *JBL* 94 (1975), pp. 4-18, the succession of the first high priests must have been: Jozedek, Jeshua, Joiakim, {Eliashib I, Johanan I}, Eliashib II, Joiada I, Johanan II, Yaddua II. On the succession of high priests during the Persian period see also M. Mor, '*hkhnym hgdwlym byhwdh btqwfh hprsyt*', *Bet Miqra'*, 70 (5738 [= 1978]), pp. 57-67.

Another way of solving the problem of the existence of Johanan, son of Eliashib, is that of considering Joiada and Johanan as brothers. In Neh. 12.11 Johanan is referred to as Jonatan, but it is the same person since he occupies the same place in the genealogy.

8.   Cf. Soggin, *Introduzione*, p. 514.

seen, though, in our analysis of the sources that memory of Nehemiah and memory of Ezra are completely separate and do not intersect at all. The attempts at harmonizing them are to be attributed to the author of the single work Ezra–Nehemiah.

In presenting the facts I have followed the chronology illustrated above, which is also the most widely accepted among scholars. The logic of the facts, to the extent that facts can have a logic, seems to confirm the hypothesis that Nehemiah's work preceded that of Ezra, even though for unknown reasons the latter did not take root.[9]

3. *Nehemiah in Jerusalem (the First Mission)*

Nehemiah was a Jew of the Diaspora who had gained affirmation at the court of Artaxerxes I. He was reached by a group of Jews from Jerusalem in 445 and he asked information on the situation in the city.

9. Most scholars are in favour of the later dating of Ezra. See, for example, H.H. Rowley, 'The Chronological Order of Ezra and Nehemiah', in S. Löwinger and J. Somogy (eds.), *I. Goldziher Memorial*, I (Budapest: Globus Nyomdai Müintézet, 1948), pp. 117-49; K. Galling, 'Ezra', in K. Galling *et al.* (eds.), *Realencyklopädie des Judentums: Die Religion in Geschichte und Gegegenwart* (7 vols.; Tübingen, 3rd edn, 1957–65), III, p. 980; Ricciotti, *Storia d'Israele*, II, pp. 120-30; Cazelles, 'La mission d'Esdras'; O. Eissfeldt, *Einleitung in das Alte Testament unter Einschluß der Apokryphen und Pseudepigraphen sowie der apokryphen- und pseudepigraphenartigen Qumran-Schriften* (Tübingen: Mohr, 3rd edn, 1964), p. 753; J. Morgernstern, 'Jerusalem 485 a.C.', *HUCA* 27 (1956), pp. 101-79; 28 (1957), pp. 15-47; 31 (1960), pp. 1-29; F. Michaëli, *Les livres des Croniques d' Esdras et de Néhémie* (Neuchâtel: Delachaux & Niestlé, 1967), pp. 281-96. The problems are clearly explained in Pelaia, *Ezra* (SBT), p. 12 and in Soggin, *Introduzione*, pp. 514-15.

The dating of Ezra–Nehemiah is followed by U. Kellermann, 'Erwägungen zum problem der Ezradatierung', *ZAW* 80 (1968), pp. 55-87; Y. Aharoni, *The Land of the Bible* (London: Burns & Oates, 1967), p. 358. For the chronology based on the 'thirty-seven' conjecture, see A. Pavlovsky, 'Die Chronologie der Tätigkeit Esdras, Versuch einer neuen Lösung', *Biblica* 38 (1957), pp. 275-305; 428-56; J. Bright, *A History of Israel* (London: SCM Press; 5th edn, 1977), p. 363; B. Reicke, *Neutestamentliche Zeitgeschichte* (Berlin: Töpelmann, 1975), p. 11. See also Soggin, *Introduzione*, p. 515.

Vermes, Renan, Torrey, Hölscher and Garbini deny the existence of Ezra.

On the problem of the book Ezra–Nehemiah, see P. Sacchi, 'La questione di Ezra', in G. Busi (ed.), *we-zo't le—Angelo* (Bologna: Fattoadarte, 1993), pp. 461-70.

> Now it happened in the month of Chislev [Nov.–Dec.], in the twentieth
> year [of the reign of an Artaxerxes, see pp. 130-35], as I was in Susa the
> capital, that Hanani, who is my brother, came from Judaea with some
> other Jews. I asked them news regarding the situation of the Jews in
> Jerusalem, 'the remnant' that had returned to the homeland from slavery,
> and concerning Jerusalem itself. And they said to me, 'The survivors of
> those who returned from slavery, there in the province are in great
> trouble and shame; the walls of Jerusalem are broken down, and its gates
> are destroyed by fire'. When I heard these words I sat down and wept...
> (Neh. 1.1-4).

The words, narrated in the first person by Nehemiah, and the way in
which he received the news, seem to indicate that a new incident had
come about in Jerusalem and that Nehemiah interpreted it as a consequence of the ancient abjection (*ḥerpâ*). The reference to the gates
that had been burned cannot allude to the destruction at the hands of
Nebuchadnezzar, that Nehemiah was well aware of, but rather to a
recent event. The expression 'the walls are broken down' demonstrates
the disillusion on the part of one who believed them to be standing.
Even Josephus's account insists on the fact that there had been recent
events that the unarmed priests had not been able to deal with.

> They said that these [the walls] were in a bad way for the walls had been
> torn down to the ground and the surrounding nations were inflicting
> many injuries on the Jews, overrunning the country and plundering it by
> day and doing mischief by night, so that many had been carried off as
> captives from the country and from Jerusalem itself, and every day the
> roads were found full of corpses (*Ant.* 11.161).

It must have been clear to Nehemiah and the circle he represented
that Jerusalem was poorly governed and that something had to be done
for the city. Just what the causes of Jerusalem's 'shame' were, according to Nehemiah, can be deduced from the policy he was to adopt. In
the meantime, according to his own account, he went before Artaxerxes
and obtained an ample mandate for re-establishing order in the city,
'the city of my fathers' sepulchres' (Neh. 2.5).

It would be impossible to establish any link whatsoever between Artaxerxes' decision to allow Nehemiah to rebuild Jerusalem's walls and
Persian policy. In other words, it is not apparent what interest Artaxerxes could have had in reinforcing Jerusalem without sending a Persian garrison or equipping the Jews as armed settlers in defence of
Persia. Bearing in mind that Nehemiah's first mission dates to 445 BCE,
Persia did not seem to be going through a particularly difficult moment;

the war against Athens was finished (the peace of Callias dates to 449), as was the satrap Megabyzus' revolt that broke out the following year. At any rate, it is unclear just exactly what advantages Persia could have received from Nehemiah's mission, given how little importance was assigned to the city; Jerusalem's occupation by Persian forces was not planned. The causes are therefore to be sought among the events of only secondary importance, which have been completely lost for us. The most probable reason is that Artaxerxes wanted to reward a functionary who had been particularly useful and faithful.

Nehemiah's goals become clear through a look at his works. He acted in the interests of the Jewish community in Babylon, and certainly enjoyed their support as well. From the capital of Judaea, he had to make Jerusalem the capital of all Judaism throughout the world. In carrying out this project Nehemiah's natural allies were all the segregationalists,[10] that is in practice the landowners. His most important enemy was the priesthood and the priesthood's universalistic policy, but the city's condition of 'shame', which could not have been acceptable to the priesthood either, played in Nehemiah's favour. But, in order to offer an acceptable alternative to the development of the priesthood's power, Nehemiah had to reorganize the administrative structure of the state, in some way damaging the *horim*. At the same time, though, some other advantages had to be offered to the *horim* too. The one group that could never have been his allies were the aliens, and those who supported them both inside and outside the city. In fact, it was among those who had returned from exile that he would find the greatest support for his reforms.

Shortly after arriving in Jerusalem as the king's special envoy for the restoration of the city, Nehemiah was able to carry out his reforms in an atmosphere of national concord. This atmosphere was perhaps more apparent than real, but it was functional. His first task was that of rebuilding the city walls (Neh. 2.11-18), an operation that was not likely to meet opposition within the city. He went to work quickly in an effort to surprise the surrounding peoples who could not have been pleased to see Jerusalem take on new strength. Opposition, therefore, came from outside, to the point that at times the Jews had to work with their weapons in hand (Neh. 4.3). Opposition to Nehemiah within the

10. The term was first used by Smith, *Palestinian Parties and Politics*; see also Smith, 'Jewish Religious Life in the Persian Period', in *CAH*, I, pp. 219-78.

city remained underground among the groups whose interests were strongly tied to outside circles.

When Sanballat, the governor of Samaria, and Tobiah, a wealthy leader of Ammon, both related to the priesthood in Jerusalem, realized that work was truly going ahead, they 'plotted together to come and fight against Jerusalem' (Neh. 4.1-2). The armed forces that the Jews had put together and the king's support of Nehemiah, which they must have known of, induced them to be more prudent.

Even some Jews were wary of Nehemiah's works. Nehemiah himself sums up the situation with words that effectively betray just how deceitful the situation was and that he himself was not sure who his enemies were and what their strength was.

'Moreover in those days the *horim* of Judah sent many letters to Tobiah, and Tobiah's letters came to them. For many in Judah were bound by oath to him, because he was the son-in-law of Shecaniah...' (Neh. 6.17-19).

Some Jews even refused to participate in the work of rebuilding the walls (Neh. 3.5), and some prophets were openly against Nehemiah, plotting against him as in the case of Noadiah[11] (Neh. 6.10-14).

All in all, though, the population of Jerusalem must have followed Nehemiah's undertakings with enthusiasm, given the fact that even the high priest Eliashib supported the reconstruction of the walls (Neh. 3.1). Eliashib must have seen this project as a means of reinforcing his own power for the future as well. Nehemiah had come to strengthen Jerusalem and Eliashib could hardly have seen the interests at work behind Nehemiah. In any case, at least officially, Nehemiah did not have anything against the high priest's authority. On the contrary, it was his interest to guarantee that authority and, in effect, his works did guarantee it.

4. *The Social Aspects of Nehemiah's Works*

As soon as work on the walls was finished, Nehemiah saw to re-ordering the social and economic situation in the city, a situation which must have been particularly grave (Neh. 5.1-13). Many were in debt to the point of having pledged their own persons or their relatives. This had led to the sale abroad of debtors as slaves and would in little time have led to a complete changeover in Jerusalem's population. It was

11. In the Hebrew text Noadiah was a woman, in the Greek text a man.

precisely this that the Jews of the Diaspora did not want; but even the *horim* must not have understood that in the long run they too would have been damaged by this situation. The Jews of the Diaspora ended up buying back the wretched in order that they could remain in Jerusalem (Neh. 5.8), but this practice could not be sustained for long. Furthermore, in this way the Jews' money often went into non-Jewish hands, thus damaging the Jews' power in Palestine.

Nehemiah imposed a moratorium on debts. This was the most delicate and difficult phase of his reforms since it went directly against constituted interests. While the ruling class, the priests and the landowners, the *horim* had been able to support the reconstruction of the walls, they were of course opposed to this second action of Nehemiah's. The two elements that allowed Nehemiah to succeed were on the one hand his authority, and on the other the fact that a greater order in the state could not displease the richest classes. The consequence of this operation was a broadening of consensus. The priesthood witnessed the consolidation of their power, because the payment of taxes was reorganized. The *horim* saw a diminution in the competitivity of many of the non-Jewish citizens of Judaea (or at least citizens considered to be non-Jews), while through Nehemiah's reform the *dallim*, the wretched, regained their human dignity.

In general Nehemiah's reforms were of a socio-economic nature, but one in particular was exquisitely political. This one became the foundation for a new Jerusalem. Nehemiah singled out contact with the aliens as the cause of Jerusalem's decadence. The atmosphere of fanaticism against the aliens and against all contact with them is illustrated by Josephus in *Ant.* 11.308. All of Jerusalem's misadventures, including even the Babylonian exile, had been provoked by the fact that '*some* had transgressed against the Law regarding marriages and had married foreign women'. The atmosphere of Neh. 13.23-30 comes to life again in these words. If the sins of only a few, as regards marriages, had been enough to bring about the ruin of Jerusalem, then the persecution of the guilty became a duty to all those who loved their country. This was the teaching that Nehemiah insisted upon and that was lived as a moral for the masses. Nehemiah's goals were essentially political; he aimed at binding Jerusalem to the Diaspora.

Having reinforced the city's walls with the support of the vast majority of the population, after having redressed the social ills and set the city on a path of greater well-being through a series of reforms that certainly met with more opposition than the reconstruction of the walls, but which also created more ardent supporters, Nehemiah reached the crucial provision of his 'mission'. In reality the provision is articulated in a series of measures directed toward the same goal. And on this last point he met with the greatest resistence and in effect divided Israel in two. Let us pass the word to him:

> The city was wide and large, but the people within it were few and no houses had been built. Then God put it into my mind to assemble the *ḥorim* [the landowners], the *seganim* [the officials/notables] and the people to be enrolled.

This would seem to be a census of all the inhabitants of the province, or at least of the Jews, but that is not the case.

> And I found the book of the genealogy of those who returned home first, and I found written in it: These were the people of the province (*bᵉnê hammᵉdînâ*) who came up out of the captivity of those exiles whom Nebuchadnezzar the king of Babylon had carried into exile... (Neh. 7.4-6).

The purpose of the assembly called by Nehemiah was that of ascertaining who were the descendants of the exiles. Those who did not belong to the lineage of the exiles, according to the list, or who could not demonstrate to belong to the lineage of an exile were excluded at least from holding offices, and in particular from the priesthood (Neh. 7.64). At the same time Nehemiah insists against mixed marriages. But in order to demonstrate the horror of these marriages, he must also insist on the Jews' need to distance themselves from foreigners. A passage from Deuteronomy is used to introduce the topic; it reads that two peoples were forever excluded from the possibility of entering into the assembly of Yhwh, that is to become Jews. 'No Ammonite or Moabite shall enter the assembly of Yhwh; even to the tenth generation none belonging to them shall enter the assembly of Yhwh forever' (Deut. 23.3). 'When the people heard the Law [that is this passage of the Law], they separated from Israel all those of foreign descent' (Neh. 13.3). Just what exactly this separation meant is not clear, but it is clear that the measure drew a precise political line of development and, in any case, divided the Jews into the two groups of those who accepted it and those who did not. In other words, it divided the segregationists whose goal was the unity of Judaism, from the universalists whose goal was the unity of the territory.

Among Nehemiah's more spectacular acts we must also include the convocation of an assembly to renew the Covenant with Yhwh, an act which I believe can be attributed to the first mission with a high degree of certainty. The scene is narrated in Nehemiah 10. This passage seems to be a contemporary document, perhaps a part of Nehemiah's memoires, even though its current position links it closely with the preceding chapter ('Because of all this...') which contains a later passage. The position should be attributed solely to the redactor. The people of Jerusalem pledge themselves in writing to Yhwh to respect all the Law, and in particular to no longer give their sons and daughters in marriage to the sons and daughters of foreigners, to respect the sabbath by not trading with the peoples of the land and to give the due offerings to the temple. The document was signed by all the notables of Israel, first among them by Nehemiah. In doing this Nehemiah placed himself in the line of the royal and Deuteronomic tradition of consecrating the relationship between the Jewish people and Yhwh with a covenant. This fact characterizes Nehemiah's ideology, to safeguard the continuity of Israel as a state by reactivating the royal tradition in republican terms. The human signatory of the Covenant was no longer the king, but all of the ruling class: the governor, the priesthood and the *ḥorim*.

5. *Nehemiah's Second Mission*

Twelve years after his departure, therefore in 433 BCE, Nehemiah returned to Susa as he had promised the king. Politics in Jerusalem were therefore completely back in the hands of the city's inhabitants and the 'anti-segregationist' party quickly regained strength, a sign that it must always have been stronger than would appear from a reading of Nehemiah's text.

Thus in an unspecified year to be placed between the end of Nehemiah's first 'mission' and the death of Artaxerxes, that is between 433 and 424 BCE, Nehemiah returned to Jerusalem to regain control of the situation. During the first 'mission' he had made the community of Judaea adopt broad, general provisions which in practice were challenged by situations and habits that had given support to the Zadokite policies. The priesthood's bonds of friendship and kinship with the surrounding peoples remained. In Judaea mixed marriages continued; they were both the foundation and the consequence of economic relations as well as simply human relations.

In the temple in Jerusalem which, like all temples of the time, had functions similar to those of our banks, an office had been made for

Tobiah (Neh. 13.4). Nehemiah had it closed, but it is hard to believe that nothing replaced the lost capital. That of the Jews of the Diaspora replaced it. That the temple played the role of a bank was not a scandal for anyone. What Nehemiah wanted to block was that foreign capital be given a permanent place in Jerusalem, foreign from Nehemiah's point of view, in other words from the point of view of the Jews of the Diaspora. Furthermore, since the Zadokites' power was essentially based on marriages into the big families of the surrounding region, Nehemiah chased out of Jerusalem a relative of the high priest (probably the son), who had married the governor of Samaria's daughter (Neh. 13.28). With these two measures Nehemiah broke the base of Zadokite power, 'foreign' capital and political marriage alliances with the powerful families of the region.

Marriages with foreign women were hindered more vigorously (Neh. 13.25); anyone keeping such a wife could be beaten and shaved. Moral persecution in the name of God and the Torah broke out in Jerusalem. Nehemiah did not reach the point, though, of condemning alien wives and their children to returning to their families of origin. This last offence, dictated by religious fanaticism and the interests of some leaders, was not to arrive until Ezra's day, and even then not everyone was willing to carry out the order.

For Nehemiah it was enough to send away a relative of the high priest who had entered the family of Sanballat, the governor of Samaria, and isolate the common people who were in a similar situation. Nehemiah was more of a politician than a theologian. He understood the risks involved in the practice of mixed marriages, but it sufficed him to break up those that effectively and immediately threatened the political situation.

Even the tithes to be paid to the temple were reorganized with a heavy hand, and drastic measures were adopted in order to ensure observance of the sabbath (Neh. 13.10 and following). Not only did Nehemiah have the city gates closed on the sabbath, but he also threatened the foreigners who dared take lodgings outside the walls on the night between Friday and Saturday (Neh. 13.21).

It is clear that during his second mission Nehemiah was much stronger than before if he was able to threaten foreign merchants and offend the family of Sanballat of Samaria. Jerusalem was by then much closer to the Jews of the Diaspora than to the aliens who lived on its territory. Jerusalem had become the capital and the reference point for the Jews of Babylon, while the sole choice left to the Jews who did not wish to bow before Nehemiah's reforms was exile. Samaria was close by and always willing to receive anyone who for one reason or another wanted to abandon Jerusalem.

The dominant tendencies in Jewish spirituality of the Early Zadokite period were inverted with Nehemiah. For Trito-Isaiah the foreigner who worshipped Yhwh would not be separated from his people (Isa. 56.3). With Nehemiah the opposite is the case. The foreigner is not only seen as something completely different from the Judaean, but he is also identified with the Moabite and the Ammonite, that is with the peoples that Deuteronomy had excluded forever from communion with Israel (Deut. 23.4-6). The Jews who did not accept this ideology found themselves excluded from the community as well.

The situation created in Jerusalem as a consequence of the measures against the aliens and the anti-segregationists is well-illustrated by Josephus. Whenever a Judaean was accused of having eaten impure foods or of having committed some similar sin, he would take refuge with the Samaritans. Samaria received the 'guilty', accentuating the rivalry between the two cities (*Ant.* 11.346-47). 'Samaritan' was to become more and more a synonym for 'traitor'. See Sir. 50.25-26 where with the greatest contempt the Samaritans are called a 'non-people', and Jn 4.9, the episode of the Samaritan at the well: 'How is it that you, a Jew, ask a drink of me, a woman of Samaria?' On the so-called Samaritan schism, see the following chapter.

6. *The Importance of the Figure of Nehemiah*

Nehemiah can be considered the founder of the second Zadokite period, which lasted until the second century BCE. The second Zadokite period differs from the first in that while the priesthood remained the structural centre of Jewish society, the passage was made from universalism to segregationalism and the Covenant was seen as having been made between God and the people through the priests and the lay leaders. The period's legislative measures, such as those regarding the sabbath, the prohibition against marrying alien women or the exclusion from Judaism of those who were not descendants of the exiles, had an essentially political value, and not an ideal one in the religious sense.

Nehemiah came from Babylon with very clear ideas and he followed their execution with lucidity, constance and at times harshness. In the first phase of his activity he sought to reinforce the structures of Jewish society. In doing so he drew to himself many elements of society, many of whom must have been the descendants of returned exiles, even though it is not likely that Nehemiah's following coincided entirely with this group to the exclusion of others.

In order to put power in the hands of this group of people Nehemiah used religious ideology, preaching against mixed marriages, a message which made sense only if the impurity of the pagan were accepted and emphasized. He interpreted the heavy sanctions placed against Moabites and Ammonites by Deuteronomy in such a way as to extend them to all foreigners. In order to grasp the scope of this interpretation of the Law, it must be seen in connection with the fact that from a certain point on Nehemiah only called assemblies of returned exiles, clearly in the sense of those belonging to that party. His political adversaries were thus excluded from the Jewish community and considered the equals of the foreigners. This explains how the Chronicler, writing in Jerusalem during the following century, was able to say that all the Jews had been deported to Babylon by Nebuchadnezzar (2 Chron. 36.20).

A piece of information given in 2 Maccabees (2.13) reveals another aspect of the figure of Nehemiah that confirms the centrality of his role in the history of Judaism. He himself had the books of his tradition collected. In other words he founded a library. Among the books in this library the text of 2 Maccabees mentions as particularly important 'the books of the kings and the books of the prophets, the books of David and the letters of the kings concerning gifts'. Let us leave aside the letters of the kings concerning gifts since we cannot establish whether they are from Jewish kings or Persian kings, even though it seems more likely that they would concern Persian kings. In that case they must have been documents, in part conserved in the first chapters of the book of Ezra, containing the various imperial privileges and authorizations regarding worship.

The other three works seem to be the Psalms (the books of David), a collection and therefore an edition of the prophetical writings and finally a work indicated as 'the books regarding the kings'. Behind this formula it is not difficult to make out a work whose central subject was the history of the monarchy. This certainly included the whole of what we today call the 'Books of Samuel and of the Kings', even though we can only hypothesize as to the real extension of this work. If we accept Noth's view, this work must have begun with Deuteronomy and included the following books. Should my thesis concerning R1 be accepted, it must have included the Tetrateuch, though in a reduced form compared to that which we possess today, since much or all of the priestly *corpus* (*Priestercodex*) would have been missing. If we accept Schmidt's thesis, this would be proof that the Yahwist was composed after the historical books were written, even though such a late date, after Nehemiah, causes many problems; the history of the patriarchs makes sense in the function of the monarchy, not of the republic.

No matter which solution is accepted regarding the formation of the Pentateuch, one datum seems certain; in this collection there was no single, unified codex. This means that Israel's legislation was not only still fluid, a fact that could appear obvious, but also that the Law did not yet occupy the central role that it would later assume. For Nehemiah the problem of the legislation either did not exist, or it was too complicated to be resolved. In any case, resolving the problem did not seem opportune. In comparison with the way of listing the texts in the tradition of Nehemiah's day, it should be noted how the Scripture was referred to in the second century BCE; the Qumran letter known as MMT mentions the books of Moses, of the Prophets and of David. Here the Torah is clearly identified.[12]

Since the laws of the Torah did not represent a unified *corpus*, someone must have seen to making one. This work is documented in the so-called *Temple Scroll* which contains a law code clearly inspired by the canonical tradition, but without contradictions. In other words the *Temple Scroll* was a real law code. We do not know why this code was not adopted in history, but the reasons must be sought in the conflicts that must have taken place with Jerusalem's ruling class. These texts themselves are our only source concerning such conflicts; there is no continuous account of Jewish history. We do not know the date of the *Temple Scroll*, but it must surely be ancient as attested both by an internal analysis and by the fact that some fragments copied around the middle of the second century BCE have been found at Qumran. It must date, therefore, to before 200 BCE. The date of the Temple Scroll is the *terminus ante quem* of the separation of the Pentateuch as the Torah. Contrary to common opinion, I believe that the most probable date for the Temple Scroll is between the fourth and third centuries BCE.[13]

12. See p. 110 n. 32.

13. The dating of the *Temple Scroll* to prior to 200 BCE has been suggested by Strugnell, but a recent study by García Martínez opts for a later dating. See

7. *Universalism and Nationalism during the Zadokite Period*

From what we have said thus far, the authors and parties of the time seem to be divisable in two groups according to whether they sustained nationalist (also called segregationalist) or universalist ideas. In the political struggle within early Zadokitism the two tendencies are easily identifiable. The groups' actions, however, are to be grasped in the positions taken regarding single problems; there is no real idealogical framework comparable to that of Deutero-Isaiah or Trito-Isaiah.

Neither the universalistic (Zadokite) current nor the nationalistic (Nehemian) one was able to rise above the level of particular interests to a wider global vision of things. Most of all this is true of the Zadokites. Ezra, who belonged to the second Zadokite period, held more precise positions on the level of thought, even though it is unlikely that he grasped all the consequences of his ideas. While for Trito-Isaiah the contingent reasons of Jerusalem's administrative necessities provided the occasion for proposing a new conception of purity, for Eliashib the political decision was never raised to the level of an interpretation of history. He accepted Nehemiah's reforms which reinforced his power, probably without even noticing that they were destroying his spirituality.

After Trito-Isaiah's great intuition, Zadokite universalism towards the peoples of Palestine became exclusively practical in nature. The great promises made to Abraham, typical of R1's thought and even more so of R2's, shrink through the years of daily adaptation.

If the question of the eunuch's impurity had been developed along the lines traced by Trito-Isaiah it would have opened new prospectives of value to the human spirit. Purity would no longer have been the chief value, but rather certain rules of life which, to use a term that was unknown to the ancient Jews, we would call ethical. The eunuch was impure, but he could come to be considered pure. R1/Yahwist's way of thinking is repeated in analogous fashion, viewing the whole earth as sacred, but justifying its use by humans because God had given it to him. It was sacred, but it could be considered profane because God had decided so (see Chapter 7, §1, pp. 439-42).

F. García Martínez, 'Sources et rédaction du Rouleau du Temple', *Henoch* 13 (1991), pp. 219-32.

Let us look at the first two chapters of Malachi. On the one hand we are presented with the pure offering made by the pagans, without any explanation of this purity (Mal. 1.11), and on the other hand the priests of Jerusalem are condemned for reasons which are clearly the opposite of those making the pagans' offering pure (Mal. 1.10). The priests have broken the Covenant. And here it is interesting to see just what Malachi considers to be the clauses of the Covenant, those rules that it is a sin to break. Fraud, adultery and oppression of the poor stand out in the list. These are transgressions that we would call ethical.

Just as the word 'universalism' holds a particular meaning in the Judaean history of the fifth century, the term 'nationalism' too takes on a particular meaning in this historical context. We are not dealing with a form of nationalism comparable to the nationalisms of the twentieth century, tied to the idea of a 'nation' that cannot be conceived of without its own territory or boundaries. The nationalism of Nehemiah and Ezra is aimed at saving the Jewish people's identity. The State of Jerusalem exists only in the function of this goal, which is felt to be the basis of all the values of the religion of Israel.

Both nationalism and universalism, the latter owing very much to contact with the Iranian world, held a common element: the exclusivity of worship of the one true God. Going along with the sound of the names of the two currents, it could seem to us today that universalism was more open towards humans, in the end more tolerant than the nationalist current. Clearly, in the case of mixed marriages it is easy to identify the anti-segregationists as the heirs to Trito-Isaiah's ideas, in turn under the influence of Deutero-Isaiah, but we should not confuse the anti-segregationists' behaviour with an image of ideas of tolerance. They too acted in defence of economic interests and in any case had lost the initial magnitude of the universalistic idea.

Yhwh was always closely attached to the affairs of his people. When around 600 BCE those who had remained in the homeland during the exile wanted to provide a juridical basis for their having taken possession of the goods of the exiles, they found no better way than the declarations of a prophet that Yhwh had abandoned the exiles (Ezek. 11.15) following the logic of the 'doctrine of the remnant'. God sifted through his people in order to arrive at the holy remnant, the true Israel. The exiles defended their rights, again through the mouth of a prophet, declaring that Yhwh had left the temple in order to follow them into exile (Ezek. 11.17).

Deutero-Isaiah saw all peoples even far off to the west awaiting the Word of Yhwh which was to reach them peacefully (Isa. 42.1-4). The Servant, which was the very Covenant of Israel with God, was also a light to the nations (Isa. 42.6). This presupposes that one day even the pagans would recognize the one God, historically revealed, Yhwh. In Trito-Isaiah accents on the peaceful spread of the true religion (Isa. 60.1-6) are alternated with visions of victory and Israel's triumph (Isa. 63.1-6).

On one point nationalism and universalism are equally intransigent and exclusivistic; the one true religion to be carried to all peoples was that of Yhwh. The difference lay in the way of conceiving relations between Israel and the Gentiles.

This double attitude was destined to last in time; both Rabbinism and Christianity have inherited it. For Christianity anyone who worships the true God in the true way belongs to Israel (obviously, opinions concerning which way is the true way vary), but all others remain excluded. For Rabbinism ethnic Israel remains the central element, but the religion holds a function that concerns all peoples and all of history.

Which of the two branches of Judaism has been more tolerant towards others is difficult to establish given the different place occupied in history by Jews and Christians. In any case, though, it is to be excluded that the universalists were any more tolerant than the others.

But perhaps this is a problem that no longer regards either Christianity or Rabbinism; it is a problem that concerns every religion that believes strongly in itself. It is probably for this reason that the most tolerant religions are the polytheistic ones and that the persecution of the Christians were, from the pagan point of view, anomalous, this because they were linked to principles such as the compulsoriness of emperor worship that seem to belong more to Mesopotamic universalism than to Greek and Latin classical pagan culture.

8. *The Elephantine Colony*

The documents (letters) from the archive at Elephantine, located in Upper Egypt at the level of the first cataract of the Nile, are very important for understanding the historical development of exilic Judaism. A military colony of Jews had been established there, probably by Cambyses, though perhaps even earlier, in order to protect Egypt's southern border. The colony had built its own temple and was in correspondence with Jerusalem over problems concerning worship, which demonstrates that union of worship, the idea that worship could only take place in Jerusalem, was an ideal which spread only in the postexilic period. The civil war between Judah and Jerusalem leading to the end of the Davidic dynasty seems the most likely cause for the unification of worship. The documents from Elephantine cover nearly the entire fifth century; the oldest dates from 495 BCE and the most recent from the beginning of the following century.

The temple at Elephantine was destroyed around 410 BCE at the instigation of the priests of the local god Khnum. One possible hypothesis explaining the Egyptian aversion to the temple of Yhwh is that the Jews made sacrifices of sheep there while the god Khnum was represented with a goat's head.

The inhabitants of Elephantine then turned to the authorities in Jerusalem, the governor and the priest, for the reconstruction of the temple. Their first letter did not receive a reply. They wrote a second letter and it would seem that their efforts paid off; the temple was rebuilt. As we can see, the ideal of a unique place of worship did allow some exceptions in practice.

The Jews of Elephantine were still polytheists. Alongside the name of Yhwh (written normally in the form *yhw*) we find the names of the divinities 'Anat Betel and Asham Bethel. These gods must have still existed in the homeland too, since mention is made of offerings for them sent to Palestine. Even the forms of the laws that appear in the correspondence are different from those that we know from the Bible. Over time, though, they evolve in the same direction as those present in the Bible, showing that contacts with the home country were quite close.[14] In any case the Elephantine letters bear witness to an extreme fluidity in Israel's religious and civil traditions. The history of Israel written from the literary documents does not correspond to the history of Israel written from day-to-day administrative documents. Perhaps, however, this is not only true of Jewish history. I remember a statement that Ugo Enrico Paoli once made during a course on the Gortyn law code: the habits and customs of a people cannot be reconstructed from their laws. It would be like reconstructing the life of the Christian peoples from the Gospels.

---

14. See I. Cardellini, 'Dalla legge alla Torah', *RSB* 3 (1991), pp. 57-81.

Chapter 5

THE SAMARITANS

1. *The Schism*

As we have seen, the rigid policy of separation from the aliens, which
had been in place in Jerusalem since Nehemiah's time, led to some
reactions. Of particular gravity was the reaction of Manasses, who
chose to leave Jerusalem and take refuge in Samaria under the protection of Sanballat, his father-in-law.

The name of Manasses has been handed down to us by Josephus in
his *Antiquities of the Jews* (11.304-12). Josephus tells us that the high
priest Jaddua (alternative spelling: Joiada) had a brother, Manasses,
who had married a certain Nikaso, daughter of Sanballat, the governor
of Samaria. The same high priest, again according to Josephus, had dis-
approved of the marriage and Manasses was forced to choose between
his wife and the priesthood. Sanballat resolved the situation by offering
Manasses the high priesthood of a new temple to be built in the territory
of Samaria. We even know the date of this event in general, though suf-
ficiently precise terms, since Sanballat was appointed governor of Samaria by Darius III, the Persian king defeated by Alexander. Therefore,
for Josephus, the episode took place during the second half of the fourth
century BCE, only a few years before the conquests of Alexander the
Great.

The event narrated by Josephus is very similar to the one narrated in
Neh. 13.28: 'And one of the sons of Joiada, the son of Eliashib the high
priest, was the son-in-law of Sanballat…therefore I chased him from
me'.

In spite of the different chronology, all appearances seem to indicate
that we are dealing with the same event in the two sources, because
Nehemiah chased away 'one of the sons of Joiada' during his second
mission (which began around 430–425), while according to Josephus,
Manasses was driven away nearly one hundred years later. Even the

family tie between the one chased away and the high priest is different in the two sources.

Although as Cross has demonstrated there was a whole dynasty of Sanballatids in Samaria,[1] it is unlikely that the same episode would repeat itself at an interval of one hundred years. We must, therefore, choose one of the two dates, and the date offered by the book of Nehemiah is preferable since the episode makes sense in the context of Nehemiah's works, and would make much less sense in a period when Nehemiah's constitution had been accepted and consolidated.

It is probable that in the sources used by Josephus, all the events regarding the various Sanballats had ended up being associated with a single person. This is more or less what happened to the Seleucids, who are present in the rabbinical tradition more as a single sovereign than as an entire dynasty.[2] Without the discovery of other contemporary documents, we would not have known that the Sanballatids had been a whole dynasty and would still be convinced that there had been only one Sanballat.

The most probable date, then, for Manasses' rebellion seems to be during the period of Eliashib's first successor, Joiada, and should therefore be placed before 409, since at that date, according to a letter from Elephantine mentioned above (Cowley no. 30), the high priest was not Joiada, but another, Johanan. Manasses was opposed to the policy of Nehemiah and refused the compromise that most Zadokites accepted: security of power in exchange for the renunciation of the ideology that had lain behind their policy during the first half of the fifth century BCE. Manasses preferred a clean break. Perhaps he hoped for a triumphal return, but if that was the case his hopes were not fulfilled by the successive course of events. The impossibility of a return led to the crystallization of the break. A Jewish community was consolidated in the North, here, too, under the guide of the Zadokites, which ended up developing its own worship on Mt Gerizim, near Shechem, and culminating in the construction of a temple analogous and rival to the one in Jerusalem. This temple had surely been completed by 328 BCE.

---

1. See F.M. Cross, 'The Discovery of the Samaria Papyri', *BA* 26 (1963), pp. 110-21; Cross, 'Aspects of Samaritan and Jewish History in Late Persian and Hellenistic Times', *HTR* 59 (1969), pp. 201-11 (205).

2. See E.J. Bickerman, 'La chaîne de la tradition pharisienne', *RB* 59 (1952), pp. 44-54 (44).

Building the temple on Mt Gerizim was justified by a passage found in Torah (Deut. 27.4), in which Moses commanded the Jews to raise a temple to Yhwh on Mt Gerizim following certain norms, as soon as they entered into the land of Canaan. The name of Gerizim is a typical variant of the Samaritan Torah compared to the Jerusalem text which reads Ebal in the same passage. Mt Ebal faces Mt Gerizim.

The text of Deuteronomy in no way opposes the construction of this temple since its author (or final redactor) desired the centralization of worship, but never claimed that such centralization had to take place in Jerusalem. It is for this reason that the Samaritans could consider the Torah a sacred book in exactly the same way as the Jerusalem community did. We shall see below just exactly what possibilities the Samaritan variant had of representing the authentic lesson.

2. *Samaritanism Stabilized*

The community of Shechem which developed into an autonomous sect over the course of the fourth century BCE following the Zadokite schism in Jerusalem, referred back to ancient local traditions which ennobled its origins and carried it backward in time. According to the Samaritan tradition, handed down to us in much later documents which may, however, contain ancient elements,[3] Israel was united up until the time of Joshua and his successor 'kings'. Joshua established the kingdom of Shechem and founded a temple on the holy mountain of Gerizim in the thirteenth year of the time of the Judges. The schism began with Eli who, having assembled a group of malcontents, founded a new sanctuary at Shilo; Phinehas, a common name among Samaritan priests, remained faithful to the tradition. Eli originated a new priesthood. During the time of Saul, who according to the Samaritan sources reigned only over the South, there was a war between the followers of Saul and those of Joshua from the North. The birth of the term *šāmᵉrîm* ('the observant', namely the Law) dates from this time; the defeated followers of Joshua took on this name and took refuge in the Basan, under the leadership of their high priest Uzzi. Those who did not flee were considered apostates just as the people of the South. The original name that the Samaritans gaves themselves, then, had nothing to do with the city of Samaria. They called themselves *šāmᵉrîm*, archaic pronunciation of *šōmᵉrîm* from the active participle qal of the verb *šmr*, 'to observe'

---

3. See P. Sacchi, 'Studi Samaritani', *RSLR* 5 (1969), pp. 413-40.

with the idea of 'to observe the law'. The fact that Shechem was very near to the city of Samaria (*šōmrōn*) and the fact that Samaria was the centre of the province, favoured the exchange *šāmᵉrîm/ šōmᵉrônîm*, also because it would have been difficult to concede the name 'the observant' to one's adversaries.

Again according to the Samaritan sources, the *šāmᵉrîm* were taken into exile at Harran by Sargon when he invaded Israel and destroyed Samaria. From there they returned to their homeland (see 2 Kgs 17.25-26) and rebuilt the temple on Mt Gerizim and remained from then on in the promised land (unlike the Jews of Jerusalem who were deported to Babylon). There is no trace of the episode regarding Manasses in the Samaritan sources.

3. *The Samaritan Torah*

The tradition of the Samaritan Torah was probably stabilized during the fourth century as well.[4] The Samaritans wrote their Law scrolls using the Hebrew characters that were in use in Palestine up until the time of the exile. The exile marked the moment when the Jews stopped using these characters, since for everyday purposes Aramaic characters were used, the so-called square writing. In this aspect Samaritanism shows a conservative tendency, at least in comparison to the latest developments in Jerusalem. The Samaritans must have rejected the new elements that had been formed in postexilic Judaism. This of course does not mean that Samaritanism did not later undergo a profound historical evolution as well.

The text of the Samaritan Torah contains roughly six thousand variants in comparison to the Masoretic text, as is apparent in the Leningrad codex reproduced in the third edition of the *BHK* and, with even more accuracy in the details, in the new *BHS*.

Many of the variants are of a purely grammatical or stylistic nature

---

4. The fact that the Samaritans hold the Pentateuch as their only canonical text shows that they accepted it as an inspired text when it had already become the Torah. This would not have been possible before or during the Nehemian reforms since the Torah did not yet exist. The Pentateuch, that is the Tetrateuch with the addition of Deuteronomy, must have come into being after Nehemiah, plausibly during the time of Ezra (fourth century BCE). In any case cultural exchanges between Jerusalem and Samaria must have continued for some time; on this point see Cazelles, 'La mission d'Esdras'.

and have only very limited influence on meaning, as is the case with most variants in all the traditions. One variant, however, is of decisive importance for Samaritanism since the legitamacy of the Gerizim temple is based on this version of the text. The passage in question is in Deut. 27.4; the altar mentioned in the biblical text is to be raised, according to the Jerusalem text, on Mt Ebal, but according to the Shechem text on Mt Gerizim. This type of variant cannot be due to a copyist's error, but rather must be a deliberate alteration of the text. As written words 'Ebal' and 'Gerizim' have nothing in common, although geographically they share a similar location; they are situated one in front of the other. Vaccari[5] favours the Jerusalem text, while Eissfeldt[6] propends for the Shechem version.

It is practically certain that the Samaritan version is the original one because in Deut. 11.29 and 27.12 Mt Ebal, which, I repeat, is in front of Mt Gerizim, is referred to as a place of curse. It is not likely that the first altar in the promised land was to be raised in such a place. Furthermore, it is obvious that the Samaritans' choice of a site for founding their temple was to fall on any place near Shechem that enjoyed the blessing of some traditionally respected person. On the contrary, for Jerusalem this place, once it had become the site of a rival temple, could only become a place of execration. It would seem therefore that in all probability Deut. 27.4 should read 'Gerizim' and not 'Ebal'.[7]

Moreover, the Samaritan text presents a number of variants in numbers, especially in those concerning years in the genealogies. To us the phenomenon could seem secondary, but in reality it is the fruit of a different conception of history. Numbers, while used in Jewish administrative documents the same way that we use them, could also hold a symbolic value as in the case of the strictly historical texts. The phenomenon's structure has not yet been entirely explained. At any rate, it should be pointed out that some of the New Testament quotations and readings of the Old Testament are based on the Samaritan text and not on the Jerusalem one. While Samaritanism was rejected by Jerusalem, from Ben Sirah to the ferocious destruction of Samaria by John Hyr-

5.   In A. Vaccari, *Institutiones Biblicae scholis accomodatae* (Rome: Pontificio Istituto Biblico, 6th edn, 1951), p. 245.

6.   Eissfeldt, *Einleitung*, p. 943.

7.   See P. Sacchi, 'Ideologia e varianti della tradizione ebraica: Deut 27, 4 e Is 52, 14', in H. Merklein, K. Müller and G. Stemberger (eds.), *Bibel in jüdischer und christlicher Tradition* (Frankfurt am Main: Hain, 1993), pp. 13-32.

canus right up to the Pharisees of the Gospels, Samaritanism continued
to be a Jewish civilization in Palestine which kept important traditions
alive up until Jesus' time, and even beyond.[8]

4. *Samaritan Messianism*

Zadokite Judaism, at least in its origins, contained a strong element of
expectation of a 'saviour', an exceptional figure who would carry the
people to victory, not through the force of arms, but through God's
blessing, in short, expectation of a figure that the Christian theology of
today would call messianic. The messiah was to be a descendant of
Jesse, anointed by Yhwh and governor of his people. Messianic hopes
had fallen on Zerubbabel, but the anointed of David soon left the scene.
Only the priestly anointed one remained. I do not know if messianic
hopes were ever focused on the priestly anointed during the Early
Zadokite period. The mediocrity of the figures probably precluded that
possibility, but the anointed of Levi did become the spiritual centre of
the nation. The covenant of Sinai, consolidating motif of the Jewish

---

8.   The Samaritan Torah has been published by von Gall. See Sacchi, 'Studi
samaritani'. On the problem of the symbolic aspect of numbers in relation to history, see Hughes, *Secrets of the Times*.
   On the New Testament quotations of the Torah based on the Samaritan text and
not the Jerusalem one, see P. Kahle, 'Untersuchungen zur Geschichte des Pentateuchtextes', *TSK* 88 (1915), pp. 399-439, reproduced in P. Kahle, *Opera
minora* (Leiden: E.J. Brill), pp. 3-37. For example, Stephen's speech before the
Sanhedrin presupposes a calculation of the ages of the patriarchs based on the
Samaritan and not the Masoretic text. In fact, if Terah, Abraham's father, had died
at the age of 205 as in the Masoretic lesson, then Abraham would have left Harran
while his father was still living, but Stephen specifies that Abraham left after his
father's death. In the Samaritan text Terah dies at the age of 145, thus allowing
Abraham to leave Harran in the same year as his father's death.
   The Samaritan tradition, however, has left clear traces in just about all the pseudepigraphical literature; its presence in the book of *Jubilees* had been ascertained, as
in *1 Enoch*, the *Assumption of Moses* and even in *4 Ezra*. See A. Dillmann, 'Bei-
träge aus dem Buche der Jubiläen zur Kritik des Pentateuchtextes', in *Sitzungs-
berichte der Berliner Akademie* (1883), pp. 337 and following, p. 339: 'Nirgends in
allen diesen Schriften sind die Zahlen des Hebräischen [that is the Masoretic text]
zugrunde gelegt, woraus zu schliessen ist, dass sie noch nicht da waren, oder doch,
dass der Glaube an ihre Rechtigkeit nicht allgemein bei den Juden durchgedrungen
war'.

people in the Deuteronomic vision, now came to be known as the covenant of Levi (Mal. 2.4, 8).

While the priesthood, recognized as legitimate, shrank from including all the sons of Aaron to including only the descendants of Zadok, for stipulating the covenant with Yhwh the entire priestly descendance was called upon. In this way emphasis was placed on the idea that the Covenant was stipulated with Moses only inasmuch as Moses was himself a priest.

Even though they preserved the priesthood's power, the ideologies of Nehemiah and Ezra completely superceded the original sense of Zadokitism. Even in their differences, both Nehemiah and Ezra proposed typical theologies of the Covenant in which there was no room for messianism. If salvation was to come to humanity through its observation of the Law, then there could be no saviour figure, or at least humans could not be allowed a central role.

The Samaritan world kept the expectation of a messiah alive (there is no reason to doubt this point even from the origins, given the particular structure of the Samaritan ideology). For the Samaritans, though, the messianic figure was very different than for the Jerusalemites. The people who broke with the power of Jerusalem clearly broke with Jerusalem's messianic tradition as well, a tradition that maintained its messianic hopes on the figure of an anointed one during the early Zadokite period. Those who had broken with Jerusalem had broken precisely with the power of the anointed, be they kings or priests. One sign of this distance is that books such as Samuel or Kings, which clearly state the promise of an eternal reign to David and his descendants, were never accepted into the Samaritan canon. Nor were the books of the prophets then in existence accepted, perhaps because some of the prophets were too closely tied to the kingdom and the reigning family, perhaps because, if, like Ezekiel, they had spoken of a reconstitution of Israel, they had not gone beyond the traditional 'king and priest' scheme.

Still, the idea of the 'prophet' did not die away among the Samaritans; it became the basis of their messianism. For them, there were only two real prophets: Moses and the future Messiah who would be equal to Moses, in following with a strict interpretation of Deut. 18.9-15:

> When you come into the land that Yhwh, your God, gives to you, do not imitate the abominations of those nations. There shall not be found among you...anyone who practices divination or foretells the future...

You shall be blameless before Yhwh, your God. These nations, which you are about to dispossess, give heed to soothsayers and to diviners, but as for you, Yhwh, your God, has not allowed you so to do. He will raise up from among you [Israel], from your brethren, a prophet like me [Moses]—him you shall heed.

The instrument of future salvation is not an anointed one, but a prophet equal to Moses. Only one who had spoken to God face to face could be called prophet (Exod. 33.11, 20; Num. 12.6-8; Deut. 34.10). Later Samaritan speculation (of Jesus' time but also even later) was focused essentially on establishing the role of the figure of Moses both in the history of salvation and in the very structure of the cosmos. In the end the figure of Moses took on superhuman characteristics and became a mediator between God and humans, with attributes that Christian thought reserves for Jesus.[9]

9.   See MacDonald, *Theology of the Samaritans*, pp. 204-206.

Chapter 6

LATE ZADOKITISM (C. 400–200 BCE)

1. *The Events and the General Circumstances*

Information regarding Jerusalem during the period running from 400 BCE up to the period of Seleucid domination, that is the beginning of the second century BCE, is relatively scarce. Information tends to be more abundant, however, for the years near the end of the period.

Until the end of the period in question, there do not seem to be any events having an effect comparable to the deep repercussions of Nehemiah's reforms on Jewish society.

It is debated whether Jerusalem took part or not in the Phoenician revolt against Persia during the middle years of the fourth century, a revolt which was put down violently. Even scholars who tend to favour the hypothesis of Judaea being involved in the revolt admit that it is only a possibility.[1]

Even an event of such great importance for all of humanity as Alexander the Great's conquest of the Persian throne does not seem to have been felt in all its importance by Jewish society, even given that Alexander surely crossed Palestine with his army in 332 BCE. A few years after the conquest there was a rebellion in Samaria and a Macedonian colony was founded there, but in Jerusalem absolutely nothing happened. It is likely that the importance of the historical transition taking place, which was to affect all the peoples of the Mediterranean, was not grasped in Jerusalem, because apparently nothing changed for the Jews.

---

1. J.W. Betlyon, 'The Provincial Government of the Persian Period and the Yehud Coins', *JBL* 105 (1986), pp. 633-42. For a very good analysis of the archaeological evidence contributing to our knowledge of the Persian period, see, G. Wildengren, 'The Persian Period', in Hayes and Miller (eds.), *Israelite and Judaean History*, pp. 489-538.

The Jewish state had become used to living under foreign domination under the Persians. The Jews paid tribute (Neh. 9.37), but they were also allowed religious freedom. According to Artaxerxes' decree for Ezra (Ezra 7.11-26) only the priests and in general those affiliated with the Temple (Ezra 7.24) were exempt from paying taxes. We do not, however, know how long this exemption remained in force. From Josephus (*Ant.* 11.297-301) we learn of a heavy tribute imposed on the Temple by the governor of Jerusalem, Bagoas, as punishment for a serious crime. The high priest Yohanan, Yoyada's successor, was said to have killed one of his brothers, who was a friend of Bagoas, inside the Temple. While the name Bagoas could have been shared by a number of people, the simultaneous presence of the names of Bagoas and Johanan in the Elephantine letters together with the information provided by Josephus that Bagoas was one of Artaxerxes II's generals allows us to date the episode to around the year 400. But even this tribute could have been modified or removed later.

The foreign king became, in the fourth century BCE, the guarantor and protector of the Law of Yhwh, but already during the exile the prophets had claimed that authority had passed from the house of David to Nebuchadnezzar, to Cyrus and to all their descendants (Jer. 27.6; Isa. 44.28; 49.1-13). It had come to be generally accepted that God exercised his authority in Israel through a foreign sovereign. Alexander, too, allowed the Jews to live according to their Law (*Ant.* 11.337-38). Josephus even recounts that Alexander made a solemn entrance into the city where he was splendidly received by the high priest. Josephus's account has been called into question because of the presence of some unlikely details, but the core of the problem that interests the historian, the concession to the Jews, under explicit request of the high priest, to be able to live under their own laws, is very highly probable.

This did not represent any sort of favourable treatment for Jerusalem, but was rather part of Alexander's general policy. He did not want to present himself to the peoples previously subject to Darius as a conqueror, but as the new emperor, the successor to Darius. Temples and systems of worship could continue to live as they had in the past. Alexander's wrath fell in all its fierceness only on the few cities that refused his rule, and the harshness of the treatment reserved for Tyre and Samaria was meant to serve as a warning for anyone who did not wish to accept his magnanimity.

After Alexander's death in 323 BCE many armies must have crossed

Palestine, given the intense warfare promoted by Ptolemy I, who had taken over Egypt. Ptolemy's armies, though, traveled along the coast and Jerusalem does not seem to have felt the effects of such movements. The continuous wars on what had been the territory of Alexander's empire must have had a negative effect on the economy, but here again perhaps Jerusalem was less affected than other cities. Jerusalem's character as a closed city led it to be poor, but autonomous. Furthermore, Egypt, on which Jerusalem depended, was not invaded by foreign armies during the third century BCE and was the most prosperous of the Hellenistic states.

In 312 Ptolemy defeated Demetrius Poliorcetes at Gaza and as a result the former's dominion of Palestine was unquestioned. Jerusalem had not taken a stance favourable to Ptolemy and, probably following the victory at Gaza, he easily conquered Jerusalem attacking it on the sabbath.[2]

At first there was a deportation (Josephus, *Ant.* 12.7). Later, the generally good conditions of the deportees led to Jewish immigration and the foundation of a sizeable and flourishing colony in Alexandria. It is possible that the Jews deported to Egypt found the land of exile agreeable, since a Jewish community made up of Jewish soldiers that had joined Alexander already existed in Alexandria. Alexander had rewarded them by allowing that they 'live in the city with rights equal to those of the Greeks' (Josephus, *War* 2.487). The state ruled over by the Ptolemies was unified, and it was also stronger and richer than the other states that had been born from the splintering of Alexander's empire. This favourable situation benefited the Jewish community, which also maintained close ties with the homeland, as did all Jewish communities of the Diaspora. This community had, however, inserted a new element into Judaism, the spread of the custom of accepting new people, who were not of Jewish descent, into the community. These people were the so-called *prosēlutoi*, the 'added ones'. This meant abandoning Nehemiah and Ezra's policy of closure to the non-Jewish world in favour of a more universalistic vision in line with the experiences of the Early

---

2.   See *Ant.* 12.4-5, where Josephus quotes Agatharchides, a Greek chronicler active in the second century BCE who lived at the Ptolemaic court. For the quotation of Agatharchides, see also *Apion* 1.205. Ptolemy I's conquest of Jerusalem is also mentioned by Appian, *Hist. Rom.* 11.50.5. It could be on this occasion that many Jews went to Alexandria (Josephus, *Apion* 1.186, who quotes Hecataeus of Abdera, a historian living at the time of the first Ptolemies).

Zadokite period, experiences which could not have been entirely vain. The religious environment of Alexandria could also have been favourable to the universalistic elements intrinsic to the Jewish religion.

It is difficult to explain just exactly what drew the pagans toward Yhwh, but the phenomenon's causes should be sought among a variety of factors. First of all, however, they should be sought in the complex sensitivity of the Hellenistic man who, especially if of Greek origin, was abandoning the traditional religion in favour of the so-called mysterious religions. This phenomenon of religious renewal did not only concern the Greeks. Ptolemy I favoured a new religion in Egypt, that of the god Serapis, alongside the traditional Egyptian religion and which was to spread even outside Egypt. In order to establish worship of the new religion Ptolemy called, together with the Egyptian Manetho, the Greek Timotheus, a Eumolpid of Eleusis.[3]

On a human level, the greatest distinguishing factor between the new Hellenistic religions and the classical ones, whether Greek or Jewish, was the image of life after death. Whether the soul went to Hades or to Sheol, it descended into a lightless world, a world with no joy, no activity, no life, and in the end with no God. The new religions promised humans a happy immortality. The soul is no longer a copy of the human destined to live a non-life in the underworld. The soul now represents a real dimension of humanity, already charged with the instruments determining his eternal destiny. The soul can by its very nature contemplate God, unlike the body, which maintains the ancient human's reduced capacities, the human who was destroyed by the presence of the divine.

While these religions promising eternal happiness for their followers grew rapidly beginning with the third century BCE, that does not mean that they originated during that century. In fact, Orphism had long existed in Greece and the West, offering its followers the possibility, through purificatory rites that they had to undergo, of avoiding descent into the mud of the underworld. Ideas of this type had even begun to circulate in Jerusalem at an unknown date, but certainly before Hellenism. These ideas were influenced both by beliefs from Greece and from Egypt, the ideas of the existence of an immortal soul and a final judgment of humans after death being long accepted in the latter. Judaism was slow to absorb this new spirituality, which must have been taken

---

3. See Cumont, *Les religions orientales*, p. 71.

up at first by a minority whose characteristics are impossible to establish. The oldest source documenting belief, among Jews, in an immortal soul, separable from the body and destined to live near God after being judged, is the *Book of Watchers*, composed before 200 BCE, and more probably, in my opinion, during the late Persian period. The books of the Jewish canon never speak of the immortality of the soul; Qohelet even denies it (Eccl. 3.18-21). The belief in an immortal soul returns, however, in the book of Wisdom and in abundance in the writings of the first century of the Christian era.

Belief in resurrection developed in Israel at roughly the same time as belief in the immortality of the soul, or not long afterward. While on a descriptive level the two beliefs are quite different one from the other, as conceptual structures of religious thought they have an identical function; both permit humans to overcome the difficulties related to the lack of terrestrial retribution for the righteous, a problem felt deeply by some Jews of the Late Zadokite period (see the books of Job and Qohelet).

The Alexandrine atmosphere must have been particularly favourable for the development of religious interests and this must have favoured the encounter and exchange between Judaism and other religions. Judaism was especially well-prepared for such an encounter, especially among those people who valued the importance of ethics in religious discourse. Furthermore, Jewish monotheism must have provided considerable material for reflection among those who no longer understood the old classical religions and were drawn to contemplate the origin of things and to reflect on ethics solely through human powers—through philosophy. Alongside such problematics, motives with a completely different matrix could also have favoured an approach to Judaism. One of these motives could have been economic, given the fact that the Jewish community was particularly prosperous and enjoyed the same rights as the Greeks, the victors.

The acceptance of a number of proselytes together with the fact that Greek was spoken in Alexandria combined to lead to the use of Greek as the common language of the Jewish community in Alexandria. Furthermore, the very fact that the community was permitted to govern itself with its own laws allows us to believe the information given in the *Letter of Aristeas* that it had been one of the Ptolemies (probably Ptolemy II Philadelphus) who had ordered that the Law be translated into Greek (Artaxerxes had had it translated into Aramaic for the same reasons). The Greek translation of the Pentateuch dates to this period.

The community in Alexandria played a very important role in Judaism's development. It was a powerful community, open to Hellenistic influences given the fact that it was surrounded by Hellenic peoples. Most of all, though, it was important because it seems to have lived in contrast to a certain underlying direction given to Judaism in Jerusalem as desired by Nehemiah. This contrast is attested to by the acceptance of large numbers of proselytes in Alexandria.

There is the impression that Jerusalem continued to be the closed and sacred city that Nehemiah and Ezra had wanted, and that the Ptolemies respected Jerusalem's desire to remain isolated. Many cities grew up in Palestine during the Ptolemaic period, and many ancient cities were revived, often under new names. Rabbath became Philadelphia and was an important Ptolemaic fortification against eventual enemies from the East. The ruins of a theatre built there can still be seen. Accho became Ptolemais and a Philoteria rose where the Jordan receives the waters from the lake of Tiberias. This was the time in which the cities that were to become the Decapolis developed. In some way, Jerusalem too must have participated in the wealth developed in the Ptolemaic state. That does not change the fact, however, that Jerusalem refused the cultural ferment of Hellenism, since not one building characteristic of Hellenistic culture was erected in the city during this period.

From his archives, it is interesting to follow the trip undertaken across Palestine by Zeno, a high-ranking royal functionary, between the years 260 and 258 BCE. His travels began in Gaza and extended to Ammanitis, clearly following the road passing through Jerusalem, then turning north toward the Decapolis and from there toward the coast at Ptolemais and then back down along the coast to Gaza. In this broad tour he does not seem to have had any contact with the authorities of Jerusalem. He did, however, have contact with a man of probable Jewish origin, at least a man with a good Yahwistic name, Tobiah (= Yhwh is good), who lived in a fortified place that Josephus calls Tyre (*Ant.* 12.233). From this place Tobiah exercised firm control over the region, considering the fact that he was the one who collected the taxes that Jerusalem owed the Ptolemies. This Tobiah lived in the same place where his family had exercised their power for centuries, and was certainly a descendant of the Tobiah whom Nehemiah had chased out of the Temple of Jerusalem. From the Preisigke papyrus no. 6709 (= *Zeno* 3) it appears that he had a contingent of Egyptian soldiers at his disposition and could even address the king with a certain familiarity, or at least with direct language. He was, therefore, a functionary recognized by Egypt, who collected taxes on behalf of the Ptolemies. Tobiah's sphere of influence must have been extremely vast. From the breadth of his authority (Zeno deals with him and not with the priesthood in all questions regarding Palestine) we can deduce that he acted as governor of Palestine, even though there are no documents precisely stating this. At any rate, Tobiah was related to the high priest in Jerusalem, having married the daughter of the high priest Onias II (*Ant.* 12.160).

The problem of a 'lay' authority alongside that of the priesthood is thus posed anew. If the authenticity of the seals discovered and published by Avigad, from which it is possible to reconstruct a series of Jewish governors in Jerusalem for the Persian period, should be confirmed, then we could consider the idea of a duplicity of power as typical of the entire period of the Second Temple, a fact that would be very important for understanding the history of the Hasmonaeans.

At any rate, Hellenism was at Jerusalem's gates. The Jews of Alexandria became aware of the values of the Western culture and sought contact with it. As we shall see, if for no other reason they sought contact with it in order to defend the originality of their own culture, or rather, in the mentality of the day, to demonstrate that the values that had been realized in Greek culture in reality had originated in Jewish civilization. It was inevitable that sooner or later the Jewish tradition should meet the new ideas from the West, and that one of two possible outcomes from such an encounter was possible: synthesis, or a clearer and clearer Jewish consciousness of their singularity in history. We shall return to this in the following pages. For the moment, though, I shall turn my attention to the Jewish civilization of the period as it appears in its most representative texts: first of all the *Book of Watchers* and the *Book of Astronomy*, both of them from the Enochic tradition which can be considered to lie at the root of apocalyptic literature, or perhaps to be an early phase of it. I shall then examine the work of the Chronicler (fourth century BCE, to be distinguished from the redactor), the book of Job and that of Qohelet (Ecclesiastes; third century BCE).[4]

---

4.   For a complete vision of the Ptolemaic state, see M. Rostovzeff, *Social and Economic History of the Hellenistic World* (Oxford: Clarendon Press, 3rd edn, 1954); in particular, with regards to Judaea.

The particular conditions of Judaea during the Hellenistic Diaspora raises many questions that remain to be approached adequately. Concerning proselytism, see

2. General Outline of Late Zadokite Thought

In spite of the fact that works such as that of the Chronicler show clear political interests, the works attributable to this period are difficult to place in the context of political history given the scarcity of information. In order to evaluate fully the political content of these works a simple approximate date is not enough; it would be necessary to know internal lines of political division as well as the nature of external support. These elements are completely unknown.

That does not mean, however, that broad trends in the history of thought cannot be drawn from the surviving works. A first line of thought is that developing the ideology of Nehemiah. This line is documented in the book of the Chronicles. While the author seems to give new form and impulse to the ideal of the Davidic state, this is done entirely within the ideology of Nehemiah and Deuteronomy. History is understood in the light of the principle of retribution, and Jewish history is the history of the Jews of the state of Judah who all went into exile with Nebuchadnezzar's conquest. The book of the Chronicler can

H.H. Rowley, 'Jewish Proselyte Baptism and Christian Origins', in *idem*, *From Moses to Qumran* (London: Lutterworth, 1964), pp. 211-35 (taken from *HUCA* 15 [1940], pp. 313-34); P.G. Bricchi, 'I proseliti' (unpublished dissertation, Turin, 1974); L. Troiani, *Due studi di storiografia e religione antiche* (Como: New Press, 1988), as well as K. Kuhn, 'προσήλυτος', in *TWNT*, IV, pp. 727-45, with the bibliography. Regarding the difficulties encountered in approaching this type of problem, see J. Le Moyne, *RevQ* 7 (1970), pp. 434-38. On the problem of proselytes in general terms, see also F. Siegert, 'Gottesfürtige und Sympatisanten', *JSJ* 4 (1973), pp. 109-68.

On the information given in the *Letter of Aristeas* and Ptolemaic initiative, see P. Sacchi, 'Il testo dei Settanta nella problematica più recente', *Atene e Roma*, NS 9 (1964), pp. 145-58, and relative bibliography. On the text of Lucian within the tradition of the LXX, see D. Barthélemy, *Les dévanciers d'Aquila* (Leiden: E.J. Brill, 1963), p. 127 and *passim*; see also P. Sacchi, Review article of Barthélemy's book, *Atene e Roma*, NS 10 (1965), pp. 135-40.

On the cities of the Decapolis, it can be said that these were cities belonging to a territory with vague boundaries located in the northeastern part of Palestine, lying on both banks of the Jordan. Most of these cities lay to the east of the Jordan and the lake of Tiberias. The Hellenistic origin of these cities led them to oppose both the Maccabees and the Hasmonaeans. Pompey recognized their independence from Jerusalem. The principal cities of the Decapolis were Scythopolis (to the west of the Jordan), Gadara, Pella and Gerasa; at least for a time, Damascus too was part of the Decapolis.

be considered representative of the ideas of the dominant class in Jerusalem.

At the current stage of our research, refusing the traditional interpretations of Ezra, although without having found a new and convincing interpretative scheme, it is difficult to assign a sure setting to the figure considered the founder of the most recent form of Judaism. His work is to be placed in line with that of Nehemiah, though the two differ considerably in the fact that Ezra places the Law rather than the Covenant at the centre of Judaism.

Some works from the previous period had opposed the basic ideas of this society and depicted a God of Israel caring for the other peoples with the same love with which he followed Israel, thus diminishing the importance of descendence from the kingdom of Judah or the exile (the book of Jonah). As for David, the founder of the eternal dynasty, he may not have had all those Jewish ancestors that the Chronicler seems to have considered essential. In the strictest sense he may not have even been a real Jew at all (the book of Ruth).

Even the question of divine retribution, considered the motive force in history by the Chronicler, was not universally seen in such clear terms as the Chronicler would have liked. Things were much more complicated than contemporary common opinion held. God does not always repay good works with happiness, nor evil with misfortune. To humans, his intervention in history seems arbitrary, just as his behaviour towards the individual seems arbitrary (Job and Ecclesiastes).

The current of thought containing the most discordant elements with respect to the majority of works is that beginning with the *Book of Watchers*. This can be taken to represent the first layer of Jewish apocalyptic literature. Here we are presented with such a different cultural world that it is hard to imagine what sort of political or even spatial relationship could have existed between it and the world of Jerusalem. It was certainly the product of educated circles, where astronomy was well known and where ancient traditions were gathered and developed in the light of the requirements of recent thought.

Contacts with the Mesopotamian world have been placed in evidence,[5] but even these are of a different nature than those of the dominant tendency in Jerusalem. Even some Egyptian influences can be

---

5.   See VanderKam, *Enoch and the Growth of an Apocalyptic Tradition*.

perceived (for example the immortality of the soul and the West as the place where the souls of the dead gather). In the case of the books of Ruth, Jonah, Job and Ecclesiastes, there are clear points of contrast with the dominant ideas, while in the case of the *Book of Watchers* there is no particular point of the dominant doctrine that is contested. We are faced with a completely different religious and cultural phenomenon.

3. *Ezra*

It is clear from the conclusions reached above (chapter 4, §1, pp. 130-35) that the historical figure of Ezra should be sought and interpreted on the basis of the texts that served as the sources for 1 Esdras (= 1E). These sources should therefore be read outside the context of 1E's ideology and even more so outside of that of the biblical book of Ezra.

From a passage of a source used by 1E (8.5) and maintained by Ezra (7.6-7), we learn that Ezra came to Jerusalem in the seventh year of an Artaxerxes, taken by most to be Artaxerxes II. From a reading of the entire text it would seem that Ezra's works did not have any immediate practical consequences, so much so that Smith[6] even speaks of his failure.

Ezra is presented as a priest and scribe who is also an expert in the Law issued by the God of Israel (1E 8.3). As a whole his ideology fits well into the general framework of Late Zadokitism and stands out only for having emphasized the centrality of the Law rather than the Covenant. This means that he had re-evaluated the Judaism of Ezekiel and of the Priestly Code over that of Deuteronomy and Nehemiah.[7] He did, however, accept the idea of segregation, radicalizing it even further, but his Judaism was centred around the Law, not the Covenant.

This could appear relatively unimportant since the Law was seen as the whole of the clauses making up the Covenant, in other words as the expression of the Covenant. In fact, it could have seemed of little importance to contemporaries, who at the most were interested in the

---

6. See Smith, *Palestinian Parties*, pp. 121-22.

7. See Cazelles, 'La mission d'Esdras'. The thesis that the Priestly Code was brought to Jerusalem only in 398 no longer seems acceptable today, though it does seem certain that Ezra is to be placed in line with the Priestly Code and Nehemiah following Deuteronomy. Some of the passages quoted by Cazelles as belonging to the law of Deuteronomy could also belong to the law of the Priestly Code.

contents of the Law. See, for example, the scene of the reading of the Law in 1E 9.37-55, placed by the author of Ezra in chapter 8 of the book of Nehemiah. Ezra's interest in the Law, though, should be seen in the light of the importance attributed to the fact that the Law that he brought to Jerusalem as 'promulgated by the God of Israel' (as emphasized by the text) had been approved by the Great King.

The Great King had accepted that the Law of Ezra be the law by which the Jews were to live. Persia accepted and, in reality, imposed a certain legislation on Judah. An event of this kind could lead to some new developments, but instead it blocked, or at least aimed at blocking, the social and political situation in Jerusalem, because from that moment onward the Law of God (that is the Jewish Law) was also the law of the king, guaranteed and imposed by Persia.

In this context the Law could no longer be seen as an expression of the Covenant. This was a political position, though, not a theoretical one. It was not possible to accept the Law as 'guaranteed' by the Great King and at the same time present it as the expression of God's Covenant. It is interesting to note, however, that the text of 1E insists that the Law had been promulgated by God (1E 8.3; Ezra 7.6). Nehemiah's position had been one of substantial autonomy, at least as far as internal administration was concerned; Ezra's, in contrast, was not.

> This is a copy of the letter which King Artaxerxes gave to Ezra the priest, the scribe, learned in matters of the commandments of Yhwh and his statutes for Israel: 'Artaxerxes, king of kings, to Ezra the priest, the scribe of the law of God of heaven. And now I make a decree that any one of the people of Israel or their priests or Levites in my kingdom, who freely offers to go to Jerusalem, may go with you. For you are sent by the king and his seven counselors to make inquiries about Judah and Jerusalem according to the law of your God, which is in your hand... Whatever is commanded by the God of heaven, let it be done in full for the Temple of the God of heaven, lest his wrath be against the realm of the king and his sons. We also notify you that it shall not be lawful to impose tribute, custom, or toll upon any one of the priests, the Levites, the singers, the doorkeepers, the Temple servants, or other servants of the Temple of God.
> 'And you, Ezra, according to the wisdom of your God which is in your hand, appoint magistrates and judges who may judge all the people in the province Beyond the River [i.e. west of the Euphrates], all such as know the laws of your God; and those who do not know them, you shall teach. Whoever will not obey the law of your God and the law of the king, let judgment be strictly executed upon him, whether for death or

for banishment or for confiscation of his goods or for imprisonment'
(Ezra 7.11-26).

Some points of this letter are of interest. The Law of Yhwh was to be imposed on all the Jews living west of the Euphrates. The law, therefore, was not only valid territorially, but within a certain space it was valid ethnically. In a way Artaxerxes' provision echoed the previous Persian provision regarding Zerubbabel who, besides the title of governor-king of Judah had also been given the title 'governor of the Jews'. The idea of a greater Israel stretching from the Euphrates to the sea, as in Josh. 1.4, a text by R1,[8] must have been derived from provisions such as these.

The situation was charged with ambiguity. For the Jews, the Persian king had accepted the Law of the Jewish God and had made himself its guarantor and protector. The Persians, however, must have seen the situation differently; they had accepted a law which was valid only inasmuch as they had approved it. But then again, some ambiguity must have existed even within the Jewish conception of the 'Law guaranteed by the king'. What would a change in the king's attitude have meant? What value did the king's will hold for the Jews? These are no small questions. In the book of Jeremiah, which had already entered into the tradition, it was written that sovereignty had left Jerusalem (Jer. 27.6), and Deutero-Isaiah had considered Cyrus anointed by God (Isa. 45.1). Such prophetic words could make outside intervention on the community more acceptable, but the idea that a number of things depended on outside events and provisions had begun to creep into people's conscience as well. This type of psychological condition was to pose a threat to Jewish society when imperial authority changed. From the postexilic point of view, just as sovereignty had passed from the Jewish kings to the Oriental kings, first the Babylonians and then the Persians, it could pass yet again into different hands. And couldn't new rulers have different desires and still represent the authority chosen by God?

On the one hand Ezra's works can appear closed within the narrow horizons of a rigid nationalism aimed at conserving the ethnic aspect of the Jewish people through the systematic application of the Torah. By the same means certain interests, and not only economic ones, of the Jews of the Diaspora were safeguarded, making Jerusalem more open

8.   See Sacchi, 'Giosuè 1, 1-9.

to the Jew living in faraway lands than to the alien living in Judah. On the other hand his works also contemplated future developments. Ezra realized that the majority of Jerusalem's population, made up of returned exiles who were used to speaking Aramaic, no longer understood the Hebrew language. Instead of going into a rage as Nehemiah had done (Neh. 13.24), he allowed the sacred texts to be translated into Aramaic, and perhaps not only oral translations.

Orally a translation was made on the day of solemn reading of the Torah (1E 9.48 ἐμφυσιοῦντες τὴν ἀνάγνωσιν 'explaining the reading' = Neh. 8.8 unclear). This explanation for the returned exiles presupposes a translation, even though it is not explicitly stated. This way of treating the Scripture, beginning with the text as it had been handed down by the tradition and rereading it in the light of what today we would call 'recent theological speculation' was to become typical of the later Jewish tradition, which made use of Aramaic translations in order to express its speculations and reflections. The *targumim*, especially the more ancient ones (see the *Targum Neofiti*), more than a translation represent a true work of interpretation in the light of the principles of the day.

The author of 1E used documents regarding Ezra in order to write a very complex story in which Ezra is only the third of three great figures, after Josiah and Zerubbabel. His story began with the Passover of Josiah and ended with the death of Ezra, today lost in 1E, but conserved in a summary by Josephus.[9] The sense of the work is to be found precisely in this beginning and end. Ezra was the heir to the Judaism of Josiah and Zerubbabel. This was in contrast to the Zadokitism of the transitional years between the Persian and Hellenistic periods. The centre of the state is to be found in the priesthood and the Temple, considered the direct heirs of the Davidic dynasty and the Davidic dynasty had been great because it had instituted the liturgy. Just as with the Chronicler, the author of 1E continues to see Israel as in some way a monarchy. He therefore allows no place in his work for Nehemiah, who depended on the Deuteronomic and republican tradition and was more desirous of controlling the Temple than of being controlled by it.

The author of Ezra, on the other hand, no longer sees Ezra as Nehemiah's antagonist, but as his guide and inspiration. This was a simple way of affirming the superiority of Ezra's Judaism over that of Nehe-

---

9.   See Sacchi, *Apocrifi*, I, p. 114.

miah. Apparently the figure of Nehemiah had reached such a level of acceptance that it could not be ignored. In Ezra's work, Josiah disappears and Zerubbabel is given a greatly reduced role. In this way two elements disappear, the sense of a dark age of Judaism following Zerubbabel and the importance of the Davidic dynasty's continuity. What interests the author of Ezra is simply seeing in Ezra a figure who had proposed a Judaism centred around the Law rather than the Covenant. At the time of the rupture between the Pharisees and the Hasmonaeans, the Pharisees considered the Covenant to be an expression of the bond between God and humans by way of the authority of the state. But the Pharisees wanted the centre of Judaism to be the Law, the eternal Law, to be distinguished from the state which pursued ends extraneous to the Law. In Ezra the Law is attributed absolute value.

Ezra's renown as a scribe is of late origin and derives from the epithet, 'a scribe skilled in the Law of Moses' (1E 8.3 = Ezra 7.6), which must have been the title given to him by the Great King, authorizing him to deal with the Law in Jerusalem. Beginning with the first century CE the Jewish tradition recalls Ezra as the scribe *par excellence*, and the first organization of the sacred books was attributed to him. See 4 Ezra 14.37-47, where the story is told that he put all the canonical and apocryphal writings in order.

Regarding the relationship between the two languages spoken by the Jews, Hebrew and Aramaic, until recently Aramaic tended to be considered the language of the people and Hebrew the language only of the most educated class. Besides the fact that only the educated would have been able to read and write Hebrew, today the opposite seems more likely, that is that Hebrew was the language spoken by the people and Aramaic the language of the upper class. According to the tradition, the Jews who returned to Palestine with Ezra were the first who needed to hear the Scripture in Aramaic. And they certainly were not the lowest class of the population.[10]

10. On the problem of bilinguism in middle Judaism, see the recent works: P. Lapide, 'Insights from Qumran into the Language of Jesus', *RevQ* 8 (1975), pp. 483-501; J.A. Soggin, 'Bilinguismo o trilinguismo nell'ebraismo postesilico: Il caso dell'aramaico e del greco', *VO* 3 (1980), pp. 209-23; P. Capelli, 'L'aramaico e l'ebraico tra il II e il III secolo secondo una fonte rabbinica e una cristiana', *EVO* 14-15 (1991–92), pp. 159-62.

4. *The Enochic Current, the Origins of Apocalyptic Literature and the Book of Watchers*

In 1976 Milik published the many large Aramaic fragments of the so-called *1 Enoch*.[11] This is a fundamental date in the history of studies on Apocalyptic; Milik dated one fragment to the middle of the second century BCE, and another as far back as the third century BCE.[12] As a result the dates previously assigned to the book of *1 Enoch*, 170 BCE for the oldest part and the end of the first century BCE for the most recent, can no longer be maintained. Since *1 Enoch* is usually considered an Apocalyptic work, this has also had consequences on our ways of thinking about the history of Apocalyptic; it must be more ancient than we once thought and its origins can be found in identifiable works. The *Book of Watchers* and the *Book of Astronomy* must necessarily be dated to the beginning of the Late Zadokite period. Since these are both very dense works as far as the thought contained is concerned, and especially the first of the two, this has led to the need to re-examine

11. The book of *1 Enoch* (*1 En.*) is a collection of five books composed in distinct periods, very distant from one another, together with an introduction and some appendices.

Chs. 1–5:	Introduction: this is not the introduction to all the Enochic pentateuch, because it was already extant in the second century BCE.
Chs. 6-36:	*Book of Watchers* (fourth century BCE).
Chs. 37–71:	*Book of Parables* (late first century BCE), the latest book of the collection, inserted in replacement of the previous *Book of Giants* which had been removed for theological reasons, perhaps because it defended the possibility of the devil's conversion.
Chs. 72–82:	*Book of Astronomy*, belonging to the same period as the *Book of Watchers*.
Chs. 83–90:	*Book of Dreams*, dated around 160 BCE.
Chs. 91–104:	*Epistle of Enoch*, dated to the first century BCE, certainly before 40 BCE.
Chs. 105–108:	late appendices.

The layers of *BW* are thus indicated: *BW* 1a(α) = chs. 6–7; *BW* 1aβ = ch. 8; *BW* 1b = chs. 9–11; *BW* 2a = chs. 12–16; *BW* 2bα = chs. 17–19, 21–22; *BW* 2bβ = ch. 20; *BW* 2c = chs. 23–36. See Sacchi, *Jewish Apocalyptic and its History*.

12. The fragment 4QEn[a] contains the fragmentary Aramaic text from 1.1 to 12.6. In other words, it contains the introduction and first chapters of the *Book of Watchers*. It has been dated to the first half of the second century BCE.

The fragment 4QEnASTR[a] contains parts of chs. 76–82 of the BA and has been dated to the end of the third century BCE.

the history of the development of Judaic thought during the entire period of the Second Temple in the light of the new dates assigned to these books.

Let us begin by presenting the most original ideas expressed in the *Book of Watchers*. The book's position in the history of Jewish thought will emerge from this analysis. As far as the labels assigned to the book are concerned (apocalyptic, Enochic, etc.), we shall deal with them only after having examined the thought expressed in the book. In the end it is only a problem of a name, and therefore not a very important problem. Names have a way, however, of hiding interpretations of history and it is because of this that it is useful to discuss them.

There are two important novelties introduced by the *Book of Watchers* into the history of Jewish thought and religion. The first of these is the idea that evil is not of human origin, and the second is that of the immortality of the soul where the soul is conceived of as an entity capable of living, disembodied, after the death of the body and in a dimension where evil does not exist. The book's interests, however, are centred around the problem of evil. Numerous explanations are given for this problem, but they all revolve around a single point of encounter; evil derives from a first transgression which took place in a higher sphere than that of human beings.

The book is characterized by a highly complex stratification, individuated in part on a purely formal level, and in part on an ideological basis. The book is the further development of a pre-existing work known in antiquity as the *Book of Noah*, containing a narration of the events leading up to the flood, events which took place during the last two or three generations before the flood. The book tells the story of some angels who descended to earth because they were inflamed with passion for women (chs. 6–7 [*BW* 1aα]). Creatures called the *nephilim* were born from the union of these angels with women. *Nephilim* was translated into Greek as *gigantes* and subsequently transcribed into modern languages as giants. These *giants* were monstrous creatures who filled the earth with mourning. These two chapters of the original *Book of Noah* were maintained with no particular interpretations.

Chapter 8 (*BW* 1aβ) is basically a parenthesis in the structure of the book as it stands today. It explains that the fallen angels damaged humanity by revealing heavenly secrets to men, those secrets being the sciences and techniques, including astronomy which was then to become the basis of all real knowledge.

Chapters 9–11 develop the ideas contained in all the preceding part. The author surely knew *BW* 1aβ, because the cause of evil is identified in the revelation of heaven's secrets, but in substance he continues the narration of *BW* 1aα. Thus *BW* 1 is the work of a single author who composed his text on the basis of the *Book of Noah*, but who already adapted it to his own ideas by the necessary insertions. Four archangels, hearing humanity's cries of suffering at the hands of the giants, invoked God to put an end to such evil. God then decided to send the flood on the earth. The text speaks of the souls of men (*1 En.* 9.3) and the souls of the dead (*1 En.* 9.10), but the latter term is a modification of the original, because the context is incompatible with the idea of 'disembodied souls' and clearly indicates that we are still dealing with living men.

First, however, before sending the flood, God ordered the archangel Raphael to close up the angel Asael,[13] who had led the revolt, underground, in the darkness together with the other rebellious angels. In some other passages the angel leading the rebellion is referred to as Semeyaza, thus confirming the duality of sources mentioned earlier. Furthermore, God ordained that the offspring of the union between angels and women should exterminate one another in fratricidal wars.

Up until this point the book's narrative presents the events as though it were a historical account. Beginning with ch. 12, however, the figure of Enoch is introduced as the author recounting his own personal experience 'with the saints and the watching angels' (clearly not the fallen ones) in the first person. While it is not explicitly stated at the outset, it is clear that Enoch's narrative concerns visions that he has had (see 13.8-9; 14.4). A typical section (*BW* 2), based on a different type of knowledge than that of the previous section, begins with ch. 12. Both heavenly and earthly matters can be known only by way of celestial visions or through directly hearing what angelic beings say.

---

13. Both the Greek and Ethiopic texts give this angel the name Azazel, while the name Asael derives from the Aramaic fragments. The lesson of Azazel seems to be a *lectio facilior* due to the influence of the name of the biblical demon mentioned in Lev. 16.8, 10. Deiana, however, has recently argued, convincingly, that it is possible that the historical process be the contrary (G. Deiana, 'Azazel in Lev. 16', *Lateranum* 54 [1988], pp. 16-33).

Section *BW* 2 can be divided into three parts, probably written each one posterior to the preceding part. This is particularly true of the last part (*BW* 2c). The author of chs. 12–16 firmly believes in the disembodied soul and the corrections to the text of *BW* 1 leading in this direction are to be attributed to him. This emerges from the way in which he develops the preceding narrative. It was true that the giants had disappeared from the earth, but not their souls, which, inasmuch as they were souls, were not mortal. The origin of evil is no longer attributed to the unveiling of heavenly secrets, nor is it seen as a simple consequence of the giants' wickedness. It is associated with a very complex category which was destined to be developed more fully later, concerning a relationship between purity and impurity, a relationship whose limits are not clear, but that rests on a very firm foundation.[14] The fallen angels had been made impure through their contact with the women, changing the natural order (see 12.4 and mostly 15.3-4). The fact that the giants' souls were still wandering the earth perfectly explained both the existence of evil spirits, that the author most certainly believed in, and the misadventures of humans attributed to those evil spirits.

> Why have you left the glorious and holy heaven and lain with the daughters of men…acted like the sons of the earth and generated giants? You, spiritual beings, saints, living eternal life, have committed impurity on the women…have done as do the men of flesh and blood, who are mortal and destructible. For this I gave them women… (*1 En.* [*BW*] 15.3-4).

The grandiose construction of *BW* 2a had the great defect of following a mythical type of logic, which was little understood in its day and which perhaps even the author had not conceived in mythical terms, but rather in historical terms. How was it possible that the origin of evil derived from events which had taken place only shortly before the flood? How was Cain's sin to be explained (*1 En.* 22.7), if it had come about before the fall?

BW 2b (chs. 17–22, with the parenthesis of ch. 20, which can be referred to as *BW* 2bβ) addresses these obvious questions. This section contains a description of both a cosmic and terrestrial 'beyond'. Enoch

---

14. This connection between evil and impurity can be found in some biblical passages as well. In particular see Gen. 3.14 (the serpent was condemned to slither on its belly, thus originally it walked on four legs and its impurity was therefore a condemnation). See below Chapter 17 §4, pp. 448-49.

envisions the great cosmic void where God relegated the first seven angels who transgressed against him when on the fourth day of the creation they carried the stars assigned to them outside of their preordained orbit (*1 En.* 18.12; 15; 21.6). The effort to make the necessities of thought and the day's scientific knowledge coincide are clear. The transgression of the angels at the beginning of time (the day of the stars' creation) brought about an alteration of the influence exercised by the stars on the earth; these were not as God had intended them. The contribution of contemporary science to this solution concerning the origin of evil is interesting. In this way the malign influence of the stars was explained.

The souls of the dead gather in some valleys of the extreme West where the good are separated from the evil following criteria which are not clarified. Here there is a source of life composed of 'water of light'. What clearly distinguishes the larvae (*'obot*) of the biblical tradition from the souls (also called 'spirits') of the *Book of Watchers* is that the larvae were all destined to the Sheol, the underworld, without being judged. All of them, both the good and the wicked, were to live the same life, sorrowful because without light. The souls of the *Book of Watchers* on the other hand go to a place where they are separated one from the other, the good from the wicked. They are therefore judged, and sent to opposite destinies.

A reaction to such revolutionary ideas can be found in the canonical book of Genesis and, in a way tending toward conciliation, in the final stratum of the *Book of Watchers* (chs. 23–36 = *BW 2c*).

The reaction in Genesis is extremely clear. At the beginning of ch. 6 the author summarizes the entire story of the fallen angels in only four verses. According to Genesis the giants never existed, or rather, they were merely 'heroes of ancient times'. This is a demythicizing interpretation of the story following a method similar to that of the Greek philosopher Euemerus. The ancient myth is not destroyed through its historicization (see the way that Genesis treats the creation myths), but through its reduction to simply an aetiological legend.[15]

A reaction against the ideas of the third and fourth strata of the *Book of Watchers* (*BW 2a* and *b*) can be found in the final stratum of the work. While the third and fourth strata concentrate their gaze beyond

15. See Sacchi, 'Historicizing and Revelation at the Origins of Judaism', in *Jewish Apocalyptic and its History*, pp. 200-10.

this world, the final one (*BW* 2*c*) looks to the earth in an attempt to blend the ideas of the first strata, as they had been received, with certain underlying tendencies of Judaism. The author of the fifth stratum has the Great Judgment in mind, but he places it in a temporal and historical context. His Great Judgment is therefore different from that of his predecessor and he is perfectly aware of this fact. This is a clear sign that he knew the work and intended to correct it, without, however, eliminating it. This work had apparently already become part of an established tradition.

The author innovates and completes. In some part of the cosmos a 'tree of life' already exists, that no one can touch until the moment for the Great Judgment arrives (*1 En.* [*BW* 2*c*] 25.4). In that moment, though, the righteous, the humble and the elect will be able to eat of the fruit of life. But just who are the righteous who will be able to eat the fruit of life? If we read *BW* 2*c* as an autonomous text it would seem that we are dealing only with those who will be alive on the final day. If, however, we view this text as an appendix to the rest of the *Book of Watchers*, it follows that the righteous are the souls of those who live in the valleys of the West. Thus the souls will return to live on the earth where they will live long lives, as long as the first patriarchs and perhaps even longer (*1 En.* 25.6). Once the earth has been regenerated in this way, humans will no longer suffer 'sickness, affliction or scourge'. In the end, though, it seems that a definitive death awaits them.

In the very same moment that the author of the final part of *Book of Watchers* seems, at least following our logic, to eliminate the idea of immortality, he also introduces the concept of resurrection, at least in embryonic form. The idea that the souls can return to life, albeit on earth and for only a limited amount of time, contains the belief that souls can be re-embodied.

In the end, what holds all the strata of the *Book of Watchers* together, guaranteeing the possibility of attributing the works to the same current of thought is the problem of evil. Evil is not interpreted simply as transgression and the consequent manifestation of suffering, but as the fruit of some guilty action which took place above the sphere of humanity. For this reason, humans are more a victim of their own evil deeds than guilty of them.[16] In effect, even in the final stratum evil is something that must be eliminated by God; human justice is hardly enough. I feel

16. This is stated categorically in *BW* (*1 En.* 10.8). God says, 'The earth has been corrupted for having learned of Asael's actions. Ascribe all sin to him'.

that the work's unity and underlying motif should be identified type of solution to the problem of evil. If the work was retouche lengthened following a problematic that was being developed b its own right and in contact with traditional Jewish thought, tha only mean that we are dealing with a group whose thought was k on an established tradition. Compromises could be sought, but the ti tion could not be abandoned.

Another clear reaction to the Enochic current of thought can be fou in the work of Qohelet, writing probably in the second half of the thi century BCE. See, for example, the negation of immortality of the sou in Eccl. 3.18-21, the negation of the possibility of acquiring knowledg except through experience (and therefore an utterance against the see of Apocalyptic) in 5.7 and 6.9, and the negation of the Judgment as a consequence of a lack of belief in the soul's immortality or in resurrection in 2.14 and the following verses.

The *Book of Watchers*, therefore, marks the beginning of a current of thought in Judaism which from its very birth was hardly linear, but which seems to have put down strong roots. In fact, the ideas presented in the *Book of Watchers* were to spread in Israel and to constitute a series of problems: acceptance, refusal and re-elaboration. The very fact that this book was handed down to us as the first volume of a Pentateuch put together during the first century BCE clearly indicates that a tradition based on this work must have subsisted for centuries. This is the tradition commonly referred to as Apocalyptic, and that could also be called, at least in this phase, Enochic, given the fact that Enoch is the seer in these works. Of course, the idea of 'Apocalyptic' is much broader than that of the 'Enochic current' and is perhaps more representative of the common interpretation of the works of this current of thought. The term 'Enochic current', however, presents the opposite advantages, that of distancing itself from any and all interpretations that have been advanced regarding Apocalyptic. In effect, the very high dating of this work allows us to see what we call Apocalyptic from a different vantage point, and a new term could aid in avoiding confusion.

5. *The* Book of Astronomy

This work, too, was certainly written prior to the year 200 BCE. We possess an Ethiopic translation of this work which, in the light of the discovery of Aramaic fragments at Qumran, seems to have been merely a summary of the original text, which must have been deemed too long (and boring) to be conserved integrally. The book contains a description of the heavens and an explanation for all the celestial phenomena. Particular attention is paid to the problems of the calendar, discussed by Enoch who narrates what he has seen during his heavenly journey.

On the level of thought, the work's predeterminism is interesting (or is it divine foresight?). The laws of the cosmos and the history of all humankind and all individuals is written in the Heavenly Tables (*1 En.* 81.1-2). Predeterminism was to touch Qohelet as well (third century BCE) and affirm itself most of all in the thought underlying the Essene *Community Rule* where it is said that God created an angel of light and an angel of darkness, one to love and the other to hate (1QS 3.26–4.1). Essenism was to seek to affirm God's omnipotence at all costs, even at the cost of denying or limiting freedom of choice for humans and the angels. And the devil was created as such by God (1QS 3.18).

What unites the *Book of Astronomy* to the *Book of Watchers* so closely, though, beyond the fact that they were bound together in the same collection, a sign that during the first century BCE the two works were recognized as having a common matrix, is the problem of the origin of evil. Even though the moment of transgression is not indicated in the *Book of Astronomy*, it is said that many angels responsible for overseeing the stars carried them out of the orbits desired by God (80.6). The author, then, follows the line of thought set forth in *BW 2b*. The real existence of an Enochic tradition is well documented by the author's insistence on Enoch's obligation to write all that he had seen for his children (81.5-6), so that 'the good shall indicate righteousness for the good'.

But there is also another interpretation of the origin of evil to be found in the *Book of Astronomy*, an origin linked to human nature as a creature.

'Explain to your son Methuselah and show to all your children [that is, the heirs to the tradition] that none of those who are of the flesh are innocent before the Lord, because He created them' (85.5).

This is an idea similar to that found in the book of Job. On the lips of Eliphaz, one of Job's friends (4.17), the expression simply meant that God is perfect and therefore he is perfect in his justice, while humanity never is. But Job picks up on this idea in order to develop it further (chs. 9 and 14) in the sense that humans are conditioned by such an impurity that they are overwhelmed before God. This points to some degree of simultaneity between the final redaction of Job and the *Book of Astronomy*. Furthermore, even the author of Job knew the myth of the fallen angels and in a way used it in developing his thought (Job 4.18).

6. *The Chronicler and his Work*

Due to the presence of numerous contradictory, or at least apparently contradictory, elements the work of the Chronicler is difficult to interpret. It is also, however, the best tool for understanding the ideas of Jerusalem in the fourth century BCE.[17] Even with its contradictions, we can sustain that the underlying ideology of the work faithfully reflects the general framework of Late Zadokite society at the moment of its greatest affirmation, before internal opposition, such as the Enochic current, and political upheaval definitively altered its nature.

Beginning with the very origins of the world, the Chronicler narrated a history of Israel that completely ignored the kingdom of the North. The true remnant of Israel was in Judah; the Jews of the North had clearly been abandoned by God who had never allowed them to return to their homeland. The Chronicler had even cancelled out the Jews who had remained in the South after Nebuchadnezzar's conquest of Jerusalem. The text of 2 Chron. 36.20 is unequivocal; Nebuchadnezzar deported all the Jews who had survived the invasion. Therefore, only those who had returned from Babylon could be called Jews. Nehemiah's political choice thus found its historical justification.

During the fourth century Samaritan Judaism began to take root in the North. For centuries the Jews of Jerusalem were to nurture the most

---

17. The dating of the book of Chronicles to the fourth century is imposed most of all by the fact that the author knows the coins called 'Darics', in use during the period of Persian domination (1 Chron. 29.7). As concerns the genealogy of the Davidians, it should be pointed out that in the Hebrew text it contains 6 generations while the Greek text includes 11. At any rate, one text is certainly an ideological rewrite of the other, since the names are the same in both. Only the family bonds vary, resulting in a different number of generations. The original list of the book of Chronicles could also have easily been added to at a later date. In the light of the most recent research, I do not believe that the Chronicler is also the author of the books of Ezra and Nehemiah. See S. Japhet, 'The Supposed Common Authorship of Chronicles and Ezra–Nehemiah Investigated Anew', *VT* 18 (1968), pp. 330-71, and H. Williamson, *Ezra and Nehemiah* (Sheffield: JSOT Press, 1987).

profound disregard for the Samaritans, and through his work the Chronicler clarified the question; the Samaritans were not even Jews at all. One of the pre-Maccabaean sources used by Josephus has been called by Motzo the 'Sacerdotale-antisamaritana' (Antisamaritan-priestly) because of the derogatory way that the Jews of the North are presented. Ben-Sira was even to define them a 'non-people' (Sir. 50.25-26). It is clear that for the Chronicler a history of Israel, the real Israel, after the period of the unified kingdom could deal only with the state of Judah and, later, with the returned exiles.

Although the Chronicler wrote a history of Israel and of the world, his interests are political and ideological rather than historical. Had he been interested in history as such, he would have continued his account well after the edict of Cyrus, the last event narrated by the Chronicler, which he placed, in our terms, in 538 BCE. The Chronicler limited himself to following the principal historical thread as drawn out by R1. Up until Saul's reign historical progress is summarized by way of genealogies, a technique which is repeated for the periods following the Edict of Cyrus.

If, then, the Chronicler's work was essentially that of rewriting a pre-existing book, this means that he did not like the way his predecessor narrated history. We have already seen how the Chronicler cancelled from his history the Jews of the kingdom of the North along with the Jews that were not exiled after the Babylonian conquest. He reinterpreted the figure of David making him appear less the founder of the kingdom and more the one who had organized worship. In this way the great figure of David was conserved in his own tradition, at the same time placing the Temple at the centre of Judaism rather than the kingdom. This does not mean that the Chronicler did not consider David king: on the contrary, he was the king *par excellence*, the figure for all successive kings.

This caused some problems for understanding the Chronicler's political thought. David was the guide, *nagid*, of his people, chosen for that role by God. But not only was David Israel's guide (1 Chron. 28.4 and 2 Chron. 6.5-6), his successors were too: 'Don't you know that Yhwh, God of Israel, gave the kingship over Israel to David and his sons by an everlasting covenant?' (2 Chron. 13.5). The Chronicler was not at all bothered by the fact that these prophecies or divine promises had not been fulfilled or maintained. Apparently for him the kingdom of David was still in existence. In the eyes of the Chronicler Israel was still a monarchy, at least by right, even in his day. If the *Temple Scroll*, which dedicates a great deal of space to the rights and duties of the king, was written during the late Zadokite period, as seems more and more probable to me, then its legislation on the king can be taken as proof that the Chronicler's ideas were widespread and shared by much if not all of society in Jerusalem.

The promise of eternal reign to David is the obvious corollary to the problem of the continued existence of Israel's monarchical constitution. On this point the Chronicler made absolutely no changes to R1's old monarchical ideology. He presents this ideology in even clearer terms, eliminating, for example, all allusions to any possible guilt on the part of the future descendants of David, who were thus idealized by the Chronicler, who was well aware of the faults of the kings of Judah. If we compare the text of 1 Chron. 17.13 with 2 Sam. 7.14, which was its source, we find that the Chronicler has omitted the sentence, 'When he commits iniquity, I will punish him with a rod such as mortals use, with blows inflicted by human beings'. The promise of eternal reign was confirmed, not denied, by history. Taking up again the text of 1 Kgs 11.36 (= 2 Chron. 21.7) the Chronicler insists, in comparison to the text used as a source, on the everlasting nature of a lamp which was to shine eternally for the descendants of David. Again, in closing Solomon's prayer, in respect to the text of his source (1 Kgs 8.52-53), he explicitly adds mention of the 'privileges of David' as a guarantee of the eternal promise made to him: 'Remember the privileges of your servant David' (2 Chron. 6.42).

On the contrary, in narrating the events prior to the exile, on several occasions the Chronicler omits an expression dear to the author of the book of Kings, 'for the sake of David'. 'For I will defend this city to save it, for my own sake and for the sake of my servant David' reads 2 Kgs 19.34, but see also 1 Kgs 11.13, 32 and 2 Kgs 20.6. For the Chronicler, Nathan's prophecy and the doctrine of the 'privileges of David' did not refer to the history of Judah under the Davidic dynasty. For him they held a different value which regarded not only the past but also the present and the future. In other terms, the Chronicler interpreted the 'privileges of David' differently than R1.

In declaring that the privileges of David were stable and eternal even though they had passed from the king to the people, Deutero-Isaiah had already inaugurated a line of intellectual behaviour capable of strong future development while safeguarding certain traditional values. For the Chronicler the 'privileges of David' were a category which by divine will was still at work in history. It is not clear, though, just who the depository was.

The Chronicler interpreted history in light of a rigid application of the principle of retribution. He had accepted the Deuteronomic teaching that saw the principle of Israel's salvation essentially in observation of the Law. He therefore considered it scandalous that a wicked king like Manasseh (seventh century BCE) could live for so long without being punished by God. Thus he remedied the situation by imagining a belated conversion on the part of the king, suffering after deportation to Assyria (2 Chron. 33.11-13). By this time the retributive principle was a reality unto itself, rooted in the author's mind and perhaps in the minds of most of his contemporaries in Palestine, with a force capable of making it a concrete reality just like any other element of daily life.

The Chronicler's thought, however, is not identical to that of Deuteronomy; while he accepts the idea of the Covenant as fundamental to Judaism, he does stand back on one fundamental point. He does not know the Covenant of Sinai. He does, however, know the Covenant with the fathers (1 Chron. 16.16-17) united to the promise of the land according to a schema deriving from a global reading of the tradition, but which seems to me to be in contradiction with the Chronicler's own theory of history. Essentially the Covenant with the fathers was an unconditional promise, while the Covenant of Sinai contained a conditional promise. For our rationalism these are irreconcilable terms, but for the ancient Jew apparently they were not, as witnessed by the entire structure of the Bible. The Chronicler, simultaneously under the influence of the Priestly Code, Deuteronomy, Nehemiah and Ezra, radicalizes the idea of salvation through 'making the Law' in the light of Ezra's ideas.

Mention of the Covenant of the fathers appears in a liturgical text which, although attributed to David, in reality reflects the ideology of the Temple. The Covenant of the fathers followed by the *'edut*, 'written testimony', at Sinai is typical of the Priestly Code, and the Chronicler claims that the tables of the Law are the tables that Moses put in the Ark at Horeb (2 Chron. 5.10).[18] But for the Chronicler the Ark was the

18. See Exod. 31.18: 'When He finished speaking with Moses on Mount Sinai, He gave him the two tablets of testimony (*'edut*)...written with the finger of God'. 2 Chron. 5.10 reads as follows: 'There was nothing in the ark except the two tables which Moses put there (*natan*) at Horeb, where Yhwh made [*karat*, 'to cut', but

Ark of the Covenant (1 Chron. 16.37; 17.1; 28.2). It is even more clear in 2 Chron. 6.11: 'And there I have set the ark, in which is the covenant of Yhwh which he made with the people of Israel'. The tablets of the Law represent the very writing of the Covenant.

The Chronicler's view of his own day is not clear, whether it was the greatest moment of messianic promises, or a transitional phase leading to better days, toward a new period. It seems, though, that even if he considered his day to be a period of transition, he was not for that unhappy with it. His view of things is serene, and messianism, interpreted as waiting for better days, is absent from his works.[19]

On the whole, Jewish society appears static in the Late Zadokite period, sure of the protection of its God and for the most part content, or rather, this is true at least of the ruling class. It can be argued that some political problems and contrasts did exist, since the formula that Judah was a monarchy without a monarch seems abstract. It must have been the result of some compromises. Apparently, however, such a solution was accepted and showed itself capable of providing stability for the little world of Jerusalem. The city certainly lived through some menacing moments with the passage of Alexander's army, and again when the wars broke out among Alexander's successors, but the city managed to stay out of the greater conflicts. When the time came for Jerusalem to take part in the affairs of the surrounding world, Zadokitism came to an end and with it one of the richest periods in Israel's history.

7. Job

The Chronicler viewed the whole of Israel's history in light of the principle of divine retribution. During his day, though, the problem of retribution was no longer seen in its social dimension, as if it regarded all of Israel, but it was also applied to the life of the individual. Since Ezekiel

here with the technical meaning indicating the stipulation of a covenant] with the people of Israel...' The text is nearly identical to that of 1 Kgs 8.9: 'There was nothing in the ark except the two tables of stone which Moses put there at Horeb, where Yhwh made a covenant with the people of Israel'. It is easy to conjecture the dropping of an 'of the Covenant' as indispensable for giving meaning to this text.

19. On this topic see Coppens, *Le messianisme royal*, p. 109, and W. Rudolph, *Esra und Nehemiah samt 3 Esra* (Tübingen: Mohr, 1949), pp. xxii-xxiii, and 'Problems on the Book of Chronicles', *VT* 4 (1954), pp. 401-409.

had declared the invalidity of the old saying that the teeth of the sons would be set on edge for the sins of the fathers, and that Yhwh now applied the new principle by which each person would either live by his righteousness or die by his evil, good or bad fortune in the life of the individual appeared to be the consequence of whether one abided by righteousness or betrayed it. The Chronicler wondered why Manasseh, a bad king, had had such a long life and found a solution by finding some merit on Manasseh's part. The theodicy did not only concern the entire people, but also the individual.

Ezekiel's principle, therefore, created a corollary; if a man is wealthy, then he is surely righteous, and if he is poor and in poor health, then he is surely paying for some sin. And while the ancient Hebrew conception of retribution in which God punished evil-doers for four generations and rewarded those who loved him for a thousand (see Exod. 20.5-6 and Deut. 5.9-10) eluded all emperical verification by humans, Ezekiel's view (ch. 18), of course, could be checked on the basis of experience. It could become the object of rational speculation.

The book of Job is to be placed after Ezekiel and more or less at the same time as the Chronicler, perhaps a bit before. It is the first book that critically approaches the problem of individual retribution. The book of Job marks the rise, though not the affirmation, of a new type of knowledge and thus demonstrates the existence of a certain critical and rationalistic spirit within Jewish society. Job, in discussing his lot with his friends, declares that he too has a brain (Job. 12.3: 'But I have a brain as you do; I am not inferior to you'). He is thus in a position to reply to the arguments presented by his three friends who rely instead on tradition: 'ask it of the past generations...' (8.8). The clearest of all is v. 13.1 read in this context: 'Lo, my eye has seen all this, my ear has heard and understood it', in other words, 'I've come to these conclusions through personal experience'.

It is interesting to note that like Job, the fourth friend, Elihu, rejects the idea of blindly accepting tradition and tries to save its values by presenting them rationally. Traditional wisdom seems solid only to the extent that it responds to rational principles. While one of the three friends falls back on a nocturnal apparition in order to support his ideas (4.13-21), Elihu never relies on such cognitive tools. This idea that knowledge is possible only on the basis of rationality and experience was later to be typical of Qohelet.

In other words, the teachings of the elders, rooted in memory, is no

longer considered infallible even by the traditionalists. The traditionalists and the rationalists seek support in opposite directions, but in both
cases outside memory: in the apparition, a close cousin to the vision
and therefore to revelation, or in human reason.

Job's response is ambiguous on the level of reason, torn between
evidence which left no doubts, and the necessity to maintain the retributory principle, considered one of the cornerstones of Jewish religiosity. Job holds that it is impossible to accept the corollary to the retributory principle; it is not true that all those who suffer are unrighteous.
He at any rate is not. His adversaries insist that if Job is suffering it is
because he must be guilty of something and he should admit to it. His
sorrows are the demonstration of his iniquity. Job upholds his inno-
cence and resists all their pressures. He will not ask forgiveness of God
for a sin that he did not commit (27.1-6). The book approaches the
problem of suffering with an acuteness that makes it a masterpiece of
human religiosity in its attempt to sound out an unfathomable God.

While the work resonates with a deep religious sensibility, it does not
provide rational answers to the questions it poses, because to answer
that one must accept without demanding to understand is not rational.
But perhaps Job did really grasp something, even though he communicates it with words that go beyond reason; Job admits that he has
spoken of things greater than he, things that he could not understand
(42.3). In this sense he retracts what he had previously said and
declares himself to repent in dust and ashes. On the other hand, in the
very same moment he adds that he has finally seen God as he is, that is,
Job claims to have understood (42.5).

And here we are presented with a surprise. In continuing our reading
of the text, up until this point the reader gets the impression that Job has
understood that he had been wrong, but the text continues by presenting
God who speaks in the first person and who claims that Job, and not
Job's friends, has spoken the truth about God's behaviour among humans. His friends must now ask Job's intercession on their behalf in
order to obtain God's forgiveness for what they had said in God's
favour (42.8). In the very moment that Job understands God and finally
declares his guilt, God intervenes confirming not this last point, but
everything that Job had said before. So, just what did Job understand
about God?

The epilogue would seem to fit with the traditionalist view of things,
since Job is rewarded for his righteousness with a great number of

material possessions. It is no longer clear, though, just what 'righteous' means. The question was to remain open for later generations.

Thus the book leaves an impression more for the questions it raises and for certain tentative solutions rather than for its conclusion. It is worth pausing for a moment to consider some of the solutions to problems that emerge, because they were destined to hold a strong influence on subsequent Jewish thought, after the Late Zadokite period had been brought to a close by the crisis of the second century BCE.

In the traditional Jewish ideology, God should be the judge between himself and humans. In other words, he was seen as humanity's counterpart inasmuch as he had established a Covenant, an agreement with humankind, but also as judge in all questions that could be raised concerning the application and respect of the Covenant's clauses. The difficulty lies here. If he is humankind's counterpart, then common sense would call for a different judge: 'For he is not a man, as I am, that I might answer him, "let us go to trial as equals". There is no umpire between us, who might lay his hand upon us both' (Job. 9.32).

Essentially God is judge, but a judge who issues his sentences without following any law, nor any pact with humankind. Either God is not the counterpart committed to the Covenant, or, if he is, he can easily neglect his obligations, supported by his own force, which in turn allows him to pass the sentences he wishes. Force seems to be God's fundamental attribute: 'With him are strength and wisdom; the deceived and the deceiver are his. He leads counsellors away stripped, and judges he makes fools' (Job. 12.16-17).

Therefore, everything depends on his strength, which is seconded by his wisdom. Wisdom belongs only to God, not to humans, not even to the elderly (12.12-13), not even if based on tradition as in the case of Job's three friends (8.8; 15.18). But Job declares, 'I have a brain, as you do' (12.3). Human intelligence has its strength and autonomy, but it is human strength and autonomy. Between intelligence and strength there is a very tight bond. To me, it seems that the meaning of vv. 12.12-13 can easily be deduced from the text itself. If we hold that Job sees human wisdom as something that grows over time, then for this very reason it is impossible that it be fully realized in humankind. And therefore we can say that only God has the strength necessary to grasp all knowledge. 'Wisdom is with the aged, and understanding in length of days. With God are wisdom and might; he has counsel and understanding'.

That being said, given the existence, however limited, of human autonomy, Job has the right to speak of God from human knowledge just as his friends do from tradition. In Job's analysis human attributes are the opposite of God's. Humanity is essentially weak, a leaf in the wind, dry chaff (13.25), its life ephemeral and unsure even during the brief time that it lasts. Another attribute of humanity is all that Job calls, with new intuition, impure. As far as the text indicates (14.1-4), impurity is no longer a contingent state in humanity. Job interprets the very fact that humanity can become contaminated as indicating that in human nature there is a sort of affinity with the impure.

> Man that is born of a woman
> is of few days, and full of trouble.
> He comes forth like a flower, and withers;
> he flees like a shadow, and does not linger.
> And do you open your eyes upon such a one
> and bring him into judgment with you?
> No one can make pure what is impure (Job. 14.1-4).

The human condition of transience, weakness and lack of means is thus summarized and synthesized in the concept of impurity.

God in his overwhelming might appears as humanity's persecutor:

> I was at ease, and he broke me asunder;
> he seized me by the neck and dashed me to pieces;
> he set me up as his target,
> his archers surround me.
> He slashes open my kidneys, and does to spare;
> he pours out my gall on the ground.
> He breaks me with breach upon breach;
> he runs upon me like a warrior...
> although there is not violence in my hands,
> and my prayer is pure (Job. 16.12-17).

And again:

> Truly I know that it is so:
> But how can a man be just [that is to prove himself right in debate] before
>   God [who is both party to the debate and judge]?
> He can ask a thousand questions
> that no one could ever answer.
> He is wise in heart, and mighty in strength,
> who has hardened himself against him, and succeeded? (Job 9.1-4)

What then is God's justice, from a human point of view, which has every right to exist, if not the force with which he imposes himself in any judgment, in any decision? With the opposite outcome the later book of Wisdom follows this same logic in understanding divine justice; God is just and we can be sure that he acts with justice precisely because he is omnipotent and nothing can stand in the way of his counsel (Wis. 12.12-18).

According to Job, God's behaviour is loathsome because he does not intervene against the wicked who can count on a long life and numerous descendants. But the most terrifying aspect of God's behaviour does not lie in the fact that he does not punish the wicked. That would simply be a lack of justice, being a bad judge and nothing more. The same punishment, pain and death, in the end awaits both the righteous and the wicked, because both the fortunate and the unhappy man 'lie down alike in the dust, and the worms cover them' (Job 21.26). The most despicable aspect of God's behaviour is elsewhere; it lies in the fact that the wicked are not such to God, but against other men. Behind every wicked action there is the suffering of another man (Job 24.1-25).

When Job ponders these things he is bewildered: 'When I think of it I am dismayed, and shuddering seizes my flesh' (Job 21.6).

A book like this could not fail to leave many problems and many questions open for the coming generations.

8. *Qohelet*

The book of Qohelet belongs to the last years of the Late Zadokite period. It is certainly a late book, even though it cannot be assigned a precise date. Lauha[20] has provided the arguments in favour of dating it to the third century BCE, and more toward the end than toward the beginning. To these arguments we could add that the book's author seems to live in a land and a period where commerce is flourishing and there are few wars. The context seems to be that of Palestine under the Ptolemies.

Many hypotheses have been put forward concerning the text's composition. According to some the book completely lacks unity and is merely derived from the combination of numerous and divergent sources, often of conflicting ideologies. This thesis, which dominated biblical studies until only recently, has prevented scholars from grasping the importance that Qohelet had on the development of Jewish thought. I feel that the book must be approached as a unitary whole.

20. Cf. Lauha, *Kohelet*, p. 3.

The author hidden behind the pseudonym of Qohelet possessed a unique temperament. In this sense, his work serves to illustrate the situation in Jerusalem only if held upside down, so to speak, paying more attention to the things that he criticizes than to what he supports.

Through its originality and its force his thought placed Judaism face to face with many if not all of its problems. With Qohelet the Zadokite period in the history of thought can be considered closed, just as the political history of Zadokitism was to draw definitively to a close only a few years after Qohelet's writings, with the passage of Palestine from Ptolemaic domination to the Seleucids of Syria.

The choice of problems to be approached by Qohelet reflects the author's formation in the Jerusalem of the Late Zadokite period. The problem of the messiah is extraneous to his work just as he does not seem to be touched by the great themes of the exile and postexilic prophets, problems such as universalism or suffering in function of salvation. In fact, the theme of salvation is flattened out in Qohelet's thought, a characteristic whose consequences can easily be seen on the level of spirituality. The book of Qohelet is quite unique in the Jewish literature of the Second Temple and the faithful can find its position among canonic literature disturbing, at least on a first reading. Qohelet's thought is rooted in the thought of Jerusalem's society as it is presented to us by the Chronicler, against whom Qohelet lifts penetrating and continuous criticism. He was also familiar with the early Apocalyptic circles for whom he felt even less sympathy. He does not argue with Apocalyptics, he only makes fun of them.

The atmosphere of Jerusalem in the third century BCE was no longer that of the early Zadokite period. All in all the city must have seemed safe and this in turn had brought about a change in its religiosity.[21] Nehemiah and the city's notables had signed a new Covenant (Neh. 10.1-2) with Yhwh; Ezra had claimed that the Jews were guilty of enormous iniquities (Ezra 9.6) for which God had punished them with exile. God had then shown mercy upon them, but now, if the Jews were to avoid certain catastrophe they had to observe God's will (Ezra 9.13-14). Jerusalem's continued salvation, which in spite of various threats had at this point lasted for a couple of centuries, seemed to prove

---

21. See E. Bickerman, *Four Strange Books of the Bible: Jonah, Daniel, Koheleth, Esther* (New York: Schocken Books, 1967); and Bickerman, 'The Generation of Ezra and Nehemiah', *Proceedings of the American Academy for Jewish Research* 45 (1978), pp. 1-28.

Israel's righteousness. Unlike the Jews who during the time of the exile were aware of their guilt, during the third century there was a widespread sensation of being at peace before God's Law. The Law, of course, had to be scrupulously observed, at least in certain parts that were assigned particular importance: perhaps those regarding purity and mixed marriages.

Let us have a look, for example, at Psalm 44, which can be dated to more or less the same time as Qohelet:

> Yet thou hast cast us off and abased us,
> and hast not gone out with our armies.
> Thou hast made us turn back from the foe;
> and our enemies have gotten spoil.
> Thou hast made us like sheep for slaughter,
> and hast scattered us among the nations.
> Thou hast sold thy people for a trifle,
> demanding no high price for them.
> Thou hast made us the taunt of our neighbours,
> the derision and scorn of those about us.
> Thou hast made us a byword among the nations,
> a laughingstock among the peoples...
> All this has come upon us,
> though we have not forgotten thee,
> or been false to thy covenant.
> Our heart has not turned back,
> nor have our steps departed from thy way...[22] (Ps. 44.9-18)

The psalm follows the same logic as ch. 9 of the book of Ezra. After the last concession of grace, the last pardon given by God to Israel, Israel will be saved only if it observes the Law. Even still, in spite of the fact that the Law has been observed (this is the author's point of view), misfortune has again struck Israel, or at least subjugation to the foreigner is seen as misfortune (see Ezra 9.9).

Alongside this psalm, let us look at the one in the fourth chapter of Joel, which, at least in the meaning and form in which it has been

22. On the dating of Ps. 44 see G. Castellino, *Libro dei Salmi* (Turin: Marietti, 3rd edn, 1965), pp. 298-99. Many scholars prefer to assign a later date to this psalm, placing it during the Maccabaean period (but see Castellino's objections). Others prefer a much earlier dating, even to the period of the kings, but without giving a precise date because there were many defeats in the history of the Jews. A margin remains open for a late dating, but not too late, based on the element, 'We have not sinned—yet we have been defeated'.

handed down to us, dates to the middle of the fourth century BCE.[23] The blood shed by the Jews is no longer the blood of the guilty punished by God, but blood of the innocent (Joel 3.19) who faithfully await the Great Judgment and the Great Vengeance.

The Jews of the exile knew that they were being punished. They suffered and it was for their guilt. The problem of why the punishment was more severe than the guilt remained an open question (Isa. 40.2) and this opened the way to the idea of a certain functionality of pain beyond punishment and, as a consequence, beyond retribution. This idea, however, does not belong to the author of Psalm 44 just as it does not belong to the final author of Joel. Deutero-Isaiah's thought long remained unproductive in Israel.

Both Psalm 44 and the fourth chapter of Joel clearly claim that punishment is not the cause of Israel's suffering. What is the cause then? According to the author of the psalm, history is entirely dominated by God and flows according to his will. Israel's victories have never been the fruit of 'their own arm' (Ps. 44.3), but always and only the fruit of God's favour. The idea of a complete separation between Israel's initial election through God's grace, and the successive history dominated by the principle of retribution was common during the Late Zadokite period and particularly clear in Ezra. In Late Zadokite society, though, we have the impression that Israel's misadventures do not depend so much on its guilt, but rather on a lack of grace. No specific reason has been determined for such a lack of grace, but this will be the object of later research. In the past guilt had been deduced from misfortune (taken as a given to be interpreted). During the fourth and third centuries BCE, in contrast, Israel's righteousness, considered to be a fact, lay at the basis of reflection and in some way caused a crisis for the principle of retribution in much the same way that Job had. The object of discourse had shifted from the individual to the collectivity while the fundamental questions remained the same.

The series of problems approached by Qohelet, then, are rooted in the Jewish society of the third century BCE, but his way of posing the questions was new. If we want to find some historical antecedents, these should be sought among some of the criticisms contained in the book of Job which could have been developed through the growing contact with the Greek and Hellenistic world. But, it is on the religious level that

23. See Soggin, *Introduction*, p. 353.

Qohelet marks a decisive shift in Judaism. He gives voice to the awareness of the impossibility of understanding God.

Apart from some affinity that Qohelet may have had with Job, there
is a clear distinction between Qohelet's thought and the rest of the Hebrew and Jewish tradition. With a freedom of spirit with regard to the
preceding Jewish tradition, he reflected on the entire world surrounding
humanity. His point of departure is the empirical observation of things
and events and his conclusions concern the relationship between
humans and God, the very sense of religion. He raised more problems
than he resolved. While it was his thought that drew the Late Zadokite
period to a close, it was also his thought that opened the tragic and
tormented period running from the removal of the high priest Onias III
to the destruction of Jerusalem.

As we have mentioned, Qohelet's point of departure is that of
observing reality. Knowledge presupposes experience, a 'seeing' or
'hearing' referred respectively to direct experience and to study. One
'sees' that water flows to the sea (1.7), just as one 'sees' that the sea is
never filled. Folly can be understood only through experience (2.3).
Qohelet does not, however, continue toward an analysis of the mechan-
ism of knowledge in the way that the classical Greek thinkers did.
Establishing how knowledge comes about in humans allows (or at least
we believe that it allows) one to judge the value of that knowledge.
Qohelet ignores problems of methodology. This means that what
appears true to him must be considered true; it is thus. This judgment
regards not only the sensory experience we have of external objects, but
also internal experience, especially concerning values. Anything that
appears as a value is a value.

All of this does not mean that he did not pose the problem of knowledge's limits. Nor that he did not try to indicate them. Since all knowledge is always derived from experience, it is clear that for Qohelet it is
impossible to know everything, because human experience is limited. It
is limited by the capability of the senses; the eye can never be filled
with what there is to see and the ear with what it can hear (1.8). It is
also limited by the limit of all limits, man's very nature as a mortal
being. Qohelet insists on this point: 'there is no work or thought or
knowledge or wisdom in Sheol, to which you are going' (9.10). 'No
one can attain new knowledge after death' (8.7), precisely because
death is the total fading away of all experience (12.2-5).

Qohelet's insistence on the motif of death as the end of all human capacity can only be explained by the circulation of opposite ideas in Jerusalem. These were the new ideas of groups known as, for lack of a better term, Enochic or Apocalyptic who were already reading the *Book of Watchers* and the *Book of Astronomy*. In 12.6 we read: 'before the silver cord is cut, or the golden bowl is broken, or the pitcher is broken at the fountain, or the wheel broken and fallen into the well'. Seen from any angle, life ends; all that remains is a slipping away toward dark waters. We see the force of Qohelet's irony when he insists that humans possess no more than the animals in 3.19-22:

> For the fate of the sons of men and the fate of beasts is the same; as one dies, so dies the other. They all have the same breath, and man has nothing over the beasts; for all is vanity. All go to one place; all are from the dust, and all turn to dust again. Who knows whether the spirit of man goes upward and the spirit of the beast goes down to the earth? So I saw that there is nothing better than that a man should enjoy his work, for that is his lot.

The very fact that each day brings with it new experience keeps humans from upholding the idea that the data they possess are *all* the data. 'What is lacking', that is that which lies beyond the senses' reach, 'cannot be numbered' (1.15), in other words, known. For this reason, any discourse that humans may undertake is destined to remain partial (1.8). Knowledge reveals itself to be a bottomless abyss or an infinite height (7.23-24). This sort of idea can be explained in terms of an open anti-Apocalyptic debate. The pretensions of knowing the cosmos and the details of the Judgment belonged to Apocalyptic. For Qohelet these were merely dreams; it was much better to stick to reality (5.6), unsatisfying as it was. Even still, Qohelet did fall under the fascination of Apocalyptic and did accept one element. That humans should aspire to globality, at least as far as knowledge is concerned, is not absurd, because it is an aspiration that actually exists in humanity and, if it exists, it is because God put it there. Qohelet knows that creation has a meaning, even if humans are incapable of grasping it all. God has given humans the principle of 'globality' (*'olam*) (3.11), but not the ability of comprehending the work of God in its entirety. Humans cannot grasp the whole of God's work (the cosmos and history), but the idea of this entirety is essential, because only in light of this entirety does the world have meaning.

> Then I reflected upon all the work of God, and I understood that man cannot discover all that occurs under the sun. However much man may

toil in seeking, he will find nothing out. Even though a wise man claims
to know, he cannot find anything out (8.17).

This is not scepticism. The fact that the wise man does not find anything does not mean that he does not know anything, since the wise
man knows a great deal about nature and about men. The fact of the
matter is that if only a single element is missing in our knowledge of
the cosmos (and Qohelet says that an infinite number of elements are
missing) then we cannot grasp the meaning of the whole. From this
point of view we can say that not even the wise man knows anything,
and Qohelet always had enough common sense not to abandon himself
to such academic consolations as, 'if I do not know, at least I know that
I do not know'.

For this reason Qohelet can state that wisdom is of great value, in the
very fact that it is wisdom. But it is also true that no one possesses it,
because human wisdom is not absolute. Wisdom is a value because it
appears as such (2.13-14), but human wisdom is destined to have to
content itself with only crumbs of truth.

This attitude distinguishes Qohelet from the Greek thinkers. He offers
a truth to humanity which is only a fragment of truth. He has no
absolute principles to propose to anyone. His importance in this goes
beyond the limits of Judaism.

Enquiring into nature, Qohelet notices that it is governed by laws,
laws that were not made by humans, but that they too must obey. For as
much as humans are capable of action, 'what is crooked', that is, what
God has made crooked for humans, 'cannot be made straight'; 'no one
has power over his life's breath, or power over the day of death' (8.8).
There is even a rule governing human psychology, which leads Qohelet
to say that in any possible future humans will do 'only what has already
been done' (2.12).

This statement is not to be interpreted in the sense that everyone
behaves in the same manner, which would be in contrast with Qohelet's
way of thinking, since he places so much emphasis on the existence of
the wise alongside fools as well as the lucky and the unfortunate.
Qohelet means to say simply that human actions are governed by their
own laws and that they cannot go beyond the limits posed by nature. In
this sense, humans cannot even know themselves completely and, most
of all, they cannot even grasp the final meaning of their own
sentiments. 'Man does not know either love or hate...' (9.1).

Alongside the laws of nature Qohelet came across another type of law, which we could call 'the law of the moment'. All humans are subject to certain laws by which they are born and die, love and hate, gain and loss. Now, the reality of birth and death can be seen from two separate points of view. It can be considered a law of the cosmos, but it can also be seen as 'my birth' and 'my death'. In this case we are no longer dealing with laws of the cosmos, but with something else. Love and hate can be seen as psychological laws valid in eternity, even though I may not understand their value or the reason for their existence, but that does not explain why I love *now* or why I hate *now*. This is even more clear when we turn to the question of gain and loss; these are things which happen in everyone's lives, but no one can know when. All of these elements fall into the category of the 'law of the moment', which, like all laws, do not depend on humans, but on God.

That the wise man should reap the fruits of his wisdom is excluded from experience. In any case, the wise man and the fool are destined to the same Sheol (2.16), but even in this life the results of our actions do not depend on our qualities, but on another factor which can only be seen as the master of the 'law of the moment'. Even the wise young man who became king did not become king because of his wisdom, but for another reason. Even if he became king *because* he was wise, he was dethroned *in spite of* his wisdom (4.13-16). God put him on the throne and God took him from it; it was neither the wisdom nor the foolishness of the man that determined his fate. History for Qohelet has no laws, it cannot constitute an object of study.

Following this line of thought, Qohelet arrives at extreme statements:

> Again I saw that under the sun the race is not to the swift, nor the battle to the strong, nor bread to the wise...but time and chance happen to them all (9.11).

In this context, the saving function of 'doing the Law' disappears.

> In my vain life I have seen everything;
> there are righteous people who perish in their righteousness,
> and there are wicked people who prolong their life in their evildoing (7.15).

> Moreover I saw under the sun
> that in the place of justice, wickedness was there...
> Thus I concluded in my heart, God judges the righteous and the wicked, for
> he has appointed a time for every matter, and for every work (3.16-17).[24]

---

24. The meaning of 'to judge' in this context is clearly 'to rule, govern, dominate'. His rule is revealed in his appointing a time for everything.

God's will dominates everything according to criteria that we cannot understand and that we do not even like, because they do not follow the principle of retribution.

Qohelet even approached the problem of God's judgment which exists before it manifests itself. His conclusions tend toward a sort of determinism: 'That which is has already been given a name [that is, its destiny], what each individual is, is already known. Man cannot dispute with one who is stronger than he' (6.10).

If Qohelet did not believe entirely in predetermination, this is due to his strong belief in human freedom and human creative capacities, qualities emphasized in the last chapters of his work. But it remains true that his work could also be interpreted in a predeterministic light and, in fact, after Qohelet the idea of predetermination entered into Judaism. This came about both in a fairly nuanced version that we could call the official version (see the book of Daniel), and in the more marked versions of Apocalyptic and in particular in Essenic Judaism (see the *Book of Dreams*, contemporary to Daniel, and Essenic thought in general).

Qohelet's ideas regarding the retributory principle undermined one of the primary elements of society in the Late Zadokite period. Jerusalem was no longer safe because of its righteousness, but for another reason. As a consequence, if 'being righteous' and 'doing the Law' were to be attributed a value (and Qohelet did not deny the value of these things, even though he did not specify just what their value was), that value, then, was not to be considered their function toward salvation. Or, at least not as a function of salvation as was generally accepted at the time, and as Qohelet himself understood it.

> The same fate comes to all,
> to the righteous and the wicked, to the good and the evil,[25]
> to the pure and the impure, to those who sacrifice and those who do not sacrifice.
> As are the good, so are the sinners;
> those who swear are like those who shun an oath.
> This is an evil in all that happens under the sun,
> that the same fate comes to everyone... (9.2-3)

But Qohelet's ideas not only shook the tranquil society of the Chronicler, they also posed the problem of the nature of the relationship between God and humans, that is of religion itself. For Qohelet, the

---

25. *and the evil*: as per the Greek text. The reading is at any rate imposed by the parallelism.

foundation of religion is fear of God. This is not a new solution in Israel, but in Qohelet it takes on a new resonance, since fear is the only bond uniting humans to their God. The relationship with God must bear the mark of knowledge of the infinite distance separating humans from their creator, 'for God is in heaven, and you upon the earth' (5.1).

In a rudimentary phase of religious experience, as seen in general in the more ancient texts, fear of God seems to be a direct consequence of experiencing the sacred. '[Jacob] was afraid, and said, "How awesome is this place! This is none other than the house of God, and this is the gate of heaven" ' (Gen. 28.17). This is the terror that pervades humans when in the presence of the sacred, the terror that overtakes Samson's father when he realizes that he has been in God's presence and believes that he will die (Judg. 13.22). The fear of God takes on a different appearance in more recent times, or, at the least, religious experience becomes more complex. It is no longer fear derived from contact with the awe-inspiring, but rather fear derived from awareness of human impotence as a creature before complete otherness, complete immensity. This experience of the fear of God is expressed well in ch. 38 of the book of Job, even though the expression 'fear of God' is not used (see also Job 37.23). Fear of God becomes the guarantor of humanity's recognition of the distance separating us from God, and it leads us to observance of the commandments (Deut. 4.10 and Ps. 119.79).

Qohelet takes up one of the motifs of the prophets, that of seeing misfortune as a warning to make the Jews fear God. But Qohelet lived in a period which for Jerusalem can be called a time of peace. Qohelet discovers that misfortunes are not absolutely necessary in order to learn the fear of God. Daily life itself already contains elements which can only give rise to the same sentiments as misfortune. A glance at all the injustice and suffering that there are in the world, which no one can relieve, is enough to lead one to exclaim :

> And I thought the dead, who have already died, more fortunate than the
>   living, who are still alive;
> but better than both is the one who has not yet been,
> and has not seen the evil deeds that are done under the sun (4.2-3).

Since the fear of God is a guarantee of giving to God that which is due, it is also a source of wisdom (Ps. 111.10). The more recent parts of the book of Proverbs follow this line of thought: 'The fear of Yhwh is the beginning of wisdom' (Prov. 9.10). In Qohelet, however, fear of God has its own particular importance, because it is the only chord played by his religion. He seems to have completely lost those parts of the religious tradition that united love and fear of God: 'So now, O Israel, what does Yhwh your God require of you? Only to fear Yhwh your God, to walk in all his ways, to love him, to serve Yhwh your God with all your heart and with all your soul...' (Deut. 10.12).

Qohelet did not lose so much the idea of the bond between love and fear of God, as he did the very concept of a love binding humans and God in some way. Hosea had used very tender words in order to convey the idea of God's love for his people:

> When Israel was a child, I loved him,
> and out of Egypt I called my son...
> It was I who taught Ephraim to walk... (Hos. 11.1-3)

Deuteronomy had placed the love that every Jew owed to his God at the very foundation of every commandment:

> Hear, O Israel: Yhwh is our God, Yhwh is one alone. You shall love Yhwh with all your heart, and with all your soul, and with all your might (Deut. 6.4-5).

Qohelet, immersed in meditation on the possibility of salvation through justice, meditation shared by nearly all during his epoch, lost this dimension of religion, which was to be rediscovered by later Judaism, Essenic, Pharisaic and Christian. In centring his attention on the retributive relationship, Qohelet not only discovered the incoherence of the theory of retribution, but also the incoherence of the very ideal of justice, considered as 'good for man'. His religious ideal, then, is placed not only beyond the norms of purity (without excluding them) (9.2), not only beyond sacrifice (without excluding it) (9.2), not only beyond the vow (without excluding it) (5.3-4), but even beyond the whole of the Law (without, however, excluding it, as can be drawn from the general meaning of his work, and the words of the Epilogist [12.13]). Thus, a new dimension of the spirit opens before him, a dimension in which the only measure possible for the relationship between humans and God is to be found exclusively in the meaning of the infinite distance between the one and the other. God and his relationship with the world can no longer be understood in the structures of the Theology of the Covenant, nor in those of the Theology of the Promise. Qohelet excludes the possibility of any philosophy and any ideology.

That being said, Qohelet's fear of God also holds a positive meaning, more intuitive than explicit. On this basis he is able to repeat with the tradition that things go well only for those who have fear of God (7.18). The meaning of this statement is nuanced, because this 'success' can not coincide with effective successes or wealth. It stands for a dimension of internal equilibrium that lies at the basis of Qohelet's exclamation that Wisdom gives life to the one who possesses it. One lives on money, but Wisdom allows one to live in any case. That, to me, is the meaning of 7.11-12, 'Wisdom is as good as an inheritance... For the protection of wisdom is like the protection of money, and the advantage of knowledge is that wisdom gives life to the one who possesses it'.

The religiosity based on fear of God that Qohelet taught in his school had vast consequences, because it opened new horizons for human spirituality. It was an opening derived, and I would say necessarily, from a new way of approaching religious discourse; the relationship between God and humans was no longer as clear as it had been in the past. It was necessary to re-examine the meaning of the Law from a new perspective, as the old one, Qohelet claimed, did not lead to salvation.

The shortcoming of the way of interpreting the Law's value in Ezra and Nehemiah's Judaism is manifested in the idea that God must be grasped, understood, beyond the Law's commandments. The Law is valid on a general level and the problem of the individual consists not only in understanding general things, but also, or rather especially, in understanding the things that regard the individual himself. Apocalyptics, in contrast, do not even seem to have posed the question. The teachers of the Law were later to try to resolve the problem by analysing every possible life situation, following the idea/ideal that the Law encompassed all of human life, from the cradle to the grave. Qohelet's thought, however, seems to follow a different path. Just as God does not reveal himself only through the unchanging laws of nature, but also and perhaps mostly through the 'laws of the moment' in which he demonstrates his unending creative capacity, thus humans must not content themselveswith knowing the Law, but must push further in order to understand (or better 'to try to understand') God's works, since no one can make straight what they have made crooked (7.13). God's *mišpaṭ* (judgment, will) is to be accepted, but not passively, humans must try to adjust to it in their freedom, understand it.

This is a purely rational movement of thought, with no love, nonetheless it represents a great opening for the human spirit. Some passages of the New Testament follow the path indicated by Qohelet. 'Be transformed by the renewing of your minds, so that you may discern what is the will of God', says Paul to the Romans (12.2). In the Gospel of Matthew (7.21), Jesus insists on the necessity of doing God's will. This is also repeated in the Lord's Prayer (6.10). The fact that God's will does not necessarily coincide with the Law, precisely because the latter has a general character and regards all men in exactly the same way, while the former requires something of each person individually, was clear to the author of the book of *Jubilees* (second century BCE) as well. According to the Law, Abraham could have returned to the land of Ur, but he was bound by God's will on this point where the Law seemed to leave him a free choice (*Jub.* 12.20-24).

9. *Hellenism*

By definition, the term Hellenism regards the civilization and history of the Mediterranean basin and the Middle East in general from 333 BCE until 31 BCE, in other words, from Alexander's departure on the conquest of the East to the battle of Actium and the beginning of the *pax Romana*.

This is not the appropriate place to make a general presentation of Hellenism, but certain aspects of the new culture which were to have an influence on Jerusalem[26] should be presented.

The very idea of Hellenism is all but clear, given the complexity of the phenomenon. From a methodological point of view, it should be pointed out first of all that Hellenism was formed by the contact between the mature and perhaps declining culture of classical Greece on one side and the civilizations of the East on the other. This in itself indicates the fluidity of the concept; the East did not house a single civilization, but many, and finding a common denominator capable of binding together the Iranian-Babylonian, the Jewish and the Egyptian cultures in order to compare them to the Greek one is not an easy task. Perhaps it is even impossible. Analyses stray from the events, from the

---

26. On the contacts between Judaism and Hellenism, see the fundamental work by M. Hengel, *Judentum und Hellenismus: Studien zu ihrer Begegnung unter besonderer Berücksichtigung Palästinas bis zur Mitte des 2. Jh.s v. Chr.* (Tübingen: Mohr, 2nd edn, 1973) (ET: *Judaism and Hellenism: Studies in their Encounter in Palestine during the Early Hellenistic Period* [London: SCM Press, 1974]) and the recent contribution to *CAH*, 'The Interpretation of Judaism and Hellenism in the Pre-Maccabean Period', II, pp. 167-86.

ideas and their interpretations and often enter into the shifting sands of 'types of logic', of mentalities. These too are variable elements within the Hellenistic world both because of the variety of cultures covered by that term and for the rapid evolution of ideas and customs during the period.

There was an encounter between Greek and oriental civilizations (from now on we shall primarily discuss the Jewish one), and this encounter led to the logical consequences of either absorption or the radicalization of each one's positions. Establishing the Eastern or Western nature of the elements in this encounter is not simple and on historical grounds it is often arbitrary. In fact, we must distinguish between the ideas that had been circulating in the Mediterranean basin before 333 BCE in a very human exchange of ideas, and what came about after 333 when the encounter between ideas no longer came about in a disinterested fashion, but instead were deeply conditioned by the social and political situation that the Greek conquest had created. When a people feels that its very existence is compromised, it is led, depending on the reactions of the single individuals, to either try to assimilate itself to the victor, or to rebel entirely, emphasizing in every possible way the distinguishing traits of its own tradition and way of living. The loss of one's culture is experienced as the worst act of tyranny. The Greeks did not impose this. In fact in the early period, under Alexander, they tried to adapt themselves to eastern customs; Alexander was struck by the idea of universal empire and dreamed of uniting Greeks and barbarians. He even tried to realize this dream by encouraging mixed marriages. The situation was soon to change, though, under the Diadochi who, each according to the particular local situation, sought to favour the Greek element of society and as a consequence blocked the fusion of Greeks and Orientals, opposing mixed marriages. If a city or a colony was founded, it was to be Greek, because only the Greeks could be trusted.

Certain ideas that had been formed in fourth-century Greece in the wake of the Persian wars must have come to mind and served as guidelines for Alexander's political behaviour. Plato wrote:

> When Greeks and non-Greeks fight, then, we'll describe this as warfare, and claim that they are natural enemies and that the term 'war' should refer to this type of hostility. But when Greeks get involved in this kind of thing with other Greeks, we'll claim that they are natural friends, and that in a situation like this Greece is diseased and in conflict, and we'll

maintain that the term 'conflict' should refer to this type of hostility
(*Republic* 5.470c).

Aristotle's ideas were not very far from these either, when he invites
the Greeks to fight against the Persians in order to enslave them (*Politics* 1.1.6 = 1252b). This must have been a widespread idea, since
according to Livy (31, 29.15) the Macedonian ambassadors to the Pan-
Aetolian Congress still used similar expressions in 200 BCE: 'Between
the Greeks and the barbarians there is and shall always be eternal war;
by their unchanging nature they are enemies'. Ideas of this sort lay at
the basis of the plan to conquer the East first envisioned by Philip and
then carried out by Alexander.

In Greece, however, there were different voices; Isocrates, who independently of his admiration for Philip had no qualms about considering
the Macedonians barbarians, still claims (*Panegyric* 50) that anyone
sharing the Greek *paideia* (that is their culture in the widest sense of the
term) was Greek in a much more profound way than those who shared
no more than common ancestors with the Greeks. The concept of 'barbarian' remains, but it tends to shift from being the opposite of 'Greek'
to being the opposite of *pepaideumenos*, that is those who know the
language and practise the customs of the Greeks. The division and
opposition are no longer made in ethnic terms, but in cultural terms. It
is still racism, but not on the crude level of one's blood. Finally, Isocrates followed Socrates' teachings (and in the end it does not matter if
the words were actually those of Socrates),[27] who thanked God 'for
being born a man and not a beast, male and not female, Greek and not
barbarian'. The only difference is that Isocrates gave a different meaning to the word 'Greek' rather than merely 'Greek by blood'. Eratosthenes, Ptolemy IV's pedagogue (third century BCE), discouraged his
pupil from maintaining the policy of discrimination, substituting the
more noble distinction between *aretē* and *kakia* (it seems that some kind
of discrimination is inevitable!) for the opposition between 'Greeks'
and 'barbarians'. This attitude did not remain closed up in philosophical
circles, but was put into practice politically when the Greeks allowed
the Phoenicians to participate in the pan-Hellenic games. Toward the
end of the century the Romans were admitted too, after their victory
over the Illyrian pirates in 229 BCE. The fusion of Greek and eastern
elements, however, was an unstoppable process. The principal instru-

27. Socrates in Diogenes Laertius 1.33.

ment in this process, alongside the power that lay in the hands of the conquerors, was the Greek language in its *koinē* form, which was spoken in many regions and became the lingua franca throughout the Mediterranean, substituting for Aramaic and Phoenician. That does not mean that some cultures did not survive; the most driven did. The most notable among these was the Jewish culture, but it is worth mentioning Egyptian culture as well, which witnessed a true renaissance with the Coptic literature of the first centuries of the Christian era.

It should be pointed out that problems similar to those afflicting Greece before 333 BCE were felt in Palestine as well, and certainly not due to Greek influence. Jerusalem during the Late Zadokite period, with its prohibition of mixed marriages and the rigid definition of 'Jew' was not much different from Athens. And as in Athens some had spoken out against the dominant mentality, thus in Israel, too, there were discordant voices. The book of Ruth cast a shadow on whether or not David could be considered a Jew according to the legal definition of 'Jew', Jonah looked on dumbfounded as the *gôyyîm* (translated as 'peoples' or 'nations', the term is in fact a synonym for 'barbarian') were the object of his God's attention and showed themselves capable of conversion more than the Jews themselves. Later, some Apocalyptic was to decidedly follow the path of universalism. Even an author who cannot be accused of being Apocalyptic, such as Aristeas, was to try to overcome the distinction between Jews and barbarians with a system reminiscent of that of Isocrates, and with the same limits. Greek culture contained the prolegomena to the true culture which was the Jewish one; in this way the distinction did not lie between Jews and barbarians, but between those who recognized the true God and his Law and those who did not. The road to union, if not to unity, has always been a difficult one and Hellenistic cosmopolitanism, shaped by the multi-ethnic and multi-cultural nature of those states, was more a phenomenon induced by such a structure than an autonomous ideal destined to survive in different socio-political situations. Religiously, Hellenistic paganism was tolerant. While some sovereigns favoured one religion over others, as in the case of the Ptolemies who protected the religion of the god Serapis beginning in about 200 BCE, they never imposed the favoured religion.

While under Hellenism religions more or less everywhere developed the more individualistic aspects of belief even against some resistance, as in the case of belief in the immortality of the soul which was no longer destined to descent to the underworld or to Sheol, but rather to

live (at least in the case of the righteous) near the divinity, this phenomenon came about entirely independently of any political pressure.
Even the pseudo-religion of sovereign worship, while publicly promoted never led to a lack of respect for the other religions. A sovereign
could have himself called 'Saviour' or even 'God', but he never
claimed to be the only one. Tolerance was a matter of fact, even though
it was not an ideal.

At any rate, it is certain that while Hellenism, from a Western perspective, was formed through contact with the East, the East in turn was
struck most by the original elements of Greek culture. In other words,
the East was influenced most by what we would call the culture of
classical Greece. From our point of view the novelty of Hellenism consists almost entirely in the absorption of eastern elements, especially in
religion as in the case of the idea of a saving divinity. From the point of
view of the East it is clear that these were not the most striking or
interesting 'Hellenistic' ideas.

First of all the different conception of 'human' must have struck the
people of the East. The Oriental is always his king's servant and even
more so the servant of his God, while the Greek, especially the Greek
of the classical period, is free. In fact he is only completely a man inasmuch as he is free, since slaves are not really men. The Greek faith in
human capacity, whether intellectual or political, is rooted in this sentiment of freedom. Western man is always more or less consciously the
measure of all things, while Eastern man, again more or less consciously, knows that the measure of all things can only be his god.

Even a deeply religious and in some aspects even prophetical discourse such as that of Socrates is clearly distinct from that of the prophets of Israel. Socrates acts according to an internal inspiration which
he attributes without a doubt to the divinity; but what is surprising is
that he does not rebel against the will of the god so politely expressed
to him. There are none of Jeremiah's pangs of suffering (ch. 20), or
Jonah's terrified flight. In short, Socrates is not 'seduced', he is aware
of his complete freedom, which he serenely puts before the will of his
god. Furthermore, from his observations on humans, on himself and his
mission, Socrates goes straight to the underlying problem: whether
death opens up to humans the possibility of living near the divinity or
whether it leads to a sleep from which there is no awakening.

The problem of judgment is thus introduced into the dilemma,
because only the righteous can live in happiness near God. But Socrates

(or Plato, it is not important) grasps another aspect of the problem of values. Values are not only such inasmuch as they are functions of salvation, but they are the real foundation of society which can only survive if the citizens respect and conserve its values. It is for this reason that even though Socrates is innocent, he cannot disobey the laws of his city, on whose basis he had been condemned. Values are therefore immanent to man, who is such only to the extent to which he respects and conserves them.

The problem of human destiny, and in the end its salvation, is approached from various directions and at times the reasoning process allows for two possible and opposite hypotheses. It is worth being righteous whether death is a transmigration from this place to another or whether death is more like an eternal sleep. Doubt, which is foreign to the Eastern author, is possible for Socrates. The Jewish prophet's truth is an intuition (and therefore experienced with the same force as with sensorial experience of the surrounding world), and intuition which he explains, and the very explanation generally follows the form of a revelation. Socrates' truth is derived from working around human experience, attempting to understand everything exclusively with human rational-discursive forces.

Beyond this, the Westerners used an adjective meaning 'beautiful' much more than the Jews had ever done. They were aware of the problems of freedom of speech and political freedom, and while they did know words that could correspond more or less to 'impure' and 'pure', they had much broader ideas on the matter, almost to the point of indifference; for example, they showed no qualms about letting themselves be seen nude.

At first the Greeks were influenced more by the Easterners than the Easterners by the Greeks. The Greeks were more open, less bound to or completely free of religious precepts in as much as their ethical system was tied to the polis and not to worship. The ease shown by Alexander in adopting oriental customs illustrates the fascination that the imperial ideology of the East held over him.[28]

The Greek conquerors were the bearers of an exceptional vitality that few historical periods have witnessed. New centres grew up just about everywhere and all of them were organized in the Greek manner, even if in the Greek manner that was being formed in contact with the East.

---

28. See G. Radet, *Alexandre le Grand* (Paris: L'artisan du livre, 1931).

In the new cities there was always a theatre and a gymnasium. The youth were given the broadest education possible under the guidance of teachers employed by the city itself. Temples were built and dedicated to many gods. The lay element of society though, that is Man, was somehow more important than the religious element. In this situation even the idea of state as founded on a common blood tended to be overcome; the uniting element in the Greek *politeia* was the participation in the common rights and duties on the same ground. This was a fairly new idea for the Greeks if we think of Clistenes' reforms in Athens in roughly 500 BCE, which at least in the realm of internal administration had shifted powers away from the *phratria*, based essentially on blood relations, to the *demos*, a territorial entity. This is a very interesting concept, because it represents a certain balance between the territorial state and the ethnic one.

The transplantation of Greek culture in the East was accompanied by a reduction in collective manifestations in favour of individualism. One of the distinguishing traits of Hellenistic society as opposed to classical Greek society is that books were particularly widespread in the former, a fact corresponding to a greater individualism in the Hellenistic man compared to his classical Greek counterpart.

Attention is shifted from thought concerning the great problems of Man to problems concerning the individual; speculation on 'Good in itself' is replaced by a search for the 'Good for man'. The way in which problems were posed moved much closer to the individual and his needs; the mystery religions replace the Apollonian one. The latter required little of humans and offered little in return while the former promised salvation beyond the life lived on this earth by way of an undying part of humanity, the 'soul'. Humanity's most authentic destiny is realized only after death. The religion of Serapis fits these requirements perfectly well, but the beliefs documented in the redaction of the *Book of Watchers* demonstrate that certain requirements had been present in the Jewish world for quite some time as well.

This world could not gain the favour of Zadokite Jerusalem, not that of Nehemiah and even less that of Ezra. It is obvious that the city tried to defend itself against the novelties that imperceptibly tended to alter the rythms of its life and cast doubt on its traditional heritage. It was, however, impossible to succeed in such resistance, even though the city's political structure sought to protect it in every way possible from outside influence.

In the third century the Hellenistic world was at the gates of Jerusalem. Philadelphia and Ptolemais were only a few kilometres away, but an even greater threat to the Zadokite city must have been represented by the contacts with the Greek-speaking Jews of Alexandria, who knew Greek culture and were taking in numerous proselytes. Even the soldiers who returned home after having served with one Hellenistic sovereign or another must have brought home with them a vision of the world very different from the one in which they were born. There is no way of knowing what these soldiers thought of the Hellenistic civilization, but one thing at least must have struck them: the technical superiority of the Greek armies. A civilization that presents itself as being stronger can only present itself as a model. A comparison between the two civilizations, the Jewish one and the Greco-Hellenistic one, was inevitable and on at least one point the Greek civilization could not help but impose itself on the attention of the other: its military might. Those who exercised power in Jerusalem could only have been attracted, or at any rate they could not avoid evaluating the problem of adapting Jewish society to the pagan one which appeared to be superior. Beginning in the first quarter of the second century BCE many influential people began to take Greek names and to absorb the logic of power according to the schema of the world surrounding them.

During the second half of the third century BCE, with Qohelet, Jewish thought entered a period of great ferment. The range of problems addressed was broadened to include questions that up until that moment it had either not known how to approach or that it had not dared to pose. The problem of human knowledge was raised along with the possibility of knowing the beginning and end of all things.

The Jewish problematic continued to spring from the roots of the Jewish tradition, but the problems posed on the basis of that problematic were new. Of greatest importance, beginning especially with the second century BCE, was the tendency of carrying all questions to their extreme consequences. It was as though there were a catalyzing agent acting on Jewish consciousness which pushed all problems towards extreme solutions. This catalyzing element must be identified as Greek thought as it came to be known to the Jews through Hellenism.

In general, it is never possible to point out just which particular aspect of Hellenism or which of its characteristic ideas provoked the rapid evolution of Jewish thought, since very few elements of Greek literature can be found in Jewish literature, and even those few elements are debatable. On the level of mentalities, though, of what the Germans call *Zeitgeist*, in the underlying orientations of the mind something happened.

Qohelet, who seeks God the creator in the laws of nature and of life does not distance himself from the Jewish tradition, but he does place his words in a new spiritual context. One gets the impression that while Hellenism led the Greeks to develop the more irrational and pathetic elements of their thought, after coming into contact with the Greeks Judaism developed the more rational and humanly independent elements of its spirit, in the search for a systematic organization of the elements composing its tradition. That is what Qohelet seeks to do. It is also what the Essene Teacher of Righteousness does, though following a very different path.[29] Covenant and Grace, the freedom of humans and the freedom of God, the meaning of retribution in the context of these problems and especially the very concept of salvation which alone sheds light on all other concepts in Jewish spirituality, are the themes most often compared, beginning especially with the second century BCE.

The answers given to these problems were many and not always compatible with one another. Judaism, which had already been broken at the time of the return from exile, over the course of two or three centuries splintered into numerous sects. Following various paths some of these sects were destined to reach our day, leaving their imprint on many aspects of the modern world. Others disappeared completely, or left only minor traces. The two giants that survived the long crisis of

29. When I wrote *Storia del mondo giudaico*, it was still possible to consider the Teacher of Righteousness the author of 1QS and therefore the founder of Essenic thought. Since then it has been shown that 1QS was composed from various sources that belong to different times. Hence, we cannot take the whole book as evidence of the origins of the sect. Besides, the text of the book is uncertain, because it varies from one manuscript to the other. Thus the Teacher of Righteousness can no longer be seen as the clear-cut figure that prevailed until the 1970s. As a consequence of this state of things, I have ususally substituted 'Teacher of Righteousness' with the more generic 'Essenic'. If on occasion the name of the Master has remained in the text, it is more to indicate an author rather than the real figure of the sect's organizer.

On the problem of the sources or the stratification of 1QS, see P. Arata Manto-vani, 'La stratificazione letteraria della *Regola della Comunità*: A proposito del libro di J. Pouilly, *La règle de la Communauté de Qumran*', *Henoch* 5 (1983), pp. 69-92 and relative bibliography.

Judaism in order to reach our own time are Pharisaism, which continues in modern-day Rabbinism, and Christianity, which has come down to us in a number of interpretations, which have greatly increased in number in the period since Humanism. Among the other minor sects that have survived the Samaritans are worthy of mention; even today they can celebrate the sacrifice of Passover on the holy mountain of Gerizim under the guide of a Zadokite priest. Karaism should be mentioned as well; while a historically distinct group only since the eighth century with Anan ben David, their doctrine contains many strangely archaic elements.[30]

30. On the problem of the survival of Essenism, see N. Wieder, *The Judean Scrolls and Karaism* (London: East and West Library, 1962); and A. Paul, *Ecrits de Qumran et sectes juives aux premiers siècles de l'Islam: Recherches sur l'origine du Caraïsme* (Paris: Letouzey et Ané, 1969). The latter is much more prudent than the former. An analytical panorama of the question can be found in a posthumous article by H. Bardtke, 'Einige Erwägungen zum Problem "Qumran und Karaismus"', *Henoch* 10 (1988), pp. 259-70. See B. Chiesa, 'Il giudaismo caraita', in *idem*, *Atti del V Congresso Internazionale dell'AISG—S. Miniato 1984* (Rome: Carucci, 1987), pp. 151-74. S. Szyszman's passionate history of his religion also merits mention: S. Szyszman, *Le karaïsme, ses doctrines et son histoire* (Lausanne: L'Age d'homme, 1980).

Part III
PALESTINE FROM THE ADVENT OF SELEUCID DOMINATION
TO THE DESTRUCTION OF THE SECOND TEMPLE

Chapter 7

PALESTINE UNDER THE SELEUCIDS: THE MACCABEES

1. *Between the Ptolemies and the Seleucids*

With the battle of Panium (later known as Caesarea Philippi), fought between Antiochus III (232–187 BCE) and Ptolemy V Epiphanes (205–180 BCE) in the year 200, Palestine entered into the Syrian orbit. The passage from one sphere of influence to another was not so very brusque, however, as could be imagined, given that it was the result of a battle. In fact, the passage was gradual and, if in the end Jerusalem was shaken in its traditional aspect and ideology, this was due primarily to the profound evolution which had taken place in the Judaic mentality of this period.

The period in which Judaea passed from Ptolemaic to Seleucid domination is a rather obscure one because of the difficulties presented by Josephus's account in the *Antiquities of the Jews*, which is the only source that speaks of the events which took place between the battle of Panium and the great crisis beginning around 175 BCE. For example, Noth brings a chapter to a close with the battle of Panium and Antiochus III's consequent decree in favour of the Judaeans, and then opens the following chapter with the documentation provided in the books of the Maccabees. Scholars have not taken the sources at the basis of Josephus's account very seriously because they seem more fit for a novel than a historical narrative; the Tobiads lie at the centre of interest of the principal source, making their story something of a historical novel.

Apart from the doubts concerning the source, the use Josephus makes of it is a separate problem. There are a number of points in Josephus's work where the chronology is confused; his chronology regarding Nehemiah and Ezra, for example, is useless. He confuses the two high priests named Simon, applying the appellative of 'Just' to the first rather than the second. He attributes construction of the Birta to

Hyrcanus while it was already in existence half-way through the third century BCE, since it was mentioned in one of Zeno's papyri (Pap. Cairo Zen. n. 59003 1.13). Josephus could have made a similar mistake regarding Joseph the Tobiad, whom he places during the reign of Ptolemy V Epiphanes (204–181 BCE), while modern scholars such as Gressman, Meyer and Momigliano prefer to place him in the time of Ptolomy III Euergetes (246–221 BCE). Momigliano, who defines Josephus's account regarding Joseph the Tobiad 'a naive construction', accepts the elements that seem most likely to him, that is the allusion to a rupture within Jerusalem between religious power and lay power, between τιμὴ ἀρχιερατική and προστασία. Momigliano also deduces that Josephus 'assumed one [the *prostasìa*] without touching the other', which is all but clear in the source, because the expression used in *Ant.* 12.167, can be interpreted (and has been interpreted) in a non-technical way: εἶναι γὰρ αὐτοῦ προστάτην.[1]

The judgment expressed by Meyer,[2] concerning Josephus's sources for the period running from Alexander's conquest to the troubles accompanying the end of Zadokitism is still valid today. There are three sources: a novel of Alexander, Aristeas and the 'Tales of the Tobiads'. These works, which are essentially novels, served to cover a period of time for which Josephus did not have any more structured material. The use of the material provided by these works in order to construct a continuing historical narrative was dangerous, since many people in this period bore the same names. At any rate, the historical events that constitute a backdrop for these stories provide a fundamental criterion for dating the events recounted, to the extent, of course, that such an operation is possible.

The argument used by Meyer to justify reassigning events strictly related to Ptolemy V and his marriage to Cleopatra, daughter of Antiochus III, to Ptolemy III Euergetes (246–221 BCE) is based on a gloss which worked its way into the tradition of Josephus's text and is, therefore, without historical value. The gloss has been identified by Niese, Reinack and Marcus. It is certain that *Ant.* 12.158 speaks of a King Ptolemy who, given the sense of the account, must be Ptolemy V Epiphanes. Some manuscripts, however, contain the addition 'Euergetes, who was father of Philopater', that is Ptolemy III. Our suspicions that this is a gloss stem from the excessive precision of the expression

1. See the Loeb edition and the note regarding this passage.
2. Cf. *Ursprung*, II, p. 128

within the body of the story and are confirmed by the problems concerning the context. The context speaks of the Ptolemies' dominion over Palestine even after the battle of Panium, when the reader would expect such dominion to have come to an end. In reality, the text explains later why Ptolemaic control over Palestine persisted, but this is difficult to grasp on first reading, hence the gloss.

On the whole Josephus's account is well structured beginning with paragraph 154 concerning the fact that Cleopatra brought income from Phoenicia, Syria and Palestine as her dowry to Ptolemy V. It is possible that in fitting his sources together Josephus confused the information regarding one Ptolemy with that regarding another, but the overall structure of the account is coherent and is based on a fact mentioned in Greek sources as well (Polybius 28.20 and Appian, *Syr.* 5). Since the story revolves around the Tobiad and not on the Jerusalem priesthood or some local king, it is up to the reader to decide when he is dealing with Onias II and when with Onias III. Even the confusion concerning the attribution of the name 'the Just' to Simon I instead of Simon II depends on the fact that his source must not have given this name to either one and Josephus must have attributed it following his own judgment. Beginning with paragraph 223 Josephus leaves the 'Tales of the Tobiads' and begins to use a source with a more solid historiographical nature. At any rate it is clear that Josephus used a variety of sources and that he established the synchronicity of events in an inductive manner, without reference to any pre-packaged history of the Jews.[3] In this manner he attributes the letter of Areios, king of Sparta, to the time of Onias III, while Areios died in 255 BCE; the Onias mentioned in Josephus's source was therefore Onias II and not Onias III. We should therefore refuse the date given for the death of Joseph and Onias II (!) as the accession of Seleucus IV to the throne (187 BCE). From the structure of Josephus's account it is clear that it is not the same source that tells of Seleucus's rise to the throne and the simultaneous deaths of Joseph and Onias II. For us, therefore, it is clear that the Onias mentioned is certainly Onias III. The juxtaposition of these deaths and Seleucus's accession to the throne is the fruit of Josephus's own chronology, which he got wrong. As concerns Hyrcanus, whom we can imagine to have been born around 190 BCE, it is difficult to believe that he could have been

---

3.   On the attention Josephus gives to chronological problems, see P. Piovanelli, 'Le texte de Jérémie utilisé par Flavius Josphus dans le X livre des Antiquités juives', *Henoch* 14 (1992), pp. 11-36.

sent to Alexandria to represent his aging father for the birth of the king's son, if that son was necessarily the successor to the throne (born in 187 BCE). Surely we are dealing with a later period. Even though the novel of Hyrcanus would have him extremely precocious (c. 190), he could not have gone to Alexandria earlier than about ten years later and the conflict with his brothers should as a consequence be placed around the crisis years of approximately 175–165.

In favour of the general chronology proposed by Josephus is the fact that the historical background for the events narrated are in concordance with the times of Ptolemy V and not Ptolemy III.

The historical account revolves around the marriage between a Cleopatra, a daughter of Antiochus (*Ant.* 12.154), with a Ptolemy, who must therefore be Epiphanes. Furthermore, the text returns a number of times to the problem of Cleopatra's dowry, which could explain the strange regime to be found in Jerusalem in the wake of the battle of Panium. It is difficult to believe that this detail was completely fictitious. This regime serves as a clarificatory background for the adventures of Joseph the Tobiad; it would seem that Josephus's source had placed the action in a precise historical atmosphere. The information regarding the dowry agreement too, besides corresponding generally to the juridical customs of the day,[4] includes complex details that have caused much debate among scholars and which cannot be the fruit of imagination (διαιρεθέντων εἰς ἀμφοτέρους τοὺς βασιλέας τῶν φόρων, 'when the tribute was divided between the two sovereigns' [12.155]). Even Onias III's (180[?]–173 BCE) refusal to pay taxes, if placed chronologically after Antiochus' edict exempting the priesthood from the payment of taxes, becomes believable. It would not be in any other historical context; Jerusalem belonged to the Seleucid state and therefore Onias had very precise juridical reasons for not paying taxes to Alexandria—he had been exempted by Antiochus. That is, Onias yes, but the people no, hence the loathsomeness of Onias' refusal to pay without opposing the levying of taxes on the people. If one thing, though, creates problems in the historical background, it is the use of exact numbers; the 22 years of Joseph the Tobiad and the 7 years of his son Hyrcanus. It is not even clear to Josephus whether the two figures are to be placed end to end or if the periods overlap. Nor is it clear from which date they begin or with which they end, since the date of Joseph's death is unknown. At any

---

4. See E. Cuq, 'La condition juridique de la Coelésyrie au temps de Ptolomée V Epiphane', *Syria* 8 (1927), pp. 143-62.

rate, the figures given by Josephus do follow their own logic. The refusal of the elderly Onias II should be placed in the year following the marriage of Cleopatra (c. 193 BCE), and therefore in the years immediately prior to 190, which can be considered the year of Onias II's death. The 22 years of Joseph the Tobiad's strong *prostasìa* in Jerusalem could even include the period of conflict with Hyrcanus and last for the rest of Joseph's life. In this case we would arrive all the way to 170 BCE, which would be confirmed by one of Josephus's sources which places Joseph the Tobiad's death in the same years as that of Onias, clearly Onias III. Regarding Hyrcanus's seven years, they must go a little beyond 170 BCE, since Hyrcanus's presence explains Jason's reaction against Menelaus (pp. 223-27).

Up until this point in time Hellenism seems to have penetrated Jerusalem only very slowly, because the city was protected by Ezra's measures against contamination with the pagans. Now, though, Hellenism breaks into the city, certainly not with its deepest values, but with its most visible manifestations: individualism, love of glory which easily becomes a thirst for power, an economy which leads to the rapid development of the most wealthy elements of society, and a trend towards syncretism which could not correspond to the most authentic principles of the Yahwist tradition. Qohelet's severe criticism of Nehemian society also weighed heavily on the Jewish society of the early second century BCE. The loss of the rigid relationship between righteousness and salvation placed spirits before a void, which inevitably attracted them.

Unlike the battle of Raphia in 217 BCE, which had been fought on the coast and ended with the defeat of Antiochus, the battle of Panium took place north of Jerusalem near Lake Tiberiad and involved the city. The Egyptians occupied the city with a garrison while the Jews awaited liberation from the Syrians. Following Antiochus' victory at Panium the Jews helped him capture the Egyptian garrison left in Jerusalem (see Polybius 16.39.4).

No great gesture in itself, it was, however, enough to enter into the good graces of Antiochus who was preparing for war against Rome and had every interest in contenting the cities left behind him. Thus, after an initial generic recognition of the restoration of the city (2 Macc. 3.2; *Ant.* 12.138-39, 143), Antiochus granted broader concessions. The Jews were allowed to take timber from the state lands free of charge, the priests and the upper classes were exempted from taxation and, in order to favour the city's repopulation, tax exemption for three years was granted to anyone who went to settle in the city. Such immigrants were to benefit from further facilitations in the future as well (Josephus, *Ant.* 12.140-42). This marked a sharp change in Jerusalem's fiscal regime since no exemptions had been granted by the Ptolemies.

The marriage arranged between Ptolemy V Epiphanes and Antiochus III's daughter Cleopatra should be placed in the context of Antiochus' desire to safeguard his Asian territories before becoming engaged in the West. Cleopatra's dowry included the revenue from all of the lands to the south of Antioch: Coele-Syria, Phoenicia, Samaria and Judaea. Sovereignty remained in Seleucid hands, but taxes were to be collected by Alexandria, with the exception of certain divisions to be made between Ptolemy and Cleopatra which are not clear (*Ant.* 12.154-55). The wedding, which probably took place in 193, was arranged in 196 BCE.[5]

On the grounds of their agreement with the Seleucids, the Egyptians requested that the Temple begin paying tribute as in the past. The high priest, who at that time was Onias II, refused on the grounds that Antiochus had exonerated the Temple from such payments (*Ant.* 12.158). Onias's position was not rebellious, it was an invitation to collect taxes from those who owed them, that is the people. The people, naturally, rioted.

The story at this point takes on a decidedly novelistic air in its details, though in broad terms Josephus's source seems credible. A nephew of Onias, Joseph the Tobiad, rose up in favour of the people and succeeded in obtaining a sort of proxy from Onias to represent him in his dealings with Egypt. Power seems to be entirely in the hands of the high priest in this period, since Josephus tells us that Onias held both the τιμὴ ἀρχιερατικὴ and the προστασία τοῦ λαοῦ. Onias (§163)

---

5. It seems to me that the text of *Ant.* 12.155, διαιρεθέντων εἰς ἀμφοτέρους τοὺς βασιλέας τῶν φόρων ('the tribute divided between the two kings'), must be interpreted as referring to the Egyptian bride and groom (see M. Holleaux, 'Sur un passage de Flavius Josèphe [*Jewish Antiquities*, xii, 4, §155]', *REJ* 39 [1899], pp. 161-76). For the opposing view see A. Momigliano, 'I Tobiadi nella preistoria del moto maccabaico', *ARAST* 67 (1931–32), pp. 165-200, but the fact that in 12.178 we find that the husband and wife could act as guarantors for one another in the payment of taxes lends support to Holleaux's interpretation.

Regarding the dates for the negotiations leading to the marriage between Ptolemy and Cleopatra and the celebration of that marriage, see CAH, VIII, p. 199. The events which followed have as *terminus post quem* the date of Ptolemy and Cleopatra's wedding (193 BCE), and must have happened very soon thereafter.

declared that he was willing to give up both of these titles, demonstrating that together the two represented the highest level of authority. Joseph the Tobiad, who was to appear with only the title of προτασία τοῦ λαοῦ (§167), called the people together in the Temple (§164), demonstrating that in some way he also had priestly authority. This confusion of powers contains its own intrinsic logic characteristic of times of crisis.

Joseph went to Alexandria in order to obtain the abolition or at least a reduction of the taxes, to consolidate his personal προστασία, and to create a role of personal power in Jerusalem following the tradition of his family. In Egypt Joseph was able to acquire the right to collect all the taxes owed by the regions, the income of which constituted Cleopatra's dowry (*Ant.* 12.175). Joseph the Tobiad was very able. At least in the hyperbole and admiration of Josephus's source, Joseph literally plundered the non-Jewish cities taking advantage of the broad autonomy and military forces available to the king's financial officials (see *Ant.* 12.180-85, and bear in mind the Tobiad of Zeno's letter). Joseph left Judaea in peace, strengthening his own position both in terms of riches and the favour of the Jews.

Jerusalem developed rapidly during the time of Joseph the Tobiad's activity, taking advantage of its unique position within the Ptolemaic state. This particularly favourable state of things, at least from an economic standpoint, lasted for some time, probably under the priesthood of Simon the Just, up until the great crisis beginning in 175 BCE (see in particular §§186 and 224). The very numerous deposits in the Temple, which became the object of the Seleucids' greed, bear witness to Jerusalem's wealth in this period.

It seems that Hyrcanus's death is to be dated to 168 BCE, thus explaining Jason's possibility of arming against Menelaus. The seven years of Hyrcanus' rule would therefore run from 175 to 168 BCE. Joseph must have died at the time of the upheavals leading first to the exile (173 BCE) and then to the death of Onias III (171 BCE).

Greater and greater tensions within Jewish society grew during this period. Following Onias II's gesture in favour of Joseph the Tobiad, power continued to slip gradually away from the high priest and the class that had ruled for centuries, in effect passing into other hands.

While Joseph was still alive conflict arose even within his family for reasons of economic interests which immediately took on political connotations. I believe that if we could know more, we would discover that ideological elements were not extraneous to the tension. One of Joseph's sons, Hyrcanus, succeeded in replacing his father in his role of tax collector. His brothers then attacked him and tried to kill him, apparently with Joseph's complicity, but they were defeated by Hyrcanus' bodyguard and two of them were even killed. Since Hyrcanus was the Ptolemies' creature, it was inevitable that the brothers sought the Seleucids' support, given the regime in which the city was basically dependent on two different capitals. The high priest Simon II, son of Onias II (§229) and perhaps most of the people sided with the brothers and the Seleucids.

The tension hidden behind these events cannot be reduced to the simple denominator of 'pro-Egyptian' and 'pro-Syrian', or that of 'traditionalists' and 'Hellenists'. These are only a few of the elements that were in ferment in Jerusalem. There were hopes for the arrival of a figure who, for the love that God bore for his people, would save Israel. This figure's characteristics were now indicated in a different way than in the past. Prophecy, which had practically disappeared in the static society of Ezra's Jerusalem, was reborn, but in a new form. At the same time the internal political situation deteriorated rapidly into one of humanity's longest and most tragic civil wars.

2. *Ethical and Political Collapse*

The first symptoms of the internal disintegration that destroyed the society of Jerusalem came about during the reign of Seleucus IV (187–175 BCE). His authority weakened, the high priest was no longer able to control the conflicts that undermined society. A typical aspect of the collapse of Jewish society is narrated in 2 Maccabees 3.

> But a man named Simon, of the tribe [in the sense of priestly family] of Bilgah,[6] who had been made captain of the Temple, had a disagreement

---

6. The reading 'of Bilgah' is from the *Vetus Latina* and the Armenian. The Greek text reads 'of Benjamin'. The priestly class of Bilgah is mentioned in 1 Chron. 24.14. It appears that the Greek lesson is to be discarded, since it does not seem likely that a layman should have a position in the Temple as high as that of Simon. But the fundamental argument is provided by the fact that one of Simon's brothers, Menelaus, was to become high priest. It is therefore most probable that it was a priestly family rather than a lay one. The claim that Menelaus was not of priestly blood therefore depends on a reading of this passage from 2 Maccabees. On this subject, see F.M. Abel, 'Simon de la tribu de Bilga', in L.C. Mohlberg (ed.),

with the high priest about the administration of the city market. Since he could not prevail over Onias [clearly Onias III], he went to Apollonius of Tarsus, who at that time was governor of Coelesyria and Phoenicia, and reported to him that the treasury in Jerusalem was full of untold sums of money, so that the amount of the funds could not be reckoned, and that they did not belong to the account of the sacrifices, but that it was possible for them to fall under the control of the king (2 Macc. 3.4-6).

Simon surely did not intend to provoke a sack of the Temple. He was simply trying to pay for an eventual nomination as high priest in place of Onias. In order to do this, he was pointing out that there were some irregularities in the Temple's administration, irregularities whose origin surely lay in the political and economic manoeuvres of Hyrcanus the Tobiad. Hyrcanus had sought to win over the high priest's trust after Onias had given asylum to Hyrcanus's surviving brothers (2 Macc. 3.11). Simon's plan failed, because Onias went personally to Seleucus and clarified things in his own favour. A path had been opened, however, which was to be trod several times in the future. The Syrian state needed a great deal of money due to the defeat at Magnesia and the heavy tribute that Antiochus III had promised to pay the Romans; and the dissidents in Jerusalem took the habit, so to speak, of trying to gain the high priesthood by buying it directly from the Seleucid king.

This event is interesting in that it illustrates a certain mentality. It is an accepted fact that the highest authority lies outside Jerusalem. If the position of high priest in Jerusalem had been in practice hereditary since the days of Persian domination, this had been able to come about because descent in the satrapies normally followed a father–son line. This was the case in the absence of particularly serious events or crises forcing the king to interrupt a dynasty. It was only because of their fidelity to the succession of kings who dominated Palestine that the priests had been able to maintain their power. Jonathan Maccabaeus, who was practically independent, still received the high priesthood from a foreign sovereign, Alexander Balas. Apparently it was felt that the high priest's authority was dependent on the foreign sovereign of the moment.

I am not sure just exactly what to think of these aspirant high priests, whether to imagine them as driven by the desire for glory, caricatures of Alexander the Great or Pyrrhus, or rather as spokesmen, representatives of the deeply rooted contrasts among the people. The glory that

Miscellanea Mercati (Rome: Biblioteca Apostolica Vaticana, 1946), I, pp. 52-58.

derives from power was a typical value of Hellenism, but it is also certain that these ambitions were supported by interests which, in turn, had to find ethical and theoretical justifications.

3. *The End of the Zadokite Period*

In the years immediately following 175 BCE, the year of Antiochus IV Epiphanes' rise to the throne, the situation in Jerusalem deteriorated rapidly. Onias III chased the Tobiad brothers from Jerusalem and they sought refuge in Antiochus (*War* 1.31-32). The rift between the high priest and the Tobiads clearly betrays the passage of Onias from the sphere of influence of Antiochus to that of Hyrcanus, a creature of the Ptolemies. This was the last link of Hyrcanus' plan to influence Onias through the gold which had been deposited in the Jerusalem Temple in an abnormal way, probably entrusted directly to the high priest rather than to the Temple. With Onias III's move, Hyrcanus's aspirations reached their fullest success in Jerusalem.

It is clear that in the struggles among the Tobiads Hellenism and theological questions were merely pretexts. Perhaps for Onias it was different, perhaps they were real problems and it would be interesting to know the motivations behind the provisions expelling the Tobiads from Jerusalem, but unfortunately we do not have this information.

I believe, however, that in order to arrive at a move of this gravity, a move whose consequences were surely foreseeable by Onias, he must have been driven by very serious considerations, and not simply of an economic order. In order to pay back Hyrcanus for the money offered him, Onias could have supported him, but he would never have done as much had his conscience not been faced with a real choice; Onias must have made a political and a theological choice. The events which followed demonstrate the scope of his gesture; one of his brothers,[7] who changed his name from Yashua to Jason, obtained the high priesthood from the Seleucid sovereign. In order to get it Jason offered the Seleucids money and committed himself to Hellenizing Jerusalem (174 BCE) (2 Macc. 4.8-9).

1 Maccabees narrates with disdain that many Jews were in favour of these innovations (1.11-15). The creation of a gymnasium, frequented

---

7.   Josephus considered Onias III, Jason and Menelaus all to be sons of Simon (*Ant.* 12.237-39). Apparently, lacking reliable information, he tried to save the legitimacy of the Jerusalem priesthood, at least up until the Hasmonaean high priests.

mostly by the sons of the upper class, and therefore the youth of the priestly caste, can be taken as a symbol of the spirit of these innovations.

The gymnasium was a sign of the new mentality which had spread in Jerusalem. Admiration for Greek culture led to disdain for one's own culture (2 Macc. 4.15). Some of Judaism's most ancient precepts, but also the most irrational ones, were seen as absurd in the light of reason. Babies were no longer circumcised and young men underwent a sort of plastic surgery in order to hide a circumcision that their nudity as athletes showed in public (1 Macc. 1.15). Zeal for the gods which were so prominent in Hellenistic culture, at least publicly, even led Jason to send money to Antiochus IV Epiphanes for a sacrifice in honour of Hercules (2 Macc. 4.19). Hellenism gained ground in Jerusalem not only because of the Syrians' efforts, but also because of the convictions of many Jews. While the author of 1 Maccabees interprets the Judaean civil war of 167–142 BCE as a war of liberation against the foreign rulers who had used Hellenism as a means of penetrating Jewish society, he also narrates in 1.11-13 that the desire to abandon living by the Torah had originated spontaneously among the Jews.

The process of Hellenization did not fail to cause a reaction among those elements of society who considered the values of the Torah as fundamental for their very existence. As in all reactionary phenomena, the ideal was radicalized. If a comparison, or even a dialogue between Judaism and Hellenism was possible, this could only take place on a very profound basis. That is, when the most authentic Hellenistic values had been understood by the Jews and on condition that it was possible to distinguish between cosmopolitan tolerance and syncretism, which has never been an easy undertaking in any historical period.

To the person in the street, or to whoever judged the situation from a first impression, Hellenism had brought Jerusalem a gymnasium, a certain degree of submission to the foreigners, money, corruption and ever-growing ambition.

Jason soon fell victim to his own means. One Menelaus, brother of the Simon who had already informed Seleucus of the 'irregular' presence of money in the Temple, introduced himself to Epiphanes in order to buy the high priesthood for which Jason had already paid a considerable amount of money. The nature of this event was such as to cause a reaction among those who considered the values of Zadokite Judaism as still fully valid. In fact, while Menelaus was a priest, he certainly was not a descendant from the Zadokites. The Temple was contaminated and the very essence of Zadokite Judaism had been destroyed. Menelaus held on through force, and had to withdraw even more money from the Temple in order to maintain his position. He also betrayed Onias III and had him killed, since he could in some way have claimed the high priesthood (171 BCE).

In 169 BCE Epiphanes tried to conquer Egypt. He launched an attack, taking advantage of the fact that since 171 Rome had been engaged in a war against Macedon. In spite of his successes in 169, Epiphanes had to return to Egypt the following year, which was also the year that the Romans liquidated Macedonian resistance at Pydna. A Roman ambassador, Pompilius Lenate, reached Epiphanes in Alexandria and entered history for the brusque way in which he treated Antiochus IV, who tried to buy time in order to conclude the Egyptian question before the Romans intervened (Polybius 29.27). Forced to return home in order to avoid a conflict with Rome, Epiphanes decided to attack Jerusalem. In this way he hoped to recuperate some of the money spent on the Egyptian invasion and put an end to what was becoming an intolerable situation. In fact while Epiphanes was busy dealing with Pompilius Lenate word had spread in Palestine that Epiphanes was dead. Jason, who had taken refuge in Ammanitis, certainly in the Tobiads' fortress, immediately took advantage of the situation. He received men and arms from Hyrcanus, who was probably at the fortress as well, and assaulted his rival Menelaus in Jerusalem. Menelaus, Antiochus' creature, took refuge in the citadel, the city was sacked and Jason's men slaughtered their adversaries (2 Macc. 5.6).

Epiphanes, who was not dead, had no choice but to intervene on behalf of Menelaus, first of all to avenge a man who had been faithful to him, but also in order to put an end to the internal conflicts within Jerusalem that risked damaging all of Syria. Jerusalem lay on the kingdom's southern border and continued internal political conflict could tempt the Ptolemies to intervene.

Jason managed to escape once more, but this time the massacres were carried out by Menelaus's followers, who sought revenge for very recent deaths (2 Macc. 5.11-14). Antiochus despoiled the Temple and imposed the complete Hellenization of the city's customs. Within a very few years Jerusalem was deprived of control over its own forces. The walls were in part dismantled and a Syrian garrison was stationed in a fortress (the *akra*) inside the city. It was forbidden by law to possess the book of the Law, circumcision was prohibited and on 15 December 167 BCE the Temple was contaminated through the introduction of 'an abomination that desolates' (Dan. 9.27; 11.31; 12.11), probably a pagan altar. The Temple at Gerizim was rededicated to Zeus Xenios (Zeus-the-Friend-of-Strangers; 2 Macc. 6.2). Religious persecution was underway.

And still, it is difficult to believe that Antiochus intended to persecute the religion. Most of all, he had to turn Jerusalem into a city that he could trust. Otherwise, it is impossible to understand why the persecution was not extended to all Jews, who must have been fairly numerous in the vast Syrian state. Events such as those narrated in 2 Macc. 6.8 seem to have been sporadic and most of all limited to the cities of Palestine. The fact of the matter is that he must not have felt safe with a state of political turmoil in Judaea, his southern border, now that Egypt was under Roman protection. He gave his support to one side in the conflict because that side was more favourable to him. And while he prohibited the circumcision of infants, many Jews in Jerusalem, as we have already seen, were ashamed of their circumcision. The sabbath could seem to be an absurdity, a superstition. In the end, Antiochus could not have had the end goal of destroying Judaism if he did not destroy the Temple of Yhwh and even left a Jewish priest in charge of it. No matter how he had been elected, the high priest had been recognized as such and had been left to exercise his role for many years. For his part, Menelaus certainly consented to the measures taken by Antiochus. The very fact that Antiochus was able to individuate precisely which Jewish practices to abolish demonstrates that the person advising him on the matter knew the Judaism of the period very well and wanted to destroy *that particular* Judaism, not *all* Judaism.

No one wants to become the high priest to a god in liquidation, not even Menelaus. What Menelaus wanted to liquidate was Zadokite Judaism and there are a number of factors that could have brought him to desire this. It is only from our point of view that Judaism is equated with the Torah, while it is clear that Menelaus considered himself a priest of Yhwh even though he discarded the Torah. Apparently for him Israel was the people of Yhwh, the people chosen by God with a Covenant and that Covenant was made concrete in a Law, and it bore no importance whether that Law was guaranteed by a force external to Israel. Ezra's goal had been that of renewing a certain legislation, but in accepting the principle by which the Law of God became the law of a foreign king, Ezra gave rise to a principle destined to bring with it many consequences. The sovereign had now changed, why shouldn't the Law change too? Jason's gesture of having the citizens of Jerusalem enrolled in the lists of Antioch (2 Macc. 4.9) should be seen, in my opinion, as part of a line of behaviour whose roots lay in this belief.

What, then, lay at the centre of Judaism? The law, any law, or the people of Israel drawn up around the Temple? Amidst the profound changes brought about in the world under the influence of Hellenism, shouldn't some changes be made in order to survive as Jews? Wasn't it enough that Yhwh survive, along with his people and his worship? The final end of the Law, according to an ancient and widespread tradition was that of giving well-being and a long life. The problem of God's judgment after death which was to give each individual soul its absolute and eternal reward was a belief which had not yet been accepted in all of Israel, at least not in Jerusalem and at least not among the upper class. Let us re-examine the words of the 1 Macc. 1.11: 'Let us go and make a covenant with the Gentiles around us, for since we are separated from them [that is, since the reforms of Nehemiah and Ezra] many disasters have come upon us'. It was possible to be Jews and believe in the Torah, in a law or even only in the Temple; Israel's problem of giving itself an identity was an ancient and complex problem.

Something in the new mentality succeeded in imposing itself. The Judaism of the Late Zadokite period, based on the Zadokite priesthood, the Covenant and the Law can be considered to have come to an end. Even those who took up arms in defence of the tradition do not seem in any way attached to the priesthood of Zadok. When the reconsecration of the Temple was celebrated in 164, with a ceremony which is repeated even today in the synagogal liturgy, the high priest recognized by all the Jews who had fought in the civil war was Menelaus. The Essenes maintained the ideal of the pure Zadokite priesthood, but their opposition, at least in the second century BCE, was not only physically removed and at a distance from Jerusalem's religious and political turmoil, but it was also absolutely inactive (or at least it appears so today).

4. *Defence of the Tradition: The Forms of Reaction*

In this complex political and ideological situation, so full of contradictions, the reaction against the Hellenizing trends took on political and religious overtones which are difficult to grasp today. To fight against the process of Hellenization was not only a cultural and religious ideal, but it also meant fighting against one power in the name of, and for, another power.

If we observe the political scene closely, we notice that in the decade running from 170 to 160 BCE two distinct attitudes are formed, one of flight and the other of armed resistance. The Zadokite movements fall under the first heading. The legitimate priesthood realized that it no longer had a following, neither among the masses nor among the powerful. Thus Onias IV fled to Egypt where he founded a temple at Leontopolis, rival to the one in Jerusalem. Other Zadokites, who were probably already in conflict with the Temple for reasons which remain unknown to us, fled to the desert. Belial had been loosed and it was necessary to take a distance both from the pagans and the other Jews, and not only a ritual separation, but a real, physical one as well. It was necessary to live under the most rigid application of the norms regarding purity. It was necessary to create the 'remnant of Israel', the true Israel that God would one day save by sending a messiah, extraordinary both in his nature and his strength.

Others chose the path of armed resistance, but they chose this option for a variety of ideals and motivations. For some it was merely a question of attaining the goal of being able to live in peace in accordance with the traditions of their forebears, to be Jews according to the traditional Law. For others, however, the problem was more radical. For this second group it was a question of substituting Menelaus with another power, in the hands of another dynasty. This was the ideal behind the Maccabee brothers' actions for decades; for them it was not enough to be able to live under the traditional Law. They wanted an independent Jewish state separate and distinct from the Hellenistic states, guaranteed and protected by its own forces. The Law for them was more of a rallying cry than an ideal; the real ideal was the seizure of power, that is both the προστασία τοῦ λαοῦ and the τιμὴ ἀρχιερατική.

This latter movement, characterized by its open opposition to the Hellenizing party which had come to power with Menelaus, dominated the political scene. But those who had 'fled' to the desert also played a considerable part in the evolution of later Judaism through the elaboration of a distinct theology, in clear contrast to that of 'those who had remained'. The people who had 'remained' developed the theologies of the Covenant, those who 'fled' developed the theologies of the Promise.

Let us examine the effect of these two fundamental tendencies on men's historical actions.

5. *Onias IV*

A movement worthy of memory more for the name of its founder and the ideal it represented, rather than for its impact on the course of historical events (practically nil), is that headed by Onias IV, son of Onias III. The last legitimate Zadokite priest, Onias III had been assassinated. Onias IV, therefore, represented the continuity of the Zadokite tradition.

Onias sought refuge in Egypt and was obviously well received by the Ptolemies, arch-enemies of the Seleucids. Ptolemy VI Philometer, who reigned until 145 BCE, granted Onias permission to build a temple at Leontopolis. It is clear that for Onias the true Israel consisted in the continuity of the priesthood and legitimate worship. This was more important than the same tradition calling for the unification of worship in Jerusalem. For Onias the Leontopolis temple was to represent the spiritual centre for all Jews, and in particular for those living in Egypt. Its purpose was that of turning the Jews of Palestine away from worship centred on Jerusalem, which was no longer in Zadokite hands and was therefore illegitimate. Most of all, though, it was to serve as a new centre for Judaism should the situation in Jerusalem deteriorate.

In reality the temple at Leontopolis had little weight in the course of events and was destroyed by the Romans out of prudence in 73 CE, after they had destroyed the one in Jerusalem. For the Pharisees, even though they placed greater importance on the continuity of worship in Jerusalem than on the continuity of the Zadokite priesthood, the Leontopolis temple was not schismatic. In fact the Mishnah (*Men.* 13.10) established that a vow made at the temple in Leontopolis had the same value as one made at the Temple in Jerusalem.

According to Josephus in *Ant.* 12.237, Onias IV was still a child when his father was assassinated. In fact he was still living around the year 100. He fled to Egypt when Demetrius named Alcimus high priest in 161 BCE; until that moment he had hoped to regain the high priesthood (*Ant.* 12.387). This passage in Josephus should be read together with 1 Macc. 7.5-32. From 2 Macc. 14.3, 13 it appears that Alcimus had already been high priest before Demetrius placed him in that position in 161; this would confirm Josephus's version, but in any case it is difficult to establish the chronology of events. If the person named *hnn* (Onias) in an Egyptian papyrus dated to 164 BCE is our Onias IV, then the date for his flight to Egypt should be anticipated.[8]

---

8.   See R. de Vaux, 'Le Temple d'Onias et Qumran', *RB* 75 (1968), pp. 204-205.

The reader should also be reminded that in *The Jewish War* (1.31-33) Josephus provides a very different account of the events from that of the *Antiquities of the Jews*. In this case, though, his account is merely a summary of events, rapidly bringing together a series of facts which can hardly all be placed in 168 BCE, as it could appear on a first reading. In this version, Onias III, after having been deposed, fled to Egypt where he himself founded the temple at Leontopolis.

6. *The* Damascus Document *and the Essenes*

Near the end of the nineteenth century a text whose introduction narrates the birth of a dissident movement was found in the *genizah* (a storage room where the manuscripts of sacred texts are kept after they have become unusable) of the Cairo synagogue. Fragments of this same text have been found at Qumran and this text, which has been known now for a century, is considered part of the corpus of the Dead Sea Scrolls. It is the so-called *Damascus Document*.[9] The problem is that of determining from which other movement the dissident group separated. Should we imagine separation from all other Jewish practices, creating a completely new ideology, or a movement which had already taken shape and that was now splintering? In the first instance the *Damascus Document* narrates the birth of Essenism. In the second the formation of a sect within the Essenic movement. In either case we are dealing with a new movement. The recent discovery of the text 4QMMT[10] lies at the basis of this interpretation of the history of Essenism.

The *Damascus Document* begins with these words:

> Hear now, all you who know righteousness, and understand the works of God; for He has come in judgment of all men [Isa. 51.7] and will condemn all those who despise Him. For when they abandoned Him and were unfaithful, He hid His face from Israel and His Temple and delivered them up to the sword [Ezek. 39.23]. But remembering the Covenant of the forefathers, He left a 'remnant' of Israel and did not deliver it up to destruction. At the end of this age of divine wrath,[11] 390 years after

---

9.   The CD was published for the first time in 1910 by Schechter. It has since been published by Rost (1933), Zeitlin (1952), Rabin (1954 and 1958). Now see also M. Broshi, *The Damascus Document Reconsidered* (Jerusalem: The Israel Exploration Society, 1992). The fragments discovered at Qumran have been published in DJD, III, pp. 128-31, 181, plates xxvi, xxxviii.

10.   See p. 110 n. 32.

11.   In classical Hebrew the term *qeṣ* means 'end', but during the time of the CD

He had given them into the hand of Nebuchadnezzar, king of Babylon, God visited them, and He caused a plant root to spring from Israel and Aaron to possess the land of Israel and to prosper on all its good things.

They perceived their iniquity and recognized that they were guilty men, yet for twenty years they were like blind men groping for the way. And God observed their deeds, that they sought Him wholeheartedly, and He raised for them a Teacher of Righteousness to guide them in the way of His heart. And he made known to the last generations that which God had done to the last generation, the congregation of traitors... (CD 1.1-12).

The text is interesting both for what it tells and for the way in which it tells it. First of all it is useful because it provides a key to an initial understanding of the mentality of those who fled Jerusalem in the second century BCE. It also tells us that 390 years[12] after the fall of Jerusalem, and therefore towards the beginning of the second century BCE, some Jews became aware that their society was losing its identity. It is the moment of Hellenism's rapid entry into Jerusalem, the heyday of the Tobiads' strength, the period of humiliation for the priesthood. Already, then, before the end of legitimate Zadokitism, a group of Jews had broken away from the community, with a gesture that must be judged more negative than positive since in fact for 20 years they did not know exactly what to do; 'they were like blind men'. Viewing their own history in hindsight, they were able to claim to be the true Israel whence the two anointed ones would come, that of Aaron and that of Israel.[13] It was therefore a traditionalist group bound to the Zadokite tradition that was familiar with the dual nature of power, τιμὴ ἀρχιε-ρατικὴ and προστασία τοῦ λαοῦ.

Twenty years after the birth of the Essenic movement, and therefore in roughly the same years as the crisis springing from the rise of Menelaus to the high priesthood and the murder of Onias III, a man known as the Teacher of Righteousness joined the movement. We too will refer

in most instances it had come to mean 'times, a period of time'. In this case, however, it appears that the former meaning re-emerges: 'at the end of the wrath' 'of the period of wrath'.

12. I am in favour of interpreting this as a real number. See P. Sacchi, 'Il problema degli anni 390 nel Documento di Damasco', *RevQ* 5 (1964), pp. 89-96. This does not mean that the number should be taken as historically exact down to the single year, since I doubt that at the time it was possible to reconstruct a chronology of the Zadokite period with such precision.

13. For the expression, 'the anointed of Aaron and Israel', see 1QS 9.9-11.

to him as the Teacher of Righteousness, since his real name remains unknown. He was a priest and a Zadokite and he gave a set of laws to the community that he reached in the desert, providing it with the structure that it was to maintain through its history. As we have already mentioned, it is not clear whether these norms were accepted by the entire Essenic community, or whether they were only adopted by a group within the larger movement.

Until recently all of the principal Qumran writings were attributed to the Teacher of Righteousness. Today we are much more cautious, for two reasons: (1) not all of the works once attributed to the Teacher of Righteousness can be dated to the same period; (2) a single work (see for example the *Community Rule*, perhaps the most important for understanding Essenism) is composed of more than one strata. Here the problem is that of individuating which stratum can be attributed to the Teacher of Righteousness.

Paralleling the changes in the way we now view the Teacher of Righteousness, we now view the sect's great adversary, the wicked priest, in a different light as well. In the past attempts were made to identify him with one of the high priests that governed Jerusalem between Jason and Alexander Jannaeus. Today we prefer to see a name referring to the high priest exercising that office in Jerusalem at any given moment. Therefore the term can refer to a number of high priests, a different one for each work or context.[14]

Following the information given in the *Damascus Document*, the Teacher of Righteousness is to be placed around the second quarter of the second century BCE, and his flight into the desert around the year 170 BCE. The most probable names for his persecutors therefore are the high priests Jason, Menelaus and Alcimus. These are all possibilities, though the most probable seems to be Menelaus both for the scope of the struggles that broke out during his priesthood, and because a combined reading of CD 1.13-17 and 8.8-11 with 1QpHab 9.9-12, 12.2-6 and especially 4Q171 (= 4QpPs 37), 2.17-20 seems to indicate that the sect's adversaries, including the wicked priest, ended up in enemy hands and were put to death. The figure of Menelaus meets the requirements.

14. On the plurality of historical figures referred to by the sole expression 'wicked priest', see A.S. van der Woude, 'Wicked Priest or Wicked Priests? Reflections on the Identification of the Wicked Priest in the Habakkuk Commentary', *JJS* 33 (1982), pp. 349-59; García Martínez, 'Qumran Origins and Early History'.

These Jews did not return to Jerusalem from the desert, at least not during the second century and perhaps much of the first. In Jesus' day at least some of them had probably re-established contact with the impure city. The new dedication of the Temple by Judas Maccabaeus in 164 BCE did not seem sufficient for them to consider the city purified; the high priest Menelaus remained. The situation cannot be said to have changed either, from this point of view, when power and the high priesthood came into the hands of Simon Maccabaeus, hero of the resistance against Hellenism and the Syrians (141 BCE).

With the passage of time the movement organized itself into a series of communities governed by very rigid norms. At times, it seems, these communities came into conflict with one another. Archaeologists have today brought to light a place where some of them had grouped together in complete isolation on the shores of the Dead Sea. The oldest artefacts should date to the time of Simon Maccabaeus. Probably, when they had the sensation that the situation had become static, they gave themselves a stable organization and tried to become as completely self-sufficient as possible, as demonstrated by the agricultural development of Ain Feshkha,[15] not far from the site of the principal settlement at Khirbet Qumran, hence the commonly used term Qumranic. If we accept the hypothesis that the Teacher of Righteousness was the founder of a dissident group within Essenism rather than of the movement itself, then the name Qumranic should be reserved solely for the dissident group.

The historic reason for the flight into the desert grew further and further away in time and was replaced by a theology of isolation and detachment based on the most rigid application of the norms of purity. For some, this detachment probably lasted until the first century CE when it appeared that the moment had arrived for the supreme battle against the forces of evil. They took the field with the Zealots against the Romans, and with the Zealots they disappeared.

While their political importance was practically non-existent, on a doctrinal level their impact was of the first order. They carried to their extreme consequences certain premises of Jewish thought which were destined to have a great role in the thought of the following century and the time of Jesus of Nazareth. Whether Essenes or Qumranics, the

15. See R. de Vaux, 'Ain Feshkha', *RB* 65 (1958), pp. 406-408.

movement that classical and Jewish writers alike (the latter only when writing in Greek) called the Essenic movement was born with them.

Just exactly when the movement took on the forms that Flavius Josephus, Philo and Pliny (to name only the most important writers) called Essenic is impossible to establish, just as it is impossible to establish the origin of the name 'Essenes', even though the traditional interpretation of 'the pious' seems the most probable.[16] Judging from Philo's and Pliny's texts, it would appear that the Essenes were an ancient group of Israel, something like the Rechabites mentioned by Jeremiah. At any rate it is clear that even if the Essenes were that ancient, they reached the vitality that was so important in Jewish thought only when they mixed with the Zadokites who had abandoned Jerusalem when the city had been contaminated with Hellenism.[17]

Henceforth we shall refer to this movement with the name 'Essenism', even though this term can cause some problems, because the Essenic movement was much broader than can be demonstrated with only the documents that have been discovered at Qumran. There were probably various currents of thought within the movement and the relationships between such currents are not always clear. In this sense 'Essenism', to some degree like 'Apocalyptic', risks becoming little more than a convenient term for referring to that part of Jewish thought that developed around the broad lines of the theology of the Promise at the beginning of the Common Era.

7. *Mattathias Maccabaeus*

The armed reaction against Menelaus and the Syrians who supported him was set in motion by Mattathias, who was not a Zadokite but who did belong to a priestly family.

Mattathias' priestly class was that of Yehoyarib. The steps in the rise of this class can be deduced from various lists of priests that have been handed down to us. In 1 Chron. 24.7 the name of Yehoyarib is even the first in the list; this list, which is the longest (24 names) and represents the final arrangement among the various priestly families, is later than the shorter lists appearing in Neh. 12. In one of the oldest lists (Neh.

---

16. See Muraoka, ' "Essene" in the Septuagint'.
17. See P. Sacchi, 'Ancora su Plinio e gli esseni', *PdP* 93 (1963), pp. 451-55.

12.1-7a) Yehoyarib (written Yoyarib) is among the last names given, in a sort of appendix. It seems worthy of note that the Chronicler's long preamble to the above-mentioned list of priests (1 Chron. 24.1-6) shows a kind of organization of the priestly families in which the Zadokites do not seem to maintain all of the prerogatives that they had been given by Ezekiel.[18]

On 15 December 167 BCE, 'the abomination that desolates' spoken of by Daniel (Dan. 9.27) was placed in the Jerusalem Temple. Immediately thereafter, the Hellenists applied more and more pressure to abolish the Law and with it all the norms regarding purity. The Law was rightly seen as traditional Judaism's most valid instrument of defence, by then almost a reactionary force. For the Seleucids, as the author of 1 Maccabees observed (1.41), it was a question of unifying the civil law of their entire empire. For the Hellenist Judaeans it was a question of giving Judaism a new face, in line with the great culture of the day; they were not advocating renouncing worship of Yhwh, centre of the Jewish nation, but *a* law which was felt to be outdated, especially in the so-called purity norms and their irrational content.

While Antiochus IV could have been interested in seeing the Jewish Judaeans apply the laws of Antioch and not the traditional Jewish Law, he could not have been interested in prohibiting particular rites such as circumcision or the particular customs regarding foods. These were fought from within, by those who knew them well and understood that it was indispensable to eliminate them in order to change Judaism into something that seemed better to them, better because more in line with the times.

> Then the king [Antiochus IV] wrote to his whole kingdom that all should be one people, and that all should give up their particular customs. All the Gentiles accepted the command of the king. Many even from Israel gladly adopted his religion; they sacrificed to idols and profaned the Sabbath (1 Macc. 1.41-43).

18. For the final redaction of the books of the Chronicles, see Eissfeldt, *Einleitung*, and K.F. Pohlmann, *Studien zum Dritten Esra* (Göttingen: Vandenhoeck & Ruprecht, 1970). This would explain the ruptures within the priesthood that appeared in such a clamourous manner only in the second century BCE. It also explains how many people were able to accept a non-Zadokite priesthood; the crisis of Zadokitism must have been rooted in the distant past, somewhere in the reorganization of the society of Jerusalem between the ideologies of Nehemiah and Ezra.

> Many of the people, everyone who forsook the law, joined them, and
> they did evil in the land; they drove the Jews [the true ones, the true
> Israel] into hiding in every place of refuge they had (1 Macc. 1.52-53).

For as much as the author of 1 Maccabees tries to emphasize the
external responsibilities over the internal ones and talks of the repres-
sive edicts of Antiochus and his inspectors, it is clear from this account
that many Jews, perhaps a very great number, took the side of Menelaus. It was they who persecuted the traditionalists and who sacrificed
in the 'contaminated' Temple.

> The kings officers who were enforcing the apostasy came to the town of
> Modein to make them offer sacrifice. Many from Israel came to them;
> and Mattathias and his sons were assembled. Then the king's officers
> spoke to Mattathias as follows: 'You are a leader, honoured and great in
> this town, and supported by sons and brothers. Now be the first to come
> and do what the king commands, as all the Gentiles and the people of
> Judah and those that are left in Jerusalem have done... But Mattathias
> answered and said in a loud voice: 'Even if all the nations that live under
> the rule of the king obey him, and have chosen to obey his command-
> ments, everyone of them abandoning the religion of their ancestors, I and
> my sons and my brothers will continue to live by the Covenant of our
> Fathers...'
> When he had finished speaking these words, a Jew came forward in
> the sight of all to offer sacrifice on the altar in Modein, according to the
> king's command.
> When Mattathias saw it, he burned with zeal and his heart was stirred.
> He gave vent to righteous anger; he ran and killed him on the altar. At the
> same time he killed the king's officer who was forcing them to sacrifice,
> and he tore down the altar. Thus he burned with zeal for the Law, just as
> Phinehas did against Zimri son of Salu. Then Mattathias cried out in the
> town with a loud voice, saying: 'Let every one who is zealous for the
> Law and supports the Covenant come out with me!' Then he and his sons
> fled to the hills and left all that they had in the town (1 Macc. 2.15-28).

Mattathias's violent act is defined and justified on the basis of the
Torah, in this case indicated as the 'Covenant of our fathers'. For Mattathias the traditional values are summed up in the Covenant, of which
the Law is the expression. For him the centre of Judaism remains the
Covenant. Whether he was already aware of it, or whether his gesture
was later interpreted as such, which is more probable, his act was an act
of 'zeal for the Law'. His act was compared to that of Phinehas who is
admired in Num. 25.6-13, for having killed another Jew, guilty of contaminating himself with a foreign woman. This passage in the Priestly

Codex, which seems to have been composed in opposition to the early Zadokite Judaism in Jerusalem, defined Phinehas' act an act of 'zeal for the Law', and the expression was brought back to life in the Maccabaean period indicating a certain way of interpreting the Law. 'Zealous for the Law' referred to all those who were willing to kill in order to make the Law respected.

Sirach had already re-proposed the praise of Phinehas made in the book of Numbers, with the difference that he considered the prophecy regarding Phinehas' priesthood as already having come about:

> A covenant of friendship was established with him,
> that he should be leader of the sanctuary [and of his people],[19]
> that he and his descendants
> should have the dignity of the priesthood forever (Sir. 45.24).

For Sirach Phinehas's priesthood is not an exceptional one. Here it only represents a step, albeit an important one, in the eternal life of Aaron's priesthood (see chs. 44–45).

At the time of the Maccabees in contrast, the prophecy contained in Num. 25.12-13 where an 'eternal' priesthood for Phinehas and his descendants is mentioned takes on a new meaning.[20] Ezekiel had chosen the Zadokites from among the descendants of Aaron, and the Maccabees apparently were not Zadokites. Thus as priests they sought

---

19. *Sanctuary*: the translation is from the Hebrew, which in this case certainly represents the original and not a re-translation; see G. Prato, *Il problema della teodicea in Ben Sira* (Rome: Biblical Institute Press, 1975), and H.-P. Rüger, *Text und Textform im hebräischen Sirach* (Berlin: W. de Gruyter, 1970). The Greek text reads προστάτης τῶν ἁγίων, a generic expression. It is difficult to recognize 'temple' in such an expression. The Hebrew text leaves no room for doubt since it uses the word *miqdaš*.

[and of his people]: through a comparison with the Hebrew text it is clear that this is an internal corruption within the Greek text (NAOϒ > ΛAOϒ). In fact, some manuscripts have ναοῦ instead of λαοῦ, but, given the presence of τῶν ἁγίων, ναοῦ should be interpreted as a simple corruption of λαοῦ. In reality we are merely faced with the confluence of two translations which are substantially correct, one of which simply had the defect of using too generic a word.

20. This could even seem to be an interpolation made during the Maccabaean period, aimed at finding some justification for the Maccabees' power in the Scriptures. This solution, however, is excluded by the Greek text's concordance. It should be noted that Origen places some of the words of v. 12 under obelum. For similar problems see B. Chiesa, 'Contrasti ideologici del tempo degli Asmonei nella Aggadah e nelle versioni di Genesi 49, 3', *AION* 37 (1977), pp. 417-48.

to reactivate the promise of priesthood to Phinehas, ignoring the restrictions made by Ezekiel. In so doing, they reached two goals simultaneously: on the one hand they associated themselves with the figure of the Law's zealot *par excellence*; on the other they drew to themselves all those who saw the way to salvation in the zealous interpretation of the Law. Furthermore, in this way they justified their rise to the high priesthood to the disadvantage of the Zadokites. The Hasidaeans were able to accept the celebration of the Temple's reconsecration under Menelaus in 164 only because they considered the Zadokite priesthood to have come to an end. Later they were even ready to accept, full of hope, the nomination of Alcimus, who was a descendant of Aaron. Apparently the Zadokite priesthood had come completely to an end because the Zadokites, for one reason or for another, had all abandoned the struggle. Zadokitism ended up in the ranks of Hellenism among Menelaus' followers, or in the dogged though apparently weak resistance movements such as that of the Essenes, or even in flight to Egypt.

Given the extremely brief time that Mattathias led the struggle (one year), it is difficult to judge his works, but the principal characteristic of the works of the Maccabee sons is the ambition to become kings of Israel (in whatever sense that word could hold during the Hellenistic period). One has the impression that the only driving force behind the Maccabaean priests in their opposition to Menelaus's priesthood was the former's desire to replace the latter. For them the Law was merely a banner for rallying all those who really did believe in the Law. As with all leaders of the day, their religion was basically that of glory; in this they were a true expression of the Hellenism that they claimed to be fighting against.

Not long after the murder of the king's emissary at Modein and the beginning of the war, a group referred to by the author of 1 Maccabees as the 'Hasidaeans', the 'pious', joined Mattathias. They were not of priestly descent, or rather, for them the authenticity of the priestly descent was not a central element of Judaism. They believed that Israel would be saved only if it respected the Law and they were willing to fight for the recuperation of Israel's religious freedom. 1 Maccabees says that they were 'the most enthusiastic for the Law' (1 Macc. 2.42). The use of the word 'enthusiastic' is not a random choice, it marks a distance between them and the true Zealots who wanted to impose the traditional Law on all. The first application of Ezra's theology, though perhaps not through a conscious decision, can be attributed to these 'enthusiasts for the Law', because they placed the Law itself at the centre of Judaism, as an absolute value independent of the state. For them, citizens living by different customs could co-exist within the same state.

The Hasidaeans were welcomed by Mattathias and probably made up the better share of his army. This forced the Maccabees to give a religious and legalistic colour to all their actions, even though some dissent between the Modein priests and the Hasidaeans was inevitable. The former embodied the spirit of the Hellenistic *condottieri* while the spirit of the latter was devoted to God according to the Law.

> And all who became fugitives to escape their troubles joined them and reinforced them. They organized an army, and struck down sinners in their anger and renegades in their wrath; the survivors fled to the Gentiles for safety (1 Macc. 2.43-44).

It is clear that the struggle began as a civil war. Later, when the Syrians gave their support to Jerusalem, as was inevitable, the conflict took on the character of a war of national liberation.

The figure of Mattathias is tied to the decision to not respect the Sabbath in military operations, a decision made after many had already joined his cause and which therefore must have been widely shared. The soldiers of Antiochus and Menelaus, who did not observe the Torah had attacked and massacred the rebels without resistance on the day of the sabbath (1 Macc. 2.29-41). Hence Mattathias's practical decision. Such rigid respect for the sabbath was already a part of the Judaic tradition, since Apollonius, Antiochus IV's general, waited until the sabbath to attack Jerusalem (2 Macc. 5.24-26). Since this *halakah* regarding the sabbath is attested to in the later book of *Jubilees* as well (*Jub.* 50.12-13) produced in decidedly pro-Zadokite circles, two things become clear: (1) the conservative nature of this type of *halakah* and (2) in consequence, the innovation desired by Mattathias.

Concerning the name of the party that took the side of the Maccabaeans, the Hasidaeans (1 Macc. 2.42), it is worth making a few observations. Historically the Hasidaeans are the precursors of the Pharisaic movement, which appears with this name only at the time of John Hyrcanus. On the contrary, their name may have survived in its Aramaic form indicating the Essenes (*ḥsy'*). In any case, the name change of the Hasidaean-Pharisaic movement seems to point to a rupture in the movement. The roots of such a rupture could lie in the ideological difficulties arising from the Hasidaeans' decision to take up the armed struggle alongside the Maccabaeans at the time of Alcimus' high priesthood (151 BCE; see pp. 242-44).

8. *Second-century BCE Apocalyptic: An Escapist Movement?*

The history of *1 Enoch*, as can now be delineated, in the light of recent discoveries, demonstrates the existence from the beginning of the Late Zadokite period of a movement whose characteristics were decidedly different from those of nomist Judaism. Shortly after the death of Antiochus IV (in 164 BCE, date of the last events known to the author) a work known as the *Book of Dreams* was produced within this movement, or at least from its ideas. Let us examine the attitude of this book's author towards the events of his day.

He can be distinguished from the author of the book of Daniel,[21] his contemporary, by the global nature of his vision of history, beginning with the origin of the world rather than the golden reign of Nebuchadnezzar. He knows that all events have been preordained by God; in a vision Enoch sees all of future history. Among other things he sees that God has condemned the Temple to destruction along with all the blind sheep of Israel. This position was therefore distinct from that of the Hasidaeans who had accepted the reorganization of the Temple under Menelaus in precisely those years (see p. 243). This brings the Enochic, or Apocalyptic positions closer to those of the Essenes. The *Book of Dreams* seems to distinguish itself from the Essenes in its greater contact with history. In spite of the common points and even their probable common origin, Essenism and Apocalyptic were historically distinct. The expectation of two messiahs, a royal one and a priestly one, that characterizes the more recent strata of the *Community Rule*, holds no place in the Enochic tradition which envisions a single messiah, clearly the royal one, as the fulcrum of future history.

In the *Book of Dreams* the crucial event in history will be a Great Judgment, seen as miraculous and absolutely exceptional in nature, which will give rise to the reign of God on earth. This brings the *Book of Dreams* closer to Daniel, but differences begin to emerge over the way the Great Judgment and future ages are conceived. For the author of Daniel there is only Israel, 'the people of the holy ones of the Most

---

21. See G. Boccaccini, 'È Daniele un testo apocalittico? Una (ri)definizione del Libro di Daniele in rapporto al Libro dei Sogni e all'apocalittica', *Henoch* 9 (1987), pp. 267-302.

High' (7.27). For the author of the *Book of Dreams* Israel is not a single unit; there are the sheep who see and the ones who do not, and the blind ones are to suffer the wrath of Judgment even before the pagans. For Daniel's author the Jerusalem of Menalaus's cultural and political compromise was acceptable while awaiting liberation from the pagans, in accordance with the Hasidaean positions. For the author of the *Book of Dreams* that situation was unacceptable.

As regards the future eon, for the author of Daniel it would be characterized by Israel's dominion over the other peoples. For the author of the *Book of Dreams* it would be the age of the Messiah King's universal rule, accompanied by the regeneration of human nature which would return to what it had been originally (*1 En.* [*BD*] 90.37-38).

It seems then that at the beginning of the Maccabaean period the Apocalyptic movement espoused positions quite close to those of the Essenes. Even though the movement's followers took part in the fighting, they did not associate the Maccabaean war with the beginning of God's reign. The real problem lay in Israel's sin, which was not even to be attributed to all, only to the blind sheep.[22]

9. *From Judas to Simon Maccabaeus*

Mattathias died in 166 BCE and his son Judas assumed leadership of the struggle against the Hellenizers. In 164 an agreement was reached between Judas and Menelaus. Documents regarding this agreement are conserved in 2 Macc. 11.13-38.

This was a compromise made by the two principal leaders under the auspices and mediation of Lysias, regent in Antioch for Antiochus IV who was then engaged in a war against the Parthians. The need for complete freedom of action against the more powerful enemy led Syria to favour the pacification of Palestine. The agreement stated that Menelaus was to retain the high priesthood, while the rebels were to be

22. On the relationship between early Apocalyptic (Enochic current) and the origins of Essenism, see F. García Martínez, 'Essénisme qumranien: Origines, caractéristiques, héritage', in B. Chiesa (ed.), *Atti del V Congresso Internazionale dell'AISG* (Rome: Carucci, 1987), pp. 37-58. The element that always distinguished Essenic spirituality compared to Apocalyptic spirituality is that the Essenes believed in a rigid predeterminism regarding both history and the individual, the Apocalyptics, in contrast, accepted predeterminism regarding history, but continued to believe in the individual's freedom.

allowed to return to their homeland and to live according to the Torah, even though, clearly, the Hellenizers were to be able to live as they pleased.

There are no documents providing direct testimony of just how the agreement was received by the Hasidaeans, but the enthusiastic celebration of Hanukkah, the new dedication of the Temple on 25 December 164 BCE, and the fact that Hanukkah became one of the principal festivities of later Judaism, lead us to believe that the Hasidaeans agreed, in this case, with the political line adopted by Judas. The Zadokite priesthood was no longer part of the tradition. This explains why Onias IV did not return to Jerusalem, why the Essenes maintained their distance and why the author of the *Book of Dreams* awaited the complete purification of the Temple by God, through its miraculous destruction and reconstruction through divine intervention (*1 En.* [*BD*] 90.28-29).

Judas's move, however, was nothing more than an expedient for re-entering Jerusalem while Syria was weakened by the war against the Parthians, in which Antiochus IV was to lose his life. In fact, once installed in Jerusalem, Judas began sending his troops in all directions, even to the far off region of Gilead (1 Macc. 5.25) in order to forcibly restore the Yahwism of the Torah and to destroy the Hellenistic influence that Menelaus based his power on. In the meantime he built a fortress in Jerusalem in opposition to the *akra* of Menelaus and the Syrians (1 Macc. 4.60).

Lysias was forced to intervene, though not without hesitation, since he was aware of the difficulties of intervening in Judaea while a child was on the throne (Antiochus V) and a pretender, Philip, was nearing. The Hellenists had been closed up in the *akra* and were under siege there when Lysias made his move. Lysias defeated Judas in open battle and forced him to retreat to the Temple hill where his fate would have been sealed had Philip not forced Lysias's withdrawal and a return to the previous terms in Judaea. For reasons unknown to us, Menelaus was made prisoner and executed. According to the author of 2 Maccabees (13.4-7) the Syrians had condemned Menelaus because they considered him incapable of controlling the situation.

In the meantime yet another pretender, not Philip, rose to the throne in Antioch, Demetrius I, son of Seleucus IV and not of Antiochus IV. He reigned from 162 to 150 BCE.

Antiochus IV had taken advantage of the favour of Rome in order to occupy the throne, even though he was the brother and not the son of

Seleucus IV. From that moment forward, the greatest source of tension within the Syrian state was the rivalry between the two branches of Antiochus III's descendants, the branch of the 'Seleucids' and that of the 'Antiochids', the descendants of Seleucus IV and Antiochus IV respectively. Demetrius I (162–150) and Demetrius II (145–138 and 129–125) were Seleucids, while Antiochus V (164–162), Alexander Balas (153–145), Antiochus VI (145–142), Antiochus VII (138–129) and Alexander Zabinas (128–122) were Antiochids.

Demetrius granted the high priesthood to one Alcimus, who was from a priestly family and who, according to 2 Macc. 14.3, had already been high priest. He had probably been named high priest by Lysias immediately after Menelaus had been executed (see 1 Macc. 7.9-10; 2 Macc. 14.3-14; Josephus, *Ant.* 12.385, 391-92). He himself had gone to Demetrius asking for support against Judas. He feared being compromised with Antiochus V and Lysias and therefore sought to protect himself by taking the initiative. Demetrius confirmed him as high priest (1 Macc. 7.9) and gave him *carte blanche* in Judaea. Demetrius had intended that Alcimus take care of things for himself and Alcimus was quite able at using the arms of persuasion and of force. The Hasidaeans were in favour of accepting him as high priest and Judas was left to carry on the struggle alone. The Hasidaeans' ideology separated them from Judas in precisely his most dangerous moment. More than anything else, they desired to live in peace according to their Law; they had little interest in the Maccabees' dreams of glory.

> Then a group of scribes [the Hasidaean notables] appeared in a body before Alcimus and Bacchides [the Syrian general] to ask for just terms. The Hasidaeans were first among the Israelites to seek peace from them, for they said, 'A priest of the line of Aaron has come with the army, and he will not harm us'. He [Alcimus] spoke peaceable words to them and swore this oath to them, 'We will not seek to injure you or your friends'. So they trusted him; but he [the subject seems to still be Alcimus] seized sixty of them and killed them in one day [1 Macc. 7.12-16].

I believe that the expression '[Alcimus is] a priest of the line of Aaron' does not so much mean that Menelaus was not from a priestly family as it does that a priest should have been trustworthy. In short, it is not to be interpreted as 'unlike Menelaus', but rather 'unlike Bacchides'. In other words, the meaning of the sentence seems to be: 'We can not trust Bacchides, but we can trust Alcimus who belongs to our priestly caste'. Josephus paraphrases it well, saying that they could trust

Alcimus because he was ὁμόφυλος, 'compatriot' (see *Ant.* 12.395).

The version of events given by Josephus is different, but on the whole more likely, and could even be based on the same source used by the author of 1 Maccabees. On the whole the text of 1 Maccabees is ambiguous and the subject of 'seized' seems to be Alcimus if only from the context presented in the author's reduction of the source. In Josephus, though (*Ant.* 12.396), the subject is explicitly Bacchides who, despising oaths, had the 60 Hasidaeans arrested and executed. In Josephus's version, Alcimus counted more on his political ability than on military force.

Bacchides' act caused more damage than good for Alcimus. Alcimus had hoped to fight against Judas by isolating him; with this in mind he imposed himself on Jerusalem through able political manoeuvring, granting everyone what they wanted as long as they recognized him as high priest. Therefore, he confirmed the permission for the traditionalists to live by the Torah.

> Alcimus, wishing to strengthen his authority [he was high priest, but he was not present in Jerusalem], and perceiving that by making the people feel friendly toward him he would govern with greater security, led them on with kind words, and speaking to everyone in a pleasant and gracious manner [and therefore promising the Hasidaeans that which they longed for the most], very soon indeed acquired a large body of men and a force behind him (*Ant.* 12.398).

In spite of Bacchides' action, which apart from its cruelty hardly seems astute, Alcimus' policy was successful, but only briefly. Once again the so-called logic of power shook both Judas and Syria. Alcimus realized that he would not be able to resolve the problem of 'pacification' in this way and he again took up arms against Judas. This provoked both the Hasidaeans' defection and renewed Syrian intervention. Judas fell in battle during the defeat at Beth-horon in 160 BCE.

After the death of Judas the leadership of the Maccabaean cause passed into the hands of Judas' brother Jonathan who was forced to retreat into the desert because all of the cities were in the hands of Alcimus and the Hellenizing party who appeared to have won the struggle with Alcimus' policy of firmness and pacification. Then, unexpectedly, Alcimus died, probably following an attack of paralysis while he was in the Temple. This event made a great impression and gave new courage to his adversaries.

In the one hundred and fifty-third year [of the Seleucid era = 159 BCE],
in the second month, Alcimus gave orders to tear down the wall of the
inner court of the Temple. He tore down the work of the prophets! But
he only began to tear it down, for at that time Alcimus was stricken (by
God) and his work was hindered (1 Macc. 9.54-55; see also *Ant.* 12.413).

It would be interesting to know why Alcimus wanted to tear down
that ancient wall (*Ant.* 12.413). Surely, this act represented a rupture
with some element of tradition. The role of a wall is to separate, and it
comes to mind that perhaps that wall was there to keep the pagans away
from the most sacred part of the Temple. Since later documents show
that the pagans were kept out of a much larger area and since the wall
was not rebuilt,[23] it is more likely that it marked a dividing line within
Judaism itself; the division between the priests and the people. In
keeping with Alcimus' policy of openness this act meant a broadening
of priestly dignity to cover all the people. The wall must have been
built according to the desires of the priesthood of the Early Zadokite
period; this would explain why the wall was so old, from the days of
'the prophets' which had long since come to an end (see 1 Macc. 9.27;
see also 1 Macc. 4.46 and 14.41). It was therefore an innovation that led
Judaism away from the Zadokite customs and which could be interpreted in two different ways, as in fact happened. It could be seen either
in terms of laicization, or the complete sacralization of the people.[24]

After the death of Alcimus, who had shown himself to be an able
leader, the Hellenizing party was faced with serious problems, probably
stemming from internal conflict arising from the lack of a recognized
leader. This favoured Jonathan.

An indication of the internal divisions among the Hellenizers can be
seen in the fact that no successor to Alcimus was elected high priest.
This is clear in Josephus's statement (*Ant.* 20.237): 'No one succeeded
him and for seven years the city had no high priest'.[25] It is true that

23. For the documentation see Garbini, *Storia e ideologia*, pp. 225-27 (ET:
History and Ideology in Ancient Israel [London: SCM Press, 1988]).

24. See P. Sacchi, 'Osservazioni sul sacerdozio presso gli ebrei nel suo rapporto
col potere e coi laici', *Testimonianze*, 297–98 (1987), pp. 26-31.

25. Modern scholars generally accept this information even though Josephus
himself writes three times that Judas was named high priest after the death of Alcimus (*Ant.* 12.414, 419, 434). The text of 1 Macc. excludes this possibility, as does
Josephus's own account. Some scholars accept the opposite view: see the recent
article by C. Saulnier, 'Le cadre politico-religieux en Palestine de la révolte des
Maccabées à l'intervention romaine', in P. Sacchi (ed.), *Il giudaismo palestinese:*

traditionally it was the king's prerogative to name the high priest, but the king must have preferred to buy time, hoping to avoid further complications in a region that already had far too many. This time Bacchides was forced to intervene against the Hellenizers in Jerusalem in order to re-establish order in the region. It is clear that the Syrians did not favour either side in particular, but aimed exclusively at maintaining the peace in the region.[26]

All of this brought Jonathan closer to Syria. From Bacchides Jonathan was able to obtain the city of Michmash, north of Jerusalem, where he established his power. Michmash must have enjoyed an unusual political situation; it was entirely in the hands of Jonathan who pledged not to disturb Jerusalem. Jonathan maintained a low profile, but he also gathered together soldiers while he waited for a favourable moment, which was not long in coming, given the weakness of the Antiochian throne. Jonathan had been able to draw together a sizable army. 1 Macc. 10.36 speaks of thirty thousand Jews that Demetrius I tried to enlist in his own army, together with their leaders. 1 Macc. 10.74 says that Jonathan was able to choose ten thousand men from his army.

A new pretender to the Syrian throne rose in 153 BCE, Alexander Balas. He needed men and Jonathan placed himself in Alexander's service; in exchange Jonathan was named high priest. For the Hellenizing party this was the beginning of the end, for the Zadokites in the desert nothing changed. Jonathan contaminated the city just as every other high priest had done since Onias III had been driven out.

Jonathan was a true mercenary leader who showed himself capable of manoeuvre between the two pretenders, managing always to be on the side of the winner. On the other hand, he had amassed such a large army that he could tip the balance in favour of one or the other contender. The conflict between Alexander Balas and Demetrius was decided by the support Jonathan gave to the former, after long negotiations and much stalling which show that Jonathan was determined to sell himself at the highest possible price and to the candidate most likely to be victorious.

Balas held power alone until 145 BCE when two pretenders emerged

---

Dal I secolo a.C. al I secolo d.C. Atti del Congresso Internazionale dell'AISG—S. Miniato 5–6–7 novembre 1990 (Bologna: AISG, 1993), pp. 199-211, in particular p. 202 n.

26. See Ricciotti, *Storia d'Israele*, II, pp. 307-308, interpreting 1 Macc. 9.58-61.

at the same time, Demetrius II (145–138 BCE) and Antiochus VI (145–142 BCE). Jonathan died in 143, victim of a trap laid by Trypho (one of Antiochus VI's generals), who had unforeseeably become a third pretender to the throne.

Jonathan was succeeded by his brother Simon, under whom Judaea became practically an independent state.

Trypho killed Antiochus VI while Demetrius II was still in arms. This brought the last of the Maccabees closer to this Demetrius who was well aware of the weight carried by the Jewish mercenaries in Syria's internal wars. Demetrius immediately bound Simon to his cause, confirming him in the role of high priest (1 Macc. 14.38), granting him complete exemption from all tributes and giving him the right to possess fortresses. This was a *de facto* independence that Simon understood perfectly well; from that point on he acted as a full sovereign, even though he never took the title of king.

> In the one hundred seventieth year [of the Seleucid period which began in 312 BCE, therefore 142 BCE] the yoke of the Gentiles was removed from Israel, and the people began to write in their documents and contracts, 'In the first year of Simon the great high priest and commander (στρατεγός) and leader (ἡγούμενος) of the Jews' (1 Macc. 13.41-42).

In giving the formula for dating with reference to Simon, Josephus attributes him the title of *euergetes*, 'benefactor', typical of Hellenistic sovereigns (*Ant.* 13.214). Simon was elected high priest by the people (1 Macc. 14.35) and Demetrius limited himself to confirming him in that position. The historical importance of this fact was grasped well by Josephus (*Ant.* 13.213).

Simon eliminated all the forces which could have posed a threat to him; the Hellenizing party was persecuted and destroyed.

> In those days he [Simon] encamped against Gazara and surrounded it with troops. He made a siege engine, brought it up to the city, and battered and captured one tower... The men in the city, with their wives and children, went up on the wall with their clothes torn, and they cried out with a loud voice, asking Simon to make peace with them; they said, 'Do not treat us according to our wicked acts but according to your mercy'. So Simon reached an agreement with them and stopped fighting against them. But he expelled them from the city and cleansed the houses in which the idols were located, and then entered it with hymns and praise. He removed all uncleanness from it, and settled in it those who observed the Law (1 Macc. 13.43-48).

Three years later Simon was sure of his kingdom. A great assembly bringing together the priests, notables and the people formulated a declaration in two parts. The first part summarized briefly the history of the Maccabaean war, leaving the lion's share of the story to Simon's actions. The war is not presented as a civil war, but as a national one against 'the enemies of their nation, in order that their Temple and the Law might be preserved; and they [the Maccabees] brought great glory to their nation' (1 Macc. 14.29). Simon did not want to be seen as the leader of a faction that had imposed itself over others, but as leader of his entire nation.

In the second half of the assembly it was deliberated that Simon 'should be their leader (ἡγούμενος) and high priest forever, until a trustworthy prophet should arise' (1 Macc. 14.41). Even in this formulation it is easy to see the lasting structure of the conception of the state held by the Jews of the Zadokite period. Since Zerubbabel's day, lay and sacred power had been kept separate, even though we do not know the precise functions of the two branches of authority. After the king and the priest came the priest and the governor, and then προστασία τοῦ λαοῦ alongside the τιμὴ ἀρχιερατική. The confines of this division could change with the international situation surrounding Jerusalem, with functions varying from one period to the next, but the division, at least theoretically, was constant (see the episodes of Onias II and Joseph the Tobiad in §1, pp. 214-21). Simon now possessed the greatest power possible in as much as both aspects of power were concentrated in a single person; he was both ἡγούμενος and ἀρχιερεύς. The measures taken by Pompey against Hyrcanus II in 63 BCE confirm this state of things. Pompey took away the royal title, but in order to allow Hyrcanus to remain leader of his people as a vassal, Pompey gave him the title προστάτης τοῦ ἔθνους. Josephus recounts that he 'permitted him to have the προστασία τοῦ ἔθνους, but forbade him to wear a crown' (*Ant.* 20.244). The substitution of ἔθνος for λαός derived from the new perspective. For the Romans the Jews were an ἔθνος, but the fact that the word προστασία remained clearly shows just what we are talking about. The προστασία of the people was a deeply rooted term in Jewish culture indicating lay authority, distinct from priestly authority.

As far as the formula 'until a trustworthy prophet should arise' is concerned, this is certainly fruit of a compromise desired by Simon himself in order to avoid further internal conflict. He knew perfectly well just how anomalous his position in Jerusalem was. He could have been contested, by the Hasidaeans, but not only them, on the grounds that he was not from a priestly family. It was also against the tradition that the high priest be elected by the people and it was against the normal Jewish tradition that the high priest exercise secular power as well, no matter how he was nominated. Then there is the fact that Simon was not only ἡγούμενος of his people, but also στρατηγός. In this case we are faced with a complete innovation that could be forgiven only of one who had fought for the Law and the Temple. If he later fought for other reasons, this could only cause unrest, especially among the Hasidaeans who had fought too, but only for the right to live according to their customs and the Law.

Recognizing his position as an anomaly, Simon, who can now be called Hasmonaean (see pp. 250-53), satisfied those who were most attached to tradition by explicitly declaring himself ready to change those things that needed changing as soon as a 'trustworthy' prophet came along. The addition of 'trustworthy' shows that Simon wanted to protect himself in case someone claiming to be a prophet really did turn up.

This formula is interesting for another reason as well; it shows that the expectation of a prophet was in some way still alive among the Jews. Prophecy had only been suspended for some reason in God's impenetrable designs, but the institution was not dead. A prophet was still awaited who would even resolve questions regarding the anointed one. And it is clear, then, that the messianic figure awaited in the future was expected to have characteristics going beyond mere unction, because Simon already had that.

Chapter 8

THE HASMONAEANS

1. *Hellenized Jerusalem: Simon*

With the first year of Simon (141 BCE) we usually begin to speak of the
Hasmonaeans rather than the Maccabees. The name change reflects a
deep transformation in the social and spiritual structures of Palestine.
Even though the word 'king' is no longer used, there is in effect a monarchy and it is not the Davidic one. While the election of the Maccabees
to the high priesthood went against tradition as it had been established
since the time of Ezekiel, their rise to the throne went against all Jewish
tradition. The kings had to be of the house of David. One supporting
point in the Scripture could be found, though, in Deuteronomy (17.15),
where it is written that any Jew could become king, but there is no evidence that the Hasmonaeans ever used this text to explain their position.

It is true that the 'privileges of David' had been given a profoundly
democratic reinterpretation and had been extended to all the people
even with Deutero-Isaiah, but the Chronicler seems to assume an ambiguous position on this topic, which does not exclude the idea that Israel
was still a kingdom. At any rate, Simon did not hazard any new interpretations of the tradition and, if he did not assume the title of 'king' it
was to avoid complications with Syria. Having brought together sacred
and lay power, not to mention command of the army, in effect he held
the same power over the Jews as a Hellenistic king. Furthermore, in this
way he avoided breaking with the most recent tradition in Israel, which
had become used to having two authorities: the τιμὴ ἀρχιερατικὴ and
the προστασία τοῦ λαοῦ.

Being on the crest of the wave of popular support, while awaiting the
arrival of a prophet who would clear up the controversial questions,
Simon could ask what he wanted of the people. Of course, with the passage of time enthusiasm for the Maccabees, now called the Hasmonaeans, waned, at least among a broad section of the population, that

part of society under the influence of the Hasidaeans, who were in the process of becoming the Pharisees. When the Hasmonaeans finally did assume the title of 'king' without an adequate reinterpretation of the tradition, this deepened the rupture with the Hasidaeans, a rupture which had existed since the very beginning of the Maccabaean period.

The Maccabees had fought for their own power and affirmation, the Hasidaeans for that of the Law. They all agreed on a form of nationalism, but a nationalism holding different values for the two groups. In the end, the Maccabees–Hasmoneans had absorbed much more Hellenism than one would expect, given the fact that they fought against it. The Hellenistic princes were always fighting among themselves, since Hellenism never led to any form of agreement among those who held its ideals. On the contrary, the logic of the glory and power of its leaders inevitably led to wars among aspirants to the throne. The war fought by the Maccabees was precisely that kind of war. Their greatest strength lay in their ability to take advantage of the Hasidaeans' nationalism, though the ideological roots of that nationalism were extraneous to the Maccabees.

The Hellenistic attitudes began to multiply under Simon; at Modein he had a grandiose monumental tomb built, and he transferred the remains of his entire family there, according to the usage of the Hellenistic kings. In fact, there were columns of war trophies and rostra, following a custom which was new to Israel (1 Macc. 13.27-30).

Even more interesting, though, is the relationship between the general and his army, which is typical of all the Hellenistic states. The first Hasidaeans that fought alongside Judas had been free soldiers, fighting for their own cause. Later we have the impression, already with Jonathan, that his forces were a personal army, with salaried, professional soldiers as with all Hellenistic kings. The army was in his hands and mention is no longer made of whether the Hasidaeans agreed with his policies or not. A new recruit was his soldier and, in a sense, those who did not join him did not belong to him. It is clear from 1 Macc. 14.32 that Simon paid his soldiers (but I believe that Jonathan had already begun this practice, given the size and strength of his army). And the money for paying the troops could only have come from the people, willingly or not. The people maintained the offices and authorities held traditionally; Simon's authority was simply superimposed over the traditional forms of power, without eliminating them. The great assembly that elected Simon high priest and ἡγούμενος of the people was formed by the traditional authorities of the nation: priests, λαός, leaders of the people (ἔθνος) and the elders of the region[1] (1 Macc. 14.28). This marks the distance between the sovereign and the people typical of Hellenistic states. Normally, the sovereign did not even belong to the nation that he ruled over; his strength was his army, which the people were called upon to support through the payment of taxes. Let us re-examine the Jews' decree in favour of Simon in 1 Macc. 14.27-47. The people had been convened and were present with all the traditional forms of authority, because the authority to be granted to Simon, which in truth he already held, was seen as something different and superior. From the text it does not appear that he was the one who convened the assembly or who presided over it formally.

His distance from the people is confirmed by the wording on the Hasmonaean coins which names two sources of authority: the sovereign and the people. The duality of power was thus formally maintained, even though the 'people' never had any form of authority without delegating someone to represent it. Under Hyrcanus, alongside coins with the phrase, 'John, high priest and the assembly (?) (*ḥbr*) of Jews', others appear with the expression, 'John, high priest and head of the *ḥbr* of the Jews'. It is clear that the political situation was precarious, but the attempt at overcoming that precariousness, at least in the formulas, is equally clear.[2]

---

1.   It is not clear just what the author means by the term λαός. In this context it must have been something different from ἔθνος. Apparently on the political and administrative level there was a distinction between the inhabitants of the city and those of the rest of the region, here referred to with the term χώρα. In this case too, we are faced with the continued existence of an ancient situation. It is the classical distinction between Jerusalem and Judah. The meaning of the text indicates two distinctions, one between priests and laymen and, within this distinction, between those of the people (Jerusalem) and those of the region. The ancient polarity between Jerusalem and Judah was maintained throughout the Hellenistic period. On the political structure of the Hellenistic states see E. Schürer, *The History of the Jewish People in the Age of Jesus Christ* (rev. and ed. G. Vermes, F. Millar, M. Black [4 vols.; Edinburgh: T. & T. Clark, 1973–87], II, pp. 86 et seq., and especially pp. 86-87 and 184-85). The πρεσβύτεροι were members of the peripheral βουλαί.

2.   The term *ḥbr* clearly indicates an assembly, perhaps the Sanhedrin. The wording on these coins confirms the continued existence of a dual conception of power. The expression *ḥbr yhwdym* also appears on the coins of later sovereigns, for example Alexander Jannaeus.

Apart from the politically inactive opposition of the Essenes, the strongest opposition to the Hasmonaean state lay within, among those who had founded it, or had greatly aided in its foundation.

2. *John Hyrcanus*

Like his brothers, Simon too died a violent death. He was assassinated by his son-in-law, Ptolemy, in an attempted *coup*. Ptolemy had laid his hopes in Antiochus VII (138–129), rival of Demetrius II, who had consecrated Simon's ultimate success. Ptolemy tried to kill all of Simon's family in Jericho, but one son, John Hyrcanus, was absent and escaped murder.

Hyrcanus was a great leader, one of the greatest of a family of leaders. He quickly forced Ptolemy to flee, but had to face the brunt of an attack in force by the Syrians. He was forced to take refuge in Jerusalem where he resisted a long siege, counting on the elements that had always played in the Jews' favour, division within the Syrian camp, attacks by the Parthians or diplomatic intervention by Rome. Once again luck was with Hyrcanus. Whether due to Roman intervention or in order to free his hands for a war against the Parthians, or perhaps both, Antiochus ended up proposing peace to Hyrcanus, who accepted. Hyrcanus agreed to once again pay tribute, hand over hostages and dismantle the walls of Jerusalem. Furthermore, he had to leave the city in order to accompany the king in a campaign against the Parthians.

This would have been the end of the Jews' independence had the Parthians not defeated and killed Antiochus. Demetrius, now a prisoner of the Parthians, became king and Hyrcanus returned to Jerusalem to rule in the same conditions as his father Simon before him. His position was even strengthened during the reign of Alexander Zebinas (128–122) when the dynastic wars became chronic in the Syrian state. Syria entered into a phase of decadence which permitted the Jewish state to become more and more autonomous.

Through taxes levied on his subjects Hyrcanus accumulated riches that Josephus claims were uncountable (*Ant.* 13.273), and which were used to maintain his army. While the armies of Jonathan and Simon had been composed of mercenaries, but only Jews, Hyrcanus systematically enlisted pagans as well (*Ant.* 13.249). This too is a sign that the Hasidaeans were taking more and more of a distance from Hyrcanus's policies. They had fought for the Maccabees in order to gain religious freedom; they were much less enthusiastic about fighting for Hyrcanus once that freedom had been reached. They could also have been kept away from arms by the fact that, with internal peace, Judaea entered a favourable period from an economic point of view, which certainly did not increase the desire to join the army. Even Hyrcanus could not have been opposed to the economic growth of the region. In short, there was a series of factors which kept the majority of the Jews, especially those whose living depended on their work, from becoming professional soldiers. In contrast, Hyrcanus, who wanted to extend Judaea's borders to where they had been under the great kings of the Jewish tradition, needed soldiers. He had to settle for pagans. This, however, created some complications for those who wanted the Law to be implemented in its entirety. The pagans in the army were impure, yet they lived alongside the pure. For the Essenes the city's impurity continued to increase, for the Hasidaeans problems of impurity arose where previously there had been none. Suspicion of the Hasmonaeans must have grown.[3]

In fact, with Hyrcanus we should stop speaking of Hasidaeans and speak instead of Pharisees. Josephus has the first open opposition between the Pharisees and the Hasmonaeans date from the reign of Hyrcanus. The Talmud, which narrates the same event with different details, dates it to the reign of Alexander Jannaeus (*b. Qid.* 66a). In as much as the dating of many episodes and works of the pre-Christian period is unsure, the date proposed by Josephus is more reliable than the later date given in the Talmud.

Josephus narrates (*Ant.* 13.288-92) that Hyrcanus, who had been educated by the Pharisees, invited a number of important Pharisees to a banquet. There he posed a question worthy of such guests, especially if they were wise to the ways of the world. Hyrcanus, who was aware of the existence of serious dissent, with the friendly gesture of the banquet hoped that the leaders of the Pharisees would declare their support of his policies, at least officially. He asked his guests to state clearly, given his love of justice and action according to the will of God, 'if they saw that he was doing anything wrong or straying from the right path'. Of course he received the desired chorus of praise. Only one Pharisee disagreed, a certain Eleazar, whom Josephus judges 'an evil-natured man who took pleasure in dissension'.[4]

---

3. On the impurity of the pagan, see Schürer, *History of the Jewish People*, II, pp. 83-84.

4. On the date of the Eleazar episode, see J. Derenbourg, *Essai sur l'histoire et*

Josephus's judgment of Eleazar was certainly informed by his source, which reveals itself to be favourable to the Hasmonaeans and therefore entirely trustworthy regarding the words put in the mouth of Eleazar. According to Josephus then, Eleazar responded to John Hyrcanus in this way:

'Since you have asked to be told the truth, if you wish to be righteous, give up the high-priesthood and be content with governing the people'. And when Hyrcanus asked him for what reason he should give up the high-priesthood, he replied: 'Because we have heard from our elders that your mother was a captive in the reign of Antiochus Epiphanes [i.e. Antiochus IV] (*Ant.* 13.291-92).

The way in which Eleazar formulates his accusation demonstrates that by that time the idea that the two forms of power, priestly and secular, could be held by a single individual was accepted. At least formally, Eleazar only attacks Hyrcanus' ability to hold the position of high priest. In fact, according to the Law (Lev. 21.14-15) the high priest had to have a pure ancestry (see *m. Qid.* 4.4) and one could suspect that the female prisoner had been violated and was therefore impure (see *Apion* 1.34-36). Even though Josephus claims that Eleazar's statement was false, it must have been a widespread rumour. Hyrcanus asked the Pharisees present what punishment Eleazar deserved for having insulted him, and the Pharisees answered that Eleazar should be beaten and put in chains. Hyrcanus, however, felt that death was the only adequate punishment and came to the conclusion that all the Pharisees agreed with Eleazar. From that moment onward Hyrcanus distanced

la géographie de la Palestine d'après les Talmuds et les autres sources rabbiniques (Paris: Imprimerie Imperial, 1867), pp. 79-82. For an opposing interpretation, see F. Parente, 'Escatologia e politica nel tardo giudaismo e nel cristianesimo primitivo', *RStIt* 80 (1968), pp. 234-96, which provides both a history of the question and an ample bibliography. In favour of the early dating given by Josephus, see *b. Ber.*, 29a, which confirms dissent between the Pharisees and the Hasmonaeans already during the times of John Hyrcanus. This date is followed by, among others, Schürer, *History of the Jewish People*, I, p. 214; Ricciotti, *Storia di Israele*, II, p. 336; M. Noth, *Geschichte Israels* (Göttingen: Vandenhoeck & Ruprecht, 5th edn, 1963), p. 347 (ET: *The History of Israel* [London: SCM Press, 2nd edn, 1983]); Reicke, *Neutestamentliche Zeitgeschichte*, p. 51; and recently by Soggin, *Storia d'Israele* (Brescia: Paideia, 1984), p. 454 (ET: *A History of Israel* [London: SCM Press, 1984]). Parente's thesis has been taken up again by Stemberger, *Pharisäer, Sadduzäer, Essener*. The entire question is discussed in P. Sacchi's review of Stemberger in *Henoch* 17 (1995), pp. 248-52.

himself completely from the Pharisees, even prohibiting the observance of their laws, and passed over to the Sadducees. The whole episode could be imaginary, but it explains the situation of the time very clearly. Eleazar's reasoning shows a particularly interesting aspect of Pharisee logic applied to behaviour. The possibility that an event of a negative nature could have happened leads to the consideration that, from the legal point of view, that event actually did take place.

In *The Jewish War* (1.67) Josephus also mentions that Hyrcanus even had to face a popular uprising as well, and that, in any case, he was able to put it down. It is clear, then, that the Pharisees, concerned about the purity of Jerusalem, either no longer sustained John Hyrcanus or they did so less and less during the expansionistic wars that lasted for all of his reign.

Among his expeditions was one to the north against Sychem, where the hated temple of Gerizim lay. The temple was torn to the ground in 128 BCE. The Judaeans despised the Samaritans and that in itself could justify the war in the eyes of many.

Hyrcanus then turned to the conquest of the other regions around Jerusalem in order to broaden the borders of the state. Among other areas, he also occupied Idumaea, the region to the south of Palestine which for centuries had been distant from Jerusalem. In his policy of conquest, Hyrcanus also imposed circumcision on the Idumaeans (*Ant.* 13.257-58), who were not Jewish, and insisted that they live by the Judaic Law. The drama of Mattathias, whom Menelaus and Antiochus IV had not wanted to allow to live according to the Torah, had been completely reversed. In so doing, Hyrcanus subjected the Idumaeans to the same law as Jerusalem, thus favouring the unity of the state. Even the Pharisees, who held sway over the people and only broke with Hyrcanus completely during the final part of his reign, in practice helped Hyrcanus by way of the synagogues and the constitution of *haburot* which helped to unify the kingdom.

> The communities and companies in which the Pharisees gathered were called *haburot*. It is well known that the word 'Pharisee' means 'separated', but from what? According to *Ḥag.* 2.7, from the *'am ha'areṣ*. The ancient interpretation is quite suggestive and seems to reflect the historical-sociological situation of the first century CE well.[5] The Essenic associations were called *yáḥad*.

5.   See ER 1.1534.

Finally, Hyrcanus turned his attention to Samaria which, after a long war, was torn to the ground. At this point his kingdom had reached nearly the same dimensions as the kingdom of David. The price to be paid for conquest was the loss of Pharisaic support. This forced the king to seek the support of the Sadducees.

The historical character of the Sadducees is elusive. According to most scholars the name indicates them as belonging to the priestly class. We should be dealing with legitimate priests, who had not abandoned Jerusalem during the crisis years that brought about the end of the Zadokite period. They appear, therefore, to be the descendants of the priests who collaborated with Menelaus and with Alcimus.[6]

The Sadducees were therefore the spiritual descendants of those priests who had not been scandalized by the reforms of Jason and Menelaus. The individuals who held the most economic power, the landowners, whom we could call nobles, must have belonged to this current. Even though they had followed the opposite path, the same spirit that animated Onias IV (see below) can be seen in their political choices. They believe in Israel, an Israel which must dominate all other

---

6.   On the Sadducees, see the vast amount of information provided by J. Le Moyne, *Les Sadducéens* (Paris: Gabalda, 1972). Concerning the origin of the name, it is generally considered to be derived from Zadok, from whom all legitimate Jerusalem priests were to have descended since the exile. The Sadducees would therefore be the priests. It should be pointed out, though, that at the time that the sect took on its historical form, reference was no longer made to the legitimate Zadokite priesthood. The hypothesis has been put forward, then, that the name derives from an adjective which has not been documented (and this is a serious handicap), *ṣadduq, analogous to the formation of *ḥannun*, 'merciful'. *ṣadduq would mean 'he who practices justice', to be understood as following a set of norms in contrast with those of the Pharisees. See also T.W. Manson, 'Sadducee and Pharisee: The Origin and Significance of the Names', *BJRL* 22 (1938), pp. 144-59, and Reicke, *Neutestamentliche Zeitgeschichte*, pp. 113-15, 153-57.

The distinction between Zadokites and Sadducees is to be made on historical grounds, no matter what the origin of the names. Most probably, the words have the same origin, just as the two groups were formed in the same priestly circles. The Zadokites were those priests (and their followers) who left Jerusalem during the final crisis of Zadokitism. The Sadducees were those priests (and their followers) who remained in Jerusalem, but maintained a set of norms different from those of the Hasidaeans–Pharisees, even though they were destined to come nearer and nearer the Pharisaic schools. During the time of Jesus of Nazareth, they distinguished themselves from the Pharisees in their political philosophy and in their not having accepted the recent doctrine of resurrection.

peoples, according to a certain interpretation of the Scriptures. They do not shy away from armed struggle and political intrigue. They are the descendants of those who were not scandalized by Hellenism's entry into Jerusalem, because it seemed to bring with it power and money. This is the reason why they now supported the warlike policies of the Hasmonaeans; an agreement with them was inevitable. If they hadn't supported the Maccabees, or if they had only done so late in the game, it was because they had believed in the eventual success of someone like Menelaus or Alcimus who were supported by Syrian might and were open to the great Hellenistic culture. They also got along well with Hyrcanus. In the end, they wanted to make Israel a reality through political struggle, through the state and its logic. When Onias IV saw a Hasmonaean in trouble during the early years of Alexander Jannaeus's reign, he did not hesitate, for purely political reasons, to support fully the Egyptian expedition sent to save him. And yet, Alexander Jannaeus was the high priest of the Temple which was, according to the Zadokites, contaminated.

3. *Aristobulus I*

John Hyrcanus died in 104 BCE and was succeeded by one of his five sons, known as Aristobulus by the Greeks, Judah by the Jews. The information we have regarding this sovereign, who governed for only one year, is not convincing and there are still many doubts regarding this figure. It seems difficult to believe that the dying Hyrcanus should leave the government in the hands of his wife (*Ant.* 13.302). Hyrcanus had not assumed the title of king (though he did have the ἀρχή) and he therefore could not have left the government to his wife since the high priesthood precluded her. Perhaps there is some confusion with an analogous situation that was created on the death of Alexander Jannaeus who left the throne to his wife (but he had been king). The information given by Josephus regarding John Hyrcanus's wife is in a sort of parenthesis which seems to have been added later in order to explain a situation that may not have been clear to Josephus either.

Again according to Josephus (*Ant.* 13.301), Aristobulus was the first Hasmonaean to take the title of king officially, though the fact remains that only the traditional inscription of 'Judah High Priest' appears on his coins. Strabo (16.2, 40) claims that the first Hasmonaean to assume the title of king was his successor Alexander. This information is

however framed by the expression: ἤδη δ' οὖν φανερῶς τυραννου-
μένης τῆς Ἰουδαίας. The only information regarding Aristobulus that
we can regard as certain is that he killed his mother (which would confirm the information given by Josephus's source) and his brother Antigonus, while his other brothers were put in prison. He carried out the
massacre in order to protect himself against future pretenders. He then
set about continuing the wars of conquest begun by Hyrcanus, trying to
extend the state's borders to where they had been during the age of the
great kings of the tradition. At that time Galilee was inhabited by Itur-
aean tribes and Aristobulus forced them to accept circumcision and the
Law, as his father had already done with the Idumaeans.

An echo of the spiritual rupture dividing the Jews during the Hasmonaean period can be found in the historiography concerning Aristobulus. On the one hand Josephus narrates his crimes, arriving at monstrous
degrees of cruelty (causing his mother to starve to death in prison), on
the other hand he repeats the opinion first given by Timagenes (*Ant.*
13.319), that Aristobulus had been ἐπιεικής, 'courteous', added to the
title 'Philhellene' (φιλέλλην).

To the Hellenistic sources, then, Aristobulus appeared as a ruler
worthy of the greatest respect, a good sovereign. This must also have
been the opinion of the Sadducees who supported him. For the Pharisees, however, he remained a monster. Josephus did not know how to
resolve the contradictions of his sources; while he substantially concords with the judgment of the Pharisees who provided his information,
he did not entirely eliminate elements of the opposite tradition.

4. *Alexander Jannaeus*

On the death of Aristobulus his wife, whom Josephus calls Salina or,
perhaps Salome in *Ant.* 13.320 (but whose name he does not mention in
War 1.85), had his brothers released from prison and married one of
them, Jannaeus for the Jews, Alexander for the Greeks. Under Alexander all of the political difficulties accumulated under his predecessors
came to the surface, all the hatred and all the rivalries. He spent his life
in arms, in a continuous struggle, at times for conquest and at other
times for the very survival of the dynasty. Alexander had to resort to
the force of his army in order to defend himself against both internal
and external enemies. At his death he had the precise sensation that the
Hasmonaean policy had failed in its fight on two fronts: against the

lesser (but not always so very small) sovereigns of the neighbouring regions who feared the growing power of the Hasmonaeans, and on the internal front against the Pharisees who abhorred the king whose goal was clearly not that of applying the Law.

The particular attitude of the religious reflection of the most enlightened Pharisee masters of half a century later was formed in contact with the totally negative experience of the Hasmonaean wars. The Pharisee teachers claimed to love peace (see the saying of Hillel, 'Love peace and hasten to follow it', *Pirqe Ab.* 1.12) and to tend to the promises made to Israel through 'doing the Law'. They also categorically refused a series of wars which to them seemed to go against the will of God and the Law. If they had been involved in an extremely violent civil war during the time of Alexander Jannaeus, it had been fought in defence of the Law. And while in all probability there were other factors at play as well, such as the revolt of the bourgeoisie against the landed nobility, the underlying ideal was not betrayed. It was even reinforced by the test.

After having eliminated one of his surviving brothers because he seemed too intelligent and active, Alexander assaulted Ptolemais with the intention of re-establishing the boarders of David's Israel. Ptolemy IX Lathyrus, however, arrived from Cyprus to raise the siege. Chased from Egypt by his mother, Cleopatra III, Ptolemy Lathyrus had set up a small kingdom on the island of Cyprus. From there he landed an army on the mainland, probably with the intention of carving out a bigger kingdom for himself. Alexander was defeated and was saved only because Cleopatra III, worried about the eventual successes of her overly enterprising son, sent help to Alexander. Two Jews, Chelkias and Ananias, sons of Onias IV, led the Egyptian army. The logic of ideology, which does not always correspond to the logic of politics, would have had the sons of Onias arch-enemies of the Hasmonaeans. It is clear that the descendants of Onias, who had become something like the princes of Leontopolis, did not see any advantage in disrupting the *status quo*. Thus Alexander was able to hold on to his throne in a Palestine which had been devastated by Lathyrus.

Having returned to Jerusalem, Alexander undertook a long series of military expeditions to recuperate lost territory and, when possible, to extend his borders. He conquered the area to the east of the Jordan (Gadara on the Yarmuk, and Amathus on the east bank of the Jordan). He then turned south, reaching as far as Raphia and Gaza, only to return to the northeast again to reconquer Amathus, pushing into the Galaaditis. Here he found his path blocked by a local petty king. Obedas, king of the Nabataeans, wished to extend his own power to the north as far as Damascus, over territory conquered by Alexander.

> The Nabataeans' principal centre was the city of Petra, more or less halfway between the Dead Sea and the Gulf of Aqaba. Their inscriptions are in Aramaic. They first appear in history in 312 BCE when Demetrius, son of Antigonus, attacked them without success. The Nabataeans were occupied primarily with commerce between the Mediterranean, the Red Sea and the Orient.

Alexander was soundly defeated and had to take refuge in Jerusalem. The cities of Judaea had become as hostile as foreign cities. In defeat, Alexander had no choice but to retreat to Jerusalem, defended by his mercenaries.

This was the occasion for the revolt of the Feast of the Tabernacles mentioned by Josephus (*Ant.* 13.372-73). While Alexander was making a sacrifice at the altar, the crowd struck him with boughs of cedar and palm branches that they had brought with them for the celebration of the feast. 'They added insult to injury by saying that he was descended from captives and was unfit to hold office [as high priest] and to perform sacrifices'. It was the same accusation that Eleazar had made to John Hyrcanus and which must have become the slogan of the Pharisaic opposition. The Hasmonaeans were impure.

According to Josephus roughly six thousand Jews died at the hands of Alexander's mercenaries during the repression of the revolt. Alexander himself realized that the rupture with the Pharisees was now complete. He had a palisade built around the Temple just as he had already done around his palace. Only the priests, that is only Sadducee elements, could regularly cross the palisade.

Sometime after this event, but we do not know the exact date, a true civil war broke out among the Jews. The event has been placed in relation, though I'm not sure just how correctly, with the popular and anti-capitalist uprising led by Mithridates of Pontus who, in 88 BCE, massacred Romans and Italics in the province of Asia.

When they realized that they could not compete with Alexander's mercenaries, the Pharisees sought help from a foreign king, Demetrius III of Syria, who was glad to accept the request. Once more Alexander was defeated, but Demetrius was unable to follow up the victory. For reasons that remain unclear he was forced to return home, probably due to some aspect of the civil wars that had wracked Syria for more than 50 years. According to Josephus (*Ant.* 13.379), Demetrius's brusque retreat was caused by the defection of six thousand Pharisees who, overtaken by a sense of 'compassion', are said to have gone over to the side of their hated adversary. It is possible that some Pharisees did desert Demetrius, fearing the passage from the yoke of a Sadducee high priest to that of a Greek sovereign. Even if that were the case, though, the flight of six thousand men could hardly have stopped Demetrius the day after the victory.[7]

At any rate Alexander was able to crush the Pharisee resistance in a short time, giving himself over to repression and revenge, as had become the custom in Palestine since the time of the struggle between Menelaus and Jonathan.

When the last members of the Pharisee resistance surrendered, they were taken to Jerusalem where 800 of them were crucified after their wives and children had been killed before their eyes. In the meantime Alexander feasted in his palace, with his women (*Ant.* 13.380). We know that in all the civil war lasted six years (*Ant.* 13.376) and cost the lives of fifty thousand Jews.

By 80 BCE the situation had been normalized. Alexander could once again concentrate on his wars of conquest in order to re-establish the borders, always forcing the vanquished to accept circumcision.

And once again in these operations Alexander came into conflict with the Nabataeans, now led by King Aretas, who had extended their borders as far north as Damascus, thus closing Israel's eastern borders. Moving then from Damascus the Nabataeans penetrated deep into Alexander's territory. A battle took place near Lydda and Alexander was defeated, but through granting concessions whose particulars remain unknown, he did succeed in making Aretas return to his own territory. At any rate, the Nabataeans remained a threat because their state extended around much of Israel and they were interested in

---

7.   Josephus claims that Demetrius III's army was made up of forty thousand infantrymen and three thousand cavalry (*Ant.* 13.377). In *War* 1.93 the number given for the infantry is much lower, fourteen thousand. We do not know what proportion of that figure were Jews, since they are counted together with the others. According to *Antiquities of the Jews*, Alexander's army was roughly half that of Demetrius, twenty thousand men, while in *War* the two armies are said to have been roughly the same size.

expanding toward the sea. Later, the Nabataeans were to intervene often in affairs regarding the Jewish state.

Before dying, Alexander advised his wife, Alexandra Salome,[8] that if she wanted to preserve the kingdom and ensure her own life and the lives of her children, she should seek the full support of the Pharisees (*Ant.* 13.399-404). He was perfectly aware of the irreparable rupture between him and the people who were either under the influence of the Pharisees, or some other opposition groups whose weight was beginning to be felt. The choice lay between continuing the war and living in a fortress, or reaching an agreement with the Pharisees.[9]

5. *Alexandra Salome*

Alexandra reigned for nine years, from 76 to 67 BCE. She was able to create an independent and militarily strong government that was not consumed by internal fighting. If her political achievements did not prove long-lasting, that was due to the violence of the tensions dividing the Jews, which were complicated by the appearance of the phenomenon of a money-based capitalism that had as an immediate consequence the formation of a proletarian class.

Alexandra gained *de facto* royal power. Having assumed command of the army she continued the siege of Ragaba 'beyond the Jordan' during which Alexander had died. Thus, in practice the army recognized her as its commander. Having ensured control of the army, she went to Jerusalem and made contact with the Pharisees, in whose

---

8. *Ant.* 13.320. *Salina, Salome*: the tradition is divided concerning these two names, whose form is similar enough to consider them two renderings of the same name. The name 'Salina' could be a Hellenized version of 'Salome', which in turn could be explained as a reduced form of Shelamzion; see Derenbourg, *Essai sur l'histoire et la géographie de la Palestine*, p. 102 n. Niese accepts the reading 'Salina'. The fact that Salome already had a Greek name, Alexandra, could cause some difficulty for this interpretation. It is possible that Salina was merely the Greek pronunciation, a bit deformed, of 'Salome'. It is also possible that the name 'Alexandra' was related to her position as queen, wife of Alexander. But these are only hypotheses.

9. On the relationship between Alexander Jannaeus and the Pharisees as given in the rabbinical sources, see Derenbourg, *Essai sur l'histoire et la géographie de la Palestine*, p. 95 n. Jannaeus's return to the side of the Pharisees is confirmed in *b.Ber.* 29a: he was wicked, but became righteous. From the context it is clear that the word 'wicked' means 'Sadducee'.

hands she 'placed all that concerned his corpse and the royal power' (*Ant.* 13.405). Josephus recounts that before this gesture the Pharisees ceased in their wrath, celebrated a magnificent funeral in Alexander's honour telling the people that 'they had lost a just king'. The civil war which had cost fifty thousand lives seems to have been forgotten along with the 800 men crucified in front of both Alexandra and the Pharisees.

Josephus explains Alexandra's success with these words (*Ant.* 13.408): 'She allowed the Pharisees to do as they saw fit in all matters and ordered the people to obey them; and whatever regulations, introduced by the Pharisees in accordance with the tradition of their fathers, had been abolished by her father-in-law Hyrcanus [sc. John Hyrcanus], these she again restored'.

Josephus's words tell us a great deal. The Pharisees had introduced certain norms concerning observation of the Law based on the so-called oral tradition, which clearly only they recognized, which John Hyrcanus had abolished, probably when he passed over from the Pharisees to the Sadducees. Alexandra once again accepted the Pharisee's interpretation of the Law and they accepted her reign, because it was the only way to impose that interpretation of the Law (and consequently a certain societal structure) on the people. Alexandra had control of the army and gave no signs of either renouncing it nor of weakening it. She even recruited more mercenaries (*Ant.* 13.409).

Josephus's expression that Alexandra held only the title of queen while real power lay in the hands of the Pharisees should be taken to mean that she gave the Pharisees control over questions regarding the laws. The Pharisees, in fact, were able to enter into the Sanhedrin, presided over by the high priest and controlled, up until that time, by the Sadducees. Thus the Pharisees began in some way to participate in the τιμὴ ἀρχιερατική, which they soon came to dominate. The Pharisees and Sadducees then began to unite their forces against a common enemy, capitalism, which on differing occasions was to penetrate both lay and priestly power.

At that time Tigranes, king of Armenia, constituted a great threat to the Jewish state. Tigranes had occupied the Syrian throne and extended his power as far as Damascus, and his future plans included an invasion of Judaea. A Jewish expedition against Damascus, led by the queen's son Aristobulus, the future Aristobulus II, did not meet with success. Jerusalem was saved, however, by the Roman attack on Tigranes led by

Lucullus. The Roman offensive was not very successful, but it did prevent Tigranes from taking the initiative in Judaea (*Ant.* 13.419-21).

In order to understand the following period, it would be essential to establish the Pharisees' degree of penetration around Jerusalem. They were very active, promoting their laws, for political as well as ideological reasons. And the masses? Given the precautions taken in the following century against the 'people of the countryside' (*'am ha-'areṣ*), their penetration into the surrounding areas must have been limited. Furthermore, the principal fortified places outside Jerusalem remained in the possession of the Sadducees. As we shall see below, this fact could explain many elements in the preachings of Jesus of Nazareth.

The Pharisees were able to allow the return of all the exiles and to free their prisoners, but when they wanted to seek revenge against the Sadducees, accused of having induced Alexander to crucify the 800 Pharisees, the queen refused (*Ant.* 13.410). She was able to do this because it was she who governed the country. If a couple of Sadducees did lose their lives, it is because they were treacherously murdered. While Alexandra's policy was favourable to the Pharisees, it was not so because she felt that Pharisaism was the authentic interpretation of Judaism, but rather because she wanted to put an end to the hatred and civil wars that afflicted the country. She did not strive to eliminate the Sadducees, but to find room for both parties.

The balance between the Pharisees and the throne was favoured by the choice of Alexandra's eldest son as high priest. This son, Hyrcanus II, was also heir to the throne. He must have had a particularly passive character (Josephus refers to him as ἀπράγμος, 'inactive'), since he accepted to renounce the throne in his mother's favour and left it up to the Pharisees to establish the norms regarding the Law. His grandfather, Hyrcanus I, had never allowed so much. It is, however, unclear just how much the power of the Sanhedrin, controlled by the Pharisees, was felt outside Jerusalem (see the situation at the time of Simon, p. 252 n. 2).

Alexandra's army made no expeditions, but it is clear that her neighbours considered her strong, since they sent her hostages. Given the particular structure of the Hellenistic states, in which the army was completely separate from the rest of the population, Alexandra had to establish a number of fortresses in the kingdom, under the command of Sadducees, as had been the custom since Simon Maccabaeus. The first among these commanders was Aristobulus II, the queen's younger son who, unlike his brother, was very active and ambitious. By sending the key Sadducean figures to the fortresses as commanders, Alexandra removed them from the threat of revenge by the Pharisees and put the army under the command of men who were accustomed by tradition to command. Thus she succeeded in creating distinct zones of power, but it is also clear that this policy created two opposing forces which were bound to attack one another at the first propitious moment. Thus under Alexandra civil wars were avoided, in spite of the Pharisees' attempts to spur her into conflict with the Sadducees. The very division of territories made by Alexandra in order to separate the leaders of the two groups, however, was destined to be the source of future problems.

Aristobulus controlled nearly all the outlying fortresses and therefore had a considerable army under his command. This worried the Pharisees who asked Alexandra's counsel, but she replied that in her old age she no longer wanted to busy herself with state affairs. She was able to calm them by reminding them that they too had an army, the one in Jerusalem (which, however, was under her command), consistent tax revenues and a healthy economy. That should have been enough to guarantee peace in the kingdom and the safety of all. She was right, in referring to the present, but a new civil war after her death seemed inevitable.

This assessment of her reign was already formulated by Josephus. He praised her positive qualities, first and foremost the desire to keep the peace among her people, but accused her of living only for the present, with a complete lack of foresight.

Alexandra died in 67 BCE. Under Pompey Rome was about to begin the *Bellum piraticum*. Pompey defeated Mithradates VI, king of Pontus, in 66 BCE and accepted Tigranes' submission. Syria thus became part of the Roman empire. Pompey sent his legate Scaurus to Syria, and in 65 BCE Scaurus had arrived at Judaea's borders.

6. *Hyrcanus II and Aristobulus II*

As was easily foreseeable, following the death of Alexandra war broke out between her two sons Hyrcanus and Aristobulus.

Hyrcanus, who was the elder of the two and already high priest, assumed the title of king, but his brother did not approve. A battle was fought at Jericho and Aristobulus won. Hyrcanus did not continue the fight, ceding all of his rights and prerogatives to his brother and accepting a pension in return (*Ant.* 14.4-7).

The conflict would probably have ended there if a certain Antipater (an Idumaean and therefore a Jew, since Hyrcanus I had forced circumcision on the Idumaeans) had not taken up the cause of Hyrcanus II. It is not clear just what Antipater's position in Idumaea was, but since his father had governed Idumaea with the title of *stratēgos* during the times of Alexander Jannaeus, it is likely that Antipater held the same position as his father.

> Antipater was afraid of Aristobulus' power as king, fearing that he could suffer because of Aristobulus' hatred for him; he therefore took to stirring up the most powerful Jews against Aristobulus, making secret contacts. Antipater claimed that Aristobulus had no right to the throne because it rightfully belonged to his elder brother (*Ant.* 14.11).

Of course, in order to become the champion of Hyrcanus's rights he needed Hyrcanus's consent. Antipater was able to obtain this by telling him that his life was in danger and that an army under Aretas, king of the Nabataeans, would have taken him back to Jerusalem as high priest. Antipater himself resolved to go to Jerusalem to win over Hyrcanus and to accompany him in his flight to Petra (*Ant.* 14.14-18; *War* 1.123-26).

It had still been possible to see traces of broader popular movements, such as those of the Pharisees and the Sadducees, in the disagreements between Hyrcanus and Aristobulus during the reign of their mother Alexandra Salome. In short, one has the impression that the discord between the two brothers reflected more general discord among the Jewish people. In the war between Hyrcanus and Aristobulus, in contrast, one has the impression that the Pharisee/Sadducee formula cannot explain the events. It appears as though the old protagonists have been pushed aside by new forces. The Pharisees and Sadducees were destined to come closer and closer together up until the time of Jesus of Nazareth, when together they represented the traditionalists.

The war between Hyrcanus and Aristobulus had culminated in the battle of Jericho, where a great many of Hyrcanus's troops had gone over to the side of Aristobulus. The Pharisees and Sadducees had not taken the field against one another; both armies were composed of mercenaries.

Antipater, as can be seen in the passage from Josephus quoted above, did not seek the support of the Pharisees in order to bring the legitimate high priest back to Jerusalem, but rather he sought the support of 'powerful men of Israel'. Within the limits of what can be reasonably argued, apparently a phenomenon similar to what was happening throughout the Roman empire was occurring in Palestine as well. Alongside what was essentially a warrior nobility, traditionally bound to the king and to its landed possessions, a new wealthy class was being formed which was equidistant from the noble Sadducees and the bourgeois Pharisees. Antipater's friends were from this new class. Governor of Idumaea, Antipater was wealthy enough to send sufficient gifts to Aretas to convince him to intervene urgently on Hyrcanus's behalf. Josephus (*Ant.* 14.17) mentions an unceasing flow of gifts, every day until Aretas decided to act.

Of course Hyrcanus agreed to give back to the Nabataeans the cities on the east bank of the Dead Sea that Hyrcanus I and Alexander had conquered. Aristobulus was defeated and forced to take refuge in the Temple with the few followers that remained faithful to him,[10] only Sadducee priests, since most of his followers had gone over to the side of the winners. Once more, things would probably have gone a certain way if a great power had not had an armed contingent in Damascus. News reached Scaurus that there was fighting in Judaea while both Hyrcanus and Aristobulus sent him gifts in order to win his support. Scaurus took Aristobulus's side because, according to Josephus, it was easier to carry out operations against a besieging army rather than against one under siege (*Ant.* 14.31). The fact of the matter is, however, that if Scaurus had preferred Hyrcanus he would simply have had to wait. If he decided to intervene it was because he was following the Roman logic of bringing aid to the weaker party (Aristobulus) against the stronger (Hyrcanus) who already had the support of Antipater and the Nabataean king.

Once Aretas lifted the siege Aristobulus pursued and defeated him. It must not have been a decisive victory, though, because Antipater continued to govern Idumaea, and he governed it for Hyrcanus.

In the meantime, near the end of 64 BCE Pompey entered Syria to winter his troops there. Here Antipater met with him in the unidentified city of Aspis (Dio Cassius 37.7) in order to present Hyrcanus' case. In his own defence, Aristobulus too sent an ambassador. Pompey stalled, and only took up the question again the following spring in Damascus.

---

10. See the prayer of Onias. The besiegers had asked Onias to damn the besieged, and when Onias refused he was stoned to death. The division between the people and the priesthood is clear from his words: 'Since those who surround me here are your *people* and those under siege are your *priests*...' (*Ant.* 14.22-24).

This time a legation of Jews was also present, who explained to Pompey that 'they were accustomed by tradition to being governed by the priests of the God they worshipped' (*Ant.* 14.41) and that they therefore wanted the monarchy to be abolished. This delegation is traditionally seen as having been sent by the Pharisees, but the fact that they speak of 'obeying their priests', at least according to Josephus, without naming any other organ of government, like the Sanhedrin, for example, gives rise to some perplexity. It is more likely that the legation represented a spontaneous wave of traditionalism reflecting the ideas of most of the Jews in Jerusalem. Tired of the Hellenizing Hasmonaean kings, they were nostalgic for a past that no longer existed.

Pompey must have realized that there was no real political force behind this group, because he did not even take them into consideration. For him the problem was that of resolving the conflict between the two princes, and he resolved it in favour of Hyrcanus, perhaps impressed by the fact that many notables (*Ant.* 14.43, mentions more than one thousand men, δοκιμώτατοι, who went to Pompey's camp in order to declare themselves) had come out in Hyrcanus's favour. This sizable group of 'notables' represents the group that Antipater had always based his power on and that we have identified as the wealthy, non-priestly class. Pompey understood this group more than the others; they were the Palestinian equivalent to the Roman *equites*. The ties between Antipater and the Roman ruling class began in that moment and from then on remained a constant in Antipater's policies. Roman consuls and praetors came and went, but Antipater continued to dominate the scene up until the rise of Caesar.

Pompey did not make an open decision in favour of Hyrcanus in order avoid the risk that Aristobulus should prepare his defences. When it was clear that Pompey was leaning toward the side of Hyrcanus, Aristobulus hastily prepared his resistance. In the end, however, convinced of the hopelessness of a fight, he surrendered personally to Pompey. Jerusalem did not give up the struggle, though, and the Roman troops advanced up to the walls of the city. At this point the majority of the city's inhabitants, pro-Pharisee and pro-Hyrcanus, decided to open the city's gates to the Romans. Only a small minority of Sadducees took refuge in the Temple and decided to hold out until the very end. This was autumn 63 BCE.

On this occasion Pompey broke into the Temple. The fact that this has been remembered in history demonstrates that it was an exceptional event, and that it was a clear act of Pompey's will. Tacitus recalls the event and forcefully describes the sense of wonder (perhaps his own as well as Pompey's) when in the Temple he saw nothing but *vacuam sedem et inania arcana* (*Hist.* 5.9).

Pompey certainly did not want to present himself as a conqueror. The day after taking the Temple, he allowed it to be purified and the normal liturgical services were resumed. As for Aristobulus, he was taken prisoner to Rome and paraded through the city during Pompey's triumph. Aristobulus's son Antigonus was taken to Rome as well, though his other son Alexander managed to escape during the voyage.

Besides being high priest, Hyrcanus assumed the title of ethnarch. Josephus (*Ant.* 20.244) recalls the event with words we have already seen: 'Pompey also restored the high priesthood to Hyrcanus and permitted him to have the προστασία τοῦ ἔθνους.[11] Judaea was no longer independent. Furthermore, Pompey separated from Judaea all of those cities that had been forcefully 'Judaized' by the Hasmonaeans, giving them back their freedom. This was the case of all the cities beyond the Jordan, including Scythopolis, which became the cities of the so-called 'Decapolis'. The Idumaean cities, in contrast, were not restored their freedom, given the nature of the bond created between Antipater and Hyrcanus II. Samaria, too, was separated from Judaea and worship on Mt Gerizim began once again.

Beyond the area around Jerusalem and southern Idumaea, Judaea now included the better part of what had once been Samarian territory, Galilee, and the cities beyond the Jordan south of Decapolis, the region known as Peraea. This latter area had been taken from the Nabataeans who were destined to come into conflict with the Romans, since the latter wanted to dominate the caravan routes leading to the east. And one of the principal routes passed through Petra, the Nabataean capital.

7. *The New Political and Social Situation*

While on the whole the political and social situation in Judaea was none too clear, it does seem that something had changed since the first half of the century when conflict could be interpreted as stemming from the differences between the ideas and interests of the Pharisees and the Sadducees. As we have seen, since the battle of Jericho in 67 BCE this

---

11. Regarding Hyrcanus's *prostasia*, see pp. 248-49, above.

explanation no longer held true. Antipater did not side with the Pharisees or the Sadducees, and it is difficult to imagine Hyrcanus as an exponent of the Sadducees even though he was high priest and heir to the Hasmonaeans dynasty, which for 50 years had based its power on Sadducee support. It is also difficult to establish just who was represented by the delegation that presented itself to Pompey in the name of the Jewish people. The priests that Pompey killed in the Temple were certainly Sadducees, but the priests that purified the Temple the next day must have been Sadducees as well, though with different political ideas than the ones who had decided to die in the Temple in spite of the fact that Aristobulus, their high priest, had already surrendered. Given the course of events, some of the Sadducees were willing to accept Hyrcanus. The social and political situation was fragmented and was becoming more and more nuanced.

Political division must have grown from two distinct, but parallel causes, one of which has already been mentioned, the formation in Palestine of a capitalistic class separate from the old Sadducee nobility. It is senseless to try to establish which sect these capitalists belonged to before Antipater showed them that they represented a precise class of people. They could have been Sadducees or Pharisees, or even Essenes, or simply opportunists; it really does not matter very much.

The other factor that influenced the politics of the day was the corresponding formation of what today we would call a proletariat, which probably hated pretty much all the religious and political movements equally: mercenaries, unemployed between one war and the next must have tended toward the Sadducees, and the Pharisee craftsmen who had been ruined and lived as they could. Rejected by the Jewish society of the day, both of these groups could do nothing but soak up the words concerning the arrival of a messiah. Variations of this message came from various groups, first of all from the Essenes and the Apocalyptics, but also from the Samaritans. Messianism united expectations of divine intervention of a cosmic and totally renovating nature with much more earthly desires of a clear political and social character. It is difficult to gauge the weight of messianism in each of the revolts that took place during the second half of the first century BCE, but it is clear that messianism could be used as a sort of anti-Hasmonaean banner. The Hasmonaeans were the ones who had usurped David's throne.

The *Psalms of Solomon*, an anonymous work written not long after the middle of the first century BCE, bear witness to this spirituality.

For if you do not give strength, who can endure discipline in poverty?...
Your testing is in his flesh, and in the difficulty of poverty (*Ps. Sol.*
16.13-14).

Lord, you are our king forevermore...
We hope in God our saviour, for the strength of our God is forever with
mercy; and the kingdom of our God is forever over the nations through
his judgment.
Lord, you chose David to be king over Israel, and swore to him about his
descendants forever, that his kingdom should not fail before you.
But because of our sins, sinners rose up against us, they set upon us and
drove us out. Those to whom you did not [make the] promise, they took
away [from us] by force; and they did not glorify your honourable name.
With pomp they set up a monarchy because of their arrogance; they
despoiled the throne of David with arrogant shouting.
But you, O God, overthrow them, and uproot their descendants from the
earth, causing a man alien to our race to rise up against them.
Reward them, O God, according to their sins...
See, Lord, and raise up for them *their king, the son of David*, so that your
servant reign over Israel[12] in the time known to you, O God. Undergird
him with the strength to destroy the unrighteous rulers, to purge
Jerusalem from gentiles who trample her to destruction...to smash the
arrogance of sinners like a potter's jar; to shatter all their substance with
an iron rod; to destroy the unlawful nations with the word of his
mouth...
He will gather a holy people whom he will lead in righteousness...He
will not tolerate unrighteousness [even] to pause among them...The alien
and the foreigner will no longer live near them. He will judge peoples
and nations in the wisdom of his righteousness... And he will have
gentile nations serving him under his yoke, and he will glorify the Lord
in [a place] prominent [above] the whole earth. And he will purge
Jerusalem [and make it] holy as it was even from the beginning...
[For] he will not rely on horse and rider and bow, nor will he collect
gold and silver for war. Nor will be build up hope in a multitude for a
day of war. The Lord himself is his king, the hope of the one who has a
strong hope in God...
He will lead them all in equality and there will be no arrogance among
them, that any should be oppressed...
The Lord Himself is our king forevermore (*Ps. Sol.* 17, *passim*).

The text of this psalm bears witness to the fact that there were people
in Judaea who had been forced to abandon their land and take refuge in

---

12. An alternative interpretation, 'to reign over Israel, your Servant', is also
possible.

the wilderness. There they awaited a man from the house of David who would come and establish the kingdom of Israel, the one promised by God. They awaited God's reign. One day that was to happen, and it was to be the work of the anointed one (a recurrent term in these psalms), whose true strength would lie in the support received from God. All social injustices were to be eliminated.

These people, who had abandoned their land and lived as they could outside the cities, represented a restless mass, ready to take up arms and follow the first one to call. But they were not to be docile with just any adventurer. At least that is what the author of *Psalms of Solomon* 17 says; he does not want to take part in a meaningless battle, but he does want to be led by the son of David, anointed by God. There was a serious problem concerning this last condition. How could they await the 'son of David', if David's line had apparently been lost through the centuries, to the point that there was not even any information regarding Zerubbabel's descendants? At least up until the third century BCE there had been genealogical lists for the house of David (see 1 Chron. 3). They have been lost for the following period, but it is possible that someone continued to keep them. In fact, it is hardly possible that the psalm was meant in an allegorical sense where 'descendant of David' meant 'a righteous king'. Usurpation of the throne is mentioned and the awaited messiah is truly the anointed one from the house of David. The tone is different from that felt in the Dead Sea Scrolls where the messiah awaited is generically the anointed of Israel. Anyone awaiting the anointed one of Israel poses no preconditions for accepting that figure; the messiah only has to present himself as such. Those awaiting the anointed descendant of David provide a precise limitation for identifying that figure.

8. *From Antipater to Herod*

In 57 BCE Gabinius arrived in Syria as proconsul. Within three years of his arrival he was faced with three Jewish rebellions, all of them provoked either by Aristobulus himself, who had been sent prisoner to Rome but who had managed to escape, or by his son Alexander, known as Hasmoneus in order to distinguish him from Alexander Jannaeus. They had decided to fight in order to regain their lost power, and there was no lack of malcontents to enlist in their support.

The first revolt took place in 57 BCE and was led by Alexander Hasmoneus. He travelled throughout Judaea and was able to put together an army of 10,000 infantrymen and 1500 cavalry, all of them Jews (*Ant.* 14.83). These men were not mercenaries, they were Jews fighting for a cause that they recognized as their own. They must have come from the ranks of the numerous displaced persons who had fled the cities during Hyrcanus's and Aristobulus's wars, victims more of capitalism than of the Sadducees and Pharisees. The expectations of a messiah mentioned earlier must have taken root among these groups of people. The author of the *Psalms of Solomon* seems to link the messiah to the house of David, considering the Hasmonaeans as usurpers, but, as we have seen, not all groups shared this conception of the messiah. They were willing to fight against Rome for anyone who could free them from the economic dominion of Hyrcanus and Antipater, and the capitalists that backed them up. In contrast, the Romans themselves, who belonged to the so-called equestrian class and whose methods of governing the provinces are well known, got along perfectly well with Antipater. They shared the same interests and, in the end, the same view of life. Antipater never did anything to harm the Romans and he came to their aid every time they were in difficulty. These were wars of independence, but they were also social wars. The two elements, love of independence and hatred of the dominant capitalistic class, were inextricably bound together. With the passage of time, though, the patriotic element of the resistance was destined to grow stronger and stronger.

Alexander was defeated and forced to take refuge in the fortress of Alexandreion, where he was saved by his mother. She was a philo-Roman and stepped in as mediator. The negotiations led to a new equilibrium in Judaea where Hyrcanus, while faithful to the Romans, saw his influence reduced even more. Gabinius took *de facto* responsibility for governing the country away from Hyrcanus, since he had proved unable to maintain the peace with his own forces. Judaea was then divided into five regions both for reasons of tax collecting and in order to make contacts among the Jews more difficult. According to the expression of Josephus, each of these regions was governed by a Sanhedrin. 'Thus the Jews, freed from a monarchical regime, passed under an aristocratic one' (*Ant.* 14.91; see also *War* 1.170).

Usually when Josephus uses terms derived from the word 'aristocracy' he is referring to the Sadducees, but in this case his meaning is not clear. He could be referring to the new moneyed aristocracy. In any case, it becomes evident in later episodes, such as the judgment of Herod (*Ant.* 14.168-84), that the Pharisees too were present in these five

Sanhedrins. Hyrcanus was weakened by this new organization of Judaea, because the Sanhedrin that he presided over as high priest held authority over only one part of the country.

The following year it was Aristobulus, with the aid of his son Antigonus, who took up arms. Once again it was not difficult to find men willing to fight for him. In fact, too many men volunteered for the weapons he had available and he had to send one thousand of them away. Josephus explains the ease with which the Jews took up arms and followed anyone willing to fight against Jerusalem and against Rome with the expression that 'they always welcomed revolutionary movements' (*Ant.* 14.93). Josephus does not explain the causes, but they can be deduced from the general context. Aristobulus was quickly defeated, taken prisoner and sent once again to Rome. His sons Alexander and Antigonus, however, remained free (*Ant.* 14.97 and *War* 1.174).

Alexander Hasmoneus again tried his hand at armed conflict, with admirable courage and tenacity. While Gabinius was engaged in Egypt putting Ptolemy XI Auletes (55 BCE) back on the throne, Alexander led a vast uprising in all of Judaea. Before setting in motion strictly military operations, Gabinius asked the faithful Antipater to try to reason with as many Jews as possible (*Ant.* 14.101). Thus, Alexander's army began to thin out, but he still had thirty thousand men at his command. He gave battle to Gabinius at Mt Tabor and was completely defeated (*Ant.* 14.102 and *War* 1.177-78).

Crassus, the new Roman governor of Syria who was seeking glory, riches and power in the East, passed through Jerusalem the following year, 54 BCE. He had a great deal of money handed over to him from the Temple, which was once again extremely wealthy due to the money and precious items sent to it from Jews throughout the world (*Ant.* 14.105-10). The Jews and other sympathizers who sent money to the Temple from around the world certainly were not proletarians; if they were not the equivalent of Antipater and Hyrcanus, at the very least they were persons who stood to gain from the current situation and sought to maintain it as it was. The Jews were present at that time throughout the Mediterranean basin, including Rome, and according to Strabo in a passage picked up by Josephus (*Ant.* 14.115), wherever they settled they were able to impose themselves. If Aristobulus's wife was able to negotiate the release of her son outside the walls of Alexandreion and one year later successfully negotiate the release of her sons taken prisoner with Aristobulus, she must have been something more

than simply pro-Roman. This type of favours, which were very dangerous for Rome (as illustrated by Alexander's third rebellion), could only
be obtained in one way at the time of Pompey, Crassus and Caesar.
Jerusalem was tied to the Diaspora, or at least to the most influential
elements of the Diaspora by a great amount of money, the same money
that separated Jerusalem from many Jews who lived in Palestine. The
Palestinian Jews were perhaps more numerous than the Jews of the
Diaspora, but they lacked political weight.

Crassus's defeat at Carrhae (53 BCE) rekindled hopes of resistance to
the Romans among the Jews of the countryside, but Cassius Longinus,
future assassin of Caesar, with the political advice of Antipater quickly
crushed all resistance. The leader of the revolt, Peitholaus, was killed
and 30,000 Jews were sold into slavery (*Ant.* 14.120-21 and *War*
1.180). That made for 30,000 less malcontents, who hindered the establishment of order desired by Antipater and the Roman equestrians.

The civil war between Caesar and Pompey broke out in 49 BCE.
Antipater, and therefore Hyrcanus as well, were allied to the latter.
Thus Caesar released Aristobulus so that he could return to Judaea and
take up arms again against Antipater and the supporters of Pompey.
Aristobulus, however, was poisoned and his son, Alexander, was captured and decapitated. Pompey was defeated at Pharsalus in 48 BCE and
fled from there into Egypt where he was killed by Ptolemy XII. Caesar
then landed at Alexandria, but found himself ill-prepared for an armed
uprising in Egypt.

Antipater was quick to seize the favourable occasion and through
Hyrcanus, the high priest, convinced the Jews in Egypt and of all the
Diaspora to support Caesar. He himself led a Jewish expeditionary
force into Egypt where he convinced the Jews of Leontopolis, who had
no particular sympathy for Caesar, to take his side. It is clear that even
in Leontopolis the Jews, or at least those who held power, were on the
side of the Roman equestrians. Antipater arrived in time to demonstrate
that they had nothing to lose, not even with Caesar.

Caesar was particularly grateful to Antipater and Hyrcanus and provisions in their favour and in favour of all the Jews of the empire did
not fail to come forth. The list of provisions in favour of the Jews is
given by Josephus in an ample section of the *Antiquities of the Jews*
(14.143-55 and 185-216) where the material is presented in a rather
confused manner. Not all of the decrees mentioned seem to date from
this period, nor have they all been handed down to us. On the whole,

though, the Jewish ἔθνος came to find itself in a particularly favourable position.

Hyrcanus was once again given the title of ethnarch that Gabinius had taken away. He also received the title 'friend of the Roman people', both of these titles being hereditary. Furthermore, the Romans did not protest if Hyrcanus had himself addressed as king in Judaea (*Ant.* 14.174).

The person who gained the most from the situation, however, was Antipater. He was given the title of 'governor' (ἐπίτροπος) of Judaea, a title which Antipater was left free to choose (*Ant.* 14.143). Judaea was exempted from paying any ordinary or extraordinary tribute (in wartime), with the sole exception of the city of Joppa, which, if the text has been interpreted correctly, continued to pay tribute to Rome. Even Joppa was, however, placed once again under Jewish authority. The city did benefit, though, from the sabbatical year and every seventh year it too was exempted from paying tribute (*Ant.* 14.202).

Caesar also took to the trouble to guarantee religious freedom for the Jews throughout the empire. See, for example, *Ant.* 14.213-16,[13] which reproduces an edict of Caesar's specifying that, while the θίασοι ('religious societies') had been prohibited (law of 55 BCE) an exception was to be made for the Jews, the only exception in the entire empire. In addition, given their norms concerning the sabbath, several edicts exonerated the Jews from military service. In this case we are clearly dealing with Jews who had obtained Roman citizenship and would therefore have been subject to serving in the legions (*Ant.* 14.240; *War* 6.333-35; Philo, *Leg. Gai.* 155-58). In many places Jews were even allowed to maintain their own legislation, impose tribute and remit sentences.[14]

---

13. Many conjectures have been made concerning the name of Caesar, here given as Ἰούλιος Γάιος. These conjectures are destined to remain such. See the Loeb edition, VII, pp. 560-61. The text could very easily have been written by Caesar, but even in the case that it was not, it still reflects a pro-Jewish atmosphere in the Roman world.

14. Willrich, basing his opinions on previous works, opposed the better part of the Judaeo-Hellenistic documentation in *Urkundenfälschung in der hellenistisch-jüdischen Literatur* (Göttingen: Vandenhoeck & Ruprecht, 1924), pp. 1-9, 38-85. He held that, on a stylistic basis, these documents were false, since where a comparison is possible the texts handed down to us are different from the originals. E. Meyer held the opposite opinion; cfr. *Ursprung und Anfänge des Christentums* (3 vols.; Stuttgart: Magnus, 1921–23), II, p. 127, especially concerning Josephus, *Ant.* 12.138. See R. Laqueur, *Der jüdische Historiker Flavius Josephus* (Giessen:

It should come as no surprise, then, when Suetonius (Divus Julius 84.5) tells us that the Jews wept for several nights after Caesar's death. Now, the problem lies in finding out why Caesar was so generous with the Jewish communities, with Jerusalem and with those who ruled in Jerusalem. Some[15] have maintained that Caesar was driven by his interest in the East, that he wished to establish Roman dominion on a solid basis. This would be an acceptable explanation if Caesar had extended the same concessions to all the peoples of the East, but, by the tone of the individual decrees, they seem to be of an exceptional nature, specifically in favour of the Jews. Furthermore, it is striking that Caesar wished to favour the Jews throughout the empire, and not simply in Palestine. It is more probable that in Caesar's time the Jews represented a political and economic force strong enough to warrant Caesar's support in religious and economic questions (the decrees regard a lot more than just religious freedom!). He insisted on the former in order to make available the latter. He must have understood the strength of Judaism, but, unlike his predecessors, he also understood that it was impossible to count on the Jews' support without respecting all of their religious requirements, no matter how strange they must have seemed to him, given his Epicurean education.

It is possible that Caesar was not at all averse to monotheism. The ideal of a god as master of all the earth and a monarch who governed over all peoples in his name was a very ancient one. It was already present in Lugalzaggisí, a Sumerian king of the twenty-fourth century BCE, who aspired to conquering the whole earth in order to govern it in the name of the god Enlil.

> [When] Enlil, king of all the earth, had granted kingship over all the earth[16] to Lugalzaggisí...after he had brought all the lands[17] under his dominion and from East to West he had subjected them to his power

Münchow, 1920), p. 221; A. Momigliano, *Prime linee di storia della tradizione maccabaica* (Rome, 1931; Amsterdam: Hakkert, 1968), pp. 151-70; *idem.*, 'Ricerche sull'organizzazione della Giudea sotto il dominio romano', *ASNSP* NS 2, III (1934 [1967]), pp. 183-222; 347-97, especially pp. 192-221; and B. Motzo, *Saggi di storia e letteratura giudeo-ellenistica* (Firenze: Felice Le Monnier, 1927), pp. 207-14.

See also the Loeb edition of the *Antiquities of the Jews* in the relevant chapters.

15. See Noth, *Geschichte Israels*, p. 366.

16. KALAM, 'the land of Sumer'; see F. Thureau Dangin, *Die sumerischen und akkadischen Königsinschriften* (Leipzig: Hinrichs, 1907), p. 154.

17. KUR KUR, *ibidem*.

[with Thureau Dangin], then from the Lower sea up along the Tigris and the Euphrates to the Upper sea He made safe the roads... From East to West all...all peoples lived in peace.[18]

The idea of universal empire re-emerges from time to time throughout all of Mesopotamian history. It was present among the Assyrians and it re-emerged forcefully in the ideology of the Persian empire that fought to extend the sovereignty of Ahura Mazda over all the earth. Alexander the Great was fascinated with this ideal. Christianity adopted it in a purely religious form, but it is a well-known fact that the idea was destined to dominate the history of the western world for a very long time.

Jewish communities flourished throughout the Mediterranean basin and became the natural vehicle for the spread of early Christianity throughout the Roman empire.

In the meantime, Antipater prepared to take advantage of his extremely influential position to overthrow the Hasmonaean dynasty and replace it with his own. He knew Hyrcanus well and was convinced that he was weak. Thus Antipater named two of his own sons στρατηγοί in two areas of Judaea: Phasael in Jerusalem itself, and Herod in Galilee (*Ant.* 14.160-61 and *War* 1.203-207). Hyrcanus did not react.

This episode, narrated by Josephus, should suffice in order to give some idea of the atmosphere in Jerusalem during the times of Antipater and Hyrcanus:

> When the leading Jews saw Antipater and his sons growing so great through the goodwill of the nation and the revenues which they received from Judea and Hyrcanus' wealth, they became hostile toward him...
>
> And so they came to Hyrcanus and now openly accused Antipater, saying, 'How long will you keep quiet in the face of what is happening? Do you not see that Antipater and his sons have girded themselves with royal power, while you have only the name of King given you?... Thus Herod...has killed Ezekias and many of his men in violation of our law, which forbids us to slay a man, even an evil-doer, unless he has first

18. This is the text indicated as 1H2b in E. Sollberger and J.R. Kupper, *Inscriptions royales sumériennes et akkadiennes* (Paris: Cerf, 1971), pp. 93-95. See also G.A. Barton, *The Royal Inscriptions of Sumer and Akkad* (New Haven: Yale University Press, 1929), pp. 2-3; and more recently H. Steible, *Die altsumerischen Bau- und Weihinschriften* (Wiesbaden: Steiner, 1982), pp. 316-17, and J.S. Cooper, *Sumerian and Akkadian Royal Inscriptions. I. Presargonic Inscriptions* (New Haven: American Oriental Society, 1986), p. 94.

been condemned by the Sanhedrin to suffer this fate. He, however, has
dared to do this without authority from you (Josephus, *Ant.* 14.163-67).

This passage illustrates the situation fairly well. I believe that Josephus is speaking of the notables of Jerusalem with the expression 'the leading Jews', the Pharisees and Sadducees who saw their influence crumbling before the new political forces. They are Pharisees and Sadducees that begin to be seen as a single element. They were aware that the masses tended to support Antipater more and more, following a schema that was taking place in Rome as well, and that Hyrcanus, who theoretically as high priest represented them, was becoming more and more simply a tool in Antipater's hands.

Antipater had learned Caesar's lesson and began to gather followers within that class of people who had initially been averse to him, probably because his money created work, and created it outside Jerusalem.

The passage quoted above confirms that Hyrcanus had himself addressed as king in Judaea and, at least in the opinion of the principal citizens of Jerusalem, he had the power to remit sentences of death, at least in certain cases, such as those involving armed rebellion. This power was normally restricted to the Sanhedrin. For the members of the Sanhedrin, Pharisees and Sadducees, there was no doubt that Ezekias was wicked, but this did not change the fact that Herod's behaviour was unacceptable. Herod had overstepped his authority. Whether his actions were justified or not, Herod had infringed on royal prerogatives and, as a consequence, on constituted authority. According to the principal citizens, who recognized that Ezekias was 'a wicked man', the king should have at least expressed his desire that Ezekias be condemned. Ezekias in fact was a Galilaean who had promoted rebellion. He was probably a representative of that current of Judaism which, beginning with the Maccabees and ending with the Zealots, saw the armed uprising as a means of making the Law triumph, or, in this case, as a means of asserting their right to independence.

Hyrcanus condescended to calling Herod before the Sanhedrin. Herod, confident in the strength of his army and his friendship with the Romans, appeared lavishly dressed and accompanied by an armed escort.

No one dared speak out against him except a certain Samaias (the term given by Josephus), commonly identified as Shemaya, a teacher belonging to the fourth pair of *tanna'im*. The expression 'a certain Samaias' used in reference to a man who was extremely well known can cause some problems. But the problem cannot be resolved by proposing, as has been done, that instead of Shemaya we are dealing with Shammai, a teacher belonging to the fifth pair together with Hillel, and no less well known than Shemaya. The fact that Josephus mentions Samaias in other points of his narrative in conjunction with Pollion, the Greek name behind which it is not difficult to identify the Hebrew name Abtalion, the second teacher of the fourth pair, seems to favour the traditional identification.

Samaias summarized the situation rapidly and concluded by saying that he did not blame Herod in the least for what he was doing, because he was doing it for his own defence. On the other hand he blamed Hyrcanus and the members of the Sanhedrin saying, 'God is great and this man, whom you now wish to release for Hyrcanus's sake, will one day punish you and the king as well' (*Ant.* 14.174).

Caesar was assassinated in 44 BCE and Cassius Longinus, who had maintained friendly relations with Antipater, returned to Syria. He needed money in order to raise an army against Marc Antony and Octavian. The Jewish ruling class, Hyrcanus and the family of Antipater, backed him completely and helped him in every way, even tolerating acts of brutality against those Jewish cities which were slow in paying the enormous sums imposed by Cassius. In this state of tension Antipater was assassinated (43 BCE) by a certain Malichus.

Having raised an army, Cassius left for the West in 42 BCE, leaving behind him a half devastated Judaea, prey to desperate waves of revolt. The last descendant of the Hasmonaeans, Antigonus for the Greeks, Mattathias for the Jews,[19] took advantage of such hopes for change. Herod attacked Antigonus, presenting himself as the champion of Hyrcanus's cause. Herod became friendly with Hyrcanus, and was even engaged to Mariamne, daughter of Alexandra and grand-daughter of Hyrcanus. Alexandra had had Mariamne by her marriage with Alexander Hasmoneus who had married Hyrcanus's daughter during one of his rebellions between 57 and 55 BCE in an attempt to win the king over. Thus Mariamne had blood from both branches of the Hasmonaean family, that of Hyrcanus and that of Aristobulus.

19. An interesting bit of information emerges from the coins minted by Antigonus. The Greek inscription presents him as 'king', while in the Hebrew inscription he is referred to as 'high priest'. Apparently the dignity associated to the high priesthood was considered the equivalent of that of kingship. In effect, the two positions had been united since Simon Maccabaeus.

The situation of the Jewish ruling class seemed to take a drastic turn for the worse after the battle of Philippi (autumn of 42 BCE), since they had all, without an exception, taken the side of Brutus and Cassius. Once again, and for reasons which are all but clear, they were able to remain in power with the support of Antony. The spiritual heirs of the Jews who had gone before Pompey in 63 BCE asking the abolition of the monarchy of Judah, now went before Antony in Bithynia hoping that their wishes should be fulfilled. This time they were not even able to have themselves received. At the same time Herod was able to clear the way for an official reconciliation of the ruling class in Jerusalem with the followers of Caesar. Josephus speaks of Herod's cunning, portraying the Jews as having been persecuted by Cassius (*Ant.* 14.301-304). This is a naive explanation, though. Antony believed Herod only because it was in his best interests to believe him, so much so that the delegation of Jews was not even received. Antony knew that he needed the rulers of Jerusalem, both for their money and for the support of the Jews of the Diaspora. He was aware of the fact that he would be able to gain the support of the latter group through the rulers of Jerusalem, and not through their adversaries in Judaea. In 41 BCE Antony gave both Herod and Phasael the title of tetrarchs of Judaea, without taking the same title away from Hyrcanus (*Ant.* 14.326 and *War* 1.244). It is not clear just how the three divided their powers.

The dominion of the descendants of Antipater was far from secure. The Parthians invaded Judaea from the East in 40 BCE, and Antigonus joined the invaders. Jerusalem itself was conquered. Herod managed to escape, but both Hyrcanus and Phasael were captured and handed over to Antigonus. Antigonus himself bit off Hyrcanus's ears, therefore rendering him incapable of holding the position of high priest since high priests had to be physically whole. Phasael committed suicide (*Ant.* 14.366-367 and *War* 1.268-271).

Herod fled to Rome to seek support. The Senate named him king of Judaea, following the desires of Antony and Octavian. In 39 BCE Herod landed at Ptolomais and began to gather troops for the reconquest of Judaea, his new kingdom (only *de jure*, of course). It was not an easy struggle, because of Antigonus's resistance, who seems to have had a large part of the population on his side, but also because of the presence of armed bands in Galilee that hindered Herod's operations. These were probably the heirs to Ezekias's movement. Finally, after having received a couple of Roman legions from Antony, Herod was able to overcome all the enemy's defences. He sent the Roman legions home with lavish gifts and proceeded to pacifying the region. The Romans had helped him to win the battles, but they had also made him unpopular with the people. Antigonus was taken prisoner and sent to Antioch where Antony, who had received money from Herod, ordered his decapitation. With the Parthians on the border, Herod did not want another Jewish king alive, especially one whom the Parthians themselves had put on the throne. He immediately married Mariamne, grand-daughter of Hyrcanus, and invited Hyrcanus himself to return to the country. Apparently Herod did not want a complete rupture with the Hasmonaean and Sadducaean party.

From 37 BCE Herod could truly be called king, both *de jure* and *de facto*, of the Jews.

Chapter 9

JUDAEA AT THE TIME OF JESUS OF NAZARETH

1. *The Reign of Herod the Great*

Information regarding the reign of Herod the Great[1] comes, for the most part, from two completely different sources: the first is Josephus who in turn draws on Nicolaus of Damascus who lived at Herod's court and naturally left a favourable image; the second is the rabbinical tradition which was sharply critical. Such a clear dichotomy in the sources has necessarily had its effects on modern historians as well. Graetz and Wellhausen can be considered the modern fathers of two schools of thought, one critical of and the other favourable to Herod. Schalit takes particular care to create an impartial historiographical approach.

Herod reigned 33 years, from 37 to 4 BCE, and apart from its difficult beginnings, between arms and palace intrigues related to international politics, only on one occasion did his reign undergo any serious risks. The dangerous moment came with the outbreak of the last civil war in Rome between Octavian and Antony.

After the defeat at Actium and the death of Antony, who had been Herod's protector, grasping the threatening nature of the situation Herod rushed to Rhodes to present himself to Octavian. He very theatrically threw his crown to the ground at Octavian's feet. Octavian, who apparently was waiting for such a gesture, placed Herod's crown back on his head and as a reward for such submission even increased the territories under Herod's control. One thing is certain, Octavian saw no reason to break with the ruler of Judaea and thought it fit to streng- then Herod's position. In this case he acted in exactly the same way as all the Romans before him. From this moment on Herod's reign, at least

---

1.   Herod was already referred to as 'the Great' by Josephus who has left us with an irreplaceable image of his time. At any rate, the title 'the Great' is attributed to Herod in only one point of the *Ant.* 18.130.

politically, can be said to have been fortunate. His private life, though, became more and more tragic.

Josephus dedicates a great deal of space to Herod in the *Antiquities of the Jews*. The source he draws on is excellent, though at times partial. Josephus draws on the work of Nicolas of Damascus, who lived at Herod's court.

There are many aspects of Herod's court which are not always easy to interpret. Given the difference in scale, he is very much in line with the great Roman military leaders of his day: rich, supported by both the big capitalists and the people, and in general hated by the traditional nobility. This was the position of Caesar and Octavian in Rome, and of Herod in Jerusalem. Unlike his Roman counterparts, though, alongside the nobility Herod also had to face the opposition of the Pharisees. The Pharisees could only accept an authority which presented itself in the name of the Law or as guarantor of the Law. They drew no economic advantage from Herod's rule and they continued to see the Sanhedrin as the most authentic expression of Israel. Furthermore, they quite simply did not like the idea of being ruled over by an Idumaean. In their opposition to the monarchy the Pharisees and the Sadducees found themselves tactical allies, while the Pharisaic legislation came to be accepted more and more by the Sadducees (*Ant.* 18.15-17). In all probability, by this time they accepted the same traditions as the Pharisees, with the exception of only a few of the most clamorous innovations of the Pharisaic ideology, such as the idea of resurrection. The Sadducees based their individuality on their vision of events which was always informed by practical considerations.[2] This led to their willingness to approach the position of the Romans and, in the end, to their disappearance from the historical scene due to the lack of a defining ideological core. For Herod it was easier to find support among the people of the countryside who were looked down upon by the Pharisees as ignorant of the Law.

Herod managed to dominate all of the groups opposed to him. He was able to hold the Pharisees in check because he understood their mentality; they always placed more faith in the Law, which Herod

---

2.   It is not clear whether the Sadducees and Pharisees agreed on which texts were to be considered sacred. The problem perhaps lay in a question of degrees of sacredness; even the Pharisees considered the Torah to be more sacred, since its writing dated from the origins, while the prophets and the *ketubim* were derived from the tradition. On the whole, one gets the impression that they based themselves only on the written Torah. See Le Moyne, *Les Sadducéens*, pp. 357-64.

always allowed them to observe, than in rebellions. This was the message preached by some of their teachers, who saw the realization of Samaias' prophecy in Herod's reign (*Ant.* 15.3-4).[3] For Herod, Samaias had shown the merit of inviting the people of Jerusalem not to resist when Herod arrived with the Roman troops in 37 BCE. Samaias had not changed his opinion concerning Herod. He merely understood the uselessness of resisting Herod, uselessness not only in political terms, but also in the much more important terms of the Law as well. The Law would not have gained any advantages from another civil war. It was not blood that would cause the Law to triumph. Samaias was perfectly aware of this and Herod took advantage of it, honouring a man that he knew was held in high esteem.

The struggle against the Sadducees was more difficult due to the fact that they found it more easy to ally themselves with the last descendants of the Hasmonaeans, to whom Herod was related by marriage. The Sadducee opposition found ready ears at court, especially in the person of Alexandra, Mariamne's mother, and on at least one occasion in Mariamne herself. The idea that the high priesthood was now the prerogative of the Hasmonaeans must have been a widespread idea and Herod had to cope with that fact. Furthermore, Cleopatra VII, who had her eye on Judaea and could take advantage of her sway over Antony, created difficulty for Herod on several occasions by supporting both the Nabataeans, who pressured Judaea's borders from outside, and the philo-Hasmonaeans on the inside. She was even able to get Antony to assign the region of Jericho to her, which she in turn rented to Herod.

At one point Herod had 45 nobles condemned to death as an example to all malcontents. But while the frontal opposition ended there, opposition continued in the form of palace intrigue.

Not being of priestly origin, and not even completely Israelite given his Idumaean descent, Herod could not assume the position of the high priesthood. He therefore sent for a certain Ananel, descendant from a priestly family (ἀρχιερατικοῦ γένους), to come from Babylon and he had him named high priest (*Ant.* 15.40). He probably intended to re-establish the old Zadokite priesthood in opposition to the Hasmonaeans' claims. But Alexandra, who maintained relations with Cleo-

---

3. The manuscript tradition of the *Antiquities of the Jews* oscillates between the names of Samaias and Pollion. The comparison with *Ant.* 14.172-76 favours the name of Samaias. The reference to 15.370 made by Marcus is too vague to be considered in favour of the reading 'Pollion'.

patra, insisted that Aristobulus, her son by Alexander Hasmoneus, be named high priest. Aristobulus should have been acceptable to those who were willing to see in him the heir to the Hasmonaeans' glories, but it was precisely for this reason that he was not acceptable for Herod. In order to please his mother-in-law for reasons that should be sought in the international situation, Herod conceded the high priesthood to Aristobulus, but in order to do this he had to take it away from Ananel, which was absolutely illegal. Shortly thereafter, Aristobulus drowned at Jericho while taking a bath, killed by those whose job it was to protect him. Ananel became high priest once more. There was still some opposition, but it was less and less openly expressed, and at any rate Herod kept it strictly under control.

The fact that the Pharisees and Sadducees both participated in the government of Jerusalem kept the two groups fairly united while the people of the countryside, derogatorily referred to as *'am ha-'areṣ* and considered impure, came more and more to be considered *extra legem* by both. Herod's rule must not have been disliked so much by the *'am ha-'areṣ* as by the Jews of Jerusalem. In fact Herod carried out many public works, such as the reconstruction of the Temple, employing great numbers of labourers who surely did not come from the ranks of the Pharisees and Sadducees, save for rare exceptions.

Herod's interest for the conditions of the poorest elements of society is also proven by the fact that in 25 BCE, during a famine, he provided foodstuffs from Egypt at his own expense.

The extraordinary number of buildings that Herod had constructed in Palestine is an indicator of his great wealth, a wealth which could hardly have been accumulated simply by bleeding the region's inhabitants as some historians would have it. He was extremely rich because he was able to make his investments pay off, and he must have had very diversified investments just as any great financier of the Roman empire.

Samaria ranks among his best-known building projects. He received the city during Augustus's reign and renamed it Sebaste ('august') in honour of the emperor. Even more spectacular, though, was the construction of Caesarea on the sea about 35 kilometres south of Mt Carmel. Caesarea is a model city of Hellenistic urban planning.[4]

He also had the Temple rebuilt, broadening the esplanade. Support bastions were built to contain a landfill, constituting the new and larger

---

4.   On Hellenistic urban planning see H.P. Kuhnen, *Palästina in griechisch-römischer Zeit* (Handbuch der Archäologie II, 2; Munich: Beck, 1990).

esplanade. In order to rebuild the Temple and avoid malcontent, he had a thousand priests instructed in building practices so that only they would touch the innermost parts of the Temple.

He was also concerned with the safety of his own family and had a number of new fortresses built and old ones strengthened as possible refuges in case he was forced to flee from Jerusalem. Most of these were built in the area around the Dead Sea: Herodium, near Bethlehem, destined to contain his tomb; Cypros, near Jericho, named for his mother; Masada on the western shore of the Dead Sea; Machaerus just inland of the eastern shore of the Dead Sea.

The placement of these fortresses leads us to believe that, in case of danger, Herod was most willing to trust the people who lived in the Dead Sea area. This was the region where the Essenes lived, and their theoretical position of condemnation is well known, but in practice they must have fully accepted constituted authority, in this case Herod's authority.[5]

While Herod's reign was particularly fortunate, his family life was, in contrast, tragic. Struggles driven by personal ambition had dominated the Hasmonaean dynasty, but up until Herod's time struggle within the ruling family had been mixed with the ambitions of other dynasties; the wars never seemed to be entirely internal and therefore in some way nobilitated the combatants. By the time Herod took the throne, though, the international scene had changed.

The hatreds and ambitions of the Jews were no longer able to blend themselves with the hatreds and ambitions of powerful foreign dynasties. Thus they found an outlet in domestic intrigue.

What had complicated Herod's life was the fact that he had sought to marry into the Hasmonaean dynasty through his marriage with Mariamne. The fact that the Hasmonaean women tended to favour the descendants of their family line pitted Herod's mother and sister, Salome, against his second wife and her mother.

After the death of Aristobulus, the elderly Hyrcanus and Mariamne were murdered as well (29 BCE). The murder of Alexandra, his mother-in-law, followed shortly thereafter. Alexandra had tried to gain control of the Temple when she heard a false rumour of Herod's death. Salome's first husband, Joseph, had fallen as did her second husband,

---

5.   On Essenism's position vis-à-vis authority, see pp. 418-19 below.

Costobar, an Idumaean who kept Hasmonaean partisans hidden in Idumaea.

After years of indecision and deceit, in 7 BCE Herod had Alexander and Aristobulus, his two sons by Mariamne, killed. These sons had been educated in Rome and in all probability he had intended to leave the throne to them. After having become suspicious of these two sons he had called for Antipater, his son by his first wife, Doris. Herod had hoped to use Antipater as a counterbalance for his other two sons, but when he became aware that Antipater, too, was plotting his death Herod had him imprisoned as well. Herod received permission from Augustus to condemn Antipater to death and had him executed shortly before his own death. In the meantime the Pharisees had turned against Herod when he had two of their teachers, Judas and Matthias, put to death for inciting the people to pull down a pagan emblem from the door of the Temple when they believed Herod to be dead. The last years of Herod's reign were truly characterized by blood and terror.

2. *Judaea in Herod's Day*

The term 'Judaea' can be used in a narrow sense to refer to the administrative district of Jerusalem, to be compared, for example, to Idumaea or Galilee, or in a broader sense it can be used to refer to all of Herod's territories.

Theoretically, under Herod Judaea was an independent country. Herod was an ally king of the Romans, bound therefore to follow Roman foreign policy and to provide for the defence of the empire's eastern borders. Judaea paid no tribute to the Romans and was not subject to control by the Roman governor of the province of Syria.

In 37 BCE Herod's state was made up of Judaea, Idumaea, Peraea and most of Galilee. Samaria and the port of Joppa, which Caesar had given to Hyrcanus, were not part of Herod's territory. Antony had reduced the size of Herod's territory by giving Joppa and the independent coastal cities in the south to Cleopatra, together with Jericho. That situation, however, did not last long. After the battle of Actium, Augustus gave back to Herod the lands that had been given to Cleopatra together with the coastal cities that had previously been independent, as well as the area east of the Jordan, north of Peraea, excluding most of Decapolis which remained independent.

3. Herod's Successors

Even though Herod had eliminated a wife and his three eldest sons, having had ten wives he left a fair number of aspiring heirs to the throne. Dissent among Herod's heirs deeply disrupted the kingdom's internal order, weakening it politically. Since many of his children were not yet of age, or were not politically inclined, the struggle for the throne revolved around the three sons he had named in his last will, written only a few days before his death. Archelaus and Herod Antipas, both the sons of a Samaritan woman, Malthace, and Philip, son of a woman from Jerusalem, Cleopatra, were the principal contenders. The continually active presence of Herod's sister, Salome, complicated the question further. Herod's plan was to leave the kingdom to Archelaus, who would be assisted by his brothers in the role of ethnarchs. Ashdod and Jamnia were to be left to Salome.

Thus, upon Herod's death the family considered Archelaus king and he was also proclaimed king by the troops in Jericho, to whom Herod's powerful sister read a letter left by Herod thanking her for her faithfulness and asking as much for his successor (*Ant.* 17.193-95). Archelaus, however, refused the title of king. He was aware that he was a dependent of Rome and did not want to make a move that could displease Augustus. He decided to go personally to Rome to clarify his position in the most favourable manner possible or, at any rate, in complete accordance with Octavian.

Thus, after Herod's funeral and burial in the Herodium in accordance with his last wishes, Archelaus went to Jerusalem and entered the Temple. Before leaving for Rome he wanted to establish contact with his subjects and personally sound out the degree of favour he could expect. His entry into Jerusalem was triumphant (*Ant.* 17.200). Seated on a golden throne he received the public, and many came to ask him favours. He granted many favours, too, such as the release of all those who had been imprisoned by Herod and the suppression of taxes.

Trying to make sense of Josephus's account (Josephus does not specify who Archelaus's enthusiastic supporters were nor who was putting forward the requests) it would appear that the most enthusiastic of those praising Archelaus were from the lower strata of society, from outside Jerusalem for the most part, while those who had access to the throne were the city's notables, Pharisees and Sadducees. It was the latter group who requested the release of political prisoners and the abolition of taxes. It was again the Pharisees and the Sadducees who, encouraged by the young king's condescension (he was 18 years old), made the bold request that Archelaus put to death those of Herod's counsellors who had suggested the execution of Judas and Matthias. These counsellors were probably also members of Archelaus's entourage. While Archelaus did not openly refuse, he answered that he would only take up the question after having returned from Rome. At that point a riot broke out which was put down with considerable bloodshed.

Archelaus, Antipas and Salome each went to Rome to negotiate the succession as much to his or her own advantage as possible. In fact, Archelaus had been named principal heir only in the final will, made just a few days before Herod's death, while in a previous will the same position was left to Antipas. While the three were in Rome, however, Judaea was once again the theatre of serious uprisings throughout the kingdom: in Judaea itself under the leadership of a shepherd, a certain Athronges; in Peraea under the leadership of Simon, a former slave of Herod's; and in Galilee under Judas, son of the Ezechias put to death by Herod.

These rebellions were entirely unrelated to the riots that had broken out in Jerusalem while Archelaus had been in the city. The violence in Jerusalem had sprung from the ruling class, while the other revolts were popular uprisings, fomented among the people 'who did not know the Law', and fought against the Roman oppressors and the Jews that supported them. These uprisings were aimed at the establishment of a new kingdom, perhaps with messianic overtones, while the rebels in Jerusalem were seeking to broaden the power of the Sanhedrin. Phenomena such as these demonstrate the great complexity of the political situation and the danger of reducing analyses to overly simplified and precise schema. There were many movements and a great number of potential alliances that could be born and dissolve again in a brief space of time. It is clear that the only supporters of Herod's dynasty were to be found among the most modest classes, but it was also among these classes that messianic revolts broke out, revolts not shared by the Pharisees and even sabotaged by the Sadducees. Let us look at the position taken by Rabbi Gamaliel as narrated in the Acts of the Apostles (5.35-39). He compares the Christians to the uprising of Judas (perhaps the son of Ezechias) and exhorts the mob to let them go in peace. It was clear that Judas had not been the true Messiah, because his undertaking had failed. As regarded the Christians, it was better to let them go in peace and await God's judgment in history. Even the Pharisees were awaiting divine intervention, perhaps even the Messiah. What distinguished them from the people of the countryside, though, was the fact that they represented an educated class that did not give itself over easily to enthusiasm. The only thing that they were sure came from God was the Law.

While the Roman army re-established order in all of Judaea, in Rome Octavian examined Herod's will. The territories were assigned according to Herod's last wishes with the sole difference, and it was a difference of considerable political import, that he refused to grant Archelaus the title of king. Archelaus received only the lesser title of ethnarch.

Judaea was thus dismembered into three or four independent parts. Archelaus was assigned Judaea proper, Samaria and Idumaea, the best part of the kingdom. Herod Antipas received Galilee and Peraea while Philip was given the area east of the River Jordan and north of the Yarmuk. Salome was granted the cities of Ashdod and Jamnia without any precise title. The cities of Hippos, Gadara and Gaza were declared free, separated from Judaea and placed within the administrative system of the province of Syria.

While the kingdom's division was being discussed in Rome, the ruling class in Jerusalem tried to have the monarchy abolished, just as they had already tried with Pompey and Antony. This time their position was clearly much stronger than in the past. This is borne out by the amount of attention given to the 50 delegates who were received by Augustus. Their strength certainly did not lie in their long speech against Herod, accused of being a cruel man and of violating the Jewish Law, nor did it lie in their discourses against Archelaus, guilty of not having met all of their requests. Their strength, and Octavian was well aware of it, lay in the community of eight thousand Jews living in Rome who all supported the delegation's requests more or less openly, depending on family relations (*Ant.* 17.299-300).

Like Caesar before him, Octavian had always sought the favour of the Jews, and he now began to realize that Archelaus did not represent the Jews' interests. He did not want to go against the royal rights of the house of Herod, deciding on what belonged to whom, nor did he want to face a sudden change in the political structure of Judaea. In fact, Augustus limited himself to sending Archelaus away without the title of king, promising him the kingdom only on condition that he were able to control Jewish affairs. Octavian would wait and watch. Should Archelaus show himself incapable of winning over the Jews of Jerusalem, who were clearly supported by the Jews spread throughout the empire, then on the first occasion his fate would be sealed.

4. *The Herods*

Of the three Herods the one whose reign was the least troubled was Philip, who was able to remain at the head of his tetrarchy until 34 CE. He remained faithful to the Romans and his government is remembered for the construction of Caesarea on the site where Paneas had once stood. In order to distinguish this city from the other Caesarea, the one built on the coast by Herod the Great, it is usually referred to as Caesarea Philippi. Philip married Salome, daughter of Herodias, who had been the cause of John the Baptist's decapitation.

Herod Antipas, whom Josephus defines a lover of tranquillity (*Ant.* 18.245), could perhaps have lived in peace like his half brother had he not met Herodias, with whom he fell in love and for whom he had to face many perils and many enemies.

Herodias had Hasmonaean blood in her veins. She was the daughter of Aristobulus Hasmoneus, son of Mariamne, both of them executed by Herod the Great. Herodias had married Herod Boethus, who was yet another son of Herod the Great, by Mariamne II, a woman of priestly descent. Thus Herodias was the sister-in-law of Herod Antipas. Boethus chose not to involve himself in politics. Herodias met Herod Antipas in Rome where the passion was born that would unite the two for the rest of their lives, even in the most adverse circumstances, since Herodias, though certainly a very ambitious woman, chose never to abandon the man whose political ruin she most probably caused.

Antipas decided to repudiate his wife, a Nabataean princess, and Herodias abandoned her husband, by whom she had had a daughter, Salome, whom Herodias took with her. Antipas' wife fled to her father without waiting for the repudiation and Antipas and Herodias were thus able to be together. All of this must have happened shortly before John the Baptist began his preaching.

John was the only Jew who, in the silent disapproval of everyone, had the courage to go before Herod Antipas and say: 'It is not lawful for you to have your brother's wife' (Mk 6.18). Antipas admired this man and held him in high esteem. Apparently he also met him a number of times (Mk 6.20). Antipas had come to know that John was admired by the people (*Ant.* 18.118), by the people of the countryside who kept their distance from the Pharisees of the city (Jn 4.1-3) and who by tradition constituted the only possible base for the Herods' government. Therefore, there were many factors calling for prudence from this man who, with the exception of his passion for Herodias, was always prudent. She, in contrast, wanted to see John dead, whether for personal hatred or for political reasons since, while it was dangerous to have him killed, letting him live implied risks as well.

According to the accounts of Mark (6.17-29) and Matthew (14.3-12), during a feast at Machaerus Salome danced so well that Herod promised to give her anything she desired. Her mother told her to ask for John's head and he was immediately decapitated.

In 36 CE Aretas, king of the Nabataeans, attacked Herod Antipas in order to avenge the old affront and Herod was defeated. He had hoped that the Romans would come to his aid, but the death of Tiberius brought the Roman army, which was already on the move to relieve Herod, to a halt. Caligula, a friend of Herodias's brother, Agrippa, granted the title of king to Agrippa. Driven by his wife who could not tolerate the insult, Antipas went to Rome to try to make up for lost ground. This, however, only worsened his situation. Agrippa accused him of negotiating secretly with the Parthians and Caligula exiled him to Lyon in Gaul.

The year 6 CE was fundamental for the Judaea of Jesus' day; the region was no longer a tetrarchy and it had been given that particular political and administrative structure that we find reflected in Jesus of Nazareth's trial. The information available regarding Archelaus' rule is quite scarce, especially in the light of how much we would like to know. This is due to the death of Nicolaus of Damascus, who up until that point had been Josephus's principal source. Josephus condenses the events of Archelaus's rule into just a few paragraphs, *Ant.* 17.339-41. We must, therefore, analyze them with the utmost attention.

As soon as he returned from Rome to Jerusalem, Archelaus deposed the high priest Joazar and had him replaced with his brother Eleazar. Joazar was accused of not being able to control the people in Archelaus's absence. It had been in the wake of the uprising that Varus had brought his troops into Judaea and had allowed the famous delegation of 50 notables to leave for Rome with their request for the abolition of the monarchy. To Archelaus, Joazar must have appeared the person most responsible for those events, hence his deposition. In his place one of his brothers was elected in an attempt to divide the family and in the hopes that the brother would have followers of his own. If in the end that was the case: the followers were few.

In order to strengthen his position Archelaus married Glaphyra, widow of Alexander Hasmonaeus and therefore his own sister-in-law. In the end Eleazar was deposed from the high priesthood as well, and replaced with Jesus, son of See. The degree of tension between the monarchy and Jerusalem's ruling class must have then reached its highest point.

Archelaus drew his support from the military and, among the civilians, the inhabitants of the area near the River Jordan. Jericho had been Herod's favourite city and now it was Archelaus's favourite too. He had a royal palace built there and provided for the irrigation of part of the surrounding plain. The area around his habitual residence and the centre of his attentions seems to have been the same area where John the Baptist preached and many Essenes lived.[6]

The most influential citizens of Jerusalem must have continued insisting with Octavian that Archelaus be removed, and in the end Augustus accepted their suggestion, convinced that Archelaus represented neither the Jews in Jerusalem nor the Jews of the Diaspora, and, as we have seen, the Romans were always eager to content the Jews, the most important ones of course.

Alongside the delegation from Jerusalem, the Samaritans sent one as well. Everyone accused Archelaus of being a cruel tyrant. Octavian called Archelaus to Rome and condemned him to exile in Vienne, in Gaul.

An unusual administrative solution was then created for the government of Jerusalem, a city which for various reasons was not easy to rule. Judaea was annexed to the imperial province of Syria and the highest authority was now, therefore, the governor of Syria. In effect, though, another imperial authority resided in Caesarea, on the sea, with the strictly administrative title of *procurator*,[7] but whose role in reality

---

6.   On the possibility that Jericho was essentially an Essenic city, see Daniel, 'Les esséniens et l'arrière fond historique de la Parabole du Bon Samaritain'.

7.   The sources do not all agree on the title of the Roman governor of Judaea. The title *praefectus* has been documented regarding Pilate in an inscription found in Caesarea in 1961 (see C. Fovra, 'L'iscrizione di Ponzio Pilato a Cesarea', *Rendiconti dell'Istituto Lombardo, Accademia di Scienze e Lettere* 95 [1961], pp. 419-34). The title of *procurator* came to be preferred later. This title was originally a

was that of commander of the troops stationed in Judaea. He was responsible both for the collection of taxes and for maintaining order. It is not clear whether the power to pass death sentences was exclusively his. It is likely that this was a prerogative reserved for him only in cases of rebellion or generically for political crimes.[8]

Following the Roman custom, the Jews were allowed to maintain their own administration and governing bodies, the highest of which was the Sanhedrin, the latest incarnation in the ongoing evolution of the 'heads of the ancestral houses of all the people' mentioned in Neh. 8.13, and the γερουσία mentioned by Josephus regarding the Ptolemaic period (*Ant.* 12.138, 142). The Sanhedrin was headed by the high priest who was nominated by the foreign sovereign, as in the Early Zadokite period and especially since the times of the Maccabaean revolt. In fact it was Quirinius, governor of Syria, who named Ananus high priest, probably because he had been one of Archelaus' most active adversaries and would therefore be a strenuous supporter of Roman dominion. He was high priest from 6 to 15 CE, after which the high priesthood passed on to other members of his family. Of note among his successors is Caiaphas, his son-in-law, who was directly involved in the trial of Jesus. At any rate, the Sanhedrin and politics in Jerusalem in general continued to be dominated by the figure of Ananus up until his death in 35 CE.

The Romans tried to respect the requirements of the Torah as much as possible. Since the Law prohibited images, the Roman soldiers did not introduce their standards into Jerusalem. The coins made in Judaea bore only the emperor's name and not his image,[9] though it should be pointed out that only bronze coins could be minted in Judaea. The more valuable coins did carry the emperor's image, since they were minted elsewhere (Mk 12.15-16); some contamination was inevitable. Unlike the inhabitants of other eastern provinces of the empire, the Jews were

---

purely administrative one, but it later came to refer to the emperor's representative. As the administration of the royal household gained the upper hand over the official state administration, use of the title *procurator* became more frequent than *praefectus*, though it was a change in name only and not in substance. Furthermore, contemporary sources use these and other titles with no clear distinction. More or less from the time of Claudius the title *procurator* seems to be the preferred one.

8.   On the powers of the Roman governors, see P.A. Brunt, 'Procuratorial Jurisdiction', *Latomus* 25 (1966), pp. 461-89.

9.   The region governed by Philip is an exception; the pagan element of the population there was quite large.

also exempted from participating in emperor worship in any form whatsoever.

In order to facilitate the collection of taxes, the Romans divided Judaea into 11 districts called toparchies and took a census of the entire population. Each head of family had to register his name and the amount of his possessions.

News of the census for purposes of taxation led once again to serious troubles. Given the efforts of the priesthood to calm the population, the rebellion did not break out in Judaea. It did, however, break out in Galilee, just outside the borders of the Roman administration, where a certain Judas, from Gamala, led a revolt with messianic overtones. Though we do not have any precise information, it would appear that Judas came down into Judaea where he was supported even by some Pharisees. At least one Pharisee, Saddok (Zadok), openly took his side.

What distinguishes this Saddok's interpretation of the Law from that of the contemporary Pharisaic interpretation was the problem of 'zeal', which we have already discussed concerning the Maccabaean rebellion, fuelled by the 'zeal' for the Law. For these men armed struggle was the only way to truly observe the Law. The Zealot movement thus has roots linking it both to the messianic movements and to Pharisaism. As Roman domination became stronger the movement of the Zealots was to rise to dominate the series of events which led to the destruction of Jerusalem in 70 CE.

The above is more a presentation of the ideas behind Zealotism rather than a history of that party. Even Josephus, when he presents the fourth Jewish sect to be added to the three classic ones, seems to have the birth of Zealotism coincide with Judas' revolt (*War* 2.118), but he limits himself at that point to illustrating only the driving ideas of the movement. Afterwards, he mentions the Zealots only in conjunction with the Jewish War (*War* 2.651). Previously Josephus speaks only of *sicarii* and not of Zealots. But beyond the names used to refer to historical movements whose defining traits will always remain blurred to us, the existence of the ideal of a struggle to the end against the Romans and their supporters seems clear. Cullmann writes: 'Without denying their differences...in keeping with the word's usage today, I attribute the name Zealot to all members of the resistance at that time'.[10] Theissen goes so far as to use the word 'partisans'.

---

10. *Jesus und die Revolutionären seiner Zeit: Gottesdienst, Gesellschaft, Politik* (Tübingen: J.C.B. Mohr, 1970), p. 15.

5. *Judaea under the Procurators*

Direct Roman administration of the territories previously ruled by the ethnarch Archelaus began in 6 CE in the forms outlined above. The rule of the tetrarchs Philip and Antipas coincided chronologically with the Roman administration of Judaea. This situation was rather confused on the level of the structures of Judaea taken in its broadest sense. This confusion was mirrored in an equally confusing situation within Judaea taken in its more narrow sense. While in theory government of the Jews had passed from Herod to Archelaus and then to the Sadducee aristo-cracy, by this point that aristocracy seems to be so decidedly pro-Roman that it could be considered more the continuation of the policies of Antipater and Herod rather than the beginning of a new political policy. In other words, the class of people both in Palestine and the Diaspora who had supported the monarchy of the Herods, now saw its interests as being represented more by the Sadducee government than by the monarchy. The Sadducee government must have seemed prefer-able because it continued to protect the economic interests of the wealthiest class and at the same time presented the advantage of better representing and guaranteeing Jewish identity. This type of choice pre-supposes a high degree of cultural and national identity, but also points to the perception of a need to protect such an identity from growing threats. The anti-Jewish uprisings in Alexandria at the beginning of Caligula's reign confirm the idea that the need for identity and pro-tection were anything but unfounded.

Furthermore, it cannot be excluded that in principle the Romans con-sidered Judaea a single cultural unit with its own dynasty. Such an ideology is documented by the fact that the Romans named two more Jewish kings, descendants of Herod and the Hasmonaeans: Agrippa I, reigning from 37 to 44, and his son Agrippa II who held on to the title until around the year 90. From the Roman point of view the Jewish state, or at least the Jewish *ethnos*, continued to exist. Even after the destruction of Jerusalem the Jews had their leader, a *nāśî'* living in Jamnia, that the Romans considered leader of the Jewish community.

The more the strength of the pagans manifested itself in all its cul-tural greatness and political superiority, the more the Jews sought strength in their tradition, emphasizing their own peculiarities, the dis-tinctions that were to be found in their way of life and, in the end, in observance of the Law. Of course, this does not mean that the Jews were always in agreement over the contents of the Law. They did not agree on the value of the oral Law which was being developed along-side the written one, nor did they agree on the interpretation to be given to many of the commandments. They argued over the possibility of simplifying the Law in terms of a few fundamental commandments. They could not all agree even on belief in resurrection. It was not clear just how divine judgment was to come about, nor was it clear to what degree death marked a clear moment beyond which salvation was impossible; the possibility of intercession on behalf of the dead was under discussion.

The norms regarding purity had been causing problems for some time; it was difficult to find some sort of rational justification for them in a world dominated by rational thought. This was not only a problem that regarded those writing apologies of Judaism, presenting Judaism to the pagans in the Greek language, but it was also a problem within Judaism itself.

In this period the problem of images became extremely complex, because it was linked to relations with the dominant nation. The Romans used images even in their military standards while the radical-ization of the norms prohibiting them had the function of defending Judaism and its peculiarities. In principle the Romans not only toler-ated, but approved of and recognized Jewish worship, as demonstrated by their acceptance of capital punishment for any pagan who dared enter the Temple in Jerusalem. This is confirmed by sporadic episodes, such as the beheading of a Roman soldier who had torn a scroll of the Law while Cumanus was procurator (48–52 CE; *Ant.* 20.115-17; *War* 2.228-31).

The problem of respect for the norms of the Law was the source of serious tension primarily in Jerusalem, and the problem that surfaces most often is that of the images, which was not easy for the Romans to comprehend and even constituted a limitation on their own habits and customs. The Roman procurators never seem to have grasped Jewish spirituality on this point and must have mistaken what for practising Jews were fundamental questions of their religiosity for mere acts of political protest. For a Roman it must have been difficult to distinguish religious necessity from provocation, since in any case this was one way for the Jews to preserve their own identity in the face of the Romans. In general the Roman governors of Judaea were profit seekers and thieves, but they were no different in this from the governors of the other provinces. That being said, however, in the first century in no other province was there as much tension as in Judaea. The example of Vitellius (*Ant.* 18.120-25) having his troops march around Jewish territory (narrowly defined) in a campaign against the Nabataeans, in order not to offend the Jews with the presence of the Roman military standards, demonstrates a degree of tolerance that to others could seem absurd. A few years later Petronius (*Ant.* 18.263-72), another governor of Syria, when ordered to place a statue of Caligula in the Temple in Jerusalem, hesitated to the point that the emperor ordered him to commit suicide.[11]

The internal situation in Palestine was characterized by serious public disorder. The region was full of various types of figures, among them many itinerant preachers.[12] Such people usually gave themselves at least the title of prophet and caused unrest among the masses with the mirage of imminent and miraculous divine intervention in favour of the chosen people. The need for a miracle and for the supernatural, expectations of the revelation of divine power, bore different, though analogous fruit in literature and in daily life. Apocalyptic literature flourished, speculating on the coming of God's reign which would bring justice, laying low the rich and the enemies of the Jewish people (see the *Book of Parables*). There was also a flourishing of fanatics who considered themselves charged by God with great missions. In 35 CE a self-proclaimed Samaritan prophet promised to make the sacred ornaments of the Gerizim temple reappear from a part of the mountain where they had remained buried since the time of Moses, only if the people would gather on the right spot (*Ant.* 18.85-89). Pilate's reaction, armed intervention and the massacre of those assembled, caused the Roman governor of Syria, Vitellius, to remove Pilate from office. Once more, while Fadus was procurator (44–46 CE), a certain Theudas[13] promised to part the waters of the Jordan on command. Another self-proclaimed prophet referred to as the Egyptian (Acts 21.38; *Ant.* 20.169-71 and

---

11. Petronius, however, did not commit suicide. The messenger bearing news of Caligula's death arrived before the one carrying Caligula's orders.

12. See O. Cullmann, *Jesus und die Revolutionären seiner Zeit*; and more importantly G. Theissen, *Soziologie der Jesusbewegung: Ein Beitrag zur Entstehungsgeschichte des Urchristentums* (Theologische Existenz heute, 194; Munich: Chr. Kaiser Verlag, 1977).

13. Concerning Theudas see Acts 5.36 and *Ant.* 20.97-99. According to the account in Acts, Theudas was anterior to Judas of Gamala.

War 2.261-63) gathered together a number of people promising that if they could reach the Mount of Olives at Jerusalem's gates, then he would have caused the walls to crumble, allowing them to easily take the city.

Alongside those who preached miracles and victory, there were also those who foretold total ruin. An ancient tradition that must have been deeply rooted in the popular mentality held that Israel was a 'hard-headed people'; it was a sinning people that had to pay for its guilty actions just as it had had to do in the past. The rupture that had shaken the priesthood in the first half of the second century BCE had led some to write that the temple would be destroyed again, only to be rebuilt by the very hand of God (see *1 En.* [*BD*] 90.28-29). John the Baptist saw the divine axe 'lying at the root' (Mt. 3.10). Jesus repeated the prophecy regarding the Temple's destruction from a different eschatological perspective, but again as a catastrophe, a function of a divine scrutiny allowing the survival of the holy remainder. Prophets of miraculous victory and prophets of doom took root in the same humus, marked by a division between those awaiting the final and victorious war and those awaiting catastrophe. Both saw the coming of a terrible war as an inevitable reality, as obvious. The sense of sin and its consequences and the sense of justice for Israel oppressed by its enemies combined to create a mentality in which war against Rome was seen as the logical consequence of a sequence of events, interpreted in the light of popular Jewish traditions.

Religious and political tensions were mixed in a confused tangle which made Roman domination very difficult (*Ant.* 20.167-68; and *War* 2.259-60). What today we call eschatology and messianism were not simply religious concepts, but they were powerful ideas at work in history. If messianism and eschatology find little room in the Judaism of the Mishnah,[14] that is due to the reaction of an element of society that was not pro-Roman, but was against any and all extremisms and infatuations.

As the years passed, the political tendencies of the Jews assumed radical positions under opposing banners. On the one side we find those who felt that friendship with Rome could not be called into question, either because they had a vested interest in maintaining the *status quo*,

14. See J. Neusner, 'Il messia nel contesto della Mishnah', *Henoch* 5 (1983), pp. 343-70, and 'Temi messianici nel periodo di formazione del giudaismo', *Henoch* 6 (1984), pp. 31-54.

or because they felt that any rebellion was doomed to fail. This was the position of the Sadducees and many of the Pharisees. On the other side the proponents of a rebellion were gaining more and more ground among the people, attracting many followers. Those in favour of an armed insurrection came to identify their enemies not only in the Romans, but also in all those Jews who for one reason or another supported the government and preached peace. The murder of pacifists by Zealot extremists became more and more common and the situation had very nearly reached complete chaos when the great revolt broke out in 66.

The priesthood grew more and more removed from the people, thus laying the political basis for its own disappearance after the destruction of the Temple in 70 CE. In that year the Temple was destroyed, but Judaism certainly was not. Essenism disappeared from the historical scene in 70 as well. Certain Essenic ideas known to us through the Dead Sea Scrolls clearly show the Zadokite origin of the movement and its aversion to armed rebellion.[15] With the passage of time, however, and the acceptance of a number of ideas spread throughout Judaism, the Essenic movement took up positions quite different from its original ones, to the point of collaborating with the Zealots in the great uprising and of being overwhelmed along with them.[16]

As we can see, the political forces at play in Judaea during Jesus' day were many, following tendencies that were not always unitary, precisely because of the variety of concepts animating them. Given the complexity of the phenomena and the lack of sufficient documentation for following the development of each individual movement, in order to better grasp the panorama of the evolution of Jewish ideology, it is better to discuss the story of the single concepts behind the movements.

---

15. On respect for authority as an expression of God's will as characteristic of the Essenes up until the great revolt, see pp. 418-19 below.

16. See M. Baillet, 'Un recueil liturgique de Qumrân, Grotte 4: "Les paroles des luminaires"', *RB* 68 (1961), pp. 191-250; A. Denis, 'Evolution des structures dans la secte de Qumrân', in J. Giblet, P. Andriessen and L. Cerfaux (eds.), *Aux origines de l'Eglise* (Bruges: Desclée de Brouwer, 1965), pp. 23-49; H. Seidel, 'Erwägungen zur Frage des geistigen Ursprungsortes der Erweckungsbewegung von Qumran', in S. Wagner (ed.), *Bibel und Qumran* (Berlin: Ev. Haupt-Bibelges., 1968), pp. 188-97; L. Moraldi, *I manoscritti di Qumran* (Turin: UTET, 2nd edn, 1986), pp. 215-18.

Part IV
THE THEMES OF MIDDLE JUDAISM

Chapter 10

INTRODUCTION TO THE PROBLEMS

1. *The General Characteristics of the Period of Middle Judaism*

As can be easily seen through the description of the political events, the nearly three centuries running from 200 BCE to the years of the Second Temple's destruction are characterized by a deep spiritual crisis. Until not too many years ago this period of Jewish history was called 'Late Judaism', emphasizing the idea that the Judaism of Jesus' time was 'late', if not entirely exhausted since in reality its underlying spirit was carried forth only by Christianity. Another and opposite wording, 'Early Judaism', was then applied to the same period to indicate that the Judaism of Jesus' day was anything but exhausted; it could be seen instead as a melting pot from which modern Judaism was born. In this case the terminology reveals an interpretation of history in which emphasis lies on the links between the Judaism of the first century, substantially identified with Pharisaism, and modern Judaism, Rabbinism.

In recent years scholars have felt the need for a new terminology which interprets history in a more objective manner, less subject to conditioning by modern theological problems and by our own religious positions. The modern age has at least the merit of approaching events (or at least trying to) in the most neutral way possible when historical ideologies and religions are concerned; it seems that humans with all their impulses, ideals and misdeeds, are coming to be placed at the centre of ideologies. The expression 'Middle Judaism' has been proposed with the intent of emphasizing the continuity between the most ancient form of Judaism, that formed with the beginning of the republic which through the rich and varied forms of Middle Judaism continues even today in both the Jewish and Christian religions. This new label attempts to overcome the limits imposed by the former ones by embracing them both; Middle Judaism, inasmuch as it presupposes a later Judaism, avoids both the idea that Judaism came to an end with the advent of Christianity and that Christianity is outside of the Jewish realm of thought.[1]

The existence of a distinct Middle Judaism is as certain as it is difficult to define. It decidedly stands out against the backdrop of the religions and cultures which surrounded it for its rigid monotheism and for its faithfulness to its traditional customs, that is, the Law as it was then interpreted, giving great importance both to the dietary norms and the impurity of the pagans. Nonetheless the numerous currents that make up its vitality also hinder a precise definition. Above all else Middle Judaism witnessed the growth of the barrier separating those who conceived of the relationship between humans and God in terms of the theology of the Promise and those who saw it in terms of the theology of the Covenant. The Law held greater importance for the latter, but radical positions on the same topic can be found among the former as well. Messianism was more important for the first group, though it is also clear that the phenomenon was taking root in many circles and in widely varied forms. Even the very conception of salvation was subject to modification according to whether the idea of life after death was accepted or not, be it in terms of the immortality of the soul, or of resurrection. The same idea can appear in groups which were ideologically opposed, but with different values depending on the group's position in the ideological constellation. Modalities of knowledge varied from group to group and were in turn linked to the relationship between the freedom of humans and the omnipotent freedom of God; predetermination, which in some way was presented as a possibility by Qohelet, gained more and more ground while others defended human freedom of choice. At the same time it became more and more clear that the truly righteous man, the only one who should benefit from observation of the Law, did not exist. For the Jew this represented a grave problem because it caused a crisis of hope in salvation which by this time meant not only salvation in this life but also, for many, for eternity. The problem of what we refer to as the rules of purity, that is all the norms of the Law which could not be traced to a rational principle, underlaid an entire range of problems. This was a problem brought to light by contact with Greek civilization. On the one hand these behavioural norms gave the Jew a sense of identity, but on the other they constituted a problem for the Jews

1. See G. Boccaccini, *Middle Judaism: Jewish Thought 300 BCE to 200 CE* (Minneapolis: Fortress Press, 1991).

themselves, given their irrationality with respect to the fundamental concepts of the Law. But did the Law have a centre, or not? Add to this the evolution of the calendar which even affected the liturgical aspects of the Jew's life and we have a first glance of the complexity of the problems of the period.

Contact and confrontation among the various groups was great and was not confined to academic and theological matters. The ideological divisions reverberated within the factions nourishing them. The unifying element in Judaism was the awareness of belonging to the same ethnic unit which could be recognized in a few common elements, even though those common elements were interpreted in different ways. Samaritanism was, of course, an exception. With their temple on Gerizim since the fourth century BCE the Samaritans maintained a structure parallel to that of the Judaism of Jerusalem. Relations with this rival were, however, socially limited and ideologically inexistent from the second century BCE onward. The tensions between Samaritans and Judaeans reached a peak with the destruction of the temple on Gerizim by John Hyrcanus.

More than any sort of religious unity or universally recognized authority, Jewish society was held together by a vast complex of historical and social factors. The Temple and the Law were the two pillars of Jewish religion, but behind worship we find the priest and behind the Law we find the scribe. It is unthinkable that the priest did not intervene in questions regarding the Law just as the scribe could, and did, intervene in questions regarding worship. This dual nature of the pillars supporting the entire religious structure of Israel is underlined by a maxim of Simon the Just, living at the beginning of the second century BCE: 'The world exists for three things: for the Law, for the Temple and for Mercy' (*m. Abot.* 1.2).[2]

Law and Temple are the two necessary yet independent pillars; the necessity of Mercy (*gmlwt ḥsdym*) is stated too, as love for one's neighbour, felt as a fact which certainly was not contrary to the other two, but ontologically different from them. The problem of the relationship between these three elements could be posed and resolved in terms of the pre-eminence of one over the others; the unity of the religious tradition lay in an intrinsic force of being Jewish, historically and culturally more than theologically. The high priest existed as a functionary of the

---

2.	The treatise *Pirqe Abot* is definitely late (no earlier than the third century CE), though certain maxims can be much older; this is certainly one such case.

Jewish religion, but he did not represent it, and there was no authority which could give an interpretation of the Law that was binding for all. The legislation contained in the *Temple Scroll*,[3] certainly already existent in the second century BCE, and the letter known as 4QMMT, which dates from the same period and discusses the body of norms, both document a reality which scholars had intuited some time ago.[4]

The existence of this ideological and theological fragmentation had led some modern scholars to use the term 'Judaisms' in the plural.[5] I prefer the old terminology of 'currents' in order to emphasize the contemporary Jews' awareness of belonging to a single ethnic and cultural unit. While there have been many ways of being Jewish, if the Jew always saw himself to be such it seems to me that we should maintain a unitary term; 'currents (plural) of Judaism (singular)': multiplicity and unity. Furthermore, we must underscore the fact that these currents were very competitive with one another, producing tensions which were in turn given political motivations of various natures, as we have seen in the historical section of the book.

The splintering of the body of norms brought about mutual exclu-

---

3.   On the dating of the *Temple Scroll*, see A. Vivian, *Il rotolo del tempio* (Brescia: Paideia, 1990). The current tendency is to date it to the second century BCE. See M.O. Wise, *A Critical Study of the Temple Scroll from Qumran Cave 11* (Chicago: Oriental Institute of the University of Chicago, 1990), and 'The Teacher of Righteousness and the Temple Scroll', *The Qumran Chronicle* 1 (1990), pp. 59-60; García Martínez, 'Sources et rédaction du Rouleau du Temple'. Some elements, though, in terms of both linguistics and contents, suggest an even earlier dating; see B.A. Levine, 'The Temple Scroll: Aspects of its Historical Provenience and Literary Character', *BASOR* 232 (1978), pp. 5-23; H. Stegemann, 'The Origins of the Temple Scroll', *VTSup* 40 (1988), pp. 235-56, esp. pp. 236, 251; J. Maier, 'The Architectural History of the Temple in Jerusalem in the Light of the Temple Scroll', in G.J. Brooke (ed.), *Temple Scroll Studies* (Sheffield: Sheffield Academic Press, 1989), pp. 23-62. If one fragment (4QTemple) is dated to the middle of the second century BCE (see B.Z. Wacholder, *The Dawn of Qumran: The Sectarian Torah and the Teacher of Righteousness* [Cincinnati: Hebrew Union College Press, 1983], p. 46) it is yet another strong argument in favour of an earlier dating, which I feel, based on the elements gathered in the above-mentioned studies, can be given as the second half of the fourth century BCE. Those who argue in favour of a later date distinguish clearly between the final version and the sources. At least for the sources, though, that is for the various sections of the work, an earlier date than the second century BCE is necessary.

4.   For the text of 4QMMT, see p. 110 n. 32.

5.   The expression was coined by Neusner, now followed by Boccaccini.

sions whose consequences on a practical level are difficult to imagine today. Even still, these internal fractures, which went beyond the simple existence of different currents of thought, never gave rise to doubts concerning the existence of the Jew, who was seen as such both in his own eyes and in those of the pagans. The distinguishing characteristic of the Jew was, in any case, not only the fact that he believed in a single God, but the application of rules concerning his daily behaviour which to the pagans seemed strange, to say the least. The Jews refused certain foods, others they ate only in certain ways, they practised ablution, on certain days of the year they abstained from work and travel. As a consequence they had special relations with the pagans which always distinguished them in some way in every situation. At times this relationship was difficult for the Jews who were unable to give rational explanations to the many questions posed by the pagans. On the other hand it gave the Jews the sense of their peculiarity in regard to others. Even though the group of norms known today as the rules of purity (for the Jews they were part of the Law with the same status as 'You shall not kill' or 'You shall not steal') were not followed in the same way by all; they were, however, known by all and everyone tried to follow them as much as humanly possible. Paragraph 182 of the *Letter of Aristeas* and the praise of Joseph for not having eaten with the pagans in *Joseph and Aseneth* are exemplary: 'Joseph did not eat with the Egyptians, because for him it was an abomination' (7.1).

The necessity of the Law was so deeply felt that some texts raise the question of how Abraham could have been called a friend of God given the fact that he did not yet know the Law. The Law was thus spoken of as being written on celestial tablets, an absolute Law, and that human law was merely an imperfect echo; according to the book of *Jubilees* the angels that guide Adam already observe the Law, as written on the celestial tablets, of course (*Jub.* 3.10, 31). This sense of the Law's necessity led Judaism to lend great importance to the question of morality, but this is modern terminology and perhaps a peculiarly modern problem as well. For the Jews the central problem was the Law and its interpretation. Since in the Law, as it is written, the commandments have no hierarchy of importance, the problem arose as to whether such a hierarchy existed or not; that is, whether it was possible or not to place one set of commandments above others in such a way as to simplify the entire system and, more importantly, to provide a rationally valid key to the system of the Torah. (See the *Testaments* of *Benjamin* and *Asher*, as well as the New Testament, Mk 12.28-34 and parallel passages.)

The splintering of the Jewish religious tradition in the two centuries before the Common Era stems from the lack of any clear relationship between religious thought and religious authority. As Jewish thought developed it became more and more evident that the Law was meaningful only if interpreted coherently, but there was no body with the recognized authority of providing a 'true' interpretation. Thus various interpretations arose simultaneously with the effect of creating greater insecurity rather than reinforcing faith. The problem of giving an authentic interpretation to the Law was felt to be so great and so far beyond human capabilities that some delegated its solution to the messiah as his fundamental function.[6] On the other hand, the lack of a central authority capable of guaranteeing the 'true' laws favoured the formation of groups which could and did argue, but without mutually excluding one another. Furthermore, the comparison of the same legal texts known to us through the Masoretic and other traditions demonstrates that not even the text of the Torah had been definitively established as yet.[7]

In the whirlwind of interests already described, the various theological positions grew more and more diversified and found reason for deepening their differences in the historical events themselves. It is therefore difficult to make the distinction, dear to modern historians, between conservative movements and progressive ones. There is in fact a profound evolution, a constant search for the clarification of the Scriptures' definitive meaning, in order to seize the secret of salvation. This search is dominated by the most irrational intuition and by the most rigid logic; while not always immediately apparent, Jewish thought is split between investigations following paths which are often diametrically opposed to one another.

I shall try, then, to present the broad challenges addressed by Middle Jewish thought. I shall proceed by themes rather than by authors for

6. See W.D. Davies, *The Setting of the Sermon of the Mount* (Cambridge: Cambridge University Press, 1964), p. 155.

7. See A. Rofé, 'Gli albori delle sette nel Giudaismo postesilico (Notizie inedite dai Settanta, Trito-Isaia, Siracide e Malachia)', in B. Chiesa (ed.), *Correnti culturali e movimenti religiosi del giudaismo: Atti del V Congresso Internazionale dell'AISG, 12–15 nov 1984* (Rome: Carucci, 1987), pp. 25-35; Cardellini, 'Dalla legge alla Torah'. See also the case of Exod. 21.22-25, regarding abortion. The law in the Hebrew text is older and, in any case, different than that of the Greek text.

two specific reasons: first, it is difficult to identify most of the authors writing during the period, and secondly (and more importantly) it is difficult to give a precise and sure date to all of the works. For the same reason we cannot make too close a correlation between the ideological themes and the single historical moments and events, which also made it necessary to present the facts and the ideas in separate sections of this book. On the other hand, in spite of the differing solutions found from author to author, the same problems present themselves throughout the period of Middle Judaism. This attenuates the importance of the relative uncertainty of many texts' dating for understanding the debate. The vast literary production which characterizes the entire period of Middle Judaism has been given a broad array of names, usually following theological more than historical criteria.

Concerning the problem of labelling this literature, I have decided to avoid giving it a name, calling it simply Jewish literature, obviously referring to the period in question. It should be borne in mind that certain names such as 'apocryphal', 'pseudepigraphic' or 'apocalyptic' derive from modern conceptualizations and not from the contemporary problematics addressed in the texts themselves. Regarding the Dead Sea manuscripts, the term is derived from the place of their discovery and has no historical value, at least as long as no particular sub-group is identified.[8] Even though it has clear historical aims, the use of the term 'intertestamentary' is derived from the strict counterposition of the New and Old Testaments, a distinction stemming from a set of problems arising decidedly later than the period in question. Furthermore, the label is chronologically erroneous since a fair portion of this literature is either anterior to the latest canonical Old Testament writings or posterior to the earliest New Testament ones. We can therefore present only the themes which were dealt with during these centuries: the problem of the Son of Man or that of the resurrection are not restricted to the book of Daniel, and the problem of the origin of evil pervades a great deal of the period's literary production.

I agree with Boccaccini that the principal cause for the difficulty in understanding the period in its totality stems from the division of

8.   According to García Martínez the Qumran manuscripts express the ideology of a specific sect which can even be placed within the Essenic current. See García Martínez, 'Qumran Origins and Early History: A Groningen Hypothesis'; García Martínez and A.S. van der Woude 'A Groningen Hypothesis of Qumran Origins and Early History', *RevQ* 14 (1990), pp. 522-41.

Middle Judaism's literature *in corpora* based on modern ideological and theological grounds.

2. Pesharim *and the Interpretation of History*

The problem of assigning relatively precise dates to the works of the period remains unresolved and satisfactory answers for our questions will perhaps never be found, given the lack of the necessary elements for precise dating. It is a well-known fact that while these texts are a gold mine of historical references, they rarely give specific information; proper names and exact indications of events are lacking.

Works of a clearly historical nature, in a modern sense of the word, are obviously exceptions to the rule: works like 1 Maccabees and the lost work of Nicolaus of Damascus, the primary source of Josephus. Both authors, however, are closely tied to the circle of the court and therefore much nearer to a Western, lay mentality than to a Jewish one. Nor was there a lack of authors in the Diaspora, authors like Jason of Cyrene of the second century BCE, with openly historical, though apologetic, intentions.[9]

The *Book of Dreams* and the book of Daniel are the exceptions among the works of a literary nature in the second century BCE due to the fact that they can be dated precisely. Unique are the first century cases of the *Psalms of Solomon*, with a *terminus post quem* of 48 BCE, date of the death of Pompey, and the *Book of Parables* with a *terminus post quem* of 40 BCE, date of a Parthian invasion. The contrast with the Dead Sea manuscripts is great; there is even a debate as to whether the frequently used term *kittim* refers to the Seleucids or to the Romans.[10]

There are two causes for the poor expositive clarity of these texts; first, the authors were writing for a group of readers who, we suppose, were able to understand the allusions made, and, secondly, the texts were not read with our mentality. In other words, they were not read for information about a fact, but rather with the aim of understanding, in

9.   A certain interest in history developed among the Jews in the hellenistic world of Alexandria in the late third and early second centuries BCE. Only a few fragments, however, remain of the works of these historiographers. Some such historiographers are: *Pseudo-Hecataeus, Demetrius, Aristeas the Exegete, Eupolemus, Pseudo-Eupolemus, Cleodemus Malchus*. See now: L. Troiani, in P. Sacchi (ed.), *Apocrif dell'Antico Testamento*, V.

10.   For a bibliography of the problems, see Moraldi, *I manoscritti*, pp. 289-90.

the deepest sense of the word, the reader's place in the history of salvation. In short, the idea was not to know history as much as to know
God's will, to seek to interpret the facts in their final and definitive
meaning.

In this way, a text written in the second century BCE condemning a
priest for having contaminated the Temple through his inability to perform his role could still be read a century later since the juridic position
of the high priesthood had not changed since the death of Onias III. The
entire work is read in terms of the present; it not only contains norms of
behaviour, but it also holds a key to understanding the contemporary
drama. Below I will demonstrate how this lack of historical sense is
common to all Jewish spirituality of the period. For the moment,
though, it will suffice to mention that a whole literary *genre*, known as
pesher, developed around the reading of a brief passage of Scripture
and its use for understanding contemporary facts and events.

> In the cave of Qumran fragments of several *pesharim* were found. The
> best known and best conserved of them is the one commenting on the
> book of Habakkuk.[11]

The following is a passage from the Habakkuk *pesher* which
illustrates the method:

> [Look at the peoples, consider them, wonder at them and be amazed. I
> shall do a work in your days that you would not believe if they] told you
> (Hab. 1.5).

> [The interpretation of this passage concerns] those who with the Liar
> have betrayed, because [they did not believe the words] of the Teacher of
> Righteousness, words which he received from the mouth of God. It
> concerns those who have betrayed...the New [Covenant], not having

---

11. For the possible Egyptian origins of the *pesher* method of reading the Scriptures, see F. Daumas, 'Littérature prophétique et exégétique égyptienne et commentaires esséniens', in M. Jourjon (ed.), *A la rencontre de Dieu: Mémorial Albert
Gelin* (Le Puy: Mappus, 1961), pp. 203-21; though this work could be carried
further. As concerns the observations of J. van der Ploeg ('Les manuscrits du désert
de Juda: Livres récents', *BO* 16 [1959], pp. 162-76 [163]), that this type of literature
in the end belonged to the *midrash*, given that the expression *pšrw*, which appears
often in this *genre* of works, does not indicate the work as a whole, but rather the
single explanation, can be considered correct. A different term is useful, however,
for indicating a literary *genre* which, even though similar to the *midrash*, offers the
distinct characteristic of being an instrument for the direct interpretation of the
Scripture. See Moraldi, *I manoscritti*, pp. 496-506.

believed in the Covenant of God, [and having profaned his [Sa]cred Na[me]. Furthermore, the interpretation of the passage concerns [all those who shall be]*tray in the future*. They are the...who will not believe, when they hear all that which [will] happen [to] the last generation, from the mouth of the priest to whom God has granted...the intelligence for interpreting...all the words of his servants and prophets...through them God has narrated all that must happen to his people (*1QpHab*. 2.1-10).

For I am about to rouse the Chaldaeans, that fierce and impetuous people (Hab 1, 6). The interpretation of this passage regards the Kittim, wh[o ar]e fast and courageous in war... (*1QpHab*. 2.12-13)

The link between the text of Habukkuk and the present is extremely subtle and all but clear. The author of the *pesher* deduces an account of contemporary history from the biblical text. A foreign people, the *Kittim*, dominate Israel. On the other hand, even the Judaeans of Jerusalem are put on the same level as the pagans since the expression, 'Look at the peoples', refers to them. Disaster has befallen them because they did not believe the preaching of the Teacher of Righteousness, who did not speak with the authority of a prophet, but as one who interpreted the prophets, with divine charisma, of course.[12]

The destruction of the unbelievers, those who follow a 'Liar', is foreseen. Rather, a destruction has already taken place, but it is not yet final because more and similar destructions will follow until the final destruction which is only hinted at here. 'Teacher of Righteousness', 'Liar' and '*Kittim*' are all terms which intentionally obscure the real historical identity of the figures. The foreign oppressors could be Seleucids or they could be Romans and, as for 'Liars' who did not follow the teachings of the 'Teacher of Righteousness', there are as many as you like. The passage's interpreter is careful to adapt the text not only to a situation which has already been clarified, but also to analogous situations which could and did re-present themselves.

It is clear that the author of this *pesher* did not have the same conception of history as we do, that is, history as being made up of events which come one after another following a logical progression. For him all of history has already been written in the Scriptures, because 'history' is not the progression of events, but rather the manifestation of God's plan. History is not read directly in God's mind; it is taken to be a product of his will, like the cosmos and its laws. Just as one can arrive

12. See Sacchi, 'Knowledge among the Jews from Amos to the Essenes' in *Jewish Apocalyptic*, pp. 168-99.

at God through the cosmos, since he created it, the same progression can be made through history. The prophet communicated God's will to humans in order that they should act in history in accordance with God's will. The wise men of this period understand God through the history he has made.

The *pesher*'s aim is not to relate facts so much as it is to understand the struggle between the righteous man and the wicked man. The former speaks in the name of God and is followed by those who have faith in God, the latter rejects the charisma of the righteous man. This world is the battleground in the conflict between good and evil following God's eternal plan, a plan which can be understood only by illuminated men. All the rest are doomed to destruction or to divine hatred, because God not only hates evil, but also the wicked, even though he created them as such in his own likeness (on this subject see Chapter 12, §1, pp. 328-33).

A certain kind of *pesher* is present also in Luke (4.16-21) where Jesus reads Isaiah and apply it directly to himself, 'The spirit of the Lord is upon *me*...' His listeners were troubled since they were accustomed to reading the Scripture in reference to the present. The same reasoning can be seen among the people who eat the bread multiplied in Jn 6.22-34, and in particular in the reference to the Scriptures in v. 31, 'He gave them bread from heaven to eat'.

The sense of history which had been characteristic of Hebrew thought was dissolving. Only two extreme elements seem to remain and they are difficult to reconcile with one another. On the one hand there are the broad metaphysical themes, the history of salvation, or rather the manifestation of the will, the realization of God's judgment of the world. On the other, humanity's eternally repeated drama, the individual faced with the problem of good and evil. Man's choice, however (whether active or passive), does not make history; it is only a function of his salvation or perdition.[13]

This new way of experiencing history and of reading the Scriptures cannot be attributed to chance, nor can it be considered extraneous to the Jewish ideological constellation of the two centuries before the Common Era. It stems from a profound modification of all that which made up the spiritual baggage first of the Hebrew and later of the Jew,

---

13. See D. Rössler, *Gesetz und Geschichte: Untersuchungen zur Theologie der jüdischen Apokalyptik und der pharisäischen Orthodoxie* (WMANT, 3; Neu-kirchen–Vluyn: Neukirchener Verlag, 2nd edn, 1962).

right up to the great crisis of 200 BCE. In the following pages the essential aspects of the new Jewish *Weltanschauung* will be outlined. The expository order is arbitrary and simply follows the internal logic of the subject matter. Each aspect is in fact very closely linked to all the others, forming the new Jewish spirituality.

Chapter 11

THE PROBLEM OF KNOWLEDGE

1. *Apocalyptic Vision and Essenic Illumination*

An examination of the mechanisms of knowledge, as they were conceived at the time, can help to provide some orientation for understanding the spirituality of Middle Judaism.

The last two centuries prior to the Common Era were characterized, in the Jewish world, by a deep desire for knowledge. The book of Wisdom (7.17-20) provides an outline of the fields that the wise man must know: cosmology and astronomy, zoology and psychology, botany and pharmacology. But even before 200 BCE, in *1 Enoch* (chs. 2–5), we find knowledge of botany already organized hierarchically as a science, and certainly before 200 BCE the *Book of Astronomy* put forth a description and explanation of heavenly phenomena.

According to an ancient tradition (1 Kgs 5.13), Solomon had a broad knowledge of botany and zoology, but the type of knowledge sought in the centuries immediately preceding the Common Era was of a different nature than that of the past. A global knowledge was sought, which is even different from encyclopaedic knowledge. The final end, or goal of knowledge, had become knowledge of the 'whole', that is not only knowledge of things, but also of their meaning and the meaning of history, history being considered an aspect of the cosmic whole rather than the autonomous unfolding of human events. In the past, wisdom and prophecy had been independent one from the other; the object of prophecy had been knowledge of the times in relation to the question of salvation. The prophet delivered God's message to men, encouraging them to convert. This was the message of a God who seemed to mix freely with human events. God punished and rewarded, and he also threatened punishment that he could later decide not to send. The existence of a true science of God was not possible, since God was seen as essentially free, in exactly the same way that humanity felt itself to be free.

The idea that God's threats are linked to and conditioned by the sins of the people is quite widespread in the Old Testament. But the sense of God's historical freedom is so strong that the Bible can even mention God being sorry, as in Gen. 6.6. See also Jer. 18.7-8; 26.3 and Jon. 3.4-10: ' "Forty days more and Nineveh shall be overthrown!"…([the king]) covered himself with sackcloth and sat in ashes…God changed his mind about the calamity that he had said he would bring upon them; and he did not do it'. Alongside God's freedom we find the freedom of the prophet. We are reminded of Jonah's flight and of Jeremiah's painful acceptance.

The eschatological world appeared before the eyes of the prophets with completely new elements with regard to the present world. Jeremiah had glimpsed such a new humanity that the Law would be written in the hearts of every person (31.33), and a later passage inserted into the book of Isaiah (11.6) reads: 'The wolf shall live with the lamb'. But the passage from this world to the eschatological one remained unexplained, a mystery shrouded in the will and knowledge of God, unfathomable by humans.

This deep fracture between God's knowledge and what is knowable by humans was deeply felt by Qohelet; if humans were able to know the beginning and end of all things, the alpha and omega of all creation, then his condition would be quite different. But God has denied humanity the possibility of knowing the alpha and omega because he wants to be feared by humans, he wants humankind to be constantly reminded that God is in heaven and that humans are on the earth. If humans could possess all knowledge, then their condition, that of fear, would perhaps be different. For Qohelet the drama of human existence lies in knowing that the alpha and omega exist, because only end terms are capable of giving meaning to the whole, and in being irremediably incapable of grasping those terms (Qoh. 3.11). Qohelet denied the possibility of overcoming the limits of human experience, precisely because certain ideas must have already been circulating; the need to surpass limits was very much alive in the spirit of Qohelet's time. In fact, the two centuries following Qohelet's lifetime are characterized by the search for and the sense of possession of this new total knowledge, which included even the alpha and omega, the beginning and the end of all things.

This new form of knowledge, which claimed to know all things, was not based on a new methodology, on something like a metaphysical discourse which gives humanity the illusion of being able to rend the veils of cosmic mystery with its own powers. Rather, it was based on a new certainty of having received a new revelation from God. In other words, through revelation humanity was given knowledge that it realized it would not have been able to attain on its own. This type of knowledge was presented in the Apocalyptic in the form of the vision, clearly sent by God only to his chosen few. In Essenism it was to take on an even more radical and different form through the idea of 'illumination', which is something more than just revelation since it consists in seeing things through God's own light.

The discourse concerning revelation, however, was not limited to knowledge of things lying beyond the grasp of human senses. Unlike Qohelet who used his own human capabilities to investigate the things of the world, the sages of the following epoch tended to attribute to divine revelation not only the knowledge of the things of the heavenly world, but also of what they knew about nature (Wis. 7.17-21). This gives a peculiar character to the discourse of the new period, an esoteric tone. It is clear that what counts is not the empirical knowledge of Qohelet, which is considered worthless, but the interpretation given to things. And interpretation is only possible in terms of divine revelation. In this way the acquisition of knowledge is always initiation into a secret.

> As I was tending the flocks…a spirit of understanding from the Lord came upon me, and I observed all human beings making their way in life deceitfully. Sin was erecting walls and injustice was ensconced in towers (*T. Levi* 2.3).

The object of revealed knowledge is often heaven or the underworld. Again in the *Testament of Levi* we read:

> I kept grieving over the race of the sons of men, and I prayed to the Lord that I might be delivered. Then sleep fell upon me, and I beheld a high mountain, and I was on it.
>
> And behold, the heavens were opened [see Ezek. 1.1], and an angel of the Lord spoke to me: 'Levi, Levi, enter!' And I entered the first heaven, and saw there much water suspended. And again I saw a second heaven much brighter and more lustrous, for there was a measureless height in it. And I said to the angel, 'Why are these things thus?' And the angel said to me, 'Do not be amazed concerning this, for you shall see another heaven more lustrous and beyond compare. And when you have mounted there, you shall stand near the Lord. You shall be his priest and you shall tell forth his mysteries to men. You shall announce the one who is about to redeem Israel' (*T. Levi* 2.4-10).

At times the author deliberately presents the vision as incomprehensible or vague, only to have it followed by an authentic interpretation placed in the mouth of an angel.

> Listen, therefore, concerning the heavens which have been shown to you. The lowest is dark for this reason: It sees all the injustices of humankind and contains fire, snow, and ice, ready for the day determined by God's righteous judgment. In it are all the spirits of those dispatched to achieve the punishment of mankind. In the second are the armies arrayed for the day of judgment to work vengeance on the spirits of error and of Beliar. Above them are the Holy Ones. In the uppermost heaven of all dwells the Great Glory in the Holy of Holies superior to all holiness.[1]
>
> There with him are the archangels, who serve and offer propitiatory sacrifices to the Lord in behalf of all the sins of ignorance of the righteous ones. They present to the Lord a pleasing odour, a rational and bloodless oblation. In the heaven below them[2] are the messengers who carry the responses to the angels of the Lord's presence. There with him are thrones and authorities; there praises to God are offered eternally. So when the Lord looks upon us we all tremble. Even the heavens and earth and the abysses tremble before the presence of his majesty. But the sons of men, being insensitive to these matters, keep sinning and provoking the anger of the Most High (*T. Levi* 3.1-10).

Between God and humans there is an enormous 'in-between world' organized in a hierarchical fashion, between the 'Glory superior to all holiness' and its opposite, represented by this world full of injustices.

The world exists on two levels, one subject to perception by human senses, but which does not let its secrets be understood except when God unveils their authentic reality to his chosen ones, and a second, higher level where things really take place, as Zechariah had already seen (see pp. 125-29). Let us look again at the above passage from *T. Levi* 2.3; the spirit of iniquity has occupied the gates of the city and

---

1.   The adjective 'holy, sacred' is generally reserved in the Qumran manuscripts for angelic beings. An exception is represented by 1QM 12.7 and 19.1 in a context that has been heavily influenced by the Old Testament, where sacrality is the ensign of the divine force that will destroy the pagans. A similar concept is documented in the text of the *Songs of the Sabbath Sacrifice*. God is the source of holiness, but he is not holy; he lives in his divinity. See 4Q400-407. i.2.

2.   'In the heaven below them…': the author's vision of the heavens' structure is not clear. First he described the heavens proceeding from low to high, and continues from high to low. It would seem then that there are only three heavens and that there are angels with different duties in each of them.

there is no escape. The people cannot see this, but it has happened all the same and for them there is no means of escape. Just as Zechariah had had no doubts concerning Joshua's salvation, since it had already taken place in the in-between world, here the certainty is one of inescapable doom, inevitable because it has already taken place in a higher world than that of men. In the in-between world angels and demons are engaged in a conflict whose consequences inevitably fall on humans.

In the book of Daniel it takes 21 days for the angel invoked by Daniel to arrive because the angel who protects Persia had blocked his way (Dan. 10.13), and only the intervention of Michael, Israel's great protector, freed the angel's way.

Revealed knowledge can be presented in a variety of ways, that in this epoch, however, can be reduced to three fundamental types. There is the apocalyptic vision which can either be a direct representation of the other world or an allegory capable of interpreting reality. The so-called 'heavenly tablets', books in which at the beginning of the world God himself wrote all of future history, represent a simplification of the apocalyptic vision; the chosen one is allowed to glimpse the tablets. The heavenly tablets correspond to a predeterministic vision of history common in certain circles during this period.

The most original development of knowledge through revelation came about in Essenism. For the Essenes knowledge of the truth was conceived of as the fruit of the human intellect which through God's grace ('Nothing is known without the will of God', 1QH 1.8 and elsewhere) was able to raise itself to where it could see the entire cosmos in the light, that is the intelligence, of God himself. In this case truth is immanent to the sage's words within the limits to which God's thought can be expressed. Again, 'From the source of his knowledge he has loosed his light that illuminates me, so that my eye has contemplated his wonders, and the light of my heart, the mystery to come and the eternal being' (1 QS 11.3-4).

In these words the process of illumination is described in detail. Knowledge is light both in God and in humans, though in humans it only exists as reflected light. And the light of knowledge is not granted to all humans, but only to a few chosen ones, or even to just one chosen one. The object of human knowledge is the same as that of divine knowledge, so that the author's mind (probably later than the Teacher of Righteousness) is able to grasp the meaning both of the cosmos (his wonders) and history (the mystery to come). In fact, what happens today is meaningful only inasmuch as it paves the way for the decisive future event.

The past, present and future, the cosmos and history, are all gathered in a union whose centre lies in God's mind. The flow of time does not lead toward the unknown; history is merely a manifestation of divine will, as is the cosmos. In this way, illumination seems to be a fact like any other, one of the elements of the cosmos itself. This radical way of seeing illumination has as a necessary correlation a conviction in pre-determination and the denial of human freedom.

There are many passages in which the Teacher of Righteousness, or whoever else the text's author may be, thanks God for the illumination received. See 1QH 3.1: 'Thank you, oh Lord, for having illuminated me with the splendour of your face'. The formulation in 1QH 4.5 is interesting: 'Thank you, oh Lord, for having illuminated my face through your Covenant... I seek you, and, like a true dawn you revealed your perfect light to me'.

The Bible tells us that God can illuminate someone's eyes (Pss. 13.4; 19.9; Prov. 29.13; Ezra 9.8), or that he can make his face shine upon someone (Num. 6.25; Pss. 31.17; 67.2; 80.4, 8, 20; 119.135; Dan. 9.17), though it never says that God illuminates someone's face.[3] The novelty of this expression is not only stylistic; the Teacher of Righteousness plays a peculiar role; his face, or rather his mind (in Hebrew *leb*, 'heart') both receives and gives light.

At any rate, even authors who don't share the ideological radicalism of the Teacher of Righteousness, like the author of the book of Wisdom, agree on conceiving of all 'true' knowledge as the fruit of some illumination, or in any case of revelation:

> For it is he [God] who gave me *true* knowledge of what exists, to know the structure of the cosmos and the force of the elements; the beginning and end and middle of times, the alternations of the solstices and the changes of the seasons, the cycles of the year and the constellations of the stars, the natures of animals and the tempers of wild animals, the powers

---

3. See J. Carmignac, *Les manuscrits de Qumrân traduits et annotés* (2 vols.; Paris: Letouzey et Ané, 1961, 1963) p. 205 n. 2. See also the text of 1QS 2.2-4: 'May [God] bless you with all good and keep you from all evil; may he illuminate your mind with the intellect of life [that is, granting you the basic understanding that leads to life]; and grace you with eternal knowledge [that is, that through his grace he grant you the highest form of knowledge]'.

> of spirits and the thoughts of human beings, the varieties of plants and
> the virtues of roots; I learned both what is secret and what is manifest,
> for Wisdom, the fashioner of all things, taught me (Wis. 7.17-22).

The adjective 'true' alongside 'knowledge' is not without its importance. Man's knowledge is in itself error; only God can teach the truth. Therefore all valid knowledge is the fruit of revelation, not research. Furthermore, supreme knowledge comes from that knowledge of all times, past, present and future that for the most part eludes human senses.

Scholars have long discussed the problem of apocalyptic knowledge, knowledge of the world and God's mysteries by vision or revelation. Most of this discussion has revolved around placing this type of knowledge in a historical perspective. Most scholars have linked it to prophetism, while others, and they are certainly mistaken, have linked it to wisdom and wisdom literature. But whatever the origin of the single elements, the cognitive system of revelations and visions did not exist before the so-called apocalyptic works. Single elements and motifs may have existed earlier, though they were bound to have a different meaning in different epochs.

The relation between this type of knowledge and gnosis have also been pointed out. And again, the same reservations remain valid, since it is clear that a sort of revelation exists in gnostic systems, but it holds a very different meaning because it is inserted in a different ideological constellation. The single element may remain the same for generations, but its meaning changes over time and in different historical circumstances.[4]

---

4. On this problem in general see K. Koch, *The Rediscovery of Apocalyptic* (London: SCM Press, 1972); and G. von Rad, *Old Testament Theology* (London: SCM Press, 1975), II, pp. 301-308. See also *TWNT*, VI, pp. 827-28 and *RGG*, I, pp. 466-67. The entry *'wr* in *ThWAT*, pp. 181-82, is of little use to us in this case.

On the relationship between the apocalyptic and gnosis, see R. Otto, *Reich Gottes und Menschensohn* (Munich: Beck, 1934), where on p. 5 he finds a truly effective way of expressing a certain spiritual stance: 'Gnosis is the spirit of the spirit of the apocalyptic'. The recent conference, *Apocalittica e gnosticismo. Roma 18–19 giugno 1993*, was dedicated to the relationship between the Apocalyptic and gnosis; the acts were published in 1995 in Rome (M.V. Cerutti [ed.], *Apocalittica e gnosticismo. Roma 18–19 giugno 1993* [Roma: GEI, 1995]).

On the methodology in general, see my *Apocrifi*, II, pp. 14-15 concerning the

In comparison to the Greek world which, with only a few rare and interesting exceptions, believed in the autonomy of human discourse, the Jewish world presented the opposite stance, intent on explaining the cognitive process as possible only by the will and grace of God. Perhaps their ideas were not all that far from those of the Stoics, but it is interesting to see ways of approaching the same questions from opposite sides. For the Greek Stoic the truth expressed by an individual held meaning only to the extent that it coincided with the will of Destiny or of the Divinity. For the Essene it was the very will of God that allowed the formulation of the truth. The Stoic discourse begins with humankind, the Jewish one with God.

There is a long history behind the complex vision of things which sees the Jewish world and Greek culture in contrast even when they are in agreement regarding single elements, and perhaps that history has not been studied enough. I shall outline its fundamental elements below. We shall also see that certain fundamental problems, such as the criterion of truth, were held in common, but the search for the truth always began from opposite points.

2. *Knowledge and the Law*

For as much as the problem of knowledge assumed a cosmic aspect in general, it was still felt to be related to the Law, and even more so to a human discourse.

---

relationship between the New Testament and the other Jewish documents. 'The overall weight that each group of sources may have remains an open problem. Leafing through Strack and Billerbeck one gets the impression that there is nothing in the Gospels that doesn't come from the rabbinical tradition; single sentences and single sayings are documented as being identical or at least similar in both bodies of literature. But, as pointed out by S. Ben Chorin (*Bruder Jesus: Der Nazarener in jüdischer Sicht* [Munich: List, 1967], p. 83), 'it is the accumulation of a certain type of saying and thought that gives the New Testament its unmistakable character in contrast to the rabbinical tradition. The comparison should not be made, or should not only be made, on the level of the single sentence, but should be extended to entire contexts and the ideas underlying them'. In other words, not only should we be wary of single sentences (that take on value from their context), but we should also be wary of single ideas. Each idea assumes the value it holds in the constellation of ideas in which it is inserted.

And now, my children, I command you:
Fear the Lord your God with your whole heart,
and walk according to his Law in integrity.
Teach your children letters also,
so that they might have understanding throughout all their lives
as they ceaselessly read the Law of God.
For everyone who knows the Law of God shall be honoured...
Acquire wisdom in fear of the Lord because if a captivity occurs,
if cities and territories are laid waste,
if silver and gold and every possession are lost,
nothing can take away the wisdom of the wise man
except the blindness of impiety and the obtuseness of sin (*T. Levi* 13.1-7).

The tone of this passage is decidedly more cautious than that of the two passages we read above. The author says that one must know the Law well, because one who knows the Law has everything that he needs in life. This knowledge does not seem to be any kind of superior knowledge. It is the natural human knowledge. The only thing that can hinder this kind of knowledge is sin, which brings about the loss of wisdom. In this case wisdom comes from neither revelation nor illumination, but is within everyone's reach, or at least within the grasp of anyone who knows how to read and write. It lies at the very foundation of religious life. The idea that the wise man possesses all things is held in common with Stoicism, but in the Jewish world it is developed following a peculiar religious value. Knowledge is accompanied by an irrational element. A certain human preparation is necessary for understanding the Law, and that preparation is nurtured through piety. In this case the anxiety regarding the acquisition of knowledge is perfectly absorbed in the traditional Jewish vision, since it is seen as a function of salvation, but through the Law. And the Law is the eternal and unchanging source of wisdom.

3. *Rational Knowledge*

There is, however, a type of knowledge based on reason which is present even in the Jewish world. The Pharisees had already begun to deduce a *halakah* from other precepts that had been confirmed through rational thought.

But even in Essenism, especially late Essenism, a rational type of reasoning has been documented. The author of the *Damascus Document* claims to 'reveal' something 'to the ears of those who listen': for example 'the ways of the wicked' in 2.2-3. He does not say anything, though, about how he learned the things he reveals to others. Yet he is aware of the problem of revelation, since he claims (CD 2.11) that God instructed those '$q^e r\hat{\imath}'\hat{e}$ *šem* men (lit: "called by name") through those anointed by his holy spirit (the prophets)'. The prophets said the truth in God's name, not because God had spoken to them, but only because they were 'anointed by his holy spirit'. In our words, 'because they were inspired by the Holy Spirit, or something like it'.

The author of the *Damascus Document* does not tell us, though, who revealed to him that the prophets had been inspired by the spirit. And if he does not say it, then it must be because it was common knowledge, at least among the members of the sect. As an idea it did not cause any problems; it was a commonly held idea derived from the very way the Bible was read. For the Essenes the Bible in its entirety was God's truth, even when it was pure historical narrative told from memory. What counts is that no matter what type of expository style and underlying cognitive premises, the Bible is always and in any case the Word of God.

But the fact that the author of the *Damascus Document* addresses only the members of the sect, because they alone are capable of understanding (1.1-2), and exposes ideas that he knows his listeners share demonstrates the rise of a new concept, that of 'tradition', or rather of the 'tradition as guarantee'. At the beginning of his work he explicitly declares that his exclusive audience is made up of 'those who know and practise righteousness (*yôd'ê ṣedeq*)', in other words the members of the sect. He can make his revelations only to those who already know righteousness, and the revelations regard only a certain development of the sect's ideology, not its foundation. Furthermore, only those who have already accepted the sect's basic truths are able to follow these new revelations which, in the end, don't really reveal anything new.

The author is aware that the Law does not foresee all possibilities and that there are some obscure commandments (*nistārôt*, already present in the *Community Rule*, 5.11). The Law is like a well which must be continually deepened until the arrival of a final Teacher of Righteousness (CD 6.3-11).

In effect, having finished the prologue, the author proceeds with two types of revelation. One concerns the fate of the wicked, only a few words built around what were certainly commonplaces for the Essenes, but also for most of the Jews of the time: 'Strength, power and great fury with fiery flames...upon all those who have strayed from the way...for them there shall be no remains, no escape' (2.5-6). This is not a revelation, it is a banality.

The author dedicates much more space and attention to the other type of revelation, but some doubt remains as to whether the author reveals or demonstrates. In 2.14 he introduces this series of revelations with the phrase 'I will open (*ᵃgalleh*) your eyes so that you can see and understand the works of God'. In other words the author seems to introduce a revelatory discourse on reality which should serve as an interpretative grid for presenting examples of upright *halakah*. In reality, however, this discourse is missing. Once it has been established that the listeners consider the Bible God's word, and that they consider the fundamental points of the sect's ideology as God's word as well, then the innovative part, which should be made up of pure revelation, is always presented in a rational manner.

'Those who marry two women in their lives' are mistaken, 'because the principle of creation is "male and female he created them" ' (CD 4.21).

Even in the second part of the work, concerning the laws, it is worth noting that while some have an apodictic form, others explain why a certain punishment is to be inflicted (see 9.1 for the first case, 9.6 for the second).

The judgment given on David's behaviour is interesting as well; in the eyes of the author David was a saint. How is it, then, that this holy man did not observe the Scripture forbidding a prince to possess many women? The answer is to be found in history, obviously, in history as the author knew it (CD 5.2-6): 'David had not read the book of the Law because it had been sealed...and was not opened again until the coming of Zadok'. Thus David's deeds were accepted by God, with the exception of the blood of Uriah, even though they were not in conformity with the Law. Therefore, even those who do not know the Law are bound by a certain moral code. Whether he explicitly states it or not, our author clearly holds a concept of what we would call natural law. Paul refers to this idea in Rom. 2.12: 'All who have sinned apart from the Law will also perish apart from the Law'. It is interesting to note that the revealed law, at least in this example, regards the topic of sexual habits.

In conclusion, it is clear to the author that he cannot aspire to convince 'the men of the Pit'; he addresses only those who already know righteousness. In practice he follows the teachings of the *Community Rule* which prohibits the members of the sect from speaking with the men of unrighteousness (9.16-17). It is useless to speak to the men of unrighteousness because there is a fundamental and irremediable error in their lives; they have not followed the Teacher of Righteousness. Only those who have faith in him can be freed from God's final judgment.

Chapter 12

PREDETERMINISM AND THE PROBLEM OF EVIL

1. *Predeterminism**

God's omnipotence and his ability to intervene freely in human events, directing them in ways known only to him, are very old ideas in Israel. God's omnipotent intervention in history was already placed in a very close relationship with his creative ability in Amos. Just as God had created all things, he could also in some way cause human events:

* The term 'predeterminism' (and other similar terms) causes problems for some people. See A. Marx, 'Y a-t-il une prédestination à Qumran?', *RevQ* 6 (1967), pp. 323-42, and F. Nötscher, *Zur theologischen Terminologie der Qumrantexte* (Bonn: P. Hanstein, 1956), which criticizes the rigidity of modern rationalistic terminology. Marx also has the merit of providing a good summary of the current positions·in the ongoing debate. In this context the term 'predeterminism' can be maintained, but I would like to make it clear that it should be understood exclusively as a historical phenomenon regarding the sect of the Essenes. In other words, Qumranic predeterminism presents specific characteristics that identify it, notwithstanding the philosophical *aporiae* that can be brought to light. This should not come as a surprise, since all terms, even philosophical ones, always take on a specific value when used to indicate the concrete thought of an individual. 'Soul' always means soul, even though it is not the same thing in Plato, in Aristotle or in Thomas Aquinas. Essenic discourse is centred more around God than around humans. They believed that humans were good or evil because God had created them that way and that God had created Belial in order to carry out his plans. Thus, even the wicked are part of the divine plan, as is their final destruction. At any rate, the fact that Josephus decided to present the Jewish sects according to their positions concerning the problem of human freedom of choice demonstrates that during his day the problem of freedom of choice was a central issue in Jewish thought. Every religion, in order to survive must believe in the freedom of humans and God, a problem which inevitably raises an infinite number of problems, as borne out by the history of theological thought. In the case at hand, the Essenes placed greater emphasis on God's freedom, to the detriment of the freedom of humanity. In this sense they were predeterministic, even if their predeterminism was unique, as with every specific historical case.

The one who made the Pleiades and Orion,
and turns deep darkness into the morning,
and darkens the day into night,
who calls for the waters of the sea,
and pours them out on the surface of the earth
Yhwh is his name,
who makes destruction flash out against the strong,
so that destruction comes upon the fortress (Amos 5.8-9).[1]

The idea that humans are completely in God's hands is expressed extremely clearly in Jeremiah as well, with the well-known image of the potter that was later to be taken up by Paul (Rom. 9.20-24):

> The word that came to Jeremiah from Yhwh: 'Come, go down to the potter's house, and there I will let you hear my words'. So I went down to the potter's house, and there he was working at his wheel. The vessel he was making of clay was spoiled in the potter's hand, and he reworked it into another vessel, as seemed good to him. Then the word of Yhwh came to me: Can I not do with you, O house of Israel, just as this potter has done? says Yhwh. Just like the clay in the potter's hand, so are you in my hand, O house of Israel (Jer. 18.1-6).

But in Jeremiah, at least in a certain Jeremiah,[2] the idea of God's omnipotence in history is tempered by recognition of human freedom: 'At one moment I may declare concerning a nation or a kingdom, that I will pluck up and break down and destroy it, but if that nation, concerning which I have spoken, turns from its evil, I will change my mind about the disaster that I intended to bring on it' (Jer. 18.7-8).

The idea of the freedom of humans is particularly clear in the works

---

1.   *The one...fortress*: the translation has been made from the Greek, which seems to have interpreted the Hebrew well. The Hebrew text is quite difficult given a number of rare words and perhaps some corruptions.

2.   Jeremiah's thought is very complex. A line of development, however, can be individuated which can hardly be attributed to the succession of editions that the text has undergone. The calling as prophet was a true burden for Jeremiah (see Jer. 20.7-10). With the passage of time he became more and more convinced of the futility of his calling if the goal behind it was Israel's conversion, because a black man cannot become white nor a leopard change the colour of its skin (13.23). The very fact that he felt the only possibility for future salvation was a new creation of human nature (31.33) shows us his lack of hope in humankind. And while he did have infinite faith in God ('Blessed are those who trust in Yhwh' and 'Cursed are those who trust in mere mortals', Jer. 17.5, 7), he was the first Jew to seriously pose the question of God's sense of justice if God did not reward men's actions in keeping with justice: 'Why does the way of the guilty prosper?' (12.1).

closer to the Theology of the Covenant. See ch. 18 of Ezekiel, which insists on the idea that humans live only inasmuch as they (freely) observe the Law, or the lapidarian sentence of Deut. 30.15: 'I have set before you today life and prosperity, death and adversity'. No one denies God the possibility of intervening in history. The problem is whether that intervention is an act of force correcting the course of history made by humans, in order to make it go in the direction he desires, or whether history itself is not simply a manifestation of God's will. Everyone knows, to use the words of Hannah's Prayer, that no one can resist God with force: 'The bow of the mighty is broken,[3] but the feeble gird on strength' (1 Sam. 2.4, a postexilic passage).[4] The question is whether the punishment threatened can be avoided through righteousness and repentance. Jeremiah felt the desperation of being prophet precisely because he doubted the possibility of repentance.

We have already seen that the idea that all men, righteous and wicked, weak and strong, are in God's hands, is one of the dominant ideas in the thought of Job and Qohelet. We could say that they simply develop and hone a theme that had already characterized the Jewish tradition for some time. What is new in Job and Qohelet then is not the idea in itself, but rather that God's omnipotence is not counterbalanced by the idea, typical of the Theology of the Covenant, that God saves the righteous and those who repent, nor by the idea that God in any case saves Israel, prevalent in the Theology of the Promise. Perhaps the primary interest of these authors, passing from meditation on the people to meditation on the individual, made them lose the liberatory and tranquilizing idea of the life of the people as being independent from the individual's life. In this way God's action can no longer be understood by humans. God's action is no longer aimed at a goal that humans can understand; it does not tend toward rewarding human's works. These authors do not seem to be interested in the final destiny of humankind as a whole.

---

3.   *Broken*: the Masoretic text uses the plural, which does not make sense here.

4.   The passage known as Hannah's Prayer has all the appearances of being a later addition, both because of the ideas it presents and because of certain expressions that it uses. In favour of its later dating see H. Stoebe, *Das erste Buch Samuelis* (Gütersloh: Gerd Mohn, 1973), p. 106: 'Man wird daraus folgern müssen, dass es sich hierbei um eine sekundäre Komposition unter Verwendung verschiedener ältere Motive handelt'. De Vaux (*Bible de Jérusalem* [Paris: Cerf, 1974], p. 314) holds the opposite view, preferring to date the passage to the period of the monarchy.

After Qohelet, the conception of God's omnipotence became more radical, at the expense of the idea of human freedom. God can do all things, God created all things, God is the author of all history. Or rather, in his omnipotence he is not so much the author of all history because he acts in it, but for the much more radical reason that he enacts over time what he already decided at the beginning of time and wrote on the heavenly tablets.

In the *Book of Dreams* (written just after the death of Antiochus IV) Enoch sees the unfolding of future history in a vision. The book of *Jubilees* tells us that God inscribed the fate of all humankind on seven tablets called the 'tablets of Heaven'.

> [Jacob] saw in a vision of the night, and behold an angel was descending from heaven, and there were seven tablets in his hands. And he gave [them] to Jacob, and he read them, and he knew everything which was written in them, which would happen to him and to his sons during all the ages (*Jub*. 32.21).

If God created all things, then all things must be as God desired them to be. The idea is expressed well in this passage from the *Assumption of Moses*:

> God has created all the nations which are in the world [just as he created] us. And he has foreseen both them and us from the beginning of the creation of the world even to the end of the age. Indeed, nothing, to the least thing, has been overlooked by him. But [rather,] he has seen all things and he is the cause of all... (*Ass. Mos*. 12.4).

Given his omnipotence, God's ability to foresee all things easily turns into predeterminism. The very close relationship between knowledge as illumination, and not simply as revelation, and predeterminism is clear. The only knowledge possible to humans is God's knowledge, and God has always known everything that he established at the beginning of time. The Teacher of Righteousness, or one of his followers, touches on various aspects of God's omniscience/omnipotence many times.

> All that is and all that shall be comes from the God of knowledge. Before men exist, He established their thoughts (*mḥšbtm*);[5] and when they come into existence as has been established, they carry out their deeds in con-

---

5. *maḥᵃšābtām*: the translation 'their thoughts' seems more natural to me. Others prefer 'their plan', that is the way of being that God has imposed on each individual. In any case the general meaning does not change.

formity with the thought of His glory, without the possibility of changing anything. Judgment (*mšpṭ*)[6] over everyone is in His hand and he provides for all beings according to their needs (1QS 3.15-17).

Everything has been preordained in the most minute detail. Man only thinks the thoughts that God wanted him to think. Man does not even have freedom of expression in his own thoughts, because even his thoughts are a product of the divine plan. The same laws govern both the movements of the stars and humans; the laws of nature and the laws of the moment are one and the same thing, just as for Qohelet, but both of them are rooted in a single law corresponding to God's will. Each of them can be known in the same way, through illumination, if God allows them to be known.

Here is another typical passage, taken from the first (now ninth) column of the *Hodayot*:

> Before you had created men,
> you already knew their works, as they would be done throughout the
>   centuries
> [And only by your will] is anything done
> and nothing can be known without your will.
> You have created every spirit
> and ma[de] every soul;
> [you gave a commandment] and a rule for all their deeds.
> You stretched out the heavens for your glory;
> every [soul] you [created] according to your will,
> the powerful spirits, according to their rule,
> before becoming angels of [...] eternal spirits in their domains,
> the luminaries according to their mysteries [that is the laws by which
>   they are regulated]
> the stars according to their paths...
> You created the earth with your strength,
> the seas, the abysses. [The heavens and...]
> their [sta]rs you have fixed through your wisdom;
> all that is in them you have established according to your will.
> [...] for the spirit of man,
> that you created placing him on the earth
> forever, for all the generations...
> [*You have fixed*] *for each generation your intervention*
> *that frees or strikes down men.* [Reconstruction of the meaning as it
>   appears in a very fragmentary part.]

---

6.   In this context *mišpāṭ* 'judgment', means 'will', or even 'manifestation of divine will'. In the end it means control over the world by God.

In the wisdom of your knowledge
you have established the role of men, before they exist;
everything occurs according to your mouth [and your words].
Without you nothing can be done.
All these things I have known from your knowledge,
because to my ears you revealed your secrets,
which are beyond the possibility of man (*pl'*)...
To you, god of knowledge (*'el hadde'ot*),
all works of righteousness belong
and the secret of truth,
while works of wickedness and laxism (*remiyyah*) are of
the sons of man.
You created the breath [of the word] on the tongue.
You know the words it pronounces.
You fixed the fruit of his lips
before the words are pronounced... (1QH 1[9].8-29)

In the following passage, taken from the *Damascus Document*, the emphasis has been shifted; more than determinism here we should speak of 'election'. The theme of God's omnipotence is seen as being close to that of election; one overlaps the other in a completely natural movement.

But strength, power and great fury with flames of fire, through [(him)][7] all the angels of destruction, will touch on those who have strayed from the way and have detested the commandment; for them there shall be no remains, no escape. In fact, God did not chose them from the beginning. Before they came into being, God knew their works; from the beginning[8] he hated [their] generations. He hid his face from the earth, from Israel [and he will keep it hidden] until their destruction. He knew the years of their existence, the number and exact date of the times... From among all he has raised up for himself men called by name [that is the elect], in order to leave a remnant for the country and to fill the world's surface with their descendants.

He has instructed them through the anointed ones of the holy spirit, which is the truth. He has established their names with precision. He makes to lose their way the ones he hates (CD 2.5-13).

7.   [(him)]: the suppression of the *waw* is both certain and necessary. Another *waw* should be suppressed at line 13; *śmw*, 'they have established', does not make sense.

8.   'from the beginning': the text reads *mdm*, 'from the blood'. Certainly a *qoph* has been let fall: *m<q>dm*.

2. *The Problem of Dualism*

If everything that takes place in the world comes about by the will of God, then the origin of evil must in some way be sought in God as well, as illustrated clearly in the passages quoted above. Prior to the Essenic movement, post-exile Judaism had always rejected the idea that evil could be directly attributed to God, even though some believed that all things that happened depended on him. A way around the dilemma had been found in developing the ideas concerning the in-between world, which became more and more densely populated with spirits placed in the various heavens. Even the in-between world, though, lost the unity that it had had for Zechariah and Job; in Zechariah the satan accuses Joshua, but he is part of the same world as the defending angels. The satan is the enemy as much in the sense that a public prosecutor could be, rather than someone who wishes evil upon us because he is intrinsically evil himself. The situation is no different in Job. With Enochism, however, we find that there are angels who deliberately rebelled against God. Thus the in-between world is divided into two opposing parts: good angels and evil ones. In Essenism, however, both types of angels, the good and the bad, appear to have been created by God in order to carry out the missions assigned to each of them directly by their creator. In this way the indivisibility of God and his omnipotence are absolutely guaranteed, but the existence of evil must be attributed to him, even though we cannot understand the logic behind God's actions. Whatever solution human thought adopts, the question of the divine and its relationship with evil remains shrouded in mystery.

Let us read, then, the fundamental passage dealing with the so-called doctrine of the two spirits by which all the angels are subordinated to two leaders, the prince of light and the prince of darkness.

> God created man to rule over the world and placed in him two spirits to accompany him until the time of his [God's] intervention. They are the spirits of good (*'mt*) and of evil (*'wl*).
>
> The generations of good are in a source of light and the generations of evil come from a source of darkness. Rule over all the children of righteousness is in the hands of the prince of light and they proceed along the ways of the light. Rule over the children of evil is completely in the hands of the angel of darkness, and they proceed along the ways of darkness. Because of the angel of darkness all the children of righteousness go astray [too] and all their sins...are in his domain, according to God's mysterious plan, until the pre-ordained time.

> All the misfortunes of men and the times of their anguish depend on
> the dominion of his [the angel of darkness'] persecution; all the spirits
> assigned to him have the role of making the children of the light waver.
> But the God of Israel and the angel of his truth aid the children of the
> light…
> God eternally loves one [spirit] and he is always pleased by his works;
> God hates the counsel and detests the ways of the other for eternity.
> These are their ways in the world… (1QS 3.17–4.2).

This passage is interesting because it points out that the Essenes were aware of the difficulties inherent in their system. If God created two clearly distinct and opposing sides, one under the protection of the angel of good and the other under the rule of the angel of evil, then as a result there should be two categories of men, the perfectly evil and the perfectly good. The fact of the matter is, though, that the angel of evil carries his attacks over into the opposing faction by making men sin. Each time that a man sins, in fact, it is because of the angel of evil, and man would be lost if he weren't protected by the angel of good and God's own intervention. After Qohelet, who had stated that there is no righteous man without sin (7.20), the problem of evil became more complicated, since the figure of the righteous man as one without sin disappeared. Sinners are no longer the only ones in need of redemption. The righteous need it as well, supposing that the term 'righteous' still means something. But we shall return to that question in Chapter 15 below.

Clearly, Essenic dualism is a peculiar dualism. It is not a metaphysical dualism, because no current of Judaism was more firm in maintaining that all things are derived from God. It cannot, however, in my opinion, be defined as a moral dualism either, since that sort of dualism is present in all forms of Judaism, and not only in Judaism: it is part of ethics in general. If we must find a label, then, we should choose something like 'dualism on the level of spirits', though I think the best solution would be to limit ourselves to simply calling it 'Essenic dualism'.

This is a profoundly pessimistic view of the world. This is not exclusive to Essenism, but rather is shared by more or less all of Jewish thought of the period, which was prevalently an apocalyptic type of thought. Evil dominates over good and, alone, humans have no means of salvation. One must wait for the measure and time of evil to run its course, because in the end God will intervene in favour of good and the good people. It should be no surprise that messianism regained vitality in this period, but that too is the stuff of a separate chapter.

The ideas expressed in the *Book of Watchers* parallel those of Essenism in its search for the origins of evil outside humans, substantially identifying evil with impurity (see Chapter 17). The two differ, however, on one fundamental point. For the *Book of Watchers* the world was not created by God as it is now, but was ruined after the creation by a freely deliberated rebellion of angels. Thus, for the *Book of Watchers*, the world is in some way different from the way God wanted it to be. The stars are not in their correct positions and they influence events on the earth in a different way than how God had planned. Faith and science (astrology) concord in this view of the world based on the idea that the world is bad, at least in part, and in any case it is different from the way God had envisioned it. Therefore, there are only remnants of God's cosmic order still in existence; the cosmic order is, in reality, disorder. For this reason the early Apocalyptic condemned all sciences, including astronomy (*1 En.* [*BW*] 8.3).

In an erratic mass within the *Book of Watchers* (ch. 8) the origin of evil is taken back to the unveiling of sciences to humans by an angel, naturally a rebel angel, a freely rebellious angel, Asael.[9] The sciences had been a heavenly secret not to be revealed to men, which again substantiates the underlying idea that the world as it is now is not the way God had planned it. It is understandable, then, how this erratic mass came to be included in the *Book of Watchers* even though it differs from the thought of the rest of the book. The underlying attitude of early Enochism, and ch. 8 of the *Book of Watchers* in particular, led to the condemnation of astronomy, which was later to become the basis of all knowledge for Enochism and the Apocalyptic. This shift had already come about with the *Book of Astronomy* and is only one of the radical changes that characterize the history of the Enochic tradition. Enoch is the man who lived 365 years, as many years as there are days in the solar year. The Enoch of the canonic book, who lived 365 years, is contemporary to a substantially later phase in Enochic thought than the one that condemned astronomy. This is an indication that the earliest Enochic traditions are early indeed, in fact they are quite ancient. It could be that we are dealing with the further development of the

---

9.   The name Asael is derived from the Aramaic fragments of Qumran. The Greek and Ethiopic texts read Azazel, the name of a demon in the Bible and therefore a *lectio facilior*. Anyhow, Deiana, has maintained the originality of Azazel with good arguments; see Deiana, 'Azazel in Lev. 16'.

creation story as told by the Jahwist, that the core of Adam and Eve's sin was knowledge of good and evil.

The idea that evil derives in some way from knowledge, which should be the exclusive prerogative of God, is taken up again in the *Book of Parables*, written toward the end of the first century BCE and now inserted into *1 Enoch*. In *1 En.* 69.9-11 the author says that the rebellious angel Penemu taught men how to write, obviously against God's wishes:

> therefore many have gone astray over the centuries up until today, because man was not created to confirm his faith in this way, with water, soot and pen. In fact men were created to be no other than like the angels, holy and righteous, and death, that destroys all things, would not touch them, but for this their knowledge, they will be destroyed...

It is interesting to note that among the evil sciences taught to humans by the rebellious angels, agriculture is never mentioned. The book of *Jubilees* (3.15) comes to our aid here. It states that God himself taught Adam this art. Behind this type of text, we seem to be able to make out a conservative agricultural world that saw the cause of much if not all evil in the development of culture and technology, a clear characteristic of the Hellenistic period.

3. *Man and Evil*

While the problem of evil, on a cosmic level, was presented in Enochism and in Essenism in the terms we have just seen, on an anthropological level it was experienced by humans in dramatic terms.

Whatever its origin and real essence, how does evil present itself before humans? What must humans do if they want to free themselves of evil, should that be possible, which is hated by God and is the source of all human suffering?

In this new vision of the universe the traditional answer to the problem is no longer satisfactory, even though there is documented evidence that that view continued to exist. Perhaps we should say that it no longer satisfied those who contemplated the world in light of the principles we have been discussing. The traditional answer can be seen in passages like the one quoted above from the *Testament of Levi*, where it says that the solution to the problem lies in better knowledge of God's Law. That view, however, assumes that the root of evil is the free will of humans who choose to either accept or to break a commandment.

This is a very old idea, but it hardly fits with the concept of knowledge as illumination or with the prevailing ideas of predeterminism.

The *Book of Parables* (*1 En.* [*BP*] 50.2), where it says that God's elect teach men 'to repent and renounce the works of their hands', sheds some light on the new positions concerning the problem of evil, not in its metaphysical dimensions, but as a daily reality in human life. The goal of 'doing penance' is not to return to the works of the Law, or at least the works of the Law are not seen as an ideal scheme to be followed. In order to be approved of by God we must do what we do *not* want to do. This is the meaning. The text does not mention the Law. Man must free himself of his own will in order to do God's will, because human will leads to perdition while God's leads to salvation. An analogous idea is to be found in CD 3.2: 'Abraham did not continue in the stubbornness of his heart and was considered a person who observed God's commandments with love, without following the impulses of his own spirit'.

That our daily decisions should not be made following the criterion of the Law, but rather in our adherence to God's plan is clearly illustrated in *Jub.* 12.19-21 as well. Abraham is uncertain whether he should return to Ur where he has been invited by the Chaldaeans. It is not a moral problem; Abraham, however, makes a religious question of it. 'May the right way in your eyes blossom in the hands of your servant, so that I may follow it without getting lost among the ravings of my heart...' Man's task is to realize God's plans; in this atmosphere 'doing the Law' is not sufficient for the religious consciousness.

An idea of this nature is the logical development of Qohelet's thought when he invites humankind to try to understand the 'work of God' (7.13).

The idea that whatever humans want is intrinsically bad is only barely hinted at in the passages of the books we have seen thus far, written by authors who more or less naively reflected the prevalent ideas of their times. Once again, though, it was the Essenes who sought to integrate the problem of evil thoroughly into their system of thought. Their conclusions are the same as those of the book of *Jubilees*, but with a great number of implications and the author's conclusions bear the mark of a radicalism that comes through long meditation and strong conviction.

The supreme goal of the righteous person, the highest level of initiate (the text speaks of the *maśkil*), is to do the will of God in every act.

He will do God's will in everything he undertakes and everything that
depends on him, as God has ordained. As for everything that happens to
him, he will find spontaneous joy in it and, beyond the will of God nothing will please him. He will pleasure in all the words of his mouth and
will not desire anything that he has not ordained, but rather will always
look to what God wants from him [moment after moment]... Even in
tribulation he will bless his creator (1QS 9.23-25).

Doing evil, therefore, for Essenism too means departing from what
God expects of one during the various moments of life. Observation of
the Law's commandments cannot and should not be sufficient for
humanity. God's will must be fully realized, as revealed, of course, to
those whom God has chosen. Anyone who acts according to his own
will can only sin, independently of the acceptability or not of his
actions according to the Law.

In order for this idea to be meaningful, there must be an intrinsically
bad principle in humanity that reveals itself in human actions, but that
is bad a priori, independently of those very actions. That principle is
humans themselves who, in the Essenic view of things, are nothing but
sin. Let us look at some passages that we believe were written by the
Teacher of Righteousness himself, and that illustrate Essenic thought
on this point.

> I am a creature of clay,
> fashioned with water,
> a foundation of shame, a source of impurity,
> a crucible of wickedness, a building of sin,
> a spirit of error and perversion,
> incapable of knowledge, fearful of righteous judgments...
> God of knowledge, to you all the works of righteousness
> and the mystery of truth belong, while the servitude of wickedness
> belongs to the sons of man... (1QH 1[9].21-27)

Humans, in and of themselves, are nothing but earth and water. Their
construction is sin itself identified with a perennial state of impurity,
where impurity is a fundamental characteristic of humanity's being.
Until this point, the Jewish tradition, in keeping with the Priestly line of
thought (Lev. 10.10), had always insisted on the need of distinguishing
pure things from impure ones. Things like blood and sex could contaminate humanity, but the idea that humans were inherently impure
had never been formulated. This idea represents a coherent development of Job's idea, mentioned above, that his weakness was nothing
other than the impurity ingrained in human nature (see Chapter 6, §7).

While on the one hand all purity and righteousness must belong to God, on the other all impurity and sin must belong to humankind.

> Man is in sin (*'awon*) from when he is in the womb
> and until old age he is in guilty iniquity.
> I know that righteousness does not belong to man, nor does the perfect
>   way belong to the son of man.
> All works of righteousness belong to the most high God,
> while the way of man is not firm,
> save through the spirit that God created for him (1QH 4[12].29-31)

Sin, evil, is ingrained in humankind, it is part of their very nature and makes them impure even before they are born. Humanity's sole hope is in divine intervention, even an exceptional act of intervention, modifying the situation by which humans would otherwise be destined to remain in God's hatred. In Essenism (and perhaps in Judaism in general) we must distinguish between *het* and *'awon*. Both words can mean sin, but while *het* contains the idea of transgression, *'awon* holds more the idea of something negative which is linked to sin/transgression without coinciding with it (see Chapter 17). In Essenism *'awon* can exist even before the conscience is formed and even be present in the individual still in the mother's womb. *'awon* is the evil aspect of impurity, or, to borrow a term from the language of computers, it is impurity's interface with sin. The concept is very similar to that of original sin; it is sin lying at the origin.

This intuition regarding the ontological nature of human impurity has a profound effect on Jewish ideology. There are, in fact, many consequences. The profane (*hol*), the most authentic essence of humanity, that which had allowed Abraham to speak freely with God while maintaining his own spiritual autonomy and freedom of choice (Gen. 18.22-33), no longer has sense. The profane has been equated with the impure and humans must no longer follow their own will, which could only lead them to sin. Humans must in some way empty themselves out, renounce themselves in order to do only the works of God, the only righteous ones.

In this way the traditional Jewish world was completely turned upside down. When the Priestly Tradition gathered the material for Leviticus, it established the parallel sacred/profane–impure/pure. It was the sacred things, the things of God, that were impure for humanity, while the things that humans could use were pure, because in some way they were theirs. Now the sacred has become the *locus* of the pure and the profane that of the impure. Thus the very nature of traditional Judaism was completely transformed. Everyone is a sinner, even the Essenic teacher who wrote the following lines; he saw nothing in himself as a human being that was better than other men:

> I belong to the wicked humanity,
> the assembly of the wicked.
> My failings, my transgressions and my sins,
> together with the perversity of my heart,
> belong to the assembly of worms [i.e. impure]
> and to those who walk in darkness (1QS 11.9-10).

However, once he has confessed his unworthiness, he attributes it to a sort of cosmic fatalism. It is part of a drama that involves him in exactly the same way that it involves all living beings, but it is neither the product of his will nor of that of other men.

> By way of His knowledge all things come into existence.
> All that exists, He has made to exist through His thought.
> Nothing is done without Him (1QS 11.11).

During the first century CE the question of evil and of sin with all of its inevitable consequences was very much alive in Israel, augmented by the country's tragic situation. The figure of John the Baptist is typical; he addressed himself to all Jews indiscriminately because he believed that they were all sinners. He knows that everyone breaks the commandments and that this is a drama because, if everyone sins, then Israel's punishment will be great. He does not seem to pay attention to the specific norms. He clearly refers simply to a commonly recognized sense of morality, giving generic practical advice such as, 'Whoever has two coats must share with anyone who has none' (Lk. 3.11), addressed especially to cases that must have seemed dubious in the eyes of common opinion, such as that of the soldier and the tax-collector (Lk. 3.12-14). The only obstacle between humankind and salvation was 'sin'. It was necessary for everyone to do penance, but even that was not enough. The repentant sinners would also have to purify themselves through a lustral bath, baptism, in order to remove something negative that lingered even after repentance. This is an interpretation of the Essenic idea of *'awon*. Sin left something behind, a particular kind of impurity that had to be removed. His work was an extreme attempt at 'forgiveness of sins', because the one who had to come would soon arrive, eliminating sin by uprooting the sinner: 'Even now the axe is lying at the root' (Mt. 3.10 and Lk. 3.9). There is an impressive vividness in the consciousness of catastrophe. The entire world is submerged in evil and seems to await salvation through divine intervention. And according to an idea common to the period, which we call apocalyptic, that intervention would essentially be destructive. As for himself, John decided to live as much as possible away from society, in a life of absolute purity.[10]

I feel that in order to understand Jesus of Nazareth in relation to this question, we must view him in the same manner as John, without, however, underestimating the differences between the two. It is the starting point that is the same: the universality of sin and the problems that depend of this state of things. Jesus refused isolation and did not wait for the sinners to come to him, but rather he went looking for them. He also did not place the same emphasis on impurity that John had, or at any rate he reinterprets the values attached to impurity (Mk 7). Jesus, unlike John, did not believe in an Israel capable of saving itself by not sinning, but rather he believed in an Israel capable of saving itself through its ability to forgive: 'the measure you give will be the measure you get' (Mk 4.24; a theme which is particularly developed in Matthew). God's kingdom is compared to a mustard seed; it already exists at the time of his preachings and is destined to grow more and more, irresistably, finally becoming a refuge for the birds of the heavens (Mk 4.30-32). But not even the advent of God's kingdom in history would be enough, sin had to be expiated in all of its aspects; the relationship with God (the Covenant) had to be renewed. This seems to me to be the sense of Jesus' life, the true generative idea of the thought behind his actions.

It could be pointed out (and it is an idea that I agree with completely) that the very idea that humankind saves itself is alien to Christianity; for Christianity man does not save himself, but rather he is saved. Still, the rule that 'the measure you give will be the measure you get' means exactly what it says and this idea of the need to forgive in function of salvation is the single most characteristic idea of Christianity. Given Jesus' discourse on forgiveness, which I believe is authentic, then the problem of forgiveness as a function of salvation is resolved on the level of human behaviour. It is true that humans are saved, but they are

10. See E. Lupieri, *Giovanni Battista nelle tradizioni sinottiche* (Brescia: Paideia, 1988), pp. 78-79. See Josephus, *Ant.* 18.117, excellently translated and commentated in E. Lupieri, *Giovanni Battista fra storia e leggenda* (Brescia: Paideia, 1988), pp. 121-24.

also required to respect a moral code that is more rigid than that of the scribes and Pharisees. James would later write, 'For judgment will be without mercy to anyone who has shown no mercy; mercy triumphs over [that is, is superior to] judgment' (Jas 2.13). The commandment to love one another, which must include forgiveness, is clear in John too, while love of one's fellow man and love of God are the same thing (1 Jn 2.3-5 and elsewhere). This love, however, does not eliminate sin from the Christian community. If nothing else, forgiveness of sins pre-supposes the existence of sin to be forgiven, and for this sin we have an advocate in Jesus Christ (1 Jn 2.1). Every Jewish current, including Christianity, tends to split. There were several ways of being a Pharisee, but also several ways of being a Christian. For all Christians salvation from sin comes from Jesus, but this does not subtract humankind from the responsibility of certain rules of conduct. Even Paul, who among the first Christians had the most severe words against the Law (as a function of salvation), protested against those who interpreted his teachings as a licence to sin (Rom. 3.8). The Christian authors can emphasize one point or another, but the fact remains that in the end the Christians in general believed more in a society where single individuals were willing to forgive one another, rather than a society where everyone followed the rules. For Jesus, even God's forgiveness and that of the Son of Man are gratuitous (see Mk 2.10), though humans are required to love their neighbour. These two fundamental ideas are not easy to fit together rationally, but they lie at the basis of all Christianity. The Gospels announce God's grace to all humans inasmuch as all humans are sinners. This is followed by the inevitable request for adequate 'good works' on the level of the individual's beha-viour. Regarding this point, the parable of the unforgiving slave in Mt. 18.23-35 is exemplary.

4. *Evil as a Will to Evil: The Devil*

Until now we have dealt with evil as transgression, or as a thing. Now, however, we shall examine it under a more disquieting light. We have already seen that in ancient Judaism the idea that there was an in-between world had developed, a world between that of humans and the divine sphere, a world populated by angels capable of influencing the course of earthly events. We have also seen that the *Book of Watchers* attributed the evil on earth to the fact that nature had been ruined at the beginning of time by a group of rebellious angels. Reflection within Judaism on the question of a rebellion among the angels continued until it arrived at the solution that the rebellion was caused by a chief angel, who was identified with the principle of evil. Under whatever name, we can easily call this angel the devil, in other words a being created as a spirit, possessing intelligence, will and consciousness, who in a specific moment rebelled against God's order and against God himself.

The figure of the devil was born in Judaism during the period when its hereditary tradition was being organized into a rigidly monotheistic religion. Prior to the exile the Jews had only been monolatric, if not polytheistic.

The figure of the devil has two fundamental characteristics during the period of the Second Temple. (1) The devil can be the principle of evil and his existence explains the origin of evil, its ἀρχή, but he is not active. In this case the devil is merely the first cause of the fact that nature has been subverted. (2) The devil can be considered as a continually active will at work in history, continually rebelling against God and harmful to humans. We shall see how the two basic conceptions can be combined or, in some authors, fade into one another to the point of creating a sort of relationship of collaboration between God and the devil. The existence of one of God's angels called satan, which is rare in the non-canonical texts,[11] contributed to this conception of the devil.

We first find a figure that in some way corresponds to our definition of the devil in the *Book of Watchers* (see Chapter 6, §4, pp. 174-80). Going against the divine plan, by which the angels were to be purely spiritual beings, a group of angels descended to the earth in order to marry women (*1 En.* [*BW*] 15.6). These angels, who with this action contaminated nature, had a chief named Asael, or Semeyaza. This chief could be the first sketch of the devil figure, and I say sketch because the myth insists on the shared responsibility of the rebellion lying at the basis of the contamination of nature. This event took place a few generations before the flood. Later, as we have already mentioned, the angels' sin was transported back in time to the creation and the sin of the seven stars, that is the angels assigned to the seven planets that rotate around the earth. The shared responsibility is even more marked here than in the first myth, because no chief is ever mentioned for the seven angels.

11. The non-canonical *Book of Parables* mentions a whole array of satanic angels whose duty it is to refer men's sins to God (*1 En.* 40.7).

The myth narrates that God enchained the rebellious angels in the darkness of the mythical desert of Dudael. He then saw to it that the *nephilim*, the offspring of the angels' union with women, destroyed one another in fratricidal conflict. Unfortunately, he could do nothing against their immortal souls. The *nephilim* disappeared from the earth, but their souls continued to wander, doing evil to men and pushing men to rebel against God. The origin and nature of evil spirits, common stock of all religions, was explained in this way, but the devil remained in the shadows. Evil among men was derived exclusively from the contamination of nature and from the disorganized presence in the world of evil spirits.[12]

The author of this text had formulated a complex philosophy aimed at providing a rational structural unity to all the information provided by his tradition and which, for certain aspects, his experience confirmed. On the other hand, he was trying to overcome certain aporias that were also present in the tradition. According to the text of the first chapter of Genesis, which I believe was composed in the priestly circle of Ezekiel (c. sixth century BCE), God created Light on the first day to counterbalance the Darkness, which already existed. In this way God's goodness was safeguarded, but something was left out of the creation. Another prophet, Deutero-Isaiah (late sixth century BCE) sought to remedy the situation by saying that God was the creator of both Light and Darkness (Isa. 45.7). In this way the unity of all creation was saved, but another problem was opened, that of God as creator of Darkness, a vague principle of evil.

In the solution proposed by the author of the *Book of Watchers* all of creation was good, and evil in a concrete sense was not a product of nature as created, but rather of nature ruined. In this way, of course, impurity took on decidedly negative connotations, since it was the consequence of the angels' sin. The author of the *Book of Watchers* thus aligns himself with the Jahwist tradition, which had always conceived of impurity as evil. The serpent that had tempted Eve was condemned to slither, that is, it had been an animal with four legs and it was condemned to become a snake, the most impure of all animals. This view was opposed to the Priestly Tradition that provocatively claimed that even reptiles had been created in their present form by God and after

---

12. Beyond the evil spirits that wandered the earth, like the *šēdim*, the *s^eîrîm* and Lilith, the feminine demon of the night, the Jews also believed in cosmic monsters like Yam, Leviathan and Behemoth.

having created them God saw that it was good (Gen. 1.24).

Another problem was that of the ancient belief in the existence of evil spirits. Like the gods, they seem to lie outside the sphere of Yhwh, but this was an idea that did not fit well with absolute monotheism. Ezekiel and the Priestly Tradition were truly embarrassed by this problem and they resolved it by prohibiting contacts with these spirits. The sorcerer was to be punished,[13] but with this solution the existence of evil spirits was confirmed.

The author of the *Book of Watchers* found a solution for this problem as well. The evil spirits were the souls of the *nephilim*; God had nothing to do with their creation.

The author of the *Book of Watchers* directs his thought toward a search for the ἀρχή, the past principle capable of explaining the present reality. Even the devil is part of this general scheme. In a certain sense, for the man of his day this devil is a distant reality, almost a metaphysical one, more or less like the water of Thales. In fact, the devil no longer acts in history, because he is closed up in hellish Darkness, bound there in eternal punishment by God. The consequences of his actions, however, impurity and evil spirits, remain in history. Thus, all reality is created, but evil does not in any way proceed from God. Furthermore, the solution based on the sin of the seven stars had the advantage of linking the problem of evil to contemporary science, astrology. The presence of negative influence coming from the stars, which did not fit well with the goodness of creation, could thus be explained perfectly.

We mentioned that in early Enochism the devil is not active. He is a principle of evil, but on earth only the band of evil spirits acts and they are inferior to the angels (since they are the offspring of angels and human women) and in any case they can be exorcised.

The situation changed around 160 BCE with the *Book of Dreams*. The author of the *Book of Dreams* was aware of the story of the fallen angels, but he felt that it could not explain the entity of the disasters that beset Israel in the second century BCE. The fallen angels were a distant ἀρχή and the evil spirits must have seemed too weak to offer any kind of explanation. Furthermore, the Israel of the exile had interpreted its history as being marked by God's punishment of an unfaithful people.

---

13. See Lev. 19.26b: 'You shall not practise augury or witchcraft'; 19.31: 'Do not turn to mediums or wizards; do not seek them out, to be defiled by them'. See also Lev. 20.6.

During the second century BCE Israel, or at least many Jews, did not see themselves as wicked, or at any rate not as any more wicked than their neighbours. There was a historical and political disaster to be explained, and that disaster seemed to have been caused by some higher order and not from the fault of Israel.[14]

Thus a new rebellion of angels was introduced, called the 'rebellion of the seventy shepherd angels'. They were 70 angels that God had assigned to protecting and punishing Israel after the exile (*1 En.* [*BD*] 89.59-65), but they abused their power, tormenting Israel. Behind the misfortune a powerful and malicious will can be seen ever more clearly. It is not just the wandering evil spirits who are assaulting Israel, it is something much more powerful. The time is ripe for developing and organizing thought concerning the great enemy.

The *Book of Dreams* tells the myth of the fallen angels in symbolic terms, but it adds that one angel had come to the earth *before* the others. Thus the first rebellion was perpetrated by a single angel; the figure of the devil begins to take shape. Nothing else is said of the first angel to fall to earth, though, except that he lived among the humans.

The story of the origins of humanity as told by the author of the *Book of Dreams* is so different from the one we know from the Genesis tradition that it can be difficult to understand. The author uses a metaphorical language that is clear only when he refers to things that we know from other sources.

In an early vision (*1 En.* [*BD*] 85) the author presents Adam and Eve coming out of the earth, followed immediately by their two sons, Cain and Abel. Adam is presented as a righteous man. This version of the creation leaves no room for the Garden of Eden. The devil appears in a later vision (*1 En.* [*BD*] 86) or in a later phase of the first vision, at any

14. While the Jewish tradition up to Deutero-Isaiah concords in considering Israel guilty and the exile as its punishment (see Ezekiel 20 and the whole historio-graphical conception of R1), later tradition tends to see Israel as unjustly persecuted (see Joel 3.19, where Judah is referred to as 'innocent blood', that is it has been unjustly made the victim of violence; see Garbini, *Storia e ideologia*, p. 158. The origins of such persecution can be seen in the mystery of God's will and Israel can be made to coincide with the suffering Servant (see the ancient gloss of the Hebrew text that adds the word 'Israel' to 'Servant' in Isa. 49.3). See also Ps. 44, certainly postexilic and probably quite late. Once again 4E, after the destruction of the temple and the ruin of 70 CE, does not modify this schema; Israel is more righteous than Babylon yet God has borne with those who sin, spared the wicked and destroyed his people (4E 3.28-33).

rate the *incipit* is clear. The devil mingles with Adam's sons, who by now are quite numerous, and lives among them, even though we are not told how the devil appeared. He was, therefore, on the earth with Cain and Abel. We can suppose that the devil had a hand in Abel's tragic end, but the text does not explicitly state this.[15]

The author then substantially repeats the myth of the fall as in the *Book of Watchers*, including the fact that the devil was placed in a sort of cosmic prison with the fallen angels. The doctrine does not seem to differ on this point, even though it is difficult to take a strong position, since the author bases his work on origin myths that do not coincide with the ones we know. In any case the devil is an inactive devil.

The book of *Jubilees* (a late second century BCE work which takes up positions similar to those of the Essenes) presents a clear evolution of thought regarding the devil. The author repeats the myth of the fall of angels during the time of Yared, though no particular mention is made of a leader. The inactive devil of early Enochism does not interest the author, who emphasizes the idea that nature was contaminated by the angelic sin. He tells how the fallen angels were imprisoned, how the *nephilim* were killed 'and bound [their souls] in the depths of the earth' (*Jub.* 5.6). Nature was renewed (5.11). The evil spirits had disappeared from the earth. The new creation was placed in the hands of the new humanity that had survived the flood (*Jub.* 5.14). After the flood, though, the souls of the *nephilim* returned as evil spirits to create turmoil among men (*Jub.* 10.1). Up to this point there is not much new compared to early Enochic thought.

Now we come to the new part. Noah saw that the works of the *nephilim* could constitute a mortal danger for his house and asked God to keep them closed up 'in the place of hellish punishment' (*Jub.* 10.5). God gave the order to his angels to bind all the evil spirits (*Jub.* 10.7), but at this point 'Mastema, messenger of the spirits' arrived at the heavenly court and on behalf of a third party makes a strange request of God. 'Lord and creator, leave some of them before me that they shall do what I tell them, because, if I am left with none of them I cannot use the power of my will in the sons of man' (*Jub.* 10.8). God then decided

---

15. Since the myth of Eden is lacking in *BD*, the devil can in no way be identified with the serpent. He descends to earth and mingles with the humans. Cain is presented as having been born a black calf, that is violent and evil, and seems to have been so from his very birth. The relationship between Cain's sin and the devil is therefore not clear.

to lock up nine tenths of the evil spirits in hell and to leave one tenth at the orders of the figure for whom Mastema acts as messenger. That figure's name appears shortly thereafter in the text: Satan.

From metaphysical principle of evil the devil has become the chief of a sort of kingdom parallel to and opposed to the kingdom of God, and to whom God himself assigns the souls of the *nephilim*, the evil spirits, as subjects. The kingdom of evil has been unified and made humanity's contemporary. Humankind is no longer surrounded by bands of evil spirits acting independently, but rather by an organized kingdom opposed to God. Somehow, though, this realm is subordinate to God if the devil is reduced to begging that not all the demons be locked away underground. It even seems that God is concerned that the devil exercise some power. In effect, this myth seems to take the problem of the relationship between God and evil, a relationship that is imagined similar to that of the oldest Jewish tradition, back to when there was no hesitation about saying that some evils came from God.

Again, in the book of *Jubilees* God uses Mastema against men, against the Egyptians for example; Mastema is a sort of rabid dog. After having struck the Egyptians he would have smitten the Jews who had escaped from slavery as well, if the angels of God had not arrived and bound him, avoiding a massacre. The example is grotesque, but the underlying problem is clear; while early Enochism had resolved the problem of God's relationship with evil by completely separating the two, now the two tend to blend together.

Thus we have met the name of Satan as the name of the devil for the first time, at the head of an evil kingdom. The name of 'satan' comes from circles that had adopted less drastic solutions to the problem of evil than early Enochism. The satan (with a small 's') was an angel at the heavenly court who had the job of referring human sins to God. 'Satan' means enemy, with very strong connotations. As a technical term it probably meant the prosecutor in trials.

This satan angel appears for the first time in Zech. 3.2, toward the end of the sixth century BCE, at the beginning of the Persian period. It is the angel that accuses the high priest Joshua before God. From the narration it is clear that the satan has a precise task which he carries out with a spirit of personal initiative. This task, then, brings him into conflict with the work of other angels. Within the limits of his attributes, he is free, he enjoys freedom of the will.

His working autonomy is even more clear in the book of Job; he discusses the problem of justice with God and it is he who proposes that Job be put to the test. Within the limits of God's authorization it is he who decides how to strike Job. Even though he is one of God's angels, he is seen to act with a fair amount of freedom and always against humans.

Toward the end of the Persian period his figure reappears in 1 Chron. 21.1, where 'satan' has become a proper name. The article has been dropped and he has become Satan with a capital 'S'. A comparison between the text as it appears in the Chronicles and its source in the books of Samuel (2 Sam. 24.1) shows us just which problems led some Jews to use this figure. In the older text, that of the source, we read, 'Again the anger of Yhwh was kindled against Israel...', in a context where no motivation for God's anger is given. Apparently the idea that God could get angry with no apparent reason and put sinful ideas into someone's heart (in this case David's) must have been repugnant to the religious sensibilities of the fourth century BCE. The Chronicler's text becomes, 'Satan stood up against Israel...'

Without the comparison to its source, the text in Chronicles would seem to refer to the devil. In comparison to the source, though, we see that it was simply a way of expressing an embarrassing idea, that God could desire someone's harm, just as in the most ancient tradition. In any case, in this book Satan is an ambiguous figure, because it is not clear just how much freedom of action he has at the heavenly court and up to just what point he can harm humankind. In this way the satan and the devil (whether Asael or Semeyaza) grow strangely closer until, as we have seen, Satan becomes without a doubt the name of the devil in the book of *Jubilees*. He no longer belongs to the heavenly court, but is ruler of his own kingdom.

The striking thing is that no mention is ever made of his nature or of his history. He is not a fallen angel. As we shall see below, in another text, the *Book of Parables*, Satan appears as unjudged and unjudgable.

During the first half of the second century BCE, when the author of the *Book of Dreams* was developing his ideas about the devil, it must have seemed a commonplace to attribute humanity's worst inclinations to him. Ben Sira provides us with proof of this when he provocatively says that, 'When an ungodly person curses the satan,[16] he curses him-

---

16. Given the use of the article before the name, it is not clear just how Ben Sira conceived of Satan. Was he an angel of the Lord, or a rebel? The problem remains open, much like the case of the book of Chronicles. In any case he incited men to

self'. For Ben Sira then, the devil does not exist; Satan is only a metaphor for our worst instincts (Sir. 21.27).

Essenism's conception of the devil was coherent with the general outline of Essenic thought. If God is omnipotent to the point that he has even predetermined the words that will come from the mouths of men (1QH 1[9].29), then he must have also determined the actions of the angels. In the very beginning God created two spirits, two angelic beings, one of whom he placed in charge of the Light, and the other in charge of Darkness (1QS 3.17-19), one to be loved and one to be hated (1QS 3.26–4.1). This prince of Darkness is yet another interpretation of the devil. This time, though, he has been created by God and given power over all those whom God assigns him, both spirits and men.

With the book of Wisdom (end of the first century BCE) the devil goes back to being the ἀρχή of evil, and of death in particular. But this is a different devil than the early Enochic one. This figure does not coincide with the leader of the fallen angels, but with the serpent of Genesis, even though the serpent is never mentioned. Anyhow, the statement that God did not create death (Wis. 1.14) and that it came into the world because of the devil (Wis. 2.24) can only be explained in reference to the story of Eden and Adam's disobedience.

The problem of Adam's sin, which was to assume so much importance in Paul's thought, thus appears for the first time in Jewish thought,[17] even though not in an explicit fashion since Adam is not even mentioned. It is precisely the introduction of Adam's sin, though, that reduces the devil's importance as tempter. In effect, the book of Wisdom never presents the devil in that light. He is the cause of death, the supreme evil. Sin, on the other hand, comes from the human soul's 'distorted reasoning', and carries humankind away from God (Wis. 1.3).

In the *Testaments of the Twelve Patriarchs* the devil is presented as malicious activity, especially if read in the first-century BCE edition. In *T. Reub.* 2.2 we read that the devil places seven spirits into man at birth, and these spirits lay at the root of 'the deeds of youth'. 'When a soul is continually perturbed, the Lord withdraws from it and Beliar [a name of the Devil] rules it' (*T. Dan* 4.7). Here, the devil lives in very close contact with man, he even enters into man. It is the devil that has given

do evil and was closer to 'Satan' than to 'the satan'. The problem is hardly important, though, because Ben Sira did not believe in the existence of this S/satan.

17. In Ben Sira the sin was not Adam's, but Eve's (Sir. 25.24).

man his every bad instinct, and it is he that enters into the individual who has lost his internal equilibrium, his serenity.

Earlier ambiguities about the relationship between God and the tempter are resolved; there is a sharp line dividing good and evil. The devil is completely extraneous to God, his will is hostile to God. 'You must take hold of God's will and refuse that of Belial' (*T. Naph.* 3.1). 'God is in the light; while Beliar is in the Darkness' (*T. Jos.* 7.20). The two kingdoms occupy two separate and distinct places. Perhaps it is even better to say two opposite more than separate places. The dominion of the two kingdoms and the struggle between them extends even to within humankind.

In the *Book of Parables* the conception of the devil is extremely complex and probably not unitary, since it at times follows other sources too closely. I will limit myself to examining a passage that was definitely written by the book's author. In ch. 54 he tells of a vision in which he saw the chains prepared for Azazel,[18] the chief of the fallen angels. Therefore, for our author the leader of the fallen angels has not yet been enchained. He is not an inactive devil, but one still at work, still at the head of the rank and file that will follow him into eternal damnation. There are no longer any evil spirits to be distinguished from the fallen angels. The demons are all of the same type, fallen angels. The devil's power has been increased.

The striking element here is the way in which the author presents the fallen angels' transgression. They are guilty of being Satan's servants and of having induced men into sinning (*1 En.* [*BP*] 54.6). Thus Azazel sinned inasmuch as he served Satan, who, therefore, already existed. As in the book of *Jubilees* nothing is said of Satan's origin.

And while two passages speak of Azazel's future punishment, which is certain, there is no mention of Satan being judged. This could hardly be an omission (see chs. 54 and 55.4). Just who is this Satan that lives beyond judgment, but who causes the ruin of anyone, human or angel, that follows him?

The devil is mentioned again in ch. 69 in a passage that does not belong to the original author. Here, however, it is interesting to note that the creation of the devil (here given a name that does not appear anywhere else, Yequn) has been pushed back in time to before the crea-

18. Azazel is the same as Asael in the Aramaic text of *BW*. In the Greek and Ethiopic texts the name always appears as Azazel. We have no fragments of *BP* in their original language.

tion of humanity. Eve's tempter was not the first sinner, but the third, named Gadriel. The serpent in Eden is clearly interpreted as a devil figure, or as a devil.

Leafing through the texts mentioned so far, then, there is a problem that comes up from time to time, especially in the book of *Jubilees*, namely the relationship between God and the devil. We have already seen that in the book of *Jubilees*, from the late second century BCE, God had shown some interest in Satan's ability to do his job properly. Therefore, the work of the devil could in some way be part of God's plan; there was some form of collaboration between the two that went beyond God's mere tolerance of the devil's actions and existence.

This vision of the devil is developed further in the *Testament of Job*, a work datable to the first century CE. Here the devil, who is referred to both as 'the devil' and as Satan, seems to be more humanity's antagonist than God's. He is 'he who deceives human nature' (3.3), in the sense that he 'tries to deceive'. As a tempter his freedom of action is limited only by human conscience, but if Satan wants to materially attack someone, he must ask God's permission (ch. 8), therefore becoming to some extent God's instrument and collaborator, similar to the satan in the canonical book of Job.

Ancient Israel, before the exile, had not hesitated to attribute all misfortunes to God (a trait still present in Deutero-Isaiah—45.7). The preferred formula by the first century BCE seems to have been 'diabolic action, divine authorization'. The two figures of God and the devil are strangely close; the devil must speak with God if he wants to carry out certain actions. It is no surprise then, that for the author humanity's greatest virtue is patience. Ben Sira, who did not believe in the devil, said that only he who has been put to the test by God could truly be called righteous: 'For gold is tested in the fire, and those found acceptable, in the furnace of humiliation' (Sir. 2.5). For Ben Sira, God could put humanity to the test without using Satan, or, as in the *Testament of Job*, without Satan's initiative.

The New Testament, too, presents a variety of versions of the devil, ranging from Jesus' tempter to Peter's raging lion that roams around us (1 Pet. 5.8) and John's first sinner (1 Jn 3.8), the cause of the terrible cosmic drama that is still with us. Again in the New Testament, in Paul, we can also find Adam's sin in the place of Satan's, with exactly the same role.

Devil and demons suddenly disappear from Jewish writings at the end of the first century CE. There are three great and extremely broad texts from this period: the Syriac *Apocalypse of Baruch*, *4 Ezra* and *2 (Slavonic) Enoch* (the oldest redaction, the so-called B or shorter recension, is from before 70 CE). The devil is not mentioned in any of these, even though the story of the fall is mentioned. In the Syriac *Apocalypse of Baruch* (56.10-13) the fall of the angels is seen as a consequence of Adam's example (therefore Adam's sin involves the angels and not vice versa!) and in *2 (Slavonic) Enoch* (7.1-3) the apostate angels stand silent and powerless in the second heaven, awaiting judgment. In this case a decision regarding their final judgment does not seem to have been reached yet. In the Syriac *Apocalypse of Baruch* and in *4 Ezra*, as in Paul, Adam's sin completely substitutes Satan's.

The devil's eclipse was not destined to last, though. A later version of *2 (Slavonic) Enoch* (the so-called A or longer recension), written a few centuries later, dedicates plenty of room to speculation on Satan.

In Middle Judaism humans experience the devil as both an external and an internal force. The devil in Middle Judaism is not 'that part of the whole called Darkness',[19] to use Goethe's words, nor is he Death, or Evil, of the ancient Canaanite myths.[20] The devil explains the continued existence of evil, which is always out of place, so to speak, because it is the force opposing cosmic order which cannot in any way be integrated into a reassuring structure of creation, such as that of Saint Augustine, for whom evil is 'non being', or Idealism where it is only a moment (antithesis) of the joyous synthesis.

19. 'Ich bin ein Teil des Teils, der Anfangs Alles War—Ein Teil der Finsternis, die sich das Licht gebar' (*Faust*, vv. 1349-50).

20. See the 'Myth of Baal and Death', published with other myths in C. Kappler, *Apocalypses et voyages dans l'au-delà* (Paris: Cerf, 1987).

Chapter 13

SALVATION

1. *General Observations*

For pre-exilic Hebraism salvation always and only regarded this world. During the period of ancient Judaism the *Book of Watchers* widened human destiny to beyond the grave. His soul was to be judged by God and, depending on the verdict, would be allowed to live eternally near him (the first delineation of Paradise), or would be chased into a place of torment, hell.

Apart from the *Book of Watchers* and the problems raised in Job, before Qohelet Judaism had always seen righteousness, 'doing the Law', as the only road to salvation. And salvation always meant 'salvation in this world'. During Qohelet's time ideas concerning the possibility of life after death must have been fairly widespread in Israel, since he firmly rejected them (Qoh. 3.18-20). In the following century the idea of life after death took root in at least a few circles where not only was the immortality of the soul affirmed, but even the idea of resurrection.[1]

Belief in life after death is clearly confirmed in the second century BCE in 2 Maccabees, even though it seems to be an exceptional fact, reserved for those who lose their life in order to avoid breaking the Law, and not necessarily as a generic reward for the righteous.

I shall return to the question of resurrection and the immortality of

---

1. It is well known that this idea is present in Dan. 12.2 and in 2 Macc. 7.9. Immortality of the soul is also clearly stated in the book of Wisdom (3.4). The Essenes believed in the immortality of the soul as well. While there are no clear statements to this effect in their texts, indirect sources bear witness to it along with the probable interpretation of some of their texts. The Essene, in fact, saw himself in a certain sense as already part of the angelic world and he therefore did not dwell too much on death as the starting point of the life of the disembodied soul. See pp. 374-75.

the soul in Chapter 16, but for now I would like to emphasize how belief that life continues after death brings about a sort of swelling of the idea of salvation. In the same way the view of the world that was growing predominant in the second century BCE, based on the idea of knowledge as revelation or illumination and of history as the field in which God's eternal will unfolds, must have brought about a different view of salvation. This new vision of salvation is particularly clear in Essenism where it is possible to grasp the close relationship running between the new view of salvation and illumination and all of its consequences.

Before examining the Essenic conception of salvation, though, let us look at the means of salvation available to the Essene.

2. *Salvation and Purification*

Since for the Essene evil is impurity, in the broadest sense of the term, it is no surprise that the road to salvation was first of all the road to purification. The only problem was that the means of purification necessary for cleansing humans of their very nature, which was impure, was not to be found among any of Judaism's traditional views on purification. Not even all the waters of the seas and rivers can purify humans of their nature. The only road to this fundamental purification lay in accepting the teachings of the Teacher of Righteousness and joining his sect, *separating oneself* from all other men, both pagans and Jews (on the need for separation see Chapter 17). Only in this way was it possible to eliminate the ontological impurity innate in human beings that impedes all contact between humans and God, all prayer, all salvation. In this way the purification deriving from adhesion to the sect was an individual's true act of salvation.

The following passage is taken from 1QS 2.25–3.9. Here I propose only the most important points:

> Everyone who refuses to enter [the Covenant of G]od, walking in the stubbornness of his heart, will not [be admitted to the Com]unity of His Truth, because he has despised the instructions about knowledge of the righteous precepts; he has not had the strength to change his life. [For this reason] he cannot be counted among the righteous...he cannot be justified for the excessive stubbornness of his heart, inasmuch as he looks towards darkness as the ways of the light... He will not be purified by atonement; he will not be cleansed by waters of purification; he will not be made sacred [by this point the word has become synonym of 'pure

inasmuch as belonging to God, holy']² by the [water of the] seas, nor by that of the rivers; he will not be made pure by the waters of ablution. He who refuses God's statutes without letting himself be taught in the Community of His Assembly shall remain completely impure for all time.

In fact, it is through the spirit of the Assembly of God's Truth that all man's actions are atoned, all of his iniquities (*'āwôn*), so that he can contemplate the Light of Life. Through the holy spirit of the Community [founded] on His Truth he is purified of all his iniquities. His sin (*ḥeṭ*) will be atoned in a spirit of uprightness and humility; with the humility of his soul before all of God's commandments his body will be purified, when it is aspersed with water of purification and made holy with the water of contrition.

Only adhesion to the sect and the will of God manifested through the sect's teachers can purify humans of their ontological impurity, but this does not mean that they lose their ability to sin. The angels of Darkness constantly tempt the children of the Light in order to lure them into sin. At this point, it is difficult to establish precisely what the sect's doctrine was, since, from our point of view, it does not seem coherent, but that could depend on the fact that we do not know how they classified sins. It is even more likely that the idea of righteousness was undergoing a change in all of Judaism, in the wake of the spread of Qohelet's notion that there is no righteous man without sin (7.20).

In fact, on the one hand, we find that anyone sinning against the Law or against the sect's own norms was severely punished and readmitted to the Community only after having expiated the consequent punishment. On the other hand, certain expressions lead us to believe that God justified the sect's members not only in regard to what we have defined as ontological sin, *'āwôn*, but also in regard to the *ḥēṭ*.

Anyone who sinned was separated from the sect. The following are some of the norms taken from the *Community Rule*:

These are the norms by which the men of [the] perfect holiness must behave toward one another: all of those who enter into the holy Assembly and walk along the perfect way as He has ordained,—anyone breaking any single one of the commandments of the Torah of Moses, whether willingly or through laxity, shall be expelled from the Assembly of the Community and shall not be readmitted. No one of the holy men is

2.   'holy': the underlying Hebrew word is always *qadoš*, which up until this point we have translated with 'sacred', but from this historical moment onwards the use of the Hebrew term broadens to include concepts that in modern English require translation as 'holy'.

to have relations of any sort with him in questions regarding his property or his counsel—with no exceptions. But if he has acted unknowingly, then he must [only] be separated from the purity and the Assembly. This norm is to be applied: for two years he shall judge no one and his counsel shall not be asked. If his behaviour should be perfect, he will be readmitted to his dwelling, to study and to the Assembly [ac]cording to the vi[ews] of the *rabbim* ['the many', the term indicates the Essenes convened in assembly], on condition that he has committed no more transgressions unknowingly up until the completion of two years to the day. In fact, for a transgression committed unknowingly one must be punished for two years, but as for one who acts willingly, he shall not be readmitted (1QS 8.20–9.1).

It is clear that there are three distinct types of transgression possible regarding the commandments of the Law. The Law can be broken 1) willingly (*b^eyad rāmāh*), 2) through laxity (*r^emîyyâ*), 3) unknowingly (*šegagah*). In the first case remission is impossible; the man is chased from the community of the pure and must return, if he feels that it is possible, to the other Jews, condemned to spend the rest of his life in the same impurity as them. In the third case, the man is suspended from his role within the community and therefore does not commune with it, but after two years, if he can demonstrate that he has not committed any more involutary transgressions, he can take up his place in the council once again. Just what exactly *r^emîyyâ* means remains to be established. Clearly, guilt for *r^emîyyâ* should be of a lesser order than for deliberately breaking the Law, given the descending order followed in the discourse. The two types of transgression are, however, punished in the same way. The expression 'sin through laxity' must refer to the position of those who followed the Law of Moses, but following a looser interpretation, at any rate following an interpretation that differed from the one imposed by the sect. It is not hard to identify these sins through *r^emîyyâ* as those committed while following a rival interpretation of the Law such as the predominant interpretation given in Jerusalem. Allusion to the Hasidaeans/Pharisees appears clear. Interpreting the Law like others interpreted it was the equivalent of breaking it, so much so that one was forever expelled from the sect.[3]

Other parts of the *Community Rule* list more punishments, even for voluntary trangressions, which are quite harsh, though which do not

---

3.   On this interpretation of *r^emîyyâ* see J. Carmignac, *Les textes de Qumrân* p. 35 n. 47.

include banishment from the sect. On the whole these transgressions seem to be less serious.

At this point it appears that the Essenes divided sins into two broad categories, forgivable and unforgivable sins. I have deliberately avoided two synonyms used in Christian teachings in order to avoid confusion regarding a possible influence of Essenism on the formation of the doctrine of 'mortal' and 'venial' sins. That does not mean that there are not some similarities between the Essenic and the Christian positions, especially if we bear in mind the rigour of the early Christians, who did exclude those guilty of grave sins from communion.[4]

For the Essenes grave transgression of the Law committed either intentionally or due to a different interpretation of the Law than theirs constituted an unforgivable sin. Forgivable sins were those committed on less serious grounds and those committed unknowingly.

The problem of the Pharisees' position in the history of Jewish law is closely related to the question of *r^emîyyâ*. As seen from the point of view of the Gospels, the Pharisees seem to rigidly enforce the norms of the Law following the oral interpretation, but the fact that they are often called hypocrites in the Gospel demonstrates that their efforts at adapting the Law to day-to-day reality could be interpreted by their adversaries as laxness. A good example can be found in the efforts of the Pharisees to save the Law calling for a sabbatical year in which all debts were to be condoned. This contrasted with the practical necessities of the economy, especially as felt by Jerusalem's ruling class, leading to the stagnation of the money market as the sabbatical year approached.[5] The idea that the Pharisee *halakah* was a more flexible version of the ancient *halakah* established by the Jerusalem priesthood was put forward by Geiger (*Urschrift und Übersetzungen der Bibel*, Breslau 1857 [1928]) and should be examined more fully. Rosso[6] has pointed out that the practice of purification by bathing before meals, seen as normal for pious Jews in the books of Tobiah and Judith, by Jesus' day had been reduced to merely washing one's hands. We could

4. See *EC* 9.1104-31.

5. On the *prozbul* annulling the effects of the sabbatical year, see J. Jeremias, *Jerusalem zur Zeit Jesu: Eine kulturgeschichtliche Untersuchung zur neutestamentlichen Zeitgeschichte* (Göttingen: Vandenhoeck & Ruprecht, 3rd edn, 1969), p. 130. See also the case of Mt. 15.6.

6. See L. Rosso Ubigli, 'Un'antica variante del libro di Tobit (Tob., VII, 9)', *RSO* 50 (1976), pp. 73-89.

add the case of Mattathias abolishing one of the prohibitions of the Sabbath (that of fighting), which was however confirmed by the book of *Jubilees* (50.12) which was the product of Zadokite circles.

The following is a series of laws regarding various situations. They give an idea of the Essenes' judgment of human behaviour and of just what the so-called Essenic rigour was.

The text as it has been handed down to us shows some traces of having been altered, a sign that the sect's norms did undergo some evolution. These alterations make translation difficult in a number of places, hence here I have sought to simplify and clarify the text.

> These are the rules by which judgment is to be made in the Community's enquiries, according to the cases.[7]
>
> If it is found that a man has lied about the quantity of his goods, and has done so deliberately, he shall be separated from the midst of the Purity of the assembly of *rabbim* for one year and shall be punished by reducing his food by one quarter.
>
> Whoever has answered a companion harshly or spoken with impatience, h[urti]ng his companion's dignity, without respecting the word of his companion who is registered before him, [and acti]ng on his own initiative, shall have a punishment of one year [...];
>
> [who]ever has spoken out against the glorious Name above all the [creatures?], and has blasphemed, whether because stricken by adversity or any other personal reason, whether when reading the Book or reciting the benediction, shall be expelled and not allowed to return to the Assembly of the Community;
>
> If one speaks with anger against any of the priests inscribed in the Book, he shall have a punishment of one year and shall be excluded from the purity of the *rabbim*, but if he has spoken unwittingly his punishment shall be of six months.
>
> Anyone who has deliberately lied shall have a punishment of six months.
>
> Anyone who has insulted a companion deliberately and for no reason shall have a punishment of one year and must remain separate.
>
> Anyone who has spoken to a companion with resentment, or who has behaved with laxness toward him, and willingly, shall have a punishment of six months.
>
> If one should show himself to be negligent toward his neighbor he shall have a punishment of three months.
>
> If one should show himself to be negligent toward the goods of the community, damaging them, he shall pay the damage personally; but if

7.   See A. Vivian, 'Il concetto di legge nel rotolo del tempio (11QTemple Scroll)', *RSB* 3 (1991), pp. 97-114.

he cannot pay the damages he shall have a punishment of sixty days.

Whoever holds a grudge unjustly against his companion shall have a punishment of one year [in its more ancient form the text reads 'six months']. The same treatment is reserved for anyone taking revenge for himself for any reason.

Anyone who has spoken foolishly, three months.

Anyone who interupts the words of another with his own, ten days.

Anyone who has lain down and fallen asleep during an assembly of the *rabbim*, thirty days; anyone who has left the assembly of the *rabbim* without permission or who has fallen asleep three times during the same assembly is to be treated in the same way: he shall have a punishment of ten days, but if they wake him and then he leaves, he shall have a punishment of thirty days.

Anyone who has let himself be seen nude by a companion, unless due to illness, shall have a punishment of six months.

Anyone who has spit in the assembly of the *rabbim* shall have a punishment of thirty days.

Anyone who has shown his penis from under his clothes, or whose clothes are so ragged that his nudity can be seen, shall have a punishment of thirty days.

Anyone who has joked foolishly, letting his voice be heard clearly, shall have a punishment of thirty days.

Anyone drawing out the left hand in order to ask to speak [?] with it, shall have a punishment of ten days. [The slight infraction, judging from the entity of the punishment, must have consisted in using the left hand for a gesture that should have been made with the right.]

Anyone slandering his companion shall be excluded from the purity of the *rabbim* for one year and shall only be punished, but if he slanders everyone, he shall be expelled and shall not be readmitted.

Anyone who has murmered against the authority [$y^esôd$, 'foundation'] of the Community shall be expelled and shall not return, if instead he has murmered against his companion with no reason, he shall have a punishment of six months.

Anyone who has strayed from the foundation of the community [$y^esôd$ *hayyaḥad* here surely indicates the sect's fundamental truths], betraying the truth and proceeding in the stubbornness of his heart, if he repents he shall have a punishment of two years. During the first [year] he shall not touch the purity of the *rabbim*, and in the second he shall not touch the drink of the *rabbim* and shall be seated after all the members of the Community. When his two years are complete, the *rabbim* will be questioned concerning him and if they decide to re-admit him he shall be inscribed according to his rank, after which he may be consulted regarding decisions to be made.

Anyone who, after having been in the Assembly of the Community for ten years, turns back, betraying it, leaving the sight of the *rabbim* in order to proceed in the stubbornness of his heart, he shall not be re-admitted into the Assembly of the Community (1QS 6.24-7.25).

As can be drawn from these rules, the guilty party had to be set apart from the 'purity' of the innocent members. In other words, it was not just a question of punishing the guilty, but also of keeping him from contaminating the 'pure', because the sinner, whether sinning against the Law or simply against the sect's own regulations, became impure during the very moment of transgression.

Apparently the state of impurity lasts for a certain amount of time, varying with the degree of the sin's gravity. Then once the period of impurity was finished, the guilty person was re-admitted to the community without, it seems, any particular rites.

A typical example of the view that the way of perfection was the way of an ever greater purity, in terms of an ever greater distance from anything that could contaminate the person, is offered by John the Baptist. The primary aim of John's preaching, at least in keeping with the information provided by the Gospels and by Josephus, is that of pushing Israel to complete conversion. Sin is rampant, therefore a way must be found for the 'remission of sins'. It is necessary to stop sinning and, once penance has been done, purify oneself through baptism. It is clear that for John sin produced an impurity that had to be removed and penitence was not enough to take away the stain caused by sin. That stain, had it remained, would have been the equivalent of the sin. This is a theological scheme similar to the one documented at Qumran, which must have been widespread among the Jews of that time; not only was there *ḥeṭ*, but there was also *'awon*.

Since sin was, or caused, impurity, then John the Baptist saw purity as the road to perfection, and that was the road he followed. He avoided populated areas and he avoided eating food that had been touched by human hands; his staples were wild honey and locusts. Eating these things meant avoiding as much as possible contact with men and the things touched by men; man's hand is always impure because of his sin. John's path toward God was one of absolute purity.[8]

8. John's clothing, made of camel skins, presents a problem in that the camel is considered an impure animal (Lev. 11.4). It seems that for John impurity never springs from the things themselves, but from humans. It could also be that the camel skin clothes, unlike linen clothing, favoured purification by immersion. See Lupieri, *Giovanni Battista fra storia e leggenda*, p. 171 n. 24; *idem*, *Giovanni Battista nelle tradizioni sinottiche*; *idem*, *Giovanni e Gesù, storia d'un antagonismo*

3. *Justification and Judgment*

One of the most lively and certainly one of the most productive themes meditated upon by the Teacher of Righteousness, becoming one of the characteristics of all of Essenism, is the problem of who is 'righteous'. In the Jewish world this question was always approached from the perspective of salvation, an idea which continued to be the matrix structuring all other ideas around it. The Teacher of Righteousness' approach was an innovative one, even though it was derived from a question whose existence was as old as the Jewish world.

Once again we must refer back to Qohelet, in whose work certain concepts, such as 'righteousness' and the lack of a retributive criterion in God's work, take shape in Jewish thought. After Qohelet, Antigonus of Socho (first half of the second century BCE) again takes up the problem of the 'righteous man' and his retribution, again resolving the question in negative terms. Antigonus, however, breaks new ground because he explains why there can be no retribution from God.

Antigonus teaches that, just as the slave should not serve his master in hopes of being repaid (and some masters could go as far as to grant their slaves repayment), humankind should not expect anything in return from God as a reward for its service.

> Antigonus of Socho received the teachings of Simon the Just. He often said, 'Do not be like the slaves who serve their master with the thought of receiving rewards (*prs*), but be like those slaves who serve their master with the thought of not receiving *prs*. The fear of God be in you' (*Pirqe Ab.* 1.3).[9]

Antigonus has thus discovered the reason why there is no retribution where human common sense would like to see it. In his justice God does grant rewards, but he will never find anything to reward in humans because the man that has done everything that he must, that has done

---

(Milan: Mondadori, 1991); *idem*, 'Giovanni Battista fra i testi e la storia', *StAns* 106 (1991), pp. 75-107.

9.   On this maxim see E.J. Bickerman, 'The Maxim of Antigonus of Socho', *HTR* 44 (1951), pp. 153-65. The accepted text reads *hyw k'bdym hmšmšym 't hrb 'l mnt šl' lqbl prs*, and in the final part emphasizes the intention of not receiving rewards. The traditional text reads *hyw k'bdym hmšmšym 't hrb šl' 'l mnt lqbl prs*, 'Be like the servants who serve their master without aiming at rewards'. See A.I. Katsch, 'Unpublished Geniza Fragments of Pirqe Abot in Antonin Geniza Collection in Leningrad', *JQR* 61 (1970), pp. 1-12.

everything written in the Law, has only done his duty. The deep-rooted idea of ancient Hebraism and Judaism that the righteous man must be rewarded for his righteousness disappears. For Antigonus 'Doing the Law' was a duty that merited no reward, but transgression of the Law was definitely still a sin and as such was to be punished.

There is a clear relationship here with Stoicism.

In Antigonus of Socho's thought, the relationship between humans and God is seen as parallel to that between the slave and the free man. During the Hellenistic period the slave was nothing more than an object in the hands of his master, and the more power the master wielded, the lower the condition of the slave in comparison. What were humans, then, when compared to God? Biblical expressions regarding the tendency toward evil inherent in man (Gen. 8.21) or his insignificance in comparison to God (Ps. 39) were now to be read with a sense of dejection that did not exist before.

Antigonus of Socho's thought and his pessimism regarding humanity certainly had an influence on the Teacher of Righteousness and on the formation of Essenic thought. Humanity became 'a crucible of impurity and sin'. What could he expect from God? What righteousness could humans claim before God?

The question seems to find its answer in the following passages, the last of which was certainly written by the Teacher of Righteousness, while the others follow his same line of thought.

> To God I say: 'My Righteousness' (1QS 10.11).

> As for me, my fate belongs to God
> and the perfection of my behavior and the uprightness of my heart are in His hands.
> He through His righteousness cancels my sins (*peša‘*).
> For from the source of his knowledge he has loosed His light [so that] my eye has contemplated His wonders, and the rays of my heart the mystery to come and the eternal being (1QS 11.2-4).

> As for me, if I waver,
> God's mercy (*ḥasdê 'ēl*) is my salvation forever,
> and if I stumble for the iniquity (*‘āwôn*) of the flesh [that is due to my being made of flesh],
> my judgment is based on God's righteousness, which is everlasting.
> If He lets made me fall into anguish,
> He lifts me from the pit and puts my steps on the [right] way.
> By His love (*raḥªmîm*) He has brought me near
> and by His mercy (*ḥªsādîm*) He judges me.

He judges me by the righteousness of His Truth

and the abundance of His goodness (*ṭôb*) he expiates all my iniquities (*'āwôn*).

By His righteousness He cleanses me of man's impurity and of the sin (*ḥēṭ*) of the sons of Adam [so that] I might praise God for His righteousness and the Most High for His glory.

Blessed are You, my God,

who have opened the heart of Your servant to knowledge.

Establish all of his works in righteousness and place [him] as a son of Your Truth,

as you have desired for the elect of Adam, that they should be always before You.

Since without You behaviour cannot be perfect and without Your will nothing can be done.

You have taught all knowledge,

and all that exists, exists because of Your will.

There is no one beyond You that can oppose Your counsel,

or that can teach all the thought of Your holiness, contemplate the depth of Your secrets and understand all of Your wonders, or the strength of Your power.

Who could understand Your glory?

And what is, in the end, the son of man among Your wondrous works?

He who is born of woman, how can he stand before You?

He who is kneaded from the dust and whose body will be bread for worms? (1QS 11.11-21)

When the wicked rose up against Your Covenant [that is against the Teacher of Righteousness' sect].

and the vicious against Your word [that is against the preachings of the Teacher of Righteousness],

I said, 'Because of my sins (*peša'*),

I have been cut out of Your Covenant'.

But, remembering the strength of Your hand

and the richness of Your love (*raḥᵃmîm*),

I gathered myself together and rose;

my spirit held its place firmly in the face of adver[sity],

because I drew support from Your mercy (*ḥᵃsādîm*)

and the richness of your love (*raḥᵃmîm*).

You cleanse evil (*'āwôn*) and fr[ee ma]n from his sins ['*ašmah*, the exact meaning is not known, similar to *ḥēṭ*] by Your righteousness. And not for man... You have done this, because You created the righteous and the wicked one... (1QH 4.34-38)

Each of these passages touches on a problem that we could call the question of justification. For each of them I have quoted more than was strictly necessary to illustrate the statement regarding justification, in order to show how illumination, predeterminism and justification are three aspects of the same reality. They are very closely linked to one another in Essenic thought and in the writings of the Teacher of Righteousness.

There is still some uncertainty if we try to establish just what type of sins the Teacher of Righteousness (or whoever the author may be) was thinking of, given that we have singled out five different types of sin for the Essenes: ontological sin; the willing transgression of a clear and important commandment of the Law, which brings about exclusion from the sect; transgression of a commandment due to a different *halakah*, which also brings about exclusion from the sect; sins committed unknowingly, which do not bring about exclusion; and finally those sins that we have called 'forgivable'. The expression, 'He cleanses me of man's impurity' (which can also be translated 'of Adam's impurity') seems to allude to the ontological purification that God grants to those who enter the sect of the New Covenant, but then the phrase continues 'and of the sin (*ḥēṭ*) of the sons of Adam'. The second part of the phrase indicates a type of sin different from ontological sin. It refers to the breaking of the Law, or of the sect's rules, or, more engaging still, transgression of God's will.

This awareness of sin, which could be committed even after the individual had entered into the Covenant with God, leads the Teacher of Righteousness to a movement of desperation when faced with persecution. According to the old saying and ways of believing, every misfortune was the consequence of guilt. Therefore, if the Teacher of Righteousness was being persecuted, then he must have felt cut off from the Covenant and God's Mercy. But he was able to avoid losing hope because he knew that 'You cleanse evil (* āwôn*) and fr[ee ma]n from his sins by Your righteousness' (1QH 4.37). If men, then, can be righteous or wicked, that depends on the mysterious plans of God's will, who created all men in one way or the other, in other words he assigned them either to the angel of Darkness or to the angel of Light. Persecution of the Teacher of Righteousness is not, therefore, a result of his guilt, but rather is part of God's *ab aeterno* plan for reasons that humans cannot understand. In spite of the illumination received, the Teacher of Righteousness himself can do nothing but accept it (this is his true and most profound illumination), because he has understood that everything that happens on earth takes place because God has so desired. Qohelet had said that everything is a gift from God and that wise is he who tries to understand his works.

It is therefore necessary to distinguish between an ontic purification and God's forgiveness of (light) shortcomings. The former takes place when the believer completely and definitively joined the sect, entering the ranks of those who belong to the Light, while the latter takes place after that original purification.

Even though the Teacher of Righteousness felt that he always received God's forgiveness, he was nonetheless not lax, nor was Essenism in general. It was quite the contrary. This emerges clearly both from the legalistic texts that regulated the life of the community and from the more personal documents that show all of the Teacher of Righteousness' abhorrence of sin-impurity.

Another novel aspect of the Teacher of Righteousness' thought is the idea that there is no such thing as a righteous man, but rather the 'justified man'.

I believe that this new idea of the righteous as 'justified' can be held to have been absorbed by all of Judaism. No one will go back to seeing the righteous in the simple terms of the Hebrew texts or with the schematization imposed by Ezekiel. Neither Christianity nor Pharisaism accepted the old idea of the righteous either.

Pharisaism, however, was to resolve the problem of justification in such a way as to avoid betraying the fundamental necessities of the Jewish tradition that had always proclaimed human freedom (closely linked to a sharp distinction between the sacred and the profane) and salvation for 'he who does the Law because of the Law', an idea expressed clearly by Ezekiel and which posed a problem for Ben Sira, who tried to save the idea by eliminating the former schematisms (see Chapter 15, §1, pp. 410-18). The element that allowed the Pharisees to save the deepest necessities of the ancient Jewish tradition was the acceptance of the idea of resurrection. This allowed them to transfer divine Judgment from this earth, where things decidedly go the way that Job and Qohelet had said, to the next world.

In the first century CE the schools of Hillel and Shammai discussed the form of Judgment in the next world.[10] It is clear that for both of them, humans did not present themselves for Judgment in order to know whether they had been righteous or not, because no human is

---

10. See W. Bacher, *Die Aggada der Tannaiten* (2 vols.; Strasbourg: Trübner, 1890, 1903).

righteous, no one is without sin. They, however, do reject Antigonus' idea that 'he who does the Law, and every time he does it' has no merit, but is like the useless slave that Jesus, too, was to speak of (Lk. 17.10).

Judgment for the Pharisees, then, should be seen as a sort of balance sheet (*ḥešbôn*) calculated by God. The details of God's method of calculation remain beyond human reach, but not the underlying criterion; acts of observance of the Law go in humanity's favour while acts against the Law count against humanity. Therefore the individual who is saved is justified, but not righteous, because every human is guilty. The Pharisees, however, admit that in the end it is the individual who allows God to justify him through his 'having done the Law'.

The clearest formulation of the guiding criterion of the final Judgment is to be found in R. Aqiba (first half of the second century CE). In the *Pirqe Abot* (3.16) we read: 'All is foreseen, but freedom of choice is given. The world [that is men] is judged by mercy, yet everything depends on the quantity of works (*sc.* good works or bad works)'. Man's freedom of choice exists alongside and equal to God's foreknowledge. In contrast, judgment is made by mercy. In other words God does not only look at transgressions against the Law, but he also takes into account acts of observance of the Law. God's mercy is not separated from his justice.

Between the school of Hillel and that of Shammai there was, on the topic of the Judgment, a slight difference, which shows that Hillel's school was more willing to give in to the spiritual pressures of its day. In discussing the case of the *benônî*, or 'middling man', who found himself with an equal number of good and bad actions, Hillel's school claimed that God's mercy would have erased a bad action from the balance, thus allowing the man to be saved. The school of Shammai, in contrast, condemned the *benônî* to a period of suffering in the other world in order to expiate the sin. This was perfectly in line with the doctrine of merits that admitted the possibility of doing penance for one's sins even in this life.

As we can see, there is a clear distinction between the Pharasaic conception of human merits for 'doing the Law' and the Christian (and perhaps Essenic) idea that having 'done the Law' man had simply done his duty and, in the words of Jesus, was like a worthless slave who had only done what he ought to have done (Lk. 17.7-10). For Paul, Judgment made following the criteria of the Law could only lead to condemnation (Gal. 3.10), since God would clearly only pay attention to one's transgressions, as in human tribunals, while for the Pharisees an individual's entire life was to be evaluated. As a consequence, for the Christian the underlying problem was to be that of avoiding Judgment (in terms of the Law); anyone going before God's Judgment was bound to be condemned, because no human is without sin.

Unlike Pharisaism, Christianity followed in the wake of Antigonus of Socho; Judgment can only regard the infraction of the Law, because there is no merit in observing it. In a tribunal we must answer for crimes committed, and we cannot hope to be acquitted of one crime for the simple reason that we did not commit others, or because we did observe one law or another. As a result, for the Christian Judgment is synonymous with condemnation. A clear formulation of this principle appears in both Paul and John, but the idea is already clear in Jesus' teachings as presented in the synoptic Gospels. John says, 'Those who believe in him are not judged; but those who do not believe have already been judged' (Jn 3.18). 'Judge' in this context is practically the equivalent of 'condemn', because no one can go before Judgment without sin. In fact, many modern versions translate this passage with 'condemn'. Paul bases his interpretation of the Judgment on the Scriptures (Gal. 3.10 and Deut. 27.26), saying that anyone who breaks even one of the commandments of the Law is cursed, according to the economy that Christianity was trying to overcome, of course.

Following this line of thought, if we do not want to arrive at the conclusion that everyone is destined for condemnation, the only possible solutions are either the abolition of Judgment, or a new interpretation of it. In the first case a shift in terms is necessary, because it is only through some sort of Judgment that it can be established who must undergo judgment–condemnation and who should not. The criteria and modalities on which this pre-Judgment are to be founded remain to be established. In the second case, which in the end is not much different from the first, emphasis is placed on the novelty of the Christian Judgment that can no longer be based on the Law. Along these lines one can compare Paul's idea of salvation through faith and James's Judgment by the 'Law of freedom'.

Jesus claims that anyone who has put into practice all the things written in the Law, following his interpretation of course, cannot for this reason alone expect anything. After having done what he had to do he is no more than a worthless slave (Lk. 17.7-10). Jesus' interpretation of the Law, on the other hand, is particularly rigorous. The disciples are perplexed and discouraged, as in the case of the rich man who, absurdly, had observed all the Law and still Jesus told him that that was not enough. 'Then who can be saved?', ask the disciples anxiously (Mt. 19.25; Mk 10.26; and Lk. 18.26). Jesus answers that humanity cannot save itself by bringing its own righteousness before God. Jesus reassures them, though, that salvation based on humanity's supposed merits is not possible because those merits do not exist. At the same time there are no limits to God's power. In other words, it is God that can justify humanity. But who is chosen by God to be justified?

Jesus does not provide a single answer, at least according to the synoptic Gospels, to this fundamental question, but rather seems to admit a number of paths leading to God's mercy. Each of these paths is presented as being possible, but the first and foremost in Jesus' thought, it seems to me, is that of forgiveness. God will judge the individual with the same measure that the individual has judged others. 'Do not judge, so that you may not be judged. For with the judgment you make you will be judged, and the measure you give will be the measure you get' (Mt. 7.1-2). This is an absolute and limitless invitation to forgiveness: 'Do not judge'. Jesus does not have in mind a humanity that no longer sins, as was the presupposition of John the Baptist's preaching. He has in mind a humanity that compensates for its wrongdoings with forgiveness. Forgiveness is therefore a fundamental element of the pre-Judgment, and unfortunate is he who is sent to Judgment.

On the other hand, the code of behaviour dictated by forgiveness as a criterion of pre-Judgment is not absolute. The man who forgives his neighbour does what he ought to do and his behaviour pushes God toward a sort of *imitatio hominis*, but God is not at all bound to it. Otherwise, we would be back to square one of the problem. The story of Jesus healing the paralytic (Mk 2) is still fundamental for understanding Jesus. The Son of Man's forgiveness is not only given freely, but without even being requested.

Another road to salvation indicated by Jesus is that of suffering: 'Blessed are those who weep, for they shall be consoled'. Even more so than in the case of forgiveness, here the way to salvation is clearly placed outside of any scheme of the *halakah*, outside of any ethical code of behaviour. Suffering in and of itself, at least if not in expiation of sin, represents a value to be rewarded. The way to salvation is primarily that of forgiveness and the acceptance of suffering. This should be compared to the *Habakkuk pesher* (8.2-3): 'God will free them from the house of judgment [in this case the 'divine tribunal'] because of their suffering and their faith in the Teacher of Righteousness'.

Other cases of human behaviour worthy of reward emerge from the reading of the blessings in Mt. 5.3-11 (and parallel passages), while it is emphasized that not only those who kill are worthy of Gehenna, but even those who offend their neighbour. I feel, however, that in the case of Christianity the expression 'human behaviour' is inadequate. More than behaviour Jesus addresses the individual's attitude. It is a different discourse whose historical roots are to be found in the way that Ben Sira approached the problem of the righteous man at the beginning of the second century BCE; Ben Sira was convinced that the righteous man did not exist. There are certain absolutely ineliminable human necessities: the fact that there is no 'righteous man without sin' does not change the fact that in some way we feel that the righteous man must exist. If we look more closely at the expression 'the righteous man without sin does not exist', we see that the existence of the subject ('the righteous man') is not denied, only a certain type of subject. (On this, see Chapter 15, §1, pp. 410-18.)

It is clear that there are elements present in this conception of salvation that we could call of a sociological type, as in the *Book of Parables* and the *Psalms of Solomon* as well. That takes us away from the discourse on the Judgment towards the question of the humble, the *'anawim* (see p. 395). The *Book of Parables* claims that the *'anawim* are already destined for salvation, once again following a path that is independent from 'doing the Law'. The *'anawim* are to receive compensation for the oppression that they have suffered.

In this context the Law is of no use for salvation, even though it remains the central pillar of human behaviour, the pillar on which society is founded and can live. Anyone in need of forgiveness needs forgiveness for having broken the Law and in so doing harmed another person.

The conception of salvation as it appears in Jn 5.24 is of particular interest. It is similar to that of the Essenes; the Christian already has eternal life within him in this world because he has passed from death to life, and he will not undergo Judgment, because he believes in God and has accepted the words of the Christ.

The Pharisees, as we have already seen, overcame the problem of the Judgment formulated in terms of transgressions, and therefore leading inevitably to condemnation, by imagining that, in Judgment, God not

only takes account of acts of transgression, but also of those of observance, the former going to our discredit, the latter to our credit.

4. *Salvation in Essenism*

It remains an open question whether or not the profound novelty of the
ideas of illumination and predeterminism in the thought of the Teacher
of Righteousness and in Essenism, together with the substitution of the
idea of retribution for one's works in favour of the idea of justification,
penetrated and involved the idea of salvation.

While everything seems to lead us to believe that even the idea of
salvation must have undergone some changes in the Teacher of
Righteousness's thought, there is no clear evidence to this effect that
can be deduced from the texts. At times salvation is spoken of in a concrete and historical sense, as was common in the ancient Hebrew and
Jewish traditions. At other times salvation is put off to the future, which
could even be an eschatological future, and seems to be linked to the
figure of the Teacher of Righteousness himself, as in 1QH 5[11].11-12,
where the text is somewhat sybilline and has been interpreted in various
ways: 'You, oh my God, have hidden me before the sons of man, you
have hidden Your law [in me], [un]til the moment of revelation of your
salvation to me'.[11]

In this text the Teacher seems to be the depository of a particular
truth, of an authentic interpretation of the Law, which, however, he is
not going to reveal to anyone until God's salvation has been revealed to
him. I am not entirely sure whether this is to be considered an eschatological text, in spite of the weight of the expression, 'you have hidden
Your law in me'. In any case it deals with salvation in the traditional
Jewish and Hebraic conception of the term.

If there is something new regarding salvation in the Teacher of
Righteousness and Essenism, I believe that is to be sought in the
position that the adept assumes in the cosmos. This is all but an isolated

---

11. The conjecture of 'in me' for filling the lacuna appears on the whole certain,
because it is based on the parallel element where we read 'salvation to me' (*yišāʿᵃkā
lî*). Some doubt may remain regarding the choice of preposition (*b* or *l*), though I
am in favour of the former, because that way the parallel style tends to repeat itself
while avoiding using the same words. The meaning, too, supports conjecture in
favour of *b*.

idea in the texts of the Teacher of Righteousness, which can be illustrated by a text that I feel to be of particular significance.

> You have freed my soul [that is 'my self'] from the pit, from the sheol of perdition you have made me rise to the eternal height [that is 'most high' and therefore 'safe'], I am roaming in a plain where the human gaze is lost.
> I have known that there is hope
> for the one that You have formed from the dust,
> in sight of the eternal Community.
> You have purified the spirit perverted by numerous sins,
> so that it could take its place in the ranks of the saints [that is the members of the sect];
> so that it could enter in communion with the assembly of the sons of heaven [the angels].
> You have assigned to man an eternal sort with the spirits of knowledge,
> so that he shall praise Your Name in the ju[bilati]ng assembly,
> and so that he shall tell of Your wonders before all Your works [the cosmos] (1QH 3.19-23).

Concerning the expression 'eternal height', I would avoid interpretations that see life after death in this 'eternity'. It is more likely that it refers to a sort of new life for the adept who frees himself from the sheol of (ontological) impurity in order to reach the eternal (cosmic) light of God's purity. See also 1QS^b 5.23: 'May the Lord raise you to eternal height, like a mighty tower on high walls'. 'Eternal height' seems to indicate a particularly safe place, from which it is possible to drive the enemy away.[12]

The author begins, then, with a personal case in mind, but his thought soon goes beyond personal limits to include all of the elect, or in other words, the members of the sect. These people are sinners and they are made of dust, just like all men, but they are also destined for justification and life in a new dimension. As such they have a 'precise place' in the angelic host, an army characterized by possession of a particular knowledge, with the goal of exalting God before the entire cosmos.

This type of superior knowledge characteristic of the angels also belongs, through God's grace, to the sect's elect who, even though

---

12. See *Odes* 29.4. In this sense see Carmignac in *Les textes de Qumran, Les Hymnes*, p. 199. In the opposite sense see J. van der Ploeg, 'The Belief in Immortality in the Writings of Qumran', *BO* 18 (1961), p. 122, which, however, is rather hazy.

made of dust, can contemplate the eternal.

It seems to me that the Teacher's thought can be synthesized as follows: 'Inasmuch as it is the supreme goal, the knowledge of the angels is salvation'. He does not believe that this knowledge leads to salvation, but that it is in itself salvation. Therefore, we are faced with a thought holding that, while emphasizing the fact that humans are dust, the object of their knowledge is total. It remains to be understood up until just what point the object of knowledge can modify human nature, once they have reached this exceptional knowledge. Humans are by nature dust and *'āwôn*, but for the Essene this is not so.

Just as there is an earthly temple, which is contaminated and has been replaced by the members of the sect, there is also a heavenly temple officiated over by the angels. The Essenes, too, participate in this angelic priesthood. They have been placed in God's eternal temple as his priests. But at this point it is more than likely that the Essenes believed that they were already in the realm of the eternal, and this explains why the idea of survival after death is lacking in their thought, at least in clear terms. The Essene does not enter into God's world through death, because he is already there. The Jewish authors writing in Greek, in fact, found no difficulty in stating that the Essenes believed in the immortality of the soul. No mention is made in the sources, however, of belief in resurrection.

The text of the *Songs of the Sabbath Sacrifice* confirms this interpretation. The choirs of angels are God's priests in the cosmic temple and offer only their praises in sacrifice. The Essenes, too, are placed in this eternal liturgy, which, in all probability alone among men, makes them eternal. For Essenism, no soul is immortal by nature, but it can become immortal by entering into the sect, which celebrates God's praises together with the angels in a single assembly.

While the Teacher of Righteousness's thought does present some aspects that could be called gnostic, it is still a unique form of gnosis, since his knowledge not only leads to salvation, but is in itself salvation. It is clear that such a position must have opened up a number of questions concerning the nature of humanity; what in humans could be made eternal. These problems, however, do not appear in the Essenic texts. The eternity frequently mentioned in the Dead Sea manuscripts was available to the adept. This was not an eternity to be reached through victory over death (the Christian position), but a state already reached. See, however, 1 Jn 3.14.

A number of scholars, from Dupont-Sommer to Michelini Tocci and recently Ménard, have maintained the presence of gnostic elements in the Teacher of Righteousness's thought. I, however, would avoid speaking of gnosticism regarding the Teacher of Righteousness, because the gnostic elements appear only occasionally and embedded with other ideas that are certainly not gnostic. For the Teacher of Righteousness salvation is a form of knowledge, but it is *also* tied to other elements. I realize that it is a 'Byzantine' problem, like all problems concerning definitions. While his dualism was a *sui generis* dualism, his gnosis was no less *sui generis*.

5. *Salvation in More Traditional Circles*

The ideas that appear to be innovative in the Teacher of Righteousness are not isolated in that time period. The distinguishing feature of the Teacher of Righteousness's thought when compared to the authors of books like the book of *Jubilees* or the *Testaments of the Twelve Patriarchs* is his greater coherence. In the other books new ideas appear right alongside traditional ones, with no clearly structured system of thought.

Still, it is worthwhile to point out some traditional and some new aspects documented in the two books.

In the book of *Jubilees* we find a certain dualistic structure of the world and a certain predeterminism. When he created the world, God assigned a line of behaviour to every thing and to every living being (*Jub.* 2.8-10):

> And on the fourth day He made the sun, the moon and the stars. And He set them in the firmament of heaven so that they might give light upon the whole earth and rule over the day and the night and separate light and darkness. And the Lord set the sun as a great sign upon the earth for days, sabbaths, months, feast days, years…so that every thing which sprouts and grows upon the earth might surely prosper.

As we can see, the role of the sun is not only that of lighting the earth, but also of marking the different moments of the year so that the feast days and sacred days can be distinguished from the profane ones. Everything is right in creation because every created thing performs the role assigned it by God. By this point Jewish thought has moved away from the position of early Enochism that considered the cosmos as flawed due to the sin of the angels, and saw the stars as being out of place and influencing the earth in a way that God had not desired.

Unlike the stars and the forces of nature, though, humans would not know what to do if God did not reveal it to them. This is the reason that God sent the angels to Adam immediately after creating him (*Jub.* 3.15) and continued sending them throughout the duration of history to let men know his commandments, as they were written in the heavenly tablets. The Law of Israel, the Torah, is none other than a transcription, made for humans, of the heavenly Laws. God does not just reveal his Laws to humanity, however, he also indicates the path for each human to follow. The problem of the range of human freedom of action is thus delicately approached and given a solution different from that of the tradition, even though at first glance it may not seem so.

Hebraism had always witnessed the phenomenon of humans being called expressly by God for particular missions, as in the case of the prophets in the canonical tradition. These, however, were exceptional cases. There was no point in trying to go toward God; if he wanted to reveal himself to someone, he knew perfectly well how to do it. During the period of Middle Judaism, it is the individual who begins to move toward God, in order that God can tell the person what is expected of him. And still, everything is written in the heavenly tablets. In *Jubilees* the freedom of humans and predeterminism exist side by side. While the Teacher of Righteousness had resolved the question concerning the law of the moment as formulated by Qohelet, in *Jubilees* it remains unsolved. On the one hand the traditional view of human freedom, which was never even put into doubt in early Enochism, is still intact in *Jubilees*; humans must not only adapt to the requirements of the Law, but also to God's will. On the other hand, though, we find the new idea that everything has already been written in the heavenly tablets. Thus, it is claimed that salvation, that is a longer life of perennial youth, without a trace of fatigue, will come to the world when evil has reached the point where 'a boy of three weeks will appear to be a one-hundred-year-old man… In that time the youth will begin to study the Law, to once again seek the commandments and to turn once again toward the way of righteousness' (*Jub.* 23.25-26). It is hard to establish whether seeking the Law and the commandments is only the fruit and sign of divine grace, or whether it has some role in salvation itself.

On the whole, though, it seems that grace and God's intervention prevail decidedly over any human behaviour.

...until I [God] come down [to the earth] to live among them [the humans] in all the ages of eternity...until my sanctuary is built in their midst for ever, and the Lord will appear in the sight of all, and everyone will know that I am the God of Israel, the father of all the sons of Jacob... (*Jub.* 1.26-28)

This passage from the book of *Jubilees* contains a problem that was imposing itself on Jewish consciousness during the second century BCE. It was slowly being discovered that while the pagans were normally polytheistic, the Greek *paideia* was aware of the existence of a single God, exactly like the Jews. Was it perhaps the same God? This was an embarrassing question, since, if there really was only one God, then anyone anywhere identifying the sole God must be referring to the same one. What was the relationship between the Jewish tradition and the Greek *paideia*?

The theme lies very clearly at the basis of the contemporary *Letter of Aristeas*. 'God is one' (§132), and his works benefit the entire world (§210) and in some way he grants his blessing (§205). So, this sole God, who takes care of the whole world and keeps it alive, is also known in Greek culture. The author of *Aristeas* even finds a further parallel between Jews and Greeks; just as the Greeks have their *paideia*, the Jews have the Torah. But there is a fundamental difference between the *paideia* and the Torah which the author does not explicitly mention, even though it lies at the basis of his thought. The Torah was revealed directly by God while the Greek *paideia* is the fruit of human efforts.

This is the mental background that allows us to understand the discourse of *Jubilees*; one day all men will have to recognize that the one God, that the best men already believe in, is the God who revealed himself to Israel, the 'God of Israel, the father of all the sons of Jacob'. Awareness of the sole God is not enough, it is necessary to recognize that God revealed himself to Israel.

In this way the Torah is given absolute value, that must be recognized by all the peoples of the world. *Aristeas* is not against an encounter between Jews and Gentiles, but they can sit together at the same table only if the Gentiles accept the dietary laws of the Jews. In other words, only if they agree to behave in accordance with the Torah. The role of the *paideia* is that of preparing the way for knowledge of the truth, but that truth can only be found in Jerusalem. *Aristeas* is happy to go to Jerusalem as Ptolemy's ambassador, so that the king can satisfy his 'determination to know the divine things' (§3).

This represents an extremely noteworthy opening toward universalism; the pagan world seems to be preparing itself for the encounter with God that leads to salvation. Such an encounter can only take place through Israel, the depository of the best laws governing life. The God that makes Ptolemy's kingdom prosper is the same one who gave the Law to Israel. The one God can only be known through Israel and the revelation made to Israel.

It is interesting to note that in *Jubilees* there is no mediation between God and humans. No messiah is coming to rule over the earth in God's name, as in the *Book of Dreams*, but God himself will descend directly to the earth. Israel's role in history, however, is clearly indicated, and it even seems that in the good world of the future the Jews will have a new nature and will be better than the other men.

> [Abraham] blessed his creator...because He created him by His goodness, for he knew and he perceived that from him there would be a righteous planting for all future generations and a holy seed from him *so that he might be like* the One who make everything... (*Jub.* 16.26).

6. *The Expansion of Salvation*

What seems clear from these texts is that changes were taking place in the concept of salvation. On the one hand it was still claimed that God gave salvation to those who 'did the Law', but alongside this traditional vision the idea of a more serious problem emerges. Rather than the problem of 'doing the Law', the question now revolves around the much more vague and complex question of doing God's will. A lack of faith in human ability to reach their own salvation through the Law seems to be spreading. Otherwise, there is no explanation for the appearance of expectations that God himself will descend to earth. A more and more marked pessimism concerning humanity's real possibilities makes headway; humanity will be saved if it observes the Covenant of Sinai, but can humanity observe it? God's intervention seems necessary, through a prophet, an anointed one or through something even greater, because the task of establishing righteousness appears decidedly beyond man's own capabilities.

On the other hand, the greater human misfortune, the greater the salvation that humanity seeks. Under the overwhelming Syrian oppression as felt by the author of 2 Maccabees, an oppression that massacred the righteous such as Eleazar and the seven brothers, as felt by the Jews who remained faithful to the Law according to the words of Ps. 44, salvation could not be derived from 'doing the Law', as was clear from all observation. Most of all, though, salvation could not be seen as consisting of rewards given in this life, since it was precisely this life that was so unjustly being taken away. If God is just, then, he must at least give life back to his martyrs; let us reread the words of the seven brothers' mother:

> I do not know how you came into being in my womb. It was not I who gave you life and breath, nor I who set in order the elements within each of you. Therefore the Creator of the world, who shaped the beginning of humankind and devised the origin of all things, will in his mercy give life and breath back to you again... (2 Macc. 7.22-23).

Resurrection is necessary in order for God to bring about the justice that does not exist on the earth. By this time humanity does not die with the idea of paying for the sins of the fathers, nor of a hidden sin. The righteous man dies unjustly for his faithfulness to God: he is sacred to God and if God allows him to die then God must restore to him somewhere the life that was taken away from him here on earth.

The concept of salvation has been expanded. A completely new vision of life has opened up before humankind, so that the salvation from the enemy mentioned by the Teacher of Righteousness, salvation from the crumbling wall or from the hidden serpent, no longer hold any value. God can easily make the righteous man die in order to fulfil his uncensurable designs, which are surely bent on the salvation of Israel (see *4 Macc.* 6.28-29; 17.21-22). God can make the righteous man die within the narrow confines of human history, but he cannot make that man disappear from his presence, destining him to Sheol. Human horizons have been broadened; humans are no longer a being living on the earth; they have become a cosmic being, called to live a wonderful and lasting life near God, or to be lost forever in a life which is no longer seen as a pale reflection of this one, but as 'wailing and grinding of teeth'.

In its expansion the theme of salvation involves the pagans as well. Closer and closer contact is made with the pagans and certain values in the Greek *paideia* are recognized by at least some Jews. God is one and he is the God of all. What is the role of the pagans in God's eternal plan for human history?

Chapter 14

MESSIANISM

1. *Forms of Messianism prior to 200 BCE*

Even though the Hebrew and Aramaic word *mašiaḥ* in the Old Testament does not indicate the figure of a future saviour, as pointed out by Coppens,[1] it is still possible to reconstruct a minimal notion of 'Messiah' from the biblical texts. This is why in the introduction to this book I proposed a differentiated use of the words 'anointed' and 'Messiah', the first indicating the *mašiaḥ* as intended in the texts, the latter indicating the saviour figure awaited in the future.

There is a category of Jewish thought that we can call messianism, which is built around two fundamental elements: the first is constituted by the certainty that at some unforeseeable future date there will be a happier world; the second element, closely linked to the first, is that the future happy world will not come about solely through the efforts of humankind, but through the mediation of a figure appointed by God for that task. I will use the term Messiah to refer to any saving mediator, whatever his nature may be.

On the other hand, expectations of a future world profoundly better than the one in which we live and perhaps even ontologically different, at least in the visions of some prophets (see the conception of the New Covenant in Jeremiah and see also Isa. 65.17, which speaks of the creation of new heavens), are not always linked to the figure of a human, prophet, king or whatever. For this reason, the problem of messianism ends up becoming a multi-faceted and at times elusive theme, given the difficulty of establishing just what is essential to messianism and what is not. While, as the name itself implies, messianism is derived from the name of a man, and implies the activity of a future man. The messianic problem is usually bound to the conception of the 'Messiah', who can

---

1. Coppens, *Le messianisme royal.*

also appear in a more abstract form, linked exclusively to faith in a saving act of God. It is therefore worth posing the question as to whether the fundamental element of messianism is the Messiah, or perhaps the messianic expectations, that is the expectation, based on the Scripture, that one day 'the wolf and the lamb shall graze together', no matter what the means necessary for reaching that new world. It could arise through God's direct intervention, creating a new world in much the same way in which he created this one, or it could be the fruit of human labour, putting the commandments of the Law into practice. It could also come about, in accordance with much of the biblical tradition, through the intervention of an exceptional figure, many times seen as a king, acting as the instrument of God. In fact, using the term messianism we mean this last type of messianism, and it is to this type, at any rate, that we will direct most of our attention.

During different historical periods and in different places messianism, therefore, took on different forms. The oldest form is royal messianism. The scriptural basis for royal messianism could today seem to be the prophecy of Nathan as it is narrated in the seventh chapter of the 2 Samuel: 'Your house and your kingdom shall be made sure forever before me;[2] your throne shall be established forever'. At least in the form that has been handed down to us, this text is certainly later than the events narrated. Essentially it mirrors the ideology of salvation belonging to the redactor of the historical books, who was a convinced monarchist.

The historical origin of royal messianism should instead be sought in Isa. 11.1-5. Here Isaiah states that a happier time will come and that the advent of that time is linked to a descendant of David possessing particular gifts. We therefore have the two fundamental elements of messianism, a better future world and the human instrument, in this case a descendant of the house of David. In this case we must speak, therefore, of Davidic messianism. In its original form messianism was both royal and Davidic.

The role of this future king shall be that of judging the *dallim*, the miserable, those whom we today would call the marginalized (Isa.

2.   *Before me*: is the reading of some Hebrew manuscripts and the Greek. Most Hebrew manuscripts, the Vulgate and the Syriac read 'before you', which limits the prophecy to the reign of David. In any case, the Chronicles read 'before me', clearly indicating an eternal reign.

11.4). He will therefore establish a kingdom where justice, in human terms, will reign; we are still a long way from the good world of the Apocalyptic, characterized by perfection and the complete absence of evil.

Later, towards the end of the seventh century BCE, we find messianic statements in Jeremiah. This is still Davidic messianism. In Jer. 23.5-6 we read:

> The days are surely coming, says Yhwh, when I will raise up for David a righteous Branch, and he shall reign as king (*umālak melek*) and deal wisely, and shall execute justice and righteousness in the land. In his days Judah will be saved and Israel will live in safety.

Here too we find the two fundamental elements of the messianic category: a radiant future and the figure who will instate it on the earth.

The Messiah will be a king of Israel and Judah and his role will be that of bringing safety with God's help. The safety that Jeremiah has in mind, though, at least in this passage, pales in comparison to later visions where the Messiah saves all the people of the earth. For others salvation not only concerns our little world, but the entire kingdom of God, both heaven and earth, and therefore even God himself, as in Paul's famous expression 'if children, then heirs, heirs of God' (Rom. 8.17). The passage from Jeremiah still betrays a conception of messianism closely tied to the house of David; it mentions the salvation of Judah and still holds some hope for Israel.

The reinterpretations, new readings of the first messianic prophecies, begin as early as Ezekiel; the royal element of messianism remains, but the Davidic element does not. Ezekiel believed, and most certainly hoped, that the Davidic monarchy had come to an end. For the future he, or his school, had in mind an Israel governed by two heads, the *nāsᶜî*, the (vassal) king, and the priest. He does not mention the dynasty of this king. On the reasons that led Ezekiel to this position, see I, 2, §4, pp. 82-86.

The historical David thus became a pure figure of the ideal king that would one day come to save Israel; that future king will be the real David. In Ezek. 34.23 we read: 'I will set up over them one shepherd, my servant David, and he shall feed them: he shall feed them and be their shepherd'. Thus David, the real one, is yet to come and he will be Israel's shepherd. First, David was an ancestor of the Messiah-king, now he is the Messiah-king's figure.

Again in 37.24-26 we find:

My servant David shall be king over them; and they shall all have one shepherd. They shall follow my ordinances and be careful to observe my statutes…and my servant David shall be their prince forever. I will make a covenant of peace with them; it shall be an everlasting covenant with them…

Mention is no longer made of the Davidic dynasty; Ezekiel is awaiting a new David who will fulfill the expectations that were once hoped for in a historical descendant of the house of David. The messianic hopes are beginning to be transformed. The first step is the passage from a descendant of David to an ideal David who is not necessarily a descendant of the historical one. The successive steps were to be even more audacious.

Around the year 20 of the sixth century Israel had the impression that its messianic hopes were being fulfilled. In 521 a great caravan of exiles arrived in Jerusalem headed by two leaders, one a layperson and the other a priest: Zerubbabel and Joshua. The Jews were clearly trying to put into practice Ezekiel's constitution, by which the Jewish people were to live under the leadership of two heads: a prince and a priest. The prince, furthermore, belonged to the house of David. The prophet Zechariah, who lived during that time, was able to declare to the people: 'These are the two *sons of the oil* who stand by the Lord of the whole earth' (4.14). Both leaders are clearly included in the sacred sphere of regality: they are both 'anointed'.

It is difficult, however, for two to govern together. Zerubbabel must have predominated in an early phase, as can be deduced from Zech. 3.8: 'I am going to bring my servant the Branch', without doubt referring to the lay leader. This is the same name[3] used by Jeremiah to indicate the great future king, the one who would establish justice and righteousness in Israel. The hopes of the prophet and part of the people must have fallen on Zerubbabel with precisely this role in mind. We know from Haggai, another contemporary, that the Temple was refounded under the joint initiative of the two, but Zerubbabel is always named first.

At the moment of the new Temple's dedication (515 BCE), however, Joshua alone of the two is present (see *Ant.* 11.79). Not only has Zerubbabel disappeared from the scene, but we do not see any of his sons in

---

3.   *Branch*: in Hebrew ṣemaḥ, is the term used in Jer. 23.5 and 33.15. Isaiah, in the passage from ch. 11 quoted above, uses the terms ḥōṭer and nēṣer. The term ṣemaḥ was also used by Isaiah, but in a context which is not necessarily to be considered messianic (4.2).

his place; a person was not eliminated, but an entire institution.[4] With the elimination of the monarchy as an institution, royal messianism no longer made sense. Messianism, however, did not disappear from Jewish culture. Through the great disappointment an idea destined to be extremely vital remained; messianism had lost the unity of the person of the saviour, because the anointed ones had become two. The wait for the Messiah could now become a wait for a number of Messiahs. Not only that, but the concept of 'Messiah' was no longer linked to a king figure; a priest, at least, could also become Messiah. The role of the Messiah, saving Israel, in becoming autonomous with regard to royalty became more open to the assumption of religious values.

There is another passage from the book of Zechariah (9.9-10) that is worth remembering:

> Rejoice greatly, O daughter of Zion! Shout aloud, O daughter Jerusalem! Lo, your king comes to you; triumphant and victorious is he, humble and riding on a donkey, on a colt, the foal of a donkey. I will cut off the chariot from Ephraim and the war-horse from Jerusalem; and the battle bow shall be cut off, and he shall command peace to the nations; his dominion shall be from sea to sea, and from the River to the ends of the earth.

The most difficult problem regarding the interpretation of this passage from the second section of the book of Zechariah, the so-called Deutero-Zechariah, is the fact that hypotheses concerning its dating range over a period of about two centuries, from the age of Jeremiah to the Maccabaean period. Most commentators today prefer dating it to the end of the fourth century, but others place it in more ancient times, even in the days of Zechariah himself.[5] To me, the identification of the humble and victorious king with Zerubbabel during the early years of his rule seems the most natural, at least when choosing from the many

---

4.   On the importance of the revolution which took place between 520 and 515 BCE, see Smith, *Palestinian Parties and Politics*, pp. 99-125. While the reconstruction of the details made by Smith is too far from the texts to be accepted, the underlying ideas are still valid. I have developed the theme further in P. Sacchi, 'L'esilio e la fine della monarchia davidica', *Henoch* 11 (1989), pp. 131-48.

5.   Chs. 9–14 were written by a different hand than the first eight. The dating of Deutero-Zechariah to the same period as the first has been sustained by Lamarche, *Zacherie IX–XIV*. While the text has undergone considerable torment by the tradition, allusions in ch. 12 to a civil war and a character whose death resolved the situation are still evident.

postexilic figures that we know of. Even though the passage was written in the context of a precise historical situation, characterized by concrete political tension, once Zerubbabel had been consigned to the past the text could only be read as referring to a distant eschatological future. It became a messianic prophecy repeating the one made by Isaiah, with the additional element of the king's humility.

The Greek translation of this book (second century BCE, approx.) emphasizes the messianic interpretation of this passage, substituting 'I will cut off' with 'he will cut off', the same verb, but in the third person. The subject therefore becomes the king. 'Victorious, saved' (*nôšāʿ*) is replaced by the active participle σώζων, 'saviour'. In the second century BCE the prophecy was certainly read in messianic terms.

After Zerubbabel's day, then, the messianic ideology lost some of its vigour. We cannot claim that it disappeared, if for no other reason because messianic texts continued to be read, but it was inactive for roughly three centuries, at least in the culture of Jerusalem's dominant class.

It is also in the light of a crisis in Davidism that the new interpretation of 'the privileges of David' in Isa. 55.3 (see Chapter 2, §5, pp. 86-90) can be explained; they make sense even in the absence of the Davidic dynasty because they refer to all of Israel. Third Isaiah, perhaps disappointed by the events regarding Joshua and Zerubbabel, speaks of a happier world of the future, which will come about without a messiah: 'I will appoint Peace as your overseer and Justice as your Taskmaster' (Isa. 60.17). In this case we have true messianism without a messiah, demonstrating that there was a force and reason for messianic expectations to be independent of any contingent situation.

The wait for a future happier time appears without intermediaries even in the works of two prophets whose work can be dated to the fifth century BCE: Obadiah and Joel.[6]

The Jews in Jerusalem may have lived a lean period after Nehemiah, but a tranquil one. The great ideals that had animated the prophets of the exile and early Zadokitism had been put aside and salvation seems

---

6. Obadiah certainly wrote after the fall of Jerusalem which is mentioned in his work. It is more difficult to establish just exactly how long afterward, because we do not know the later events that he alludes to. The dating of Joel is particularly controversial, but on the whole the fourth century seems the most probable period. The state of the question has been summed up well by Soggin, *Introduzione*, pp. 424, 436-38.

to have been limited to that of the proper inner workings of a small vassal state, Jerusalem. The book of Chronicles mirrors this attitude well.
Expectations of a better world were not lacking in this society either,
though. The restoration of Jerusalem was awaited and glorified, but
attention was directed for the most part towards human activity. Now,
messianic expectations based on human beings marked a complete
reversal of traditional messianism's values.[7] It was for these expectations that Judith fought successfully (Jdt. 9.8-13). And for Ben Sira
these hopes have already clearly been realized:

> How shall we magnify Zerubbabel?
> He is like a signet ring on the right hand [of God],
> and so was Jeshua son of Yozedeq;
> in their days they built an altar[8]
> and raised a holy temple to the Lord,
> destined for everlasting glory (Sir. 49.11-12).

If a traditional messianic idea still existed, it should be sought in the
North, among the Samaritans, even though their messianism was not
based on an anointed one, but on a prophet (see Chapter 4, §4, pp. 157-
59).

2. *The Rebirth of Messianism in the Second Century* BCE

With the profound political crisis that struck the Palestinian world during the second century BCE messianic expectations underwent a strong
and sudden rebirth. The way had already been paved by the penetrating
internal criticisms that appear in the work of Qohelet, which questioned
a number of traditional values underlying Late Zadokite society. Messianism's flourishing coincided with the end of Zadokitism.

Faced with the uncertainty, injustice and massacres rampant everywhere, human hopes were raised from the earth and turned towards the
heavens. The Scriptures were read with a new spirit and a group of
illuminated wise men explained the meaning which lay therein, adding
visions of the 'in-between world' to the ancient tradition. These visions
explained the reasons behind the current tragedies and gave hope that
God himself would soon bring about a better world dominated by
righteousness.

---

7. See A. Barucq, *Le livre des Proverbes*, p. 23; A. Caquot, 'Ben Sira et le
messianisme', *Sem* 16 (1965), pp. 43-68, in particular p. 63.

The wise men of the Zadokite period already believed in a presence of God among human beings that was to be fully realized only through the mediation of a more or less hypostatized Wisdom, which would carry out the role of bringing happiness into the human world, judging the wicked (see Prov. 1.20-32; 8.1–9.6). It now seems necessary, however, that God himself come and live among the human beings, because only he seems able to guarantee the contents of what we call messianic hopes.

This movement of messianic hopes is documented in its most complete formulation in the book of *Jubilees*. One day God himself will come down among the humans in order to set about totally renovating the cosmos:

> Until I [God] shall descend [to the earth] and dwell with them (the human beings) in all the ages of eternity...[9]
>
> And the angel of the presence...took the tablets of the division of years from the time of the creation of the law and testimony according to their weeks, according to the jubilees, year by year throughout the full number of jubilees, from the day of the new creation[10] when the heaven and earth and all of the creatures shall be renewed according to the powers of heaven and according to the whole nature of earth, until the sanctuary of the Lord is created in Jerusalem upon Mount Zion. And all the lights will be renewed for healing and peace and blessing for all the elect of Israel and in order that it might be thus from that day and unto all the days of the earth (*Jub.* 1.26, 29).

The new creation will be a complete renewal of the entire cosmos, from the sanctuary of Jerusalem to the heavens and their stars, which will finally stop sending their evil influence to the earth.

Awaiting God's descent to earth could seem an inheritance of messianic expectations without the Messiah, since there does not appear to be an intermediary between divine intervention and human salvation. In reality, though, this conception stems from a different spiritual attitude

---

8.   *an altar*: with the Hebrew; the Greek text reads 'a house'.

9.   The idea that God would come down to the earth one day and re-establish justice himself, or even remain in the earth among the humans, is documented in *Jub.* 1.17 and is particularly frequent in the *Test. XII Patr.*; see the clear passage in *T. Sim.* 6.5 ('Then Shem will be glorified, because God the Lord, the Great One in Israel, shall appear on the earth in order to save Adam—all human beings—men through himself'); *T. Levi* 2.11; 5.2; *T. Naph.* 8.2-3; *T. Zeb.* 9.8. The passages of *T. Levi* 8.11; *T. Jud.* 22.2; *T. Ash.* 7.3 are less clear.

10.   See Isa. 66.22.

than that of the messianism without the Messiah found in the preceding centuries. The earlier belief had been that justice would have come to the earth as a gift of God, characterizing the world to come, but that world was still a distinctly human one. In the new conception God's intervention is imagined as being so complete that he himself will come and live among the humans. In other words, he becomes the mediator between himself and human beings, almost as if to emphasize the idea that the task is so great that no human could perform the messianic anointed one's functions. Following this line of thought, the role of the Messiah can only be carried out by God himself; he and he alone can be the Messiah. The ideology of the early Apocalyptic certainly lies behind this sort of conception, casting its gaze on the entire cosmos and not only on the earth.

At any rate, this idea was never very widespread, because the Later Apocalyptic, the Apocalyptic or Enochic *Book of Dreams* (approx. 163 BCE), was still more interested in history than in the cosmos; God will guide history up to the Great Judgment that is to renew the world. Humanity will be entrusted to the Messiah only after the Judgment, and the Messiah will govern in God's name. The idea that God will come down to the earth to live among men remained more in an embryonic stage, an extreme possibility rather than a fully elaborated theory. The idea, however, lay at the basis of a new form of messianism that would develop over the course of the second century BCE, continuing through the first century and reaching its greatest expression in Christianity.

3. *Superhuman Figures in Ancient and Middle Judaism*

Even before 200 BCE, there were two men present in traditional Jewish culture who held a peculiar status inasmuch as they had not died and, therefore, lived in some part of heaven: Elijah and Enoch. Elijah had been carried to heaven in a chariot of fire (2 Kgs 2.11). Genesis says of Enoch, 'Enoch walked with God; then he was no more, because God took him [with him?]' (Gen. 5.24).

The figure of Elijah was already active in the tradition; an addition to the end of the book of Malachi (3.23-24), whose date cannot be established precisely, says that Elijah will return to the earth one day to bring peace in Israel and to invite people to convert before the Great Day of Yhwh, in order to prevent God from striking Israel. The task assigned Elijah is relatively limited; he will not establish the kingdom of Israel, but he will have a part in its salvation even without being a king or a priest. His role is something more, and, with regards to salvation, his role is of a messianic nature.

Enoch has the same messianic characteristics as Elijah (he was born, but he did not die) as is described in Genesis as a figure linked to astronomy; he lived 365 years, as many as there are days in the solar calendar first proposed in Israel in the *Book of Astronomy* (in substitution of a previous solar calendar of 360 days). Unless we want to lower the date for Genesis, the *Book of Astronomy* must be assigned an early date. I believe that it should be attributed to the Persian period. Enoch is the great revealer of the *Book of Watchers* and the *Book of Astronomy*, along with many other later works. With the exception of the *Book of Parables*, where he is identified with the Son of Man (*1 En.* 71.14), who is in turn called the Messiah (*1 En.* 48.10 and 52.4), most of all Enoch is presented as one who reveals hidden truths. These truths hold a saving value for human beings, though in this early phase it is difficult to see in Enoch a true messiah. He was a superhuman, revealing figure. His role was that of intermediary, but not of salvation, at least not directly.

Enoch's position is extremely high, even higher than that of the angels; he acts as mediator between them and God. He carries messages to God from the fallen angels, who ask for forgiveness, and he takes God's negative response back to them (*1 En.* [*BW*] 12–13).

Enoch was also the first Jew to visit the underworld, in the extreme West, where he visited (*1 En.* [*BW*] 22) the souls of the dead, who had already been judged individually (the good separated from the evil) and were awaiting the collective and final Great Judgment.

A third superhuman figure is Melchizedek. Until recently, the existence of this superhuman Melchizedek was unknown, or rather, he was believed to be a later phenomenon related to the origins of Christianity. His existence was witnessed by only two texts; the first is the letter to the Hebrews (7.3): 'Without father, without mother, without genealogy, having neither beginning of days nor end of life, but resembling the Son of God, he remains a priest forever'. The other text is the apocryphal *2 (Slavonic) Enoch*,[11] contemporary to the letter to the Hebrews, where

11. *2 (Slavonic) Enoch* (*2 En.*) is an apocryphal text belonging to the second half of the first century CE (recension B). A fuller version, probably from the fifth century (recension A) also exists. It has been handed down to us only in Palaeo-Slavic.

we are told that he was the son of Nir, an otherwise unknown person in the Jewish tradition, son of Methuselah, son of Enoch. He is therefore an antediluvian character born, according to this text, of a virgin birth to Sophonim, wife of Nir, after the latter had already been proclaimed high priest by the people. The baby is born with the signs of the priesthood and already able to speak like an adult. He is 'priest of priests forever' (*2 En.* 71.29). With the approach of the flood, the archangel Michael descended from heaven, took the baby and carried him to safety in Eden, where he still lives and shall live forever.

A fragment has emerged from the discoveries at Qumran, 11QMelch, materially written around the middle of the first century BCE, that shows that the myth of Melchizedek was already active much earlier than had been believed earlier. In fact there is a rather strong negative clue going back as far as the second century BCE; the book of *Jubilees*, a *midrash* of Genesis, in spite of its usual tendency to expand on numerous details, completely omits the episode of Melchizedek as narrated in Gen. 14.17-20. Apparently the author preferred not to mention the figure of Melchizedek, or even to lead readers to believe that he had never existed.[12]

A fourth and later superhuman figure, but the most grandiose of all, is the 'Son of Man' of the *Book of Parables*. These characters all act by direct order from God and their works hold a saving function for Israel. In some way, therefore, they play the same role once attributed to the anointed king. We can justifiably speak of messianic functions.

I will not speak here of Daniel 7 because, contrary to what I claimed in my previous *Storia del mondo giudaico*, I do not believe that it refers to a particular person. The figure of the Son of Man that appears there is only the figure of the chosen people, as the author himself clearly states. I therefore believe that the truly autonomous figure of the Son of Man as he appears in the *Book of Parables* is derived from a reading of Dan. 7.13-14 taken out of its context (Dan. 7.27). The grandiosity of the image, which in Daniel is manifestly and purely symbolic, favoured the

12. See M. Testuz, *Les idées religieuses du livre des Jubilées* (Geneva: Librairie E. Droz, 1960). Enoch also has priestly functions; see L. Rosso Ubigli, 'La fortuna di Enoc nel giudaismo antico. Valenze e problemi', *Annali di storia dell'esegesi* 1 (1984), pp. 153-64. In *Jub.* 7.38 Enoch gives instructions for worship (*Yom kippur*) and for behaviour (*Jub.* 21.10). In *Jub.* 4.25 Enoch evens acts as a priest. Contrary to the biblical tradition, *Jub.* 7.39 establishes that Enoch died.

formation of a belief in the Son of Man as a real individual with extremely broad powers, as we shall see below.

4. *Superhuman Messianism*

In the book of Daniel there is no superhuman figure with messianic characteristics, since the references made to an eschatological time regard Israel. This is true for the stone cut out from the mountain by no human hands, becoming itself a great mountain (Dan. 2.34-35), and for the Son of Man, destined to hold eternal power.

There is, however, a contemporary book, the *Book of Dreams*, datable with certainty to the years immediately after 164 since the last event mentioned is the battle of Beth-sur,[13] which presents an interesting messianic doctrine of the superhuman type, even though its messiah's powers could be called more 'exceptional' than 'superhuman', in the way that we have used this term to refer to Elijah and Enoch. The *Book of Dreams* contains a history of Israel that the author presents as being narrated by Enoch to his son Methuselah after having seen it in a vision. The vision also regards future history. Naturally, the author knows the future well right up to his own time, but after that he knows nothing. That does not mean, however, that his discourse stops at the year 164, only that up until that point he speaks of events that were well known, but from that point on it is pure prophecy. The author is able to do this because he is awaiting something that he believes in with the utmost certainty. He is waiting for God to descend to the earth and judge (1) the sinning angels, (2) the blind sheep (the 'bad' Jews, those who do not believe as he does), and (3) all the peoples.

Having completed his Judgment, God will make the Temple disappear and will build a new one. The new temple (*1 En.* [*BD*] 90.29)[14] will mark the beginning of a new world where an ox with great horns will appear. In the author's metaphorical language the Jews are always referred to as sheep, the angels as humans and foreign peoples as wild or unclean animals. In the middle, between angels and human beings, or in the author's language between humans and sheep, there are the oxen, figures of the biblical tradition particularly blessed by God. Adam and Noah, for example, are oxen, the latter being the only living

13. See J.T. Milik, *The Books of Enoch* (Oxford: Oxford University Press, 1976), p. 44.
14. See *Jub.* 1.27.

creature to be transformed into a man, that is into an angel (*1 En.* [*BD*] 89.1, 9). Shem, Abraham and Isaac are oxen as well, though Jacob is presented as a sheep, as are the fathers of the 12 tribes of Israel. Moses and Aaron are sheep as well (*1 En.* [*BD*] 89.17-18), and not oxen.

The ox awaited by the author of the *Book of Dreams* is a man who will have the same blessing from God as Adam and the patriarchs up until Isaac. He will govern over all peoples (*1 En.* [*BD*] 90.37). The author's line of thought is as follows: history is destined to go worse and worse until God intervenes to punish the wicked, Jews and non-Jews alike. After the Great Judgment God will build a new temple and there will finally be a reign of righteousness under this exceptional being, who becomes the Messiah in the sense of the 'king', but with no link to the house of David. In fact he will be of a superior nature to the men of his age, until all men become like him. The Messiah will come after the Judgment and will have the role of administering the order and righteousness desired by God on earth.

The book of *Jubilees*, as we have seen, betrays a strong dislike of the figure of Melchizedek, eliminating him from its story while normally additions abound. At first, this dislike could be attributed to the fact that the figure of Melchizedek could in some way justify the position of the Hasmoneans who, in contrast with the Jewish tradition, were both kings and priests. But the discovery of the Qumran fragment 11QMelch shows that the author of *Jubilees* could have had more precise and more serious cause for making the figure of Melchizedek disappear from his work. Melchizedek was one of Enoch's antagonists and presented the marked characteristics of a saviour figure.

11QMelch is very fragmentary and its meaning is not always clear. A few phrases, however, no matter what the context, are disconcerting and are in any case of the greatest interest. Lines 5-6 read: '[Melchize]dek will make them come back to themselves and will proclaim an amnesty, freeing them from [the debt of] all their iniquities...', and at l. 8: 'when expiation for all the [sons of the light(?)] and the me[n] of Melchizedek's part will be completed'. Psalm 82.1 is referred to him and at l. 10 we read: 'Elohim has taken his place in the [assembly of El]'. At l. 13: 'Melchizedek will carry out the venge[ance] of the judgments of El'. In l. 16, Isa. 52.7 is referred to him as well: 'Your elohim [reigns]'. His reign is extended over those who belong to his group: '[Z]ion is [the assembly...of those] who uphold the Covenant' (l. 24). He also seems to be indicated as '[anoin]ted of the spiri[t]' (l. 18). And in the end his shall be the role of freeing the Jews from the hand of Belial (l. 25).[15]

In another Qumranic text (4QAmram[b]) God's great antagonist is called *Mlkrš'*. Behind this otherwise unknown name it is hard not to see a name based on the reversal of Melchizedek, the devil, the 'wicked king' in contrast to the 'righteous king'.

A number of things can be deduced from this text: (1) Melchizedek is a superhuman being, an *'elohim*.[16] (2) His task is that of bringing the Jews back onto the right path, that of converting them. (3) It is he who shall announce the forgiveness of past sins. (4) He also has the task of carrying out God's vengeance, if not that of Judgment itself (the text is not clear). These are typically messianic functions, because they are related to salvation. It must be pointed out, though, that the importance of these functions has grown enormously when compared to more ancient forms of messianism. And along with the growth of the functions we see a growth, so to speak, of the messianic figure's nature, assuming characteristics which are more and more superhuman. While the future Messiah of the *Book of Dreams* is to have the nature of the patriarchs, Elijah, Enoch and now Melchizedek belong to a decidedly higher plane than the human one; they were born, but they did not die.

The greatest development of superhuman messianism in the period prior to the preachings of Jesus and the rise of Christianity is seen in the figure of the Son of Man in the *Book of Parables* (approx. 30 BCE). The figure, as such, was certainly derived from the book of Daniel, but it has become a truly autonomous figure identified with Enoch (*1 En.* [*BP*] 71.14) and also declared to be the Messiah (*1 En.* [*BP*] 52.4). Son of Man therefore seems to be a title[17] belonging to a mysterious and

15. See E. Puech, 'Notes sur le manuscrit de XIQMelkisedeq', *RevQ* 12 (1987), pp. 483-513.

16. See C. Gianotto, *Melchisedek e la sua tipologia* (Supplementi alla Rivista Biblica, 12; Brescia: Paideia, 1984), p. 64.

17. Vermes holds that, at least in the Gospels, 'Son of Man' does not represent a title. In one sense he is right, because, as we have seen, the expression 'Son of Man' in the end merely indicates a character. In more concrete terms, though, it is difficult to distinguish between the character and his functions, especially given the fact that they are indicated through the use of the same term. In order to put a chronological distance between the 'Son of Man' and Jesus, Vermes must postdate *BP*, which would thus become a Christian work. The identification of the Son of Man with Enoch, however, makes this interpretation quite improbable (*1 En.* 71.14). See G. Vermes, *Jesus the Jew: A Historian's Reading of the Gospels*

superhuman figure with messianic functions. The identification of this figure with Enoch in the *Book of Parables* may be an addition, but certainly not by a Christian hand (*1 En.* [*BP*] 71.14).

In the *Book of Parables* we see that certain traits of the royal Messiah have been attributed to the superhuman Messiah and that he is said to have existed near God since before the creation. His mission shall regard all people and righteousness shall characterize the world governed over by him.[18] The messianic character is given three different titles in the book: the first is 'the Righteous One', then 'the Chosen One', and finally 'Son of Man'.

The following is a passage that illustrates the new messianic concept. The Son of Man's existence had been willed by God *ab aeterno*, but unlike the other creatures that came into existence, even though foreseen and willed *ab aeterno*, the Son of Man's existence began in the moment when his name was first pronounced. From that moment he has been hidden, whether in some part of the cosmos or even earth is not clear.[19]

> In that place I saw the fountain of righteousness, which does not become depleted and is surrounded completely by numerous fountains of wisdom. All the thirsty ones drink [of the water] and become filled with wisdom. [Then] their dwelling places become with the holy, righteous, and elect ones. At that hour, that Son of Man was given a name by the Lord of the Spirits,[20] even before the creation of the sun and the moon, before the creation of the stars, he was given a name in the presence of the Lord of the Spirits. He will become a staff for the righteous ones in order that they may lean on him and not fall. He is the light of the gentiles and he will become hope of those who are sick in their hearts. All those who live upon the earth shall fall and worship before him; they shall glorify, bless, and sing the name of the Lord of the Spirits. For this purpose he became the Chosen One; he was concealed by Him prior to

(London: 2nd edn, SCM Press, 1983), pp. 160-86, and P. Sacchi, 'Gesù l'ebreo', *Henoch* 6 (1984), pp. 347-68. Milik's opinion that *BP* was written toward the end of the third century is completely unfounded; see Sacchi, *Apocrifi*, I, p. 424.

18. See P. Sacchi, '*Ethiopic Enoch* 91. 15 and the Problem of Mediation', in *Jewish Apocalyptic*, pp. 140-49.

19. See Aune, 'Problem of the Messianic Secret'.

20. 'By the Lord of the Spirits': literally reads 'before the Lord of the Spirits'. This is based on a Hebrew expression used in passive verb constructions when the agent is God. See J. Carmignac, 'Le complément d'agent après un verbe passif dans l'Hébreu et dans l'araméen de Qumran', *RevQ* 9 (1978), pp. 409-28, pp. 421-24.

the creation of the world, and will be before Him [that is do His will] for eternity (*1 En. [BP]* 48.1-6).

The fulcrum of the world ruled over by the Son of Man is righteousness, and wisdom itself is derived from that righteousness in a descending movement towards humanity. Individual human beings, in contrast, can reach righteousness only through wisdom, moving along the same lines but in the opposite direction. Heavenly righteousness is reserved for only the righteous ones or the chosen ones, but there will come a time when all of humanity, through the messianic works of the Son of Man, will partake in the drink of wisdom.

Again in the *Book of Parables* we read:

In that place[21] my eyes saw the Elect One of righteousness and of faithfulness, and righteousness shall prevail in his days, and the righteous and elect ones shall be without number before him and forever and ever. And I saw a dwelling place underneath the wings of the Lord of the Spirits; and all the righteous and the elect before him shall be as intense as the light of fire. Their mouths shall be full of blessing; and their lips will praise the name of the Lord of the Spirits, and righteousness before him will have no end; and uprightness before him [probable meaning, 'because of him'] will not cease.

There [underneath the wings of God] I wanted to dwell; and my soul [that is I] desired that dwelling place, because my portion is already there; for thus has it been reserved for me by the Lord of the Spirits (*1 En. [BP]* 39.6-8).

One of the tools to be used by the Son of Man in establishing righteousness on earth will be his absolute knowledge of the Law. At the time of the *Book of Parables* in Israel there were already several different interpretations of the Law, different *halakot*. The question of which interpretation was the true one must have been very much alive. Only the Messiah, according to this book, will know the precise meaning of each norm.

[The Elect One] is mighty in all the secrets of righteousness, and oppression will vanish like a shadow having no foundation. The Elect One stands before the Lord of the Spirits [that is does his will]; his glory is forever and ever and his power is unto all generations (*1 En. [BP]* 49.2).

The Son of Man's principal task is that of carrying out the Great Judgment in God's name. He shall overthrow the wicked, whom the

---

21. 'In that place': with ms. c. The rest of the tradition reads 'in those days'.

author identifies primarily with those with political power, or at any rate those who hold some form of power, while the good by definition are the poor, the humble and the marginalized in general. He will throw down kings from their thrones and break the teeth of the sinners. His judgment will be severe. He alone will carry out all the functions that the *Epistle of Enoch* had attributed to all the Watching Angels (*1 En.* [EE] 91.15). Thus he will set up God's reign on earth. In this text the coming of God's reign coincides with the messianic figure, unlike the text of the *Book of Dreams*, where the Judgment precedes the advent of the Messiah.

Regarding the reign of the Son of Man—Messiah, it is not only a future reality, as in earlier apocalyptic works, but it already exists. It is already reality in the 'in-between world'. The 'in-between world', however, plays a different role in the *Book of Parables* than in the thought of Zechariah. It is not the place of formation of a reality destined to be reproduced on earth. The reality of the 'in-between world' in some way communicates with our world *already, now*. The righteous (or the chosen ones) who have left this world *already* live together with the angels in the world of the Messiah. What others foresaw for the future, in the *Book of Parables* becomes both future and present. It is a further development of the cosmic ideology of the ancient *Book of Watchers*, now structured in such a way as to depict a kingdom with its king. What in the end distinguishes the *Book of Parables* from the ideology of the Essenes is the fact that the Essenes believed that they could sing God's praises together with the angels already here on this earth. For them, eternity had already begun on earth; there was no passing away of this world in order to usher in the new one. When the adept arrived at the 'eternal Good' (1QS 4.3) and at contemplation of 'eternal being' (1QS 11.5-6)[22] he was already in the eternal world.

The influence of the ideas contained in the book of *Enoch*, and the *Book of Parables* in particular, on Christianity is clear. The influence on some books of the New Testament on a literary level has been acknowledged for some time,[23] but I feel that this book is most important because it provides a cultural context very similar to the one in which the men and women of the New Testament lived. On several occasions Jesus claims to have the same functions as the Son of Man in the *Book*

22. See also the work known as *Songs of the Sabbath Sacrifice* (4Q400-407 and 11Q17).

23. See Sacchi, *Apocrifi*, I, pp. 425-31.

of Parables. But since he refers to the Son of Man without referring to the *Book of Parables*, this means that the people must have known who the 'Son of Man' was independently of the book. He was the super-human figure of the eschatological judge. It is for this that Jesus can say in Mk 2.10-11: 'But so that you may know that the Son of Man has authority on earth to forgive sins... *I* say to you, stand up, take your mat and go home'. If we want to hold that the people understand Jesus' words and that they make sense, then we must admit that both he and the people knew that the Son of Man was the great eschatological Judge.

In Christianity we see, furthermore, that Jesus presents himself as the absolute interpreter of the Law. Taking, for example, the Sermon of the Mount, the formula 'Verily, verily I say to you' are words of charisma and authority, and not of an interpretation of the texts following human logic.[24]

5. *Dual Messianism*

Between the second and the first centuries BCE another particular type of messianism developed. This form was derived from the dual mes-sianism of Zechariah, but the link was only a literary one, not a his-torical one. We will call this form 'dual' messianism, or perhaps it would be better to say 'priestly' messianism for the reasons we shall mention below. There are two anointed ones, the anointed of Aaron or of Levi, and the anointed one of Israel or Judah. No mention is made of David or of Zadok; an even broader denominator is being sought. The fundamental element of this type of messianism is the clear distinction between the civil and religious functions, both of them being saving functions projected into the future. The two Messiahs are yet to come, and when they do come they will present themselves hierarchically with the priestly Messiah occupying the higher position. This is a dual messianism, which can also be defined as priestly messianism because of the primacy of the priestly Messiah over the lay one. This type of messianism has been documented both in Essenism and in the *Testa-ments of the Twelve Patriarchs*, where it is particularly developed.

> They [the Essenes] shall be governed according to the first rules, those used to instruct the members of the Community, until the coming of the prophet and the anointed ones of Aaron and of Israel (1QS 9.10-11).

24. See Davies, *Setting of the Sermon of the Mount*.

The community admits that the rules it has given itself may not be perfect and therefore awaits someone who can indicate the perfect *halakah*. Not only the two Messiahs are awaited for this function, but also a prophet who is to precede them. It is the same schema that Christianity applied to John the Baptist with regards to Jesus. There must have been some differences of opinion on this matter within Essenism itself and perhaps there was some internal evolution.[25]

At any rate, that a prophet was awaited in order to put an end to political and juridical problems is also documented in 1 Maccabees (14.41). When Simon found himself in a juridically rather confused situation, having concentrated religious and civil authority in his own hands and having assumed the high priesthood without being of Zadokite descent, he found a suitable expedient for buying time in putting the problem off until 'a trustworthy prophet should arise'. For the people the solution was acceptable, so the possibility of a mediator capable of referring to God's will must have been commonly acknowledged.

While in the Essenic text the superiority of the anointed one of Aaron over the anointed one of Israel can only be deduced by the fact that the one precedes the other, the motif is much more developed in the *Testaments of the Twelve Patriarchs*. In *T. Jud.* 21.4 we read: 'Just as the heavens are superior to the earth, thus the priesthood of God is superior to the kingdom on earth'. See also *T. Reub.* 6.8.

The priestly Messiah's tasks not only include the final interpretation of the Law in all the points where the *halakah* is uncertain,[26] but he is

25. See also J. Starcky, 'Les quatre étapes du messianisme à Qumran', *RB* 70 (1963), pp. 481-504, in particular p. 482. The text mentioning the prophet and the two anointed ones is clearly legible in the MS. 1QS, which was the first one discovered and which includes practically the entire work. It is, however, relatively late (late first century BCE). The fragment 4Q259 from the early Hasmonaean period (late second century BCE) does not contain the section between vv. 8.15 and 9.11. It is not clear whether this is an omission or rather an earlier and shorter *stratum* of the work. The latter possibility seems to be the more probable. Regarding the fragment 4Q258, which is a bit older than 1QS, it contains part of the passage omitted by 4Q259 and, while it ends in a lacuna in col. 2 with the words corresponding to the middle of l. 10 of 1QS, there is enough space for us to consider it certain that the entire sentence mentioning the prophet and the two anointed ones was present. The idea of a prophet who was to precede the two Messiahs must have risen then around the middle of the first century BCE.

26. This is how I interpret *T. Levi* 18.2: 'To whom [that is to Levi] all the words

also to bind Satan ('Beliar shall be bound by him', *T. Levi* 18.12). Here Satan is given an importance that he is not afforded in the canonical texts. As in Essenism, the world is divided into two parts, two *goralim*, one of Light and one of Darkness. One is under the guide of the angel of Light, generally interpreted as Michael, and the other under the guide of the angel of Darkness, referred to with a variety of names, but it is always the devil (see 1QS 3.15-21). The high priest will have a saving function and will free the world of Satan, that is of evil.

This future priest, however, has nothing in common with the historical priesthood of Israel, not even with its most authentic representatives. It is to be a new and exceptional priesthood. In *T. Levi* 18.1-12 we read:

> When vengeance will have come upon them from the Lord, the priest-hood will lapse.
> And the Lord will raise up a new priest to whom all the words of the Lord will be revealed [therefore he will be able to teach the true *halakah*].
> He shall effect the judgment of truth over the earth for many days...
> This one will shine forth like the sun in the earth;
> he shall take away all darkness from under heaven,
> and there shall be peace in all the earth.
> The heavens shall greatly rejoice in his days
> and the earth shall be glad;
> the clouds will be filled with joy...
> And the glory of the Most High shall burst forth upon him.
> And the spirit of understanding and sanctification shall rest upon him [in the water].
> For he shall give the majesty of the Lord to those who are his sons in truth and forever...
> In his priesthood sin shall cease...
> and he will grant to the saints to eat of the tree of life...
> And Beliar shall be bound by him...

On the whole we have the impression that the author of the *Testaments of the Twelve Patriarchs* expected a new world that was to be ushered in by the Messiahs of Levi and Judah. It is interesting that while the name of David has disappeared, replaced by the broader Judah, the author still awaits the Kingdom of Israel's restoration as prophesied in the old Davidic messianism. In *T. Jud.* 22.2-3 we read:

of the Lord shall be revealed'. On the need for particular revelation in order to know the true *halakah*, see also 1QS 9.10-11.

My rule shall be terminated by men of alien race, until the salvation of Israel comes, until the coming of the God of righteousness, so that Jacob may enjoy tranquility and peace, as well as all the nations. He [the descendant of Judah] shall preserve the power of my kingdom forever. With an oath the Lord swore to me that the rule would not cease for my posterity, forever.

The following passage merits particular attention:

And now, my children, be obedient to Levi and to Judah. Do not exalt yourselves above these two tribes, because the salvation of God will come out of them. For the Lord will raise up from Levi someone as high priest and from Judah someone as king, God and man. He will save all the gentiles and the tribe of Israel (*T. Sim.* 7.1-2).

This passage provides a good example of the problems in textual criticism that surround the apocryphal works which have been handed down to us by Christian circles. Just how much may the Christian scribe have adapted the text to correspond to his own faith we cannot know.

While in disagreement with those who hold this text to be written entirely by a Christian hand, in his edition Becker suppresses the part between 'For the Lord' and 'Israel', because he considers them Christian. I do not agree at all. The 'God and man' is obviously Christian, but I doubt very seriously that a Christian of the second century CE could have expected a high priest from Levi and a king from Judah. If there is something Christian in this part of the text, I feel that it should be seen in the addition of 'as' before the terms 'priest' and 'king' in order to attenuate the concept. For the Christians the sentence makes sense only interpreted metaphorically, that there is only one Messiah combining the functions of priest and king, but first of all who is a descendant of David. In fact the expression 'God and man' is added to the Davidic Messiah. The last part of the text too, 'He will save all the gentiles and the tribe of Israel', could also be Christian, but it could also belong to a phase in Judaism which witnesses an opening toward universalism, as seen in the *Psalms of Solomon*, 17.30-31 for example, where it says that the Messiah will rule over all peoples and that they all will come, in keeping with the ancient prophecies, to honour him in Jerusalem. Universalism, however, had already appeared in the *Book of Dreams* and was also to reappear later in the *Book of Parables*.

Another element in favour of our hypothesis that the text is not the product of Christian hands, but that it was simply re-elaborated by them, is the variant οὕτως, 'thus', in the place of οὗτος, 'he'. 'Thus' marks the Jewish text; the subject of 'will save' is clearly God, in keeping with the scheme presented elsewhere in the book by which the two Messiahs are functions of the saving, but in the end it is only God who saves. The Christians have changed οὕτως to οὗτος making the subject of 'will save' become the Messiah of David. This is a fairly subtle operation, but it is still detectable.

In the text quoted above the two Messiahs and God's salvation are closely related, but they do not completely coincide.

The following is a passage from the *Testament of Naphtali* where the complex relationship between the Messiah and salvation can be seen better:

> Command your children that they be in unity with Levi and Judah, for through them will arise salvation for Israel, and through them Jacob will be blessed. Through their tribes God will appear [dwelling among men on the earth], to save the people of Israel, and to assemble the righteous from among the nations (*T. Naph.* 8.2-3).[27]

Salvation is to come through Levi and Judah, but it will be made complete only by the apparition of God himself who will satisfy the messianic hopes. At any rate, while awaiting the parousia of the anointed high priest, the children of Israel must follow the *halakah* established by the sons of Levi.

> It is for this reason that I command you to give heed to Levi, because he will know the law of God and will give instructions regarding justice and will make sacrifices in Israel until the consummation of times, until the advent of the anointed high priest indicated by the Lord (*T. Reub.* 6.8).

And even more clearly:

> The Most High has given heed to your prayer that you be delivered from wrongdoing, that you should become a son to him, as minister and priest in his presence. The light of knowledge you shall kindle in Jacob, and

---

27. The text presented here is the reconstructed text. The manuscripts give the Christian re-elaboration, substituting 'through them' with 'through him', drawing all attention to Judah while Judah is clearly in the second position. As regards 'dwelling among men', this is certainly an interpolation, because it is not in keeping with the rythm of the text; the two parallel parts are 'to save the people of Israel' and 'assemble the righteous'. This is not necessarily a Christian interpolation, though, because, as we have seen, there were also other universalistic currents of Judaism.

> you shall be as the sun for all the posterity of Israel. Blessing shall be
> given to you and to all your posterity until through his son's mercy the
> Lord shall visit all the nations forever (*T. Levi* 4.2-4).

Still, the current priest possesses the same dignity as the highest
angels (those of the Face of God) and while the people await the great
divine intervention, it is up to the priest to proclaim the right *halakah.*

6. *The Rebirth of Davidic Messianism*

In the *Testament of Judah* some mention is made of the everlasting
kingdom. Apparently this is the kingdom once ascribed to David, but
now understood in more generic terms as the kingdom of Israel. There
is a very strong eschatological tone to the text and perhaps the text is
more polemical with the immorality of the times in general than with
the Hasmonaean dynasty in itself.

> Those who rule shall be like sea monsters,
> swallowing up human beings like fish...
> The Lord will instigate among them factions set against each other
> and conflicts will persist in Israel.
> My rule shall be terminated by men of alien race,
> until the salvation of Israel comes,
> until the coming of the God of righteousness,
> so that Jacob may enjoy tranquility and peace, as well as all the nations.
> He shall preserve the power of my kingdom forever. With an oath the
>   Lord swore to me [to Judah] that the rule would not cease for my
>   posterity, forever (*T. Jud.* 21.7 and 22.1-3).

There were also, however, people who took up decidedly more political positions against the Hasmonaeans, accused of usurping the throne
of Israel which by right could only belong to a descendant of David.
The *Psalms of Solomon*, written just after the middle of the first century
BCE, witness the rebirth of Davidic messianism. The work is usually
attributed to Pharisaic circles, but this responds more to a need to apply
a label at all costs to works which in the end present only the individual
author. We know the Pharisaism of the day only through the *Pirqe
Abot*, a decidedly late work which presents Pharisaism according to its
own ideals. For this reason, its presentation is certainly if not false at
least selective. The period of the *Psalms of Solomon* was dominated by
the figures and the teachings of Shemaya, Abtalion and, later, Hillel.

Withdrawal from political life, understood in terms of acting in the
world with the means of the world, begins with Shemaya. This ten-

dency was later to become characteristic of Pharisaism, especially after the disaster of 70 CE. Among Shemaya's teachings the *Pirqe Abot* conserves the following, which their author must have found quite interesting: 'Love manual labour, hate grandeur, do not let yourself be known to authority' (*Pirqe Ab.* 1.10).

The fundamental problem about how to interpret this passage revolves around the value to be given to the expression *śn' 't hrbnwt,'l ttwd' lršwt*, 'hate grandeur, do not let yourself be known to authority', which is interpreted as an exhortation to humility, to renounce all honours and in the end to give up all power.[28] Others see in this passage an invitation not to neglect manual labour. In this case the individual should keep away from public offices in order to have more time to dedicate to manual labour.[29] It should be pointed out that the verb 'to hate' is very strong and, most of all, the final invitation not to let oneself be known to authority is perplexing. It seems to be an open invitation to believe exclusively in the authority of the Law, and therefore the Sanhedrin, and to oppose, even passively, all other authority.

The author of the *Psalms of Solomon* holds the opposite point of view; he believes in the struggle and awaits salvation with victory. Faced with the overwhelming power of the Romans he sees the only possibility of victory in an exceptional leader, sent by God and fighting in God's name. This leader must be from the line of David and, for that reason, be an anointed one. The Davidic descent of the Messiah is thus reconfirmed in Israel, alongside the more generic messianism which merely mentioned descent from the tribe of Judah.

The text of one of these psalms, no. 17, has already been reproduced above. The author insists that the only legitimate sovereign of Jerusalem must be a descendant of David, and cannot, therefore, be a Hasmonaean. 'Lord, you chose David to be king over Israel, and swore to him about his descendants forever, that his kingdom should not fail before you...'

On the one hand, in this text we find faith in the eternal reign of David, but on the other we have the impression that the eschatological tension has slackened. The author of the *Book of Dreams* seems to have expected the Great Judgment which would have inaugurated the Messiah's reign in the near future, perhaps even in his own lifetime. The

---

28. See V. Castiglioni, *Mishnayot* (3 vols.; Rome: Tipografia Sabbadini, 3rd edn, 1962-64), at the verse.

29. See Marti and Beer, *Pirqe Abot (Giessener Mischna)*, at the verse.

author of the *Psalms of Solomon* experiences his hope with a certain detachment. He is aware of the fact that he does not know the time, and he uses a formula leaving ample room for God's patience: 'in the time known to you' (*Pss. Sol.* 17.21).

The final destination of history, though, can only be this. The function of David's descendant, when he comes, will be that of bringing about justice on earth, justice understood as social equality, according to a type of thought also documented in the *Book of Parables*, written only a short time afterwards: 'You will lead them in equality' can be found in the same psalm (17.46). This is the second element of the messianic category: the realization of a reign of justice.

Assuming that the author was a Pharisee, the events of his life brought him closer to the Jews of the countryside, to the despised *'am hā'āreṣ*. He certainly shared much of the Pharisees' ideology. He believed in resurrection, reserved for the righteous, and in the destruction of the wicked (*Pss. Sol.* 13.9-10, if it is not an interpolation; but also 3.12). He also believed in and vigorously proclaims human freedom of choice, against those who would deny it (*Pss. Sol.* 9.7). The fact that the righteous, in practice identified with those who fear God (*Pss. Sol.* 15.13), can suffer tribulation is explained by the principle of paternal correction (*Pss. Sol.* 14.1);[30] but he also took up a position against all those who had been able to remain in Jerusalem, Pharisees and Sadducees alike. He had been driven from his land and lived in poverty (*Pss. Sol.* 17.5 together with 16.13). Poverty is the most severe correction that God can inflict on those he loves. Anyhow, the author felt that his situation was profoundly unjust and placed his hopes in the coming of the anointed of God, who would re-establish justice.

Hopes in impending salvation arriving on the heels of a war were very strong in the *War Scroll* (perhaps the second half of the first

---

30. The author of the *Psalms of Solomon* searches for the solution to the problem of the righteous man who suffers, following the same path as Ben Sira (2.1-6). The misadventures of the righteous are not punishment, but correction: 'The Lord is faithful to those who truly love him, to those who endure his discipline, to those who live in the righteousness of his commandments' (*Pss. Sol.* 14.1-2). This idea is expressed in even more radical terms in the book of Wisdom; the righteous must be put to the test. His reward for this 'brief trial' cannot be compared to the pain suffered: 'For when they were tried, though they were being disciplined (παιδευόμενοι) in mercy...' (Wis. 11.9a). 'They were troubled for a little while as a warning (νουθεσία), and received a symbol of deliverance to remind them of your Law's command' (Wis. 16.6).

century BCE), but here they rest essentially on God, who, through his strength consisting more in the array of angels than of men, will bring victory to his poor and his humble. In the *War Scroll* the role of the anointed one is quite peculiar. In 1QM 11.7-8 all the illuminated wise men seem to be defined as anointed ones: 'By way of your anointed ones, those who know your decisions, you have let us know the times of the wars...' Here 'anointed one' does not mean 'messiah', but rather indicates the particular charisma of illumination, not supreme authority.

We can conclude that beginning with the second century BCE messianic expectations had again risen forcefully in Israel. Such expectations took on a wide variety of forms, the only common denominator being the expectation that God would in some way finally bring salvation to Israel. The essence of dual messianism then creates some problems. While the fact that for a very brief period in history there had been two anointed ones in Israel may have justified the theory, it is still difficult to believe that dual messianism was born solely for that reason.

The division into two figures follows an idea of power by which, in modern terms, civil and religious functions were separated. This reflects the long-standing contrast in Judaism between τιμὴ ἀρχιερατική and προστασία τοῦ λαοῦ. Dual messianism is the eschatological projection of a historical situation, and furthermore bears witness to the priesthood's desire to affirm its superiority over civil authority.

It should also be noticed that in the Essenic texts, and in those close to the Essenic movement, salvation is seen as a process over time. Before the anointed ones of Aaron and Levi are to appear a prophet must appear first. But even the role of the illuminated wise men, in the end anointed ones too, is a tangible sign that God has a plan regarding human history. Even in the midst of much difficulty and a widespread sense of impending doom (for example the prophecy of the destruction of the Temple [*1 En.* [*BD*] 90.28; *Jub.* 1.27] and the danger of a new exile foreseen by Abtalion [*Pirqe Ab.* 1.11])[31] God lays the basis of future hope in history.

31. 'Wise men, be wary of your words, because you could be condemned to the punishment of exile and wander in lands of bad water. Your students could drink of them and die. The name of Heaven [that is of God] would be profaned'. Formally this text is addressed to the masters, but since the consequences of their lack of faith in the Law fall on the disciples as well, it seems to me that we can take it to refer to all of Israel. Abtalion had the idea that society was falling apart. See *REJ*, at the entry.

Even in some of the Qumran fragments we find documentation of expectations of a descendant of David as anointed one (see especially 4QpGen[a], commenting on Gen. 49.8-10), but even though there are some texts which only mention the royal messiah and others mentioning only the priestly one, Essenic messianism should be considered dual. The basic text remains 1QS 9.11; see also CD 12.22-13.1; 14.19; 19.1-11; 20.1.[32]

On the whole the messianic movements were viewed with suspicion by the ruling class in Jerusalem, because they were seen as politically dangerous, for both the complications that they could bring to relations with the Romans and for the egalitarian and populistic doctrines that often animated them. The Pharisees must also have been very suspicious of the bellicose spirit behind some messianic movements, very far removed from the most characteristic Pharisaic thought.

7. Christian Messianism in the Judaism of the Day

As far as Christian messianism is concerned, I believe that it is best understood in terms of superhuman messianism, and especially the figure of the Son of Man, and not the royal messianic ideology.[33] The texts of the New Testament themselves seem to reject the interpretation of Jesus as the royal, Davidic Messiah (see Jn 6.15 and the problem of the messianic secret). If Jesus' kingdom exists, it is not on this earth. This problem is clearly felt by John who has Jesus clarify the question before Pilate (Jn 18.36). Besides, beginning with the Messiah of the *Book of Dreams*, the superhuman Messiah is also king of an eschatological kingdom. I am convinced that Jesus was sure to have a particular relationship with God. See the parable of the wicked tenants (Mk 12.1, which immediately follows Jesus' discourse on the authority with which he speaks). Here 'son' of the landowner is a meaningful word, because this son is the sole heir.[34] In Jesus' day, expectations of an

32. The messianic fragments from Qumran have recently been presented by F. García Martínez, 'Nuevos textos mesiánicos de Qumrán y el Nuevo Testamento', *Communio* 26 (1993), pp. 3-31.

33. See F. Ardusso, *Gesù Cristo figlio del Dio vivente* (Cinisello Balsamo: Edizioni Paoline, 1992), p. 125.

34. On the value of the parable of the wicked tenants, see J.H. Charlesworth, 'The Righteous Teacher and the Historical Jesus: A Study of the Self-Understandings of Two Jewish Charismatics', in W.P. Wearer (ed.), *Perspectives on Christol-*

eschatological judge, of a superhuman saviour, of the Son of Man had been widespread in Judaism for some time.

The Gospel of Mark places the healing of the paralytic among the first episodes recounted; Jesus forgives his sins before healing him. ' "But so that you may know that the Son of Man has authority on earth to forgive sins"—he said to the paralytic—"I say to you, stand up, take your mat and go to your home" ' (Mk 2.10-11). Note the shift from the third person to the first. The meaning could be summarized as follows: 'So that you understand that the Great Judge (the people must have understood in these terms) not only has the power to condemn, but also to forgive, *I*, in order to demonstrate that I have this power, say to you...'

8. *The Reduction of the Messianic Tasks*

After the catastrophe of 70 CE messianism began to decline, even though it remained alive within Judaism for another century.[35] The importance of the Messiah begins to diminish with the Syriac *Apocalypse of Baruch* (late first century CE), though the figure still remains greater than the normal human. The Messiah's task is that of preparing the world for the Great Judgment; the relationship between the Great Judgment and the Messiah has thus been reversed in comparison to the *Book of Dreams*. The Messiah's role is that of preparing the way for God's kingdom, not that of ruling over it himself.

This Messiah is a human being. It is said, however, that he is revealed (2 Bar. 29.3; 39.7) by God and that after he has performed his task he will return (2 Bar. 30.1), it seems, to heaven. He will bring justice to the pagans and stability to Israel; his final act will consist in judging and executing the last king of the Gentiles (2 Bar. 40.1-2). His duties will then be complete and he will reign until the end of the world, until the moment when 'the world of corruption has ended' (2 Bar. 40.3). The kingdom of incorruptibility will begin then.

The function assigned to the Messiah in *4 Ezra* is similar to this. The Messiah again shows decidedly human traits, though he is clearly of a superior humanity compared to common mortals. The Messiah in *4 Ezra* is again presented as a descendant of David (12.32). He will

ogy (Nashville: Exodus Press, 1988), pp. 73-94.

35. See W. Horbury, 'Messianism among Jews and Christians in the Second Century', *Augustinianum* 28 (1988), pp. 71-88.

preside over the Great Judgment and will apply justice to the pagans. He will live for 400 years. At the end of his 400 years he will die and with his death history will be drawn to a close. From that point on the world will return to its primordial silence; for seven days, seven just as in the creation, there will be total silence. Then there will be a new creation, a new world, finally the one with no evil.

Chapter 15

THE RIGHTEOUS

1. *The Righteous in Ben Sira*

After Qohelet, a second fundamental moment in Jewish thought is represented by Ben Sira. His importance in the history of Jewish thought is
much greater than is usually thought even in the light of important
recent works dedicated to his book, such as those by Prato and
Schnabel, who have pointed out the complexity of the underlying
thought. Boccaccini's *Middle Judaisms* (pp. 77-98) should also be singled out for its demonstration of the importance of Ben Sira's thought,
not only within the book itself, but for the further development of
Middle Jewish thought.

We have many Hebrew fragments of Ecclesiasticus found in two different locations, Qumran and the *genizah* of Cairo. The Hebrew text
presents many variants in comparison to the Greek, which seems to
respect the original more closely, at least with regards to the thought,
than the Hebrew. For this reason the Hebrew is only used when necessary for correcting the Greek text in single expressions. When the
Hebrew variants give a very different meaning, this creates a number of
problems concerning the history of the text, which are quite difficult to
resolve. The Hebrew text seems to have been transmitted in Essenic
circles which were interested in weakening the force of some of Ben
Sira's statements in favour of humanity's complete freedom of choice.[1]

As we have seen several times, righteousness, that is the condition of
the man who 'does the Law', from Ezekiel to the Chronicler was considered a fundamental element in salvation in the Jewish world. We
have also seen that some authors, Job and Qohelet, spoke out against
this conception of righteousness.

Ezekiel not only held that man can live only inasmuch as he observes

1. See n. 6 below.

the Law, but he also felt that the man who repented his errors and went back to 'doing the Law', could continue living because of the Law that he went back to observing. This was a vision of things that could not hold up to the rational criticism of Job and Qohelet.

Qohelet brought the whole system to a crisis, because the subject that was supposed to benefit from the arrangement, the righteous man, seemed to disappear. Qohelet did not believe in the existence of the righteous person for the simple reason that there is no righteous person without sin (Qoh. 7.20). In Ezekiel's system, the existence of a wicked man who did not observe the Law yet continued to live was possible, though this creates a contradiction with the assertion that the righteous man 'lives through the Law': 'For the righteousness which he has done he shall live' (Ezek. 18.22). At any rate, for Ezekiel the two moments, one of righteousness and one of iniquity, are two distinct phases within the same individual. Qohelet's discourse is not only innovative in that it excludes the possibility of a person without sin, but because he claims there is no 'righteous person' without sin. For Qohelet, the word 'righteousness' loses its meaning when applied to human beings. The 'righteous' exist, at least on a theoretical level; in practice Qohelet believed in the existence of the 'righteous within certain limits'. This idea, however, did not fit well with the commonly held idea that salvation was reserved for the righteous, and no one else. Qohelet's solution became possible when he separated the problem of righteousness from that of salvation. God sends the various 'moments' of one's life following a plan that we cannot know, supposing one exists, but which in no way corresponds to the retributory principle. In Qohelet's thought righteousness did not cause a problem, because God's action is not based on retribution. If such a problem existed, and the tradition demonstrates that it continued to exist, for Qohelet it was a matter of pure theory.

We have already seen the radical solution that the Teacher of Righteousness and Essenism gave to the problem many years later. Human beings are always sinners and sin is a sort of impurity inherent in human flesh. Man can be freed of the impurity only through a gratuitous act of God. This idea was to be particularly fruitful in Christianity, but it did not bear fruit, at least not immediately, in Israel. At any rate, the problem of just who was righteous and what righteousness was continued to be one of the central problems of Middle Judaism. The value to be given to the Law and to God's behaviour towards human beings depended on the problem's solution, and these were also central themes in Jewish speculation. In a system of thought no element is independent of the others and reflection on the limits and values of human righteousness occupied a very important position in the thought of Middle Judaism.

While Ben Sira reflected on more or less all the themes being debated in his day, his thought is centred around the theme of righteousness. He was a product of his time and therefore strongly attached to the Late Zadokite tradition. Ben Sira defended the values linked to that tradition, even though he was aware of the weight of some of his criticisms. The underlying problem for Ben Sira can be summarized more or less as follows: what is the relationship between God's omnipotence and omniscience, which were deeply felt at the time, and human freedom of choice? He knew that knowledge, in the fullest sense of the word, that is the full understanding of the meaning of things, belonged only to God. It was the Wisdom, God's first creation, that lived in the 'in-between world'.

> All wisdom is from the Lord
> and with him it remains forever…
> Wisdom was created before all other things,
> and prudent understanding from eternity…
> There is but one who is wise, greatly to be feared,
> seated upon his throne—the Lord.
> It is he who created it;
> he saw it and took its measure;
> he poured it out upon all his works,
> upon all the living according to his gift;
> he lavished it upon those who love him…
> To fear the Lord is the beginning of Wisdom (Sir. 1.1-14).

Ben Sira learned from Qohelet that the only true knowledge, the only one worthy of that name, is knowledge of the whole, but that intelligence is God's alone. Even though he is aware that human capacity for comprehension is derived from God's gift of wisdom, he still inserts these new ideas into the old value system, and defends both the value of the Law and human freedom of choice.

Ben Sira knows that the differences between one human and another do not depend on the individual human beings, but on God. He also knows that the best of fortune can change quickly for no apparent reason (see the passage reproduced below). The influence of Qohelet's doctrine of the 'moments' is clear, and Ben Sira blends it with other elements of Scripture in order to demonstrate its truth. He also felt the truth of the idea of human freedom of choice, without which he knew that Judaism would have lost some of its fundamental values. Ben Sira had a perfect grasp of the tradition's weak point; it wasn't so much a question of insisting on God's omnipotence and omniscience, but of insisting on them without confirming the principle of human freedom and responsibility for one's own actions. 'When an ungodly person curses Satan, he curses himself' (Sir. 21.27). The critique of the early Enochism emerges clearly; it is not true that all sin comes from the devil (see *1 En.* [*BW*] 10.8). Confirming human freedom meant placing an obstacle in the way of the mixture of the sacred with the profane. This meant defending the Deuteronomic tradition, the one which held that it had been Israel that chose between serving God or other gods. It is no mere coincidence that the words of Deut. 30.15 reappear only slightly paraphrased in Sir. 15.17: 'Before each person are life and death, and whichever one chooses will be given'. Ben Sira accepts the two ideas even though rationally they are difficult to reconcile. He develops his reflection in such a way as to make them appear valid in a new dimension where they could co-exist. God is omnipotent and his action in the individual's life is arbitrary, but human freedom also exists. That made it necessary to investigate the essence of the Law, though in constant reference to the structure of the entire cosmos. The meaning and value of human righteousness can be grasped only if the individual is considered against this backdrop.

For Ben Sira the sacred and the profane were two clearly distinct realities. He understood that in losing awareness of the freedom of choice, the individual also lost his autonomy before the sacred.

> Why is one day more important than another,
> when all the daylight in the year is from the sun?
> By the Lord's wisdom they were distinguished,
> and he appointed the different seasons and festivals.
> Some days he blessed[2] and hallowed,
> and some he made ordinary days.
> All human beings come from the ground,
> and humankind was created out of the dust.
> In the fullness of his knowledge the Lord distinguished them
> and appointed their different ways.
> Some he blessed and exalted,
> and some he made holy and brought near to himself;
> but some he cursed and brought low,

---

2.   *blessed*: with the Hebrew ברך. The Greek reads ἀνύψωσεν.

and turned them out of their place.
Like clay in the hand of the potter,
to be moulded as he pleases,[3]
so all are in the hand of their Maker,
to be given whatever he decides.
Good is the opposite of evil,
and life the opposite of death;
so the sinner is the opposite of the godly.
Look at all the works of the Most High;
they come in pairs, one the opposite of the other (Sir. 33.7-15).

This is the structure of creation and it places human beings in an ambiguous condition; free to choose between good and evil, they have no choice regarding the position in which they find themselves. There is the one that God has chosen to keep near to himself (the priest?), the exalted one (the one having authority?), but there is also the one brought low. There are the pious and the sinners, because opposite evil there is good. All of this is in God's design. What Ben Sira does not say is whether 'good' and 'evil' indicate two opposite categories that do exist, desired by God without having pronounced a single individual's name. In other words, whether the individual creates his or her own destiny, choosing freely between life and death (see Sir. 15.17), or whether God from the very beginning assigns every human to one of the two categories. The influence of Enochic ideas is clear, as is clear the desire to avoid all the consequences.

At any rate, contemplation of the world divided between good and evil does not create the drama for Ben Sira that it does for the Teacher of Righteousness. For Ben Sira it is liberating to know that if the world was made as it is, then it was certainly done so according to God's will. Qohelet too had made an invitation to try to understand God's work (Qoh. 7.13). He had understood that it was necessary to go beyond rationalism and human schemes of thought. Ben Sira was able to make considerable progress along this difficult path, which consisted in recognizing the limits of human knowledge. Qohelet had understood this rationally, but does not seem to have applied it to religious experience. 'The works of the Lord are wonderful, and his works are concealed from humankind' (Sir. 11.4). In rational terms this makes no sense, but it shows Ben Sira's profound religious experience.

---

3.   *to be moulded as he pleases*: with the Latin and one Greek MS, now confirmed by the Hebrew.

Wisdom is placed very high between God and human beings, and somewhere below Wisdom is the Law. God grants Wisdom to those who love him (Sir. 1.7-8). And for Ben Sira those who love God are those who observe, or better, as we shall see, who try to observe the Law. The Law therefore has a pedagogical function for arriving at Wisdom, but the two are not to be identified with one another.[4] For Ben Sira the Law, or rather observance of the Law, is the road to Wisdom. This makes his conception of righteousness ambiguous, because righteousness is both the way to Wisdom and to some extent a gift of Wisdom. This contradiction, however, exists merely on the level of logic. On the level of religious experience Ben Sira's intuition holds true value. The truly righteous are those who have received the gift of Wisdom and who have prepared themselves for this gift through observance of the Law. Observance of the Law, therefore, is not the highest form of righteousness. One becomes wise; the acquisition of Wisdom comes through a process made of acts of observance of the Law, until the moment of the gift of Wisdom. And it is not even necessary to think of the gift of Wisdom as being a single moment; it could be imagined more as a long progression. The fear of the Lord in a person with little intelligence is worth more than a great mind that offends the Law (Sir. 19.21).

The Law is the only road towards Wisdom. Oracles and dreams are only valid as warnings. As far as knowledge goes they are only the vain pursuit of fools (Sir. 34.1-8). The anti-Enochic position is perfectly clear, repeating analogous statements made by Qohelet (6.9).

Ben Sira forcefully affirms the individual's freedom of choice:

> Do not say, 'It was the Lord's doing that I fell away';
> for God does not do[5] what he hates.
> Do not say, 'It was he who led me astray';
> for he has no need of the sinful.
> The Lord hates all abominations;
> such things are not loved by those who fear him.

---

4.   With Boccaccini and in disagreement with E.J. Schnabel, *Law and Wisdom from Ben Sira to Paul* (Tübingen: J.C.B. Mohr, 1985).

5.   *For God does not do*: is a conjecture by R. Smend, *Die Weisheit des Jesus Sirach erklärt von R. Smend* (Berlin: G. Reimer, 1906), at the verse, accepted by A. Rahlfs, *Septuaginta; id est Vetus Testamentum Graece iuxta LXX interpretes* (2 vols.; Stuttgart: Privilegierte Würtenbergische Anstalt, 1935), II, at the verse, against the tradition that would have humankind as the subject. The hypothesis is no longer simple conjecture, as it has been confirmed by the Hebrew text.

It was he who created humankind in the beginning,
and he left them in the power of their own free choice.[6]
If you choose, you can keep the commandments,
and to act faithfully is a matter of your own choice.
He has placed before you fire and water;
stretch out your hand for whichever you choose.
Before each person are life and death,
and whichever one chooses will be given (Sir. 15.11-17).

The idea of retribution is put forth vigorously. We read:

He did not forgive the ancient giants
who revolted in their might.
He did not spare the neighbours of Lot,
whom he loathed on account of their arrogance.
He showed no pity on the doomed nation,
on those dispossessed because of their sins [an allusion to the
Canaanites];
or on the six hundred thousand [Jewish] foot soldiers
who assembled in their stubbornness.
Even if there were only one stiff-necked person,
it would be a wonder if he remained unpunished (Sir. 16.7-11).

This affirmation of retribution fits extremely well with the Late
Zadokite Jewish tradition. Below we shall see the rewards that await
the righteous person, and which the righteous will surely have.

The righteous and the wicked for Ben Sira form two clearly opposed
groups. He seems not to have learned from Qohelet's reflections on the
question:

If you do good, know to whom you do it,
and you will be thanked for your good deeds.

6.   *Power of their own free choice*: διαβούλιον. The Hebrew text presents a
completely different meaning for this passage, constituting one of the most
noteworthy variants in the whole Catholic Bible. The following is the Hebrew text,
which also has some variants, but which have little effect on the meaning.

'lhym mbr'šyt br' 'dm	From the beginning God created humanity
wyštyhw byd ḥwtpw	and placed it in its enemy's hand
wytnhw byd yṣrw	he [God] handed it over to its nature.
'm tḥpṣ tšmr mṣwh	If you want, you can observe his commandment
wtbwnh l'śwt rṣwnw	and doing his will is intelligence.

On the idea that humankind is in the hands of his enemy, the devil, an idea that is
absolutely foreign to Ben Sira, see *T. Reub.* 2.2, a part belonging to the first century
BCE.

> Do good to the righteous,[7] and you will be repaid—
> if not by them, certainly by the Most High...
> Give to the good, but do not help the sinner.
> Do good to the humble, but do not give to the ungodly;
> hold back their bread, and do not give it to them... (Sir. 12.1-5).

The righteous and the wicked, therefore, belong to two clearly distinct categories and each one will be rewarded according to his actions. But things are not so simple. The idea of righteousness cannot be summed up in a precise formula. To begin with, in the fullest sense of the word only God is just (Sir. 18.2), because even a just person can sin: 'Remember that we are all sinners',[8] so much so that the exclamation 'Happy are those who do not sin' (Sir. 14.1) seems to be merely a speculative one. The idea of righteousness is not opposed to sin, because even the righteous man sins. It is possible to be righteous and still sin. Ezekiel too had seen this possibility, but for him it was a question of two distinct moments in the individual's life. For Ben Sira there is a single state of righteousness that also includes the moment of sin.

Ben Sira gives no explicit explanation of this conviction, which is the fulcrum of all of his thought. Boccaccini argues that for Ben Sira the acts of observance of the Law in some way cancel out the sins: 'The idea that a person's merits can somehow compensate for inevitable transgressions in the eyes of God is stated here for the first time in the history of Jewish thought' (*Middle Judaism*, p. 117). Besides acts of observing the Law, though, Ben Sira also recognizes repentance (17.20-24; 18.21), prayer (21.1; 28.2) and sacrifices made at the Temple (7.31; 35.4-6). The righteous person, as Ben Sira conceives him, is aware of his sins, knows that the Law is the greatest instrument for salvation and *tries* to put it into practice. In this sense the righteous man clearly distinguishes himself from the wicked one.

But even Ben Sira's sharp statements in defence of the retributory principle, that God always rewards human beings (Sir. 11.17),[9] are given some nuances, making them conform better to the new problems. Suffering cannot always be interpreted as punishment. It could be a form of teaching:

7.   *To the righteous*: with the Hebrew. The Greek reads 'pious'.
8.   *Sinners*: with the Hebrew. The Greek reads 'in punishment'.
9.   The Hebrew text uses the term 'righteous' while the Greek reads 'pious'. Formally the Hebrew text is different and longer, but the meaning does not change much.

My child, when you come to serve the Lord,
prepare yourself for testing.
Set your heart right and be steadfast,
and do not be impetuous in time of calamity.
Cling to him and do not depart,
so that your last days may be prosperous.
Accept whatever befalls you,
and in times of humiliation be patient.
For gold is tested in the fire,
and those found acceptable, in the furnace of humiliation... (Sir. 2.1-5)

Ben Sira accepts the doctrine of retribution, but he removes all schematism from it. He is aware that good fortune can change to its opposite for no apparent reason (Sir. 20.9-10) and he also knows that everything is in the hands of a God that we cannot understand. He also knows that life's misfortunes are not necessarily a form of punishment, but they can also be a warning from God. God educates his people for salvation through the Law, but also through trials; pain is never senseless.

It remains to be established just what the reward awaiting the righteous person was for Ben Sira, since he did not believe in any form of life after death. First of all there was Wisdom (Sir. 15.1). But is Wisdom an end in itself, or is it in turn a tool for something else? Once again Ben Sira takes up a position outside of all schemata, because he feels that Wisdom is both. On the one hand those who have Wisdom are destined to affirm themselves in life (Sir. 15.4-5), and on the other he insists on the joy that comes from the simple fact of possessing Wisdom (Sir. 4.11-14). Once again echoes of the stoic philosophers can be heard in the Middle Jewish authors.

Given the value assigned to the trial in forming the righteous person, the theme of poverty, considered one of the most difficult tests, assumes a certain importance in Sirach (Sir. 2.4). While richness is considered good in itself, Ben Sira is still wary of it. It is linked to power, and power and riches end up being two evils that one should beware of. This is a new idea destined to much further development in Middle Jewish thought, in Essenism, in the *Book of Parables* and in Christianity. In all probability Ben Sira's lack of trust in riches reflected a condemnation of the affairs of Jerusalem, where the intrigues of the first Hellenized capitalists, the Tobiads, were on the verge of leading to ruin and a long civil war.

By their very nature the rich and powerful seem to belong to the same category as the wicked. For Ben Sira power is rooted in wealth and the rich become overbearing, because they obtain power.

> Do not lift a weight too heavy for you,
> or associate with one mightier and richer[10] than you.
> How can the clay pot associate with the iron kettle?
> The pot will strike against it and be smashed.
> A rich person does wrong, and even adds insults;
> a poor person suffers wrong, and must add apologies.
> A rich person will exploit you if you can be of use to him,
> but if you are in need he will abandon you.
> If you own something, he will live with you;
> he will drain your resources without a qualm.
> When he needs you he will deceive you,
> and will smile at you and encourage you;
> he will speak to you kindly and say, 'What do you need?'
> He will embarrass you with his delicacies,
> until he has drained you two or three times [that is many times],
> and finally he will laugh at you... (Sir. 13.2-7).

The parallel between wealth, strength, power and evil is clear. The powerful have become so because of their wealth, and they maintain their power by making the others perceive them as being above even God's Law.

2. *The Righteous and the Wicked in the Teacher of Righteousness: Poverty Re-evaluated*

We have already seen that the Teacher of Righteousness considered all men impure–wicked until God granted them purification–justification, if they adhered to his teachings.

Even among the Essenes, though, there was a less theoretical, more practical way of seeing human beings, and here too disdain for those who hold authority appears. The words of the Essenes are forceful in a way not seen in Sirach. The author is indignant and prays to God to help him remain humble before those who hold power, because one must be humble in the face of power: 'Before the proud I will answer with humbleness and with a spirit of submission to those who hold power [literally: men with the sceptre], who point their finger, whose word is evil, whose [only] desire is money' (1QS 11.1-2).

---

10. The word 'mightier' is lacking in the Hebrew. The Greek clarifies the meaning of the single word *ʿāšîr* in this context.

The desire to remain humble and obedient to those in power, even when they are evil, is explained by a piece of information regarding the Essenes provided by Josephus (*War* 2.139-40): 'The Essene makes terrible oaths...to always be faithful towards everyone, and especially towards those who are invested with authority, because no one receives it without God's will'. This is an idea that we also find later in Paul: 'Let every person be subject to the governing authorities; for there is no authority except from God, and those authorities that exist have been instituted by God' (Rom. 13.1).

Thus the traditional opinion concerning the value of riches was being overturned. Wealth was no longer a positive value, a good thing desired by God, as was still the case for Job and for Qohelet (Job 42.12 and Qoh. 7.12; 11.1-2), but rather it was becoming a sign of the presence of evil and it is interesting to note that the idea of authority is always associated with wealth. In certain Jewish circles they noticed that the wealth of Jerusalem had grown, and especially among the most Hellenized elements of society, like the Tobiads, whose criterion for evaluating their principles was success. 'Let us go and make a covenant with the Gentiles around us, for since we separated from them many disasters have come upon us' (1 Macc. 1.11). In the end this was the golden rule of the past, applied to the present. If prosperous business was a sign of God's blessing, of his favour, then there was no reason not to draw nearer to the Hellenistic world, a world that was superior to the Jewish one in productive and economic techniques as well as in military technology.[11] There was an abyss between the new wealth of the Hellenistic-style capitalists and the old patriarchal wealth, not only in quantity, but also in terms of the type of lifestyle that it implied. Once acquired money brought with it the need for fighting and intrigue in order to maintain it. It was a political tool, that is, of internal struggles. In this light wealth seemed more the fruit of evil-doing than a gift of God, and the authority attained by the Maccabee-Hasmoneans seemed the fruit of ambition, abuse and love of money.

3. *The Righteous as a Social Category in Texts of the Second Half of the First Century BCE*

The idea that all of humanity is divided into two parts, the good part and the evil part, was given a theoretical basis by Essenic predetermin-

---

11. See Hengel, *Judaism und Hellenism*, pp. 6-57.

ism. On the one hand there were the children of the Light, on the other the children of Darkness (see Chapter 12, §2, pp. 334-36 above). The idea, however, is also present in a less philosophical, more immediate form in other works of the second half of the first century BCE. The most radical presentation is to be found in the *Book of Parables*, where humankind appears divided into good and evil, into righteous and wicked. In practice, the wicked are identified with those who hold power, the rich. A deeply felt sentiment of social protest can be seen at the basis of this type of idea.

At the beginning of the first parable we read:

> When the congregation of the righteous shall appear, sinners shall be judged for their sins, they shall be driven from the face of the earth, and when the Righteous One[12] shall appear before the face of the righteous, those elect ones whose deeds are hung upon the Lord of Spirits. He shall reveal light to the righteous and the elect who dwell upon the earth, where will the dwelling of the sinners be, and where the resting place of those who denied the name of the Lord of the Spirits. It would have been better for them not to have been born! When the secrets of the righteous are revealed, the sinners shall be judged and the wicked ones will be driven from the presence of the righteous and the elect. From that time, those who possess the earth will neither be rulers nor princes, they shall not be able to behold the faces of the holy ones, for the light of the Lord of the Spirits will appear on the face of the holy, the righteous and the elect. At that moment, kings and rulers shall perish, they shall be delivered into the hands of the righteous and holy ones, and from thenceforth no one shall be able to induce the Lord of the Spirits to show them mercy, for their life shall be annihilated (*1 En.* [*BP*] 38).

It is clear that for the author of the *Book of Parables* only the kings and the powerful, the wicked by definition, will go to hell. In 46.4-5 we read again:

> This Son of Man...would remove the kings and the mighty ones from their comfortable seats and the strong ones from their thrones. He shall loosen the reins of the strong and crush the teeth of the sinners. He shall depose the kings from their thrones and kingdoms. For they do not extol and glorify him, and neither do they obey him, the source of their kingship.

---

12. This is the first name given to the mysterious character, created before time, the protagonist of the *Book of Parables*. The other names are the Elect One and Son of Man.

He will become a staff for the righteous ones in order that they may lean on him and not fall. He is the light of the gentiles and he will become the hope of those who are sick in their hearts (*1 En*. [*BP*] 48.4).

In these pages the righteous are often identified with the elect, like the figure of the great judge and saviour, the Son of Man. The righteous are not declared such for having observed the Law, not even in the less rigid sense that Ben Sira had given to the expression, but simply because they have been chosen and placed among the ranks of those who suffer. This latter group, apart from a few expressions like 'all those who suffer in their souls', is identified with those who have neither wealth nor power. They are placed on the same plane as the saints, that is the angels. No mention is made of paradise, but we are dealing with a kind of thought similar to that of the Essenes; those who belong to the ranks of the angels already live in the angelic assembly. In the *Book of Parables* the scene seems to regard only a future moment on earth, but the schema does not change; there will be an assembly of the righteous and the angels together, the ones equal to the others. It is the heavenly assembly. See also the words of Jesus: 'They will be like angels in heaven'.

In the *Epistle of Enoch* the righteous form a clearly distinct category, so much so that the protagonist, Enoch, is able to address the righteous alone. It is to them that he directs the invitation, 'Do not walk in the evil way' (*1 En*. [*EE*] 94, 3), because they too would be destroyed. 'Woe unto you, O rich people, for you have put trust in your wealth'. The category of the righteous is not identified with the poor with the same rigidity as in the *Book of Parables*, but there is a solid link between evil and wealth.

This interpretation of righteousness, which we could call a sociological interpretation, is not foreign even to the author of the *Psalms of Solomon*, at least in the sense that he conceives of righteousness as social justice. He is convinced that Pompey's conquest of Jerusalem had been caused by the transgressions of the city's inhabitants. He had appealed to God to liberate the city and had hoped that his prayer would be answered, because he knew he himself was righteous, but apparently he was not aware of his compatriots' sins (*Pss. Sol.* 1).

The dominant motif of the *Psalms of Solomon* is the hope that God, who has used a foreign people in order to punish the Jews, should punish the foreigner as well, because 'they have not done it in zeal, but following their own soul's desire' (*Pss. Sol.* 2.24). The author has been driven from Jerusalem by his political foes (*Pss. Sol.* 17.6) and has placed his hopes in the anointed one of God to restore justice. And with justice re-established he envisions not only Israel ruling over the other peoples, but also an egalitarian Israel. This must have been the dream shared more by the disinherited masses than the ruling class in Jerusalem, no matter which party they represented: '[The anointed one] will lead them all with equality and there will be no arrogance among them so that no one will be oppressed' (*Pss. Sol.* 17.41).

While avoiding the populistic tones of the *Book of Parables*, the author of the *Psalms of Solomon* also believes that the only authority capable of governing without oppression is the Messiah. The author of the *Psalms of Solomon* betrays a lack of faith in human authority that could only lead to a negative attitude towards authority itself. In those who held office the Essenes saw only ambition, greed, individuals to be accepted with humility only because nothing comes about without God's will. In the *Book of Parables* we have seen an even more drastic stance, with no mediating idea that all authority has come about through God's will. Condemnation of those who hold power is absolute, with no differentiation between Jews and Gentiles. Romans and Hasmonaeans, the Sanhedrin and the temple priests are all part of the same lot. Works such as these show us that at the turn of the era the division between the ruling class and the population was growing deeper and deeper.

4. The *ᵃnāwîm, the 'Humble'*

We have seen that beginning with the second century BCE the traditional values concerning wealth were overturned. Being rich was no longer seen as a sign of God's blessing. The idea that God rewarded human actions had disappeared, both in Qohelet's radical form and Ben Sira's more attenuated form. This necessarily brought about a search for new contents for society's value system; the rewards for the wise and righteous ones were to be found in inner peace or, more generically, in the acquisition of Wisdom itself. Wealth, in contrast, was tied to authority and seen as an tool of Belial. In this sort of atmosphere it is only natural to expect the contemporary attribution of a certain value to poverty, closely associated with everything that wealth avoids: a low social position and persecution.

Isaiah had already assigned a fundamental value to the virtue of humility, though without giving it any social value. With Third Isaiah humbleness had taken on social and political connotations as well.

> The spirit of Yhwh is upon me,
> because Yhwh has anointed me;
> he has sent me to bring good news to the oppressed,
> to bind up the brokenhearted,
> to proclaim liberty to the captives, and release the prisoners;
> to proclaim the year of Yhwh's favour,
> and the day of vengeance of our God;
> to comfort all who mourn...
> to give them a garland instead of ashes (Isa. 61.1-3).

Third Isaiah was thinking of all the Jews, who should not look for safety through the use of arms, but in salvation as an act of God. This was an idea whose roots lay in the theology of the Promise and which well adapted to the political situation of the Early Zadokite period. Following the logic of the *pesharim* the passage must have been read differently during the Maccabee-Hasmonaean period. The freedom announced by Third Isaiah no longer regarded all of Israel and it was no longer freedom from foreigners, or at least not only from foreigners. The reader knew that there would even be a time when evil, by that time Belial, would triumph. Only when the measure of evil was full could salvation from God be expected. According to this mentality being *'anaw*, 'humble and unfortunate', seemed to be a sign of God's predilection, because the promise of future glory and dominion over all peoples, as seen further on in the passage from Third Isaiah quoted above, was reserved for those who had renounced all force and all the tools of constituted authority, like wealth. *'anawah* was a state of grace and, in a certain sense, of strength. Its fundamental principle is the recognition of God's omnipotence.[13]

In the *Book of Watchers* we already find the humble as synonymous with the righteous: 'No being made of flesh has the power to touch this sweet smelling tree until the Great Judgment. When He shall take vengeance on all and conclude forever. This [tree] shall be given to the righteous and the humble' (*1 En.* [*BW*] 25.4).

---

13. There are two words meaning 'the humble person' in Hebrew: *'nw* and *'ny*, plur. *'nwym* and *'nyym*. Since the difference between the yod and the waw was often not marked at Qumran, and since the two words are essentially synonymous, it is often difficult to distinguish the two in specific cases. For *'nw* BDB gives the meanings 'poor, 'afflicted, humble, meek'.

It is in the *Community Rule*, however, that we find the best description of what *'anawah* is: it is the basic virtue of the man of the sect. In 1QS 4.3 there is a list of the practical virtues of the adept. In ascending order they are *ruaḥ 'anawah, 'orek 'appaym* and *rob raḥamim*, that is humility, patience and overabundant charity. The starting point on the path to perfection is humility, which draws nourishment from its surroundings when put in its natural place, marginalization.

The spirit of humility allowed the Teacher of Righteousness to accept any trial, because he knew that his real strength lay in being humble: 'You have saved the soul of the poor man (*'ebion*), that they thought they could destroy by shedding his blood' (1QH 2.32). The 'poor man' here stands for the humble and the oppressed. Once again it is the book of Isaiah in a late passage (25.3) that foresees future salvation for the poor, the *'ᵉbyônîm*, following a line of thought parallel to that of Third Isaiah when he sees salvation reserved for the *'anawim*, so much so that in Middle Judaism the two terms seem substantially to be synonyms, as further attested to by the *Damascus Document* where they appear together (3.21 and 14.13).

The state of *'anawah*, of the poor and the marginalized, is a state of grace, token of God's help since man can recognize in this condition the fact that he belongs to the elect, since in Essenic predeterminism examining one's own life simply means trying to understand how God's will has been manifested in the life of each individual. Towards the end of the period, when it seemed to the Essenes that God had decided on the final, conclusive battle against evil and the enemies of the true Israel, they saw the victory come about at the hands of the *'ᵉbyônîm*:

> Indeed you will deliver [the ene]mies of all the regions into the hands of the *'ᵉbyônîm*, into the hands of those who are bent over in the dust, to humiliate the mighty peoples, to let the reward of the wicked fall [on the head of your enemies]... (1QM 11.13-14; see also 11.9).

> Who is similar to you, o God of Israel? The hand of your might is with the poor... (1QM 13.13-14).

The definition given of the *'ᵉbyônîm* in 1QM 14.7 is particularly interesting; they are called *'ny/wy rwḥ*, which it is difficult not to translate into the Greek used by Matthew (5.3), πτωχοὶ τῷ πνεύματι, usually translated as 'poor in spirit'. *'ᵃnāwat rûaḥ* is a deeper level of *'ᵃnāwâ*; it is the moment in which each person becomes fully aware of all the underlying values.

The *ᵃnāwē rûaḥ* are the little people, those destined to serve as pedestals for politicians, instruments of gain for capitalists, those destined to remain in obscurity and poverty in the broadest sense of the word. Essenism and Enochism preach the strength of these people: 'With Your might You cause the fallen to be raised, and you bring down those who are high' (1QM 14.10-11).

This is the theme of the Song of Hannah and the 'Magnificat', and one of the issues that most influenced the thought of Jesus. Few periods in history have more forcefully underscored the human drama of recognizing the need for power and at the same time its execrability. In Essenic and Enochic thought there is no remedy for this situation which in the end can be traced to Belial. It must be borne out within the limits in which God himself bears with it. The world will know no justice until it is ruled over by God's anointed one.

Chapter 16

LIFE BEYOND DEATH: THE IMMORTAL SOUL
AND THE RESURRECTION OF THE BODY

1. *Death as a Question*

Before the exile death did not represent a problem for the Jews. Dying was a necessity of nature and dying meant ending up in Sheol, a subterranean world without light, and I would add without life, where the larvae (*'ôbôt*) lived distant from Yhwh without being able to regale him with praise. The effective expression 'fully depotentiated life' has been used to indicate this type of life in Sheol.[1]

Sheol is underground: 'So they with all that belonged to them went down alive into Sheol; the earth closed over them, and they perished from the midst of the assembly' (Num. 16.33). In the human mind Sheol is the antithesis of the heavens where God resides: 'For a fire is kindled by my anger, and burns to the depths of Sheol' (Deut. 32.22).

Just what the Jews thought Sheol was is not very clear. The fact that one descends into Sheol indicates a real descent into a real place, not into a void. This can be confirmed by the existence of necromancy and by stories like the one of the medium of Endor who evokes the ghost of Samuel for Saul (1 Sam. 28). The view of the other world is similar to the Mesopotamic or Homeric vision. Sheol awaits everyone, the powerful and the poor, the good and the bad, Samuel and Saul. Everyone, with no distinctions, is destined (Isa. 14.11) for a life between putrefaction and worms, at any rate distant from Yhwh:

> For Sheol cannot sing to you,
> death cannot praise you;
> those who go down to the Pit cannot hope
> for your faithfulness.
> The living, the living, they thank you… (Isa. 38.18-19).

1.   E. Jacob, *Théologie de l'Ancien Testament* (Neuchâtel: Delachaux & Niestlé, 1958, 2nd edn, 1968), p. 243.

In the very same way all people descend into Sheol. There is no Judgment distinguishing one destiny from another.

Again in Ezekiel, in a passage that has been dated to 587 BCE, the conception of Sheol appears unchanged:

> All this is in order that no trees [metaphorical expression] by the waters
> may grow to lofty height...and that no trees that drink water may
> reach up to them in height.
> For all of them are handed over to death,
> to the world below;
> along with all mortals,
> with those who go down to the Pit (Ezek. 31.14).

Not even Job sees anything beyond death, even though in his words death begins to appear more as the greatest sign of human limitation, covering a vague need to overcome it.

> But mortals die, and are laid low;
> humans expire, and where are they?...
> If mortals die, will they live again? (Job 14.10-14).

Sheol is the only place where the awesome hand of God does not reach and Job would like to hide in Sheol in order to escape God: 'O that you would hide me in Sheol, that you would conceal me until your wrath is past' (Job 14.13).

The immortality of the soul appears with the *Book of Watchers* (see Chapter 6, §4, pp. 174-80), though this belief was late in affirming itself. Qohelet fought against it, saying that it was an illusion. At any rate the possibility of life after death had presented itself to the Jewish mind and as a result the drama of death, linked with this possibility, no matter how remote, became more acute. Discussions began concerning just what death is. The idea of a possible victory over death presented itself in Jewish thought again and again.

I use the expression 'victory over death' because death came to be seen less as a fact and more as a force, obviously an enemy of human-kind. This idea fits well with the spiritual context of the Second Temple, which tended to hypostatize both the functions and facts of human life. In the Song of Songs (date very uncertain) death is an immense force which serves as a term of comparison for the strength of love (Song 8.6): 'love is strong as death', while jealousy is as 'over-whelming as Sheol'. Sheol and death have by this point become synon-ymous indicating an inexorable force; the place that Samuel's ghost was made to rise from can no longer be recognized in this Sheol. No mention is made of worms and putrefaction, but death is associated with complete disappearance. Sheol becomes the literary synonym for death and the land of the dead comes to be called by Job *'ᵃbaddôn*, 'destruction' (Job 26.6; 28.22; Prov. 15.11; 27.20), and *dûmâ*, 'silence' (Ps. 94.17; 115.17). The idea of the nothingness of death becomes more and more clear, reaching Qohelet's lucid meditations on death.

Qohelet is opposed to belief in the immortal soul. He dwells on it at length; a rationalist and an empiricist he avoided viewing death as a force external to human beings and, therefore, in some way superable by humans. He saw death as annihilation. Death, even the good death of old age, is nothing more than the final act of the weakening process that is old age. Death appears as nothing but the fading away of the individual's vital capacities until their complete disappearance. We experience death internally while we are still alive:

> Whatever your hand finds to do, do with your might; for there is no work or thought or knowledge or wisdom in Sheol, to which you are going (Qoh. 9.10).

Death is the absolute incapacity to love, to hate, to have ambition:

> But whoever is joined with all the living has hope, for a living dog is better than a dead lion. The living know that they will die, but the dead know nothing; they have no more reward, and even the memory of them is lost. Their love and their hate and their ambition have already perished; never again will they have any share in all that happens under the sun (Qoh. 9.4-6).

Death as a weakening process of the vital forces until their utter disappearance is described in a passage full of cool pathos. Expression is controlled. Qohelet indulges in metaphors and symbols, in the literary construction. This creates an impressive air of lucid detachment:

> Remember your creator in the days of your youth,
> before the days of trouble come,
> and the years draw near
> when you will say, 'I have no pleasure in them';
> before the sun and the light
> and the moon and the stars are darkened
> and the clouds return after the storm...
> before the silver cord is cut,
> and the golden bowl is broken,
> and the pitcher is broken at the fountain,
> and the pulley broken and fallen into the well (Qoh. 12.1-6).

Seen from the end, life is a series of events that comes to an end (the cord that snaps). It is its entirety, as perceived by humanity in the succession of instances throughout a lifetime, that breaks (the golden bowl). The water is the symbol of life which, once its container is broken falls into the darkness of the well, an image whose exceptional charge escapes rational explanation.

Qohelet was certainly aware, though, of different ways of seeing death.[2] Otherwise his insistence on the problem and his irony in saying that humans have nothing on the animals would be incomprehensible. His polemical stance is also, however, a demonstration that the ideas born with the *Book of Watchers* were spreading. By the third century BCE the problem of death existed. It no longer appears, or at least not only as the conclusion of the vital process, but rather as a force extraneous to human nature, derived from a distortion of the cosmic order. Death came to be seen as against nature.

Not long after Qohelet, during the first years of the second century BCE, Ben Sira wrote that 'from a woman sin had its beginning, and because of her [or because of sin, the expression is ambiguous both in Hebrew and in Greek, but the meaning does not change] we all die' (Sir. 25.24). Ben Sira does not believe in a form of life after death either:

> Give and take, and deceive your soul,
> because in Sheol one cannot look for pleasure.
> All living beings become old like a garment,
> for the decree from of old is, 'You must die!'
> Like abundant leaves on a spreading tree
> that sheds some and puts forth others,
> so are the generations of flesh and blood:
> one dies and another is born.
> Every work decays and ceases to exist,
> and the one who made it will pass away with it (Sir. 14.16-19).

By this point Sheol has disappeared even as a literary motif; death is annihilation.

For Ben Sira the problem of death clearly exists. He accepts the idea that nothing exists beyond death, but he considers it against nature, at least in the sense of against 'nature before history', to the extent that the

---

2.   See L. Rosso Ubigli, 'Qohelet di fronte all'apocalittica', *Henoch* 5 (1983), pp. 209-34.

current order of the cosmos, the order described in the passage quoted above, does not correspond to the way God had desired the universe, even though it was he who established things in this way. The world is as it is because God had to punish Eve's sin (or simply sin). The most profound nature of death is not to be sought, then, in the nature of things, but in the nature of sin. At least in theory, if sin could be overcome, so could death.

It is interesting to note that in the *Book of Dreams*, written shortly after Sirach, Adam appears to be created as a righteous man, without being placed in the Garden of Eden. In this way, his sin disappears while that of the devil remains. In the wake of sin human life may have been shortened, but death is part of nature. If there is to be a resurrection, it depends entirely on an act of God. See *1 En.* [*BD*] 90.33.

During the second half of the first century BCE two books approach the problem again, though with differing intensity: the *Book of Parables* and the book of Wisdom.[3]

> Human beings were not created but to be like angels, to live holy and righteous, and death, which destroys everything, would have not touched them… (*1 En.* [*BD*] 69.11).

The author's statement is not argumentative. For him it is established doctrine.

The problem of the origin of death was taken up again and given more ample treatment in the book of Wisdom. Death entered the world exclusively because of the devil's envy. Not only was humanity's death not created by God, but God did not create death for any living creature, or for any thing. It is sin that brings death, because righteousness in itself is immortal. Since sin does not come from God, death does not come from him either. On the other hand, opening the problem of death up from humans to all living creatures and even the cosmos itself, places the problem in a whole new light. According to this new idea, evil is not simply transgression, but a cosmic force, a spirit. Evil is the devil, who will keep this world under his control until he is

---

3.   Some assign an even later date to the book of Wisdom. Using good arguments Scarpat places it around 40 CE, but on the whole this date seems too late. See G. Scarpat, *Il libro della Sapienza*, I (Brescia: Paideia, 1989). For a generally more balanced dating of the book of Wisdom, see now L. Mazzinghi, *Notte di paura e di luce esegesi di Sap. 17, 1–18, 4* (Rome: Editrice Pontificio Istituto Biblico, 1995). The author dates the text to after 30 BCE. See also David Winston, *The Wisdom of Solomon* (AB; Garden City: Doubleday, 1979), pp. 20-25.

defeated. The eschatological world presupposes not only a new humanity but also an entirely regenerated universe:

> God did not make death,
> and he does not delight in the death of the living.
> For he created all things so that they might exist;
> all creatures belong to salvation,
> and there is no destructive poison in them,
> and the dominion of Sheol [here too the personification of Death] is not
>   on earth.
> For righteousness is immortal (Wis. 1.13-15).

The expression 'righteousness is immortal' is usually understood as meaning that the righteous person will live eternally near God.[4] The sentence says something more, though. It says that the righteous person can live eternally near God, because they participate in righteousness; they have righteousness which is by nature immortal.

In an old book Cornely approaches the problem of just what type of righteousness the author of the book of Wisdom has in mind.[5] He establishes a certain parallel with Paul's *caritas quae numquam excidit*, where *caritas* cannot be a human virtue. In this text 'righteousness' indicates neither the cosmic order nor human righteousness prior to original sin. It is a righteousness that *causa est immortalitatis*. My impression is that the argumentation is carried out on the basis of an additional hemistich, considered authentic by many, in the Latina Vetus. The half line of verse is added at the end and does seem to be the missing parallel of 'For righteousness is immortal'. The hemistich reads: *iniustitia autem mortis est acquisitio*.

This is a rather optimistic vision of life, contrasting sharply with the prevailing pessimism of the first century BCE; death cannot touch the righteous. This immortality is possible because human beings have a soul, and only sin can destroy the soul.

If he does not enter into (or belong to?) the sphere of the devil (Wis. 2.24), the individual maintains his original immortality. The surprising thing about this work is that it completely ignores the entire debate concerning the possibility that a truly righteous person exists, regardless of whether it is really possible to maintain or recuperate the state of

4.   See J. Weber, *Le livre de la Sagesse* (Paris: Letouzey & Ané, 1951), at the verses, where there is a long exposition.

5.   R. Cornely, *Commentarius in librum Sapientiae* (Paris: Lethielleux, 1910), pp. 71-72.

righteousness from before Adam's sin. The author speaks of the righteous and the wicked as two clearly distinct categories, but it is not clear what measure he uses for determining a person's righteousness. The wicked are clearly those who violate the Law (Wis. 4.20), but a contrasting and parallel definition of the righteous cannot be found in the book of Wisdom.

In effect, the author's primary interest is not righteousness, but immortality. He is a firm believer in immortality. He knows that the nature of righteousness is immortality, but, in contrast, he also knows that righteousness is derived from having Wisdom. For this reason he is able to say that immortality is already present in a person living in union with Wisdom (Wis. 8.17). But Wisdom is obtained only through grace, it is not a human achievement (Wis. 8.21). And the gift of Wisdom from God does not teach the Law to those who receive it; it teaches what pleases God (Wis. 9.10), which does not exactly coincide with the Law, though it does not exclude it either.

> For who can learn the counsel of God?
> Or who can discern what the Lord wills?
> For the reasoning of mortals is worthless,
> and our designs are likely to fail;
> for a perishable body weighs down the soul,
> and this earthy tent burdens the thoughtful mind.
> We can hardly guess at what is on earth,
> and what is at hand we find with labour;
> but who has traced out what is in the heavens?
> Who has learned your counsel,
> unless you have given wisdom
> and sent your holy spirit from on high?
> And thus the paths of those on earth were set right,
> and people were taught what pleases you,
> and were saved by wisdom (Wis. 9.13-18).

2. Resurrection

The idea that physical death does not represent the end of the individual, but only the destruction of the body, took shape in Israel in two initially distinct conceptions: the immortality of a part of us, the soul, which is spirit, or immortality through the resurrection of the body. The two concepts were blended in Jewish culture more instinctively than rationally. In many texts it is unclear which of the two versions the author believed in. Images are used that at times recall one conception and at times the other, without distinguishing between the two human conditions.

The oldest text that mentions resurrection is the so-called Apocalypse of Isaiah, that is chs. 24–27 of the book of Isaiah. It is practically impossible to establish a precise date for this composition; hypotheses vary from the fifth to the second century BCE.[6] The manuscript 1QIs[a] found at Qumran contains the passage in question and therefore provides a *terminus ad quem* of the second century BCE. There is also a whole series of themes in the Apocalypse of Isaiah that prevent us from assigning the text too early a date, because they contain apocalyptic ideas such as: the 'poor' (Isa. 25.4 and 26.6), the idea that men learn to understand God through his judgments on earth and history (Isa. 26.9), the idea that humanity's works are done by God (Isa. 26.12) and the idea that before humans can overcome death (25.8) God must visit, that is punish 'the host of heaven' (24.21). This last idea betrays a certain degree of development of angelology and the in-between world. I therefore believe that the composition should be dated to before the crisis of Zadokitism, but not before Qohelet. Had Qohelet known this work it is difficult to believe that he would not have commented on it, since he contested the idea of life after death, and not only in the form of the immortal soul. He knew the *Book of Watchers*, but he did not know the Apocalypse of Isaiah.

In the Apocalypse of Isaiah resurrection is reserved only for those who belong to God, an expression which seems to indicate more the Jews than the righteous. For all others physical death marks the complete end. No indication can be drawn from the text regarding the type of life that awaits those whom God will raise from the grave:

> Your dead shall live, their corpses[7] shall rise [the verb *qwm*, 'to rise',
> was to become the verb meaning resurrection in Hebrew].
> Those who lie in the dust
> shall wake[8] and sing for joy!
> For your dew is a dew of light,
> and the earth will give birth to the shades (*refa'im*) (Isa. 26.19).

6. See Soggin, *Introduction*, p. 264.

7. *Their corpses*: the Hebrew text reads 'my corpse', which does not make sense.

8. *Shall wake*: the form *hqṣw* causes some difficulty in this context, where all the verb forms are in the imperfect. The conjectured reading *yqyṣw* has now been confirmed by the Scroll A of Isaiah discovered at Qumran.

The dead who belong to the Lord will come back to life after the earth has been flooded with a miraculous dew, called dew of light, with a terminology that recalls the water of light of *1 En.* [*BW*] 22.9.

The same text tells us that the enemies of Israel will not rise. There is nothing like a Last Judgment in this text:

> The dead [sc. of the enemies] will not live;
> shades (*repha'im*) will not arise—
> because you have visited and destroyed them,
> and wiped out all memory of them (Isa. 26.14).

The idea of the resurrection in 2 Maccabees is to be placed along this same line. The mother of one of the seven brothers says:

> I do not know how you came into being in my womb. It was not I who gave you life and breath, nor I who set in order the elements within each of you. Therefore the Creator of the world, who shaped the beginning of humankind and devised the origin of all things, will in his mercy give life and breath back to you again, since you now forget yourselves for the sake of his laws (2 Macc. 7.22-23).

Resurrection in this text is reserved for only a few, to those who belong to God in a special way. In this case, too, resurrection is independent from the Judgment; it seems to be more of a reward for extraordinary merit than a fact that concerns all. It is a question of giving back that which was unjustly taken away and, most of all, that which was taken due to faithfulness to God.

The new ideas regarding life after death do not seem to have been accepted in Maccabee-Hasmonaean circles, though. The author of 1 Maccabees, who certainly lived after Simon and therefore at the Hasmonaean court, makes no mention of resurrection, not even in the words placed in the mouth of the dying Mattathias in 2.49-68.

The doctrine of resurrection is, however, documented in the second century BCE in the book of Daniel:

> At that time Michael, the great prince, the protector of your people, shall arise. There shall be a time of anguish, such as has never occurred since nations first came into existence. But at that time your people shall be delivered, everyone who is found written in the book. Many of those who sleep in the land of dust shall awake, some to everlasting life, and some to shame and everlasting contempt. Those who are wise shall shine like the brightness of the sky, and those who lead many to righteousness, like the stars forever and ever (Dan. 12.1-3).

In this text resurrection seems to await everyone, but with two diametrically opposed outcomes. I say 'seems', because the text reads
'Many of those who sleep' and not 'all of those who sleep'. Nothing is
said about where the wicked will end up; it does not appear that they
are to be annihilated, but rather destined for a life of infamy. The wise,
the righteous, will shine with a special light, which is probably the
same light mentioned in the Apocalypse of Isaiah where it speaks of the
dew of light that will free the dead from the earth.

We can conclude that in the second century BCE the idea of the resurrection had made its appearance in Jewish culture with a certain
impetus, but it had not been universally accepted. Besides, there are no
precise statements about the all-inclusiveness of the resurrection. Even
the book of Daniel is not clear on this point.

In the following century resurrection is mentioned in the *Psalms of
Solomon* (3.12) in a passage that has raised some questions of attribution. It is uncertain whether the verse is by the author or if it is an
interpolation.

> The destruction of the sinner is forever,
> and he will not be remembered when [God] looks after the righteous...
> Those who fear the Lord shall rise up [will be resurrected] to eternal life
> and their life shall be in the Lord's light, and it shall never end (*Pss. Sol.*
> 3.11-12).

In this case too, resurrection is a privilege of the righteous. For
everyone else death coincides with the end. The idea of resurrection for
all the dead without distinction, only becomes clear with the *Book of
Parables*:

> In those days, Sheol will return all the deposits which she had received
> and hell will give back all that which it owes. And he [the Elect One]
> shall choose the righteous and the holy ones from among [the risen
> dead], for the day when they shall be saved has arrived. In those days
> [the Elect One] shall sit on his throne, and from the intelligence of his
> mouth shall come out all the secrets of Wisdom, for the Lord of the
> Spirits has given them to him and glorified him. In those days, mountains
> shall dance like rams; and the hills shall leap like kids satiated with milk.
> All of them shall be angels in heaven. And their faces shall shine with
> joy, because on that day the Elect One shall arise. And the earth shall
> rejoice; and the righteous ones shall dwell upon her and the elect ones
> shall walk upon her (*1 En.* [*BP*] 51).

Resurrection, therefore, will be universal. It will be followed by the Judgment and after the Judgment only the righteous will have life. This passage does not speak of hell, but see *1 En.* 56.1-4:

> Then I saw there an army of the angels of punishment marching, holding nets of iron and bronze. And I asked the angel of peace, who was walking with me, saying to him, 'To whom are they going, these who are holding [the nets]?' And he said to me, '[They are going] to their elect and beloved ones in order that they may be cast into the crevices of the abyss of the valley. Then the valley shall be filled with their elect and beloved ones.

3. *The Immortality of the Soul*

As we have seen (Chapter 6, §4, pp. 174-80), belief in the immortality of the soul entered Israel much earlier than believed until recently. The idea was quite late in imposing itself, however. It was openly contested by Qohelet and even denied by Ben Sira in the second century BCE. Josephus (*War* 2.164-65) informs us that the Sadducees did not believe in the soul's immortality even in his day. Luke tells us (20.27) that they did not believe in resurrection. It is possible that Josephus had not wanted to mention belief in the resurrection since it must have sounded strange, to say the least, to his Greek audience. The fact of the matter is, however, that the difference between the two ideas must have gone unnoticed, or at least the difference was not given the weight that our rationalism would expect. The texts that speak of the immortality of the soul, for example, normally do not even pose the question of its relationship with the body. The sole exception is the book of Wisdom (late first century BCE to early first century CE), which emphasizes the contrast between the incorruptibility of the soul and the body's corruptibility, to the point that the body is seen as weighing down the soul, following a conception that until this point had been completely foreign to Judaism (Wis. 9.15).

After the *Book of Watchers* the soul's immortality reappears only in a few passages of the book of *Jubilees*. *Jubilees* 23.31 is clear enough, but the idea is not developed at all: 'Their bones [of the righteous] will rest in the earth and their spirits will increase in joy'.

See the passages at 7.29 and 36.10 as well, where punishment of the wicked is mentioned. It seems that they are to be punished both in this life and after death.

In the *Psalms of Solomon* of the following century the theme of life after death surfaces several times, giving a reason of hope for the righteous being persecuted. But if we look for some description of the type of life the author expected, we will be disappointed, because we find only expressions which lend themselves equally well to belief in resurrection or in the immortality of the soul. See the following passages: 3.12, 'Those who fear the Lord shall rise up again for eternal life and their life will be in the light of the Lord and will have no end'; 9.5, 'The one who does what is right saves up life for himself with the Lord, and the one who does what is wrong causes his own life to be destroyed'; 13.11, 'The life of the righteous is eternal, but the sinners shall be taken away to destruction'; 14.9-10, 'Therefore their inheritance is death...and they will not be found on the day of mercy for the righteous; but the devout of the Lord will inherit life in happiness'; 15.12-13, 'And sinners shall perish forever in the day of the Lord's Judgment... But those who fear the Lord shall find mercy in it and shall live by their God's mercy'.

The expression used in 3.12 seems to allude to life through resurrection. The same verb translated here as 'shall rise up again' could also be translated directly as 'will be resurrected'. 13.11, however, seems to refer more to the immortality of the soul. And does the Judgment referred to in 15.12 concern all humankind, or only those living in that particular moment? It would seem that the problem was not perceived as such, and that most of all they had faith in the fact that *in some way* God would have given life after death.[9]

The doctrine of the immortality of the soul is most clearly expressed in Wis. 3.1-8:

> But the souls of the righteous are in the hand of God,
> and no torment will ever touch them.
> In the eyes of the foolish they seemed to have died,
> and their departure was thought to be a disaster,
> and their going from us to be their destruction;
> but they are at peace.
> For though in the sight of others they are being punished,
> their hope is full of immortality.
> Having been disciplined a little, they will receive great good,
> because God tested them and found them worthy of himself;
> like gold in the furnace he tried them,
> and like a sacrificial burnt offering he accepted them.

9. See M. Lana, *Salmi di Salomone*, in Sacchi (ed.), *Apocrifi*, II, pp. 39-146 (54).

In the time of their visitation they will shine forth,
and will run like sparks through the stubble.
They will govern nations and rule over peoples,
and the Lord will reign over them forever.

The righteous will be like the highest angels in the service of the Lord and, like the angels in the *Epistle of Enoch*,[10] they will take part in the judgment of the pagans.

10. See Sacchi, *'Ethiopic Enoch* 91.15'.

Chapter 17

THE SACRED AND THE PROFANE, THE IMPURE AND THE PURE

1. *The Sacred in the Hebrew Period*

The conception that the Jews had of the sacred (*qadoš*) underwent a slow though profound evolution throughout their history. In the beginning the sacred was only a cosmic force, linked in some way to the divine. By the time of Middle Judaism it had become a deep religious value. In the evolution of the conception of the sacred and, consequently, in the idea of other closely related concepts, the labour of religious consciousness placing itself before the cosmos and before God can be seen.

The most characteristic category of Jewish thought, in any case, is the one used to interpret and classify reality, that of 'Sacred–profane/ impure–pure'. Writing the history of the evolution of the contents of this category of thought, and the relationship between the terms that make it up, is the same as writing a very large portion of the history of Jewish thought. One of the most innovative parts of Jesus' preaching regards the interpretation of this category. The consequences of this revolution have been considerable, even though it is difficult to evaluate it with precision, because the exact contents of Jesus' interpretation were not even clear then, and are not clear today.

A sure starting point for our examination are the passages from Ezekiel (44.23) and Leviticus (10.10), where we find a formulation of the category in the terms and thought of the sixth century BCE. The text from Ezekiel assigning the priest the role of teaching how to distinguish the sacred from the profane and the impure from the pure reads as follows: '[the priests] shall teach my people the difference between the sacred and the profane, and show them how to distinguish between the impure and the pure' (Ezek. 44.23).

It is clearly a category divided into two sub-categories, capable of allowing for the interpretation and classification of all reality. Everything that is real can be seen as belonging to one of the four elements in the category.

There are two closely interrelated problems to be solved. What things are to be assigned to each element, and what is the relationship between the elements of one sub-category and those of another. Should the terms be read in a parallel or in a chiastic manner? Which is parallel to the sacred, the impure or the pure? Given the lack of an explanation in the text, we must look for clarification elsewhere, referring to other texts, even from different periods, that shed some light on the most ancient period of Jewish history.

It can practically be taken for granted that the sacred was in some sort of relationship with the divine and that it was opposed to the profane, which belonged to the realm of human things. The uncertainties arise when we try to establish more precisely the relationship between the divinity and the sacred. Was it a force inherent to and controlled by the divinity, or was it an independent cosmic force, with both the divinity and the sacred on a higher plane than humankind? The texts that refer to the Hebraic period do not provide a single answer to these questions; we can find both solutions.

The following passage is taken from Exodus and is part of a very ancient context, certainly from before the exile, because it says that altars can be built anywhere.

> You shall not make gods of silver alongside me, nor shall you make for yourselves gods of gold. You need make for me only an altar of earth and sacrifice on it your burnt offerings and your offerings…But if you make for me an altar of stone, do not build it of hewn stones; for if you use a chisel upon them you profane them (Exod. 20.23-25).[1]

The human who touches an object in order to shape it as he or she desires, profanes it; by exercising his or her power over the object the object is profaned, it enters the realm of human things, the realm of the profane. God does not tolerate that an altar dedicated to him should be built of stones profaned by humans. For the ancient Hebrew, then, things were sacred if they belonged to an order of things considered higher than the human plane of existence. The sacred was seen as a

---

1.   *Them…them*: this is an approximate translation. The Masoretic text presents a third person singular femminine pronoun, therefore used as a neutral referring to both the stones and the altar. The Samaritan Hebrew uses the masculine and refers only to the profanation of the altar.

terrible force, capable of killing anyone who entered into direct contact with it or with the things manifestly linked to it.

The idea that in its most direct manifestations the sacred could kill can be seen in the episode, certainly quite ancient, of the annunciation of Samson's birth by a *mal'āk Yhwh*, an 'angel of Yhwh'. When Samson's father realizes that the being in front of him is not human he exclaims, 'we shall surely die, for we have seen God' (Judg. 13.22). Samson's mother replies that had God meant for them to die he would not have promised them a son. This shows that (1) the apparition of a divine being was considered lethal, but (2) that it was also plausible that the divinity could control and even suspend such a power of the sacred.

These two approaches to the sacred, as a force that either could or could not be controlled by the divinity, are documented in several texts. In Exod. 19.12-13, for example, God teaches the Jews how to defend themselves from the sacred, seen as a blind, rigid and superhuman force emanating from God's presence, though independent of him. God is not able to block this force's action. This cosmic force's existence is also foreseen by certain rites, such as oaths, curses and blessings. See the description of the scene of the Covenant between God and Israel as narrated in Exod. 24.3-8, a passage once attributed to the Eloist, but which now lacks a sure attribution. Moses binds God and the people through a Covenant sanctioned by blood. God promises to protect his people if they obey his laws; the blood, as an element that contaminates, makes the Covenant binding both for the Jews and for God. This means that there must have been a force capable in some way even of binding God. It is precisely the loss of this conception of the sacred, as capable of binding the divinity, which leads to Job's doubts (fifth–fourth century BCE) regarding the existence of such a Covenant. Given the existence of such a Covenant,[2] God could violate it whenever he saw fit. Regarding a force capable of creating an irresistible guarantee that everyone would respect an oath, see the case of Jephthah (Judg. 11.29-40), and Micah's mother (Judg. 17). Whatever the epoch of these text's composition, they tell ancient stories of ancient deeds.

In Exod. 24.11, on the contrary, we see that God can let himself be seen by the elders of Israel, without 'lay[ing] his hand on the chief men of the people of Israel'. In other words, God controls the power of the sacred and can suspend it when he so desires. This story, too, antedates

2. See P. Sacchi, 'Giobbe e il Patto (Giobbe 9, 32-33)', *Henoch* 4 (1982), pp. 175-84.

the exile and is as ancient as the other, opposing accounts. It is difficult to establish which conception is the older of the two. Following an abstract line of thought, it would seem that the idea which holds the sacred to be a mere cosmic force, above the gods, is the oldest. In reality, however, the two ideas existed side by side in Israel.

In the ancient texts collected by the court author that I refer to as R1, the problem of agriculture can be grasped. In light of the general conception of the sacred, agriculture would appear to be a profanation. These texts sought to explain why humans were able to use such things without profaning them. This type of problem is typical of a society which has reached a certain degree of progress and is capable of reflection on its own condition. Either the society recalls the passage from nomadism to settled agriculture, or at any rate poses the problem of the relationship between two ways of life, comparing its own way of life with that of the nomads that were always present in Israel. In this case the question not only concerns the group's own behaviour but also the need to justify and explain its civilization. The latter reason, which does not exclude the former, is much more probable, since the question was still an open one at the time of the Priestly Code (see below, pp. 449-52).

A solution to the problem was found in the idea that God had given certain things to humans, rather than establishing an ontological difference between the various things to be found in the cosmos. The things given to humans, therefore, were ontologically sacred, but anthropologically profane.

I feel that this is the meaning to be given to some of the passages concerning the creation as told by R1 (the Jahwist for most scholars), for example where God leads all the animals before Adam so that Adam could name them (Gen. 2.19-20), symbolizing their consignment to humanity, a sort of lordship by concession. Concerning plants, then, the Priestly Code is even more clear in saying that God has given to humankind 'every plant yielding seed and every tree bearing fruit' (Gen. 1.29). Raising animals and, most of all, agriculture are in principle possible without any profanation. The idea, however, that all things belong to God is clearly perceived in the norms regarding first fruits.

2. *Impurity during the Hebraic Period*

Some orientation concerning what impurity meant is provided by the lists of impure animals, the longest of which is the classic ch. 11 of

Leviticus. All those things that are defined as impure in other contexts should be added to this list. The animals defined as pure can be touched and can be eaten; those classified as impure can never be eaten, since contact with them, if they are dead, generates impurity. Contact with living impure animals does not generate impurity (Lev. 11.25, 28, 31). Leviticus 11.26, however, gives us the impression that some amount of impurity can be contracted even from contact with the live animal (see the *Letter of Aristeas* 149).

The general principle for determining whether an animal is pure or impure can be found in Lev. 11.41, 42:

> All creatures that swarm upon the earth are detestable; they shall not be eaten. Whatever moves on its belly, and whatever moves on all fours, or whatever has many feet, all the creatures that swarm upon the earth, you shall not eat; for they are detestable.

The serpent, therefore, is most impure, then the lizard, and so forth. Among fish, those with no scales are impure. Apparently this is a classification by analogy; fish without scales are seen as the equivalent of snakes. Among the large quadrupeds in general terms those with a cloven feet are pure, those having a less compact contact with the earth. There is also a second condition that quadrupeds must meet in order to be considered pure; they must be ruminating animals. This principle seems to be of a different nature than the main rule.

As far as birds are concerned, whether a particular bird is considered pure or not seems to depend on what they normally eat. Birds of prey are impure, because they eat meat together with blood. Blood is among the most impure of all things. Even the meat of pure animals must be eaten only after the blood has been drained from it.

From the general rule governing the classification of animals as impure, contact with the ground, we can deduce that impurity was considered a consequence of contact with the earth. Since we have already seen that the earth was sacred, it follows that impurity must have had some affinity with the sacred. We must therefore read Ezekiel's category in a parallel and not in a chiastic fashion. Sacred is parallel to impure and profane is parallel to pure.

In continuing the list of impure things we have to mention the entire life cycle. This is based on blood, where life resides ('For the life of the flesh is in the blood', Lev. 17.11). All of the primary manifestations of the life cycle are considered impure, from the woman who has just given birth, to sexual intercourse and in some way the sexual organs themselves (see the priest at the altar in Exod. 20.26), to the cadaver.

A concept that could be useful in linking these two series of impurities is that of the 'life principle', seen as belonging to the realm of the divine[3] and present in the earth's fertility.

As further proof of the affinity between the sacred and the impure, it can be observed that impurity is a hostile force to humankind, as is the sacred. What distinguishes it from the sacred is simply the lesser degree of harm it does to humankind. Impurity is a diluted version of the sacred, so to speak. Contact with the impure is not lethal, but it does weaken the human being. See, for example, the episode of Laban's pursuit of Jacob in search of the idols that had been stolen from him. He does not look under the saddle of Rachel's camel when she tells him, 'the way of women is upon me' (Gen. 31.35). Laban is travelling and is in particular need of purity in order to face the dangers of his journey. He cannot run the risk of contaminating himself by touching a menstruating woman or the objects she has touched.

If purity was important for the traveller, it was even more so for the soldier. When David, fleeing from Saul, was asked by the priest at Nob whether he was in a state of purity, so that he could approach the things near the altar, he was able to guarantee his purity by explaining that he was leading a military expedition (1 Sam. 21.5-7); the soldier needed purity. A law in Deuteronomy (23.10-15) states that a soldier in a state of impurity must be expelled from the camp. From these examples we can see that impurity was considered a sort of fluid, or something similar, capable of being passed from one body to another through contact. Impurity was a physical thing and therefore to be treated with caution, as with any dangerous physical thing.

Given the logic by which impurity is a force that weakens, those who had to face the greatest risks were those who needed purity the most. For this reason the priests were required to maintain the highest degree of purity. According to Ezekiel's theology, as well as that of the Priestly Code, the layperson could not be contaminated by sweat, while the priest had even to beware of sweat during the liturgical offices (no

---

3.   In the Syro-Mesopotamian world there was a widespread belief that only the gods do not die. In the fullest sense of the word, life is their prerogative alone and they are jealous of it. We are reminded of Gilgamesh's vain efforts to reach life, and the last verse describing Adam and Eve's expulsion from Eden: '[God] drove out the man; and at the east of the garden of Eden he placed the cherubim, and a sword flaming and turning to guard the way to the tree of life' (Gen. 3.24).

woollen clothing, only linen). The priest was also forbidden to drink wine, though the reasoning behind this restriction is not clear (Ezek. 44.17-18 and Lev. 6.3-4). The priest must be as pure as possible in order to face the sacred, not to be in harmony with it, as would seem natural to a modern observer. We shall see below, however, that even during Ezekiel's day things were not as clear as they seem in this text.

A third type of impurity comes from mixing things that are not to be mixed. At first sight this kind of impurity seems to stem from a different series of principles than those discussed so far. For example, 'A woman shall not wear a man's apparel, nor shall a man put on a woman's garment' (Deut. 22.5); or, 'You shall not sow your vineyard with a second kind of seed... You shall not plough with an ox and a donkey yoked together. You shall not wear clothes made of wool and linen woven together' (Deut. 22.9-11). Some associate this prohibition with the commandment not to cook a kid in its mother's milk (Exod. 23.19; 34.26; Deut. 14.21), or not to sacrifice mother and son together (Lev. 22.28). But while it is possible to find a common denominator in the laws regarding the sacrifice of mother and son together, or even of ploughing with an ox and a donkey, in a sort of pity to be shown even to animals, it is impossible to apply this line of reasoning to the prohibition of wearing the other sex's clothes or planting two kinds of seeds in the same field. Here we are dealing with a kind of impurity that comes from disorder; failure to keep distinct things separate would be like returning to the shapelessness typical of the sacred earth. We have seen that settled agriculture raised some problems. It was necessary to avoid recreating the sacrality found in nature prior to the order imposed by human intervention.[4]

3. *The Relationship between Humans and God in the Theology of the Covenant*

As organized by Ezekiel, the 'sacred–profane' category creates a specific relationship between God and humans, between the sacred and the profane. Human beings on the one side, God on the other. Nature is

---

4.   M. Douglas, *Purity and Danger: An Analysis of Concepts of Pollution and Taboo* (London: Routledge & Kegan Paul, 1966), tends to explain all phenomena of impurity by linking them to the idea of disorder. For a critique of this interpretation of impurity, at least concerning the Hebraic world, see P. Sacchi, 'Il puro e l'impuro nella Bibbia: Antropologia e storia', *Henoch* 6 (1984), pp. 65-80.

sacred, but God gave it to humankind, in some cases with limiting conditions and in some cases without. Human beings face God with a very strong sense of dignity, freedom and ability to judge. Human profanity faces God's sacrality, but God cannot dispose of the human will. Human beings are held to be free and in some way able to stand comparison with God. It is true that before God humans are only dust and ashes, passing shadows, but people can also debate with God over what is righteous and what is wicked.

In a story which is usually held to be quite ancient, apart from a few universalistic touches added even after R1, Abraham contests God's right to destroy an entire city in order to punish the wicked, when that punishment would also fall on the righteous. I quote what seem to me to be the most important elements of the story, avoiding the universalistic interpolations: 'Yhwh said, 'Shall I hide from Abraham what I am about to do…?'

Yhwh continues, revealing his intention to destroy Sodom and Gomorrah.

> While Yhwh remained standing before Abraham,[5] Abraham came near and said, 'Will you indeed sweep away the righteous with the wicked? Suppose there are fifty righteous within the city; will you then sweep away the place and not forgive it for the fifty righteous who are in it? Far be it from you to do such a thing, to slay the righteous with the wicked, so that the righteous fare as the wicked! Far be that from you! Shall not the Judge […] do what is just?'
>
> And Yhwh said, 'If I find at Sodom fifty righteous in the city, I will forgive the whole place for their sake'.
>
> Abraham answered, 'Let me take it upon myself to speak to the Lord, I who am but dust and ashes…' (Gen. 18.17-32).

Abraham is aware that he is only dust and ashes, but if he knows that he is right he does not give in. This idea of human autonomy even before God is typical of the theology of the Covenant and, apart from the problems raised by the theology of the Promise, characterizes Jewish spirituality until Middle Judaism, that is until the Hellenistic crisis.

---

5.   This is a typical case of *tiqqun sopherim*, or 'correction by the scribes'. The Hebraic tradition has preserved a record of some cases where the scribes altered the sacred text in order to avoid profanation of the Name. In this case the Name would have been profaned by God's humble attitude toward Abraham. The structure of the corrected text is the opposite of the original, having Abraham stand before God rather than vice versa. On the *tiqqun sopherim*, see Barthélemy, *Les dévanciers d'Aquila*.

At that point much of Judaism lost the sense of human autonomy, in other words the sense of the profane before the sacred, the clear distinction between the two realms. Pharisaic and Rabbinic Judaism reacted to this process by returning to a strong insistence on the distinction between the sacred and the profane. I believe that Otto[6] gave too much weight to the expression 'dust and ashes', and not enough weight to the context. Abraham is aware that he is a creature, but this does not stop him from defending what is just, not even before God.

This is also the spiritual background for the passage from the Song of Deborah, perhaps one of the oldest pages of the Bible, cursing those Jews who 'did not come to the help of Yhwh' when the war broke out (Judg. 5.23). Joshua's discourse to the Jews belongs to this same atmosphere as well: 'Now if you are unwilling to serve Yhwh, choose this day whom you will serve, whether the gods your ancestors served in the region beyond the River or the gods of the Amorites in whose land you are living' (Josh. 24.15).

God chose his people once, now it is the Jews' turn to choose; they are given complete freedom of choice. This sense of human freedom even in the face of God is the primary characteristic of most Hebraic and Jewish thought, and is rooted in the clear separation between the realms of the sacred and the profane. The discordant voices that did exist in Hebraism and even more so in Middle Judaism held that the distinction was more blurred, when they did not deny it outright.

Just as the sense of human freedom was strongly felt, so was the idea of God's freedom, to the point that to us it appears to be conceived of in human terms, since it was felt to be bound in time and not eternal. God is free to choose; he has chosen his people and he chooses the number of generations to reward for good actions and how many to punish for evildoing (Exod. 20.5-6 = Deut. 5.9-10). God has made no eternal decrees of destruction and threatens no irrevocable punishment unless the measure is full. In Hosea we find both the certainty of punishment relative to the sins committed together with an invitation to repent, bringing God's favour back to Israel (14.2-3). According to Gen. 6.6, God can even show remorse for what he has done. At times God addresses humankind grieving, at times full of wrath, so that the people should return to him, avoiding his punishment. He lives his great role among humans, perfectly integrated in history, that is in time, which

6.   *The Idea of the Holy*, p. 9.

seems to be the dimension in which his decisions flow. The image of an absolute thought, God's having thought and willed everything from the beginning of time in such a way that his actions were limited to his own plan, did not present itself to the pre-exilic Hebrew, but it did haunt the later Jew of the Hellenistic age.

4. *Impurity and Sin in some Pre-exilic Texts*

While in most of the pre-exilic biblical texts, or at any rate those reporting events or ideas from before the exile, impurity appears to be a negative force to humanity, but with no link to sin, there are some texts constituting an exception. It is worth discussing these texts, given the importance they were to have on the development of Jewish thought.

In the second account of the creation, usually attributed to the Yahwist, God is said to have punished the serpent, condemning it to slither on its belly (Gen. 3.14). It must, therefore, have originally been a four-legged creature, condemned to becoming impure through contact with the soil. The animal was not created impure, but was condemned to become so. If, then, impurity was a punishment, that means that it is to be considered as bad, even as a physical quality. In history it becomes innate in an evil being. In the first account of the creation, the priestly one, the serpent is, on the contrary, created by God in its present form and God explicitly declares that it is good (Gen. 1.25). In this case impurity is seen as a force of nature completely independent of the idea of evil.

The idea that there is an affinity between impurity and sin (understood as transgression) was developed in ch. 6 of Isaiah. This was to be of fundamental importance in the formation of one current of Jewish thought. On the one hand he clearly states that the sacred is the essence, or the fundamental attribute of the divine (God is three times sacred), while on the other he establishes that transgression of the divine will, sin, is also a source of contamination. I am not sure how Isaiah arrived at this conclusion, but the conclusion is there for all to see. In his vision Isaiah thinks that he is in Yhwh's presence and fears to be lost, because he knows that he is in a state of impurity. Nothing new so far. What is new, however, is the conception of impurity that emerges from Isaiah's discourse. An angel comes to help Isaiah and purifies him. This purification, though, does not remove Isaiah's impurity as we would expect, but his *'āwôn* and his *ḥēṭ*, 'guilt' and 'transgression'. 'Now that this [the live coal] has touched your lips, your guilt has departed (*šār*) and your sin is blotted out'. Purity is reached through the expiation of sin (an abstract concept) and the expulsion of '*āwôn*, where the terminology presupposes that '*āwôn* is a thing, something evil and concrete that can be found in humans the same way that impurity can be in humans. In any case the angel's action removes the impurity from Isaiah that had made him fear for himself in his encounter with God. This idea of '*āwôn* as akin to impurity was to receive its fullest development in Essenism.

Therefore, sin too (or the consequence of sin) can in like manner be seen as a thing, perhaps even coinciding with impurity. And as a thing, sin could even exist outside humanity. A step in this direction can be found in Gen. 4.7. It is not a very sure step, but the image of sin as an autonomous reality is clear; it is something monstrous 'whose desire is for you'. The Hebrew signifier here translated as 'desire' is *tešuqah*, the same word used to express a woman's sexual desire for a man. Sin seems to exist outside the human being, an autonomous reality desirous of uniting itself with the person as a woman with a man. We could consider this simply a literary image, but the fact remains that the Hebraic imagination was able to conceive of sin as something external, yet possessing an autonomous reality. In any case, guilt could also be considered by other Jews as a thing similar to impurity which, like impurity, could be removed and sent away.

5. *The Priestly Legislation: Impurity as a Strictly Physical Force*

It is certain that there was some tension within Jewish thought concerning the nature of impurity. There was a tendency to link impurity, as something negative for human beings, with the idea of evil (in the ethical sense of the word, as we use it today). At the same time efforts were made to fit impurity, considered something that really did exist, into a system which could keep it under control, without identifying and assimilating it with evil. The group that made the greatest efforts to give a structured formulation to all the traditional beliefs regarding impurity was that of the priests. They had certainly already begun their work before the exile, but it was during the exilic period that they gave the system a good organic, though not always perfectly clear form. The two tendencies, the one linking impurity to sin and the one keeping it separate, gave rise to two contrasting conceptions of impurity. The former found its natural place in the theology of the Promise and the latter in the theology of the Covenant.

The early prophets (late eighth century BCE) had insisted on the need to do good, because God's wrath falls on those who do evil. Their discourse apparently uses the terms good and evil in line with the period's common moral sense, without worrying about the actual contents of good and evil, except in the most generic way. Amos (5.14-15) writes: 'Seek good and not evil, that you may live... Hate evil and love good'. In this phase norms regarding the realm of purity did not exist yet. This confirms the idea that impurity was considered a thing, in itself neither good nor bad, that one should be wary of since it weakens one, but without moral implications. If Laban avoided touching Rachel (Gen. 31.35) it was not out of respect for a law, but out of fear. Applying one of Paul's thoughts to this way of seeing things, we could say that in the sphere of human behaviour, regarding impure things 'All things are lawful, but not all things are beneficial' (1 Cor. 10.23).

The priestly circles sought to put order into the array of moral conceptions in existence in Israel by assigning objective contents to the generic concepts of good and evil. In this operation they also sought to give structure in a coherent system of thought to all the beliefs concerning impurity. The priest's fundamental task of teaching how to distinguish between the impure and the pure and between the sacred and the profane stem from this. In fact, all of the Priestly Code's moral thought is derived from a single central concept, God's sacrality: 'I am sacred'. See, for example, Lev. 19.2, 'You shall be sacred, for I Yhwh your God am sacred'. This idea is expressed in a lapidary fashion in Exod. 19.5-6, clearly inserted in the theology of the Covenant: 'Now therefore, if you obey my voice and keep my Covenant, you shall be my treasured possession out of all the peoples. Indeed, the whole earth is mine, but you shall be for me a priestly kingdom and a sacred nation'. A strong ambiguity is created, because Israel is boldly placed in the realm of the sacred, which remains lethal, however, or at least dangerous to humankind. See all the precautions listed by Ezekiel for protecting oneself from contact with the sacred (Ezek. 44). The concept of the sacred is undergoing change. It is no longer applied solely to a cosmic force, but it is also a reality in history. It begins to penetrate the realm of the human and the profane.

Sacrality seen in this way, indicating one's belonging to God through his intervention in history rather than merely through creation, comes to distinguish people according to the degree of sacrality that each person possesses. A scale of human values is created, running from the most to the least sacred, the priest and the pagan occupying the extreme positions in the hierarchy. A lesser degree of sacrality is considered impurity, since it reduces the possibility of contact with God. A scheme of thought tends to emerge where a lesser degree of sacrality is considered impure in relation to a higher one; only the priest may touch the altar, the layperson must remain at a certain distance and the pagan is completely excluded.

The interpretation of impurity could hardly avoid being involved in the same ambiguity that affected the sacred. Since impurity weakened one and as a result precluded contact with the sacred, with God, it took on more and more of a negative value. We have already seen this in the condemnation of the serpent in Genesis and we have seen the idea developed by Isaiah. On the other hand, the traditional view of impurity permeated every aspect of life to the point that it became necessary to distinguish between licit impurities and illicit impurities. Hence the new value assigned to the category 'sacred–profane/impure–pure', which became an ethical question controlled by the Law. Thus impurity, as such, remained a strictly physical thing, while its moral value was shifted towards the transgression (or not) of the commandments regarding one's behaviour toward impure things. The greatest difficulties were met in the sphere of sexual ethics, where the distinction between licit impurities and illicit ones was inevitable, marriage and procreation belonging to the former category, eating meat with blood belonging to the latter. In effect, in the past the sex act generated impurity, and it continued to do so quite independently of its admissibility. It became necessary to create a system of obligatory purification for all the cases in which impurity was allowed. In these cases transgression only began with omission of the required purification.

The category of impure things was thus placed under the Law. This meant excluding the idea that there was something inherently bad in impure things. Animals that slither, as we have seen (Gen. 1.25), had been declared good by the Priestly current, even though it was formally forbidden to eat them. On the contrary, it is sufficient to purify oneself after the entirely licit act of childbirth. The rite of '*rientrare in santo*' in use in the Catholic Church (at least in Italy) up until the Second Vatican Council is the direct continuation of that element of the Priestly Law.

Let us examine the structure of the Holiness Code (Lev. 17–26).

Moses pronounces norms and principles which are fundamental for Israel. First he gives the norms governing sacrifices, then he prohibits even foreigners in Israel from eating meat with blood (17.12). He prohibits incest, approaching a menstruating woman, committing adultery, altering scales, stealing, lying, committing fraud, and making false oaths in order not to profane God's name. One must love one's neighbour as oneself; it is forbidden to sow two different kinds of seed in the same field... (Lev. 17–19).

As we can see, the rules on purity are mixed with those which we would call ethical; the value of each kind of norm depends on the same divine will. The distinction between norms of purity and ethical norms is strictly ours, because we live in a time after the experiences of Judaism between the second century BCE and the first century CE.

On the other hand, the Priestly Code's idea of sin was decidedly different from Isaiah's. For the Holiness Code, sin is going against the will of God as it is clearly expressed in the Law. Transgression against the Law, God's will, leads to the profanation of God's name. For Isaiah sin is still transgression against God's will, but the consequence is our own impurity. The Holiness Code forbids transgression, even with regards to impurity. Isaiah sees impurity as the consequence of transgression. Isaiah lies at the root of a conception of morality which is very different from the one expressed in the Holiness Code, in the Priestly Code and in Deuteronomy. Even though his idea lay fallow for some time, it was full of consequences for the period in Israel's history when the distinctions between the sacred and the profane, between the pure and the impure, were lost.

6. Ezekiel and a Coherent Theology of the Sacred

While the Holiness Code has provided us with a coherent framework for the idea of impurity in the Priestly Code's circles, it is Ezekiel who gives an organic order to the entire category of 'sacred–profane/impure–pure'. From the premisses provided Ezekiel draws the necessary consequences:

> Thus says the Lord Yhwh: 'O house of Israel, let there be an end to all your abominations in admitting foreigners, uncircumcised in heart and flesh, to be in my sanctuary, profaning my temple...'

> Thus says the Lord Yhwh: 'No foreigner, uncircumcised in heart and flesh, of all the foreigners who are among the people of Israel, shall enter my sanctuary' (Ezek. 44.6-9)[7].

This norm is a further restriction in comparison both to the Holiness Code, which allowed the *ger*, the foreigner living in Israel, to make sacrifices to Yhwh (Lev. 17.8), and to the legislation of Num. 15.14, both written in the Priestly circles. According to the royal ideology, Solomon in his prayer to Yhwh joyously foresees a time in which the foreigners will render homage to Yhwh in the temple of Jerusalem (1 Kgs 8.41-43).

With Ezekiel, however, the foreigner has become manifestly impure, but even the Jewish laymen are seen as impure in comparison to the priests.

> When [the priests] enter the gates of the inner court [that is the sacred part of the temple], they shall wear linen vestments; they shall have nothing of wool on them; while they minister at the gates of the inner court, and within.[8] They shall have linen turbans on their heads, and linen undergarments on their loins; they shall not bind themselves with anything that causes sweat.[9]
>
> When they go out into the outer court to the people, they shall remove the vestments in which they have been ministering, and lay them in the holy chambers; and they shall put on other garments, so that they may not make the people sacred with their [liturgical] vestments (Ezek. 44.17-19).

There is a precise topographical limit between the sacred and the profane, marked by the gates separating the temple's inner and outer courts. Beyond the line of demarcation there is a level of sacrality that the profane person could not bear, but even the profane people standing outside the Temple gates are more sacred than the pagans, who are not allowed even to come near the Temple.

---

7.   Some scholars feel that this text alludes only to the practice of using foreign slaves in the service of the Temple, a practice attested to by Ezra 8.20 (from G.A. Cooke, *A Critical and Exegetical Commentary on the Book of Ezekiel* [ICC; Edinburgh: T. & T. Clark, 1936], p. 479). In that case, here Ezekiel prohibits that practice.

8.   *Within*: the Hebrew text uses a form indicating motion from place to place, which cannot be justified.

9.   *With anything that causes sweat*: the Hebrew text reads simply, 'they shall not bind themselves with sweat'. With or without the conjecture, the meaning is clear.

The officiating priest must leave his profane clothing outside the gates of the inner court, in order not to bring any impurity in with him. And when he goes out again among the people he must leave behind in the Temple his liturgical vestments, in order not to contaminate them. Otherwise God would be profaned and the people would be contaminated by contact with a higher level of sacrality than they could bear. The expression translated here as 'make...sacred' is the same one used in Deuteronomy to indicate the vineyard where different kinds of plants have been planted.

7. *The Sacred during the Early Zadokite Period*

Ezekiel spoke of the future temple. The organization that he foresaw, though, was not put in place until much later. During Jesus' day there were Greek and Roman inscriptions forbidding pagans from crossing the *soreg*, or the boundary of the outer court (*m. Mid.* 2.3). We are reminded of the incident concerning Paul narrated in Acts 21.28-30.

The situation in Jerusalem prior to Nehemiah's reforms (see Chapter 3, §2, pp. 117-24) did not allow a clear separation between Jews and pagans. This led to a certain neglect of the norms on purity, not so much out of negligence as from the fact that Jewish thought in Palestine placed greater emphasis on Israel's universal mission. The foreigner was not meant to feel cut off from Jewish society (Isa. 56.3-6). His offerings to Yhwh could be even more pleasing than those of the priests (Mal. 1.11). Impurity lost, or rather had not yet assumed, its most terrible aspect, the capacity to threaten the very essence of a human being or of Israel; not even the most debilitating of physical deformations, that of the eunuch, could exclude one from the community (Isa. 56.4-5).

Political and ideological reasons combined to form a kind of Judaism that did not have time to affirm itself, because it was blocked by Nehemiah's reforms, which imposed a sharp distinction between Jews and aliens. This was especially true a century later with Ezra's reforms, which even imposed, or at least proposed, repudiation of 'foreign' wives and of children had by 'foreign' wives.

8. *Between the End of the Persian Period and the Hellenistic Age: The Crisis of the Category*

The first canonical book that puts the category of 'sacred–profane/impure–pure' in doubt is Job. Until the beginning of the Persian period human beings were the typical profane reality, they had no *inherent* impurity, but were immersed in a world where contamination was always possible. Being impure, however, had nothing to do with the fact of being human. Job contemplates human weakness, 'a windblown leaf...dry chaff' (Job 13.25), and interprets it as proof of humankind's natural impurity.

> A mortal born of woman, few of days and full of trouble, comes up like a flower and withers, flees like a shadow and does not last. Do you fix your eyes on such a one? Do you bring me into judgment with you? Who can bring a pure thing out of an impure? No one can (Job 14.1-4).

The human condition, frailty, weakness and ignorance are expressed in terms of a sort of ontological weakness, expressed well by the ancient idea of impurity as something that causes weakness. Job sees this weakness as being innate in human beings and, as a consequence, impurity too is a part of human nature.

Job's innovation has wide-ranging effects; it completely overturns the structure of the 'sacred–profane/impure–pure' category, giving it a chiastic structure where it had previously been parallel. The sacred comes to be associated with the pure and the profane with the impure. Impurity enters the realm of the profane in an ontological manner while purity, as a force, becomes a divine attribute. Purity becomes the aim of religious life, with complex consequences. In ancient Israel the greatest purity was required of the priest only when and because he officiated. In contrast, in a world with a growing sense of spirituality, where contact with God was no longer simply a momentary event, purity tended to become the very foundation of religious life. It was no longer seen as something that gave one the strength to approach the altar, essentially seen as a danger, but rather as something that allowed one to come closer to God.

While a greater value was given to purity, at least in the sphere of religious life if not that of morality, there was a corresponding tendency to diminish the value attached to impurity, seen more and more as having an affinity with evil. In roughly 160 BCE the *Book of Dreams* claimed that Enoch was able to have his visions only before he married (see *1 En.* [*BD*] 83.2). Of course, marriage was not forbidden, but in some way it was seen as an obstacle to being near God, because it was a source of impurity. We shall return to this negative idea of sex below, an idea that was to become ever more widespread during later centuries.

Further confirmation of the new structure assumed by the category 'sacred–profane/impure–pure' can be found in Qohelet where he divides humankind into 'the righteous and the wicked, the good and the evil,[10] the pure and the impure' (Qoh. 9.2). 'Righteous', 'good' and 'pure' are three adjectives referring to the same members of humankind. At the same time 'wicked', 'evil' and 'impure' refer to the opposing side. If 'pure' is not a synonym of 'good', it at the very least has some affinity to it.

9. *Impurity as a Cause of Sin in Man*

An even greater revolution concerning the idea of impurity can be found in the *Book of Watchers*. The author (see Chapter 6, §4, pp. 174-80) poses the question of the origins of evil, and arrives at a new solution to the problem. Evil came into the world as a result of an angelic sin (I shall examine the most radical, and probably the latest form of the myth) which took place on the fourth day of creation when the angels assigned to guiding the seven planets in heaven put them in different orbits than those desired by God. This transgression brought about a contamination of all of nature, humankind included. Man was created in a world that had already been contaminated. Therefore, the impurity that exists in the world is the result of a sin, following Isaiah's idea which had been let fall, and it is simultaneously the cause of an infinite number of later sins. The initial transgression took place on a plane above humanity and brought about terrible cosmic consequences for humankind.

This underlying idea in the book must belong to its most ancient *strata*, as can be concluded by the words put in God's mouth (see *1 En.* [*BW*] 10.8): 'Attribute all sin to Asael'. Following this vision of things the human being becomes more a victim than a cause of the evil he commits. The reverse side of this pessimistic view of human nature, however, is a new element capable of giving humankind hope beyond all limits. The individual possesses an immortal soul that survives the body. The soul of the righteous person, though it is not clear just who that is, is destined to live in a world without evil, somewhere in the extreme West, where it awaits God's Great Judgment in peace. There the soul will live forever near God.

10. *And the evil*: with the Septuagint. The word is missing in the Hebrew text, but the parallel structure requires its presence.

10. *Impurity and Sacrality among the Essenes*

It was in Essenism that the conception of impurity as an evil force, basically coinciding with sin and with evil, reached its most radical extreme. Impurity and sin coincide and are part of human nature. Freedom from sin is the same as freedom from impurity. Purification is liberation from sin.

'Man is in *'awon* ['sin', but not as transgression] from when he is in the womb' (1QH 4.29-30).

'awon is a thing, a stain attached to humanity from when he was conceived; it is part of his nature. Some people, though, can purify themselves of this innate impurity, but not through the traditional means of purification:

> Anyone who declines to enter [the Covenant with Go]d [that is, into the sect] in order to walk in the stubbornness of his heart…shall not be counted with the righteous… He *lo' yisdaq* ['shall not be just/righteous' where 'just/righteous' can only mean 'justified']… He will not become clean by the acts of atonement, nor shall he be purified by the cleansing waters, or shall he be made holy[11] by the seas or rivers, nor shall he be purified by all the water of the ablutions. *Impure, impure* shall he be… For it is by the spirit of the Council of the Truth of God that human deeds and sins are atoned so that he can look at the light of life (1QS 2.25-3.9).

Of course, practice of this exceptional purification does not mean that the Essenes stopped practising the purification rites of the priestly tradition. The rites remained, but only for the purification of 'historical' states of impurity, contracted during the various occasions of one's life. The individual can be purified of his innate impurity only through joining the sect, that is through an act of faith: 'God will free them from Judgment[12] on account of their sufferings and of their faith in the Teacher of Righteousness' (1QpHab. 8.2-3).

---

11. *Lo yitqaddeš*: 'will not make himself sacred', but the word 'sacred' has taken on a different value by this time. It now means 'pure' or 'holy'; see the use of 'impure' as its opposite!

12. 'God will free them from Judgment': this is how I translate *yaṣṣilem 'el mibbet hammišpat. Bet hammišpat* is (God's) tribunal. The text is a comment on Hab. 2.4: 'The righteous person shall live by his faith, *be'emunato*'. In the Essenic commentary the meaning of *'emunah* has shifted from 'faithfulness' to 'faith'. The interpretation of *'emunah be* as 'faithfulness to' seems difficult to me due to the

Summing up, we can say that for the Essenes impurity and sin coincide. It should be emphasized, however, that sin in this case is '*awon*, which in this type of context indicates more of a stain, independently of the individual's will, than sin as transgression. Other terms are used for sin as transgression.

For the Essenes, the human being is no longer the seat of the profane, but of impurity. With this development, profanity and all the values attached to it become meaningless. With the profane the sense of human freedom to collaborate with his creator within the limits of the Law disappears as well. Essenism was predeterminist both in its conception of history and in its interpretation of the life of the individual. The world is dominated by impurity/evil; the neophytes are still impure, as are the Jews who refuse to join the sect. Jerusalem is impure as all the pagans are impure. If there is anything that binds the Jews (with the exception of the Essenes) to the pagans it is their common impurity and condemnation, a sort of reverse universalism.[13]

structure of Essenic thought in general, but also, in this case, because of the construction of *'emunah* with *be*, which is not an Old Testament construction. Regarding faith that frees one from Judgment, see Jn 3.18: 'Those who believe in him are not judged'. In both cases salvation means being exonerated from Judgment because of one's faith, rather than being considered righteous at the Great Judgment. Therefore, for both John and the author of 1QpHab, if there were no supplementary grace the Judgment would consist in the examination of one's sins. Since there is no such thing as a righteous person without sin, in order to be saved Judgment must be avoided. If there were a Judgment everyone would be condemned. The Pharisees resolved the problem in a different way; Judgment regarded all the actions in a person's life. In his goodness God justified the person who had done more works in keeping with the Law than transgressions against it. R. Aqiba's (early second century CE) formulation is perfectly clear: 'All things are foreseen. Freedom of choice is given. The world is judged with goodness [that is God does not examine only the evil committed]. Everything depends on the number of works [good or bad]' (*Pirqe Ab.* 3.15). The meaning is that God grants justification to those who, based on the number of their merits or demerits, allow him to justify them. Justification in this case is based on works, but it is still justification, even for the Pharisees.

13. For the novitiate, see *War* 2.137-38, 150; 1QS 6.13-22 (8.10-11). From the Qumran texts it is impossible to reconstruct the number of years that the novitiate lasted. There was a trial period, after which the neophyte took his place alongside the members, but not their drink (1QS 6.16-17 and 20-21); apparently there were various degrees of purity, which imposed caution in contact with others. The existence of differing levels of purity is documented for the Pharisees as well. See

In order to maintain this exceptional purity the Essene had to avoid contact with many things that could cause contamination, in a life which would seem bearable only to a fanatic.

> Anyone who has let himself be seen nude by a companion, unless due to illness, shall have a punishment of six months…
>
> Anyone who has shown his penis from under his clothes, or whose clothes are so ragged that his nudity can be seen, shall have a punishment of thirty days (1QS 7.14-16).

Even defecating was cause for worry among the Essenes. Josephus narrates (*War* 2.147-49) that the Essenes avoided doing it on the sabbath. What seems incredible at first assumes a meaning if we compare different norms from the *War Scroll* and the *Damascus Document*. The author of the *War Scroll* gave orders for building the camp prior to the great battle for the final liberation. Taking up a passage of Deut. 23.13-15 ordering the Jews to dispose of their excrement outside the camp, he adds the distance for preparing the pit, 2000 cubits away (1QM 7.6-7).

We learn from the *Damascus Document* (10.21), however, that the Essenes could not cover more than 1000 cubits on the sabbath, hence the dilemma illustrated by Josephus. Apparently a comparison between the two norms made it impossible to apply the rule regarding excrement on the sabbath.

Alongside the identification of the impure with human nature, in Essenism the division between the sacred and the profane was lost as well. Through ascesis a person could reach the highest purity, identified with the very sacrality of God. To be pure in the fullest sense meant being in the realm of the divine. We gather from the *Community Rule* that the novice could not touch the members of the sect, because they apparently had a higher degree of purity. In like manner, a member being punished had first of all to leave the purity of the other members.

---

m. Ḥag. 2.7. The first level was that of the layperson (*ḥaber*, member of the *ḥaburah*), then the priest who could consume the *terumah*, followed by the priest who could take part in the holy things. The highest level was occupied by the priest who could prepare the ashes of the red cow. The disappearance of the priesthood, however, eliminated the value of such distinctions. See also the discrimination within Jewish society concerning marriages (see Jeremias, *Jerusalem*, pp. 360, 401). On the impurity of the pagans during Jesus' day, see Acts 10.28: 'You yourselves know that it is unlawful for a Jew to associate with or to visit a pagan'; and Jn 18.28: 'They did not enter the *praetorium* so as to avoid ritual defilement'. See also Boccaccini, *Middle Judaism*, pp. 251-56.

> If he [the postulant] is included in the Community council, he must not
> touch the purity of the members of the council while they test him about
> his spirits and about his deeds until he has completed a full year (1QS
> 6.16-17).

The men of the Essenic Community are at times referred to as 'sacred
men' (though at this point in English we should say 'holy') and their
exceptional level of purity is mentioned once as 'glorious purity' (1QS
4.5), literally 'purity of glory', which is the great epithet of God. In the
sabbath liturgy, as it appears in the *Songs of the Sabbath Sacrifice*, the
Essene sings God's praise from inside the heavenly temple along with
the angels; he is already living in the eternal dimension.

The overturning of the category 'sacred–profane/impure–pure' corresponds to a new type of religiosity. The traditional interpretation of
the category had been that the two principles were autonomous. God
and human beings were at opposite poles of the cosmos and each was
free in his own realm. In this sense, the Law was a tool of freedom,
because it indicates the limits within which humankind must keep its
own creativity. The Law is a system that does not impose anything on
the individual as such, but only in as much as the individual is a human
being.

With the new spirituality the place for the profane disappears. Mankind's highest aspiration is to do God's will integrally, a will which is
now directed toward the individual, asking and imposing what God
expects of each person (see Chapter 12, §3, pp. 337-43). Mankind's
aspiration is to penetrate into the realm of the divine while still on the
earth.

11. *Impurity and Sex in Middle Judaism*

In the book of *Jubilees* we read: 'There is no sin greater than fornication...' (33.20). This statement, which can seem strange to us today
and which in any case is fruit of a different moral sensitivity than the
classical Jewish one, dates from the second century BCE, probably
toward the end of the century. It can already be seen, though, documented in the Jewish tradition which lay at the base of the Septuagint;
in the series of the three great commandments that regard one's neighbour, the first place is not occupied by 'Thou shalt not kill', but by
'Thou shalt not commit adultery'. This is the case both in Exodus and
in Deuteronomy. Something has changed in the scale of values. The

greatest offence that can be made against a man concerns his woman more than his very life.

The shift in the scale of values did not depend on a different evaluation of the seriousness of the offence in itself, but rather in viewing adultery in the light of the problem of impurity. The angels who descended to earth, desirous of women, committed a sexual sin (Gen. 6.1-4 and most of all the *Book of Watchers*). The contamination of the earth was the result of a sin that some myths associate with sexuality. The idea that sex was a source of impurity was well-known even before the exile, but it was an impurity that was not normally identified with evil. We have seen, though, that even in ancient times some authors had seen a relationship between impurity and evil/sin. In the Hellenistic age, the roots of evil and impurity were seen in sexuality.

The commandment that reads 'Thou shalt not commit adultery' was openly taken to mean, 'Thou shalt not commit fornication' (in Hebrew z^e*nût*, in Greek πορνεία), as reads the text from *Jubilees* quoted above. And fornication is pointed out as the greatest impurity. The entire text of the passage in *Jubilees* quoted above says:

> There is no sin greater than fornication...because Israel is a sacred nation to the Lord...a people of priests... Such an impurity cannot appear in a sacred nation.

Any and all things that can harm the priest's purity becomes *zenut*, in other words impurity/sin/evil for the entire Jewish people.[14]

In the *Testament of Simeon* (5.3), z^e*nût*/πορνεία is called the 'mother of all evils'. In the list of the spirits of error in the *Testament of Reuben* (2.2–3.3) πορνεία occupies the first place, as it does in the *Damascus Document* (4.17), where it says that z^e*nût* is the first of Belial's three nets. πορνεία can even makes its home in a marriage. In Tob. 8.7 the protagonist declares that he is getting married ἐπ᾽ ἀληθείας, and not διὰ πορνείαν, not for πορνεία, but for truth, that is for correct behaviour. In a fragment of the *Damascus Document*[15] we can read, 'He

---

14. The tendency to extend the rules of purity regarding the priesthood to cover laymen as well is typical of all of Judaism until the fall of the Second Temple. This is a widespread opinion. See M. Newton, *The Concept of Purity at Qumran and in the Letters of Paul* (SNTSMS, 53; Cambridge: Cambridge University Press, 1985), pp. 80-81, and E. Lupieri, 'La purità impura: Giuseppe Flavio e le purificazioni degli esseni', *Henoch* 7 (1985), pp. 15-44.

15. See L. Rosso Ubigli, 'Il documento di Damasco e l'etica coniugale: A proposito di un nuovo passo qumranico', *Henoch* 14 (1992), pp. 3-10.

who approaches his woman *liznût* ["for fornication", which corresponds exactly to the διὰ πορνείαν of Tobit] and not according to the rule, shall be expelled and shall not return [to the sect]'. The *Testament of Asher* (5.1) mentions ἀσωτία (dissoluteness) in marriage.

So far we could say that the question only regards the proper role of marriage; for example, limiting the sex act to the sole aim of procreation. Some texts, however, go further. It is only said of the spirit of πορνεία that it separates one from God and brings one closer to Belial or to idols (*T. Reub.* 4.6 and *T. Sim.* 5.3). The spirit of πορνεία is the first impulse towards sin (*T. Reub.* 3.3). Thus from the sin of πορνεία narrowly interpreted, we pass step by step to unrighteousness. In a sense, πορνεία is the unifying principle of all sins; fighting against indecency means attacking man's worst inclinations at the root. And in just the same way that πορνεία is bound to sex and the body, the idea of impurity is linked to sex in a particular way. Impurity, though, while linked to πορνεία on the one hand, on the other is identified more and more with evil, to the point that evil spirits can be called either bad or impure interchangeably (see *T. Benj.* 5.2; *1 En.* 53.3; *Jub.* 10.1 and frequent passages in the New Testament).

We read in the *Testament of Issachar* (2.1), 'An angel of the Lord appeared to Jacob and said: "Rachel shall bear two children, because she despised intercourse with her husband chosing rather continence".' Seeking sex even within a marriage is evil. God grants children as a reward to those who renounce seeking sex. Beyond the immediate content, the text reveals a certain horror for the sex act. In the same *Testament* (3.5) Issachar declares that he had married at the age of 35 (the average life was much shorter then than it is now!), 'because hard work consumed my energy, and pleasure with a woman never came to my mind; rather sleep overtook me because of my labour'. This complex category begins to lead towards pleasure as being linked to impurity, evil and sin.

The idea that the root of evil lay in sexuality as pleasure is clearly present in Philo as well. In *De opificio mundi* he writes:

> The principle of guilty life was [for Adam] woman, because as long as he was alone, by his unicity he was like the world and like God and he had the character of the two natures impressed in his soul. But when woman was created, seeing a figure similar to him and with a similar shape to his own he was happy and, coming near her, he greeted her affectionately. And she, seeing no other being that was more similar to her, rejoiced and returned his greetings with modesty. And thus love

(ἔρως) was born; joining, so to speak, the separate parts of a single being, it unites them by planting in both of them the desire (πόθος) for union, with the goal of procreating a being similar to them. This desire, however, also generates physical pleasure, which is the principle of injustice and transgressions. It is due to pleasure that human beings barter bliss and immortal life for mortal life and misfortune (*Op. Mund.* 151-52).

Through pleasure sex is the cause of sin, of every sin, from Adam until the present. In Paul (1 Cor. 6.16-18), πορνεία, here meaning prostitution, is a singular and particularly terrible sin. 'Shun πορνεία! Every sin that a person commits is outside the body; but πορνεία sins against the body itself'. Impurity exists and reveals itself primarily, even in Christianity, through sins linked to sex.

An ideology and a sensitivity like the one we have just described could not avoid addressing the question of marriage. In the Hebrew and ancient Jewish world fertility was a benediction and a joy; virginity represented a misfortune. When Jephthah's daughter finds out that she must die she seems saddest at the thought of dying a virgin. 'She departed, she and her companions, and bewailed her virginity on the mountains' (Judg. 11.38).

The barren woman could be held in contempt, as Sarai was by Hagar (Gen. 16.4), or Hannah by Penninah (1 Sam. 1.6). The eunuch was considered extremely impure and was not allowed into the assembly of Yhwh (Deut. 23.2).

In this atmosphere no position is taken up in favour of marriage, because it was so much a part of the normal rhythm of life, such a normal practice that there was no need to recommend it. Such a position does appear, though, in the rabbinical period, where it is even established that anyone who has not married by the age of 20 has broken a commandment (*b. Qid.* 29b). Between biblical times and rabbinical Judaism lies the problematic regarding sex in Middle Judaism, which apparently took its toll on marriage.

It is with the Essenes, of course, that we find the clearest contempt for marriage, and they won the admiration of writers like Philo and Josephus.

> Foreseeing that marriage would be an obstacle both in itself and for community life, the Essenes have banned it, imposing on themselves practice of perfect continence. No one among them marries, because they hold women to be selfish, jealous and her seduction a snare for the husband (Philo, *Hypoth.*, para. 14).

> The Essenes reject pleasures as being evil, while they view temperance and resistence to the passions as a virtue. Marriage is held in disdain, but they adopt the children of others while they are still susceptible to teaching. They consider them members of the family and mould them according to their customs. Still, they have not abolished marriage...but they are wary of women's lasciviousness and are convinced that no woman is faithful to a single man (Josephus, *War* 2.120-21; see also *Ant.* 18.21).

Even Pliny, in his *Natural History* (V, 17, 4), mentions this strange people that had survived 'for thousands of centuries', in spite of having given up women and love.

Leaving aside Philo's hyperbolic presentation of this information, it is certain that marriage raised a number of problems for the Essenes and some of them must have given it up. Besides the norms regarding sexual behaviour, which we have already mentioned, it was also forbidden to marry a sterile woman, even though their method for establishing a woman's sterility was less than scientific. After mentioning that there were Essenes who married, Josephus adds that 'they examine their women for three months and they marry them only after they have been purified three times [that is they have had their period three times], thus giving proof that they are able to bear children' (*War* 2.161).

12. *The Problem of Impurity and Pagan Morality*

Mosaic Law was a morality based on divine commandment. Among the norms included in that system of Law there were a number that seem to us to belong to a particular sphere of human existence, which we call 'norms of purity', following the example of the author of the *Letter of Aristeas* (probably the second century BCE). That work's author was the first to conceptualize this category in the Law (142), a category which the Greeks had some difficulty understanding, just as we do today. In particular these are the norms concerning food, the purifications necessary after performing certain licit acts and perhaps circumcision. However Aristeas defined them, and whatever we make of them today, any distinctions lie outside the Law, because for the Jews all the commandments were the product of God's will. Historically, the norms of purity were all the Jewish laws that pagan morality, essentially following a rational structure, did not accept, in spite of any admiration for Judaism, for its faith in the one God and for the high value attached to ethical behaviour.

The author of the *Letter of Aristeas* felt the need to explain the norms of purity in rational terms in order to explain them to the Greeks. He approached the question in two ways: first, that the norms of purity were symbols and, secondly, that they were a preventive defence, so to speak, against the moral pitfalls that are always lying in wait. 'To prevent us from being contaminated or from being perverted by the company of unworthy persons, the Legislator protected us on all sides with norms of purity' (142). 'Everything has been set...to spur us towards pure reflection and to give us upright moral direction for the sake of righteousness' (144). The way of proceeding by pairs should be noted; a term indicating purity is followed by a term indicating its function for the end goal of justice, an end which the Greeks could easily understand.

The symbolic argumentation, however, prevails:

> By means of the impure animals the Legislator has handed down to intelligent beings that they must be righteous and achieve nothing through violence, nor take advantage of their own strength in order to oppress others. In effect, in the cases where it is not allowed to even touch the aforementioned birds because of their own nature, how would it be possible to not take all precautions against letting our own customs degenerate in that same way? We must come to the conclusion that the rules regarding our conduct toward these animals as mere beasts have been set out symbolically (*Ep. Arist.* 148-50).

In the end the norms of purity revolve around justice.

13. *The Norms of Purity as a Problem for the Jews Themselves*

In the *Letter of Aristeas* we see that eating with the king did not pose a problem for the Jews, as long as he accepted their dietary customs (184). Whatever the explanation given for the norms of purity regarding food, the author of the *Letter of Aristeas* is sure of one thing, that they are part of the Law and are to be followed like any other command-ment. *Aristeas*'s discourse is aimed exclusively at defending the existence of the norms of purity, or at least those regarding food, in the face of objections raised in non-Jewish circles. Later, though, the prob-lem came to be felt even within Judaism. The Jews themselves began to question these norms. The problem became particularly acute in the first century CE and we meet it again and again, with various solutions to the problem.

The solutions were sought in two opposite directions: on the one hand there was the tendency to make purity coincide with good in absolute terms (in Essenism it is even made to coincide with sacrality), and on the other there is a tendency to deny purity any real value, following the norms simply because it is God's will. Jesus took a precise position on this question; he did not deny the reality of impurity, but he expressed its contents in a new way.

Philo follows in *Aristeas*'s steps, clarifying his arguments and carrying them further. He also makes use of concepts borrowed from Greek thought. In *De specialibus legibus* we read:

> Impure is the unrighteous or the wicked person [therefore impurity coincides with what is morally wrong], who has regard for neither human nor divine things, who soils and joins everything with no sense of measure of his passions and with the excesses of vice... On the contrary the actions of the good are praised as they are shaped by the virtue of the one who achieves them, because that which is done is similar to the one who does it (3.209).

In this passage Philo clearly tends to subsume the idea of 'pure/ impure' into morality (in the modern sense of the word). Immediately prior to the passage quoted above, though, Philo had just said that the impurity that comes from touching a corpse had been established by the Legislator, so that 'no one be παραίτιος, that is, concurrent in the cause of another's death' (3.205). And this even when the person had died of natural causes. With this statement we return to the idea of the norms of purity as protection against immorality.

This is why, explains Philo, purification is necessary even for those who have simply entered a house where there is a dead person. Philo is aware that there is still an obstacle to be overcome in his rational way of explaining things. He knows that 'even the objects in a house where there is a dead person become impure'. At this point he brings the idea of impurity back to the realm of the most authentic Jewish tradition, but by way of a concept that the Greeks of his day could understand; the soul is a divine image and impurity is a thing, produced by the soul's departure from the body. It is the lack of the divine that causes impurity. Philo accepts more or less all the possible explanations for impurity; what is important to him is to preserve the concept of impurity in the broad sense that the term held during his day, without taking anything away from Mosaic Law.

Another characteristic figure in the theme of the 'pure/impure' is John the Baptist, active during the earliest period of Jesus' preaching. John must have had some relationship with Jesus, even though in this case Jesus' position was very different from the Baptist's. The primary goal of John's preachings, as far as we can tell from the Gospels and from Josephus, is the total conversion of Israel. Sin is everywhere, a way must be found for the 'remission of sins'. First it is necessary that people stop sinning and, having done penance, that they purify themselves through baptism. It is clear that for John sin produced impurity which had to be removed, and penance alone was not enough to remove the stain that sin had produced. That stain, had it remained, would have been the equivalent of the sin. This is a theological schema similar to the one documented at Qumran, which must have been quite widespread among the Jews of the period.

Since sin either was impurity or generated impurity, John the Baptist saw purity as the high road to perfection, and that is the road he followed.

14. *Christianity and the Radicalization of Isaiah's Ideas on Impurity*

As we all know, Jesus left John and was not afraid to mix with people in a possible state of impurity, nor to eat foods touched by others. He took a very different path and had no objections if his disciples failed to respect the norms regarding meals, be they norms established simply by tradition or by the Law. According to Mark (ch. 7), Jesus abolished the norms of purity regarding food (7.18-19). If we read the text carefully, though, Jesus used the norms on food in order to reach a series of conclusions that go well beyond the rules regarding meals, even though it is not clear just how far beyond.

'There is nothing outside a person that by going in can defile, but the things that come out are what defile' (7.15). The question posed by the Pharisees had only been on whether one could eat something without having performed the traditional ablution. The very first words of Jesus' answer go beyond the question, 'nothing...by going in can defile'. This not only addresses the question of how one should eat, but also what. The second part ('the things that come out') leads to even vaster consequences and in a way articulates a general principle. The only thing that can contaminate a human being (and here 'contaminate', 'defile', must hold the meaning that the Jews of the period gave it, that is more of a spiritual weakening than a physical one, something that kept one from coming near to God) is transgression against the Law, as Jesus taught it, naturally. Mark's interpretation, 'Thus he declared all foods pure' (7.19), is reductive and indicative of a certain unease in the early Christian tradition in the face of Jesus' teaching.

In other words, Jesus maintains the idea that impurity is extremely negative, but the contents of impurity are not those taught by the tradition. We must remember, however, that the tradition considered any transgression against the norms of purity as a sin. If Jesus said that only 'the things that come out...defile', it means that he reduced the contents of the Law to what we would call ethics, but this was an idea that the Jews of the time were unaware of, or at least they had not yet formalized it. Saying that there is nothing impure in nature can be a valid and understandable principle (see the *Ep. Arist.* 143;[16] Rom. 14.14), but to Jesus' listeners the step from the general principle to its effective contents must have been very difficult. For the Jew of that epoch all parts of the Law were Law to the same degree. It is clear that Jesus abolishes the norms regarding foods, but other similar norms were potentially eliminated as well. The text is not precise. The norms of purity also concerned worship, sexual relations and contact with the pagans.

The question of the actual contents of the principle expressed by Jesus remained an open question. It is clear that for Jesus the traditional Law was to be considered valid, with the exception of the cases where impurity derived from external things, that is, the norms grouped together under the vague heading of norms of purity. It is certain that Jesus abolished all the norms concerning foods, but which other norms were to be considered invalidated? For example, the period's common sense of morality certainly condemned prostitution and other unclean things related to sex, but once the norms of purity had been abolished, on what basis could prostitution be prohibited? The ancient Law did not prohibit it directly. Another example: what was the message to be gathered from Jesus' general principle in ethical questions regarding marriage, or relations with the pagans? The precepts set forth by the so-called 'Council of Jerusalem' (Acts 15.28-29) provide abundant evidence of the first Christians' uncertainty. We are reminded of Peter's doubt as to whether he should enter the house of the centurion Cornelius (Acts 10), and also of Peter's behaviour in Antioch (Gal. 2.12). Peter knows that he can enter the pagan's house because in a dream he

---

16.   'In general, according to the natural principle all things are equal since they are governed by a single power, but a deep meaning, specific to each thing, is linked to abstention from some things and to the use of others'.

was offered unclean foods; the parallel between being permitted to eat unclean foods and being permitted to have contact with the pagans, in other words the purity of both the one and the other, is clear. The question of the impurity of foods as a point of reference also shows, however, that this was a question that was considered easy to overcome. This must have been a result of Jesus' teaching, which had been received, but not applied: 'You can eat' is certainly not an obligation and foods considered impure must have been avoided. Jesus' discourse on the purity of foods was not a response to questions regarding the foods themselves, but the way of eating foods that were in themselves pure. But just how far did Jesus want to go with the abolition of the norms of purity? Or better, just where did Jesus place the boundary between ethical norms and norms of purity?

The question of the relationship between purity and ethics becomes particularly acute in Paul. It has already been pointed out[17] that Paul found it difficult to preach the moral of the Gospels without basing himself on some kind of code. In 1 Corinthians he seems to put love at the centre of Christian life (ch. 13). But love is a charisma, or even above the charismas, not a law. And even if it can be taken as the basis of a set of rules for behaviour, there will clearly always be a subjective hiatus between the principle and the infinite occasions of daily life. On the one hand, Paul was a Pharisee and the study of the Law lay at the basis of his moral education. His sureness about what is right and what is wrong stem from that education. On the other hand, though, according to Paul the Law could not save anyone. He did maintain the Law's historical value, though, as a guide leading to the Christ, and he also upheld it as a moral paradigm (Rom. 7.16 and 22; Gal. 3.24-25).

Here we are faced with yet another problem, because Paul was well aware that Jesus had modified the Law, and therefore referring back to the Law had lost meaning, at least as long as we do not mean referring to the Law that even the pagans observe, what we could call natural morality, or, more correctly historically, the period's common sense of morality. In this case, though, it is obvious that the idea of the Law

17. See Booth, *Jesus and the Laws of Purity* and Newton, *Concept*, as well as García Martínez's article, 'Les limites de la Communauté: Pureté, et impureté à Qumrân et dans le Nouveau Testament', in T. Baarde *et al.* (eds.), *Text and Testimony: Essays on New Testament and Apocryphal Literature in Honour of A.F.J. Klijn* (Kampen: Kok, 1988), pp. 111-22.

becomes extremely feeble: 'All who have sinned without the Law will also perish without the Law' (Rom. 2.12).

It should come as no surprise that some interpreted Paul's preaching as though he did not care about sin. Awareness of this fact (see Rom. 3.8)[18] must have led Paul to root his new morality in more solid and clear-cut principles. Or perhaps not even he was aware that his conception of sin was no longer that of his Pharisaic up-bringing. Paul writes:

> We know that the Law is spiritual; but I am of the flesh, sold into slavery under sin. I do not understand my own actions. For I do not do what I want, but I do the very thing I hate. Now if I do what I do not want, I agree that the law is good. But in fact it is no longer I that do it, but sin that dwells within me (Rom. 7.14-17).

What Law is Paul referring to? To the historical one? No, because he considers it surpassed. The new one had not been written, though, and perhaps not even thought of. Anyhow, he felt the need for an ideal paradigm as a point of reference. Not only but, as I said earlier, not even Paul's idea of 'sin' corresponds to the idea held by those who saw salvation in 'doing the Law'. In the Pauline context 'sin' in no way means transgression; sin is a reality that lives within humankind, and not the abstract concept of transgression. It is therefore a reality with very strong affinities to impurity. In Rom. 1.24 Paul writes, 'God gave them up [those who do not recognize him] in the lusts of their hearts to impurity (ἀκαθαρσία), to the degrading of their bodies among themselves'. Impurity, too, is a real thing to which one can be given up or condemned, like the ancient serpent. The presence of impurity in humankind is revealed in his every vile action, especially if in the realm of sex.

In the sixth chapter of Paul's 1 Corinthians, mentioned above, echoes of the book of *Jubilees'* ideology can be heard: 'There is no sin greater than fornication...' Paul writes:

> The body is meant not for πορνεία, but for the Lord... Shun πορνεία! Every sin that a person commits is outside the body; but he who commits πορνεία sins against the body itself. Or do you not know that your body is a temple of the Holy Spirit within you, which you have from God? (1 Cor. 6.13, 18-19).

18. See R. Penna, 'I diffamatori di Paolo in Rom 3, 8', *RSB* 1 (1989), pp. 43-53.

Even from the quickest of glances at these texts it appears that for Paul the basis of moral life consisted in keeping oneself pure, that is in keeping oneself like a new temple following the same rules used to safeguard the purity of the Temple.[19] The problem, however, had only been postponed, because the old Temple could be contaminated by the presence of a pagan, while the new temple could not. The old Jew could be contaminated by foods, but the new Jew could not. In the case of a marriage between a Christian and a pagan, the pagan did not contaminate the Christian (and here Paul follows a very Jewish line of reasoning), but it was the Christian that purified the pagan (1 Cor. 7.14). Therefore the problem of purity remained in Paul in spite of Rom. 14.14.[20] We do not know, though, just how many of the Torah's norms Paul was willing to consider abolished inasmuch as they regarded a form of impurity that no longer had to be considered impure. We have invented the terms 'legal or cultural impurity', but these are our terms that we use to explain why the ancient Jews posed the problem of certain laws, which were seen as being different from the others. But we do not know what contents should be used to fill the concept of 'legal impurity'. The problem of the precise extension of πορνεία remains an open question as well.

Leaving aside Paul and examining a few facts that contributed to shape the early Church, we see that the problem of defining the 'impure which must no longer be considered such',[21] must have been quite serious. The so-called Council of Jerusalem forbade few things to the pagans (Acts 15.20), indicating them among those things that apparently were not commonly recognized as sins in the morality of the age. The majority of the prohibitions were understood, since it was well known that the pagans already shared them. Among the explicit prohibitions we find that it was forbidden to eat the meat of animals that

19. See Newton, *Concept*, p. 53: 'The point is that the language of the Temple, sacrifice and purity pervades Paul's letters and frequently influences the way he thinks about himself, his converts and his behaviour'.

20. From the context it seems clear that here Paul is only talking about foods.

21. See the formula used in Acts 10.15. Peter has the vision of the foods traditionally considered impure that are sent to him from Heaven with the order to eat them. He refuses. A voice then tells him: ἃ ὁ θεὸς ἐκαθάρισεν, σὺ μὴ κοίνου, 'What God has purified, you must not call profane'. The expression, 'What God has purified', perplexes me. What event does the text allude to? I believe, and I am not alone, that ἐκαθάρισεν should be understood as 'has declared pure', sc. in the vision. God intervenes to declare that there are no longer any impure things.

had been strangled. It does not seem to me, though, that Paul ever recommended the application of this rule to the Church of the Gentiles. It must have been clear to him that food never contaminated people, not even meat, no matter how it had been butchered.

The Council of Jerusalem did, however, prohibit πορνεία, but we do not know exactly what the Church's first fathers were referring to, since we do not know the definition given to πορνεία by the common morality of the day. As far as marriage was concerned, in 1 Corinthians Paul advised couples not to neglect sexual relations (7.2-5), unless by common consent and in order to concentrate on prayer. He does not seem to impose any other limitations, even though marriage is seen here as a *remedium concupiscentiae*, 'so that Satan may not tempt you'.

Justin, however, around the year 165, wrote, 'We Christians, while we do marry, it is only in order to raise children'. This could be taken as a general statement, if we didn't also have Athenagoras' very clear words, written in 177. He explained to Marcus Aurelius that the Christians only married in order to have children, explaining that as a consequence they avoided having sex during the wife's pregnancy.[22] It is clear that in this case there would have been πορνεία even within marriage, a possibility already admitted in Tobit and that we also find documented in a fragment from Qumran.[23] Athenagoras follows the same line of reasoning as Philo, advising repudiation of sterile wives, though it was not obligatory, in order to avoid sowing one's seed uselessly. At the same time Philo (*Spec. Leg.* 3.34-36) strongly condemned marrying a woman that was known to be barren (a widow or divorcée with no children, or in advanced age?). Through the centuries some vestiges of this way of seeing things has been handed down to us; the history of the Church's stance on sexuality is a good example.[24] This depends on the fact that we do not know the exact connotations of πορνεία in Jesus' teachings; Paul and Athenagoras seem to have very different ideas on the subject.

22. On Justin and Athenagoras, see J.L. Flandrin, *L'église et le contrôle des naissances* (Paris: Flammarion, 1970), p. 28.

23. See n. 15 of this chapter.

24. See J.L. Flandrin, *Le sexe et l'occident* (Paris: Editions du Seuil, 1981); idem, *Un temps pour embrasser: Aux origines de la morale sexuelle occidentale (VI–XI siècle)* (Paris: Editions du Seuil, 1983).

15. *Other Responses to the Question of Impurity in First-Century Judaism*

Hanina ben Dosa, who was perhaps only a bit younger than Jesus, has gone down in history primarily for a single act; he walked through his village holding a snake that had bit him in his hand. He said, 'It is not the serpent that kills, but sin'. But holding a snake in one's hand was itself against the Law. It would seem, therefore, that he held a position similar to the one held by Jesus. Unfortunately we know very little about Hanina ben Dosa.[25]

The solution offered by Yohanan ben Zakkai, the man who took the destiny of the Palestinian Jews in hand after the catastrophe of 70 CE, was extremely clear and coherent with the fundamental elements of Pharisaic thought. He set up an academy at Yamnia and set about reorganizing Judaism and gathering together its historical writings. Under his guidance Judaism came more and more to be identified with Pharisaism. 'The cadaver does not contaminate and the ashes of the red cow do not purify; it is God who has ordained that these things be done'.[26]

16. *The Sacred and Oath-taking*

According to Josephus, one of the fundamental elements of the Essenes' theology was the prohibition of oaths. It is worth examining the motives that brought the Essenes to that position.

> Their every word [of the Essenes] is stronger than an oath. They refrain from taking oaths, because they consider it worse than perjury... (*War* 2.135)

> Still, before being able to touch the common food [the adept] takes terrible oaths. In the first place he must be pious towards the divinity, then he must observe justice towards men...With such oaths they ensure the faithfulness of those who enter the sect (*War* 2.139-42).

In comparing these two passages it emerges that the Essenes, as Josephus knew them, forbade oaths, but only with regards to

---

25. See *b. Ber.* 33a.

26. See *Tanḥ. Ḥuqqat* §8. While this is a decidedly late text, the information regarding ben Zakkai fits so well in the context of the first-century questions that it can be considered reliable. See also *Pes. K.* 4.7.

unimportant things. Furthermore, in the lack of any sort of case history, from these two passages it would seem that the only kind of oath that the Essenes practised was swearing by God.

In general, the Essenic texts that we have today confirm the information provided by Josephus. They also shed light on some details.

> He [the adept] shall pledge on himself with a binding (formally valid) oath to revert to the Law of Moses according to all he has decreed, with whole heart and whole soul, in compliance with all that has been revealed concerning the sons of Zadok, the priests who keep the covenant and interpret His will (1QS 5.8-9).

This is the same fundamental oath that one of the *Hodayot* refers to: '[I] have known thanks to the wealth of Your goodness and with an oath I have enjoined on myself not to sin against You' (1QH 14.17).

It is worth noting that in this basic pledge neither the verb 'swear' (*nšb'*) nor the name of God appears; the Essene swears by himself. In Deut. 10.20 it is written: 'by his name you shall swear'. The Deuteronomic legislator was more worried about idolatry; he wanted to be sure that no one swore by entities other than God. Deuteronomy 6.13 is even more explicit, repeating the same formula as before, but adding the word 'alone': 'by his name alone you shall swear'.

In Essenism the verb 'to swear' has disappeared and been replaced by *hqym 'l npšw*, 'pledge on one's own soul, life, on oneself'. That this is the intended meaning of the expression is confirmed by the existence of the simple pronoun in place of *npšy* in the same formula (see CD 15.6).

On the other hand, oaths too existed among the Essenes, but they were used very cautiously, and only in tribunals.

> Concerning the oath (*šbw'*)—as for what is written: 'You shall not do justice with your [own] hand', but whoever forces the making of an oath in the open field, not in the presence of judges or at their command, has done justice for himself with his hand [therefore private oaths are forbidden] (CD 9.8-10).

Swearing before a judge was not only allowed, but it was imposed. At the beginning of col. 15, unfortunately with many *lacunae*, there is a list of the cases of the particular forms of oaths.

> [No one shall sw]ear by *Aleph* and *Lamed*, nor by *Aleph* and *Daleth* [that is neither by God, written with the characters *Aleph* and *Lamed*, nor by one of his appellatives, Adonai, written *Aleph Daleth*], but [he] shall make the oath by the curses of the Covenant, without mentioning the

Law of Moses because [with this he would pro]fane the [Name](?). And
if he swears [by God] and transgresses, he would profane the Name. But
if he sw[ears] by the curses of the covenant [before the] judges, if he
transgresses, he will be guilty and will have to confess and make amends
but he shall not be liable [for sin and shall not] die (CD 15.1-5).

If I am not mistaken concerning the meaning of the rest of the text, it
means that it was forbidden to swear in daily life, but one had to swear
before a judge. Neither God nor the Law was to be mentioned, but only
the curses given in the Covenant. Not even the neophyte entering the
sect pronounces a real oath, because he only pledges on himself. Even
though the idea is the same, the verb is different. Anyhow, this pledge
is referred to as an 'oath' in CD 15.6. In front of a judge, however, one
swore, one pronounced an oath using the verb 'to swear'. The rule
against mentioning the Law in oaths must depend on the fact that it was
considered an expression of divine will and therefore, in a way, a name
of God. This same line of reasoning can be found in Pharisaism and in
Christianity. The Pharisaic logic appears in the Gospel of Matthew in
relation to the same problem:

Woe to you, blind guides, who say 'Whoever swears by the sanctuary is
bound by nothing, but whoever swears by the gold of the sanctuary is
bound by the oath'. You blind fools! For which is greater, the gold or the
sanctuary that has made the gold sacred? And you say, 'Whoever swears
by the altar is bound by nothing, but whoever swears by the gift that is
on the altar is bound by the oath'. How blind you are! For which is
greater, the gift or the altar that makes the gift sacred? (Mt. 23.16-19).

The Pharisees allowed oaths even outside the tribunals, but they did
not want people to swear by God directly, or by things that were too
close to him and therefore, in a word, too sacred. It was possible to
swear by things that were sacred enough to make for a binding oath, but
not so sacred as to profane the Name. At least that was the Pharisaic
reasoning during Jesus' time. It seems clear that Middle Jewish society
saw reality as distributed across several different planes, according to
each thing's degree of sacrality.

We do not know whom Jesus' argumentation on the sacred, as developed in the Sermon on the Mount, was directed against. It is, however,
apparent that his adversaries followed the same logic that in this case
the Pharisees and the Essenes held in common. Jesus forbids the use of
oaths, and in his explanation mentions the formulas then in use.

But I say to you, Do not swear at all, either by heaven, for it is the throne of God, or by the earth, for it is his footstool, or by Jerusalem, for it is the city of the great King. And do not swear by your head [that is on yourself], for you cannot make one hair white or black (Mt. 5.34-36).

Jesus' doctrine takes the idea that the world is sacred, inasmuch as it belongs to God, and carries it to its extreme consequences. This conception of things fits perfectly well with the idea that there are no impure things in all creation; impurity is nothing other than sin. On the other hand, if everything is pure and sacred, there is no room left for oaths; no matter what one swears by, in the end they swear by God. The prohibition also covers swearing by oneself, the formula used by the Essenes for their most serious pledges. In Christianity the profane seems to disappear completely. There is no precise limit between God and humankind, a conception that strongly emphasizes the idea that human beings belong to God. The expression 'Thy will be done' indicates a conception of the relationship between God and humans which is not simply different from, but opposite to, the conception expressed in the dialogue between Abraham and God on what is righteous and what is not. In Christianity the role given to freedom of the will cannot be defined in exact terms, as demonstrated by the numerous splits that have taken place within the Church over the question of the freedom of will's extension. In Christianity there is a very deep, though subtle relationship between freedom of the will and grace. It is easy to lose sight of that relationship, which is, in any case, difficult to express in rational terms.

Chapter 18

THE TWO CALENDARS

1. *The Structure*

There is no doubt about the fact that at the time of Jesus there were two different calendars in Palestine.[1] One is called lunar-solar and the other solar.

The months of the lunar-solar calendar coincided more or less with the phases of the moon. There were 12 months made up of either 29 or 30 days each, given the fact that the lunar cycle lasts roughly 29 days and a half. The 12 months thus constituted a year of 354 days, destined therefore to fall behind the solar calendar by about 11 days a year. In order to avoid this, every two or three years an additional month was added at the end of the year in such a way that the first full moon after the vernal equinox fell during the first month of the year, in Nisan. The day of the full moon was the fifteenth of Nisan, the principal Jewish holiday, Passover, which coincided with the day of the full moon regardless of the day of the week.

The solar calendar in use during Jesus' time had 364 days divided into 8 months of 30 days each and 4 months with 31. The months with 30 and 31 days were arranged in such a way as to obtain four equal periods, each made up of two months with 30 days and one of 31. This way of dividing time was undeniably more attractive on the level of numerical speculation. The year could be divided perfectly into four seasons each with 91 days. Each of the seasons could be divided into 13 weeks. The year always began on a Wednesday, the day the stars were

1.   If there were any doubts, they have been cleared up by the publication of the text 4Q321, which contains a synopsis of the two calendars regarding the succession of sacerdotal families in the service of the Temple. The basis for computation is clearly the solar calendar and not the lunar one which is used for comparison. See S. Talmon and I. Knohl, 'A Calendrical Scroll from Qumran Cave IV, Mish. B[a] (4Q 321)', *Tarbiz* 60 (1991), pp. 505-21.

created, therefore the day that historical time was created. Liturgically the beginning of the year actualized the creation of the stars. According to this calendar all years were equal, not only because every year was 364 days long, but because each day always fell on the same day of the week. As a result the holidays always fell on the same day of the week. Following this calendar, too, Passover was always the fifteenth of the first month, always a Wednesday, liturgically the most important day. The days of the week were the same in both calendars; Wednesday was Wednesday for all the Jews, and Saturday, the sabbath, was always Saturday.

With respect to the solar year this calendar fell a little more than a day behind each year. It is not clear how it was periodically brought up to date, which must have been necessary. It can be excluded that a day or two was added each year, because this would have brought about a shift of the days of the week within the calendar, and they remained fixed. The only plausible hypothesis is that approximately every five years a whole week was added, an embolic week, outside of the computation of the year.

The existence of the lunar-solar calendar has always been known. With the exception of some bits of information regarding the pre-exilic period,[2] this was thought to be the only calendar of the Bible. In any case it was believed that the differences regarded only the names of the months, and not the calendar's structure. Concerning the Hebrew period this solution remains the most probable, apart from the date for the beginning of the year, which must have been set at the first of Nisan during the exile.

It was also known that there was a solar calendar, since it is mentioned in the book of *Jubilees* and in *1 Enoch*, but little importance was given to this fact. With the discovery of the Dead Sea manuscripts, however, scholars had to begin to take the question into serious consideration. These manuscripts refer only to the solar calendar.

This fact poses a number of problems: which of the two calendars is the oldest in Israel and how was the use of the two calendars distributed in Jewish society? In other words, who used the one and who used the other? The presence of two calendars has also shed some light on the

2.   A.G. Gaster, 'The Feast of Jeroboam and the Samaritan Calendar', *ExpTim* 24 (1913), pp. 198-201, had already noticed that one biblical passage could only be explained by the existence of some differences between the calendars in use in the North and the South.

study of Christian origins. It is well known that according to the three synoptic Gospels Jesus celebrated Passover before his arrest, and therefore before his death and resurrection. For the synoptic Gospels, Pilate held Jesus' trial on the occasion of the 'holiday' (Mt. 27.15; Mk 15.6; Lk. 23.17). John, on the other hand, does not say that Jesus celebrated Passover at the supper, but only that it was a special supper. Jesus' death took place on a Friday before Passover (Jn 18.39). The narration of events is substantially the same, but the names given to the celebrations are not. This had always raised a number of questions, but the answers had always been sought elsewhere, while the most simple, and therefore most probable explanation is the existence of two calendars.[3]

2. *The History and Distribution of the Calendars' Use*

It is clear that during Jesus' day the lunar-solar calendar was used in all civil documents. This is the calendar used by Josephus to date events not many years later. Josephus gives the Greek names for the months; for him the only difference between the Greek and Jewish calendars was the names of the months; the Temple had not fallen on the ninth of Ab, but on the ninth of Loos. This was also the calendar used by the Pharisees. We do not know whether the Sadducees used it as well, but by Jesus' time they had accepted the ideological structure of Pharisaism (see *Ant.* 18.15-17), with the exception of a few noteworthy new elements, like the resurrection of the dead. In fact, the lunar-solar calendar corresponded to the calendars used by the Babylonians and the Greeks; it was the international calendar of the time inasmuch as Caesar's innovations seem for the moment not to have been accepted.

On the contrary, the solar calendar as described above was not in use among any of the nearby peoples. Only in Babylon, at the time of the exile, was there a comparable solar calendar, the Babylonian one being composed of 12 months of 30 days each, for a total of 360 days. This was a 'scientific' calendar whose days were not really days, but rather the 360 degrees of the horizon. In practice such a calendar could be used, and with notable commercial advantages, if only a few intercalary days were added.[4]

---

3. See the classic though often criticized work of A. Jaubert, *La date de la cène* (Paris: Lecoffre, 1957).

4. After the discovery of a 360-day calendar at Ebla (See G. Pettinato, *Ebla, un impero inciso nell'argilla* [Milan: Mondadori, 1979], p. 142), it is certain that the

The fact that this calendar had an influence on the formation of the 364-day Jewish calendar results from the *Book of Astronomy*, which seems to address polemically those who use (apparently everyone) the 360-day calendar, without taking the four 'powerful' days of the solstices and equinoxes into account.

> Blessed are all the righteous ones; blessed are those who walk in the street of righteousness and have no sin like the sinners in the computation of the days in which the sun goes its course in the sky. It [the sun] comes in through a door[5] and rises for thirty days together with the chiefs of the thousands of the orders of the stars, together with the four which are added to determine the intervals within [the year, that is, the intervals] between the four seasons of the year; those that lead them along come in on four days. On this account people err because they do not count them [the four days] in the computation of all time: for the people make error and do not recognize them accurately; for they belong to the reckoning of the year... The year is completed in three hundred and sixty-four days (*1 En.* [*BA*] 82.4-6).

The 4 days to be added are 'true additions'. Therefore, the 'true' month was made up of 30 days, as in the tradition, but these 4 days had to be calculated in the year. They were truly special days, but not for this were they to be left out of the computation. Errors regarding the position of these 4 days were serious (in the tradition they probably disappeared among the embolic days necessary at the end of each year), because a lag between the heavens and the earth, between the cosmic structure and human time, would cause the religious holidays to fall in the wrong time. This calendar responds to the cosmic needs of early Enochism.

The Babylonian origin of the 360-day calendar, easily hypothesized on a historical basis, is confirmed by the polemical remarks in chapter

---

12-month year owes its formation to practical reasons; only in a later period was it based on astronomical speculation. B.L. van der Waerden writes ('History of the Zodiac', *AfO* 16 [1952–53], p. 218): 'There are 12 signs, because there are 12 months in the schematical year of mul Apin. The signs were made of equal length in order to get months of equal duration: they were divided into 30 degrees each, because the schematical months were supposed to contain 30 days each'. See F.H. Cryer, 'The 360-Day Calendar Year and the Early Judaic Sectarianism', *JSOT* 1 (1987), pp. 116-22.

5. The sky was imagined as having many openings, or doors. The variations in the sun's path during the different seasons was explained by the sun's entrance into the sky through different doors.

80, addressed to those who mistake the stars for gods (v. 7).

The author of the *Book of Astronomy* is in open debate with the pre-existent 360-day calendar, which should be substituted with the 364-day one. In later texts the 360-day calendar is not even mentioned; it must have been completely replaced by the new one. Since we have an Aramaic fragment of the *Book of Astronomy* from the third century BCE[6] which shows that the work already contained the 364-day calendar, it is beyond doubt that the innovation dates at least to the third century BCE.

It is noteworthy that the author of the *Book of Astronomy* is opposed to another solar calendar which is different from his own more in principle than in substance, but he makes no mention at all of the lunar-solar calendar. This raises some questions, since we have always believed that the lunar-solar calendar in use during the time of Jesus was Babylonian in origin and dated from the time of the exile.

In her famous *La date de la cène* Jaubert claims that the solar calendar was extremely ancient, because it is already documented in Ezekiel and parts of the Hexateuch. Even leaving the Hexateuch aside, there is still the firm point of reference in Ezekiel, whose visions always take place on either Friday or Sunday, that is either just before or just after the holy time of the sabbath.[7] Jaubert also claimed that the lunar-solar calendar came into use with Nehemiah.

Unfortunately, the nature of the two calendars is such that while we can say that certain dates come from the solar calendar, we cannot do

6. See Sacchi, *Jewish Apocalyptic*, pp. 136-37.

7. See Ezek. 1.1, 'in the fourth month, on the fifth day', is Sunday. 3.19 refers to seven days later. 8.1, 'in the sixth month, on the fifth day of the month', is Friday. 24.1, 'in the tenth month, on the tenth day of the month', is Friday. 29.1, 'in the tenth month, on the twelfth day of the month', is Sunday. 31.1, 'in the third month, on the first day of the month', is Sunday. 32.1, 'in the twelfth month, on the first day of the month', is Sunday. 33.21, 'in the tenth month on the fifth day of the month', is Sunday. 40.1, 'on the tenth day of the [seventh] month', is Friday.

The Septuagint presents three variants, but two are to be considered errors in the Greek, because the numbers that are different from the Hebrew are the same as another number in the date. In the case of 29.1 we lack the criteria for a precise choice on a historical basis. The two readings are historically adiaphoretic. Even on a literary basis it is difficult to choose, because the day given by the Septuagint (the first day of the tenth month) falls on a Wednesday, which is a liturgically strong day. In this case I accept the Hebrew text following the criterion of similarity with the other cases.

the same for the lunar-solar calendar. In effect, the use of the solar calendar is clear when we have a series of coincidences showing the importance of the day of the week. In the case of isolated dates, however, with no liturgical reference, it is absolutely impossible to establish which calendar was being used. We would need to find an event dated to an embolic month (short Adar), but that never happens. In other words, we can neither exclude nor confirm a particular calendar for the majority of dates. Another problem is raised by the fact that the author of the *Book of Astronomy* claims that the 364-day calendar is his own innovation. While the date of the *Book of Astronomy* is not known, still it cannot be contemporary to Ezekiel. We can establish, however, that Ezekiel's dated visions all take place on either Friday or Sunday, which is possible only with the 364-day solar calendar. If therefore, again according to the author of the *Book of Astronomy*, previously a 360-day calendar had been in use, which would not allow the constant coincidence of the days of the week with the months, then we would have to admit that the embolic days were regulated even before the *Book of Astronomy* in such a way that the beginning of the year coincided with a particular day of the week. In fact, the *Book of Astronomy*'s author does not so much claim that the four 'powerful' days exist, as he does that they should be part of the calculation of the year, in other words that they are not embolic. This is where the four 31-day months come into being.

While it is possible to find a convincing answer to that question, it is more difficult to establish when the lunar-solar calendar came into use in Israel. In general it is believed that when we find the Babylonian name for a month rather than a simple ordinal number then we are faced with the lunar-solar calendar. It is easy to object, however, that the use of names for the months could have come into use independently of the lunar-solar calendar. In other words, the Pharisaic custom of calling the months by name (the Babylonian name) can not necessarily be linked, lacking more precise information on the subject, to the use of the lunar-solar calendar.

Given the *Book of Astronomy*'s silence regarding the lunar-solar calendar, we must suppose that it came into use sometime after the third century BCE. Since this is an *argumentum ex silentio*, it is of only relative worth, even though it is hard to imagine that someone who defends a particular way of calculating 4 days would have nothing to say about a real lag of 10 or 11 days. The book of Daniel, however, confirms our hypothesis. In 7.25 the author accuses Antiochus IV of having changed 'the times and the Law'. The accusation of changing the Law refers to Jason, who had the citizens of Jerusalem enrolled in the lists of Antioch (2 Macc. 4.9), so that they were no longer subject to Jewish law. The accusation of having changed the times, though, can only refer to a change in the calendar, which could only mean the substitution of the Jewish one for the Greek one.[8] The Greek calendar was the same as the Babylonian one, that is it was a lunar-solar calendar. The only plausible explanation of the information provided by Daniel is that the lunar-solar calendar substituted the pre-existent solar one.

The book of *Jubilees* confirms Daniel, defending the use of the solar calendar against the lunar-solar one, considered a recent pagan innovation. In the second century BCE the author could hardly have had the Babylonians in mind; his polemic is against the Greek calendar.

> They shall forget the feasts of the Covenant and walk *in the feasts of the gentiles*, after their errors and after their ignorance. And there will be those who will examine the moon diligently because it will corrupt the times and it will advance from year to year ten days. Therefore, the years will come to them as they corrupt and make a day of testimony a reproach and a profane day a festival, and they will mix up everything, the holy days with the impure[9] ones (*Jub.* 6.35-37).

Here there can be no doubt that the calendar under attack is the 354-day lunar-solar calendar, attributed to recent pagan influence. The book of *Jubilees* has been dated to the end of the second century BCE.

The profound changes in the social structures brought about under Jason and Menelaus easily explain the change in calendars as well, but some problems are raised when, with the compromise reached in 164 BCE between the traditionalists and the Hellenizers, use of the solar calendar is not re-established.[10] It is possible that given the practicality of the lunar-solar calendar, due to its international use, it was maintained at least for secular affairs. But the book of *Jubilees*' attack is certainly later; the fact of the matter is that both calendars were probably

---

8.   J.C. VanderKam, '2 Maccabees 6, 7a and Calendrical Change in Jerusalem', *JSJ* 12 (1981), pp. 52-74; *idem*, 'The Origin, Character and Early History of the 364-Day Calendar: A Reassessment of Jaubert's Hypothesis', *CBQ* 41 (1979), pp. 390-411.

9.   Note the use of 'impure' as a synonym of 'profane'.

10.   See P. Davies, 'Calendrical Change and Qumran Origins: An Assessment of VanderKam's Theory', *CBQ* 45 (1983), pp. 80-89.

in use in Israel even for liturgical purposes, varying from place to place. The solar calendar must have remained in use in the Temple, though. According to the Rabbinic tradition, when Hillel arrived in Jerusalem from Babylon he was asked whether the law of the Passover sacrifice was stronger than the sacrifice of the sabbath, because it was said that the relevant rule had been forgotten. It is impossible that they had forgotten the tradition, because Passover falls on the sabbath fairly often. Unless we decide to dismiss the tradition as false, we must allow the possibility that at a certain point a problem was faced which previously had not existed. This could only have come about because of the change in calendars; with the solar calendar Passover always fell on a Wednesday.[11]

Judaism during the time of Jesus was divided into many different sects and currents that clashed with one another over a number of underlying normative and ideological questions. In this context, the existence of the solar calendar alongside the lunar-solar one is merely one more element to be added to the general situation. It created, however, a particularly divisive difference, because it broke up the liturgical community.

11. See F. Manns, *Pour lire la Mishna* (Jerusalem: Franciscan Printing Press, 1984), pp. 50-51 and various references. In particular see *t. Pes.* 4.13 and *y. Pes.* 6.1 (33a).

Chapter 19

JESUS IN HIS TIME

1. *The Historical Problems*

The reader should not expect to find any explanation of the mystery of Jesus or an illustration of the origins of Christian doctrine in such a brief space. I feel, however, that we are still unable to write the history of the origins of Christianity, given the lack of historical studies which take on the problem in all the vastness of its documentation, constituting a reference point for future historians. Among other things, we do not have the instruments necessary for dominating all the literatures derived from the cultures of the day. I use the plural 'literatures', because the Jews used a plurality of languages and their literature is divided into different *corpora*, kept apart by the differing historical fates of each *corpus*, a problem which is also reflected in the various specializations of modern scholars.

The only source that allows us to know Jesus' thought, although it is difficult to distinguish between what really comes from Jesus and what comes from the earliest Christian community, is the New Testament. When we try to reconstruct the historical context for his thought, however, the social and cultural world that Jesus inhabited and from which he drew his language, we are faced with numerous texts written in various languages.

There is the Mishnah, which is useful for individuating ideas in circulation during Jesus' time, especially in Pharisaic circles. This is a text that should be used only by specialists, at least for the present, because it dates to about a century and a half after the period we are interested in, and the studies regarding its stratification have only just begun. Alongside the Mishnah are a few less studied yet interesting works from Palestine, that simultaneously paraphrase and comment the text of the Bible. These are the Palestinian *targumin*. Among these the *Targum Neofiti* is worthy of the greatest attention due to its probable antiquity (second century) and the richness of the thought expressed in it. There are also the Old Testament pseudepigraphical texts which, while most them are contemporary to or older than Jesus, have been handed down to us in translations made by Christians into various languages, some of which can be read by only a very few scholars. Generally speaking, the Christian scribes may have retouched the texts, adapting them to the needs of the Christian community. I do not believe that the problem of the Christian interpolations is as serious as some people think, because in general they are easily identifiable and while the dubitative method works well in philosophy it does not fit so well with philology. There is also the vast amount of literature found at Qumran which presents the advantage that most of it is written in Hebrew and none of it is later than 70 CE. These texts do present some difficulties, but they are related to the fact that many of the manuscripts are unique and may present copying or writing errors that are hard to detect. Many of the texts have *lacunae* and many are only fragments. We must also bear in mind the information given to us by the Jewish authors writing in Greek, Josephus and Philo of Alexandria. This is indirect documentation, but the ideas and facts are already presented along a line of interpretation. There is room for debated, but this does constitute a starting point. For the history of this period, seen as a series of interrelated events, Josephus is the principal source.

The problem of weighing each group of sources against the others remains. Reading Strack and Billerbeck[1] one gets the impression that there is nothing in the Gospels that has not also been handed down by the rabbinic tradition; individual sentences and maxims are documented in identical or similar form in both *corpora*. But as Ben Chorin[2] points out, it is the accumulation of a certain type of thought and a certain type of maxim that give the New Testament an unmistakable air when compared to the rabbinic tradition.

My aim is more limited, in keeping with the spirit of this book, to reflections on a few topics rather than putting together a global presentation of the history of events and ideas. To the preceding reflections I would like to add some others, following the centre of my research, since I began reading the New Testament in Greek while writing the thesis for my first university degree.

1.   For Strack and Billerbeck, see bibliography.
2.   See Ben Chorin, *Bruder Jesus*, p. 83.

For the believer Jesus is the son of God, as all four Gospels write, even though there are deep differences between the prologues of Mark and John. Born of a virgin birth for Luke and Matthew, he descended to earth to save mankind from the grip of sin. For the non-Christian, Jesus was a man who preached a radical doctrine of love, the importance of which lies in the historical success of Christianity.

The historian, whether a believer or not, looks at facts and ideas, approaching his theme with as few preconceptions as possible, trying to make the epoch's various characters speak with the logic of the day according to the mental categories of the day. If, by chance, he is also Christian, he will look for some reflection of the divine in Jesus' very human face. Some can be found in the condition of those who followed him after having listened to him , because they found that only he had words of eternal life (Jn 6.68). This, however, is a personal question, which cannot interfere with method; his prayer to God is only that his method be valid *iuxta principia sua*.

Jesus was a Jew who believed that he had a particular relationship with God[3] and who taught a doctrine whose origins are to be sought in the questions and ideas in circulation in the Palestine of his day. While it is not new (this was already Reimarus' approach in the eighteenth century),[4] this way of approaching our studies is very widely accepted

3.   The value of the expression 'Son of God' is not as clear in Jewish culture as it would be in a Western language. Angelic beings are already called sons of God in the Bible (Gen. 6.1-4; Ps. 29.1; Dan. 3.25 = LXX 3.92) as are the Jews as a whole (Exod. 4.22; Hos. 11.1, Jer. 31.20; Deut. 32.5-6, 18, 19). Even the kings were sons of God. See Ps. 2.7 for the expression 'today I have begotten you', in reference to the enthronement. Besides, 'son of...' could also indicate merely belonging to a class or species, with nuancing that varies from one case to the next; see the expression 'sons of the prophets' or 'son of man' in Ezekiel. In the book of Wisdom, fairly close to Jesus chronologically, 'son of God' is applied metaphorically to the righteous (2.16-18). For Jesus, 'son of God' held more than a merely metaphorical meaning, beyond the meaning of category, comparable perhaps only to the ancient royal use (but who would have understood it in Middle Judaism!). Proof of this is to be found in the parable of the wicked tenants found in all three of the synoptic Gospels (Mk 12.1-12; Mt. 21.33-41; Lk. 20.9-19). See Charlesworth, 'The Righteous Teacher and the Historical Jesus'.

4.   See H.S. Reimarus, *I frammenti dell'anonimo di Wolfenbüttel* (ed. F. Parente; Naples: Bibliopolis, 1977). See also F. Parente, 'Il problema storico dei rapporti tra essenismo e cristianesimo prima della scoperta dei rotoli del Mar Morto', *PdP* 86 (1962), pp. 333-70, esp. pp. 333-34. Jesus is to be understood in the context

today. The works and ideas of Jesus should therefore be studied and interpreted within the context of the questions that that society posed and in the light of the categories used by that society to express its thoughts. Once the question of research concerning Jesus has been formulated in this way, his message appears somewhat less novel. Since the discovery of the Dead Sea manuscripts and a rereading of the so-called Old Testament Pseudepigrapha, it is easy to see that many ideas that were once held to be Christian innovations were in reality part of the heritage if not of all of Judaism at least of some groups within it.

The problem of Jesus' singularity must today be posed in a more global manner than in the past. I have already pointed out that trying to establish an affinity of thought based on single maxims and statements is very nearly impossible. The fact of the matter is that every individual is singular, and must be viewed against the backdrop of their period's ideologies. The degree of innovation can only be measured through a comparison of the underlying constellation of ideas against the innovative element.

There is a general level of ideas distinguishing the Jews from the pagans, true ideological matrices in Judaism such as faith in one God who has revealed himself in history, God's judgment of the world, the importance of the Law and of impurity, a deeply felt sense of sin and the problem of the origin of evil, expectation of a messiah. Then there is a lower level which we can suppose marks the differences between one group and the next, regarding the particular solutions given for some of the general problems. Messianic expectations can be spasmodic and directed towards the near future, or they can be considered a secondary element in Israel's tradition, where the advent of the Messiah is not a daily possibility; evil can be seen as depending exclusively on the free transgression of human beings, or as tied to some mysterious event which took place in extremely remote times. Besides, each of

of the history of his time. The underlying supposition of this principle is that the Gospels are four historical works in the fullest sense of the word. See Reimarus, *I frammenti*, p. 358 (ET: *Fragments* [ed. C.H. Talbert; London: SCM Press, 1971]): 'Since there are four of these historians and since they all four agree on Jesus' essential doctrine, there can be no doubt about the exactitude of the information provided nor that they withheld or forgot any important and essential point of that doctrine'. I agree with this evaluation of the sources. The fact that each author also presents his own theology (that is, his own ideas) is a common aspect of all historical works.

these solutions has repercussions on the entire ideological constellation in such a way that there is a first and fundamental division between the two poles of the theology of the Promise and the theology of the Covenant. But even within the two essential ways of being Jewish, an infinite number of solutions was given to the various problems.[5]

2. *Jesus and the Theology of the Promise*

There is hardly need to mention Jesus' fundamental Jewishness. No Greek could ever have spoken about God or about sin the way he did. It is, however, worth posing the question as to which of the ways of being Jewish Jesus belonged to, even though the answer is obvious. The origin of Jesus' thought is to be sought in the theology of the Promise. Expressions such as the following clearly place Jesus in line with the theology of the Promise: 'You did not choose me but I chose you'(Jn 15.16), or, from the context, with a clear allusion to justification, 'For mortals it is impossible, but not for God. For God all things are possible' (Mk 10.27; Mt. 19.26; Lk. 18.27).

Jesus' thought should always be read against this background. The dividing line between Jesus' theology and that of the Pharisees is the same that runs throughout Israel's history up to the end of the first century, dividing the theology of the Promise from that of the Covenant. Later, the two theologies were to take shape in two different forms of Israel, each one claiming to be authentic.

This dividing line runs deep; at times on a more superficial level attitudes reflecting one way of thinking can also been seen in the other, but what is important are the underlying attitudes. It is an old idea that James is the most Jewish of the New Testament authors. Luther even considered him as being on the margins of the canon, defining his letter a 'straw epistle'. In the light of what we have said, it is difficult not to consider the entire New Testament as Jewish, more in contrast with the theology of the Covenant and its first-century incarnation, the Pharisees, than with Judaism as such. Beyond this, however, the idea remains that James is closer than Paul to the theology of the Covenant, identified with Pharisaism and later with Judaism. Some place not only James but also Jesus in opposition to Paul; according to these scholars Jesus was a rather peculiar Pharisee, but at any rate closer to Pharisaism

---

5. See Boccaccini, *Middle Judaism*, pp. 213-28.

than to any other Jewish current of the day.[6] Christianity, in this case, was born with Paul. Judgment depends on the level of depth referred to.

Boccaccini has recently pointed out[7] that in the only point where James explicitly mentions the Law he uses the same terms as Paul. James says, 'Whoever keeps the whole Law but fails in one point has become accountable for all of it' (Jas 2.10), which corresponds to Paul's, "All who rely on the works of the Law are under a curse; for it is written, 'Cursed is everyone who does not observe and obey all the things[8] written in the book of the Law"' (Gal. 3.10). Most of all, though, James is close to Paul in his opposition to the Pharisees' thought, stating that 'judgment will be without mercy to anyone who has shown no mercy; mercy triumphs over judgment' (2.13), in other words, man's use of mercy in his lifetime leads God to use mercy in his judgment. As a result God's Judgment is no longer Judgment by the Law as commonly held, but rather judgment following the Law of liberty (2.12). Man is no longer to be judged according to the law commonly known as the Law. James follows in the wake of Jesus' words: 'the measure you give will be the measure you get' (Mt. 7.2) expresses the same idea found in Paul, both of them derived from Jesus.

We have already seen that for the Pharisees judgment could not be based exclusively on divine justice, since in that case no one would be saved. For the Pharisees there was a fundamental balance between God's justice and his mercy, in the sense that God's mercy did not justify the individual gratuitously, nor did it justify those who had forgiven others. God's mercy justified those who had become worthy of justification through their own acts: 'Everything depends on the number of [good or bad] works'.[9] Paul's discourse does use more radical expressions, but in the end the meaning is the same as James'. Mercy can triumph over judgment, because the latter will not be carried out according to the Law, as commonly understood. The presence of the question of Jesus' death is greater in Paul than in James, but this is an internal question within Christianity, to be taken on a less profound level than

6.   See the provocative title to the book by H. Falk, *Jesus the Pharisee* (New York: Paulist Press, 1985). The idea, however, is fairly widespread even outside academic circles.

7.   See Boccaccini, *Middle Judaism*, pp. 213-28.

8.   Paul refers to Deut. 27.26. It is worth noting that he has added the word 'all', which is not in the original.

9.   For R. Aqiba, see Chapter 13, §3, p. 368.

the question of Judgment (on this point see §5 below, pp. 495-96). Even John's view of the Judgment is different from that of James (see Chapter 4, §3, p. 369), but the basic motif is the same, because for James the Judgment will be based on the Law of liberty.

3. *Jesus' Point of Departure*

Jesus' point of departure (or generative idea) is that sin leads to destruction and therefore a road to salvation is necessary. This was the problem posed by John the Baptist, but then again it was the problem posed by an entire epoch. For Jesus salvation and purity did not coincide, as they did for John the Baptist and for the Essenes, even though he did maintain the sense of impurity's destructive nature, in keeping with an idea that had a long history behind it.

He had no difficulty keeping the company of people considered bad or impure. He held new ideas on impurity (Mk 7 and Mt. 15), even though they responded to problems which were particularly pressing in that time. Changing the concept of impurity, Jesus removed one of traditional Judaism's linchpins. Jesus gave an interpretation to the Law which in practice brought it closer to ethics, in the Greek and modern sense of the term. This is true in spite of the fact that he found no words for conceptualizing this choice. The formulation is ours, but the concept is his.

The Law is valid, but only under those aspects that come from man's heart. This was a vaguely expressed principle, but it is one of the few points where Jesus was a true innovator, where he cut across the deepest structures of Jewish thought. He stated that there were in fact laws with no value, norms that were not Law. The underlying criterion seems to be that of distinguishing between things that can come from man's heart and things that by nature can only touch, or at most enter, the body. This did not depend on a particular Christian idea of liberty, it is as though the entire question of good and evil could be reduced to an attitude of the human heart, by the simple fact that impure things (or at least foods) do not exist. For Jesus this fact was stronger than the Law, in contrast to *Aristeas*, who had had similar intuitions regarding the purity of things (see *Arist*. 143, see p. 468 n. 17).

In this case Jesus' thought brings about a type of innovation that we would call a conceptual or philosophical innovation, because it involves the way of viewing man and things. Once again, however, it can be noted that Jesus' innovation was produced within and on the basis of the theology of the Promise. Jewish thought comprehended two ways of conceiving impurity, both of them derived from pre-exilic Hebraic thought. On the one hand there was the idea expressed in the priestly tradition which viewed impurity as neutral, and on the other was the idea expressed in Genesis 3 and in Isaiah by which impurity was linked to sin and to evil. Jesus can be placed firmly in the second camp, because he sees impurity as truly evil, and not as a relationship between man and certain things, as was later to be clarified in Rabbinism.

4. *The Son of Man and Justification*

Those who heard Jesus preach noticed that he spoke with a particular sense of authority (Mk 1.22; Mt. 7.29). This was certainly a result of his conviction that he had a special relationship with God, by which he considered himself the son of God, even though it is not clear in just what terms he saw this sonhood. John's prologue does not contain the words of Jesus, and the Creed was written three centuries later.

Jesus, however, also presented himself as the Son of Man. The Son of Man is known to us through the *Book of Parables* as the most characteristic name attributed to a mysterious figure, created before time and called 'the Righteous One', 'the Chosen One' and only at the end 'the Son of Man'. This Son of Man, who knew all the secrets of righteousness, was to be the great and inexorable Judge of the last days. We could think that the book was the product of an isolated dreamer. But this is not the case if the people who heard Jesus never posed the question as to who this character was; apparently they understood. The people may ask who the Son of Man is, but not what he is (Jn 12.34). Further proof of this is in the gesture of the high priest, tearing his clothes, when Jesus answered that not only was he the Messiah, but also that the Son of Man would soon be seen on the clouds of heaven (Mk 14.63). His blasphemy could not have been his claim to be the Messiah. If the majority of the Sanhedrin, representing the Pharisees, did not consider Jesus' statement blasphemy, forcing those who wanted to eliminate him for fear of worse things to send him to Pilate with a different accusation, that is another question. For the Pharisees the Son of Man did not exist and therefore Jesus' statement could not be blasphemous. What is certain, however, is that whether they believed in him or not, everyone knew what 'Son of Man' meant.

The Son of Man, according to Jesus, as supreme judge also had the power to forgive sins and, as we have seen, Jesus believed that he had this function. '"But so that you may know that the Son of Man has authority on earth to forgive sins"—he said to the paralytic—"I say to you, stand up, take your mat and go to your home"' (Mk 2.10-11). It is no mere coincidence that Mark places this passage at the beginning of Jesus' preaching, since it contains the nucleus of all later Christian speculation on justification. Jesus' idea is not expressed in rational terms, it underlies his act. And Jesus' gesture is absolutely radical; he acts without being asked to do so. Not only does he give forgiveness freely, but he even gives it to a man who has not requested it. If we try to conceptualize the thought behind the gesture, using Paul's terms we find that justification can lie beyond faith and, in Matthew's and James' terms, that justification can even be independent of having been forgiven.

Once again, when his disciples were disheartened after having listened to his dialogue with the young rich man, Jesus says, 'For mortals it is impossible, but not for God; for God all things are possible' (Mk 10.27). Even though the Son of Man had the power to forgive everything, Jesus was not lax. His dialogue with the rich man is a good example of this. In the Sermon on the Mount Jesus gives a radical definition of the seriousness of sin: not only does the murderer merit hell, but so does one who insults; not only is the adulterer guilty, but so is the man who lusts *in his heart* after another's woman (Mt. 5.27-28).

Jesus did not believe in a sinless society capable of saving itself. His golden rule regarding human behaviour, his distinguishing trait within the Jewish world, was his insistence on the necessity for forgiveness beyond all limits. The theme of forgiveness is particularly strong in Matthew. Forgiveness must be radical (Mt. 18.21), because man will be judged with the same measure he has used to judge. Forgiving puts God, by way of a sort of *imitatio hominis*, so to speak, in the condition of having to forgive.

We must be careful not to read this idea in a Western fashion, in the light of cause and effect. Ancient Jewish culture only knew the principle of relationships. Therefore, God's *imitatio hominis* makes sense only to the extent that, having forgiven, humans imitate God, thus reducing the absolute nature of the principle by which James saw the Judgment as being based on the Law of liberty, whose yardstick lies in the individual's not having measured. We are reminded of Jesus' aphorism that God has it rain on the righteous and the wicked alike, and precisely for this reason he is perfect (Mt. 5.45, 48).

5. *Jesus and his Death*

If this was to be law for human beings, Jesus also had a particular law for himself. At the basis of his preachings there was not so much a new and different set of laws concerning daily life as there was his awareness that his own death was necessary in order to triumph over sin. His awareness of his own death is so insistently present in the Gospels that it is impossible even to pose the idea of later additions to the tradition. In its memory of the events the early Church had a clear perception that Jesus had wanted his own death.

Jesus was aware that according to the liturgy of the Temple a sacrifice could expiate sin, an idea that both the Essenes and the Pharisees, for different reasons, were leaving behind. The Essenes were substituting the blood sacrifice with an offering from the mouth while the Pharisees had come to see salvation as a result of one's works. In fact, for many Jews the Temple was losing its role in salvation; it had become simply a place of prayer.

Jesus saw freedom from sin as possible only through a sacrifice, with the difference that, as he had made innovations regarding the contents of purity while maintaining the underlying idea, he made an innovation regarding the appropriate victim of the sacrifice. He appeared to be the only possible victim suitable for taking 'the sin of the world' onto his own shoulders, to say it with John (1.29), precisely because he believed in his special relationship with God which he called sonhood. This and this alone led him to the cross.

The importance of the sacrifice on the cross comes out in all, or nearly all, the New Testament writings; the four Gospels are all structured around the sacrifice's narration. Paul and John insist on this in a particularly strong way, since they insert it into a theological construct. But even before the various theological formulations, the fact remains: Jesus wanted to die and he wanted it for a reason. His preaching, therefore, only makes sense when seen in the light of the frightful sacrifice, of the awareness that he was the sacrificial victim made necessary according to God's will. It is not up to a historian to judge whether this was just a marvellous utopia of love for humanity, lived to the very end, or whether the effects of that death were destined to be felt in the lives of souls, since it is easy to observe that sin is still a part of the world even after Jesus took it onto his shoulders. This is the mystery of Christianity. It is no coincidence that John has Jesus say that his kingdom is not of this world (Jn 18.36).

Even those who do not accept the idea of Jesus' particular relationship with the Father and the effective worth of his sacrifice, however, must still see the historical weight of an idea of love which, even though betrayed regularly, has remained a stimulus to mankind. Jesus' parables of the yeast and of the mustard seed (Mt. 13.33 and Lk. 13.20; Mk 4.30-32 and parallel passages) make me think that he must have been aware of this too.

BIBLIOGRAPHY

This bibliography is divided into two parts. The former is the translation of the bibliography of the Italian edition, that was finished in spring 1993. The latter is an addition containing works that came out in the following years.

BIBLIOGRAPHY UNTIL 1993

A. *General Works*

1. *Bibliographies*

Book List: Society for Old Testament Study.
Elenchus of Biblica (until 1984 *Elenchus biblicus bibliographicus*), Rome. Extensive and well-constructed, but not uniform.
Internationale Zeitschriftenschau für Bibelwissenschaft und Grenzgebiete (Paderborn).
Old Testament Abstracts (Washington) and *New Testament Abstracts* (Cambridge, MA). It contains the abstracts of the articles of many journals and allows continuous updating on the various problems.

2. *Concordances*

Even-Shoshan, A., *A New Concordance of the Bible: Thesaurus of the Language of the Bible: Hebrew and Aramaic Roots, Words, Proper Names, Phrases and Synonyms* (Jerusalem: Kiryat Sefer, 2nd edn, 1989).
Hatch, E., and H.A. Redpath, *A Concordance to the Septuagint and the Other Greek Versions of the Old Testament (including the Apocryphal Books)* (2 vols.; Oxford: Clarendon Press, 1897; repr. 1954).
Kuhn, K., *Konkordanz zu den Qumrantexten* (Göttingen: Vandenhoeck & Ruprecht, 1960).
Lisowsky, G., *Konkordanz zum hebräischen Alten Testament, nach dem von Paul Kahle in der Biblia Hebraica edidit R. Kittel besorgten masoretischen Text* (Stuttgart: Deutsche Bibelgesellschaft, 1958).
Mandelkern, S., *Veteris Testamenti concordantiae Hebraicae atque Chaldaicae* (Berlin: Schocken, 1937).
Schmoller, A., *Handkonkordanz zum griechischen Neuen Testament* (Gütersloh: Bertelsmann, 1913).

3. Catalogues

Braun, H., *Qumran und das Neue Testament* (2 vols.; Tübingen: Mohr [Paul Siebeck], 1966).

Grande lessico dell'Antico Testamento (Brescia: Paideia, 1987); original title: *Theologisches Wörterbuch zum Alten Testament* (Stuttgart, 1973).

Grande lessico del Nuovo Testamento (16 vols.; Brescia: Paideia, 1965–92; original title: *Theologisches Wörterbuch zum Neuen Testament* [10 vols.; Stuttgart: Kohlhammer, 1933–1974]).

Strack, H.L., and P. Billerbeck, *Kommentar zum Neuen Testament aus Talmud und Midrasch* (6 vols.; Munich: Beck, 1922–28).

4. Encyclopaedias

Dictionnaire de la Bible (Supplément au) (commencé par L. Pirot et A. Robert, continué sous la direction de M. Viller, assistée de F. Cavallera et J. de Guilbert; Paris, 1936 sgg.; 5 vols. + 12 of *Supplémemts*).

Enciclopedia della Bibbia (6 vols.; traduzione italiana dell'*Enciclopedía de la Biblia* compilata sotto la direzione di A. Díez Macho, S. Bartina, J.A. Gutiérrez Larraya; direttori dell'edizione italiana: A. Rolla, F. Ardusso, G. Ghiberti, G. Marocco; Turin: LDC, 1969–72).

Galling, K. *et al.* (eds.), *Realencyklopädie des Judentums: Die Religion in Geschichte und Gegegenwart* (7 vols.; Tübingen, 3rd edn, 1957–65).

Nola, A.M. di *et. al.* (eds.), *Enciclopedia delle religioni* (6 vols.; Florence, 1970–73).

Paschini, P. (ed.), *Enciclopedia cattolica* (12 vols.; Rome, 1948–53).

Pauly, A.F. von, and G. Wissowa (eds.), *Real-Encyclopädie der classischen Altertumswissenschaft* (Stuttgart: Metzler, 1893–).

Theologische Realenzyklopädie (Berlin, New York, 1977–).

5. Books and Articles concerning General Themes and Jewish History and Thought

Abel, F.M., *Géographie de la Palestine* (2 vols.; Paris: Lecoffre, 1933, 1938).

—'Alexandre à Jérusalem', *RB* 44 (1935), pp. 48-61.

—'Simon de la tribu de Bilga', in *Miscellanea Mercati* (Rome: Biblioteca Apostolica Vaticana, 1946), I, pp. 52-58.

—*Histoire de la Palestine depuis la conquête d'Alexandre jusqu'à l'invasion arabe. I. De la conquête d'Alexandre jusqu'à la guerre juive* (Paris: Lecoffre, 1952).

Ackroyd, P.R., *Israel under Babylon and Persia* (Oxford: Oxford University Press, 1970).

Aharoni, Y., *The Land of the Bible* (London: Burns & Oates, 1967).

Albright, W.F., *From the Stone Age to Christianity: Monotheism and the Historical Process* (Baltimore: Doubleday, 2nd edn, 1957).

Arata Mantovani, P., 'La stratificazione letteraria della *Regola della Comunità*: A proposito del libro di J. Pouilly, *La règle de la Communauté de Qumran*', *Henoch* 5 (1983), pp. 69-92.

—'Circoncisi e incirconcisi', *Henoch* 10 (1988), pp. 51-68.

Ardusso, F., *Gesù Cristo figlio del Dio vivente* (Cinisello Balsamo: Edizioni Paoline, 1992).

Aune, D.E., 'The Problem of the Messianic Secret', *NovT* 11 (1969), pp. 1-31.

Avigad, N., *Bullae and Seals from a Post-exilic Judean Archive* (Jerusalem: Institute of Archaeology—The Hebrew University of Jerusalem, 1976).

Bacher, W., *Die Aggada der Tannaiten* (2 vols.; Strasbourg: Trübner, 1890, 1903).

Baillet, M., 'Un recueil liturgique de Qumrân, Grotte 4: "Les paroles des luminaires" ', *RB* 68 (1961), pp. 191-250.

Barbaglio, G., 'Rassegna di studi di storia sociale e di ricerche di sociologia sulle origini cristiane', I and II, *RivB* 36 (1988), pp. 377-410, 495-520.

Bardtke, H., 'Einige Erwägungen zum Problem "Qumran und Karaismus" ', *Henoch* 10 (1988), pp. 259-70.

Barker, M., *The Lost Prophet: The Book of Enoch and its Influence on Christianity* (Nashville: Abingdon Press, 1989).

Barr, J., *Semantics of Biblical Language* (Oxford: Oxford University Press, 2nd edn, 1962).

Barthélemy, D., *Les dévanciers d'Aquila* (Leiden: E.J. Brill, 1963).

Bartlett, J.R., *Jews in the Hellenistic World* (Cambridge: Cambridge University Press, 1985).

Barton, G.A., *The Royal Inscriptions of Sumer and Akkad* (New Haven: Yale University Press, 1929).

Barucq, A., *Le livre des Proverbes* (Paris: Cerf, 1964).

Baumgarten, J.M., 'Recent Qumran Discoveries and Halakhah in the Hellenistic-Roman Period', in S. Talmon (ed.), *Jewish Civilization in the Hellenistic-Roman Period* (Sheffield: Sheffield Academic Press, 1991), pp. 147-58.

Ben Chorin, Sch., *Bruder Jesus: Der Nazarener in jüdischer Sicht* (München: List, 1967).

Berger, R.P., 'Der Kyros-Zylinder mit dem Zusatzfragment BIN II, nr. 32 und die akkadischen Personennamen im Danielbuch', *ZA* 64 (1975), pp. 192-234.

Betlyon, J.W., 'The Provincial Government of the Persian Period and the Yehud Coins', *JBL* 105 (1986), pp. 633-42.

Bettenzoli, G., 'Lessemi ebraici di radice -shabat-', *Henoch* 4 (1982), pp. 129-62.

—'La tradizione del shabbat', *Henoch* 4 (1982), pp. 265-93.

Bianchi, F., 'Monete giudaiche di età ellenistica', *RSO* 63 (1989), pp. 213-29.

—'Zorobabele, re di Giuda', *Henoch* 13 (1991), pp. 133-50.

Bickerman, E.J., 'The Edict of Cyrus in Ezra I', *JBL* 65 (1946), pp. 249-75.

—'The Maxim of Antigonus of Socho', *HTR* 44 (1951), pp. 153-65.

—'La chaîne de la tradition pharisienne', *RB* 59 (1952), pp. 44-54.

—*Four Strange Books of the Bible: Jonah, Daniel, Koheleth, Esther* (New York: Schocken Books, 1967).

—'The Generation of Ezra and Nehemiah', *Proc. of the American Acad. for Jewish Research* 45 (1978), pp. 1-28.

—*The Jews in the Greek Age* (Cambridge, MA: Harvard University Press, in cooperation with the Jewish Theological Seminary of America, 1988).

Boccaccini, G., 'È Daniele un testo apocalittico? Una (ri)definizione del Libro di Daniele in rapporto al Libro dei Sogni e all'apocalittica', *Henoch* 9 (1987), pp. 267-302.

—*Middle Judaism: Jewish Thought 300 BCE to 200 CE* (Minneapolis: Fortress Press, 1991).

—'History of Judaism: Its Periods in Antiquity', in J. Neusner (ed.), *Judaism in Late Antiquity* (Leiden: E.J. Brill, 1995), pp. 285-308.

Bokser, B.Z., *Judaism: Profile of a Faith* (New York: Knopf, 1963).

Boman, T., *Das hebräische Denken im Vergleich mit dem Griechischen* (Göttingen: Vandenhoeck & Ruprecht, 1965).

Booth, R.P., *Jesus and the Laws of Purity: Tradition History and Legal History in Mark 7* (Sheffield: Sheffield Academic Press, 1986).

Boschi, B.G., 'Alle radici del giudaismo', in B. Chiesa (ed.), *Correnti culturali e movimenti religiosi del giudaismo: Atti del V Congresso Internazionale dell'AISG, 12–15 novembre 1984* (Rome: Carucci), pp. 9-23.

Bousset, W., *Die Religion des Judentums im späthellenistischen Zeitalter* (Tübingen: Mohr, 3rd edn, 1926), title of the first edition: *Die Religion des Judentums im neutestamentlichen Zeitalter*.

Brekelmans, C.H.W., 'Eléments deutéronomiques dans le pentateuque', *Recherches Bibliques* (Journées du Colloque Biblique de Louvain) 8 (1966), pp. 77-91.

Bricchi, P.G., 'I proseliti' (unpublished dissertation, Turin, 1974).

Bright, J., *A History of Israel* (London: SCM Press, 5th edn, 1977).

Broshi, M., *The Damascus Document Reconsidered* (Jerusalem: The Israel Exploration Society, 1992).

Brunt, P.A., 'Procuratorial Jurisdiction', *Latomus* 25 (1966), pp. 461-89.

Buccellati, G., 'Gli israeliti di Palestina al tempo dell'esilio', *BeO* 2 (1960), pp. 199-209.

Cagni, L., 'Le fonti mesopotamiche dei periodi neo-babilonese, achemenide e seleucide (VI-III sec. a.C.)', *RivB* 34 (1986), pp. 11-53.

The Cambridge Ancient History (12 vols.; Cambridge: Cambridge University Press, 1965–71; repr. 20 vols.; Cambridge 1969–73).

Canfora, L., *Ellenismo* (Bari: Laterza, 1987).

Capelli, P., 'L'aramaico e l'ebraico tra il II e il III secolo secondo una fonte rabbinica e una cristiana', *EVO* 14-15 (1991–92), pp. 159-62.

Caquot, A., 'Ben Sira et le messianisme', *Sem* 16 (1965), pp. 43-68.

Cardellini, I., 'Dalla Legge alla Torah', *RSB* 3 (1991), pp. 57-81.

Carmignac, J., *Les manuscrits de Qumrân traduits et annotés* (2 vols.; Paris: Letouzey et Ané, 1961, 1963).

—'Le complément d'agent après un verbe passif dans l'hébreux et dans l'araméen de Qumran', *RevQ* 9 (1978), pp. 409-28.

Castellino, G., *Libres dei Salmi* (Turin: Mariette, 3rd edn, 1965).

—'Scriba velox', in J. Schreiner (ed.), *Wort, Lied und Gottesspruch: Festschrift für Joseph Ziegler* (Würzburg: Echter, 1972), pp. 29-34.

Cazelles, H., 'La mission d'Esdras', *VT* 4 (1954), pp. 113-40.

Cazeneuve, J., *Sociologie du rite: Tabou, magie, sacré* (Paris: Presses Universitaires de France, 1971).

Cerutti, D., *Vecchi e nuovi approcci per lo studio del rapporto tra Pentateuco e libri storici: Il contributo dell'analisi della cronologia* (unpublished diss.: Torino, 1991).

Cerutti, M.V., 'Tematiche encratite nello zoroastrismo pahlavico', in U. Bianchi (ed.), *La tradizione dell'enkrateia: Motivazioni ontologiche e protologiche: Atti del colloquio internazionale: Milano, 20–23 aprile 1982* (Roma: Edizioni dell'Ateneo, 1985), pp. 637-70.

Charlesworth, J.H., 'The Concept of the Messiah in the Pseudepigrapha', in W. Haase (ed.), *Religion (Judentum: Allgemeines; palästinisches Judentum)* (Aufstieg und Niedergang der römischen Welt II.19.1; Berlin, New York: W. de Gruyter 1979), pp. 188-218.

—'Biblical Interpretation: The Crucible of the Pseudepigrapha', in T. Baarda *et al.* (eds.),

Text and Testimony: Essays on New Testament and Apocryphal Literature in Honour of A.F.J. Klijn (Kampen: Kok, 1988), pp. 66-78.

—'From Jewish Messianology to Christian Christology: Some Caveats and Perspectives', in J. Neusner *et al.* (eds.), *Judaisms and their Messiahs at the Turn of the Christian Era* (Cambridge: Cambridge University Press, 1988), pp. 225-63.

—'The Righteous Teacher and the Historical Jesus: A Study of the Self-Understandings of Two Jewish Charismatics', in W.P. Wearer (ed.), *Perspectives on Christology* (Nashville: Exodus Press, 1988), pp. 73-94.

—*Jesus within Judaism: New Light from Existing Archaeological Discoveries* (London: SPCK, 1989).

—'Qumran in Relation to the Apocrypha, Rabbinic Judaism, and Nascent Christianity; Impacts on University Teaching of Jewish Civilization in the Hellenistic-Roman Period', in Sh. Talmon (ed.), *Jewish Civilization in Hellenistic-Roman Period* (Sheffield: Sheffield Academic Press, 1991), pp. 168-80.

Charlesworth, J.H. (ed.), *Jesus's Jewishness* (New York: American Interfaith Institute, 1991).

Chiesa, B., 'Contrasti ideologici del tempo degli Asmonei nella Aggadah e nelle versioni di Genesi 49, 3', *AION* 37 (1977), pp. 417-48.

—'Il giudaismo caraita', in *Atti del V Congresso Internazionale dell'AISG—S. Miniato 1984* (Roma: Carucci, 1987), pp. 151-74.

Collins, J.J., *The Apocalyptic Imagination: An Introduction to the Jewish Matrix of Christianity* (New York: Crossroad, 1984).

Conzelmann, H., and A. Lindemann, *Arbeitsbuch zum Neuen Testament* (Tübingen: Mohr, 7th edn, 1983).

Cooper, J.S., *Sumerian and Akkadian Royal Inscriptions*, I: *Presargonic Inscriptions* (New Haven: American Oriental Society, 1986).

Coppens, J., *Le messianisme royal: Ses origines, son développement, son accomplissement* (Paris: Cerf, 1968).

Cornely, R., *Commentarius in librum sapientiae* (Paris: Lethielleux, 1910).

Cortese, E., *Da Mosè ad Ezra: I libri storici di Israele* (Bologna: EDB, 1985).

—'Gios. 21 e Giud. 1 (TM o LXX ?) e l'abbottonatura del "Tetrateuco" con l'opera deuteronomistica', *RivB* 33 (1985), pp. 375-94.

Cross, F.M., *The Ancient Library of Qumran and Modern Biblical Studies* (Garden City, NY: Doubleday, 1958, 2nd edn, 1960).

—'The Discovery of the Samaria Papyri', *BA* 26 (1963), pp. 110-21.

—'Aspects of Samaritan and Jewish History in Late Persian and Hellenistic Times', *HTR* 59 (1969), pp. 201-11.

—'A Reconstruction of the Judaean Restoration', *JBL* 94 (1975), pp. 4-18.

Cryer, F.H., 'On the Relationship between the Yahwistic and the Deuteronomistic Histories', *BN* 29 (1985), pp. 58-74.

—'The 360-Day Calendar Year and the Early Judaic Sectarianism', *JSOT* 1 (1987), pp. 116-22.

Cullmann, O., *Jesus und die Revolutionären seiner Zeit: Gottesdienst, Gesellschaft, Politik* (Tübingen: Mohr, 1970).

Cumont, F., *Les religions orientales dans le paganisme romain: Conférences faites au Collège de France en 1905* (Paris: Librairie Orientaliste Paul Geuthner, 2nd edn, 1929 [1906]).

Cuq, E., 'La condition juridique de la Coelésyrie au temps de Ptolomée V Epiphane', *Syria* 8 (1927), pp. 143-62.

Daniel, C., 'Esséniens, zélots et sicaires et leur mention par paronymie dans le NT', *Numen* 13 (1966), pp. 88-115.

—'Une mention paulienne des esséniens de Qumran', *RevQ* 5 (1966), pp. 553-68.

—'Les hérodiens du NT, sont-ils des esséniens?', *RevQ* 6 (1967), pp. 31-54.

—'Les esséniens et l'arrière-fond historique de la parabole du bon Samaritain', *NovT* 11 (1969), pp. 71-104.

—'Les esséniens et l'arrière fond historique de la Parabole du Bon Samaritain', *NovT* 11 (1969), pp. 71-104.

—'Nouveaux arguments en faveur de l'identification des hérodiens et des esséniens', *RevQ* 7 (1970), pp. 397-402.

Daumas, F., 'Littérature prophétique et exégétique égyptienne et commentaires esséniens', in M. Jourjon (ed.), *À la rencontre de Dieu: Mémorial Albert Gelin* (Le Puy: Mappus, 1961), pp. 203-21.

Davies, P., 'Calendrical Change and Qumran Origins: An Assessment of VanderKam's Theory', *CBQ* 45 (1983), pp. 80-89.

Davies, W.D., *The Setting of the Sermon of the Mount* (Cambridge: Cambridge University Press, 1964).

Davies, W.D., and L. Finkelstein (eds.), *The Cambridge History of Judaism*. I. *Introduction; The Persian Period*. II. *The Hellenistic Age* (Cambridge: Cambridge University Press, 1984, 1989).

Deiana, G., 'Azazel in Lev. 16', *Lateranum* 54 (1988), pp. 16-33.

Del Verme, M., *Giudaismo e Nuovo Testamento: Il caso delle decime* (Napoli: M. D'Auria, 1990).

Delitzsch, F., *Babel und Bibel* (Stuttgart: Hinrichs, 1905).

Denis, A., 'Evolution des structures dans la secte de Qumrân', in J. Giblet, P. Andriessen and L. Cerfaux (eds.), *Aux origines de l'Eglise* (Bruges: Desclée, De Brouwer, 1965), pp. 23-49.

—*Introduction aux Pseudépigraphes grecs d'Ancien Testament* (Leiden: E.J. Brill, 1970).

Derenbourg, J., *Essai sur l'histoire et la géographie de la Palestine d'après les Talmuds et les autres sources rabbiniques* (Paris: Imprimerie Imperial, 1867).

Devoti, D., 'Sociologia e/o psicoanalisi del movimento di Gesù', *Henoch* 4 (1982), pp. 87-96.

Dodds, E.R., *The Greeks and the Irrational* (Los Angeles: University of California Press, 1951).

Donner, H., *Geschichte des Volkes Israel und seiner Nachbarn in Grundzügen* (2 vols.; Göttingen: Vandenhoeck & Ruprecht, 1984, 1986).

Douglas, M., *Purity and Danger: An Analysis of Concepts of Pollution and Taboo* (London: Routledge & Kegan Paul, 1966).

Durkheim, E., *Les formes élémentaires de la vie religieuse: Le système totémique en Australie* (Paris: Presses Universitaires de France, 4th edn, 1960).

Edwards, D.R., 'First Century Urban/Rural Relations in Lower Galilee: Exploring the Archaeological and Literary Evidence', in D.J. Lull (ed.), *Society of Biblical Literature Seminar Papers* (SBLSP, 27; Atlanta, GA: Scholars Press, 1988), pp. 169-82.

Eissfeldt, O., *Einleitung in das Alte Testament unter Einschluß der Apokryphen und Pseudepigraphen sowie der apokryphen- und pseudepigraphenartigen Qumran-Schriften* (Tübingen: Mohr, 3rd edn, 1964).

Eliade, M., *Das Heilige und das Profane: Vom Wesen des Religiösen* (Hamburg: Rowohlt, 1957).

—*Myth and Reality* (New York: Harper & Row, 1963).

Eph'al, I., 'On the Political and Social Organization of the Jews in Babylonian Exile', *ZDMG* suppl. 5 (1983), pp. 106-12.

Falk, H., *Jesus the Pharisee* (New York: Paulist Press, 1985).

Ferguson, E., *Backgrounds of Early Christianity* (Grand Rapids: Eerdmans, 1990).

Flandrin, J.L., *L'Eglise et le contrôle des naissances* (Paris: Flammarion, 1970).

—*Le sexe et l'occident* (Paris: Éditions du Seuil, 1981).

—*Un temps pour embrasser: Aux origines de la morale sexuelle occidentale (VI–XI siècle)* (Paris: Éditions du Seuil, 1983).

Fovra, C., 'L'iscrizione di Ponzio Pilato a Cesarea', *Rendiconti dell'Istituto Lombardo, Accademia di Scienze e Lettere* 95 (1961), pp. 419-34.

Frankfort, H., H.A. Wilson and T. Jacobsen, *Before Philosophy* (Chicago: The University of Chicago Press, 1946).

Freedman, R.E., *The Exile and Biblical Narrative: The Formation of the Deuteronomistic and Priestly Works* (Harvard Semitic Monographies, 22; Chico: Harvard University Press, 1981).

Frye, R.N., 'Iran und Israel', in *Festschrift für Wilhelm Eilers: Ein Dokument der internationalen Forschung zum 27. September 1966* (Wiesbaden: Harrassowitz, 1967), pp. 74-84.

Gabba, E., 'La Palestina e gli ebrei negli storici classici fra il V e il III sec. a. C'., *RivB* 34 (1986), pp. 127-41.

Galling, K., *Studien zur Geschichte Israels im persischen Zeitalter* (Tübingen: Kurt Mohr [Paul Siebeck], 1964).

Garbini, G., 'L'iscrizione di Balaam Bar Beor', *Henoch* 1 (1979), pp. 166-88.

—'I sigilli del regno di Israele', *OrAnt* 21 (1982), pp. 163-76.

—'Universalismo iranico e Israele', *Henoch* 6 (1984), pp. 293-312.

—*Storia e ideologia nell'Israele antico* (Brescia: Paideia, 1986).

—*History and Ideology in Ancient Israel* (trans. J. Bowden; London: SCM Press, 1988).

García Martínez, F., 'Essénisme qumranien: Origines, caractéristiques, héritage', in *Atti del V Congresso Internazionale dell'AISG* (Rome: Carucci, 1987), pp. 37-58.

—'Les limites de la Communauté: Pureté et impureté à Qumrân et dans le Nouveau Testament', in T. Baarda *et al.* (eds.), *Text and Testimony: Essays on New Testament and Apocryphal Literature in Honour of A.F.J. Klijn* (Kampen: Kok, 1988), pp. 111-22.

—'Qumran Origins and Early History: A Groningen Hypothesis', *Folia Orientalia* 25 (1988), pp. 113-36.

—'¿La apocalíptica judía como matriz de la teología cristiana?', in A. Piñero (ed.), *Orígenes del Cristianismo: Antecedentes y primeros pasos* (Cordoba: El Almendro, 1991), pp. 177-99.

—'Sources et rédaction du Rouleau du Temple', *Henoch* 13 (1991), pp. 219-32.

García Martínez, F., and A.S. van der Woude, 'A Groningen Hypothesis of Qumran Origins and Early History', *RevQ* 14 (1990), pp. 522-41.

Gaster, A.G., 'The Feast of Jeroboam and the Samaritan Calendar', *ExpTim* 24 (1913), pp. 198-201.

Gese, H., 'Wisdom Literature in the Persian Period', in W. Davies and L. Finkelstein (eds.), *The Cambridge History of Judaism* (Cambridge: Cambridge University Press, 1984), I, pp. 189-218.

Gianotto, C., *Melchisedek e la sua tipologia* (Supplementi alla Rivista Biblica, 12; Brescia: Paideia, 1984).

Gnoli, G., 'Politica religiosa e concezione della regalità sotto gli Achemenidi', in A. Forte (ed.), *Gururajamañjarika: Studi in onore di G. Tucci* (Napoli: Istituto universitario orientale, 1974), pp. 31-43.

—*Zoroaster's Time and Homeland* (Naples: Intercontinentalia, 1980).

Golb, N., 'L'origine des manuscrits de la Mer-Morte', *Annales* 40 (1985), pp. 1133-79.

—'Who Hid the Dead Sea Scrolls', *BA* 48 (1985), pp. 68-82.

—'Hypothesis of Jerusalem Origin of the Dead Sea Scrolls—Synopsis', in Z.J. Kapera (ed.), *Mogilany 1989 Papers on the Dead Sea Scrolls* (Cracow: Enigma Press, 1993), pp. 53-58.

Greenfield, J.C., and Shaffer, A., 'Notes on the Akkadian-Aramaic Bilingual Statue from Tell Fekherye', *Iraq* 45 (1983), pp. 109-16.

Grelot, P., *Les poèmes du Serviteur: De la lecture critique à l'herméneutique* (Lectio divina, 103; Paris: Cerf, 1981).

Gunneweg, A.H.J., 'Die aramäische und die hebräische Erzählung über die nachexilische Restauration: Ein Vergleich', *ZAW* 94 (1982), pp. 299-302.

Ha, J., *Genesis 15: A Theological Compendium of Pentateuchal History* (Berlin: W. de Gruyter, 1989).

Hackett, J.A., 'Some Observations on the Balaam Tradition at Deir 'Alla', *BA* 49 (1986), pp. 216-23.

Hausmann, J., *Israels Rest: Studien zum Selbstverständnis der nachexilischen Gemeinde* (Stuttgart: W. Kohlhammer, 1987).

Hayes, J.H., and J.M. Miller, *Israelite and Judaean History* (London: SCM Press, 1977).

Hengel, M., *Judentum und Hellenismus: Studien zu ihrer Begegnung unter besonderer Berücksichtigung Palästinas bis zur Mitte des 2. Jh.s v. Chr.* (Tübingen: Mohr, 2nd edn, 1973).

—*Juden, Griechen und Barbaren: Aspekte der Hellenisierung des Judentums in vorchristlicher Zeit* (Stuttgart: KBW Verlag, 1976).

—*The 'Hellenization' of Judaea in the First Century after Christ* (London: SCM Press, 1989).

Herrenschmidt, C., 'Désignation de l'empire et concepts politiques de Darius Ier d'après ses inscriptions en vieux-perse', *StIr* 5 (1976), pp. 33-65.

—'Les créations d'Ahuramazda', *StIr* 6 (1977), pp. 17-58.

Herrmann, W., 'Das Aufleben des Mythos unter den Judäern während des babylonischen Zeitalters', *BN* 40 (1987), pp. 97-129.

Hoftijzer, J., *Die Verheissungen an die drei Erzväter* (Leiden: E.J. Brill, 1956).

—'The Prophet Balaam in a 6th Century Aramaic Inscription', *BA* 39 (1976), pp. 11-17.

Hoftijzer, J., and van der Kooj, B., *Aramaic Texts from Deir Alla* (Leiden: E.J. Brill, 1976).

Holleaux, M., 'Sur un passage de Flavius Josèphe [*Jewish Antiquities*, xii, 4, § 155]', *REJ* 39 (1899), pp. 161-76.

Hölscher, G., 'Komposition und Ursprung des Deuteronomiums', *ZAW* 40 (1922), pp. 161-225.

Horbury, W., 'Messianism among Jews and Christians in the Second Century', *Augustinianum* 28 (1988), pp. 71-88.

Hughes, J., *Secrets of the Times: Myth and History in Biblical Chronology* (Sheffield: Sheffield Academic Press, 1990).

Jacob, E., *Théologie de l'Ancien Testament* (Neuchâtel: Delachaux & Niestlé, 2nd edn, 1968 [1958]).

Janssen, E., *Juda in der Exilszeit* (Göttingen: Vandenhoeck & Ruprecht, 1956).

Japhet, S., 'The Supposed Common Authorship of Chronicles and Ezra-Nehemiah Investigated Anew', *VT* 18 (1968), pp. 330-71.

—'Shesbazzar and Zerubbabel', *ZAW* 94 (1982), pp. 66-98; 95 (1983), pp. 218-29.

Jaubert, A., *La date de la cène* (Paris: Lecoffre, 1957).

Jeremias, J., *Jerusalem zur Zeit Jesu: Eine kulturgeschichtliche Untersuchung zur neutestamentlichen Zeitgeschichte* (Göttingen: Vandenhoeck & Ruprecht, 3rd edn, 1969).

Jossa, G., *Gesù e i movimenti di liberazione della Palestina* (Brescia: Paideia, 1980).

—*Dal Messia al Cristo* (Brescia: Paideia, 1990).

Jung, C.G., *Die Beziehungen zwischen dem Ich und dem Unbewussten* (Darmstadt: Reichl, 1928).

—*L'io e l'inconscio* (Torino: Boringhieri, 1948).

Kahle, P., 'Untersuchungen zur Geschichte des Pentateuchtextes', *TSK* 88 (1915), pp. 399-439.

Kaiser, O., *Einleitung in das Alte Testament* (Gütersloh: Gütersloher Verlagshaus, 4th edn, 1978).

Kappler, C., *Apocalypses et voyages dans l'au-delà* (Paris: Cerf, 1987).

Katsch, A.I., 'Unpublished Geniza Fragments of Pirqe Abot in Antonin Geniza Collection in Leningrad', *JQR* 61 (1970), pp. 1-12.

Kaufman, S.A., 'The Aramaic Texts from Deir 'Alla', *BASOR* 239 (1980), pp. 71-74.

Kellermann, U., 'Erwägungen zum problem der Ezradatierung', *ZAW* 80 (1968), pp. 55-87.

Kindler, A., 'Silver Coins Bearing the Name of Judea from the Early Hellenistic Period', *IEJ* 24 (1974), pp. 73-76.

Kippenberg, H.G., *Religion und Klassenbildung in Judäa: Eine religionssoziologische Studie zum Verständnis von Tradition und gesellschaftlicher Entwicklung* (Göttingen: Vandenhoeck & Ruprecht, 1978).

Koch, K., *Ratlos vor der Apokalyptik* (Gütersloh: Gütersloher Verlagshaus Mohn, 1970).

Köster, H., *Einführung in das Neue Testament im Rahmen der Religionsgeschichte und Kulturgeschichte der hellenistischen und römischen Zeit* (Berlin: W. de Gruyter, 1980).

Labat, R., 'L'Assiria e i suoi vicini dal 1000 a.C. al 617. Il regno babilonese fino al 539 a.c.', in E. Cassin, J. Bottéro and J. Vercoutter (eds.), *Storia Universale Feltrinelli* (Milan: Feltrinelli, 1969), IV, pp. 7-114.

Lamarche, P., *Zacharie IX–XIV: Structure littéraire et messianisme* (Paris: Lecoffre, 1961).

Lapide, P., 'Insights from Qumran into the Language of Jesus', *RevQ* 8 (1975), pp. 483-501.

Laqueur, R., *Der jüdische Historiker Flavius Josephus* (Giessen: Münchow, 1920).

Lauha, A.L., *Kohelet* (Neukirchen–Vluyn: Neukirchener Verlag, 1978).

Le Déaut, R., *Introduction à la littérature targumique* (Rome: Institut Biblique Pontifical 1966).

Le Moyne, J., *Les Sadducéens* (Paris: Gabalda, 1972).

Lemaire, A., 'Le sabbat à l'époque royale israélite', *RB* 80 (1973), pp. 161-85.

Levine, B.A., 'The Temple Scroll: Aspects of its Historical Provenience and Literary Character', *BASOR* 232 (1978), pp. 5-23.

Levi-Strauss, C., *Anthropologie structurale* (Paris: Plon, 1958).

Liverani, M., *Antico Oriente: Storia, società, economia* (Bari: Laterza, 1988).

Loretz, O., *Qohélet und der alte Orient* (Freiburg: Herder, 1964).

Lupieri, E., 'La purità impura: Giuseppe Flavio e le purificazioni degli esseni', *Henoch* 7 (1985), pp. 15-44.

—*Giovanni Battista fra storia e leggenda* (Brescia: Paideia, 1988).

—*Giovanni Battista nelle tradizioni sinottiche* (Brescia: Paideia, 1988).

—'Giovanni Battista fra i testi e la storia', *STAns* 106 (1991), pp. 75-107.

—*Giovanni e Gesù, storia di un antagonismo* (Milano: Mondadori, 1991).

MacDonald, J., *The Theology of the Samaritans* (London: SCM Press, 1964).

Maier, J., 'The Architectural History of the Temple in Jerusalem in the Light of the Temple Scroll', in G.J. Brooke (ed.), *Temple Scroll Studies* (Sheffield: Sheffield Academic Press, 1989), pp. 23-62.

—'Rivelazione, tradizione e autorità religiosa nel giudaismo palestinese e babilonese', *Augustinianum* 31 (1990), pp. 73-92.

—*Zwischen den Testamenten: Geschichte und Religion in der Zeit des zweiten Tempels* (Würzburg: Echter Verlag, 1990).

Mancini, I., *Archaeological Discoveries relative to the Judaeo-christians* (Publications of the Studium Biblicum Franciscanum. Collectio minor, 10; Jerusalem: Franciscan Printing Press, 1970).

Manns, F., *Essais sur le Judéo-christianisme* (Jerusalem: Franciscan Printing Press, 1977).

—*Pour lire la Mishna* (Jerusalem: Franciscan Printing Press, 1984).

Manson, T.W., 'Sadducee and Pharisee: The Origin and Significance of the Names', *BJRL* 22 (1938), pp. 144-59.

Margalith, O., 'The Political Role of Ezra as Persian Governor', *ZAW* 98 (1986), pp. 110-12.

Marti, K., and G. Beer, *'Abot (Väter); Text, Übersetzung und Erklärung von* (Giessen: Töpelmann, 1927).

Marx, A., 'Y a-t-il une prédestination à Qumran?', *RevQ* 6 (1967), pp. 323-42.

Mayer, B.F., 'Jesus' Ministry and Self-Understanding', in Chilton and Evans (eds.), *Studying the Historical Jesus*, pp. 337-52.

Mayer, E., *Ursprung und Anfänge des Christentums* (3 vols.; Stuttgart-Berlin, 1921–23).

McCarter, P.K., 'The Balaam Texts from Deir 'Alla', *BASOR* 239 (1980), pp. 49-60.

McEvenue, S.E., 'The Political Structure in Judah from Cyrus to Nehemiah', *CBQ* 43 (1981), pp. 353-64.

—*Il messaggio della Salvezza: Antico e Nuovo Testamento* (5 vols.; Turin: LDC, 1985).

Meyer, Ben F., 'Jesus' Ministry and Self-Understanding', in B. Chilton and C.A. Evans (eds.), *Studying the Historical Jesus: Evaluation of the State of Current Research* (Leiden: E.J. Brill, 1994), pp. 337-52.

Meyer, E., *Die Entstehung des Judentums: Eine historische Untersuchung* (Halle, Hildesheim: Olms, 1965).

—*Ursprung und Anfänge des Christentums* (3 vols.; Stuttgart: Magnus, 1921–23).

Michaëli, F., *Les livres des Croniques d' Esdras et de Néhémie* (Neuchâtel: Delachaux & Niestlé, 1967), pp. 281-96.

Michaud, R., *Qohélet et l'hellénisme* (Paris: Cerf, 1987).

Milik, J.T., *Ten Years of Discovery in the Wilderness of Judaea* (London: SCM Press, 1959).

—*The Books of Enoch* (Oxford: Oxford University Press, 1976).

Millard, A.R., and Bordeuil, P., 'A Statue from Syria with Assyrian and Aramaic Inscriptions', *BA* 45 (1982), pp. 135-43.

Mölle, H., *Genesis 15: Eine Erzählung von den Anfängen Israels* (Würzburg: Echter, 1988).

Momigliano, A., 'I Tobiadi nella preistoria del moto maccabaico', *ARAST* 67 (1931–32), pp. 165-200.

—'Ricerche sull'organizzazione della Giudea sotto il dominio romano', *ASNSP* NS 2 III (1934 [1967]), pp. 183-222; 347-97.

—*Prime linee di storia della tradizione maccabaica* (Rome, 1931; Amsterdam: Hakkert, 1968).

—*Alien Wisdom: The Limits of Hellenization* (Cambridge: Cambridge University Press, 1975).

Moraldi, L., *I manoscritti di Qumran* (Turin: UTET, 2nd edn, 1986).

Morgenstern, J., 'Jerusalem 485 a.C'., *HUCA* 27 (1956), pp. 101-79; 28 (1957), pp. 15-47; 31 (1960), pp. 1-29.

Motzo, B., *Saggi di storia e letteratura giudeo-ellenistica* (Firenze: Felice Le Monnier, 1927).

—*Ricerche sulla letteratura e la storia giudaico ellenistica* (ed. F. Parente; Roma: Centro Editoriale Internazionale, 1977). (It includes the reprint of the preceding volume).

Müller, H.P., 'Phönizien und Juda in exilisch-nachexilischer Zeit', *WdO* 6 (1970–71), pp. 189-204.

Muraoka, T., ''Essene' in the Septuagint', *RevQ* 8 (1973), pp. 267-68.

—'The Tell Fekherye Bilingual Inscription and Early Aramaic', *Abr-Nahrain* 22 (1983–84), pp. 79-117.

Musanti, *Fax chronologica* (Pistorii, 1706).

Myers, J.M., 'Edom and Judah in 6th–5th Centuries B.C'., in H. Goedicke (ed.), *Near Eastern Studies in Honor of W.F. Albright* (Baltimore, MD: The John Knox Press, 1971), pp. 377-92.

Neusner, J., *From Politics to Piety: The Emergence of Pharisaic Judaism* (New York: Ktav Pub. House, 1979).

—'Il messia nel contesto della Mishnah', *Henoch* 5 (1983), pp. 343-70.

—*Major Trends in Formative Judaism* (Chico: Scholars Press, 1984).

—'Temi messianici nel periodo di formazione del giudaismo', *Henoch* 6 (1984), pp. 31-54.

—*From Testament to* Torah: *An Introduction to Judaism in its Formative Age* (Englewood Cliffs: Prentice-Hall, 1988).

—*Il giudaismo nei primi secoli del cristianesimo* (Brescia: Morcelliana, 1989).

Newton M., *The Concept of Purity at Qumran and in the Letters of Paul* (Society for New Testament Studies. Monograph Series, 53; Cambridge: Cambridge University Press, 1985).

Nickelsburg, G.W.E., 'The Qumran Fragments of I Enoch and Other Apocryphal Works: Implications for the Understanding of Early Judaism and Christian Origins', in Sh. Talmon (ed.) *Jewish Civilization in the Hellenistic-Roman Period* (Sheffield: Sheffield Academic Press, 1991), pp. 181-95.

Noort, E., *Das Buch Josua; Forschungsgeschichte und Problemfelder* (Darmstadt: Wissenschaftliche Buchgesellschaft, 1998).

Norelli, E., 'Sociologia del cristianesimo primitivo: Qualche osservazione a partire dall'opera di Gerd Theissen', *Henoch* 9 (1987), pp. 97-123.

Noth, M., *The History of Israel* (London: A. & C. Black, 1958).

—*Geschichte Israels* (Göttingen: Vandenhoeck & Ruprecht, 5th edn, 1963).

Nötscher, F., *Zur theologischen Terminologie der Qumrantexte* (Bonn: P. Hanstein, 1956).

Nyberg, H.S., 'From a Theocratic Imperialism to an Imperium', in A. Aadahl (ed.) *Iran through the Ages* (Stockholm: Norstedt, 1972), pp. 11-19.

O'Brien, M.A., *The Deuteronomistic History Hypothesis: A Reassessment* (Freiburg, [Schweiz]: Universitätsverlag; Göttingen: Vandenhoeck & Ruprecht, 1989).

Oestreicher, T., *Das Deuteronomische Grundgesetz* (Gütersloh: C. Bertelsmann, 1923).

Otto, R., *Das Heilige: Über das Irrationale in der Idee des Göttlichen und sein Verhältnis zum Rationalen* (Stuttgart/Gotha: Verlag Friederich Andreas Perthes A.-G., 1923).

—*Reich Gottes und Menschensohn* (München: Beck, 1934).

Parente, F., 'Il problema storico dei rapporti tra essenismo e cristianesimo prima della scoperta dei rotoli del Mar Morto', *PdP* 86 (1962), pp. 333-70.

—'Il problema storico dei rapporti fra essenismo e giudeocristianesimo prima della scoperta dei Rotoli del Mar Morto', *PdP* 100 (1964), pp. 81-124.

—'Escatologia e politica nel tardo giudaismo e nel cristianesimo primitivo', *RStIt* 80 (1968), pp. 234-96.

—'Die Entstehung des Judentums: Persien, die Achämeniden und das Judentum in der Interpretation von Eduard Meyer', in W.M. Calder (ed.), *E. Meyer—Leben und Leistung eines Universalhistorikers* (Leiden: E.J. Brill, 1990), pp. 329-43.

Paul, A., *Ecrits de Qumran et sectes juives aux premiers siècles de l'Islam: Recherches sur l'origine du Caraïsme* (Paris: Letouzey et Ané, 1969).

—*Le monde juif à l'heure de Jésus: Histoire politique* (Paris: Desclée, 1981).

—'Les supports structurels de l'orthodoxie dans le système juif et dans le système chrétien', *Concilium* 212 (1987), pp. 29-40.

Pavlovsky, A., 'Die Chronologie der Tätigkeit Esdras: Versuch einer neuen Lösung', *Biblica* 38 (1957), pp. 275-305; 428-56.

Pedersen, J., *Israel, its Life and Culture* (4 vols.; London: G. Cumberlege; Copenhagen: B.Og Korch, 1926–40).

Penna, A., *Geremia* (Turin: Marietti, 1964).

Penna, R., *L'ambiente storico culturale delle origini cristiane* (Bologna: Dehoniane, 2nd edn, 1986).

—'I diffamatori di Paolo in Rom 3, 8', *RSB* 1 (1989), pp. 43-53.

Pettinato, G., *Ebla, un impero inciso nell'argilla* (Milan: Mondadori, 1979).

Piovanelli, P., 'Le texte de Jérémie utilisé par Flavius Josèphe dans le X livre des Antiquités juives', *Henoch* 14 (1992), pp. 11-36.

Ploeg, J. van der, 'Les manuscrits du désert de Juda: Livres récents', *BO* 16 (1959), pp. 162-76.

—'The Belief in Immortality in the Writings of Qumran', *BD* 18 (1961), pp. 118-24.

Pohlmann, K.F., *Studien zum Dritten Esra* (Göttingen: Vandenhoeck & Ruprecht, 1970).

Prato, G., *Il problema della teodicea in Ben Sira* (Rome: Biblical Institute Press, 1975).

—'Cosmopolitismo culturale e autoidentificazione etnica nella prima storiografia giudaica', *RivB* 34 (1986), pp. 143-82.

Puech, E., *La croyance des Esséniens en la vie future: Immortalité, résurrection, vie éternelle? Histoire d'une croyance dans le judaïsme ancien* (2 vols.; Paris: Gabalda, 1993).

—'Notes sur le manuscrit de XIQMelkisedeq', *RevQ* 12 (1987), pp. 483-513.

—'Le texte "ammonite" de Deir 'Alla: Les admonitions de Balaam (première partie)', in P. Grelot (ed.), *La vie de la Parole: De l'Ancien au Nouveau Testament* (Paris: Desclée, 1987), pp. 13-30.

Pury, A. de (ed.), *Le Pentateuque en question: Les origines et la composition des cinq premiers livres de la Bible à la lumière des recherches récentes* (Genève: Labor et Fides, 1989).

Qimron, E., and J. Strugnell, 'An Unpublished Halakhic Letter from Qumran', in J. Amitai (ed.), *Biblical Archaeology Today: Proceedings of the International Congress on Biblical Archaeology, Jerusalem, April 1984* (Jerusalem: Israel Exploration Society, 1985), pp. 400-407.

Qimron, E., and J. Strugnell, in consultation with Y. Sussman and with contributions by Y. Sussman and A. Yardemi, *Qumran Cave 4. V. Miqsat ma'ase ha-torah* (DJD, 10; Oxford: Oxford University Press, 1994).

Rad, G. von, *Théologie de l'Ancien Testament* (Geneva: Labor et Fides, 1967 [based on the fourth German edition, 1965]).

Radet, G., *Alexandre le Grand* (Paris: L'artisan du livre, 1931).

Rahlfs, A., *Septuaginta; id est Vetus Testamentum Graece iuxta LXX interpretes* (2 vols.; Stuttgart: Privilegierte Würtenbergische Anstalt, 1935).

Reich, N.J., 'The Codification of the Egyptian Laws by Darius and the Origin of the "Demotic Chronicle" ', *Mizraim* 1 (1933), pp. 178-85.

Reicke, B., *Neutestamentliche Zeitgeschichte* (Berlin: Töpelmann, 1975).

Reimarus, H.S., *I frammenti dell'anonimo di Wolfenbüttel* (ed. F. Parente; Naples: Bibliopolis, 1977).

Renan, E., *Histoire du peuple d'Israël* (4 vols.; Paris: E. Levy, 1893).

Rendtorff, R., *Das Alte Testament: Eine Einführung* (Neukirchen–Vluyn: Neukirchener Verlag, 1983).

—'Esra und das "Gesetz" ', *ZAW* 96 (1984), pp. 165-84.

—'Zur Komposition des Buches Jesaja', *VT* 34 (1984), pp. 295-320.

—'L'histoire biblique des origines (Gen 1–11) dans le contexte de la rédaction "sacerdotale" du Pentateuque', in A. de Pury (ed.), *Le Pentateuque en question: Les origines et la composition des cinq premiers livres de la Bible à la lumière des recherches récentes* (Geneva: Labor et Fides, 1989).

Ricciotti, G., *Storia d'Israele* (2 vols.; Torino: Società Editrice Internazionale, 1932, 1934). A one-volume edition appeared in 1997.

Rofé, A., 'Gli albori delle sette nel Giudaismo postesilico (Notizie inedite dai Settanta, Trito-Isaia, Siracide e Malachia)', in B. Chiesa (ed.), *Correnti culturali e movimenti religiosi del giudaismo: Atti del V Congresso Internazionale dell'AISG, 12–15 nov 1984* (Roma: Carucci, 1987), pp. 25-35.

Rose, M., *Deuteronomist und Jahwist: Untersuchungen zu den Berührungspunkten beider Literaturwerke* (Zürich: Theologischer Verlag, 1981).

Rossi, A.V., 'I materiali iranici', *RivB* 34 (1986), pp. 55-72.

Rössler, D., *Gesetz und Geschichte: Untersuchungen zur Theologie der jüdischen Apokalyptik und der pharisäischen Orthodoxie* (WMANT, 3; Neukirchen–Vluyn: Neukirchener Verlag, 2nd edn, 1962).

Rosso Ubigli, L., 'Un'antica variante del libro di Tobit (Tob., VII, 9)', *RSO* 50 (1976), pp. 73-89.

—'Il Documento di Damasco e la halakhah settaria: Rassegna di studi', *RevQ* 9 (1978), pp. 357-99.

—'Alcuni aspetti della concezione della "porneia" nel tardo giudaismo', *Henoch* 1 (1979), pp. 201-45.

—'Qohelet di fronte all'apocalittica', *Henoch* 5 (1983), pp. 209-34.

—'La fortuna di Enoc nel giudaismo antico: Valenze e problemi', *ASE* 1 (1984), pp. 153-64

—'Il Documento di Damasco e l'etica coniugale: A proposito di un nuovo passo qumranico', *Henoch* 14 (1992), pp. 3-10.

Rost, L., *Einleitung in die alttestamentlichen Apokryphen und Pseudepigraphen einschließlich der großen Qumran-Handschriften* (Heidelberg: Quelle & Meyer, 1971).

Rostovzeff, M., *Social and Economic History of the Hellenistic World* (Oxford: Clarendon Press, 3rd edn, 1954).

Rowland, C., *The Open Heaven: A Study of Apocalyptic in Judaism and Early Christianity* (New York: Crossroad, 1982).

Rowley, H.H., 'Jewish Proselyte Baptism and Christian Origins', in *idem, From Moses to Qumran* (London: Lutterworth, 1964), pp. 211-35.

Rudolph, W., *Esra und Nehemiah samt 3 Esra* (Tübingen: Mohr, 1949).

Rüger, H.-P., *Text und Textform im hebräischen Sirach* (Berlin: W. de Gruyter, 1970).

Russell, D.S., *The Method & Message of Jewish Apocalyptic 200 BC—AD 100* (Philadelphia: The Westminster Press, 1964).

Sacchi, P., 'Ancora su Plinio e gli esseni', *PdP* 93 (1963), pp. 451-55.

—'Il problema degli anni 390 nel Documento di Damasco', *RevQ* 5 (1964), pp. 89-96.

—'Studi Samaritani', *RSLR* 5 (1969), pp. 413-40.

—*Ecclesiaste* (Rome: Edizioni Paolini, 1971).

—*Storia del mondo giudaico* (Turin: Società Editrice Internazionale, 1976).

—(ed.) *Apocrifi dell'Antico Testamento* (2 vols.; Turin: UTET, 1981, 1989).

—'Giobbe e il Patto (Giobbe 9, 32-33)', *Henoch* 4 (1982), pp. 175-84.

—'Gesù l'ebreo', *Henoch* 6 (1984), pp. 347-68.

—'Il puro e l'impuro nella Bibbia: Antropologia e storia', *Henoch* 6 (1984), pp. 65-80.

—'Enoc Etiopico 91, 15 e il problema della mediazione', *Henoch* 7 (1985), pp. 257-67.

—'Osservazioni sul sacerdozio presso gli ebrei nel suo rapporto col potere e coi laici', *Testimonianze* 297–298 (1987), pp. 26-31.

—'Il più antico storico di Israele: Un'ipotesi di lavoro', in *Le Origini di Israele* (Convegno Fondazione Caetani Roma 10–11.2.86; Roma: ANL 1987), pp. 65-86. (First sketch of the unitary theory 'Pentateuch-Historical Books'; subsequently modified especially for what concerns the book of Deuteronomy.) See also *Henoch* 13 (1991), pp. 101-108.

—'L'eredità giudaica nel cristianesimo', *Augustinianum* 28 (1988), pp. 23-50.

—'Esquisse du développement du messianisme juif à la lumière du texte qumranien 11QMelch', *ZAW* 100 (1988), pp. 202-14.

—'La conoscenza presso gli ebrei da Amos all'essenismo', *RSB* 1 (1989), pp. 68-77.

—'L'esilio e la fine della monarchia davidica', *Henoch* 11 (1989), pp. 131-48.

—*L'apocalittica giudaica e la sua storia* (Brescia: Paideia, 1990).

—'Giosuè 1, 1-9: Dalla critica storica a quella letteraria', in D. Garrone and F. Israel (eds.), *Storia e Tradizioni di Israele* (Scritti in onore di J. Alberto Soggin; Brescia: Paideia 1991), pp. 237-54.

—'Das Problem des »wahren Israel« im Lichte der universalistischen Auffasungen des Alten Orients', *JfBT* 7 (1992), pp. 78-100.

—'Ideologia e varianti della tradizione ebraica: Deut 27, 4 e Is 52, 14' in H. Merklein, K. Müller and G. Stemberger (eds.), *Bibel in jüdischer und christlicher Tradition* (Frankfurt am Main: Hain, 1993), pp. 13-32.

510   *The History of the Second Temple Period*

—'La questione di Ezra', in G. Busi (ed.), *We-zo't le-Angelo* (Bologna: Fattoadarte, 1993), pp. 461-70.

—'Il sacro profano/impuro puro: Una categoria ebraica perduta', in E. Guerriero and A. Tarsia (eds.) *I segni di Dio* (Cinisello B.: S. Paolo, 1993), pp. 25-53.

—'*Ethiopic Enoch* 91. 15 and the Problem of Mediation', in *Jewish Apocalyptic*, pp. 140-49.

—'Historicizing and Revelation at the Origins of Judaism', in *Jewish Apocalyptic*, pp. 200-210.

—*Jewish Apocalyptic and its History* (Sheffield: Sheffield Academic Press, 1997).

—'Knowledge among the Jews from Amos to the Essenes', in *Jewish Apocalyptic*, pp. 168-99.

Saldarini, A.J., 'Political and Social Roles of the Pharisees and Scribes in Galilee', *SBLSP* 27 (1988), pp. 200-209.

Sanders, E.P., *Paul, the Law, and the Jewish People* (Philadelphia: Fortress Press, 1983).

Saulnier, C., 'Le cadre politico-religieux en Palestine de la révolte des Maccabées à l'intervention romaine', in P. Sacchi (ed.), *Il giudaismo palestinese: Dal I secolo a.C. al I secolo d.C. Atti del Congresso Internazionale dell'AISG—S. Miniato 5–6–7 novembre 1990* (Bologna: AISG, 1993), pp. 199-211.

Scarpat, G., *Il libro della Sapienza* (vol. I; Brescia: Paideia, 1989).

Schäfer, P., *Geschichte der Juden in der Antike: Die Juden Palästinas von Alexander dem Grossen bis zur arabischen Eroberung* (Stuttgart: Verlag Katholisches Bibelwerk, 1983).

Schiffman, 'The New Halakhic Letter (4QMMT) and the Origins of the Dead Sea Sect', *BA* 53 (1990), pp. 64-73.

—'The New Halachic Letter (4QMMT) and the Origins of the Dead Sea Sect', *The Qumran Chronicle* 1 (1990), pp. 47-48.

Schmid, H.H., *Wesen und Geschichte der Weisheit* (Berlin: Töpelmann, 1966).

—*Der sogenannte Jahwist* (Zürich: Theologischer Verlag, 1976).

Schmökel, H., *Kulturgeschichte des alten Orients* (Stuttgart: Kohlhammer, 1961).

Schnabel, E.J., *Law and Wisdom from Ben Sira to Paul* (Tübingen: Mohr, 1985).

Schürer, E., *Geschichte des jüdischen Volkes im Zeitalter Jesu Christi* (3 vols.; Leipzig: Hinrichs 1898–1902).

—*The History of the Jewish People in the Age of Jesus Christ* (rev. and ed. G. Vermes, F. Millar and M. Black; 4 vols.; Edinburgh: T. & T. Clark Ltd, 1973–87), IV.

Schweitzer, A., *Geschichte der Leben-Jesu-Forschung* (Tübingen: Mohr, 9th edn, 1984).

Seidel, H., 'Erwägungen zur Frage des geistigen Ursprungsortes der Erweckungsbewegung von Qumran', in S. Wagner (ed.), *Bibel und Qumran* (Berlin: Ev. Haupt-Bibelges., 1968), pp. 188-97.

Severino, E., *Interpretazione e traduzione dell'Orestea di Eschilo* (Milan: Rizzoli, 1985).

Siegert, F., 'Gottesfürtige und Sympatisanten', *JSJ* 4 (1973), pp. 109-68.

Sierra, S.J., 'Le condizioni spirituali degli ebrei prima della distruzione del II santuario', in A. Vivian (ed.), *Biblische und judaistische Studien: Festschrift Paolo Sacchi* (Frankfurt am Main: Lang, 1990), pp. 257-70.

Simon, M., and A. Benoit, *Le judaïsme et le christianisme antique d'Antiochus Epiphane à Constantin* (Paris: Presses Universitaires de France, 1968).

Smend, R., *Die Weisheit des Jesus Sirach erklärt von R. Smend* (Berlin: G. Reimer, 1906).

Smith, M., 'II Isaiah and the Persians', *JNES* 22 (1963), pp. 415-20.

—*Palestinian Parties and Politics that Shaped the Old Testament* (London: SCM Press, 1971).

—*Gli uomini del ritorno* (Verona: Essedue, 1984).

Snaith, N.H., 'The Language of the Old Testament', in *The Interpreter's Bible*, I (Nashville, New York: Abingdon Press, 1952).

Soggin, J.A., 'Bilinguismo o trilinguismo nell'ebraismo postesilico: Il caso dell'aramaico e del greco', *Vicino Orienta* 3 (1980), pp. 209-23.

—*Introduction to the Old Testament: From its Origins to the Closing of the Alexandrian Canon* (Philadelphia: Westminster Press, 1980).

—*Storia d'Israele* (Brescia: Paideia, 1984).

—*Introduzione all'Antico Testamento* (Brescia: Paideia, 4th edn, 1987).

—*An Introduction to the History of Israel and Judah* (London: SCM Press, 1993).

Sollberger, E., and J.R. Kupper, *Inscriptions royales sumériennes et akkadiennes* (Paris: Cerf, 1971).

Spinoza, B., *Trattato teologico-politico* (Introduzione di E. Giancotti; traduzione e commenti di A. Droeth and E. Giancotti; Turin: Einaudi, 1972).

Starcky, J., 'Les quatre étapes du messianisme à Qumran', *RB* 70 (1963), pp. 481-504.

Stegemann, H., 'The Origins of the Temple Scroll', in J.A. Emerton (ed.), *Congress Volume Jerusalem* (VTSup, 40; Leiden: E.J. Brill, 1988), pp. 235-56.

—'The "Teacher of Righteousness" and Jesus: Two Types of Religious Leadership in Judaism at the Turn of the Era', in Sh. Talmon (ed.), *Jewish Civilization in the Hellenistic-Roman Period* (Sheffield: Sheffield Academic Press, 1991), pp. 196-213.

Steible, H., *Die altsumerischen Bau- und Weihinschriften* (Wiesbaden: Steiner, 1982).

—*Pharisäer, Sadduzäer, Essener* (Stuttgart: Katholisches Bibelwerk, 1991).

Stemberger, G., *Pharisäer, Sadduzäer, Essener* (Stuttgart: Katholisches Bibelwerk, 1991).

—*Einleitung in Talmud und Midrasch* (München: Beck 1992).

Stoebe, H., *Das erste Buch Samuelis* (Gütersloh: Gerd Mohn, 1973).

Stone, M.E., 'The Book of Enoch and Judaism in the Third Century B.C.E.', *CBQ* 40 (1978), pp. 479-92.

—*Scriptures, Sects and Visions: A Profile of Judaism from Ezra to the Jewish Revolts* (Philadelphia: Fortress Press, 1980).

Szyszman, S., *Le karaïsme, ses doctrines et son histoire* (Lausanne: L'Age d'homme, 1980).

Talmon, S., 'The Internal Diversification of Judaism in the Early Second Temple Period', in S. Talmon (ed.), *Jewish Civilization in the Hellenistic-Roman Period* (Sheffield: Sheffield Academic Press, 1991), pp. 16-43.

Talmon, S., and I. Knohl, 'A Calendrical Scroll from Qumran Cave IV, Mish. B^a (4Q 321)', *Tarbiz* 60 (1991), pp. 505-21.

Testuz, M., *Les idées religieuses du livre des Jubilées* (Geneva: Librairie E. Droz, 1960).

Theissen, G., *Soziologie der Jesusbewegung: Ein Beitrag zur Entstehungsgeschichte des Urchristentums* (Theologische Existenz heute, 194; Munich: Kaiser, 1977).

—'Gruppenmessianismus: Überlegungen zum Ursprung der Kirche im Jüngerkreis Jesu', *JfBT* 7 (1992), pp. 101-24.

Thompson, T.L., *The Historicity of the Patriarchal Narratives* (Berlin: W. de Gruyter, 1974).

Thureau Dangin, F., *Die sumerischen und akkadischen Königsinschriften* (Leipzig: Hinrichs, 1907).

Torrey, C.C., *Ezra Studies* (Chicago: The University of Chicago Press, 1910).

Tosato, A., 'Israele nell'ideologia politica del Cronista', *RSB* 1 (1989), pp. 257-68.

Tresmontant, C., *Essai sur la pensée hébraïque* (Paris: Cerf, 1953).

Troiani, L., *Due studi di storiografia e religione antiche* (Como: New Press, 1988).

Vaccari, A., *Institutiones Biblicae scholis accomodatae* (Rome: Pontificio Istituto Biblico, 6th edn, 1951).

Van Seters, J., *Der Jahwist als Historiker* (trans. H.H. Schmid; Theologische Studien, 134; Zürich: Theologischer Verlag, 1987).

VanderKam, J.C., 'The Origin, Character and Early History of the 364-Day Calendar: A Reassessment of Jaubert's Hypothesis', *CBQ* 41 (1979), pp. 390-411.

—'2 Maccabees 6, 7a and Calendrical Change in Jerusalem', *JSJ* 12 (1981), pp. 52-74.

—*Enoch and the Growth of an Apocalyptic Tradition* (Washington: Catholic Biblical Association of America, 1984).

Vaux, R. de, ''Ain Feshkha', *RB* 65 (1958), pp. 406-408.

—*Les institutions de l'Ancien Testament* (2 vols.; Paris: Cerf, 1958, 1960).

—'Le Temple d'Onias et Qumran', *RB* 75 (1968), pp. 204-205.

Vermes, G., 'The Etymology of "Essenes" ', *RevQ* 2 (1960), pp. 427-43.

—*Jesus the Jew: A Historian's Reading of the Gospels* (London: Collins, 1973).

—'Methodology in the Study of Jewish Literature in the Graeco-Roman Period', *JJS* 36 (1985), pp. 145-58.

—*Jesus and the World of Judaism* (London: SCM Press, 1986).

Virgilio, B., 'Strutture templari e potere politico in Asia Minore', in B. Virgilio (ed.), *Studi Ellenistici* (Pisa: Giardini, 1987), II, pp. 199-207.

Vivian, A., 'La crisi del sacerdozio aaronita e l'origine della Mishna', in *Atti del Congresso Internazionale dell'AISG 1984* (Roma: Carucci, 1987), pp. 105-20.

—*Il rotolo del Tempio* (Brescia: Paideia, 1990).

—'Il concetto di Legge nel Rotolo del Tempio (11QTemple Scroll)', *RSB* 3 (1991), pp. 97-114.

—'I movimenti che si oppongono al tempio: Il problema del sacerdozio di Melchisedeq', *Henoch* 14 (1992), pp. 97-112.

Wacholder, B.Z., *The Dawn of Qumran: The Sectarian Torah and the Teacher of Righteousness* (Cincinnati: Hebrew Union College Press, 1983).

Waerden, B.L. van der, 'History of the Zodiac', *AfO* 16 (1952–53), pp. 216-70.

Weber, J., *Le livre de la Sagesse* (La Sainte Bible, 6; Paris: Letouzey et Ané, 1951), pp. 401-528.

Weidner, E.F., 'Jojachin, König von Juda in babylonischen Keilschrifttexten', in *Mélanges Syriens offerts à M. René Dussaud, secrétaire perpétuel de l'Académie des inscriptions et belles-lettres, par ses amis et ses élèves* (Bibliotheque archéologique et historique, 30; Paris: Paul Geuthner, 1939), II, pp. 932-35.

Weippert, H., 'Das deuteronomistische Geschichtswerk: Sein Ziel und Ende in der neueren Forschung', *ThRund* 50 (1985), pp. 213-48.

Welch, A.C., *The Code of Deuteronomy* (London: J. Clarke, 1924).

—'When Was the Worship of Israel Centralized in the Temple?', *ZAW* 43 (1925), pp. 250-55.

—*Deuteronomy, the Framework to the Code* (London: Oxford University Press, H. Milford, 1932).

Wellhausen, J., *Die Composition des Hexateuchs und der historischen Bücher des A.T.s* (Berlin, 2nd edn, 1889, 3rd edn, 1899).

—*Prolegomena zur Geschichte Israels* (Berlin: Reimer, 6th edn, 1927).

—*Israelitische und jüdische Geschichte* (Berlin: W. de Gruyter, 9th edn, 1958).

West, M.L., *Early Greek Philosophy and the Orient* (Oxford: Clarendon Press, 1971).

Widengren, G., 'The Persian Period', in J.H. Hayes and J.M. Miller (eds.), *Israelite and Judaean History* (Philadelphia: Trinity Press International, 1990), pp. 489-538.

Wieder, N., *The Judean Scrolls and Caraism* (London: East and West Library, 1962).

Williamson, H., *Ezra and Nehemiah* (Sheffield: Sheffield Academic Press, 1987).

Willrich, H., *Urkundenfälschung in der hellenistisch-jüdischen Literatur* (Göttingen: Vandenhoeck & Ruprecht, 1924).

Winston, D., 'The Iranian Component in the Bible, Apocrypha and Qumran: A Review of the Evidence', *HR* 5 (1965), pp. 183-216.

—*The Wisdom of Solomon* (AB; Garden City: Doubleday, 1979), pp. 20-25.

Wise, M.O., *A Critical Study of the Temple Scroll from Qumran Cave 11* (Chicago: Oriental Inst. of the Univ. of Chicago, 1990).

—'The Teacher of Righteousness and the Temple Scroll', *The Qumran Chronicle* 1 (1990), pp. 59-60.

Woude, A.S. van der, 'Wicked Priest or Wicked Priests? Reflections on the Identification of the Wicked Priest in the Habakkuk Commentary', *JJS* 33 (1982), pp. 349-59.

Zadok, R., *The Jews in Babylonia during the Chaldean and Achaemenian Periods according to Babylonian Sources* (Studies in the History of the Jewish People and the Land of Israel Monograph Series, 3; Haifa: the University, 1979).

Zeron, A., 'Pseudophilonic Parallels to the Inscriptions of Deir 'Alla', *VT* 41 (1991), pp. 186-91.

B. *Works concerning Single Themes*

As for this section, see my *Jewish Apocalyptic and its History* (trans. W.J. Short; JSPS, 20; Sheffield: Sheffield Academic Press, 1997), pp. 250-80. In this book the main part of the bibliography is structured according to single themes. Though it focuses on Apocalyptic, it actually concerns the whole Second Temple period. The bibliography is divided into the following sections: 1. General Works (Historical Works, Collections of Texts in Translation, Introductions). 2. Histories of Research. Bibliographies. 3. The Origin of Apocalyptic and its Relation to Other Jewish Currents or to Non-Jewish Societies. 4. History and Structure of Apocalyptic Thought. 5. The Enoch Tradition. 6. Life after Death: Immortality of the Soul and Resurrection. 7. Superhuman Figures, Messianism and Mediation. 8. The Son of Man. 9. Evil and the Devil. 10. The Angelic World. 11. The Pure and the Impure. 12. The Calendar (In the Ancient Near East; Among the Jews). 13. The Problem of Knowledge. 14. Pseudepigraphy and Forgeries.

RECENT BIBLIOGRAPHY

Hebrew Texts

Qumran Texts

Charlesworth, J.H., *The Dead Sea Scrolls*. I. *Rule of the Community; Photographic Multilanguage Edition* (Philadelphia: American Interfaith Institute/World Alliance, 1996). The *Community Rule* appears translated into six modern languages.

García Martínez, F., *The Dead Sea Scrolls Translated: The Qumran Texts in English* (Leiden: E.J. Brill, 1994).

García Martínez, F., and C. Martone, *Testi di Qumran* (Brescia: Paideia, 1996). The original Spanish edition of García Martínez has been translated by Martone into Italian from the Hebrew directly, with introductions and notes to each text.

García Martínez, F., and E.J.C. Tigchelaar, *The Dead Sea Scrolls: Study Edition* (2 vols.; Leiden: E.J. Brill, 1997, 1998).

Ibba, G., *La regola della guerra* (Torino: Silvio Zamorani, 1997). A critical edition.

Martone, C., *La Regola della Comunità* (Torino: Silvio Zamorani, 1994). A critical edition.

Jewish Texts in Other Languages

Chialà, S., *Libro delle Parabole di Enoch* (Brescia: Paideia, 1997).

Moraldi, L., *Le antichità giudaiche* (2 vols.; Torino: UTET, 1998). A translation with notes.

Troiani, L., *Letteratura giudaica di lingua greca* (Brescia: Paideia, 1997). As 5th volume of the *Apocrifi dell'Antico Testamento*, edited by P. Sacchi.

Studies

a. *History, Culture, and Religion of Second Temple Period*

Albertz, R., *A History of Israelite Religion in the Old Testament Period. II. From the Exile to the Maccabees* (Louisville: Westminster/John Knox Press, 1994).

Boccaccini, G., *Beyond the Essene Hypothesis: The Parting of the Ways between Qumran and Enochic Judaism* (Grand Rapids: Eerdmans, 1998).

Cerutti, M.V. (ed.), *Apocalittica e gnosticismo. Roma 18–19 giugno 1993* (Roma: GEI, 1995).

Davies, P.R., *In Search of Ancient Israel* (Sheffield: Sheffield Academic Press, 1992).

—'Scenes from the Early History of Judaism', in Edelman (ed.), *The Triumph*, pp. 145-84.

Donner, H., ' "Wie geschrieben steht": Herkunft und Sinn einer Formel', in *idem*, *Aufsätze zum Alten Testament aus vier Jahrzehnten* (Berlin: W. de Gruyter, 1994).

Edelman, D.V. (ed.), *The Triumph of Elohim: From Yahavisms to Judaisms* (Grand Rapids: Eerdmans, 1995).

Feldman, L.H., *Jew and Gentile in the Ancient World: Attitudes and Interactions from Alexander to Justinian* (Princeton: Princeton University Press, 1993).

Grabbe, L.L., *Judaism from Cyrus to Hadrian* (2 vols.; Minneapolis: Fortress Press, 1992, 1994).

—'What was Ezra's Mission?', in Eskenazi and Richards (eds.), *Second Temple Studies*

Jaffee, M.S., *Early Judaism* (Upper Saddkle River, NJ: Prentice Hall, 1997).

McKenzie, S.L., and M.P. Graham, *The History of Israel's Traditions: The Heritage of Martin Noth* (Sheffield: Sheffield Academic Press, 1994).

Neusner, J., *Judaism in Late Antiquity* (2 vols.; Leiden: E.J. Brill, 1995).

Nodet, E., *A Search for the Origins of Judaism: From Joshua to the Mishnah* (Sheffield: Sheffield Academic Press, 1997 [French edn 1992]).

Noort, E., *Das Buch Josua: Forschungsgeschichte und Problemfelder* (Darmstadt: Wissenschaftliche Buchgesellschaft, 1998).

Pury, A. de (ed.), *Israel construit son Histoire* (Genève: Labor et Fides, 1996).

Schiffman, L.H., *From Text to Tradition: A History of Second Temple and Rabbinic Judaism* (Hoboken: Ktav Publishing House, 1991).

—*Texts and Traditions: A Source Reader for the Study of Second Temple and Rabbinic Judaism* (Hoboken: Ktav Publishing House, 1998).

b. *Exile Period*

Jullien, C., and F. Jullien, *La Bible en exil* (Neuchâtel: Recherches et Publications, 1996).

Sacchi, P., 'The Pentateuch, the Deuteronomist, and Spinoza', *Henoch* 20 (1998), pp. 259-71.

c. *Zadokite Period*

Davies, P.R., 'Scenes from Early History of Judaism', in Edelman (ed.), *The Triumph*, pp. 145-84.

Gosse, B., *Structuration des grands ensembles bibliques et intertextualité à l'époque perse* (Berlin: W. de Gruyter, 1997).

Eskenazi, T., and K.H. Richards (eds.), *Second Temple Studies. II. Temple Community in the Persian Period* (Sheffield: Sheffield Academic Press, 1994).

Graham, M.P., K.G. Hoglund and S.L. McKenzie, *The Chronicler as Historian* (Sheffield: Sheffield Academic Press, 1997).

Japhet, S., 'Composition and Chronology in the Book of Ezra–Nehemiah', in Eskenazi and Richards, *Second Temple Studies*, pp. 189-216.

Laperrousaz, E.M. (ed.), *La Palestine à l'époque perse* (Paris: Cerf, 1994).

Lemaire, A., *Histoire et administration de la Palestine à l'époque perse*, in E.M. Laperrousaz (ed.), *La Palestine à l'époque perse* (Paris: Cerf, 1994), pp. 11-53.

Smith Christopher, D., 'The Mixed Marriage Crisis in Ezra 9–10 and Nehemiah 13', in Eskenazi and Richards (eds.), *Second Temple Studies*, pp. 243-65.

d. *From the Maccabees to the Herods*

Baumgarten, A.I., *The Flourishing of Jewish Sects in the Maccabean Era: An Interpretation* (Leiden: E.J. Brill, 1997).

Charlesworth, J.H., 'The Date of the Parables of Enoch', *Henoch* 20 (1998), pp. 93-98.

Chilton, B., and C.A. Evans, *Jesus in Context: Temple, Purity and Restoration* (Leiden: E.J. Brill, 1997).

Chilton, B., and C.A. Evans (eds.), *Studying the Historical Jesus: Evaluation of the State of Current Research* (Leiden: E.J. Brill, 1994).

Dianich, S., *Il messia sconfitto* (Casale: Piemme, 1997).

Fittschen, K. and G. Foerster (eds.), *Judaea and Greco-Roman World in the Time of Herod in the Light of Archaelogical Evidence* (Göttingen: Vandenhoeck & Ruprecht, 1996).

Grabbe, L.L., *An introduction to First Century Judaism: Jewish Religion and History in the Second Temple Period* (Edinburgh: T. & T. Clark, 1996).

Laperrousaz, E.M. (ed.), *Qoumrân et les manuscrits de la Mer Morte* (Paris: Cerf, 1997).

Mayer, B.F., 'Jesus' Ministry and Self-Understanding', in Chilton and Evans (eds.), *Structuring the Historical Jesus*, pp. 337-52.

Mazzinghi, L., *Notte di paura e di luce: Esegesi di Sap. 17, 1–18, 4* (Rome: Editrice Pontificio Istituto Biblico, 1995).

Nodet, E., *Essai sur les origines du Christianisme: Une secte éclatée* (Paris: Cerf, 1998).

Passoni Dell'Acqua, A., 'Innovazioni lessicali e attributi divini: Una caratteristica del giudaismo alessandrino?', in R. Fabris (ed.), *La parola di Dio cresceva (At 12, 24). Omaggio a C.M. Martini* (Bologna: EDB, 1998), pp. 87-108.

Penna, R., 'Kerygma e storia alle origini del cristianesimo: Nuove considerazioni su un annoso problema', *ASR* 2 (1997), pp. 239-56.

Sacchi, P., 'Il problema del male nell'ebraismo precristiano', in M. Raveri (ed.), *Del Bene e del male* (Venezia: Marsilio, 1997), pp. 137-62.

—'Qumran e Gesù', *RSB* 9 (1997), pp. 99-115.

Saulnier, C., 'Le cadre politico-religieux en Palestine de la révolte des Maccabées à l'intervention romaine', in P. Sacchi (ed.), *Il giudaismo palestinese: Dal I secolo a.C. al I secolo d.C. Atti del Congresso Internazionale dell'AISG—S. Miniato 5–6–7 novembre 1990* (Bologna: AISG, 1993), pp. 199-212.

Stemberger, G., 'Il contributo delle baraitot babilonesi alla conoscenza storica della Palestina prima del 70 d.C. (Shabbat, 13b-17b: le diciotto halakot e tradizioni connesse)', in P. Sacchi (ed.), *Il giudaismo palestinese: dal I secolo a.C. al I secolo d.C. Atti del Congresso Internazionale dell'AISG—S. Miniato 5–6–7 novembre 1990* (Bologna: AISG, 1993), pp. 213-30.

Taylor, J.E., *The Immerser: John the Baptist within Second Temple Judaism* (Grand Rapids: Eerdmans, 1997).

Troiani, L., 'La profezia e la letteratura giudaico-ellenistica', in M. Sordi (ed.), *Profezia* (Milano: Vita e Pensiero, 1993), pp. 21-30.

Troiani, L., 'Giudaismo ellenistico e cristianesimo', in *'We-zo't le- Angelo': Raccolta di scritti in memoria di A. Vivian* (Bologna: Fattoadarte, 1993), pp. 555-72.

—Introduction to the 5th vol. of the *Apocrifi dell'Antico Testamento* (Brescia: Paideia, 1997), pp. 17-72, containing the Judaeo-hellenistic texts. This introduction is an original reflexion on the importance of Egyptian Judaism in the development of Middle Judaism and Christian Origins.

INDEXES

INDEX OF REFERENCES

BIBLE

Old Testament		31.35	444, 450	11	39
Genesis		49.8-10	406	11.4	362
1.24	346			11.25	443
1.25	448, 451	*Exodus*		11.26	443
1.29	442	3.12	74	11.28	443
2.19-20	442	4.22	487	11.31	443
3	492	12	85	11.41	443
3.14	177, 448	12.40	95	11.42	443
3.24	444	19.5-6	450	16.8	176
4.7	449	19.6	39	16.10	176
5.24	388	19.12-13	441	17–26	451
6	178	20.5-6	104, 187,	17–19	452
6.1-4	461, 487		447	17.8	453
6.6	317, 447	20.11	85	17.11	443
8.21	34, 72,	20.23-25	440	17.12	452
	364	20.26	444	19.2	450
9	98	21.22-25	309	19.26	346
12.1-3	35, 121	23.19	445	19.31	346
12.3	98	24.1-2	102	20.6	346
14.17-20	390	24.3-8	36, 101,	21.14-15	255
15.13	95		441	22.28	445
15.18	62	24.9-11	35, 102		
16.4	463	24.11	441	*Numbers*	
17	102, 103	31.18	185	6.25	321
17.4	103	32.11-14	105	8.9	132
17.6	103	33.11	159	10.39	124
17.7	103	33.19	35	12.1	123
17.8	103	33.20	159	12.6-8	123, 159
17.9	103	34.26	445	15.14	453
17.10	103			16.33	426
17.14	103	*Leviticus*		24.17	30
18.17-32	446	6.3-4	445	25.6-13	236
18.22-33	340	10.10	38, 339,	25.12-13	237
28.17	200		439	25.12	237

Deuteronomy

1.7	62
1.15-17	87
3.23-27	106
4.10	200
5.3	87, 101, 114
5.9-10	104, 187, 447
5.15	85
6.4-5	201
6.13	474
7	121
7.3-4	122
7.9-11	105
7.9-10	107
7.15	121
7.16	121
10.12	201
10.20	474
11.24	62
11.29	156
14.21	445
15.12-18	89
16.18	115
17.8-9	115
17.9	117
17.14-15	86
17.14	86, 87
17.15	115, 250
17.19	87
18.1	115
18.9-22	30
18.9-15	158
18.20-22	116
18.22	74
21.10-14	123
22.5	445
22.9-11	445
22.9	39
23.2	463
23.3-4	122
23.3	142
23.4-6	145
23.4	119
23.10-15	444
23.13-15	459
24.1	89
27.4	154, 156
27.12	156
27.26	369, 490
30.15	36, 108, 330, 412
32.5-6	487
32.18	487
32.19	487
32.22	426
34.10	159

Joshua

1.4	62, 171
24.15	108, 447

Judges

3.4-6	123
5.4	82
5.23	447
11.26	96
11.29-40	441
11.38	463
13.22	200, 441
17	441
21.25	91

1 Samuel

1.6	463
2.4	330
4.4	126
13.1	95
21.5-7	444
28	426

2 Samuel

7	54, 83, 88
7.14	184
24.1	350

1 Kings

2.11	95
5.13	316
6.1	95
8.9	186
8.41-43	453
8.52-53	184
11.13	89, 184
11.32	89, 184
11.36	184
11.42	95
15.13	93
15.34	93

2 Kings

2.11	388
17.25-26	155
19.15	126
19.34	89, 184
20.6	89, 184
23.2	88
23.3	98
23.23	93
24.9	89
24.13-14	47
24.16	47
25.6-7	48
25.11	49
25.12	49
25.13-15	48
25.22	48
25.27	51, 56

1 Chronicles

3	273
3.17	60
3.18	60
5.27-41	130
5.40	133
16.16-17	185
16.37	186
17.1	186
17.13	184
21.1	350
24.7	234
24.14	221
28.2	186
28.4	183
29.7	182

2 Chronicles

5.10	185
6.5-6	183
6.11	186
6.42	184
13.5	183
21.7	184

33.11-13	185	772	132	26.6	428
36.5-8	46	8	170	27.1-6	188
36.20	50, 146,	8.8	172	28.22	428
	182	8.9	135	37.23	200
		8.13	296	38	200
Ezra		9.37	161	42.3	188
1	60	10	143	42.5	188
1.7-8	60	10.1-2	192	42.8	188
1.8	60	10.28	125	42.12	419
2.2	134	12	234		
2.70	115	12.1-7	234	*Song of Songs*	
3.2	91	12.10-11	135	8.6	420
4.8-23	124	12.11	136		
5.14	60	12.22	135	*Psalms*	
6.3	63	12.23	136	1.1	32
6.7	61	12.26	135	2.7	487
7.1	91, 133	13.3	142	13.4	321
7.6-7	169	13.4	144	18.11	126
7.6	170, 173	13.10	144	19.9	321
7.11-26	161, 171	13.21	144	29.1	487
7.24	161	13.23-30	141	31.17	321
8.20	453	13.23	121	39	364
9	193	13.24	172	44	110, 193,
9.6	192	13.25	144		194, 347
9.8	321	13.28	144, 152	44.3	194
9.9	193			44.9-18	193
9.13-14	192	*Job*		46.5-6	54
10.6	136	4.13-21	187	67.2	321
		4.17	181	80.4	321
Nehemiah		4.18	182	80.8	321
1.1-4	138	8.8	187, 189	80.20	321
1.5	109	9	181	82.1	392
2.5	138	9.1-4	190	94.17	428
2.11-18	139	9.32	189	111.10	200
3.1	140	12.3	187, 189	115.17	428
3.5	140	12.12-13	189	119.79	200
4.1-2	140	12.16-17	189	119.135	321
4.3	139	13.1	187		
5.1-13	140	13.25	190, 455	*Proverbs*	
5.8	133, 141	14	181	1.20-32	387
5.15	68, 116	14.1-4	190, 455	8.1–9.6	387
6.10-14	140	14.10-14	427	9.10	200
6.14	116	14.13	427	10.1	103
6.15	129	15.18	189	10.24	104
6.17-19	121, 140	16.12-17	190	10.27	104
7.4-6	142	21.6	191	10.30	104
7.64	142	21.26	191	11.8	104
7.72	115	24.1-25	191	11.19	104

Proverbs (cont.)

14.34	104
15.11	428
22.16	103
27.20	428
29.13	321

Ecclesiastes

1.7	195
1.8	195, 196
1.15	196
2.3	195
2.12	197
2.13-14	197
2.14	180
2.16	198
3.11	196, 317
3.16-17	198
3.18-21	164, 180
3.18-20	355
3.19-22	196
4.2-3	200
4.13-16	198
5.1	200
5.3-4	201
5.6	196
5.7	180
6.9	180, 414
6.10	199
7.11-12	202
7.12	419
7.13	202, 338, 413
7.15	198
7.18	202
7.20	335, 357, 410
7.23-24	196
8.7	195
8.8	197
8.17	197
9.1	197
9.2-3	199
9.2	201, 456
9.4-6	428
9.10	195, 428
9.11	198
11.1-2	419

12.1-6	428
12.2-5	195
12.6	196
12.13	201

Isaiah

1.13-15	90
2.2	121
2.3	120
4.2	383
4.3	71
5.3	100
6	82, 83
6.1	93
6.13	71
9.7	90
10.20	71
11	89, 383
11.1-5	381
11.1-2	89
11.1	30, 35
11.4	382
11.6	317
11.9	35
14.11	426
19.1	82
24–27	433
24.21	433
25.3	424
25.4	433
25.8	433
26.6	433
26.9	433
26.12	433
26.14	434
26.19	433
37.15	126
37.16	82
38.18-19	426
40.2	106, 109, 194
40.3	100
40.10	100
40.24	89
42.1-4	150
42.2-3	99
42.3-4	99

42.6	98, 99, 150
44.28	161
45.1	171
45.7	345, 353
49.1-13	161
49.3	347
49.6	98
51.7	230
52.7	392
55.3	385
55.8-11	127
55.8	106
56.1-8	119
56.2	120
56.3-6	454
56.3	145
56.4-5	454
56.4	120
56.6	120
60.1-6	150
60.17	385
61.1-3	423
63.1-6	150
65.17	380
66.20-21	120
66.22	387

Jeremiah

1	83
1.1-3	69
12.1-2	74
12.1	329
13.23	71, 329
17.5	329
17.7	329
18.1-6	329
18.7-8	317, 329
20	207
20.7-14	105
20.7-11	74
20.7-10	329
20.8	73
20.10	74
22.15	70
23.5-6	382
23.5	383
23.25	74

23.33-34	75	4–5	82	39.23	230
24.1-10	76	8.1	84, 481	40.1	84, 481
26.24	48	10	54	44	450
27	73	11	54	44.3	78, 79
27.1-6	73	11.1	54	44.6-9	453
27.3	73	11.15	53, 149	44.15	63, 64
27.6	161, 171	11.17	54, 149	44.17-19	453
27.14	74	13.4	54	44.17-18	445
28.4	47	15	54	44.17	78
30.1-10	69	16	81	44.23	38, 78,
30.7	73	16.3	77		439
31.20	487	16.7	77	45	64
31.25-28	106	16.8	81	45.8	79
31.28	64	16.49	81	45.9	54, 83
31.29-30	80, 106	16.59	81	45.16	79
31.29	71, 105	18	109, 187,	45.18	79
31.30	71		330	46.8-10	79
31.31	109	18.2-4	80, 107	47.22	119
31.33	317, 329	18.2	105		
31.34	72	18.22	80, 107,	*Daniel*	
32.18-19	80		410	1.1-2	47
32.18	107	20	54, 97,	2.34-35	391
33.15	383		347	3.25	487
37.1-10	69	20.10-11	77	3.92	487
39.10	49	20.25-26	77	7	390
41.5	49	20.37	81	7.13-14	390
51.59	47	20.42-43	78	7.25	483
52.28	47	22.6	54	7.27	241, 390
52.29	48	23.5	54	9.17	321
52.30	48	24.1	84, 481	9.27	226, 235
		29.1	84, 85,	10.13	320
Lamentations			481	11.31	226
1.4	49	31.1	84, 481	12.1-3	434
1.8	108	31.14	427	12.2	355
3.40	108	32.1	84, 481	12.11	226
4.22	108	33.21-27	49		
		33.21	84, 85,	*Hosea*	
Ezekiel			481	1.11	487
1	54, 83	34.16-17	107	11.1-3	201
1.1	47, 84,	34.23-24	54	14.2-3	447
	126, 318,	34.23	83, 382		
	481	34.24	57	*Joel*	
1.2	47	37	83, 109	3.19	194, 347
1.14	84	37.24-26	55, 382		
1.21	84	37.24-25	83	*Amos*	
2.8	86	37.25	57	3.6	74
3.16	84	38	54	5.8-9	74, 126,
3.19	481				329

Amos (cont.)		2.21	61	8.20-23	120
5.14-15	450	2.23	61	9–14	384
5.15	71			9.9-10	384
		Zechariah		12	65, 384
Jonah		1.9	128	12.2	66
3.4-10	317	2.8-9	65	12.5	66
		3	65, 66	12.6	66
Micah		3.1-8	128	12.9	66
4.7	71	3.2	349	13.1-6	116
		3.4-5	66		
Habakkuk		3.8	68	*Malachi*	
1.5	312	4.6-7	64	1.8	116, 118
		4.6	122, 124	1.10	149
Haggai		4.10	68	1.11	118, 149,
1.1	61	4.11-14	63		454
1.15	63	4.14	61, 383	2.4	118, 158
2.2	61	5.5-11	127	2.7	118, 124
2.7	256	6.9-15	67	2.8	101, 158
2.10-14	64	6.12	61	2.11-12	121
2.10-13	102	8.9-13	65	2.11	122, 123
2.15-19	64	8.16-17	120	3.23-24	388

APOCRYPHA

1 Esdras		1.13-15	431	4.11-14	417
1.26	46	1.14	351	7.31	416
2.8	60	2.16-18	487	11.4	413
2.23-26	124	2.24	351, 431	11.17	416
3–4	99	3.1-8	437	12.1-5	416
5.40	134	3.4	355	13.2-7	418
6.24	63	7.17-22	322	14.1	416
8.1	133	7.17-21	318	14.16-19	429
8.3	169, 170,	7.17-20	316	15.1	417
	173	8.17	432	15.4-5	417
8.5	169	8.21	432	15.11-17	415
9.1	136	9.10	432	15.17	412, 413
9.37-55	170	9.13-18	432	16.7-11	415
9.37	115, 132	9.15	436	17.20-24	416
9.48	172	11.9	404	18.2	416
		12.12-18	191	18.21	416
Tobit		16.6	404	19.21	414
8.7	461			20.9-10	417
		Ecclesiasticus		21.1	416
Judith		1.1-14	411	21.27	351, 412
9.8-13	386	1.7-8	414	25.24	351, 429
		2.1-5	417	28.2	416
Wisdom of Solomon		2.4	417	33.7-15	413
1.3	351	2.5	353	34.1-8	414

Ecclesiasticus (cont.)
35.4-6	416	
44–50	130	
44–45	237	
45.24	237	
49.11-12	386	
50.25-26	145, 183	

1 Maccabees
1.11-15	223	
1.11-13	224	
1.11	227, 419	
1.15	224	
1.41-43	235	
1.41	235	
1.52-53	236	
2.15-28	236	
2.29-41	239	
2.42	238, 239	
2.43-44	239	
2.49-68	434	
4.9	483	
4.46	245	
4.60	242	

5.25	242	
7.5-32	229	
7.9-10	243	
7.9	243	
7.12-16	243	
9.27	245	
9.54-55	245	
9.58-61	246	
10.36	246	
13.27-30	251	
13.41-42	247	
13.43-48	247	
14.27-47	252	
14.28	252	
14.29	248	
14.32	251	
14.35	247	
14.38	247	
14.41	245, 248, 398	

2 Maccabees
1.18-36	130	

2.9-12	130	
2.13	146	
3	221	
3.2	218	
3.4-6	222	
3.11	222	
4.8-9	223	
4.9	227	
4.15	224	
4.19	224	
5.6	225	
5.11-14	225	
5.24-26	239	
6.2	226	
6.8	226	
7.9	355	
7.22-23	379, 434	
11.13-38	241	
13.4-7	242	
14.3-14	243	
14.3	229, 243	
14.13	229	

NEW TESTAMENT

Matthew
3.10	301, 341	
5.3-11	371	
5.3	424	
5.27-28	493	
5.34-36	476	
5.45	494	
5.48	494	
6.10	203	
7.1-2	370	
7.2	490	
7.21	203	
7.29	492	
13.33	495	
14.3-12	294	
15	491	
18.21	493	
18.23-35	343	
19.25	370	
19.26	489	

21.33-41	487	
23.16-19	475	
27.15	479	

Mark
1.22	492	
2	370	
2.10-11	397, 407, 493	
2.10	343	
4.24	342	
4.30-32	342, 495	
6.17-29	294	
6.18	293	
6.20	293	
7	342, 467, 491	
7.15	467	
7.18-19	467	
7.19	468	

10.26	370	
10.27	489, 493	
12.1-21	487	
12.1	406	
12.15-16	296	
14.63	492	
15.6	479	

Luke
3.9	341	
3.11	341	
3.12-14	341	
4.16-21	314	
13.1-5	106	
13.20	495	
17.7-10	368, 369	
17.10	368	
18.26	370	
18.27	489	
20.9-19	487	

Luke (cont.)
20.27 436
23.17 479

John
1.29 494
3.18 369, 458
4.1-3 294
4.9 145
5.24 371
6.15 406
6.22-34 314
6.31 314
6.68 487
9.2 106
12.34 492
15.16 489
18.28 459
18.36 406, 495
18.39 479

Acts
5.35-39 291
5.36 300
10 468

10.15 471
10.28 459
13.21 95
15.20 471
15.28-29 468
21.28-30 454
21.38 300

Romans
1.24 470
2.12 326, 470
3.8 343, 470
7.14-17 470
7.16 469
8.17 382
9.20-24 329
12.2 203
13.1 419
14.14 468, 471

1 Corinthians
6.13 470
6.16-18 463
6.18-19 470
7.2-5 472

7.14 471
10.23 450
13 469

Galatians
2.12 468
3.10 368, 369, 490
3.24-25 469

James
2.10 490
2.12 490
2.13 343, 490

1 Peter
5.8 353

1 John
2.1 343
2.3-5 343
3.8 353
3.14 374

PSEUDEPIGRAPHA

1 En.
1–5 174
1.1 174
2–5 316
3 421
6–36 174
6–7 174, 175
7.3 389
8 174, 175, 336
8.32 336
9–11 174, 176
9.3 176
9.10 176
10.8 179, 412, 456
12–16 174, 177
12–13 389
12 176
12.4 177

12.6 174
13.8-9 176
15.3-4 177
15.6 344
17–22 177
17–19 174
18.12 178
18.15 178
20 174, 177
21–22 174
21.6 178
22 389
22.7 177
22.9 434
23–36 174, 178
25.4 179, 423
25.6 179
32.6 20
37–71 174
38 420

39.6-8 395
40.7 344
46.4-5 420
48.1-6 395
48.4 421
48.10 389
49.2 395
50.2 338
51 435
52.4 389, 393
53.3 462
54 352
54.6 352
55.4 352
56.1-4 436
69 352
69.9-11 337
69.11 430
71.14 389, 393, 394

72–82	174	*Ep. Arist.*		*Pss. Sol.*	
76–82	174	3	377	1	421
80.6	181	132	377	2.24	421
81.1-2	181	142	464, 465	3.11-12	435
81.5-6	181	143	468, 491	3.12	404, 435,
82.4-6	480	144	465		437
82.7	481	148-50	465	9.5	437
83–90	174	182	308	9.7	404
83.2	455	184	465	13.9-10	404
85	347	205	377	13.11	437
85.5	181	210	377	14.1-2	404
86	347			14.1	404
89.1	392	*Jos. Asen.*		15.12-13	437
89.9	392	7.1	308	15.12	437
89.17-18	392			15.13	404
89.59-65	347	*Jub.*		16.13-14	272
90.28-29	242, 301	1.17	387	16.13	404
90.28	405	1.26-28	377	17	272, 273,
90.29	391	1.26	387		403
90.33	430	1.27	391, 405	17.5	404
90.37-38	241	1.29	387	17.6	422
90.37	392	2.8-10	375	17.21	404
91-104	174	3.10	308	17.30-31	400
91.15	396	3.15	337, 376	17.41	422
94	421	3.31	308	17.46	404
105–108	174	4.25	390		
		5.6	348	*T. Job*	
2 En.		5.11	348	3.3	353
7.1-3	354	5.14	348	8	353
71.29	390	6.35-37	483		
		7.29	436	*T. Ash.*	
2 Bar.		7.39	390	5.1	462
29.3	407	10.1	348, 462	7.3	387
30.1	407	10.5	348		
39.7	407	10.7	348	*T. Benj.*	
40.1-2	407	10.8	348	5.2	462
40.3	407	12.19-21	338		
56.10-13	353	12.20-24	203	*T. Dan*	
		16.26	378	4.7	351
4 Macc.		21.10	390		
6.28-29	379	23.25-26	376	*T. Iss.*	
17.21-22	379	23.31	436	2.1	462
		32.21	331	3.5	462
4 Ezra		33.20	460		
3.28-33	347	36.10	436	*T. Jos.*	
12.32	407	50.12-13	239	7.20	352
14.37-47	173	50.12	360		

T. Jud.		5.2	387	2.2	351, 415
21.4	398	8.11	387	3.3	462
21.7	402	13.1-7	324	4.6	462
22.1-3	402	18.1-12	399	6.8	398, 401
22.2-3	399	18.2	398		
22.2	387	18.12	399	*T. Sim.*	
				5.3	461, 462
T. Levi		*T. Naph.*		6.5	387
2.3	318, 319	3.1	352	7.1-2	400
2.4-10	318	8.2-3	387, 401		
2.11	387			*T. Zeb.*	
3.1-10	319	*T. Reub.*		9.8	387
4.2-4	402	2.2–3.3	461		

QUMRAN

1QH		2.25–3.9	356, 457	*4Q171*	
1.8	320	3.15-21	399	2.17-20	232
1.8-29	333	3.15-17	332		
1.21-27	339	3.17–4.2	335	*4Q259*	
1.29	351	3.17-19	351	8.15	398
2.32	424	3.18	181	9.11	398
3.1	321	3.24–4.1	181		
3.19-23	373	3.26–4.1	351	*11QM*	
4.5	321	4.3	396, 424	5–6	392
4.29-30	457	4.5	460	8	392
4.34-38	365	5.8-9	474	10	392
4.37	366	5.23	373	13	392
4.29-31	340	6.13-22	458	16	392
5.11-12	372	6.16-17	458, 460	18	392
14.17	474	6.20-21	458	24	392
		6.24–7.25	362	25	393
1QM		7.14-16	459		
7.6-7	459	8.10-11	458	*CD*	
11.7-8	405	8.20–9.1	358	1.1-12	231
12.7	319	9.9-11	231	1.1-2	325
14.10-11	425	9.10-11	397, 399	1.13-17	232
19.1	319	9.11	406	2.2-3	325
		9.23-25	339	2.5-13	333
1QpHab		10.11	364	2.5-6	326
2.1-10	313	11.1-2	418	2.11	325
2.12-13	313	11.2-4	364	2.14	326
8.2-3	370, 457	11.3-4	320	3.2	338
9.9-12	232	11.5-6	396	3.21	424
12.2-6	232	11.9-10	341	4.17	461
		11.11-21	365	4.21	326
1QS		11.11	341	5.2-6	326
2.2-4	321			5.11	325

6.3-11	325	11.9	424	15	474
8.8-11	232	11.13-14	424	15.1-5	475
9.1	326	12.22–13.1	406	15.6	474, 475
9.6	326	13.13-14	424	19.1-11	406
9.8-10	474	14.7	424	20.1	406
9.16-17	327	14.13	424		
10.21	459	14.19	406		

JOSEPHUS

Ant.		12.237	229	14.41	269
6.378	95	12.288-98	20	14.43	269
10.143	95	12.387	229	14.83	274
11.26-31	124	12.395	244	14.91	274
11.32	61	12.396	244	14.97	275
11.79	66, 383	12.398	244	14.101	275
11.111	68	12.413	245	14.102	275
11.147	136	12.414	245	14.105-10	275
11.161	138	12.419	245	14.115	275
11.297-301	116, 161	12.434	245	14.120-21	276
11.297	135	13.213	247	14.143-55	276
11.304-12	152	13.214	247	14.143	277
11.308	141	13.249	253	14.160-61	279
11.337-38	161	13.257-58	256	14.163-67	280
11.346-47	145	13.273	253	14.168-84	274
12.4-5	162	13.288-92	254	14.172-76	286
12.7	162	13.291-92	255	14.174	277, 281
12.138-39	218	13.301	258	14.185-216	276
12.138	277, 296	13.302	258	14.193	275
12.140-42	219	13.319	259	14.202	277
12.142	296	13.320	259, 263	14.213-16	277
12.143	218	13.372-73	261	14.240	277
12.154-55	219	13.376	262	14.301-304	282
12.154	216, 217	13.377	262	14.326	282
12.155	217, 219	13.379	262	14.366-367	282
12.158	215, 219	13.380	262	15.3-4	286
12.160	166	13.399-404	263	15.40	286
12.163	219	13.405	264	15.370	286
12.164	220	13.408	264	17.193-95	290
12.167	215, 220	13.409	264	17.200	290
12.175	220	13.410	265	17.299-300	292
12.180-85	220	13.419-21	265	17.339-41	294
12.186	220	14.4-7	266	18.15-17	285, 479
12.223	216	14.11	267	18.21	464
12.224	220	14.14-18	267	18.85-89	300
12.229	221	14.17	268	18.117	342
12.233	165	14.22-24	268	18.118	294
12.237-39	223	14.31	268	18.120-25	300

Ant. (cont.)		*War*		2.135	473
18.130	284	1.31-33	230	2.137-38	458
18.245	293	1.31-32	223	2.139-42	473
18.263-72	300	1.67	256	2.139-40	419
20.97-99	300	1.85	259	2.147-49	459
20.115-17	299	1.93	262	2.150	458
20.167-68	301	1.123-26	267	2.161	464
20.169-71	300	1.170	274	2.164-65	436
20.237	245	1.174	275	2.228-31	299
20.244	248, 270	1.177-78	275	2.259-60	301
		1.180	276	2.261-63	301
Apion		1.203-207	279	2.487	162
1.34-36	255	1.244	282	2.651	297
1.186	162	1.268-71	282	6.333-35	277
1.205	162	2.118	297		
		2.120-21	464		

OTHER ANCIENT REFERENCES

Classical		*Leg. Gai.*		Suetonius	
Appian		155-58	277	*Divus Julius*	
Hist. Rom.				84.5	278
11.50.5	162	*Op. Mund.*			
		151-52	463	Tacitus	
Syr.				*Hist.*	
5	216	*Spec. Leg.*		5.9	270
		3.205	466		
Aristotle		3.209	466	Mishnah	
Politics		3.34-36	472	*Ab.*	
1.1.6	205			1.2	306
		Plato			
Dio Cassius		*Republic*		*Ḥag.*	
37.7	268	5.470c	205	2.7	459
Diogenes Laertius		Pliny		*Men.*	
1.33	205	*Nat.*		13.10	229
		5.4	464		
Isocrates		5.17	464		
Panegyric				*Mid.*	
50	205	Polybius		2.3	454
		16.39.4	218		
Livy		28.20	216	*Qid.*	
29.15	205	29.27	225	4.4	255
31	205				
		Strabo		Ostraca, Papyri	
Philo		16.2	258	and Tablets	
Hypoth.		16.40	258	*P.Cairo Zen*	
14	463			59003.1.13	215

P.Cowley
30   116, 135,
                  153

P.Preisigke
6709   165

Talmuds
b. Ber.
29a   255, 263
33a   473

b. Qid.
29b   463
66a   254

Midrashim
Pirqe Ab.
1.3   363
1.10   403
1.11   405
1.12   260
3.15   458
3.16   368

Pes. K.
4.7   473

Tanḥ. Huqqat
8   473

Early Jewish
Ass. Mos.
2.4   331

INDEX OF AUTHORS

Abel, F.M. 221
Aharoni, Y. 137
Albertz, R. 12, 13
Alt, A. 57
Amitai, J. 110
Andriessen, P. 302
Ardusso, F. 406
Aune, D.E. 394
Avigad, N. 14, 116, 166

Baarde, T. 469
Bacher, W. 367
Baillet, M. 302
Bardtke, H. 212
Barr, J. 33
Barthélemy, D. 167, 446
Barton, G.A. 279
Barucq, A. 386
Baumgarten, A.I. 19
Baumgarten, J.M. 110
Beer, G. 403
Ben Chorin, S. 323, 486
Benoit, A. 29
Berger, R.P. 59
Betlyon, J.W. 160
Bettenzoli, G. 85
Bianchi, F. 61, 116
Bianchi, U. 125, 131
Bickerman, E.J. 59, 153, 192, 363
Billerbeck, P. 323, 486
Black, M. 252
Boccaccini, G. 16-19, 29, 42-44, 240,
    305, 307, 408, 414, 459, 489, 490
Bokser, B.Z. 16
Boman, T. 32, 33
Booth, R.P. 469
Bordeuil, P. 56
Boscherini, E.G. 91

Bricchi, P.G. 167
Bright, J. 137
Brooke, G.J. 307
Broshi, M. 230
Brunt, P.A. 296
Busi, G. 15, 137

Capelli, P. 173
Caquot, A. 386
Cardellini, I. 151, 309
Carmignac, J. 42, 321, 358, 373, 394
Castellino, G. 193
Castiglioni, V. 403
Cazelles, H. 110, 155, 169
Cazeneuve, J. 40
Cerfaux, L. 302
Cerutti, D. 95
Cerutti, M.V. 125, 322
Charlesworth, J.H. 21, 23, 42, 406, 487
Chialà, S. 21
Chiesa, B. 212, 237, 241, 309
Chilton, B. 21
Cooke, G.A. 453
Cooper, J.S. 279
Coppens, J. 30, 186, 380
Cornely, R. 431
Cortese, E. 13
Cross, F.M. 29, 136, 153
Cryer, F.H. 480
Cullmann, O. 297, 300
Cumont, F. 37, 163
Cuq, E. 217

Daniel, C. 28, 295
Daumas, F. 312
Davies, P. 483
Davies, P.R. 10, 14-16
Davies, W.D. 309, 397

Deiana, G. 176, 336
Delitzsch, F. 92
Denis, A. 302
Derenbourg, J. 254, 263
Dianich, S. 21
Dillmann, A. 157
Dodds, E.R. 37
Donner, H. 13, 50
Douglas, M. 445
Droeto, A. 91
Durkheim, E. 40
Edelman, D.V. 10, 14
Eissfeldt, O. 137, 156, 235
Eliade, M. 40
Eph'al, I. 53
Eskenazi, T. 14, 15
Evans, C.A. 21

Falk, H. 490
Flandrin, J.L. 472
Fovra, C. 295
Frye, R.N. 125

Galling, K. 59, 137
Garbini, G. 20, 59, 94, 96, 137, 245, 347
García Martínez, F. 18, 147, 148, 232,
        241, 307, 310, 406, 469
Garrone, D. 13
Gaster, A.G. 478
Gianotto, C. 393
Gilet, J. 302
Goethe, J. von 354
Golb, N. 19
Gosse, B. 11
Grabbe, L.L. 9, 11, 14, 15, 20
Greenfield, J.C. 56
Grelot, P. 96

Hackett, J.A. 96
Hayes, J.H. 50, 57, 160
Hengel, M. 203, 419
Hoftijzer, J. 86, 88, 96
Holleaux, M. 219
Hölscher, G. 114, 137
Horbury, W. 407
Hughes, J. 95, 157

Israel, F. 13

Jacob, E. 426
Janssen, E. 50
Japhet, S. 14, 15, 182
Jaubert, A. 479, 481
Jeremias, J. 359, 459
Jourjon, M. 312
Jullien, C. 11
Jullien, F. 11
Jung, C.G. 40

Kahle, P. 157
Kaiser, O. 59
Kapera, Z.J. 19
Kappler, C. 354
Katsch, A.I. 363
Kaufman, S.A. 96
Kellermann, U. 137
Kindler, A. 117
Knauf, E.A. 12
Knohl, I. 477
Koch, K. 322
Kooj, B. van der 96
Kuhn, K. 167
Kuhnen, H.P. 287
Kupper, J.R. 279

Labat, R. 56
Lamarche, P. 65, 384
Lana, M. 437
Laperrousaz, E.M. 10, 18, 19
Lapide, P. 173
Laqueur, R. 277
Lauha, A.L. 191
Lemaire, A. 14, 85
Le Moyne, J. 167, 257, 285
Lévi-Strauss, C. 40
Levine, B.A. 307
Liverani, M. 56
Loretz, O. 103
Löwinger, S. 137
Lupieri, E. 342, 362, 461
Luther, M. 111

MacDonald, J. 30, 159
Maier, J. 62, 307
Manns, F. 484
Manson, T.W. 257
Mantovani, P.A. 103, 211

Marti, K. 403
Marx, A. 328
Mazzinghi, L. 430
McCarter, P.K. 96
Merklein, H. 156
Meyer, B.F. 21
Meyer, E. 215, 277
Michaëli, F. 137
Milik, J.T. 29, 174, 391, 394
Millar, F. 252
Millard, A.R. 56
Miller, J.M. 50, 57, 160
Mohlberg, L.C. 221
Momigliano, A. 215, 219, 278
Mor, M. 136
Moraldi, L. 302, 311, 312
Morgenstern, J. 137
Motzo, B. 183, 278
Müller, K. 156
Muraoka, T. 29, 56, 234

Neusner, J. 16, 29, 42, 301, 307
Newton, M. 461, 469, 471
Nodet, E. 11
Noort, E. 10
Noth, M. 11, 12, 51, 86, 94, 146, 255,
    278
Nötscher, F. 328

O'Brien, M.A. 94
Oded, B. 50, 57
Oestreicher, T. 114
Otto, R. 39, 322, 447

Parente, F. 255
Paul, A. 212
Pavlovsky, A. 137
Pederson, J. 33
Penna, R. 42, 69, 470
Pettinato, G. 479
Piovanelli, P. 130, 216
Ploeg, J. van der 312, 373
Pohlmann, K.F. 235
Prato, G. 237, 408
Puech, E. 29, 96, 393
Pury, A. de 12, 13

Qimron, E. 110

Rad, G. von 322
Radet, G. 208
Rahlfs, A. 84, 414
Reicke, B. 137
Reimarus, H.S. 44, 487, 488
Renan, E. 137
Rendtorff, R. 13
Ricciotti, G. 10, 50, 137, 246, 255
Richards, K.H. 14, 15
Rofé, A. 309
Rössler, D. 314
Rosso Ubigli, L. 359, 390, 429, 461
Rostovzeff, M. 166
Rouillard-Bonraisin, H. 10
Rowley, H.H. 137, 167
Rudolph, W. 73, 186
Rüger, H.-P. 73, 237

Sacchi, P. 12, 13, 21, 22, 42, 69, 92, 132,
    137, 154, 156, 157, 167, 171, 172,
    231, 234, 245, 255, 311, 313, 384,
    394, 396, 438, 441, 445, 481
Saulnier, C. 245
Scarpat, G. 430
Schiffman, L.H. 16, 110
Schmid, H.H. 103
Schnabel, E.J. 408, 414
Schürer, E. 252, 254
Seigert, F. 167
Seters, J. van 91, 92
Severino, E. 37
Shaffer, A. 56
Simon, M. 29
Smend, R. 414
Smith Christopher, D. 14, 169, 384
Smith, M. 65, 139
Snaith, N.H. 32
Soggin, J.A. 50, 103, 136, 137, 173, 194,
    255, 385, 433
Sollberger, E. 279
Somogy, J. 137
Spinoza, B. 90, 91
Starcky, J. 398
Stegemann, H. 307
Steible, H. 279
Stemberger, G. 20, 156, 255
Stern, E. 57, 60
Stoebe, H. 330

Strack, H.L. 323, 486
Strugnell, J. 110, 147
Sussman, Y. 110
Szyszman, S. 212

Talmon, S. 110, 477
Testuz, M. 390
Thompson, T.L. 92
Thureau Dangin, F. 278, 279
Tocci, M. 375
Torrey, C.C. 137
Tosato, A. 114, 133
Tresmontant, C. 33
Troiani, L. 22, 167, 311

Vaccari, A. 156
VanderKam, J.C. 12, 168, 483
Vaux, R. de 132, 229, 233, 330
Vermes, G. 23, 29, 42, 137, 252, 393
Vivian, A. 307, 360

Wacholder, B.Z. 307
Waerden, B.L. van der 480
Wagner, S. 302
Wearer, W.P. 406
Weber, J. 431
Welch, A.C. 114
Wellhausen, J. 50
Widengren, G. 57
Wieder, N. 212
Wildengren, G. 160
Williamson, H. 182
Willrich, H. 277
Winston, D. 430
Wise, M.O. 307
Woude, A.S. van der 232, 310

Yardeni, A. 110

Zeron, A. 96